The Sabbath Complete

The Sabbath Complete

AND

The Ascendancy of First-Day Worship

Terrence D. O'Hare

WIPF & STOCK · Eugene, Oregon

THE SABBATH COMPLETE
And the Ascendancy of First-Day Worship

Wipf & Stock
An Imprint of Wipf and Stock Publishers
199 W. 8th Ave., Suite 3
Eugene, OR 97401

www.wipfandstock.com

ISBN 13:978-1-60899-257-7

Manufactured in the U.S.A.

Dedicated to two modern heroes of the faith:

Richard M. Lewis (1924–2007)
who held to the view of a fulfilled Sabbath despite opposition within his denomination,

and

George Knevelbaard (1942–),
a righteous man, whose life of integrity and devotion to Scripture has been an inspiration to me.

Contents

Acknowledgments

First of all, I would not have considered this a topic for intense study over the past decade unless convinced that the Lord wanted it so. He ordained the circumstances that jettisoned my initial inquiry into the relationship of the Sabbath and the Lord's Day for Christians. That is the real reason for the publication of this book. My hope is that many readers will be blessed by the theology of the Sabbath and Lord's Day that is presented herein.

There is a Jewish saying, "You can eat alone, but you cannot work alone." Fortunately, I did not have to do either. I have been blessed by many people, but my wife, Patty, has served me well in both capacities. Thank you Patty for letting me spend precious hours reading and researching in preparation for the publication of this book and for listening to my every discovery while you cooked away. Time is valuable and you looked beyond the time you could have had more of a husband and saw the benefit for countless others who need a biblical view of the Sabbath. Along with many other friends, you encouraged me to remain focused on this project and prayed with me that the Lord would ultimately bless this work.

There are others who deserve special mention who helped launch the thesis and improve the manuscript. Thank you, David Vaughn for your assistance in finding a publisher. This was a crucial step, more difficult than I understood, and the Lord used you to open the door to this respectable publisher. Along with my wife, you were an encouragement in the first stage by attributing worth to the ideas presented in this volume and for the initial reading of my excessively long and disjointed manuscript. Thank you, Hannah Selleck and Christine Pickering, for doing an outstanding job editing the manuscript. I thank you for all the fine detail work and countless suggestions to improve clarity and readability. Finally, I appreciate my friends Duane Daniels and Jake Rosen for also reading the manuscript and giving me valuable advice; my friend Zachary Perkins for lightening my load at Biola library; and my friends Paul Bringard and Jim LaPorte for whole-heartedly encouraging me along, and for the kind remarks of Jerry Smith.

Introduction

Prosabbaton

THE DAY PRECEDING THE Sabbath is Prosabbaton. It seemed a fitting word to use as an introduction to this work. The day before the Sabbath was a day of preparation and anticipation, hence, my goal in this introduction is to prepare the reader for the workmanship ahead and to arouse anticipation for what will be learned. Regardless of your present views, we may all agree that the Sabbath means so much to so many people. Jews consider it at home in their religion and culture, and they experience a special sense of shared history and togetherness with it, just like an aged and respected parent in the home. They don't argue about the Sabbath; they just write recipe books and devotionals to help each other stay focused upon the delights of that day. On the other hand, the Christian church has made the Sabbath a point of controversy. While Christian authors today write their share of encouraging books on the topic advancing some form of Sabbatarian practice for the church, actually few books have been written "against" the Sabbath. For the past 600 years, the church has had difficulty defining its relationship to the Sabbath of the fourth commandment, proposing everything from strict seventh-day Sabbath-keeping to occasional attendance at Sunday church services.

This was not a topic of interest to me until I started attending an Orthodox Presbyterian Church where various Sabbath-keeping applications were stressed. A specific event sparked my interest further. I was a board member of a crisis pregnancy center and a dispute arose about whether or not to accept a donation from a church that raised funds via recreation at a business on Sunday, the Christian Sabbath. The arguments for the continuation of the Sabbath commandment for today's church were made passionately and uncompromisingly. Of course, the counter-argument that the Sabbath was not repeated in the NT seemed weak and minuscule beside the voluminous and ardent Sabbatarian teachings. I was challenged to study the topic further. After reading a variety of articles, chapters, and books supporting the Christian Sabbath, it became apparent to me that these authors were inconsistent in their analysis, varied in their interpretation of key passages, and derived a wide range of applications from Sabbath law. Not only this, there were presuppositions that were not acknowledged and more probing questions that were not asked and answered. I then embarked on a thorough examination of every text on the Sabbath and Lord's Day in the Bible. While I have not read everything in print on this topic, I have studied the perspectives of Roman Catholics, Reformed, Evangelicals, Christian Identity, Messianic Christians, and Seventh-day Adventists. After formulating a framework for understanding this topic, I searched for authors who seemed to share my view. I became familiar with D. A. Carson's anthology *From Sabbath to Lord's Day* (1982, 1999), which is an excellent, scholarly contribution to the topic that corroborated my historical findings and provided additional evidence for the church's early adoption of the phrase "the Lord's Day." Just before editing the manuscript, I discovered *Sabbath in Christ* (2003), by Dale Ratzlaff, a former Adventist pastor, whose approach to the topic is similar to this book, but from an evangelical perspective of the law. Finally, another recent book, *Sabbath, Circumcision, and Tithing* (2002), by Michael Morrison, explores the matter of the continuity and fulfillment of biblical law, devoting a third of the book to the Sabbath. So, why introduce another book? I believe I have material to present that 1) addresses the presuppositional roadblocks to a Christian consensus, 2) answers Sabbath-Lord's Day questions that have not previously been explored or explained, and 3) advocates a renewed dedication to the external badge of Christendom: a commitment to the word of God alone in congregational worship on the first day of the week, Sunday, the Lord's Day as ordained by the Lord in type and through apostolic decree. Besides this, I endorse a covenantal view of the law.

This book is not against the Sabbath any more than it is against the New Moon or circumcision, or any other fulfilled ceremonial commandment from the Mosaic covenant. It is about the *fulfillment* of the Sabbath by Jesus Christ, and so it is a book that is for the glory and power of God over creation, through history, and in redemption. I think this book will be easier for a Sunday Sabbatarian to read if he holds in his mind this one thought: the Sabbath and the Lord's Day are not the same. It has been my observation that any argument "against" the Sabbath is uniformly understood as an argument against the Lord's command to engage in weekly congregational church worship. This is certainly not the case. A fulfilled Sabbath does not remove the obligation to assemble weekly in the Lord's presence.

The reluctance of Sabbatarians to consign the Sabbath to the long list of fulfilled ceremonial laws is rooted primarily in the following postulates: 1) its association with the creation account seems to displace it from an exclusively Jewish context and endow it with a comprehensive duty upon humanity, 2) its presence in the Ten Commandments seems to afford it special status as a bearer of moral force, and 3) the teachings of our Lord during His earthly ministry on the topic seem to support its ongoing practice for the church. In addition, other factors influence the resistance to accept the Sabbath as a fulfilled, ceremonial command; and these are the forces of long-practiced traditions, the subscription to denominational standards, and the sense of piety associated with Sabbath-keeping.

Interestingly, the same pastor who ignited my interest to search out this matter, also gave a memorable and stirring sermon on Mary's prodigious worship—pouring upon the head of our Lord Jesus the expensive unguent contents of an alabaster flask. This pastor drew attention to the fact that it was not only Judas who objected to her act of worship, seeing it as a waste of a valuable asset that could better serve the ministry of the church, but that other disciples criticized her sharply as well (Mark 14:4–5). After all, giving to the poor is a sacrificial act of worship that benefits the giver as well as the recipient, and brings glory to Christ. But what sounded good on the surface to some of the disciples, was flatly rejected by Jesus, because in His mind, *everything else took a secondary place to the significance of His coming suffering and death for the redemption of His people.* We are reminded through this event how easy it is to jump on a bandwagon that serves our personal sense of piety. We are also encouraged by Mary's willingness to put her love for Christ on the line and to do something that was risky, in which her fear of the disapproval of others was superseded by her love of Jesus Christ and her passion to honor Him. By way of application, this pastor rightly urged his congregation to beware of the tendency to espouse ideas and practices that are based on tradition and arouse feelings of piety, while being shocked at that which is actually honoring to the Lord.

This book proposes that Sabbatarianism is a form of traditional pietism and that the acceptance of the fully ceremonial nature of the Sabbath, though shocking to some, is actually Christ-honoring. Every ceremonial law is foremost about Christ and the redemption of His church. Sabbatarianism is more about our interests in our personal well-being and sense of religiosity—how particular we can be in ordering our day of worship, how our body and mind are refreshed by a twenty-four hour hiatus, and how righteous we are to refrain from subsidizing the cruelty of employers—than about the primacy of Christ's fulfillment of the Scriptures (Luke 24:25–27). As Calvin warned, "the man that calls back the ceremonies into use . . . robs Christ of his excellence."[1]

Now let us put this controversy to rest.

1. Calvin, *Commentaries*, 21:193 (Col 2:17).

1

Sabbatic Prototypes in Genesis

THE PLACE OF REST

The Appeal of Rest

JUST AS IT IS the pleasure of God to provide shade for the sun-soaked brow (Jonah 4:6; Isa 25:4–5) and cool water for the wind-parched lips (Exod 17:6; Isa 44:3), so it is for God, in beneficence to us, to provide rest for the overworked body (Deut 5:14; Isa 11:10). Yet our experience with physical limitations, discomforts, and inner yearnings is but a subtle reminder of our more abysmal spiritual condition; and the goodness of God's provision for our physical need is but a token of a more transcendent remedy for our spiritual privation. The appeal of physical rest should never overshadow the more significant need for spiritual rest, nor should the appeal to cease from labor ever overshadow the need to cease from self-justifying and self-serving works. This is not to say that physical rest is inconsequential, for the redemption of mankind includes the material substance of which he is made, but the call of God is primarily to the inner man (Eph 3:14–19).

No man or woman, child or elder, throughout all the generations of humanity has been free from the heavy loads of sin and guilt; fear, anxiety and uncertainty; and difficult, imposing circumstances. These burdens of our frame are present from the moment of conception and loom unceasingly over each day of our life (Ps 51:5; 2 Cor 5:4). The inner turmoil of living a life displeasing to God cannot help but work out the exhausting struggle in our very flesh and bones (Ps 38:3–8). Furthermore, even in our quest for a pious life, we impose upon ourselves and others rigorous religious exercises in a futile effort to gain the approval of men or the approbation of the Most High God (Matt 23:4; Col 2:20–23). From these burdens of sin and selfishness, Jesus offers blessed relief in the assuring words "Come to Me . . . and you will find rest for your souls" (Matt 11:28–29). The rest provided by Jesus is available to peoples from every nation, every culture, and every era. His beckoning rest begins in the present and continues into eternity, "for the Gentiles shall seek Him, And His resting place shall be glorious" (Isa 11:10). How we enter into His rest—by grace through faith alone—implies a cessation from our own works and a counting upon the Lord's ability to provide that rest. Faith is that spiritual frame of mind that responds to the grace and goodness of God and receives by imputation divine righteousness for human unrighteousness. The complete removal of accusing sin and the unrestrained reception into the family of God are among the benefits of entering into His rest. While in this rest, yet living on earth, we are yoked as bond-servants to do the will of our Master, working for the glory of God, just as Adam was prepared to do from the beginning.

Rest Means Completion

The first occurrences of the word "rest" are found in Genesis 2:3–4, describing the course taken by God following creation. It cannot be said that He rested because He tired in His work, nor that He needed a respite from His creative activity; for a supremely omnipotent God who neither slumbers nor sleeps (Ps 121:3–4) simply has no need. God's rest was specifically defined as the *completion* of His six workdays of creation.[1] While the creation account has symbolic meaning, it should not overshadow the obvious historic fact that His creation *ex nihilo* was *complete*. It was finished and it was a work that God Himself completed. In its most fundamental intent, the creation rest simply means that He completed all His creative activities in the beginning. The hexaemeron was a one-time event, spanning the space of six ordinary days; so there was nothing cyclical about His creative work or His ensuing rest that must be interpreted as a recurring pattern. The creation rest presented in Genesis does not mean that God ceased from all activity (Neh 9:6; John 5:17), nor does it mean that God rests one in every seven days *ad infinitum*.

Yet, the seventh day was set apart from the previous six days as a day of rest and given *significance* equal to the creation itself. It is because of the significance of the seventh day that rest takes on a *symbolic* meaning rather than merely conveying the historic terminus of the creation. As a summary of the beginning of time, the creation account not only demonstrates such obvious facts as God's preexistence and His power over the material universe, but reveals the subtle truth that events in God's revelation have meaning. Hence, writers of the NT view the reality of creation with Christ and His redemption in mind (Jn 1:1–4, 10–13; 1 Cor 15:46–49; Col 1:13–18; 3:10). To be sure, the Scriptures reveal actual history, but the fact that God's history has meaning allows us to comprehend that God's rest not only existed on the seventh day but that it continues onward at the same time (Heb 4:3–5). Pipa agrees "that the seventh day of creation is a picture of the eternal rest . . . however, [this significance] does not necessarily preclude that the day is a literal day."[2] The pattern of six days work plus one day rest emphasizes that God Himself engages the world without the help of man, purposing to bring about His work in a progressive fashion to a predictable place of completion. God so worked in the beginning of creation that it may speak of a more glorious redemptive work that He intended to complete. To imbue the seventh day with meaning and to emphasize that His work ended with the desired result, the

1. Howard and Rosenthal, *Feasts*, 15; Duncan and Hall, "24-Hour View," 33; Yang, *Jesus and Sabbath*, 23–24.

2. Pipa, "Chaos to Cosmos," 166.

Lord blessed and sanctified the seventh day. Since this seventh day of perfection followed the apex of His creation—Adam and Eve—it represents the first day in which He actually enjoyed all that He had created. Thus His seventh-day rest was a day of holy fellowship with sinless mankind within a pristine cosmos. This particular day was sanctified so long as Adam remained obedient and lived in consonance with the image that he represented of God.[3] But the immediate record of Adam's fall intimates that the symbolic rest was but one day and that the image of God in man was promptly marred. However, God knowing the end from the beginning sees in Adam and Eve His Christ and the redeemed, and so this idea of a day of rest remains until the consummation when that seventh-day rest is eternally realized and unshaken by sin so that the image of God is fully realized in man (Rom 8:29). Therefore, the blessing of the seventh day and its sanctification look forward to the eternal rest when God will fellowship with His people from every nation in Christ. The seventh day is a redemptive type.

God's Rest Was Not a Sabbath

Moses wrote Genesis shortly after the Sabbath was given to Israel, yet he did not use the word "Sabbath" at all in that significant book of beginnings. The immediate audience—the first generation of Israelites to escape the snares of Egypt by the sovereign might of God—would have been emotionally prepared to receive instruction about how the initial creation rest was disrupted by sin and Satan, how their own troubles were an extension of the curse of Adam and Eve, and how the Creator was now making good on His promises to the patriarchs. The word from which "rest" is translated in Genesis 2:3–4 is *shabath* (note the single "b"). Used seventy-one times in the OT, it is usually translated "cease" or "rest." In Genesis, *shabath* is used only three times, twice in the record of creation (Gen 2:3–4) and once during the lifetime of Noah (Gen 8:22). Other Hebrew words are translated "rest." For example, *nuach* is used in Deuteronomy 5:14 to describe the rest allowed the servants of Israelites on the Sabbath day, and in Exodus 20:11 to state that God rested on the seventh day. During the first 2,000 years of recorded biblical history, the Hebrew words for rest or cessation (*shabath* and *nuach*) are used only seven times, and none of the uses implies a recurring weekly cessation from labor. Not until the exodus from Egypt's womb was Israel introduced to the Sabbath institution: "Tomorrow is a Sabbath rest, a holy Sabbath to the Lord" (Exod 16:23).

Derived from *shabath*, the doubled "b" in *shabbat* has "an intensive force, implying a complete cessation or a making to cease."[4] The Sabbath was a neologism for the Israelites. The author of Hebrews mentions the creation rest as a type of the promise of heaven (Heb 4:4), but he does *not* say "spoken in a certain place of the *Sabbath* day." If the seventh day of creation was anything other than the seventh day, this would have been a logical place to mention the Sabbath, but forgoing that, the

3. Berkhof, *Systematic Theology*, 209.

4. *Vine's Dictionary*, 542; Hamilton, "shabbāt," TWOT, 2:902.

author is consistent with the historic Jewish understanding that the Sabbath was not given until Mount Sinai.

God Rested, Not Man

The rest following creation was the Lord's rest of beatitude, to be enjoyed within the Godhead and graciously shared with mankind in perfect fellowship. For this reason, God blessed the seventh day because it represented the moment when "all was right with the world." All things being perfect, man would have commenced his effortless work even though God rested from His work. Man's sinless occupation in exercising dominion would have been accomplished during that blessed eternal rest. It was the Lord who had worked six days, not man; God's work was complete, whereas man's work was just beginning. Adam did nothing to contribute to the creation so he had nothing from which to rest. The need for physical rest—as later defined by the Mosaic dispensation as a ceasing from back-breaking labors—was absent. Since work was prescribed for man on the sixth day, the day of his creation, it becomes difficult to support the claim of a Sabbath commandment *for man* the following day, for it would have given a Sabbath rest to Adam after a single day of sweatless work. As R. J. Rushdoony asserted, "The purpose of God's Sabbath rest was that man should now work."[5] Thus, the seventh day was the first full day in which Adam exercised his stewardship over the created realm while God "was refreshed."

God preexisted the creation and was already complete in Himself. He did not need the creation to fulfill Himself. The first day alone demonstrates the magnificence of His power, but the following days reveal the intelligence, purpose, and prerogatives of His omnipotence. Therefore, the seven days of that first week were predetermined to be a symbolic expression of His completeness and perfection. Secondly, the week was a sum of six days of creative work and a final day of blessed rest—a predetermined expression of His will in relation to the cosmos and specifically toward man. The perfection and completeness inherent in the week is the consequence of combining two things: the eternal self-existent God and the created cosmos, including the image-bearers. Again, the seventh-day rest was appointed because of its intended symbolic meaning—perfection through unity. Once perfection and completeness were achieved, every following day should have been a repetition of the seventh day of God's rest with man. God ceased His creative work and man engaged in dominion work, propelling the blessed state of rest between God and man from one day to the next.

The seventh-day rest is an artifact of the creation; it is not an eternal attribute of God's character. The creation week could not have served as an example for Adam to imitate. Being fashioned on the sixth day, he had only a portion of that day to work before the seventh day. So, if Adam was morally bound from the beginning to rest from his labors in a seven-day pattern, then he could not legitimately rest until he first completed six consecutive days of labor. Furthermore, what would compel Adam to

5. Rushdoony, *Salvation and Godly Rule*, 98. While Rushdoony erroneously labels the seventh day of creation as a Sabbath, he correctly realizes that the dominion mandate left Adam no option but to work.

emulate the Lord's first week of time and not the days and weeks following? That is, if the Lord's rest continued forever, why should Adam return to work after his first seventh-day rest? And if the Lord's work continued forever, why should Adam interrupt his work with a weekly rest? The Lord's command to take dominion was not confused with an unstated moral obligation to convert the Lord's six workdays and one rest day into a cyclic pattern for mankind. The week of creation was a unique event that ended with Adam's calling to take dominion on a daily basis in perfect harmony with God.

Rest Interrupted

Given the lack of a closing statement that the seventh day of creation had an evening and a morning, there is the intimation of an indefinite continuation of God's rest. However, its endurance would be measured in days. In a sense, Adam was responsible for *maintaining* God's rest through obedience each day. Therefore, it is conceivable that a day could come that Adam and Eve rebel, as did Satan, disturbing the state of God's rest. And so it is that the Genesis account continues in greater detail, first recapitulating the creation of Adam and his wife (Gen 2:7–25), and secondly documenting the temptation and fall of our federal head (Gen 3:1–13), the curse and clothing of mankind and the curse of Satan (Gen 3:14–21), and finally, our parents' expulsion from Eden (Gen 3:22–24). Interestingly, the dominion commandment and the seventh-day rest are not repeated in this recapitulation, and the narrative leaps months forward to the births of Cain and Abel (Gen 4:1–2). If there were a moment when God could have plainly ordained a Sabbath practice for all peoples and all aeons, it would have been at the curse when mankind was condemned to work by sweat and toil, through pain and grief; however, not a hint of repose or respite was allowed for the guilty man. As Adam and Eve stood before God in judgment, there is no indication that there would be any rest for mankind until the head of the serpent was bruised by the forthcoming seed of Eve. Indeed, through their disobedience they were banished from that rest.

Thus, the first creation account (Gen 1:1—2:3) presents an overview of God's purposes and design in creation, concluding in a perfect rest. This is the idyllic creation before the fall. The second account (Gen 2:4—3:24) highlights the marring of God's rest by man's sin through the temptation of Satan. The Lord's post-creation rest was to be shared with man, but man excluded himself from that rest through sin. The rest following creation was a reality lost, however, as the story of redemption is developed through the nation Israel, that rest became a figure of a future and more enduring rest made available through the blood of Jesus Christ. As the author of Genesis, Moses knew what the Sabbath was, yet he did not mention the Sabbath at all, neither in the first creation account ending in rest, nor as a consolation of weekly rest after the documentation of the fall. The sequence of days presented in creation was not about the institution of Sabbath day worship, but about the demonstration that God's work began and ended in perfection, and that He deigned to enjoy the work of His hands in holy pleasure.

When Moses recounted the institution of the Sabbath in the wilderness, it was described as "a holy Sabbath to the Lord" (Exod 16:23). The reason for its holiness was later explained to Moses on Mount Sinai, that a relationship existed between the creation week and Israel's ritual week, "Therefore the Lord blessed the Sabbath day and hallowed it" (Ex 20:11). Using the language of the seventh-day rest, the Lord set apart the Sabbath for Israel as a means to engender the hope of restoration. This brought the history of the creation week to the present day experiences of the nation Israel in order to help them comprehend the meaning of sin and redemption through their weekly Sabbath (Rom 2:4). The source of their troubles in terms of slavery, bondage, and death was related to the sin principle deriving from the fall of Adam and Eve. They could make no claim based upon the holiness of their lives to enjoy a holy rest with God. Indeed, because of their sin they had no more right to enjoy any type of rest with God than did Adam and Eve who were banished from the creation rest. Therefore, it was only by God's grace that Israel was given the Sabbath whereby they could externally model a token of that lost rest. Israel's attention to the creation week should have focused on the disruption of harmony with God, the ejection of our first parents from the garden of Eden, and the promise of restoration through the work of some distant righteous male descendent (Isa 51:2–3). The creation rest could have been a continuous experience of beatitude; however, the Sabbath was but one seventh of the week, a single day sanctified by the grace of God, and a mere token of that former day. Thus, in spite of the reminder that they had no right to the seventh-day rest, by grace they were allowed to reenact the blessedness of the seventh day of creation. What grace was extended to the Jews that they received God's favor in spite of their sin! For Israel, the hope of a reestablished rest with God was further related to the land of Canaan, the tabernacle, and multiple sabbatic rituals. Though God's rest after creation is a type of everlasting rest yet to come, it is more certainly a type of Jesus Christ, who has come, in whom the faithful rest in salvation.

The Typological Rest

Theologians have postulated that God could have created everything all at once, and some have even taught this despite the enumeration of the succession of creative days. But God did not create everything all at once and instead chose to accomplish His work over a period of time, a sum of six days work and one day rest—seven days. There is a reason behind this pattern. It was not a full course of seven days work, or five days work and two of rest, or any other number and combination of days. Within the Bible, the recurring pattern of work and rest and the redoubling number seven portray both purpose and design. Any theory that calls into question the historicity of the creation week and the natural length of its days at once positions itself against the eschatological and typological intentions of God through that narrative. As Fairbairn aptly defined typical interpretations, "They indispensably require the reality of the facts or circumstances stated in the original narrative."[6] As will be obvious below, designating

6. Fairbairn, *Typology of Scripture*, 2–3.

the creation sequence as a biblical type requires one to understand the creation week as seven literal, real days.

The concept of biblical typology has long been with the Christian church, given Paul's specific nomination of it in his letter to the Romans, identifying Adam as "a type of Him [Jesus] who was to come" (Rom 5:14). Paul also identified the wilderness experiences of the Israelites as prefiguring examples (*tupoi*) of the church with the paraenetic intent "that we should not lust after evil things" (1 Cor 10:6). Paul conceived of himself to be a type or pattern (*hupotuposis*) of and for future converts ("for this cause") of how even the worst of sinners can be redeemed through the riches of God's grace (1 Tim 1:16). Peter also interprets OT history typologically (1 Pet 3:18–22) as well as the author of Hebrews (Heb 8:4; 9:25). Jesus correlated for Nicodemus the healing power of the brazen serpent described in Numbers 21:4–9 and the saving power of His forthcoming crucifixion as type and antitype (John 3:14–15). Christ's association of Jonah's entombment within the great fish for three days to His burial is no different than His association of thematic rest to the finality of His redemption (Jer 6:16; Matt 11:28–29). Jonah did not just happen to be engulfed by a great fish and later ejected as a random biological event, but this occurred as *designed* by the Lord to shadow forth the death, burial, and resurrection of our Lord. Likewise, the seventh day rest was not a random terminus of creation but a purposed end point to shadow forth the inevitable results of God's work in redemption. A type foreshadows something different than what it is, so there is a conceptual similarity or correspondence between the type and antitype. A type is a real person, event, or institution that represents a forthcoming real person, event, or institution; and highlights specific redemptive patterns or themes through *intended* similarities. That is, a type occurs by God's design—it is not that a situation arises in history and God uses it as an analogy at a later period to express some truth or object lesson. A type is an outworking of the sovereign will of God in history and it is recorded in Scripture to provide both a sign (mark) of His future intentions and an authentication of His sovereign power over all worldly events. As Greidanus simply put it, "Without the biblical teaching of God working sovereignly in history, typology is sheer nonsense."[7] What better place is there than at the creation of the world and setting in motion the course of history for God to display, in type, the greatest themes of redemptive history?

> Certainly, God has rested from His world-building work ever since the seventh day, and in that sense [His rest] continues. God does do other things, of course, so in another sense He continues to be active. Moreover, Genesis 1 is not merely a record of creation; it is also a typology of history, and the final sabbath will be endless.[8]

7. Griedanus, *Preaching Christ from the Old Testament*, 249.

8. Jordon, *Creation in Six Days*, 102. Jordon is thankfully unabashed in his acceptance of the overriding typology of the creation week. If his mention of a "final sabbath" is metaphorical, then he correctly states that our final rest will be endless, as typified by the seventh-day rest of creation and by the Jewish Sabbath. Since the context of his statement is with regard to the creation type, he may have better said, "and the final seventh-day rest will be endless."

The creation rest typifies both a person (Jesus Christ) and a thing (everlasting life). In the latter days of God's plan, the reality has been revealed and bestowed in the person of Jesus Christ and in the present possession of eternal life, a promise to be enjoyed in two stages—on earth and in heaven. The seventh day of fellowship was broken. In the Lord's curse He assured Adam and Eve of a day yet future when a seed should come to deal with the treachery of the Serpent. This promise initiated the anticipation of a day when such a One should be born and ultimately complete His work of settling the conflict between man and God. Anticipation and expectation of that day is the theme of the OT, but once that day arrived, all following days are subsumed to it, hence, "Today, is the day of salvation." The creation rest, besides documenting the cessation of God's work of creation, is a type of the exalted purposes of God in redemption and foreshadows the work of Christ in defeating Satan and providing reconciliation between God and man.

The Rest Followed Creation, Not the Fall

Adam was created before the seventh-day rest, and the seventh-day rest existed prior to the fall of man. So when Jesus asserted, "The Sabbath was made for man, and not man for the Sabbath," (Mark 2:27) it was not because the Jews were confused about the sequence of creation but because Jews made keeping the Sabbath superior to the interests of man. Thus, the Lord merely established the primacy of man over Sabbath ritual. He did not elevate the Sabbath to the status of a moral command.

Mankind was created to be holy, as God is holy (Lev 19:2; 1 Pet 1:15–16). Moral law, based upon the holiness of God, pre-exists man whom He has created. Moral law is before man in order and in primacy. Expressions of God's will, as contained in ceremonial laws, do not necessarily convey this deep-seated and intrinsic morality. Ceremonial commands follow the creation of mankind, and serve mankind through obedience to them, to enable him in his worship of and service to God, and to set him apart as a true worshiper.[9] As far as order is concerned, the seventh-day rest followed the creation of mankind; the fall of mankind followed the seventh-day rest; and the Sabbath followed the fall of mankind. The seventh-day rest of God was not given as a commandment to Adam but as a description of their holy fellowship before the fall. The Sabbath, on the other hand, was specifically given by commandment to Israel on account of the fall. As Jesus correctly observed, the Sabbath did not preexist (fallen) man. Therefore, the Sabbath command was ceremonial in essence because it followed not only the creation of man but his fall. If sin had not marred the landscape of human existence and we had been born into a world of trouble-free work and daily fellowship with the living God, what would a weekly Sabbath offer? The need for physical rest and weekly worship would be nonexistent as each day's work would be an act of worship and each week a continuation of the enjoyment of God's rest. It would be nonsensical to prohibit any work save those rendered for mercy's sake, for what famished mouth

9. Scripture distinguishes between "righteous" and "ritual" commands within the Mosaic Law. This two-fold construct is developed further in chapters 4 and 8.

would beg food, what infirmed body would require salve, or what prisoner would yearn visitation? What necessities of work would militate against keeping the Sabbath in a perfect world? The Sabbath was made for man—a sinful man—not a prelapsarian man. The Sabbath commandment was predicated upon the fact that Adam's sin put God's rest out of reach. Not only must man have been created before the proclamation of the Sabbath commandment, but the disruption of God's rest had to first occur also. The Mosaic Sabbath could not have any meaning otherwise. So, both order and precedence argue against any supposed intrinsic morality of the Sabbath or any form of a universal obligation to observe the Sabbath ritual.

God's Work During the Rest

Yet the stroke of Moses' pen presents us with wonderment, for "on the *seventh* day God ended his work which he had done (*asah*)" (Gen 2:2). One would expect His work to have been complete on the sixth day considering His statement of full acceptance and satisfaction with everything that He had made. Indeed, the New English Bible translation apparently perceived this as an error and records, "On the *sixth* day God completed all the work he had been doing," substituting the word "sixth" for "seventh."[10] However, most translations retain the number "seven" despite the apparent contradiction, though some publish "*By* the seventh day . . ." If God completed the creation on the sixth day and abstained from all creative work on the seventh day, why does the Scripture imply a work of God on His day of rest? Scripture advances that the sixth day ended with a sinless man and woman, because "God saw every thing that He had made, and, indeed it was very good" (Gen 1:31), but interestingly, the seventh day does not warrant such an affirming conclusion. This poses the possibility of one more, non-creative work on the seventh day. Heschel and Kaplan suggest that the blessing of the seventh day itself was the special work accomplished.[11]

The naming of Eve as "the mother of all living" (Gen 3:20) was recorded after the pronouncement of the curse, indicating Adam's understanding that she had or would become pregnant after they had sinned against God. Since all successors of Adam and Eve incurred the curse of death (Rom 5:12; Ps 51:5), it follows that the conception of Cain ensued the fall. The days that passed must have been few because the first commandment to our first parents was to be fruitful and multiply.

Also present in the garden was the devil who should not be expected to allow Adam and Eve to enjoy Eden for days before deciding to overthrow their peace and harmony with God. Though the time they spent in the garden of Eden is open to conjecture, the presence of Satan in the garden, Eve's fertility, the dominion mandate, and the fact that Cain was conceived in sin, point to a rather brief period of time. Not only that, the contextual timetable describes the disruption of the seventh-day rest and their immediate banishment. Therefore, it is not only possible, but probable, that

10. NEB, 2.

11. Heschel, *Sabbath*, 22. Heschel proposes that *menuah* was created on the Sabbath. This word is taken to mean tranquility, serenity, peace, repose, happiness, stillness, and harmony. Kaplan, *Sabbath*, 20.

Adam and Eve sinned upon the seventh day, that is, the day following their creation.[12] In this proposed scenario, God is expected to speak to the offense before the day ended (Eph 4:26) and contingent upon their humility and repentance, provide a bloody sacrifice for their sins. Thus, on the seventh day in which He "rested," God the Savior also performed a work of redemption for Adam and Eve. Instead of enjoying God's rest in obedience, Adam and Eve were expelled, albeit with two divine statements in which to put their confidence: the promise of a Seed and their sin-covering skins (His word and a sign). That Adam and Eve sinned so soon following their creation is not a novel thought, for the Jewish rabbis conjectured that Adam must have sinned just prior to the commencement of the seventh day, for, on account of their lofty view of the Sabbath, God would not have executed the death penalty on that day.[13] In a recent work, James Jordan demonstrates a relationship between the first sin and the seventh day (which he calls the Sabbath) in his analysis of the chiasmatic parallels of Genesis 1 and Genesis 2.[14] A disrupted rest rectified by redemption is the repetitive type in the OT. Furthermore, it is possible that there is a dual meaning to the absence of the phrase, "The evening and the morning were the seventh day; and God saw all that He made and it was very good," that followed the previous six days. Commentators already note that without the statement "evening and morning" we are justified in proposing that the character of the seventh day was intended to last forever. Likewise, the omission of "God saw that it was good" indicates that upon the end of the seventh day, it was no longer "very good." Based upon the scriptural implication of a non-creative work on the seventh day (Gen 2:2) and the likelihood that Adam and Eve sinned upon the seventh day, thus requiring the redemptive work of God, the seventh day of rest is charged with even greater redemptive meaning.

The creation account (Gen 1:1—2:3) and the account of the fall (Gen 2:4—3:24) are *separate* redemptive types that, though proximate, should not be confused. 1) The creation account highlights the pattern of dark/light during six days work culminating in the Lord's satisfaction with His work on the seventh day of rest. On the first day, darkness is marvelously answered by the light of His word. His work and His alone, over the course of time and under His sovereign design, results in the perfection symbolized by the seventh day of rest. This state of blessed rest is a type of the *vita aeterna*, an unending and holy fellowship of God and man and nature. 2) The *lapsus* account introduces the darkness of heart that calls for the redemptive work of God. The fall of Adam on that seventh day (dark) is answered by the redemptive work of the Lord (light) that same day through the provision of two coats of skins, ending, of course, in the Lord's propitiatory satisfaction with the erring humans. As with creation, redemption is God's work to accomplish, so the feeble effort on the part of Adam and Eve to deal with their guilt was rejected and His own provision was accepted.

12. Primus, "Sunday," 102. Primus documents Luther's determination that the fall took place on the seventh-day.

13. Edersheim, *Temple*, 130 (his footnote number one).

14. Jordan, *Creation in Six Days*, 153. A chiasmus is a literary structure of inverse parallelism, which in its most basic form follows the pattern A B B' A'. This is further discussed in Chap. 12.

As the creation story unfolds, the splendor and magnificence of God's handiwork is quickly spoiled by sin, requiring the Lord to immediately "do the dirty work" of slaying two animals (in prefigurement of Christ) for the first two sinners, and expelling them from their former exalted status. No sooner did the Lord complete the work of creation that He began the work of redemption. This was not a surprise, for from the beginning, Christ was to be slain for the sin of mankind (1 Pet 1:20; Rev 3:1–8). The post-creation rest of God served as a type of the final redemption, which has now been accomplished by Jesus Christ (Rom 5:14).

THE CREATION SABBATH?

Jewish Thought Correlates the Sabbath with Genesis

Marva Dawn quotes from Chaim Grade's memoirs in which he recalls the admonition of a Hassidic Jew to cherish the Sabbath regardless of circumstances that hinder obedience. Upon hearing that Chaim had studied the Torah, the zealot resumed, "Since the young man once studied the Torah, he surely knows that the Sabbath is a secret token between the Jewish people and the Master of the Universe."[15] Chaim Raphael, after dismissing a theorized connection between the Jewish Sabbath and the Babylonian Shappatu, exclaims "It is more natural to see the Sabbath as wholly at home among the Hebrews themselves."[16] The Sabbath was coeval with the Decalogue, not creation. The Jews correctly understand the Sabbath to have had its inception following the exodus, but ascribe special weight to it on account that the Lord followed a similar pattern Himself in the first creation week. While Jewish writers may sometimes refer to the seventh day of creation as God's Sabbath, it is done metaphorically. "There are good reasons to avoid calling the seventh day a Sabbath in Genesis 2," says Samuel Meier, "Most important is that although the seventh day is a rest for God, it marks a day of labor for humans."[17]

With a rather superficial understanding of the connection between the Sabbath and the seventh-day rest, the example of God in creation merely provides the impetus to take Sabbath-keeping more seriously. Heschel notes that time was the first thing to be hallowed by God after the creation, specifically the seventh day (Gen 2:3), but the uniqueness of the hallowed seventh-day rest is that it was the last 24-hour period in the beginning. The text does not state that God hallowed every *seventh* day following the creation, only that particular seventh day of the first week. Furthermore, were there not created things, there would not have been a sanctification of the seventh day. That is, if six days transpired without the creation of a single thing, then God would not have sanctified the seventh day. The sanctification is not based simply on the passage of time but on the fact that the material universe was spoken forth over the course of six days culminating in the creation of mankind, made in His image and in a holy relationship with the Creator.

15. Dawn, *Keeping the Sabbath*, 106.

16. Raphael, *Festivals*, 61.

17. Meier, "Sabbath and Purification Cycles," 5.

Leo Trepp concurs with the idea that the Sabbath is a celebration of time and adds the element of social justice.

> The version in Exodus emphasizes the call for cessation from work in order that we may celebrate God's sacred time. The version in Deuteronomy places emphasis on the ethical implications: equality of man, man's stewardship over nature . . . The key to the second version is social justice. The servant is to rest 'as you do;' he is equal to yourself . . . The Sabbath is the road from slavery to freedom.[18]

Unfortunately, Trepp fails to notice that the servant of the Jew remained a servant in spite of having rested with his owner on the Sabbath, thus he is never really "free" in the same sense as his master. In fact, the first ordinances mentioned after the Decalogue involve master and servant relations; therefore, the Sabbath commandment itself does not pave a road toward freedom and equality among men—it merely shared the temporal blessing of the master with the slave. But if sharing blessings between owners and slaves meant anything, it should be that the Sabbath rest prefigured ultimate freedom by the coming of the Messiah who would redeem all Israel, including those foreigners who owned the God of Israel. Thus, the slave as well as his master could cherish a sense of hope for universal freedom through Sabbath observance, but the Sabbath itself did not provide freedom. If the Sabbath is the road from slavery to freedom, then the Sabbath must begin in slavery. The reality is that the seventh day of creation began in freedom but ended in slavery to sin, so the Sabbath was but a token of that freedom lost and a shadow of the everlasting freedom to be regained. Indeed, as Job observed, it was only in death that a slave achieved real and final freedom (Job 3:19).

Later, Trepp describes a modern day servant of the Jewish household: "a *Shabbes Goy*, a Gentile with whom it was arranged beforehand to turn out the light, heat the stove in the morning, milk the cows, and perform the essential chores."[19] Apparently, those who employ such a person do not take seriously the command to allow the servants to "rest as well as you" (Deut 5:14). This apparent contradiction elicits a recurring question among practicing Jews: Why are Gentiles disallowed from keeping *Shabbat*? The answer is based on a Talmudic rendering (b. Sanh. 58b) of Genesis 8:22, "From now, all the days of the world, sowing and harvesting, cold and heat, summer and winter; day and night they [the sons of Noah] shall not rest."[20] In other words, the world population may never enjoy a day of rest. However, the gift of the Sabbath to the Jews provided temporary relief from this perpetual curse. Thus, the Rabbis, for the most part, held that the Sabbath was not intended for the Gentiles and traced its obligation to Mount Sinai.[21] Since Gentiles were not required to obey the fourth commandment, the servant mentioned in Deuteronomy 5:14 is believed to be a Jewish slave rather than a Gentile slave.

18. Trepp, *Book of Jewish Observance*, 67.

19. Ibid., 71. The Christian Sabbatarian will perform these works himself, citing the "works of necessity" exemption.

20. Adler, "Sabbath Observing Gentile," 7–18.

21. Edersheim, *Temple*, 120.

The Jews properly took note that the Sabbath institution directed their attention to creation, but they have mistakenly taught that the reason for this is to promote a respect for time. Also, since the Law demands the Jew to respect his slave in Sabbath-keeping, they have piously made the Sabbath stand for "social justice."[22] These proposed meanings do no justice to the glory of God in proclaiming redemption to His chosen people, both Jew and Gentile. There really is no Sabbath in Genesis—neither a set schedule for a release from labors, nor a weekly regulation for the worship of God—only a shadow or prototype of the Jewish Sabbath to be given millennia later, which would be accompanied by eleven other ceremonial laws of time, which, in turn, are types of the person and work of Jesus Christ in redemption.

Sabbatarian Arguments for the Sabbath in Genesis

Worship is a matter of our createdness and consciousness. Because we are living souls, we are compelled intrinsically to worship something and as a practical matter to do so at set times. It is only through the enlightenment of the Holy Spirit that we can know *whom* to worship and through the written revelation of God that we know *when* and *how* to worship. The day, time, and frequency of worship are not matters of natural law, but of God's revelatory law. There is no evidence that fallen mankind, apart from special revelation, ever understood how to worship God in spirit and in truth, let alone to rest from his labors on the seventh day of the week, or one day in seven. As we would expect, the patriarchs occasionally set aside time for the worship of God (Gen 4:3; 8:20), but there is no indication of Sabbath-keeping or any inchoate sabbatism.

Yet Sabbatarians begin with the assumption that the moral imperative for worship cannot take place outside the context of the Sabbath. Francis Turretin, a sixteenth-century theologian, listed the basic requirements of the moral aspect of the Sabbath command: "to celebrate the memory of the creation, contemplating the works of God, and the public worship of God," to which he added later, "for the rest of man like the rest of God."[23] However, he could not assign morality to the day of the week or to the sequence of days, as if one specific day of the week (i.e. Saturday) is in itself more holy or good than any other day. Turretin honestly notes that there is no mention of the Sabbath in the lives of the patriarchs, but assumes that they must have engaged in some form of public worship. However, regular worship of a public nature does not require the Sabbath institution to validate it. That is, we would expect the patriarchs to have worshipped the Lord, and indeed, Scripture records such instances, but their worship is never described in terms of Sabbath-keeping for the simple reason that there was no Sabbath commandment. Unsatisfied with the possibility that the ancient saints could worship God without a Sabbath, some authors, like Dabney, make much of the appearance of the pattern of seven days in pre-Mosaic times, such as Noah waiting seven days for the rain to begin to flood the earth (Gen 7:10); Noah waiting seven day intervals for the return of the dove (Gen 8:10,12); and the remaining family of Joseph mourn-

22. This is echoed by Joseph Ratzinger (a.k.a. Pope Benedict XVI) in "'In the Beginning . . .'" 31.

23. Turretin, *Elenctic Theology*, 2:82, 83.

ing his death for seven days (Gen 50:10), claiming that "the seventh day was evidently observed for religious worship and oblation by the human family."[24] Dabney asserts that the day on which Cain and Abel offered their sacrifices "was most likely the end of the week, the Sabbath day,"[25] but it is his zeal for the Lord's Day that prejudices this conjecture. These verses do not state on what day of the week the measure of seven days began or ended. They do not hint at worship, either congregationally or familially.

If there was ever a time that the Sabbath could have been mentioned, it would have been during Joseph's fourteen years as prime minister in Egypt (Gen 41:46—42:5). The description of Joseph's work for Pharaoh gives every indication that they reaped seven days a week during harvest the first seven years and that they sold grain seven days a week in the latter seven years. Noah worked on the construction of the ark for 120 years and there is no indication that his work was interrupted by a weekly Sabbath rest. Even aboard the ark, tending to the needs of the animals, Noah did not observe a Sabbath. Justin noted that none of the early saints from Adam to Noah and up until Moses ever kept Sabbaths.

> Therefore to you alone this circumcision was necessary, in order that the people may be no people, and the nation no nation; as also Hosea, one of the twelve prophets, declares. Moreover, all those righteous men already mentioned, though they kept no Sabbaths, were pleasing to God; and after them Abraham with all his descendants until Moses.[26]

These considerations do not deter Sabbatarian authors and pedagogues from envisioning the Sabbath on the seventh day of creation.[27] One could call it a Sabbath rest for God, but God does not call it so. Marva Dawn quotes Genesis 2:3 as the opening verse for the first chapter in her book and eisegetically replaces the word "seventh" with "Sabbath."[28] O. Palmer Robertson made the same mistake,[29] but not the author of Hebrews (Heb 4:4).

Despite the want of Sabbath observance in Genesis, European Christians accepted the theory of a creational sabbatic worship and became convinced that anthropological studies would confirm that the Sabbath was practiced among primitive nations. It was supposed that the Sabbath was the original model of the human consecration of time to God and that all pagan calendar observances devolved from a sabbatic structure. Hence, any similarities between pagan and Hebrew ceremonies were taken as evidence of a creational Sabbath. However, the claim that other nations practiced a Sabbath before the birth of Israel has never been confirmed.[30] This is consistent with the biblical record that Israel was given the Sabbath and other ceremonies of time after the exodus

24. Dabney, "Sabbath of the State," 2:611.
25. Dabney, "The Christian Sabbath," 1:503.
26. Justin, *Dial.* 19 (*ANF* 1:204).
27. Williamson, *Shorter Catechism*, 41–45.
28. Dawn, *Keeping the Sabbath*, 2.
29. Robertson, *Christ of the Covenants*, 68.
30. Rordorf, *Sunday*, 19.

by divine revelation. The biblical record also demonstrates the development of faithless will-worship among the sons of Cain in rebellion to the truth. Even secular inquiries into the origin of rest days among primitive peoples demonstrate their association with superstition and fear, hardly the underpinnings of a divinely decreed calendar of holy days. The attempts to discover similarities between pagan and Hebrew rituals has led secular anthropologists to view the rituals of the Hebrews as evolving from the taboos and traditions of those cultures surrounding them.[31] Drawing upon the custom of Tongans to proscribe work during their first fruits ceremony, Hutton Webster determined that Israel's feasts were similar in origin.

> Since a like restriction was attached to the Hebrew Day of Firstfruits, we may surmise with some probability that abstinence from labour at this time was observed by the early Hebrews as a primitive taboo long before the festival was definitely consecrated to Jehovah. It is difficult to avoid the same conclusion with respect to the sabbatarian rules which invested other agricultural festivals of the Hebrews.[32]

Dismissing the possibility that God gave the Jews specific calendar holy days and their associated duties with a mind to their spiritual and eschatological significance, modern critics assume that the roots of Jewish holy days are in ancient and primitive taboos. Instead, the Lord prescribed set worship for the Jews based on historical events that He decreed and that prefigured future events that He also decrees.

By placing the Sabbath at creation and giving it the primary meaning of physical rest and worship, Reformed authors have limited their vision of the typology of the first seven days of creation (and other sabbatic types) and reduced it to an analogy for ethical behavior, i.e., to work six days and to rest one day. That is, by mistakenly placing the Sabbath at creation, the redemptive and Christocentric type has been preempted in favor of what Christians must do. For example, John Murray imagines a Sabbath presence in Genesis and diminishes the association between the seventh-day rest and redemption.

> [The Sabbath] belongs, therefore, to the order of things which God established for man at the beginning. It is relevant quite apart from sin and the need of redemption.
>
> As an institution it antedated the fall of man and would have been, therefore, a feature of man's obedience in a perfect state of integrity and bliss.[33]

Thomas Shepard (1605–1649) completely dissociates God's rest from redemption: "[The Sabbath] did not typify either our rest in Christ from sin in this life, or our rest with God in heaven in another life."[34] James Durham (1622–1658) claimed it is

31. To this I would add Kline's comparison of the Decalogue to suzereignty treaties in the ancient Near East. Kline, "The Two Tables of the Covenant," *WTJ*, 22:133–46.

32. Webster, *Rest Days*, 91.

33. Murray, *Collected Writings*, 1:206, 208. Also, Downey, "The Sabbath," n.p. "It has no specific redemptive element..."

34. Shepard, *Theses Sabbaticae*, 171. Less discerning Sabbatarians relate the pre-fall seventh-day rest of God to redemption. For example, Tangelder says, "The seventh-day Sabbath as [a] day of rest has a

"hard to show" any foreshadowing of Christ.[35] The proleptic placement of the Sabbath at the end of the creation week leads to the untenable position that the seventh-day rest of God had nothing or little to do with redemption. This misconstruction diminishes from the glory of God and is inimical to disciplines of Reformed interpretation and theology. What is presented at the end of the creation week is the historical reality of God's rest, which, by design, is a type of Christ's redemption. Secondarily, the creation week provided the impetus for the generations of man to measure time in periods of seven days as a symbol of God's perfection.

Origins of the Week

Worldly historians propose that the week was necessary to provide a unit of measurement of time between the day and the month, but without the biblical perspective on human origins, they have a proclivity to propose a paganized explanation for the week. There may be an intellectual reluctance to acknowledge the ancient use of the week, for it lends credence to the biblical record of creation. If the religion of the Jews was mythologized, then *a priori*, they would have assimilated their beliefs from other cultures. The implication is that if the Jews borrowed the week from the Chaldeans, then their story of the creation must have been derived later as a popular myth. The biblical account presents cultures as having derived from the descendants of Noah, scattering across the globe and moving away from the history and context of biblical truth. The week, therefore, would be best preserved in the Hebrew culture and only weakly preserved in cultures that strayed from their origins.

Genesis mentions the week (*shabua*) prior to the rise of national Israel (Gen 29:27); therefore, the concept of the week, or seven-period, predates the exodus and Judaism. Though the creation of the heavenly bodies was specifically given to measure the time of man's work (Gen 1:14), the week is not directly related to the movement of the stars or planets. Certainly, the fact that the week exists is a testimony to the historical creation of the world and the transmission of the Genesis record via oral tradition through early peoples. However, the mention of a week in Genesis no more indicates Sabbath-keeping than the mention of a month indicates observance of the New Moon. Moses' precision in the selection of words to delineate the passage of time during the Genesiac epoch tells us that time was measured, but not revered. It is only reasonable that, as pagan cultures distanced themselves from their godly roots, their concept of the week became distorted: shortened or lengthened, memorialized or regarded as common, and based on half-truths or false religion. Thus, from a biblical perspective, the week would have been best preserved among Adam's godly line as a memorial of the creation week. Any pagan memorialization approximating the number seven would be a corruption of the creation week.

David Duncan states that the Romans were already friendly to the idea of a seven day week because they believed each of the seven then-known planets affected a day of

vital place in the history of redemption," in "Celebrating the Lord's Day," part 1, 13.

35. Durham, *Exposition of the Ten Commandments*, 214.

the week, but that the belief actually originated with the Babylonians in 700 BCE.[36] The biblical record demonstrates a possible connection when the Jewish culture influenced the Babylonians. At the time of King Hezekiah's reign, three kingdoms were vying for power: the Hebrews, the Assyrians, and the Babylonians. From 732 to 721 BCE the Assyrians assaulted Israel and Judah, eventually taking captive the inhabitants of the Northern Kingdom and dispersing them throughout Assyria and Medo-Persia (2 Kgs 17:1–6; 18:9–11). Hezekiah, King of Judah, resisted the Assyrians and defeated the Philistines during the early years of his reign (2 Kgs 18:7–8). A succeeding Assyrian king, Sennacherib, led two assaults against Judah. During the first invasion, Hezekiah relied upon his allies to help, so the Lord allowed defeat, and Hezekiah was forced to make annual payments of gold and silver. When the second invasion mounted, Hezekiah sought the counsel of the prophet Isaiah and put his confidence in the Lord, who, for the sake of a remnant of Israel, smote 185,000 Assyrian soldiers (2 Kgs 19:35). No doubt the news of this devastating loss of lives and the subsequent murder of Sennacherib by his own sons reached the home of the Babylonians, a rising power in the East. News too, of Hezekiah's sickness and miraculous recovery made its way to Berodach-baladan, son of Baladan, King of Babylon, who sent letters and a present to Hezekiah (2 Kgs 19:12), circa 703 to 701 BCE. The interest of the Babylonians in Hezekiah's recovery from a sickness to death was not merely that he appeared to be a viable confederate against Assyria. Remembering the miracle of the reversal by ten degrees of the shadow on the sundial, the Babylonians may have deducted that Hezekiah gained favor with their sun-god, Shamash. When Hezekiah allowed a Babylonian embassy to witness the strength and grandeur of his kingdom (2 Chr 32:31), the occasion arose to influence the early Babylonian culture with Jewish concepts of time. Thus, the Babylonians may have adopted the weekly pattern from the Jews and assigned names to each of the days of the week, beginning with Sun-day.

The influence of pagan cultures on the Jewish tradition appears to be unilateral as Scripture notes with dismal regularity the failure of the Jews to remain focused on the commandments they were given in the wilderness (Ezek 8:7–15). However, Israel had a mandate to be a light to the world, which was partly fulfilled (Isa 26:15). The power of influence did not lay directly on the righteousness of Israel to affect other societies, but with God who works all things after His sovereign will. Yet the Jews were compelled from time to time to engage and enlighten pagan societies with their knowledge of the God Most High. For example, Duncan states that Roman legend attributes their calendar to Romulus who founded the city in 735 BCE. Originally based on ten lunar months with no accounting for the week, somehow the Romans transitioned to a calendar system that employed seven days in the week. From an excavation of Pompeii, a hexagonal diagram was discovered that provided an explanation for the naming of the seven days of the week.

> The order of the day names themselves comes from ancient Mesopotamian astrologers' attaching a planet-god to preside over each hour of the day, arranged

36. Duncan, *Calendar*, 45.

> according to their correct cosmological order. For instance, Saturn controlled the first hour of Saturn's day (Saturday), followed in its second hour by Jupiter, then by Mars, the Sun, Venus, Mercury, and the Moon. In the eighth hour, the cycle started again with Saturn, and the progression repeated until the 24th hour of the day, which happened to fall to Mars. Because the next hour in the cycle—the first hour of the new day—belonged to the sun god, the day after Saturday was called Sunday.[37]

While Duncan does not attempt to explain why the early Romans adopted a *seven-day* week, the only culture that accounted for a cycle of seven days, spanned the centuries from early Mesopotamia to Rome, and interacted with these cultures while retaining its own identity was Judaism. Duncan mentions that various cultures across time and continents have had weeks of five to ten days, but it is the Jewish week that traces its origin to the beginning of creation, and is so deeply imbedded in Jewish custom that it has affected surrounding cultures. The early use of the concept of the week in civilized history, coupled with the profound Jewish influence through Sabbath practice, demonstrates that the week is a testimony to the creation of God. It is to the discredit of pagans to have become accustomed to the week yet at the same time deny the creation. This is why Christians must not waver on a literal understanding of the creation week, on its beginning by the spoken word of God, and our knowledge of this through special revelation.

THE GIVER OF REST

Noah, the Second Prototype of the Sabbath

A second prototype of eternal rest is evident in the life of Noah. At his birth, Lamech's patriarchal blessing forecasted Noah's life work: "And he called his name Noah, saying, 'This one will comfort us concerning our work and the toil of our hands, because of the ground which the *Lord* has cursed'" (Gen 5:29). Lamech was aware of the reality of the curse, perhaps even tired of fighting for his livelihood over a course of centuries, for his hope was that Noah was chosen to restore the creation rest, thus ending the toil of mankind. Various commentators suppose Noah's name is derived from *nuach*, the Hebrew word for "rest." Interestingly, the first occurrence of this word (*nuach*) is when Noah's ark comes to rest (*nuach*) upon the mountain (Gen 8:4), indicating the completion of God's judgment upon sin and the renewal of fellowship with God. Perhaps Lamech's expectation was that Noah was the promised seed who should reverse the curse of the ground, but little did Lamech know that the world would increase in wickedness, requiring God to eventually curse the ground a second time with a judgmental deluge. Noah himself was a second Adam, repopulating the cleansed earth through his three sons and reestablishing a garden through which God would bless his labors. Considering the ark as a type of Christ, those in Him are kept safe from the flood of God's judgment and are assured to eventually come to a place of redemptive rest. The

37. Ibid., 47.

holiness of the seventh day was recapitulated in the sacrificial elements of Noah's offering (Gen 8:20–21).

For the patriarchs, each birth brought them back to the sixth day, as it were, because it reenacted the creation of mankind, restoring the hope that this new man would bring rest—an eternal rest—the next day. Noah's birth was such an event, for his life's work brought redemption and restoration. In a sense, the flood returned the physical earth to an empty sphere, without form and void, whereas before, it was filled with violence and corruption (Gen 6:11). Then the Spirit of God went over the face of the earth, again distinguishing land masses and bodies of water, just as He did in the first creation. As Noah emerged from the ark, it was another "sixth day" in which the Lord repeated the command given to Adam, "Be fruitful and multiply, and fill the earth" (Gen 9:1). On the next day, Noah's sacrifice of thanksgiving was a smell of "rest" to God (Gen 8:21), who in turn, made promises of blessings to Noah and his successive generations. Then again, the ark as a type of salvation was the result of the selfless work of Noah, some one hundred twenty years,[38] and eventually ended its purpose on Mount Ararat by coming to "rest" (Gen 8:4; another six plus one pattern). The very curse that brought catastrophic death to man and animal alike was the means by which Noah and his family were saved (1 Pet 3:20). Likewise, the baptism of death suffered by Christ is the means by which we obtain eternal life (Matt 20:23). Not only was Noah the preserved remnant through whom came the promised rest (Luke 3:36), he foreshadowed the work and saving efficacy of Christ from catastrophic judgment.

It could be said that the changes following the flood, such as a shortened life span, edible animals, and predictable seasons, were a blessing to mankind and a partial fulfillment of Lamech's prophecy; but Noah was not the one through whom eternal rest would come, for he too, would succumb to sin or be subject to sin by the fruits of his garden, and through Ham's indiscretion and rebellion, curse Canaan to a life of servitude.

> So Noah awoke from his wine, and knew what his younger son had done to him. Then he said: "Cursed be Canaan; A servant of servants He shall be to his brethren." And he said: "Blessed be the *Lord*, The God of Shem, And may Canaan be his servant. May God enlarge Japheth, And may he dwell in the tents of Shem; And may Canaan be his servant." (Gen 9:24–27)

Not only would the blessed sons continue to experience the sweat of their brow and the thorns of the field in their labors, but the descendants of Canaan would be cursed to endure servitude to fellow man, an exacerbation of the curse of the ground. The need for reconciliation between men, for the removal of the curse of the ground, and for an enduring and personal fellowship with God became even more evident. Alas, Noah could not provide comfort or rest for humanity, but Christ Jesus the Lord, prefigured in Noah, would ensure a lasting rest to His people and an abiding comfort from all their sin (Isa 40:1–2). Unlike Noah, Christ would drink from the vine but would not be subverted from His mission by its charms (Matt 27:33). The earlier chapters of

38. (2 x 10 x 6) Second Adam, Tenth Generation, of Man (a six).

Genesis focus on the curse and the hope of restoration through the coming Savior, and the later chapters follow the life of Abraham and the promise of a land of rest in Canaan—the land of Noah's cursed grandson—indicating, in shadow, that blessings of rest will come through One who is cursed for our sakes (Gal 3:13–14). It is Christ who will be the giver of rest.

2

The First Sabbath in the Wilderness

SABBATH ORIGINS

THERE ARE ALWAYS QUESTIONS and controversies about origins. Genesis instructs us about the origins of mankind, their charge, and their tragic sin. Exodus discloses the origins of the nation Israel, her covenant with Jehovah, and her failures in the wilderness. Genesis ends with the death of Israel, the person; and Exodus begins with the birth of Israel, the nation. It is in the history of the redemption of the nation Israel that the Sabbath was instituted, after her redemption from Egypt but before her arrival at Mount Sinai to receive the Law (Exod 16:23–29). The focus of this chapter is the redemptive significance of the Sabbath as it was first presented to Israel. It is necessary, though, to review the hasty departure of Israel from Egypt to provide the backdrop for the initial Sabbath commandment in the wilderness.

The day before the exodus the Lord told Moses, "This month shall be your beginning of months; it shall be the first month of the year to you" (Exod 12:2). Patterned after the new beginnings of Noah (Gen 9:1–17) and Abraham (Gen 13:1–12), these words conveyed to Moses a daybreak of hope and a bright future for the Israelites. As the gestation period was then ended, Egypt was about to experience its final labor pains as God delivered Israel, His firstborn, from its womb. Yet in this promise of new beginnings is the ordinal number *first*, indicating that God would be regulating and ruling His people. The Lord then proceeded to describe the *first* of three rituals that the Israelites were to observe from one generation to the next. The Passover service was explained to Moses and Aaron to replay the following year with the selection of an unblemished yearling male lamb on the tenth day of that month (Exod 12:3–5). Then God commanded the Feast of Unleavened Bread: seven additional days to memorialize the redemption of Israel, beginning and ending with holy convocations in which *no manner of work was to be done* (Exod 12:14–20). These feast days with work restrictions are Sabbaths, and they were given to Israel before the weekly Sabbaths (Ex 16). Finally, the Lord delivered the law of the firstborn (Exod 13:11–16), completing a triad of preliminary signal ordinances that commemorated their redemption (Exod 12:13; 13:8–10).

After residing in Egypt 430 years, the Lord commanded the Israelites to journey on the fifteenth of Nisan from Rameses to encamp beside Pihahiroth near the Red Sea, giving the appearance to Egyptian scouts that they were stranded in the desert (Exod 14:1–3). The Egyptian army gathered against Israel, but the pillar of the Lord kept the two nations apart during the night, while the great sea was divided (Exod 14:20–22). By dawn, the Israelites crossed the Red Sea upon dry land (reminiscent of Noah's safety from the flood), and the Egyptians were drowned by the returning waters during their futile pursuit (Exod 14:23–31). The elapsed time from the exodus on the fifteenth of Nisan to the crossing of the Red Sea is not explicitly stated in Scripture, but Jewish tradition holds that it was seven days.[1] The Feast of Unleavened Bread (Exod 13:6–10; Lev 23:6–8) commemorates four aspects of the flight of Israel from Egypt: 1) a holy convocation commemorates the departure from Egypt (Lev 23:7; Num 33:3), 2) eating unleavened bread for seven days memorializes the seven day journey in the desert (Exod 12:15; Lev 23:6), 3) an "offering made by fire" consecrates this redemptive memorial to the Lord who brought death to the Egyptians but life to them (Exod 13:21; Lev 23:8; Num 28:19–24; 2 Cor 1:9–10), and 4) a second holy convocation commemorates the safe crossing of the Red Sea (Exod 14:29–31; Lev 23:8). The Israelites were given the Feast of Unleavened Bread to commemorate throughout their generations the "day" that the Lord brought them out of the land of Egypt (Exod 12:17). The Feast of Unleavened Bread is a ceremonial law, commemorative of redemption, and it begins and ends with sabbatic "holy convocations" during which no manner of work may be done (Exod 12:16; Lev 23:7–8; Num 28:25; Deut 16:8). This was the first time Israel was introduced to a sabbatic observance. Even though these days are not named "Sabbaths," they are regarded as Sabbaths in every sense of the word.[2] These first sabbatic rituals were redemptive, not creational. More importantly, the work restriction was a profound reminder that the Lord Himself performed the work of redemption on their behalf. Their doubled escape from the clenches of Egypt (the exodus and the Red Sea) made them doubly indebted to the Lord; they acknowledged this debt with a doublet of Sabbath days. These two annual Sabbaths of the Feast of Unleavened Bread were revealed to Israel *prior* to, and served as a conceptual *prelude* to, the weekly Sabbaths. If the Israelites knew what a Sabbath was, Moses could have penned the proper word for these two days, but the Lord did not introduce the word "Sabbath" until He commanded the weekly Sabbath weeks later.

After the Israelites crossed the Red Sea, "they went three days in the wilderness and found no water" (Exod 15:22). After thirty days of following the cloud and forlornly entering a wilderness area, they murmured about what they should eat. The Lord answered that He would provide quail at night and manna in the morning on a daily basis, except for the double portion on the sixth day, in order to reaffirm that it was He who brought them out of Egypt, that He had heard their complaint and would

1. Trepp, *Book of Jewish Observance*, 172.

2. Kurtz, *Offerings, Sacrifices, and Worship*, 356; Howard and Rosenthal, *Feasts*, 66.

supply their every need (Exod 16:6–7; cf. Ex 13:14). Not until the sixth day of the test was the weekly Sabbath introduced.

> Then he said to them, "This is what the Lord has said: 'Tomorrow is a Sabbath rest, a holy Sabbath to the Lord. Bake what you will bake today, and boil what you will boil; and lay up for yourselves all that remains, to be kept until morning.'"
>
> So they laid it up till morning, as Moses commanded; and it did not stink, nor were there any worms in it.
>
> Then Moses said, "Eat that today, for today is a Sabbath to the Lord; today you will not find it in the field.
>
> Six days you shall gather it, but on the seventh day, the Sabbath, there will be none."
>
> Now it happened that some of the people went out on the seventh day to gather, but they found none.
>
> And the Lord said to Moses, "How long do you refuse to keep My commandments and My laws?
>
> See! For the Lord has given you the Sabbath; therefore He gives you on the sixth day bread for two days. Let every man remain in his place; let no man go out of his place on the seventh day."
>
> So the people rested on the seventh day. (Exod 16:23–30)

The Sabbath, like the heaven-prepared manna, was a new experience for them and was predicated, first of all, on their worry about daily bread. The ritual of preparing food beforehand symbolically attested to the Lord's miraculous provision for their daily physical needs in the wilderness. There is no reference point for meal preparation the day before the Sabbath unless the manna was real manna and a double-portion of it was given on the sixth day. As presented to the Israelites only a month following the exodus, the heart of the Sabbath was to rest at home; they could not go out on the seventh day, at least not to go out and provide for their sustenance. They were not informed about the Sabbath until the sixth day when the double-portion of manna was prepared for them. Moses' personal and instructional manner regarding their Sabbath duties indicates the freshness and novelty of this ritual. The Israelites had to be instructed to remain inside because they were not habituated to a weekly rest. Resting was not something the Israelites were accustomed to—for over three hundred years of bondage the Israelites could not have practiced a Sabbath (Ex 5:5). This is unlike the Lord's chastisement of Moses for not being circumcised, in which the sign of the covenant with Abraham was expected to have been remembered and practiced (Exod 4:24–26). There was no rebuke for a forsaken Sabbath.

The Lord even commanded the preservation of an omer of manna as a physical testimony that He fed them in the wilderness after redeeming them from Egypt (Exod 16:32). Yet the portion of manna maintained in the ark did not putrefy or grow stale, shadowing forth the everlasting Bread of Life. As Moses reviewed the forty years of wilderness life, he understood the spiritual intent of manna: to cause those blessed by its honey taste and sapid texture to reflect upon the necessity of living by God's word (Deut 8:3). The important concern with the manna was its spiritual intent and foreshadowing essence. The miraculous preparation of it, the satisfying abundance of it, and the comforting, forty-year supply of it certainly accords with the daily need to partake of and depend upon God's word. But the manna was more than an ethical lesson for the daily life of Israel. Our Lord Jesus denied that it was the "true bread" from heaven (John 6:32–51), for if it were, it would have granted the recipients everlasting life! One need only believe in Jesus as the True Manna from heaven in order to live forever. The double-portion shadowed forth Christ, the manna of imperishable quality.

The Jews did not really labor for the manna; they neither sowed nor reaped to obtain it. It was sown in the graciousness of God, nurtured through His loving care, and miraculously delivered to the Israelites from God's heavenly abode. The only work related to the manna was the gathering and cooking of it, which was to be done before the Sabbath. The Israelites were already introduced to sabbatic days on which cooking was allowed (Exod 12:16), but these *weekly* Sabbaths, newly introduced by Moses, differed in that respect. He instructed them that there should be no cooking on the seventh day, so the Lord, in order to ready them for obedience, provided the day before the Sabbath manna sufficient for two days. At this institution of the weekly Sabbath, the Lord intimated a creation connection (prior to the explicit statement of such in the fourth commandment) simply by following the pattern of six days of work and one day of rest. But in terms of ensuring that the Israelites rest on the seventh day, the miraculous work of God in creation is hardly analogous to the mundane work of man. If the creation should be a model for how the Israelites should keep the Sabbath, then observe the behavior of Adam and Eve. They were not instructed to pick what fruit they desired on the sixth day and lay some of it aside for the following day. Indeed, they were able to eat freely from all legitimate trees every day of the week. As Ratzlaff pointed out, the commands to cook on the sixth day and to abide in their dwelling on the seventh day "would have been completely meaningless to Adam and Eve on that first seventh day *before sin entered*."[3]

The connection between the dispensation of the manna and the first week of creation must be along other lines of thought. Since Moses explained the spiritual intent of the manna to be the necessary element for spiritual life, and Jesus explained that the manna represented Him, then the correlation of the manna with the creation week must involve these same themes. Indeed, the manna of God's word was instrumental in the first week of creation, but on the sixth day came a double-portion of His word. Three possible explanations exist for a Genesiac sixth day double-portion. First of all, on the sixth day of creation, the Lord continued the progression of animals, but in Adam God created one to rule over the created world. Adam received a double-portion of God's creative attention because he was made in the image of God. He was above and separate from the rest of creation. Not only was he given life, but he received the breath of God and became a living soul. Adam was an extraordinary work, a double-portion in his own right (Gen 1:27). Secondly, Adam typified Christ who should descend from heaven and take on human flesh. Both through Adam's humanity and through Adam's typological intent, Christ should come. Adam was a

3. Ratzlaff, *Sabbath in Christ*, 74 (emphasis in the original).

double-portion because he represented all of humanity and he represented the second Adam. Lastly, when Adam was created, he contained within himself a double-portion of humanity, as it were, the female species, for out of his rib, the Lord fashioned Eve to be his helper, the mother of all living. The two were united into one, prefiguring the marriage of Christ to His believing church. Each of these sixth day double-portion ideas has a bearing on the nature of redemption.

The Israelites perhaps never asked themselves why they could not cook food or stray from their abodes on the Sabbath. They merely accepted that it epitomized unlawful work. And modern Sabbatarians seem not to ask themselves why they cook and leave their homes on their Christian Sabbath, simply accepting the notion that these commands must have been ceremonial. However, if these two commands are ceremonial, then so is the seventh-day rest that these commands are intended to sanctify. The Lord established a connection between the Sabbath and creation in order to cause the Israelites to reenact the prelapsarian garden experience of Adam and Eve when there was no need to prepare meals and no need to leave the garden of Eden. The Israelites were "playing out" the pre-fall history that prefigured the objective of Christ's work of redemption. Given to Israel for the first time in wilderness, the seventh-day rest and the requisite duties to secure that rest were clearly ceremonial.

Four ceremonial commandments were given to Israel before their arrival at Mount Sinai to receive the Law: 1) redemption of the firstborn (Exod 12:29; 13:12–15), 2) Passover (Exod 12:25–27, 42–47; 13:5–8; 23:17; 34:23–25), 3) Feast of Unleavened Bread (Exod 12:15, 17; 13:6–16; Lev 23:6–8), and 4) the weekly Sabbath (Exod 16:23–26, 29–30). Each one of these was specifically based on the redemption of Israel from 430 years' forced labor in Egypt and intended to ensure the remembrance of God's mighty deeds throughout the generations of Israel, and to serve the concealed purpose of foreshadowing the redemption of both Jew and Gentile through Jesus Christ. These rituals involved the Jews on an intense emotional and physical level. The reality of the exodus was to be remembered by every succeeding generation as if they themselves had just left. As received from the Lord in the "beginning of months," none of these rituals were mentioned prior to the exodus; none were demanded of the generations of man from Adam to Abraham, the Sabbath included. All of these ordinances were unique to the Jewish religion. Rest, then, commemorated two aspects of their redemption from Egypt: 1) freedom from grueling slave labor, and 2) internal rest from confidence in anything other than the Lord. This disposed the Israelites to look back in history with a thankful heart and to look forward in time with the confidence that God would sustain them and bring them into His presence. By engendering such trust, God proclaimed that He was able to deal with the greater needs of mankind: to erase the effects of sin in the world and to usher in an everlasting kingdom of creational rest. Of the feasts, the Sabbath takes the theme of redemption back to creation, and hence, it arises in prominence as the quintessential ceremony of the forthcoming redemption in Christ.

ARGUMENTS FOR A CREATION SABBATH

Swissman Francis Turretin

Turretin's arguments for the Sabbath's origination at the creation and the congruent ceremonial and moral essence of the Sabbath were influential in later Reformed analysis. Turretin asserted that the Sabbath originated prior to the wilderness on the basis of several points, which are answered as given.

> 1) "For God cannot be said to have blessed the seventh day and sanctified it unless by the institution of the Sabbath."[4]

Turretin advances a causal proposition, that God instituted the Sabbath by blessing and sanctifying the seventh day of creation. That God blessed the seventh day is not disputed, for the Scripture plainly states the fact, but it is difficult to state without prejudice that such a blessing instituted the Sabbath when the Sabbath is not even mentioned. Turretin excludes the possibility that God had any other purpose in blessing the seventh day than what he proposes. If the blessing of the seventh day effectively commanded Sabbath-keeping, why is there no mention of the Sabbath for the next 2,000 years of recorded history, especially given the monumental profile of weekly worshipping the God of creation? By disallowing any alternative explanation for the blessing of the seventh day, Turretin has set up a false disjunctive against any other exegesis. The previous chapter advances an alternative explanation for the blessing of the seventh day.

> 2) Exodus 16:23 "could not have been said unless the Sabbath had already been instituted and commanded by God."[5]

Turretin proposes that the language of Exodus 16:23–25 supports the conclusion that the Sabbath existed prior to that time. In reality, the text demonstrates that this is the first occurrence of the word Sabbath, and that it is clearly associated with the giving of manna, which began only six days prior. If the Sabbath was already understood by the Jews, why did Moses have to tell them not to gather manna on the morrow and why, despite Moses' warning, did some venture out to gather manna on the seventh day? The reason for the first Sabbath was because of the sequence of God's provision of manna. There was no Sabbath prior to the manna; only when God gave them two days worth of manna did He institute the Sabbath (Exod 16:29).

> 3) "The words of the fourth commandment ("Remember the Sabbath day, to keep it holy") plainly imply that this law was not then given for the first time."[6]

4. Turretin, *Elenctic Theology*, 2:79.

5. Ibid., 80. To this could be added the argument that Ex 16:29 uses the past tense, "the Lord gave you the Sabbath," implying its origin at creation. However, this verse occurs the day *after* the Sabbath was explained to Israel and after the Sabbath was profaned (while it was still the Sabbath), so the past tense is perfectly understandable for those circumstances.

6. Ibid.

Since the Israelites were given the Sabbath in the wilderness, it was certainly a day they could remember after they arrived at Mount Sinai to receive the Ten Commandments. When the Israelites were given the ritual in the desert, the Lord did not tell them to remember it. They had no greater notice for the Passover, which occurred the very night they were so commanded to obey it (Exod 12:42). The command to keep the Feast of Unleavened Bread was heralded by Moses, on the very day it commemorated, with these words, "Remember this day in which you went out of Egypt" (Exod 13:3). There is no compelling reason to propose that the Sabbath or any other ceremonial law existed *before* its first mention in the Bible simply because the Jew was asked to remember it.

> 4) That "the piety and religion of the ancient fathers confirm this very thing . . . [they] must have had some sacred and stated days in which to worship God and remember his blessings in the creation of heaven and earth."[7]

Turretin proposes that the piety and religion of the ancients confirm that the Sabbath began at creation, but advances no scriptural examples. Scripture gives several examples of the patriarch's form of worship prior to the exodus and none mention a day of rest, a pattern of recurrence, or a call to remember creation. Cain and Abel brought offerings of their work to the Lord in process of time (Gen 4:3–5), Enosh and others called upon the name of the Lord (Gen 4:26), Noah expressed gratitude to God by offering a sacrifice (Gen 8:20–21), and Abraham offered a ram atop a wooden pyre as an act of worship (Gen 22:5, 13). Turretin's assumption is that the patriarchs were unable to worship God outside the context of a Sabbath. This assumption has biased his exegesis.

> 5) "Monuments are extant among the heathen, both of the number seven in general as sacred and of the recurring seventh day held sacred among them."[8]

He quotes fragments of Clement of Alexandria, Philo, Josephus, Eusebius and others, several of which will be discussed in chapter 10. The quotes are merely opinions of the authors at their point of history (at or after the time of Christ) and offer no clear evidence of a recurring seventh day or Sabbath origins prior to the exodus of Israel. This proposition is invalid without archeological evidence. As will be discussed in other chapters, the number seven *is* divinely significant. Therefore, we expect the number seven and the measurement of time with a week to be popular in pagan cultures; but neither of these may be equated to Sabbath observance or provide unquestionable evidence that the Sabbath was practiced prior to the exodus.

Scottsman Charles Dabney

The late 1800s in American culture was a time of philosophical and political turmoil as anti-religionists battled for their own rights against what they deemed unnecessary and restrictive laws held over from America's Puritan heritage. Dabney's defense of

7. Ibid., 81.
8. Ibid., 82.

the Sabbath is but one part of a larger response to the humanistic and communistic assaults of the National Liberal League, led by Robert G. Ingersoll, which called for the taxation of church property, state control of education, the total separation of church and state, and the repeal of Sabbath laws. The atheists espoused a natural law of morality as opposed to any revelatory law, hence Dabney's attempt to defend the Sabbath as a natural law that existed from the creation of mankind. In order to defuse the argument that the Sabbath is a religious institution, Sabbatarians fervently postulated that the Sabbath existed in culture before the Jewish nation was born.

> By proving that the Sabbath command was anti-Levitical, was moral, was universal, and was perpetual, we effectually dispose of the false position, that it was abrogated with the shadows of the old dispensation . . . And our thesis as to the original institution of the Sabbath will be established by three proofs: ancient tradition, sacred history, and the physiologic and psychologic testimony of man's nature itself.[9]

Beginning with the assumption that the Sabbath originated at creation, Dabney expects to discover among the pagan cultures of antiquity the practice of seventh day rest and worship. His citation of the Greek philosopher Hesiod writing of the sacredness of the first, fourth and seventh day does little to support the theory of a universally observed Sabbath, even in rudimentary form. Nor does the menagerie of examples he offers make any mention of a recurring day of rest, but they do demonstrate the obvious: that religious peoples inevitably select a day or a string of days, on a recurrent or solitary basis, for the worship of their gods.

Archeology has determined that the ancient Babylonians observed a day called Shappatu, meaning "rest," but it is improbable that Shappatu was some Sabbath-relative since this *lunar* observance was based upon the notion that unlucky circumstances would befall those who ventured out.[10] With respect to this speculation, Chaim Raphael exclaims,

> It is safe to say that this kind of derivation for the Sabbath has little persuasiveness today. One would need firmer evidence for a connection. It is more natural to see the Sabbath as wholly at home among the Hebrews.[11]

Recognizing the historical uniqueness of the Sabbath, Reformed theologian Rushdoony flatly asserts, "A weekly day of rest is unknown to other cultures. Only where Biblical faith and culture have brought it about does it exist to this day."[12] His assertion is corroborated by Josephus, who mentions the influence of Judaism on "host" nations:

9. Dabney, "Sabbath of the State," 2:608.

10. Trepp, *Book of Jewish Observance*, 69. Heschel explains that the "Babylonian seventh day was observed on every seventh day of the lunar month" in *Sabbath*, 104.

11. Raphael, *Festivals*, 61.

12. Rushdoony, *Institutes of Biblical Law*, 128.

> There is not any city of the Grecians, nor any of the Barbarians, nor any nation whatsoever, whither our custom of resting on the seventh day hath not come.[13]

Neither archeology nor history has demonstrated the existence of a Sabbath practice prior to the Jewish state or outside of Jewish influence.

Contrary to Dabney's second line of proof, the sacred history of the church denies the existence of the Sabbath prior to the birth of the nation Israel. For example, second-century polemicist, Justin Martyr, explained that there was no Sabbath-keeping before Moses.

> For if one should wish to ask you why, since Enoch, Noah with his sons, and all others in similar circumstances, who neither were circumcised nor kept the Sabbath, pleased God, God demanded by other leaders, and by the giving of the law after the lapse of so many generations, that those who lived between the times of Abraham and of Moses be justified by circumcision and the other ordinances—to wit, the Sabbath, and sacrifices, and libation, and offerings.[14]

It was the distinctiveness of the ceremonial ordinances that separated the Hebrew nation to the God of their redemption, being endowed with great importance to the Jew in his duty to observe them as well as in his attitude when remembering them. As Kaplan summarized, "Without the Sabbath, the Jew would have vanished. It has been said that as much as the Jew has kept Shabbos, so has Shabbos kept the Jew."[15] Jewish theology denies the practice of Sabbath-keeping prior to the giving of the Law. Indeed, this theory was not advanced until after the Reformation, as will be demonstrated in chapter 10.

Dabney's third line of proof for an early Sabbath history is the supposed testimony of man's inherent need for cyclic rest, citing that travelers travel farther, armies march farther, and beasts of burden work better if they rest every seventh day. In fact, Sabbatarians have claimed that machines work more efficiently and razors keep their glimmering edge better if given a rest every seventh day. Of course, this argument doesn't say which day of the week must be the day of rest for the mechanical world because any day will do if "rest" is *all* that a Sabbath day entails. Nor does this argument say why living organisms perform more efficiently, are more healthy, and are longer-lived with a rest one day in seven as opposed to one day in six, or one day in eight. A non-Sabbatarian does not deny that occasional rest is beneficial for the mind and body, but if that is all that Sabbatarians want for humanity, working animals, and machines, then why must this be enforced with religious fervor? The more obvious physical need for cyclic rest is that which our body demands *daily*, yet Sabbatarians do not ask for civil legislation to force people to sleep every night. Since when does a physiologic need connote a moral obligation? The point is that if a cyclic rest is constitutional to our frame, then all humanity will ensure they achieve it regardless of statist or religious compulsion. However, despite the perceived benefits of a weekly low-stress

13. Josephus, *Against Apion* 2:40, 811.

14. *Justin, Dial.* 92 (*ANF* 1:245).

15. Kaplan, *Sabbath*, 5.

day, the universality of such a weekly physiologic need cannot be demonstrated in history or science. And even if someone felt they were more productive having rested one day in seven, then they may not really understand the character of the Sabbath, for as Lauren Winner surmised, "Rest for the sake of future productivity is at odds with the spirit of Shabbath."[16]

The implications of a moral Sabbath is that society should be made to rest by force of law, for as Dabney concludes, the state has the right "to enforce that outward observance of the Sabbath rest which alone makes the inculcation of God's fear and of public and private virtue practicable."[17] Dabney's arguments may have been effective in protracting the demise of Sabbath "blue laws," but within a hundred years most have been repealed or remain unenforced due to practical, economic, and constitutional concerns.[18] At the same time, the influence of Sabbatarianism on America's work ethic is indisputable, including the benefit of a culturally accepted six-day workweek, extra pay for working on Sunday, and non-discrimination of those who refuse to work on their day of worship. Nonetheless, the practice was based on a faulty premise, and with every benefit based on spurious premises there are untoward corollaries.

Dutchman J. Douma

Douma begins his contemporary exposition of the fourth commandment by acknowledging the hurdles facing the Sabbatarian viewpoint. First of all, he admits that the Sabbath is not mentioned until the exodus of Israel in the wilderness. He correctly admits that the concept of the week was understood by the patriarchs but cautions his readers from injecting the Sabbath into that period of time. Indeed, a search has been made for the Sabbath institution in other cultures, but to no avail. There simply was no Sabbath prior to the exodus. Secondly, he states that an honest exegesis of Genesis does not permit the discovery of the Sabbath for man—only God's rest on the seventh day. Yet, even after retracing these difficulties, Douma notes that when the Sabbath was given to Israel there is an "impression" that the Israelites already knew about it when the Lord said, "See! For the Lord has given you the Sabbath" (Exod 16:29). But this verse hardly gives reason to doubt the historic accuracy of the institution of the Sabbath for Israel in the wilderness. Knowing the weakness of this defense he continues:

> Nevertheless, taking into account all the data, it seems correct to speak of a Sabbath given *to Israel*, and incorrect to view it as a universal human institution, given in the beginning (after the Creation), which then later became an observance limited to Israel.[19]

At this point, his readers would expect him to conclude that the Ten Commandments contain a ceremonial institution for Israel alone; and that makes

16. Winner, *Mudhouse Sabbath*, 11.

17. Dabney, "Sabbath of the State," 2:616.

18. Harline, *Sunday*, 313–15.

19. Douma, *Ten Commandments*, 130 (emphasis in the original).

suspect all efforts to inculcate the Sabbath as an abiding institution for the church and for the world. Yet, Douma immediately cautions that "this does not yet mean that therefore we are free from the fourth commandment."

Douma also discusses the reference within the fourth commandment to the Genesis account of creation. He first states that Genesis "does not clearly indicate that God commanded Sabbath observance already in Paradise," and follows by acknowledging that the text of the fourth commandment does not affirm that the Sabbath was instituted at creation. Again, the unspoken conclusion is that the fourth commandment is not a universal dictum and did not find expression prior to the exodus of Israel. Notwithstanding, Douma cautions his readers that this fact "in no way restricts the validity of the fourth commandment to the nation of Israel." He acknowledges each biblical proof advanced by non-Sabbatarians, yet maintains that the fourth commandment is still universally relevant.

> If the Sabbath was not instituted at Creation, the fourth commandment is not therefore just a typical Jewish custom whose validity is restricted to ancient Israel. In order to defend the universal significance of the fourth commandment for the church and the world, we must not try to invoke the help of "natural reason."[20]

While he mounts up scriptural proofs against the very position he is defending, one wonders if he has a *coup d'éclat* to make sense of his irrationality. But there is none. He says, "it would be strange if before Sinai there was nothing reminding us of the fourth commandment." But why would it be strange when he just proved that the Sabbath was a Jewish institution? Why would it be strange that the Lord gave the Sabbath when He did, and not when Douma supposes it should have been given? It is only strange because he presupposes that the fourth commandment is essentially about worship, and that this Sabbath essence transcends time in both directions. It is strange because he presupposes that the fourth commandment is a moral commandment, a sort of gift to the human race that also embraces the occasional worship of the patriarchs and the weekly Sunday worship of Christians. In the end, Douma does not prove the validity of these presuppositions. However, he does rightfully acknowledge that the "Sabbath is described for us as a sign of the covenant between Yahweh and Israel (Exod 31:12–17; Ezek 20:20)."[21] While he misses the significance of this statement, it is for this very reason that the Sabbath was incorporated into the summary of the covenant as the fourth commandment.

SIGNS AND MEMORIALS

Signal Commandments

The word "sign" is translated from derivatives of Hebrew (*owth*) and Greek (*semeion*) and has a semantic range of meanings: "mark," "miracle," "prophecy," "token," "evi-

20. Ibid., 132.

21. Ibid., 130.

dence," and "monument." In Genesis, the mark for Cain was a reminder to him and others of God's gracious protection of his life even though he murdered his brother Abel (Gen 4:16). The rainbow was a sign to Noah and continues to be a sign to successive generations of God's promise not to flood the earth again (Gen 9:16–17). Circumcision was a sign to Abraham of his covenant with the Lord (Gen 17:11). The exodus and journey to Mount Sinai were a sign to the Israelites that Moses was indeed sent by the Lord (Exod 3:12). The blood on the door posts was a sign to God where the believing families were residing (Exod 12:13). The Feast of Unleavened Bread (Exod 13:9), the law of the firstborn (Exod 13:16), and the Sabbath (Exod 31:13, 17) were all signs of God's power to redeem Israel from Egypt. A sign established or identified by God is usually a visual or tangible reminder or representation of a historical experience in order to stir up action, belief, or caution. Signs communicate ideas associated with the sign and demand a response (Exod 4:8–9). In other words, a sign takes second place to the idea or event that it signifies or represents. Notwithstanding Jesus' apparent denigration of signs to the Pharisees, He essentially identified Himself as the fulfillment of the signs of Scripture. He fulfilled the sign of Jonah, not only in His preaching repentance to Israel (Luke 11:29–30), but in His forthcoming resurrection and preaching the kingdom of God to the Gentiles due to widespread Jewish unbelief (Matt 12:39–41). It is well-known that signs of the old covenant "had respect to and shadowed forth Christ who was to come," and, "were to continue until the time of reformation or the advent of Christ," but new covenant signs "regard Christ as having come," and, "continue until the end of the world."[22] The Sabbath was a sign of the old covenant (Exod 31:13, 17) that shadowed forth the glorious redemption in Jesus Christ and, having fulfilled that purpose, is no longer binding in any of its exterior rites.

The Sabbath Sign

The Jews then, kept the feast days and observances over the centuries in simple obedience, and when they slackened in attitude or failed in obedience, the faithful prophets of that day would call upon the people to repent and start afresh (Isa 56:1–7; Jer 17:24–25, 27; Neh 13:15–18). Of the calendar feasts, only the Feast of Unleavened Bread (Exod 13:8–10) and the Sabbath (Exod 31:13, 17; Ezek 20:12, 20) are specifically identified as signs by the Lord. Essentially, the Sabbath is no different than any of the other memorializing holy days of Israel's calendar that are integral to the Law (Exod 31:13). They were signs of Israel's participation in the Lord's covenant. It was as if each Israelite were affixing his signature to the covenantal document again and again, ratifying what was signified in the calendar rituals. However, the Sabbath, of all Jewish feasts, was the foremost sign of Israel's redemption. It not only memorialized their history of slavery in Egypt (signifying their spiritual separation from God), but it memorialized the fall of man through the creation connection (enlarging the significance of the need for spiritual redemption). Furthermore, the Sabbath memorialized

22. Turretin, *Elenctic Theology*, 3:370.

the miracle of the manna (signifying their need to hunger after the incarnate Word of God) and set in motion the recurring cycle of seven days (signifying the perfection of His answer to their need). Thus, it was the most frequent ceremonial law for the populace and had the most comprehensive set of rituals that foreshadowed redemption. All of this elevated the Sabbath ritual as the premier sign of Israel's redemptive covenant with the Lord.

Sabbath Memorializes Past Slavery

The memorialization of the exodus is most obvious in the Deuteronomic command that all Israelites remember from what they were redeemed: slavery in the land of Egypt.

> And remember that you were a slave in the land of Egypt, and the *Lord* your God brought you out from there by a mighty hand and by an outstretched arm; therefore the *Lord* your God commanded you to keep the Sabbath day. (Deut 5:15)

The emphasis is on what the Lord had done to rescue them, otherwise they would still be in Egypt toiling day after day for a less gracious ruler. Though remembrance is an introspective act, Jewish Sabbath liturgies encourage obedience to this command by the vocal acknowledgement that the Lord preserved Israel for her sanctification. To prevent a feeling of remoteness as a result of the centuries gone by, faithful Jews to this day consider themselves to have been slaves in Egypt so they may share the same sense of wonder and awe experienced by Israel, causing them to break out in song (Exod 15:1–18).

Furthermore, remembering past slavery is not so much about the problems of trafficking human flesh as it is about slavery to sin, a condition that still affected the Israelites in spite of their redemption from actual slavery. Free Israelites were allowed to maintain slaves themselves because the Lord wanted them to know that slavery to sin was still the prevailing issue; and their treatment of their slaves on the Sabbath was a sign that spoke of the day when the Lord should save them from their sins (Ps 130:7–8). The Sabbath commandment was based on the actual experience of deliverance from bondage in Egypt, but it was a sign of true redemption from sin. With the arrival of the Messiah and the fulfillment of the sign, it is no longer necessary to "act out" true redemption from sin by releasing a slave from work one day per week. Even as the slave was allowed to rest on the Sabbath, he was still a slave! But the Christian has been redeemed from sin, and on the basis of that truth, he can evangelize the slave so the slave could enjoy true spiritual freedom in the Lord, and not just give him a "day off" (1 Cor 7:20–22).

Sabbath Memorializes the Manna

Preparation of food prior to the Sabbath is an important aspect of Sabbath-keeping that memorializes the double-portion of manna provided in the wilderness. The remainder of the double-portion of manna given on Friday did not putrefy overnight, thus foretelling a better, eternal Manna that would never become corrupt, nor see corruption. Once the better Manna is eaten, there is no need for anything else—it is everlasting in its effect: "Whoever eats My flesh and drinks My blood has eternal life" (John 6:54). Jesus does not ask us to eat His body weekly, saving a double portion on the sixth day, like the physical manna that represented His body; this is a once-for-a-lifetime repast. During a discussion between Jesus and would-be disciples about the focus of their heart, the subject of miracles and signs arose.

> Therefore they said to Him, "What sign will You perform then, that we may see it and believe You? What work will You do?
>
> Our fathers ate the manna in the desert; as it is written, 'He gave them bread from heaven to eat.'" (John 6:30–31)

To which Jesus replied emphatically that He is the true Manna from heaven, from whom if anyone eats, shall never hunger. Jesus claimed to be the fulfillment of the manna sign. Therefore, by inference, because the Sabbath was predicated on the manna, Jesus fulfilled the Sabbath sign. He is both the Bread of Life and the Rest of God, and in each capacity He both feeds us and works for us. However, Jesus may benefit only those who come to Him on God's terms. The men who went out to look for manna on the seventh day were not only empty-handed, but had sinned against God. They had no part in the Sabbath. Likewise, the unbelieving have no part in that which the Sabbath foreshadowed: the heavenly rest. We are reminded that in the death of Jesus, He too, remained incorruptible. The cup-full of manna stored for the posterity of Israel in the ark of the covenant served as a type of the Manna from heaven, held in reverential storage, fresh as when the first manna dropped from heaven. Jesus is the true Manna from heaven, precious to God the Father, everlasting in His newness.

Sabbath Memorializes God's Redemption

The demand for rest, the suspension of all labor, and the prohibition from conducting business are defining aspects of the memorialization of Israel's redemption from Egypt.

> And Moses said to the people, "Do not be afraid. Stand still, and see the salvation of the Lord, which He will accomplish for you today. For the Egyptians whom you see today, you shall see again no more forever. The Lord will fight for you, and you shall hold your peace." (Exod 14:13–14)

The Sabbath rest is predicated on the work of God in redemption. It required no effort on the part of the Israelites, except that they held their peace and stood still. The Israelites could have taken matters into their own hands—scattering for their lives to the north or south, or risking their lives in battle to save a few—but to emphasize the single-handed work of redemption, the Lord admonished them to be still and observe Him in action. This signal rest of redemption could have been commanded as an annual memorialization, but given the redemptive significance of this sign, the Lord installed it as a weekly commemoration. God's work and man's rest: the same pattern of redemption foreshadowed on the seventh day of creation. Rest as a human act is a redemptive sign of faith and is not a reenactment of the Lord's creation timeline. That is, rest, as the benefit for having worked, is anti-redemptive (Rom 11:6). God did the work of creation and rested; God did the work of redemption for Israel and rested; man merely rests or trusts in God's work. Ceasing, as a requirement of the Sabbath, was not meant to cause the Jews to reflect on the created order or the meaning of time, to regain their strength after a weeks' labor or to consider their accomplishments during the past week, but to remind them of the circumstances of their redemption and sanctification. Indeed, as Israel stood between a wall of military might and a wall of nature, facing the possibility of decimation, the Lord compelled them to cease, to "stand still," so that He could save them. From the exodus of the chosen nation to the arrival of the chosen One, the theme of the old covenant is resting in the salvation of the Lord.

Signs Fulfilled

Circumcision was also designated as a covenantal sign between the Hebrew male and God, "between Me and you," to signify participation in the covenant with Abraham. Circumcision was a living sign, instituted during God's covenant with Abraham (Gen 17:11), practiced by the Jews during their captivity in Egypt (Josh 5:5), inseparably joined to the Passover (Exod 12:44, 48), commanded in the Law to Moses (Lev 12:1–3), and adhered to during the time of Christ (Phil 3:5). The importance of circumcision in the liberation of Israel from Egyptian bondage was highlighted when the Lord sought to kill Moses, only to release him after his son was circumcised (Exod 4:24–26). God did not command Moses to keep a forgotten Sabbath commandment, only to observe a ceremonial law that identified him as a Hebrew. Jewish believers from the sect of the Pharisees found it difficult to separate circumcision from spirituality and therefore demanded the circumcision of Gentile converts as a testimony of their salvation and their love for the law.[23] This teaching was hotly contested by the apostles and elders in Jerusalem—James, Peter and Paul included—and it was described as burdensome, subversive and troubling (Acts 15:24, 28). Such is the course when the sign is made greater than the reality. As Calvin surmised,

> For the abolishing of it has this effect—that the mystery which had been previously conveyed under it, does not now any longer belong to it: nay more, it is now no longer a sign, but a thing of no use.[24]

Since these living signs, or memorializing ordinances, were shadows of a greater reality, they are not binding upon Gentile converts, but may be optionally observed under certain circumstances for the purposes of evangelism and peace-keeping (Acts 16:3;1 Cor 7:19).

23. This is the same course of reasoning used by Sabbatarians who question the non-Sabbatarian's commitment to the moral law of God if they won't keep the Sabbath sign.

24. Calvin, *Commentaries*, 20:247 (1 Cor 7:19).

The Sabbath was regarded in much the same way. Early Jewish believers continued to meet at the synagogue on the Sabbath, but eventually their presence was detested and they were forced to meet at a different time of the week (John 16:2).[25] As the Gentile contingent grew, the apostles realized the signal charter of the Sabbath (a sign of Christ's death and burial) and were directed by the Lord to gather on the first day of the week (a sign of the resurrection). If the Sabbath were not a fulfilled sign, Jewish Christians would never have tolerated shifting their weekly worship to a non-Sabbath day without explicit apostolic revelation directing such a change. Calvin lucidly explained that the signs of the old covenant are nothing when we consider that Jesus Christ has come and is ours to enjoy.

> Moreover, it is not enough to allude to the fact that the ancient fathers possessed the ceremony in order to incite them, or that it served them as a hope, for we have far more than the external and visible sign since our Lord Jesus Christ has appeared to us, in whom all that was prefigured in shadows has been fulfilled. Therefore it is highly inappropriate for us to keep asking for those things which were under the law.[26]

What are the external and visible signs of Sabbath-keeping? The weekly physical rest signified the believer's complete trust in His perfect redemption. The prohibition from work signifies that it is the Lord's work of redemption and not our own. The restraint from business signifies that His redemption cannot be bought or sold like merchandise. Abiding and no cooking signify that our redemption is a restoration of the original garden paradise. The Lord identified the Sabbath as a sign and it is defined by the external rites performed upon that day. As a sign of the old covenant, the Sabbath "had respect to and shadowed forth Christ" and is no longer pertinent as a sign under the new covenant. The sun went down on the Sabbath, but we have in this new day the Lord Jesus Christ, the Person to whom pointed the Sabbath signs.

25. Rordorf, *Sunday*, 124–25.

26. Farley, *Calvin's Sermons*, 102.

3

The Sabbaths and the Decalogues

TWO TABLES

Ten Words

THREE MONTHS AFTER LIBERATING Israel, the Lord brought the nation into the Wilderness of Sinai and assembled them at the foot of Mount Sinai (Exod 19:1, 4). Crowning the mountain top with clouds of smoke and embellishing the sky with lightning, the Lord announced with the voice of thundering trumpets the Decalogue. These Ten Words were prefaced with a reminder of their redemption, both to inspire rejoicing at the freedom obtained by the mighty works of God alone and to evoke trembling for the ownership claimed as the supreme authority over all creation. God Himself directly purchased the Israelites, giving Him the authority to direct their lives in humble submission to His commandments. Yet these commandments were initially spoken (Exod 20:1–3). The Lord continued to instruct Moses about worship, sacrifices, slave ownership, personal injuries by man and beast, property rights, personal offenses against God's character, the keeping of times, their conduct in the conquest of Canaan, and lastly, how to further approach Him on the mount (Exod 20:22—24:2). Moses then descended the mount, "wrote all the words of the Lord" (Exod 24:4), and mediated the covenant with blood (Exod 24:8). It was not until Moses, the priests, and the seventy elders approached the Lord a second time on the mount that the Lord mentioned His intention to produce the tables of stone (Exod 24:12). Moses tarried on the mount in the cloud of God's glory for six days, and on the seventh day was called up higher into the fiery mount, remaining there forty days and nights (Exod 24:15–18). While in communion with the Lord of Glory, Moses received detailed instructions regarding the ceremonial aspects of the law regarding worship and the tabernacle, concluding with the Sabbath (Exod 25–31). Then Moses received the "two tablets of the Testimony" (Exod 31:18).

> And Moses turned and went down from the mountain, and the two tablets of the Testimony were in his hand. The tablets were written on both sides; on the one side and on the other they were written.
>
> Now the tablets were the work of God, and the writing was the writing of God engraved on the tablets. (Exod 32:15–16)

The Ten Commandments are unique in that they were written on stone by the finger of God Himself.[1] Yet their uniqueness continues in the didymous nature of their history. First, the Ten Commandments were spoken and then written by Moses. The Lord told Moses He would make the tables of stone and subsequently they were delivered to him. The Ten Commandments were written on not one, but two, tablets; and each tablet was written upon both sides. Moses broke the first set of tablets and God commanded Moses to make two more tablets like the ones he destroyed, so God could inscribe them with the same words of the former tablets (Exod 34:1). After a second forty days and nights, Moses returned with the second set of the Ten Commandments on stone (Exod 34:28). The Lord's interest in replacing the tables of stone rests in His previous command that they be kept in the ark of the covenant (Exod 25:16). This Moses did when the tabernacle was erected on the first day of the first month of the second year (Exod 40:20).

Of course, breaking the tablets of stone dramatically portrayed the failure of the Jews to obey God's law-covenant, and the new set remained as a testimony against Israel of their rebellion. Though broken so quickly after arriving at Mount Sinai, this did not alter God's providential intentions with that nation—His law was still binding upon the Israelites and His faithfulness to them was unchangeable. Yet more importantly, the law written on tables of stone represented the lifelessness and hardness of the Israelites to God's law when it was His intention that His word make men alive and affect them from deep within their souls (Ezek 11:19; 2 Cor 3:2–3). As the Apostle Paul considered the meaning of this historic event, he realized that it presented a contrast with his ministration of the gospel to the world (2 Cor 3:6–18). Referring specifically to the radiance of Moses' face upon descending with the second set of Ten Commandments (Exod 34:29–30) Paul sees at once the glory of that covenant and its ephemeral quality (2 Cor 3:7–11). The covenant, symbolized in the face of Moses, began with such radiance that it was too difficult to sustain a focused gaze upon it, but in time was regarded as a common thing. In this phenomenon, Paul sees a contrast between the Mosaic covenant, old and fading away (v. 13), and the new covenant, which surpasses it in glory and ministration (v. 11). Under the veil of typology, the Lord revealed at Mount Sinai that the covenant would be a fading covenant (the two faces of Moses) and a replaceable covenant (the second set of tables). Thus, the ultimate reason for replacing the law on stone was to foreshadow a future day, when Jesus, following Moses' pattern, would cancel the "handwriting of requirements that was against us, which was contrary to us," (Col 2:14) and replace it with a new law written upon our hearts (2 Cor 3:3; Heb 10:9). The glory in Moses' face was a token of the glory of the Only Begotten Son who is the singular topic of the Mosaic law and was the glory any Israelite could have experienced in his heart if he saw in the law the hope of Messiah's descent from heaven. The glory in Moses' face faded, but the law remained the same, for it is the faded laws (ceremonies) that must give way to the glorious revelation of

1. We must not forget the second record of the Lord's handwriting on stone, the "handwriting on the wall" to the pagan king Belshazzar (Dan 5:1–9), which also condemned the recipient of the divine message.

Jesus Christ. Paul is clear in his second letter to the Corinthians: we (Christians) are not those who corrupt the word of God (old covenant) but those who, in the sight of God, speak in Christ (2 Cor 2:17). Thus, the new covenant is in large part the old covenant unveiled to reveal the glory of Christ (2 Cor 3:14). The historical record of the administration of the Ten Commandments is a shadow of Christ administering His new covenant.

The Lord had every right to terminate His relationship with Israel; however, through Moses' intercession, the Lord preserved many and promised to bring them into the land, yet He would not accompany them (Exod 33:1–3). This implied that without His presence, there could be no rest in Canaan. Moses pleaded again, and the Lord graciously replied, "My Presence will go with you, and I will give you rest" (Exod 33:14). The pleading of Moses typifies the Lord Jesus Christ interceding for His beloved people, yet Moses' prayer actually begs for the presence of Christ as a token of God's redeeming grace. Any symbol of rest is empty without the presence of the giver of rest. Canaan was but a morsel of the expectation of rest, but Moses soon tasted of a complete rest that was more satisfying than a land, a tabernacle, or a seventh day. This pericope is nestled between the records of the first and second sets of the Ten Commandments and helps to define Sabbath rest as a symbol of God's presence.

Deuteronomic Decalogue

Deuteronomy records the rehearsal of the Ten Commandments at the end of forty years of wandering to prepare Israel to cross the Jordon River into Canaan. Slight variations occur in the syntax of several of the commandments, but the fourth and fifth[2] contain additional information and the fourth alone omits previous information. Since Moses appears to directly quote the Lord (Deut 5:4–5) and since the Lord directed Moses to instruct the people of the contents of the tablets (Exod 24:12), it is peculiar that this variation exists. The differences between the two passages are displayed below:

Exodus 20:8–11	**Deuteronomy 5:12–15**
Remember the Sabbath day, to keep it holy.	Observe the Sabbath day, to keep it holy,
	as the Lord your God commanded you.
Six days you shall labor and do all your work,	Six days you shall labor and do all your work,
but the seventh day is the Sabbath of the Lord your God.	but the seventh day is the Sabbath of the Lord your God.

2. Paul loosely quotes the Deuteronomic rehearsal of the fifth commandment in his letter to the Ephesians. The author of Hebrews references the exodus version of the fourth commandment.

Exodus 20:8–11	Deuteronomy 5:12–15
In it you shall do no work: you, nor your son, nor your daughter, nor your male servant, nor your female servant, nor your cattle, nor your stranger who is within your gates.	In it you shall do no work: you, nor your son, nor your daughter, nor your male servant, nor your female servant, nor your ox, nor your donkey, nor any of your cattle, nor your stranger who is within your gates,
	that your male servant and your female servant may rest as well as you.
For in six days the Lord made the heavens and the earth, the sea, and all that is in them, and rested the seventh day.	
	And remember that you were a slave in the land of Egypt, and the Lord your God brought you out from there by a mighty hand and by an outstretched arm;
Therefore the Lord blessed the Sabbath day and hallowed it.	therefore the Lord your God commanded you to keep the Sabbath day.

These variations have intrigued theologians and scholars for centuries because it troubles our concept of the accuracy of Scripture.[3] First of all, the opening words are different. Jewish authors Trepp and Heschel note:

> The dual injunction addresses the two poles of the Jewish soul, revealing the basic character of Judaism in general. *Zakhor*, "Remember," speaks to our emotion. The Jew is to embrace the Sabbath with his soul, celebrating it in joy, peace of mind, through meditation and festive meals. *Shamor*, "Observe," bids the Jew to observe with great care the concrete laws through which Sabbath rest is fully implemented. The two go together: the law, by restraining action, releases the soul to find its attunement.[4]

> According to an old mystic text, "Remember" is a reference to the male principle, "Keep" to the female principle . . . This we may assume suggested to Rabbi Shimeon the idea that the Sabbath was the bride and Israel the bridegroom.[5]

Whether or not these theories are correct, the intent of the command to "remember" and "keep" the Sabbath is to not forget to set this day apart every week and follow all the other instructions applicable to the special day. It is understandable that the Lord would enjoin Israel to remember the Sabbath at Mount Sinai (Exod. 20:8)—even

3. Compare the Lord's quotation of Himself, first to Moses (Exodus 19:3–6) and later to Jeremiah (Jer 7:21–23).

4. Trepp, *Book of Jewish Observance*, 68.

5. Heschel, *Sabbath*, 109.

though it was given to them only weeks before—for, as Calvin noted, they already forgot the tyranny of Egypt from which they had been redeemed!

Secondly, the stated rationale for observing the Sabbath is the most significant difference between the two versions: one invokes the creation of the cosmos, the other, the exodus from Egypt. Jewish authors approach the differences synoptically, allowing both texts to contribute their own voice to a more comprehensive understanding of the Sabbath. Leo Trepp suggests that

> The version in Exodus emphasizes the call for cessation from work in order that we may celebrate God's sacred time. The version in Deuteronomy places emphasis on the ethical implications: equality of man, man's stewardship over nature.[6]

Westerners tend to approach the differing texts more analytically, hoping to understand why God wasn't more accurate. Gleason Archer admits the difficulty with the variations but nonchalantly explains it in terms of making a partial quotation.[7] Archer's theory addresses the loss of information by ellipsis, and the addition of information by cut-and-paste, however, his theory does not account for novel information. That is, the slavery basis for obeying the Sabbath was not already recorded in Exodus nor presented earlier in Deuteronomy; it is a new idea connected with the Sabbath when it suddenly appears in the Deutoronomic Decalogue.

But the differences between the two records of the fourth commandment are not problematic. Moses explained in Exodus that the reason the Lord blessed the Sabbath is because He blessed the seventh day of the creation week; and in Deuteronomy, the reason the Israelites were to keep the Sabbath is because they were redeemed from slavery. In Exodus, the Israelites were commanded to remember (to keep) the Sabbath, and in Deuteronomy they were commanded to remember their history of slavery when they kept the Sabbath. The Israelites were not to remember the creation, as if they were there (Job 38:4ff), but to remember a weekly rest as a blessing of their release from years of labor, just as God Himself had "labored" in creation and then rested. There is no contradiction of information. Furthermore, it is likely that the Sabbath commandment written on stone was as brief as the other commandments and that Moses simply added parenthetical material in its retelling under the inspiration of the Holy Spirit. What Moses added to the Exodic passage (the creation connection) and what he added to the Deuteronomic passage (the slavery experience) were drawn from the colloquies with God as an amplification of the basic command to keep the Sabbath, though not necessarily directly quoted elsewhere in his writings nor necessarily quoted during the initial declaration of the Ten Commandments.[8] John Reisinger concurs.

> The two reasons together combine the creation rights and redemptive claims of God over his chosen nation and furnish a double obligation for obedience to the covenant sign and thus the covenant for which the sign stands. This makes for great preaching; we must consider, however, the strong probability that neither

6. Trepp, *Book of Jewish Observance*, 67.

7. Ibid., 146.

8. Kaiser, *Toward Old Testament Ethics*, 180.

> of the two different reasons given by Moses for keeping the seventh day holy were part of the actual commandments, or covenant terms, that God wrote on the tablets of stone. Both reasons are commentary added by Moses to enforce the great significance of the covenant sign (sabbath) that had just been given to Israel.[9]

While Moses remained on the mount, not yet having received the tablets (Exod 31:18), the Lord amplified the fourth commandment with these words:

> Speak also to the children of Israel, saying: Surely My Sabbaths you shall keep, for it is a sign between Me and you throughout your generations, that you may know that I am the Lord who sanctifies you.
>
> You shall keep the Sabbath, therefore, for it is holy to you. Everyone who profanes it shall surely be put to death; for whoever does any work on it, that person shall be cut off from among his people.
>
> Work shall be done for six days, but the seventh is the Sabbath of rest, holy to the Lord. Whoever does any work on the Sabbath day, he shall surely be put to death.
>
> Therefore the children of Israel shall keep the Sabbath, to observe the Sabbath throughout their generations as a perpetual covenant.
>
> It is a sign between Me and the children of Israel forever; for in six days the Lord made the heavens and the earth, and on the seventh day He rested and was refreshed. (Exod 31:13-17)

This passage iterates the creation account (v. 17) and identifies the Sabbath as a sign for Israel of their dedication to the God who brought them to Mount Sinai (v. 13, 17) to set them apart from all other nations to receive the Law. The covenant was made with a people who were just rescued from bondage (Exod 20:2); therefore, it was appropriate to relate the significance of the exodus to the signal function of the Sabbath. Those who were about to cross the Jordan were not slaves themselves in Egypt (excepting Joshua and Caleb), yet in his apopemptic discourse to his brethren, Moses urged them to recall as if they were slaves because they were the children of those who were slaves. The history of their fathers was their history. This relationship signifies that the children of Adam are sinners as much as Adam was a sinner. With their servitude and hardship a thing of the past, the ceremony became even more pertinent of the fact that each Israelite had to overcome inner slavery to sin through the sanctification of the Lord. The ceremony recalled history, but, more importantly, it was meant to be understood spiritually.

Two reasons were given to obey the Sabbath. The newly rescued Israelites heard the creation-connection at Mount Sinai and the second generation heard the exodus-connection in the plains at Moab. In terms of an ongoing tenet for Israel, it behooved them to put the two voices together. The creation rest and their freedom from slavery were two "witnesses" to the Sabbath institution, as it were, corroborating the intention of the Lord that their Sabbath-keeping reenact and encompass the story line of redemptive rest from the beginning, through their own experiences, and into a future,

9. Reisinger, *Tablets of Stone*, 33.

completed state of rest. It is fitting, then, as a ceremonial practice of the Israelites to base the Sabbath on both the creation and the exodus, for both symbolize the consummation of the work of God with an ensuing rest for man. Redemption is the work of God, not of man. Physical rest signifies the appanage of God having worked for them (Deut 4:33–35). The creation and the exodus were not pointing to the Sabbath as an end in and of itself, but they were pointing, along with the Sabbath, to the eternal rest merited by the perfect work of Jesus Christ.

Covenant Contents

Forty years after the giving of the Decalogue, in the final words of Moses before the nation crossed the Jordan River, he recalled the divine origin of the covenant in stone.

> And He wrote on the tablets according to the first writing, the Ten Commandments, which the Lord had spoken to you in the mountain from the midst of the fire in the day of the assembly; and the Lord gave them to me. (Deut 10:4)

The two divine lithoglyphs were a representative summation of all the commandments, statutes, ordinances, laws, and judgments delivered to Moses and recorded in the Pentateuch for the children of Israel to reverently obey (Exod 21:1; 34:27; Deut 31:9, 24–26). The equality and unity of both the Ten Commandments and the law of Moses with the covenant is strongly supported in Scripture (Deut 1:3; 4:2, 5–8, 13–14; 44–45; 5:1–2; 30:16; 31:10–12; Num 36:13; Lev 27:34; Ps 147:19–20).

> I am the Lord your God, who brought you out of the land of Egypt, that you should not be their slaves; I have broken the bands of your yoke and made you walk upright.
>
> But if you do not obey Me, and do not observe all these commandments, and if you despise My statutes, or if your soul abhors My judgments, so that you do not perform all My commandments, but break My covenant . . . (Lev 26:13–15)

The placement of the Pentateuch beside the Ten Commandments within the ark of the covenant demonstrates its equality in terms of divine origin, authority, and covenantal essence. Moses specifically recalled that the two tablets held tightly in his two hands were representative of the covenant (Deut 9:15). Yet the value of this compendium is better comprehended if one knows the particulars from which it is derived. Therefore, the details of the covenant are more important judicially than is a summary. The Ten Commandments, though unique in delivery, do not hold a higher position of authority than the rest of the Law, or of the Scriptures in general any more than the words of Jesus in the NT made distinct by red type. The tables of stone epitomized and represented the Lord's covenant with Israel which included not only moral law, but ceremonial law as well.

There was little reason for the Jews to distinguish various types of laws because ceremonial laws were allied to moral duties and incurred the same dreadful consequence of God's wrath when disobeyed. As Douglas Moo emphasizes, the Jews regarded the Law of God as a unity.

> Because the point is so important and so easily obscured by the history of interpretation, we must insist again: First-century Jews viewed the law as a unity. It was the *tôrâ*, given by God through Moses to the people of Israel as their guide for the whole of life. Jews did not make any fundamental distinction between "moral" and "ceremonial" laws or "moral" and "redemptive" laws.[10]

Yet, as Bahnsen notes, the Jews had an inkling of a difference between laws of righteousness and laws of reconciliation (Ps 50:12–13; Prov 31:3; Hos 6:6; cf. Matt 9:13; 12:7).[11] That is, the more spiritually inclined Jew would have agreed that it is better to obey God's righteous laws than to disobey and have to rely on the sacrificial system to restore peace between him and God. That being said, when Christ chastised the Pharisees to "go and learn" what Hosea meant (Matt 9:13), the message was that the sacrificial requirements of the Law would be esteemed by God only if the offerer recognized his sinfulness and need of repentance. Thus, redemptive laws were close to the heart of God as the gateway of reconciliation between God and man, and of even greater importance as forerunners to the Messiah who would perform the work of reconciliation in an absolute and effective way. It is not as it appears that sacrifice is antithetical to mercy, but that heartless and insincere devotion to redemptive laws is antithetical to the divine mercy that God displays in them. The performance of the laws of reconciliation was meant to inculcate personal humility and interpersonal grace among the Israelites. The nuance between righteous and ritual laws is present in the OT, but it is the teachings of the NT that bring this distinction to light. Regardless of just how much the Jews understood as to a distinction between moral and ceremonial laws, it is certain that through the advent of Jesus Christ this distinction was made palpable.

NEW ATTITUDE

Preeminent Commandments

The Jews engaged in debates regarding the classification of all the commandments of their covenant with God. The Ten Commandments were venerated, but they did not overshadow the rest of the ordinances, precepts, and judgments. Scripture records an aspect of this thinking when the Pharisees posed this question to Jesus: Which is the great commandment in the Law? (Matt 22:34–40). Jesus' answer is profound in several ways. When asked to identify the one commandment that preceded all others, He answered with *two* commandments; both positive, and when taken together, they summarize the whole moral or righteous law. Jesus did not quote any of the Ten Commandments, nor did He pretend to summarize the Ten Commandments. His selections came from two different books and are not directly associated with the Decalogue. By selecting outside the Ten Commandments for a synopsis of man's moral duty, He elevated the remainder of the Pentateuch to the same level of superiority supposed to exist in the Ten Commandments. This was in contrast to the Essenic belief

10. Moo, "Response to Greg L. Bahnsen," 167.
11. Bahnsen, "Theonomic Reformed Approach," 103–4.

that the Ten Commandments were the only essential part of the Law.[12] Like the Essenes, Sabbatarians attach special status to the Ten Commandments, an attitude at odds with esteeming the whole word of God as a unity. One of the foundational arguments for the universal obligation of the Sabbath is its inclusion in the Ten Commandments, as summarized by Walter Chantry:

> As we have noted before, the weekly Sabbath law is to be found in the midst of the Ten Commandments. Everything else about that code of law is entirely moral, nothing else being of a judicial or ceremonial nature. This summary of moral righteousness is in the New Testament (Matt 5:17–48, Rom 13:8–10, Jas 2:10–11, to mention but a few such places) upheld as the Christian standard of morality.[13]

First of all, none of Chantry's references substantiate his thesis that the NT categorically recognizes the Decalogue as a summary of moral law, and none of them even mentions the Sabbath. Secondly, Chantry's conclusion, that the fourth commandment is moral because it is in the Ten Commandments, is contained in his premise that the Ten Commandments contain only moral commands. This is nothing more than circular reasoning. Finally, a hermeneutical technique that makes determinations of morality or ceremoniality based upon textual proximity is certainly suspect. Authors McCartney and Clayton review the challenges to understanding the differences between the types of laws within the old covenant.

> The second type of distinction, that between civil, ceremonial, and moral laws, is more difficult. There is no easy way to tell whether a law is in one category or another. There are no typical linguistic forms that mark off one type from another, and the different types are all mixed together.[14]

There must be a more reasonable method for distinguishing between ceremonial and moral commandments than their juxtaposition. A review of all passages related to the Sabbath in the Pentateuch will quickly show that it is listed with moral laws only in the Ten Commandments (Exod 20; Deut 5); otherwise, it is listed with ceremonial laws (Exod 31; 35; Lev 16; 23; 24; 25; Num 28). For example, in Exodus 34:18–23 the Sabbath is baptized in a list of ceremonial laws containing the Feast of Unleavened Bread, Redemption of the Firstborn, Feast of Weeks, First Fruits, and the Feast of Ingathering.[15] Obviously, the relationship of the Sabbath command with other cer-

12. Edersheim mentioned this briefly when describing the practices of priestly duties during temple service. Following the prayer for the casting of the lot to choose which priest should burn the incense, a privilege that Zechariah received (Luke 1:8–10), the Ten Commandments were repeated. This practice was discontinued, "lest the Sadducees should declare them to be the only essential part of the law." Edersheim, *The Temple*, 112.

13. Chantry, *Call the Sabbath a Delight*, 100; McIlhenny, "Literal, Six-Day Creation," 35.

14. McCartney and Clayton, *Let the Reader Understand*, 228.

15. Other passages where the Sabbath is listed with the other feasts: Exod 34:18–23; Num 28–29; 2 Kgs 4:23; Isa 1:13–14; 66:23; Ezek 46:1–17; Hos 2:11. Of note is Kaiser's determination that the Deuteronomic Decalogue is repeated and expanded in chapters 12–25. Though he understands the Decalogue to contain moral laws, its expansion in Deut 14:28—16:17 covers only ceremonial laws, such

emonial or moral commandments is not uniform throughout the OT, so proximity is an unsatisfactory means to distinguish the various types of law. Therefore, the mention of the Sabbath in the Ten Commandments says nothing about its essence as a moral or ceremonial command.

Instead, Acts and the Epistles should hold a paramount position in defining a Christian's viewpoint of and relationship to ceremonial law. It should be a serious consideration that there is not one post-resurrection Scripture that endorses the observation of the Sabbath as a moral duty for Christians. In fact, there is not one post-resurrection Scripture that endorses the Ten Commandments as a whole, though nine of the ten individual commandments are repeated in the pastoral Epistles. The post-resurrection Scriptures that specifically mention the Ten Commandments as a whole occur in only four places: 2 Corinthians 3:2–3, 2 Corinthians 3:6–11, Galatians 4:21–26, and Hebrews 9:1–10. In none of these passages are the Ten Commandments presented as a living document that capsulizes the new covenant ethic or essence, but rather as a tombstone marking the demise of a previous age, made invalid by a more glorious economy. The Decalogue, when taken as a unity, can only be considered less glorious if it is inexorably joined with ceremonial law or if it is a type or shadow itself. The Ten Commandments that summarized the Law, even God's covenant with Israel, were actually a continuing means of bondage (*douleia*) or an imposition (*epikimai*). As Paul made clear, the old covenant is practically unintelligible without the new perspective of the new covenant (2 Cor 3:12–18); that is, it only makes sense as it is interpreted through the ministration of the Holy Spirit who testifies of Christ. It is ironic then, that in comparison to the liberty in Christ, the covenant formalized with Israel after being liberated from the house of bondage, becomes itself a form of bondage in order to manifest the greater and more enduring Jubilee in Christ. Yet within the Decalogue was the typological promise of real freedom, refreshingly contained in the Sabbath commandment. Again, ironically, the ceremonial command that bound Israel was the typological promise of freedom from sin in Christ. Now, it is certainly proper to describe the Ten Commandments as a summary of the Lord's covenant with Israel (Deut 4:13). That covenant contained both moral and ceremonial commandments as a unity. So, it is fitting that the quintessential ceremonial commandment, the one with the most to say typologically, be included in the Decalogue as a sign of that covenant.

In the absence of any particular apostolic injunctions to observe the Sabbath, Richard Barcellos attempts to demonstrate the inference of such a command via the following syllogism:

- The Ten Commandments are a functional unit in the old covenant
- Paul mentions several of the Ten Commandments in lists of functioning commands in the new covenant; therefore,
- The Ten Commandments still function as a unit in the new covenant

as triennial tithes, the Sabbatic Year, perpetual slavery, laws of the firstborn, Passover, Feast of Weeks, Feast of Booths, and the tri-annual appearances of males to Jerusalem. Kaiser, *Toward Old Testament Ethics*, 127–37.

The spuriousness of this line of reasoning may be easier to detect in this syllogism:

- The Seven Dwarves are a functional unit at the diamond mine
- Witnesses saw Doc, Grumpy, Happy, Bashful, Sneezy, and Dopey at the castle; therefore,
- The Seven Dwarves were a functional unit at the castle

The logical conclusion is actually the opposite since Sleepy was not at the castle. Since the Sabbath is not included in any NT lists of OT commands, Sabbatarians must entertain the possibility that the Sabbath is not a viable command under the new covenant.

Beginning with his "natural assumption" from Jeremiah 31:33 that the law written on the hearts of believers under the new covenant is the same law as the Ten Commandments, Barcellos expects to find the Ten Commandments *as a unit* endorsed in the NT. To this end he cites three NT verses: 2 Corinthians 3:3, Ephesians 6:2–3, and 1 Timothy 1:8–11.[16] In Paul's second letter to the Corinthians, the metaphor of heart-writing begins as a tribute in the lives of the Corinthians to the superior ministry of Jesus Christ, through Paul, as opposed to the ministry of Moses. As a defense of his apostleship, the metaphor evokes in Paul the contrast between the old and new covenants, the latter being a superior form of ministry since it represents the fulfillment of several old covenant prophecies involving the work of the Holy Spirit (Jer 31:33; Ezek 11:19; 36:26). While Paul makes a clear reference to the tables of stone, the thrust of his argument is to elaborate on the contrast between two covenants rather than to identify the specific laws written on the hearts of believers in Jesus Christ. Furthermore, Paul's metaphor about written laws is broader than what was written on the tablets of stone, for Paul alludes not only to Exodus 31:18, 32:15–16, and 34:1, but also to the matter of Moses' face in Exodus 34:29–35. Within the motif of the giving of the law under Moses, Paul also drew upon this passage (Exod 34:29).

> Then the Lord said to Moses, "Write these words, for according to the tenor of these words I have made a covenant with you and with Israel."
>
> So he was there with the Lord forty days and forty nights; he neither ate bread nor drank water. And He wrote on the tablets the words of the covenant, the Ten Commandments. (Ex 34:27–28)

While the Lord wrote His words on the tablets, He commanded Moses to write the words of His covenant on parchment which included: 1) His commands to destroy the religious systems of the pagans whom they would defeat, being careful not to covenant with them through marriage (Exod 34:10–16), 2) to refrain from making idols (Exod 34:17), and 3) to observe the Feast of Unleavened Bread, the laws of the firstborn, the Sabbath, the harvest feasts, and the Passover (Exod 34:18–23, 25). In addition, they were not to mix the sacrificial blood with leaven, or to cook a young goat in its mother's milk (Exod 34:25–26). Thus, the written law of Moses

16. He does not mention 2 Corinthians 3:6–11, Galatians 4:21–26, and Hebrews 9:1–10, which categorically depreciate the Ten Commandments as a unit.

included both moral and ceremonial laws. Barcellos makes no qualifications about the meaning of the written law—especially as Paul interprets the old covenant from the perspective of the new covenant—and sees only the Ten Commandments. Because of this assumption, he asserts that it is the Ten Commandments that are written on the hearts of believers.[17] This is not the thrust of Paul's instruction—to assert that the Ten Commandments when written on stone were a death sentence, but when the same Ten Commandments are written on flesh, they convey life. God's law is literally understood from the written Scriptures on parchment or the preached word. Paul is concerned with the symbolic contrast between the old covenant that was sown in rocky soil (written on stone, a fading glory on Moses' face, Israel's stony reception of it) and the new covenant that is sown in fertile soil (written on flesh, an exceeding glory of the Spirit, believed by Gentiles). The contrast is between the inanimate and the living, with Jesus as the reference point. While I agree with Barcellos that the new covenant does not usher in a new moral law, this is not the purpose of Paul's illustration to the Corinthians. While I agree with Barcellos that "it is simply not true that only those things from the Old Testament repeated in the New are still binding,"[18] it is also not true that all the commands in the OT continue in the New unless specifically annulled. I believe the Sabbath *is* specifically annulled in texts that Barcellos does not consider, but it is even more problematic to assert that when one commandment in a series is mentioned that the whole series is regarded as a functioning unit. Where is the exegetical basis for such a claim?

Barcellos presents 1 Timothy 1:8–11 as another text supportive of his view that the NT assumes the continuing functionality of the Ten Commandments as a whole outside the old covenant. Based upon the *partial similarity* between Paul's list and the Ten Commandments, Barcellos attempts to demonstrate *identity*. I agree with Barcellos that Paul presents the law as an ethical guide for humanity, but the passage does not indicate that Paul is building his ethical list entirely from the Ten Commandments. The following chart demonstrates the connections Barcellos makes. From the word "profane" (*bebelos*) he imagines a command to keep the Sabbath.

Decalogue	1 Tim 1:8–11	Could Have Said	Found In
	for the lawless and insubordinate,		
shall have no other Gods	for the ungodly	haters of God	Rom 1:30
shall not make idols	and for sinners,	idolaters	1 Cor 5:11; 6:9; Eph 5:5
shall not take name in vain	for the unholy	blasphemers railers	2 Tim 3:2 1 Cor 5:11

17. Barcellos, *Defense*, 20. See also 61.

18. Ibid., 40, 86.

keep the Sabbath	and profane,	Sabbath-breakers	John 5:18: Rom 1:31; 2:25
Decalogue	**1 Tim 1:8–11**	**Could Have Said**	**Found In**
honor your father and mother	for murderers of fathers and murderers of mothers,	disobedient of parents	Rom 1:30; 2 Tim 3:2
shall not murder	for manslayers,	murderers	Rom 1:29; 13:9
shall not commit adultery	for fornicators, for sodomites,	adulterers fornicators	1 Cor 6:9 1 Cor 5:11; 6:9
shall not steal	for kidnappers,	thieves	1 Cor 6:10
shall not bear false witness	for liars, for perjurers	deceiver	Rom 1:29
shall not covet		the covetous	1 Cor 5:11; 6:10
	or any other thing		

At first it must be acknowledged that Paul does not directly quote from or mention the Ten Commandments in this passage, so any similarity with the Ten Commandments comes from the flow of Paul's thought rather than his determination to follow the set order of the Ten Commandments. Three couplets of nouns begin the flow of descriptions of those the law is intended to curtail (highlighted above). Barcellos admits that the first couplet (lawless and insubordinate) does not refer to any single commandment; furthermore, a cursory comparison does not allow a match with any of the first four commandments. The second course of descriptors (murderers through perjurers) finds similarity with the sixth through ninth commandments, though the first couplet (father and mother) may be related to the fifth commandment. The tenth commandment is not even mentioned, and Paul offers a caveat that encompasses anything not mentioned, again confirming that he was not expressly duplicating the content and order of the Ten Commandments. Of course, if Paul resolved to identify sins against each of the Ten Commandments in order, he could have used terms in several instances that better reflected that purpose, as indicated in the table above. What began as a series of couplets describing those for whom the law is meant to restrain, Paul transitioned with "murderers of fathers and murderers of mothers" to a repetition of the sixth through ninth commandments, and a final catch-bag for any other sins that violated God's moral disciplines for mankind.

Barcellos attempts to draw a strong connection between the word "profane" and the command to remember the Sabbath, by citing eleven select passages in the Septuagint that use the word *bebelos* in association with the Sabbath (Exod 31:14; Neh 13:17; Ezek 20:13, 16; 21, 24; 22:8, 23:38; 23:39; Isa 56:2, 6). However, a closer examination shows his analysis to be lopsided. In the Septuagint, *bebelos* is used to translate two different Hebrew words, *chalal* (defile, profane, pollute) and *ma'ac* (abhor, despise, disdain). *Chalal* is translated roughly 67 times as defile, profane or pollute, and is applied to sins against the Lord's name, His sanctuary or services, the land (Jer 16:18), as well as the Sabbath.[19] In the NT, Hebrews 12:16 applies *bebelos* to Esau who sold his birthright for scanty orts. Without faith, Esau despised his sacred privileges, preferring instead to fill his aching belly. In contrast, Moses esteemed the reproaches of men rather than the treasures of Egypt, demonstrating his faith in God (Heb 11:24–26). Disobedience of the Sabbath was not Esau's wrongdoing. Adam Clarke informs us that the construction of the Greek word *bebelos* pertains to those who were not allowed to enter sacred grounds or to participate in its ceremonies because they despised the religious order. They are mockers of God and His religion, but lovers of themselves. The Latin word, *profanus*, means "far from the temple," signifying an irreligious person.[20] Considering the meaning of the word "profane," Calvin surmised,

> Profane then are all they in whom the love of the world so reigns and prevails that they forget heaven: as is the case with those who are led away by ambition, or become fond of money or of wealth, or give themselves up to gluttony, or become entangled in any other pleasures; they allow in their thoughts and cares no place, or it may be the last place, to the spiritual kingdom of Christ.[21]

Paul's other uses of *bebelos* do not hint at Sabbath-breaking: "profane and old wives' fables" (1 Tim 4:7) and "profane and idle babblings" (1 Tim 6:20; 2 Tim 2:16). Jesus used the word *bebelos* to describe the work of the priests in their Sabbath work, a profanation of the Sabbath that He claimed for Himself without guilt (Matt 12:5). Finally, Paul was falsely accused of bringing a Gentile to the temple, and was charged with profaning the temple (Acts 24:6). There is no reason to force the idea of Sabbath-breaking on the word *profane* in 1 Timothy 1:9 when 1) its use in the Pauline epistles and Hebrews carries no such sense, 2) its other uses by Matthew and Luke show a wide range of application, and 3) its use in the old covenant applies to those who disregard a myriad of sacred things, such as the ceremonies of place-worship and time-worship, the Lord's Name, His covenant and His law, even His commands against adultery, murder and treachery. Paul only means to identify the impious and the scoffer to Timothy. In the Epistles, nine of the Ten Commandments are given the weight and significance of moral law, but not the Sabbath. To designate the Sabbath as a ceremonial law does no damage to the Ten Commandments as a summary of God's law-covenant with Israel, only to the assumption that the Ten Commandments are all moral laws. On the ethical level, the new covenant does not make the old covenant irrelevant and inapplicable to believers; however, the old covenant must be understood from the perspective of the gospel of Christ.

19. His Name (Lev 18:21; 19:12; 20:3; 21:6; 22:6, 32; Ps 74:7; Isa 48:11; Jer 34:16; Ezek 13:19; 20:9, 14, 22, 39; 22:26; 36:21, 22, 23; Amos 2:7; Mal 1:2), His sanctuary or services (Lev 21:12, 23; 22:15; Num 18:32; Ezek 23:38, 39; 24:21; 25:3; 28:18; 44:7; Dan 11:31; Zeph 3:4), the land (Jer 16:18).

20. Clarke, *Commentary*, 6:780 (Heb 12:16).

21. Calvin, *Commentaries*, 22:326 (Heb 12:16).

Moral-Ceremonial

Absent in the NT are any explicit categorizations or matured terminologies that assist us in differentiating the various commands of the old covenant, specifically the laws given to the nation Israel. It does not appear that the NT writers had a way to classify the Law into subsets of moral and ceremonial because the Law was primarily comprehended as a unity (Gal 5:13; Jas 2:10). To complicate matters, Paul's contrast between law and grace, the variety of meanings attached to the word "law," and the apparent contradictions within the NT corpus have led to the development of a marshland of interpretations. When considering the contemporary theses on this topic, in exasperation, Kaiser exclaimed, "There is such a veritable Babel of voices and positions that one wonders what the waiting and watching church must think and make out of all this confusion on the part of her scholars!"[22] There must be a stone path somewhere.

There is no disagreement within the church that a biblical paradigm shift took place between the crucifixion and Pentecost, as this was documented in the apostolic epistles during the first seventy years of the church age. New covenant writers identified specific laws of the old covenant as ineffective and unnecessary for members of the new covenant, such as circumcision (Gal 6:15), bloody sacrifices (Heb 10:4), the Levitical priesthood (Heb 7:27; 8:4), the Day of Atonement (Heb 9:7), and feast days, New Moons, and Sabbath days (Col 2:16). The apostles taught the *futility* of performing these rituals as strictly commanded under the old covenant, as with circumcision which avails nothing (Gal 5:6; Col 2:23; Heb 9:9). They taught the *temporality* of these laws for the people of God, as with their gifts and offerings brought before the temple, which were imposed until the time of Christ (Heb 9:9–10; Gal 3:19, 23–25; Eph 2:15; Heb 8:13; 10:9). Finding their end in Christ, the apostles underscored the *intentionality* of these laws, as with the duties of the high priest which shadowed forth the greater reality in the ministry of Jesus Christ in heaven on our behalf (Heb 8:1–6; 9:9; 10:1; Col 2:16). Lastly, because these laws served such a significant role in preparing the Jews for the advent of the Messiah, the apostles drew upon their spiritual meaning as metaphors under the new covenant economy, giving them a new and spiritual *applicability* (Rom 12:1; Gal 4:28; Phil 2:17; 4:18; Heb 13:15–16). For example, the Feast of Unleavened Bread is continually "kept" by a sincere life in truth (1 Cor 5:7–8); our "gifts and offerings" are now acts of love and good works in the full assurance of faith, brought to God through Christ, our High Priest; and not to the physical temple, but to our weekly assembly as one body (Heb 10:19–25). Our new birth, as a "circumcision" made without hands, resulted in the removal of the condemning list of sins against us, making us alive to God, yet our "circumcision" is only by virtue of Christ's fulfillment of the law of circumcision in His death on the cross, as He was bloodied by the hands of men and punished by the hand of God for our sins (Col 2:11–14). Our entrance into the Canaan rest is effected by Christ, the new "Joshua," who effectually delivers on His promise: a rest received by faith and not by works (Heb 4:1–10).

22. Kaiser, "The Law as God's Gracious Guidance," 180.

First of all, are we justified in making a distinction between moral and ceremonial laws? Paul gives a clear example of this distinction in Romans 2:26, where the commandment to be circumcised is contrasted with the "righteousness of the law." Circumcision was a shadow law not only of the Mosaic covenant, but of the Abrahamic covenant. To Paul, circumcision is no longer a "righteous" commandment (i.e., a morally binding law). It may be part of the Law proper, but it is not a part that must be adhered to literally any longer. The commandment to perform the outward act of circumcision is "taken away" (i.e., ceremonial) but the symbolism of cutting away uncleanness from our heart is retained (i.e., new spiritual application in Christ). The shadow contained in circumcision was fulfilled by the promise of the Holy Spirit indwelling a believer's heart, so, under the new covenant, the believer is spiritually "circumcised" without having to be physically circumcised. The shadow of physical circumcision is supplanted by the reality of the new birth in Christ so that even Gentiles are properly called "the Circumcision" (Rom 2:26; Phil 3:3). And Paul concludes that a Gentile is as good as circumcised if he obeys, in faith, God's righteous, or moral, law, "if an uncircumcised man keeps the righteous requirements of the law" (Rom 2:26), and "who also walk in the steps of the faith which our father Abraham had while still uncircumcised" (Rom 4:12). Paul distinguished the ritual of circumcision from "keeping the commandments of God" (1 Cor 7:19). Its meaning of membership in the covenant community of Israel was worthless since not all Israel is Israel (Rom 9:6; 1 Cor 10:18). But for true believers in the blood of Jesus Christ, the circumcision is completed in a spiritual sense without the help of man. After the resurrection of Christ, there was no more morality in it, nor any obligation to obey it, otherwise the apostles would have urged the circumcision of Gentiles. Any Jew who advised or commanded circumcision had either the *mistaken* view that it was moral or the *heretical* view that circumcision, along with the performance of other moral laws, was necessary for salvation.

The Belgic Confession acknowledges the distinction between righteous and shadow laws by asserting that "the ceremonies and symbols of the law have ended with the coming of Christ, and that all foreshadowings have come to an end, so that the use of them ought to be abolished among Christians."[23] Yet what is said of these specific ceremonial laws is also said of the Mosaic law and of the old covenant as a whole. While it is easy to comprehend that specific laws given to Israel under Moses are no longer literally applicable to the people of God, it is more difficult to imagine how the whole old covenant is done away when it also contains moral laws: "My salvation will be forever, And My righteousness will not be abolished" (Isa 51:6). But what we are presented with in the apostolic writings is both the continuity of old covenant moral laws as it pertains to the ethic of the people of God in relationship to Christ, and the discontinuity of the Law and the covenant as symbols of a pre-Christ relationship between God and His people. As Paul expounds salvation by faith apart from works, he curtails any thought that righteous laws no longer have any meaning for the believer: "Do we then

23. *Ecumenical Creeds and Confessions*, 103. (Belgic Confession, Art. 25).

make void the law through faith? Certainly not! On the contrary, we establish the law" (Rom 3:31). In other words, the moral laws contained in the old covenant continue to apply to believers in the same way they applied to theocratic Israel, because we are now in a saving relationship with God, and Christ's work has affected our understanding and motivation for obeying them. Paul also addressed the topic of salvation by faith and not by works with the Galatians, referencing 1) the law as administrated by the hand of angels through a mediator (Gal 3:19), 2) the law that followed the promise to Abraham (Gal 3:21), and 3) the law of righteousness that identifies the sinfulness of mankind (Gal 3:22); yet he concluded that the law was a tutor that no longer maintains any authority over the people of God (Gal 3:24). The Belgic Confession cites this very verse as pertaining to the abrogation of ceremonial law. However, the context is not about a specific ceremony, but the law-covenant as a whole. This is because Paul is describing the law in a general, symbolic way. The shadow characteristic of the old law was that it was mediated by Moses; the fulfillment of which is the mediation of the new law by Christ. The old law seemed to be all about works but Scripture demonstrates that Abraham was declared righteous by faith in God's promise, so the gospel of Christ removes the obscurity of the old law and proclaims ecstatically that we "are all sons of God through faith in Christ Jesus" (Gal 3:26). The old law condemned Israel and made them slaves, but the new law brings redemption and adoption through Christ (Gal 4:5). Because of these decisive and symbolic contrasts, Paul concludes that the old law is done away at the advent of Christ (Gal 2:19; 4:30; 4:24).

This treatment of the Law as a pre-Christ symbol defining the relationship between God and the redeemed finds the *auctor ad Hebraeos* abrogating the Law as a whole in favor of a new law. He does not treat the law as a metonym for ceremonial law, but as a prefiguring device in and of itself in the same way that ceremonial laws shadowed forth future, more glorious realities. The law contains shadows, yet it is not merely the shadows that are taken away, but the law as a whole. This is because the law itself, *understood in a symbolic way*, is a shadow of good things to come (Heb 10:1–10). The author of Hebrews explains that the bloody sacrifices were a shadow *within the Law*, or Calvin's "rude lineaments" of good things to come, to forecast or "set forth in living colours" the sacrifice of Jesus Christ for the complete remission of sins.[24] The old covenant required them, and since they were truly ineffective as a permanent remedy for sin, the Law with its sacrifices required replacement. Those who approached God through the Law could never be made perfect by its sacrifices. Quoting earlier from Jeremiah 31:31–34, and here from Psalms 40:6–8, this apostle proves that within the old covenant record there were adumbrations of this covenantal change, now made manifest with the advent of the Messiah. For the forgiveness of sins, the first (Mosaic) law required animal sacrifices and decried human sacrifices, but the second (Messianic) law required alone the sacrifice of God's only Son. Prior to the Mosaic covenant, the Lord provided a prototype of the new covenant sacrificial law in the everlasting covenant made with Abraham which called for a human sacrifice

24. Calvin, *Commentaries*, 22:221–22 (Heb 10:1).

(Gen 22:1–14; Gal 3:15–18; Heb 11:17–19). Building upon the previous conclusion that with the new priesthood comes a new law—the former priesthood is deposed and the law is changed—the author reaffirms that one law is taken away and another established (Heb 10:9). A second reading of the larger context will show that the first-second statement regards the covenant, since he already provided the identity of the "first" in a previous verse: "Therefore not even the first covenant was dedicated without blood" (Heb 9:18 with verse 20). The dedication of the second covenant was with the singularly effective blood of Christ.

On the practical level, the duty to obey moral laws has not been altered by Christ. Instead, we are taught that the excellence of moral law surpasses in glory what can even be written down! It is comprehended in the love of God, which is immeasurable, and in the holiness of God, which is perfect. Moral laws continue in full force as the absolute and universal standard of right and wrong; laws that God imprints even on the hearts of the unregenerate (Rom 2:14). Before giving the Mosaic covenant, the Lord held mankind to a righteous standard (Gen 6:5; 11:4–5; 12:11–13; 18:19–20; 19:34–36), so there was a "law of God" that applied to both the wicked and the faithful.

The cross of Jesus Christ was not so circumscribed in its effect on the old covenant that it merely replaced the priesthood of Israel and those laws connected with it. Conversely, the advent of Jesus Christ did not so much as dismantle the old covenant to suggest that "the Christian's moral conduct has nothing to do with the Decalogue or with any other part of the old covenant."[25] The apostles paved the way for removing the veil from the old covenant so that it reveals the glories of Jesus Christ and the righteousness of God, both of which are integral topics for the life of the church. Christ's fulfillment of moral laws satisfies God on our behalf, but it does not eliminate our duty to obey them. However, Christ's fulfillment of shadow laws for the sake of our redemption does eliminate our duty to obey them. The distinction between moral laws (which reflect the righteousness of God) and ceremonial laws (which foreshadow Christ and His work of redemption) was necessary to define the church's relationship to redemptive history and contemporary culture; to determine the applicability of old covenant demands on church polity, ethics, and behavior; and to package our obligation to God's law-covenant as a doctrine for church identification and education.

DYNAMIC DUOS

Dynamic Duos

The didymous nature of the law continues in Deuteronomy. The major portion of Deuteronomy comprises the second discourse of Moses to the *new* generation of Israelites as an *iteration* of the Law of God (Deut 5–26). The name for the fifth book of the Pentateuch is taken from the Septuagint translation of Deuteronomy 17:18, wherein the Lord instructs future kings to make a fresh copy of the law for themselves. This second law, or repetition of the law, was the personal copy of the king that he was to make his delight and pursuit every day of his life. After forty years in the wilderness,

25. Badenhorst, "What Are New Covenant Ethics?" 16.

Israel came to the Jordan River for the *second* time (Deut 27). By then, a second generation arose to cross the Jordon and Moses instructed them to assemble and *rehearse* the covenant for themselves. The twelve tribes were to divide in half, six (three pairs) tribes to congregate at the foot of Mount Gerizim and six (a second three pairs) tribes at a second elevation, Mount Ebal. Mount Gerizim was the mount from which blessings were announced and from Mount Ebal, cursings. On Mount Ebal were two structures: first, large stone monuments that were plastered and written upon plainly with the words of the law (*another duplication* of the Ten Commandments), and second, an altar of whole stones upon which peace offerings and burnt offering were made. The significance of this is that the Law—when all is said and done—transmits cursings; and without the sacrificial altar, there could be no basis for mercy (Lev 16:14–15). The cursings are treated separately under the rubric of the sacrificial altar in anticipation of a perfect sacrifice (Gal 3:10–13). The blessings of the Law were predicated upon faithful obedience (Deut 28:1–14)—the missing piece in Israel's history—yet the Law anticipated One who would do the Lord's will perfectly (Ps 40:7–8). Those blessings should come, of course, with the arrival of the new covenant embodied in Jesus Christ, who would proclaim with authority (Matt 7:28–29) from an ordinary hill outside Capernaum, those anticipated blessings and a proper understanding of the Law to the lost sheep of Israel (Matt 5–7).

In Scripture, pairs often have meaning, and when there are two objects or ideas, we compare or contrast, unite or divide. As Bullinger noted, "Two affirms that there is a difference—there is another; while One affirms that there is not another!"[26] When the Lord created Adam, he was another, yet it was God's desire that he be one with Him (Amos 3:3). He designed Eve to be in relation to Adam in a way that typified how redeemed mankind is to be in relation to God. The earthly relationship has the imprint of a desired future heavenly relationship between Christ and the church. The basis for typology is in the heavenly design of copies that have in mind an original (Heb 8:5; Exod 25:40).We process this through the language of simile and metaphor, antithesis and contradistinction, and type and antitype. When pairing occurs in Scripture, it may connote on the negative side division and enmity, and on the positive side harmony and assistance. The Lord's covenant employs the number two as a symbol of law, judgments, and witnesses. God and His covenant were two witnesses against Israel to justify His judgment of them (Deut 31:26), as were heaven and earth (Isa 1:2). Yet God promised and swore on His own Name to display the two-fold surety of His word to people of faith (Heb 6:17–20). The Law and the Prophets were witnesses to Christ (Matt 5:17; Acts 28:23; Rom 3:21), and on the basis of the testimony of two, the truth will be established (Exod 31:18; Deut 17:6).

The Ten Commandments were first spoken and *secondly* written. During Moses' second assent of Mount Sinai the Lord gave him the *two* tables of the covenant. Moses spent *two* periods of forty days in the presence of God. The Decalogue was written on *two* tables, symbolic of the two parties to it and the dividing nature of God's law. The

26. Bullinger, *Number in Scripture*, 92.

Decalogue was broken and then replaced, it is recorded *twice* in the OT, and there are *two* writings of it by God and by Israel, a *copy* of the Law was for the king, and the Law was *rehearsed* to Israel before entering the promised land. It is representative of God's covenant with His redeemed people and it foreshadows a better covenant made manifest by Christ's appearance. Christ, as the ideal Lawgiver and Mediator of a new covenant, fulfilled the dual role of Moses' ministry to Israel. Appendix 1 reviews the didymous nature of the Decalogue as well as its septenary perfection. The glory of the Decalogue was reflected upon Moses' face, but it faded, symbolizing the forthcoming sustained glory of the antitypical Christ. The glory of the old covenant that was veiled, as typified in Moses' face, was the system of ceremonial laws that shadowed forth the ultimate glory of Christ's redemption. In Christ, the Law is One. Therefore, from the perspective of the new covenant, the Decalogue is understood *not* as a summary of moral law but as a symbol of a pre-Christ relationship between God and His people *and* a type of the more glorious new covenant. In its veiled form, the Decalogue was a symbol of slavery from which Israel needed to be redeemed. When the apostles address ethical considerations regarding the life of the Christian, they do not once call upon the Decalogue as a unified moral voice. However, they freely reference nine of the Ten Commandments in their hortatory letters, but never the Sabbath as an ethical norm.

The Decalogue is a summary of the Mosaic covenant that contains both "righteous" and "shadow" laws. The Sabbath was an appropriate ceremonial law to include in the Ten Commandments because it was a sign of the covenant and the foremost of its shadow laws. It was the most experienced ceremony of the inhabitants of Israel and it has the most to say typologically regarding the means and results of redemption. As Leonhard Goppelt surveyed the many themes of typology, he concluded: "The Sabbath is interpreted as an eschatological type more than any other OT institution."[27] The Sabbath was given *two* redemptive reasons for its institution from the typic record of creation and the typic history of God's people. In Exodus 20, where the example of God in creation is highlighted, Moses presents the *problem* of the lost rest through sin. God is the creator of all things; it is His world to share with mankind, but man excluded himself from that rest through rebellion. In Deuteronomy 5, Moses presents the *solution* and its implications for the Israelite: mankind begins in slavery to sin, from which the Lord must redeem him at a costly price, thereby returning to a position of rest.

27. Goppelt. *Typos*, 37.

4

Sabbath Law

SEVEN OCCUPATIONS OF THE SABBATH

After the deliverance of Israel from the whips of Egyptian taskmasters, the Lord gave the Sabbath commandment and defined it with a list of positive and negative injunctions (Neh 9:14). The obedient Jew was responsible for pleasing God by adhering to the particulars of Sabbath law, taking the observance seriously, and determining to apply it fully each week (Deut 5:12–15). As important as the Sabbath was as the signal ordinance of the covenant and a typical ceremony of God's salvation and righteousness (Isa 56:2, 6), there is only spotted reference to Sabbath-keeping during Israel's long history (1 Sam 21:6; 1 Chr 9:32 [Saul]; 1 Chr 23:29–31 [David]; 2 Chr 2:4; 8:13 [Solomon]; 2 Chr 31:3 [Hezekiah]; 2 Kgs 4:23 [Shunnamite woman]). The first recorded infractions of the Sabbath (Exod 16:27–29; Num 15:32–26) foreshadowed a national disposition to despise the Sabbath (Jer 17:21–23; Amos 8:5). The direct consequence of their repetitious failure to obey the Law that was delivered to them at Sinai, specifically the Sabbatic Year, was the dispersion and a second captivity under Babylonia. The Jews, after returning in 471 BCE from exile, took Sabbath-keeping more seriously and codified what could or could not be done on that day.

Redacted from oral traditions, some of which originated from the days of Ezra, the Mishnah represents the height of rabbinic erudition on all matters of faith and praxis. The regulations concerning the Sabbath occupy 24 chapters of serious discussions of innumerable case problems concerning the minutest details. Raphael explains that the ritualization of the Sabbath began with the hope to recapture the glory of the quondam temple and kingdom.

> From this point on, Sabbath observance began to grow into the major base on which the rabbis later built. Whatever the Sabbath's origins, it had clearly been strengthened during the Exile, like the institution of the synagogue, as a way of restoring the pride that had been linked earlier to the monarchy and the Temple.[1]

The rabbis made good and necessary inferences based on their understanding of God's word. Though the Sabbath regulations eventually became preposterous and

1. Raphael, *Festivals*, 63.

ponderous, they began with the spiritual intention to avoid the Lord's judgment in the future.

> In their illustrious fear of desecrating the spirit of the day, the ancient rabbis established a level of observance which is within the reach of exalted souls but not infrequently beyond the grasp of ordinary men.[2]

In other words, it was a burden for the ordinary Jew to observe. Initially, the Jews were guilty of profaning the Sabbath by failing to observe it at all or blending it with idolatry, and in later centuries by lading the day with pious, but excessive, traditions. Both show the unwillingness of the Israelites to see in the Sabbath commandment the beautiful and captivating typology of salvation as prophesied by Ezekiel—they "have hidden their eyes from My Sabbaths" (Ezek 22:26).

And it is not that the Sabbath command in its pristine form was not already a challenge to obey. The general precept was that Israel was to keep a Sabbath. They were commanded to remember (*zakar*—Exod 20:8), keep (*shamar*—Exod 31:13,16; Lev 19:3,30; 26:2; Isa 56:2,4,6 *asah*—Deut 5:15), observe (*asah*—Exod 31:16), hallow (*qadesh*—Exod 20:8; Ezek 20:20) and sanctify (*qadesh*—Neh 13:22) the Sabbath. The intent of these verbs is that the Sabbath should be observed with the same vigor as all the other commandments delivered to Israel. Sabbath-keeping presents the adherent with not just a moment of obedience, but a whole day of obedience. Putting aside the onerous Pharisaic rules that developed in post-exilic times and focusing only upon what the law requires, keeping the Sabbath kept the Israelites occupied. A study of all Sabbath legislation arrives at seven principal aspects of Sabbath observance. The fulfillment of these laws is summarized in Appendix 2.

- When: sixth day of the week, sunset Friday to sunset Saturday
- Where: within boundaries of home and city
- Why: remembrance of past slavery, consideration of God's rest
- How: with no manner of work, but rest
- How: with no kindling of fire; instead, prepare beforehand
- Priests: sacrifice of two additional lambs, twelve cakes of showbread
- Consequences for breaking the Sabbath: cut off from Israel, death by stoning

This list coincides very closely to the work of Maimonides, a Jewish scholar of the twelfth century, who compiled a list of 613 commandments derived from the Pentateuch, of which six were devoted to particulars of Sabbath-keeping. These instructions were: 1) to rest on the seventh day (Exod 23:12), 2) not to do prohibited labor on the seventh day (Exod 20:10), 3) that the court not inflict punishment on *Shabbat* (Exod 35:3), 4) not to walk outside the city boundary on *Shabbat* (Exod 16:29), 5) to sanctify the day with Kiddush and Havdalah (Exod 20:8), and 6) to

2. Heschel, *Sabbath*, 17.

bring two additional lambs as burnt offerings on *Shabbat* (Num 28:9). The death penalty for profaning the Sabbath is not specifically mentioned by Maimonides; however, due to the numerous instances where stoning is commanded, he simply affirmed the legality of capital punishment by stoning under a general heading (making the seventh category).

Reformed analyses of Sabbath law have been restricted to those features that seem to proximate the behaviors desired of Christians on the Lord's Day. For example, the Heidelberg Catechism lists twenty-two scriptural citations for its answer to the question, "What is God's will for you in the fourth commandment?" and only two passages have anything to do with the Sabbath. The Heidelberg understands the fourth commandment to teach the necessity of Christian education, attending church on the first day of the week, learning God's word, participating in the sacraments, praying publicly, and bringing offerings for the poor, in addition to rest.[3]

Historically, Reformed theologians have admitted at least some ceremoniality of the Sabbath,[4] but beyond acknowledging that the physical rest speaks of the spiritual rest of salvation, they have not explored the typological meaning of any of the Sabbath laws that they believe are abrogated. For example, Barcellos simply asserts "in one way or another, the non-weekly Sabbaths pointed to Christ."[5] Other Reformed theologians, who argue the complete morality of the fourth commandment, think it is difficult to demonstrate any typological associations with Sabbath law.[6] So, what was the Jewish Sabbath really all about? And how is each Sabbath law a foreshadowing of the glorious details of redemption in Jesus Christ?

The Unmovable Sabbath (the Promise)

In order to observe the Sabbath, to sanctify it and keep it holy, the Jew had to know when the Sabbath began and when it ended. As Maimonides pointed out, the Jews ensured the sacredness of the day by beginning and ending it with short, reflective ceremonies that have endured to this day (Kiddush and Havdalah). They embraced the twenty-four hour period with rituals in the home as opposed to a congregational meeting or two in the middle of that period. Patterning the Sabbath day after the days of creation, i.e.—"the evening and the morning were the first day—" the Jews started the Sabbath at sundown of the sixth day. The Sabbath on the Day of Atonement was celebrated "from evening to evening" (Lev 23:32) and Nehemiah mentioned the need to shut the gates to Jerusalem because it "began to be dark before the Sabbath" (Neh 13:19). Therefore, the Jewish *religious* day roughly begins at 6 p.m. and ends the following day at 6 p.m.

3. *Ecumenical Creeds and Reformed Confessions*, 61. (Heidelberg Catechism, Q. 103)

4. Fairbairn, *Typology*, 2:450–51; Calvin, *Institutes*, 339 (2.8.28); Turretin, *Elenctic Theology*, 2:13:20, 84.

5. Barcellos, "Old Testament Theology of the Sabbath," 39.

6. Durham, *Exposition on the Ten Commandments*, 214.

> The beginning of the Jewish day should not be confused with the beginnings of the Sabbath, holidays, or fast days. For religious purposes, these are set to begin at sunset and to end with the appearance of the stars on the following evening, or, if the holiday has two days, on the subsequent evening.[7]

Of course, faithful Jews have been observing the Sabbath day assiduously since its inception, which means on a *weekly* basis on the seventh day of each week as prescribed in the fourth commandment. The law of the Sabbath is not simply about any sequence of seven days, but about a specific day each week.

Picture again the tri-partite sequence of the Sabbath: it begins at twilight, endures a season of darkness, and is renewed on a new day. The ceremonial meaning of *crepuscular* events, that is, events beginning in twilight, is that they are shadows and incomplete figures of other realities. When you live in a perpetual gloaming, you really have no idea just how bright the world can be! The Sabbath, though, is not just about light and darkness, but about living in shadow lands, digressing into darkness, and waking to the fullness of God's glory on a new and better day. It is a rehearsal of the fall, the plunging to greater depths of sin, and our rescue from darkness into God's marvelous light. Without the great and merciful salvation of the Lord, faithless masses live twilight lives and are eventually expelled to the outer darkness (Ps 39:5–6). Only the redeemed will wake to the light of God's glory (Isa 9:2).

The New Moon is also ceremonial because of what it signifies. Unlike the Sabbath, which moves through three distinct stages, the New Moon is a *crescive* event, and ceremonially highlights "increasing." The New Moon celebration begins with the unveiling of a thin crescent of moonlight and instills the expectation that it will become fuller as the days (i.e., nights) go by. Both the New Moon and Sabbath are types of redemption, and through their unique relationship to light and dark, they symbolize specific qualities of the Lord's work of redemption of mankind. The New Moon, like a leavened cake, describes the kingdom of God in its unstoppable progress toward full disclosure. The Sabbath, on the other hand, describes the sequence of redemption from a troubled estate, through increasing difficulties and finally into the state of divine blessedness. The Jews began their existence as toiling slaves, and as redemption neared, the difficulties increased both from the hands of Pharaoh and climactically by the angel of death at midnight. Finally, they were ushered into a new life with the treasures of Egypt and the protection of the Lord in the light of a new day.

Not only does the three-part transition through the Sabbath have typological meaning but the starting and ending points as well (Kiddush and Havdalah[8]). The tradition of the Jews to specifically acknowledge the beginning of the Sabbath in the evening on the sixth day and the completion of the Sabbath in the evening on the seventh day underscores the importance of this feature. Scripturally, the Jews have only two reasons to begin the Sabbath on the evening of the sixth day: 1) God alludes to beginning a day with the evening of the previous day with the creation phrase,

7. Zinberg, *Jewish Calendar*, 26.

8. Dawn, *Keeping the Sabbath*, 34, 140, 213. She encourages Christians to duplicate these Jewish traditions.

"the evening and morning were the [nth] day," and 2) since God specifically commanded that the *ceremonial* initiation of the Sabbath on the Day of Atonement be from "evening to evening" (Lev 23:32), then, by extension, what is required of the greatest Sabbath observance is required of the weekly Sabbaths. The first basis from the creation paradigm seems to define the parameters of a day, but the phrase is so puzzling that Jordan remarks, "This question has divided exegetes for decades, and no consensus is in sight."[9] Instead, the general biblical description of a "day" is that which comprises the time from waking up to going to sleep, or the time of light from dawn to dusk, rather than "evening and morning." In respect to setting the beginning and end of the Sabbath, this phrase presents several small difficulties. The first has to do with being consistent in assigning morality to the example of God in creation. If the Sabbath is taken as a "creation mandate" because of the example of God, then God's definition of the beginning and end of a day must also be taken seriously. This is the path Seventh-day sects have chosen. The second hurdle is that the phrase "the evening and the morning" is not used to define the seventh day. In fact, the omission seems intentional for symbolic reasons.

The second basis for establishing the beginning of the Sabbath on the evening of the sixth day comes from the explicit command to celebrate the sabbatical Day of Atonement "from evening to evening" (Lev 23:32). The Jews understand this to be the *ritual* definition of a day when observing certain calendar festivals. In other words, the seventh-day Sabbath is begun *ceremonially* in the evening of the sixth day (the evening of the sixth day is *not* the seventh day). One could argue that only the Day of Atonement was to be celebrated "evening to evening;" however, 1) the sabbatic cooking prohibition implies that no work was to be done after sunset on the sixth day of the week (Exod 16:23), 2) the gates of the city were closed before the onset of the Sabbath (Neh 13:19), 3) the review of feasts in Leviticus 23 begins with the Sabbath and 4) the unifying feature of the calendar is the Sabbath, which by definition, runs "evening to evening."

Sunday Sabbatarians want a Sabbath that is partly moral and partly ceremonial—moral enough to demand its observance by Christians and ceremonial enough to dispense with such details as when it begins and ends. Therefore, they appeal to the creation to give the Christian Sabbath the moral force of God's example, and they appeal to the ceremonial law to dispense with the timing of the Sabbath.[10] However, if God's example of taking rest carries any moral force, then His definition of when the Sabbath begins and ends should also be taken seriously. And if the beginning and ending of the Sabbath are ceremonial, then why aren't the Sabbath hours in between also ceremonial? Without a typological explanation for the onset and close of the Sabbath,

9. Jordan, *Creation in Six Days*, 203.

10. This exegetical tension is difficult to maintain and leads either to a return to the complete legal requirements of the Sabbath (as with Seventh-day sects) or the complete abrogation of the Sabbath as a ceremonial law (as with Evangelicals). As such, the Sunday Sabbatarian view is contradictory and confusing.

Sabbath-keeping Christians have no reason to change the Sabbath from an evening-to-evening observance to a midnight-to-midnight observance.[11]

When God set apart the seventh day at creation, Scripture provides little indication that He began His seventh-day rest in the evening of the sixth day. So, it is curious that the Sabbath, which solemnizes the "seventh day," actually begins on the evening of the sixth day, resulting in a ceremony of rest that comprises only eighteen hours of the seventh day. Compared to God's seventh-day rest, the Sabbath truncates the seventh day by ending, as it does, in the evening, rather than continuing until midnight. This discrepancy between the timing of the Sabbath and its reference to the seventh-day rest begs explanation.

Actual historical events are the bases for types, and the details of ceremonies have spiritual and symbolic meaning. The Sabbath, rather than celebrating God's seventh-day rest, instead celebrates the original holy union between God and humanity, which began in the evening of the sixth day and ended in the evening of the seventh day. The apex of creation was not in Adam alone but Adam with Eve, who was one flesh with Adam, foreshadowing the union of Christ and His bride. God's rest from creation may have comprised the seventh day, but His fellowship with a completed and honorable humanity began the evening of the sixth day. His true delight was in the representative union of Adam and Eve. Jordan proposes that Eve's fabrication occurred late afternoon on the sixth day,[12] so this event could be the reason behind the sixth-day evening commencement of the Sabbath. Either Eve was created later toward the evening, or another event occurred that better symbolized the oneness of God and man (i.e., the consummation of their marriage). By the evening of God's seventh-day rest, His holy fellowship with mankind was interrupted by sin about twenty-four hours after Eve's creation. While God's seventh-day rest continued for the remainder of the day as a true rest from the work of creation, as a symbol of His fellowship with Adam and Eve, the seventh-day rest came to an end near evening. The Sabbath ceremony recounts the events of the sixth and seventh days of that first week to symbolize the beginning and end of holy fellowship between God and man in the garden. The day of Sabbath joy

11. Greg L. Price argues that the Jewish tradition of beginning the Sabbath in the evening of the sixth day is unscriptural in order to deal with this tension. Without understanding the fulfillment of Sabbath law by Christ's resurrection, Sabbatarian thinkers must engage in the debate as to when to begin and end their Christian Sabbath. If the fourth commandment is a moral law, then the matter of timing is equally moral, as Greg Price intuits in his booklet, *When Does The Sabbath Begin?* He asks, "When does the first day of the week begin? Does it begin Saturday evening or Sunday morning? This question has both theological and practical implications. Theologically, all unnecessary work and employment of people is to cease on the Sabbath. Does working Saturday evening or Sunday evening constitute Sabbath breaking? That depends upon when the Christian Sabbath begins." The practical implications for the church are for elders to know who to discipline for breaking the Sabbath, and, of course, for members to know what behaviors are worthy of discipline. Price supports Sunday worship beginning in the morning, but since it is a Christian *Sabbath*, he goes to great lengths to re-interpret OT passages dealing with reckoning the day, eventually implicating the Jews for erroneously beginning their Sabbath on Friday evening instead of Saturday morning. This sort of exercise is embarrassing for the church and an affront to Christ, who fulfilled the Jewish ceremonial laws of time and instituted a new form of congregational worship with His resurrection in the morning of the first day of the week.

12. James Jordan, *Creation in Six Days*, 47.

ends with approaching darkness, thus intimating that the whole week is symbolically dark[13] until the next Sabbath; and the whole week of human history is in the darkness of sin until the final redemption. The Sabbath ceremony calls its observers to redemption from the curse of the fall.

There is another possible explanation for beginning the Sabbath in the evening of the sixth day and completing it in the evening of the seventh day. As described in the three-part unfolding of the Sabbath hours—twilight, darkness, and morning (new day)—the Sabbath ceremony duplicated the course of Israel's redemption from Egypt. Beginning with the application of blood on the doorposts of their home, the Jews remained in their homes and ate their evening meal. The following Passover ceremony conformed to this historic timing by requiring the lambs to be sacrificed "at twilight, at the going down of the sun, at the *time* you came out of Egypt" (Deut 16:6). Though they did not depart until very early the next morning, the evening events of the prior day are presented as a unit with their physical departure from Egypt. The evening of the exodus finds Israel a day's journey from Ramses and encamped in Succoth (Exod 13:20). The evening of this day concludes the "day" of their exodus that began the evening of the previous day. Their redemption began in one home (in Egypt) and concluded in a new home (encamped around the Lord).

The Sabbath was given to Israel as a "perpetual covenant," to be observed throughout all their generations forever (Exod 31:16). It shares this promise of perpetuity not only with the covenants of old but with other ceremonial laws, such as the burnt offering (Lev 6:13), showbread (Lev 24:1–8), Jubilee (Lev 25:23), New Moon (Isa 66:23), Passover (Exod 12:14,24), Feast of Unleavened Bread (Exod 12:17), Feast of Tabernacles (Lev 23:41), the temple (Ezek 37:26–28) and its artifacts (Num 18:7ff), the Aaronic priesthood (Exod 40:13–15; Num 25:11–13), their holy garments (Exod 28:43), their dietary laws (Lev 10:9), and their foot and garment washings (Exod 28:21; Num 19:21). Thus, it takes its place beside those laws that speak of better things. The Sabbath sacerdotal duty to prepare bread-cakes and incense is the outworking of the "everlasting covenant" with Israel (Lev 24:8), and the Sabbath was a visible sign of Israel's covenant with the Lord at Mount Sinai (Exod 31:17). This continuing observance requires a continuing people, and this ensures that new life will ascend before the finality of death. The Sabbath is a unifying force for Israel through the unending iteration of life and death, but it symbolizes that there is more to be hoped for: the salvation of God and the revelation of His righteousness (Isa 56:1–2), the personal escort of God to His holy mountain to be filled with joy (Isa 56:6–7), and ascendancy and satisfaction in the rewards of life and the fellowship of God (Isa 58:13–14). From the Jewish perspective, the Sabbath did not and cannot change. It reflects the revealed will of God and His unchanging and trustworthy character (Jer 31:35–37). The stamp

13. Jewish tradition endeavors to explain the origin of fire, usually attributing it as a gift from God upon their exile from the garden. If fire was a gift, it was also a terrible reminder of the judgment of separation from God as viewed from the "flaming sword," the first mention of fire (Gen 3:24). If their sin and banishment happened toward the end of daylight on the seventh day, God at the same time typified the need for His light while sojourning in a hostile and darkened land.

of perpetuity on the Sabbath commandment confers no more morality on it than the perpetuity of other ceremonial laws. However, in covenantal language, the "forever" feature can be true only if both parties live forever. Only the Lord can vow in His own name that His promises are sure forever. Only the Lord can assign an unchangeable status to ceremonial rites because they reflect better, more enduring promises. The perpetuity of the Sabbath is not for the sake of Sabbath, but to symbolize an unending relationship between God and His people. It intimates a time when all is a continuing and abiding Sabbath. As Kaplan expresses, "On every Sabbath, we partake of the Future world—of the peace and harmony of the Messianic Age."[14] The intimation of an eternal Sabbath is symbolic of a greater reality to be fulfilled with the advent(s) of the Messiah. Sabbatarians cite this passage to claim either an ongoing Sabbath for the church or an eternal observation of the Sabbath in heaven. However, the context of the passage is about the quality of God's redemption, that even eunuchs—who represent the outcasts of society—will share completely in God's grace if they display trust in the Lord by adhering to the old covenant. Besides the Sabbath, the text also refers to God's house and mountain, the altar and sacrifices, all of which symbolize faith in God's promises. It is a myopic interpretation to single out the Sabbath star as a literal commandment while ignoring the other players in the field.

Based on the sabbatic theme, Isaiah prophesied of the day when the existing cosmos will be brought to an end and the worlds will be made afresh for the saints of God.

> "For as the new heavens and the new earth which I will make shall remain before Me," says the Lord, "So shall your descendants and your name remain.
>
> And it shall come to pass that from one New Moon to another, And from one Sabbath to another, All flesh shall come to worship before Me," says the Lord. (Isa 66:22–23)

The weekly Sabbath and the recurring New Moon are inseparably linked together in this passage to describe the perpetual holy worship of the Lord during timeless eternity. It cannot be describing a heavenly worship that is limited to weekly and monthly rituals reminiscent of the foreshadowing figures of the old covenant (Rev 21:23). The symbolic use of the New Moon and the Sabbath speak of the salvation and restoration of the cosmos, themes that will inhabit the praises of God's people throughout eternity. What these two ceremonial laws typify will be the eternal topic of God's people: a complete redemption that brought us to a new creation and the increasing glory of God's kingdom. This verse no more supports observation of the Sabbath for the Christian than it does the New Moon. As Heather McKay notes, "scholars who claim the dominance of the Sabbath worship seem oblivious to the equality of the New Moon and Sabbath in this text."[15] The equality of the Sabbath and New Moon are in their ceremonial status, and therefore, in their typological prefigurement of Christ's redemption. The text clearly depicts the Sabbath as a type of eternal rest and the New

14. Kaplan, *Sabbath*, 24.

15. McKay, *Sabbath and Synagogue*, 33. Though noting the contextual equality of the Sabbath and New Moon, McKay was still unable to offer a reasonable explanation for their partnership in this text.

Moon as a type of the re-creation. This is the experience of Christians now, for Christ came in the "fullness" of time (Gal 4:4). The former glass of time was emptied with the advent of Christ, and a new epoch began with the Lord's Day in which we celebrate the super-abundance of the new birth and the resurrection.

Jesus Christ is the Sabbath fulfilled. We no longer taste of eternity in the Sabbath, but drink profusely of that promise through Jesus Christ Himself (1 John 5:12), who is the beginning and the end, the Alpha and Omega, the Faithful and True. He is the full expression of the Godhead in bodily form and gloriously resides in heaven awaiting His cherished bride. The sense of God's unalterable promises to a stiff-necked nation, His enduring faithfulness to an unfaithful people, and His continuing welfare across multiple generations as portrayed in the Sabbath, is now manifested gloriously in Jesus Christ, His Son. In Jesus Christ, the promises of God find their hearty "Amen" (2 Cor 1:18–22) and of His kingdom there shall be no end. The Sabbath served its ceremonial and signal functions for the Jews and found its fulfillment in Jesus Christ, through whom the promises of God are sure, immutable, and everlasting.

The Bound Sabbath (Fellowship)

Resisting the social pressures to attend a particular church while concurrently pretending to be a religious person, Emily Dickinson wrote, "Some keep the Sabbath going to Church, I keep it, staying at home." Ironically, she probably did not realize that the Bible teaches that the Sabbath was originally centered in the home. When the Sabbath was first given to Israel, the Lord commanded, "Let every man remain in his place; let no man go out of his place on the seventh day" (Exod 16:29). The obvious intent of this command was to keep the Sabbath a day of rest in and around the home, a matter of personal and family observance, rather than of corporate worship. Rushdoony concurs:

> *First*, the Sabbath in the Old Testament law was not primarily a day of *worship* but a day of rest. The pattern of weekly worship did not exist in the Old Testament law. The synagogue introduced it [congregational worship] in the inter-testamental period, and the New Testament clearly practiced it and urged it (Heb 10:25). In the Old Testament, worship was family-centered, and woven into the fabric of daily life.[16]

The OT provides no rules that define the scope of Sabbath travel restrictions; however, barring other necessities of life, the Jew was expected to abide on the Sabbath. Were travel over a Sabbath or sabbatic feast day necessary, it would certainly be logistically difficult since most of their kinsmen were themselves occupied with Sabbath-keeping. Despite the clarity of the command, it became necessary to delineate the extent of home-boundedness required, as it conflicted with other commands that involved travel, such as taking an eight-day-old baby to the priest to be circumcised (John 7:22–24). Post-captivity scholarship on this matter gave rise to a complex system of rabbinic laws formulated to avoid the possibility that one's travel could be regarded

16. Rushdoony, *Institutes of Biblical Law*, 130 (emphasis in the original).

as Sabbath-breaking, hence the concept of a "Sabbath day's journey,"[17] which Luke used to describe the distance from the Mount of Olives to Jerusalem (Acts 1:12). The Pharisees were obsessed with defining private and public spheres of activity, probably from an interpretation of Jeremiah's charge to Sabbath-breaking Israelites not to "carry a burden out of your houses on the Sabbath day" (Jer 17:22). Edersheim prefaces his discussion of Sabbath regulations of the Mishnah with a description of the concept of "commixtures" (*erubin*), a legal machination designed to make daily activities less burdensome by connecting what may be considered a public domain with a private domain so an individual could have more freedom.

> Similarly, an extension of what was allowed as a 'Sabbath journey' might be secured by another 'commixture,' the 'Erubh' or 'connection of boundaries.' An ordinary Sabbath day's journey extended 2,000 cubits beyond one's dwelling. But if at the boundary of that 'journey' a man deposited on the Friday food for two meals, he thereby constituted it his dwelling, and hence might go on for other 2,000 cubits.[18]

The strictness applied to Sabbath travel was not exclusive to the Pharisees. Archeologist Yigael Yadin comments upon the peculiar and unnecessary severity with which the Essene community sanctified the Sabbath.

> For example, in Deuteronomy 23:12–14, we are told there is to be a place outside the camp in the wilderness for defecation. The Essenes applied this injunction literally to the entire city of Jerusalem. The Temple Scroll forbids the building of toilets in the city. "You shall make a place for the hand (a toilet) outside the city to which they shall go out . . . 3,000 cubits [outside the city] in order that it will not be visible from the city. A similar rule is found in another Dead Sea Scroll known as the War Scroll. Because three thousand cubits is beyond the limit of permitted walking on the Sabbath, Essenes who lived in Jerusalem could not walk to the latrines on the seventh day—and they therefore refrained from relieving themselves on the Sabbath.[19]

Regardless of what we think of these ascetic interpretations of the Law, the Sabbath was understood by the Pharisees and Essenes as a day selected by the Lord to ensure a weekly abiding within their dwellings and within their own community.

> Six days shall work be done, but the seventh day is a Sabbath of solemn rest, a holy convocation. You shall do no work on it; it is the Sabbath of the Lord in all your dwellings. (Lev 23:3)

Yet, the Pharasaic and Essenic Sabbath regulations are a sober reminder that the quest for increased purity and sanctification can bring people to the most draconian practices.

17. Five furlongs or 2,000 paces equal a Sabbath day's journey, a furlong being 600 feet, thus 3,000 feet or three-fifths of a mile.

18. Edersheim, *Life and Times*, 1046.

19. Yadin, "The Temple Scroll," 102.

As presented in the OT, the Sabbath was a day of family oriented rest. This had the practical benefit of promoting the sanctity of home life as the building block for national, religious, and civil unity and solidarity, following years of slavery. But this kept the Jews to themselves, observing, as it were, a microcosm of temple place-worship in all their dwellings throughout the land. The Jews were accustomed to place-worship, having received from Moses the Lord's command to erect an altar on Mount Ebal in Samaria (Deut 27:4) and later at Jerusalem. The promise to Israel as they took up residence in Canaan was to enjoy a rest of peace and safety because the Lord chose to place His name in their land.

> But when you cross over the Jordan and dwell in the land which the *Lord* your God is giving you to inherit, and He gives you rest from all your enemies round about, so that you dwell in safety, then there will be the place where the *Lord* your God chooses to make His name abide. (Deut 12:10–11)

Place-worship and rest are conceptually linked through old covenant ceremonial law, and both are fulfilled in Jesus Christ. The hour predicted by Jesus *has* come (John 4:21), in which the worshippers of God are not restricted by place. Beneficiaries of the new covenant enjoy the spiritual rest of peace and safety, not because God places His name at their physical residence or above the church door, but because He places His name on His saints, the pillars of the new Jerusalem (Rev 3:12; 14:1). A new abode has been chosen, a new place for God's name, and it is in the believer's heart, made a temple for the living God (2 Cor 6:16). With the fulfillment of the Sabbath comes the advent of a new[20] household of faith, a new family for those called out from pagan religions and outdated Judaism. No longer tethered to the family dwelling, the believer in Jesus becomes the abode of the Lord, "that Christ may dwell in your hearts through faith" (Eph 3:17). This is not a weekly experience, but a daily experience of soulical rest in Christ and in His truth (John 15:4; 2 John 9). The distance one travels is not an issue when the Lord of the Universe has taken up residence in the believer's heart.

Yet the most likely typological understanding of the command to abide in the home and the related concepts of domains, boundaries, and travel is that it pictures the Edenic or primal abode of man on the seventh day. In addition to the legal association between the Sabbath and remaining in one's dwelling, the semantic link implies a symbolic meaning, as Kaplan pointed out.

> In a sense, G-d descended to the world on the Sabbath of creation. It is interesting to note that the word *Shabbos* is related to the word *Sheves*, to dwell. On the Sabbath, G-d made the world His dwelling place.[21]

20. "New" in this sense means "expanded" in that the universal church is not a different entity from the collection of saints prior to Christ, but that the gates are opened to bring in *goyim* on a larger scale.

21. Kaplan, *Sabbath*, 21. In my references, the Hebrew is *moshab* or *yashab*. The first association between *shabbos* and *yashab* is in the law (Lev 23:3), not in Genesis. As Kaplan states, however, the archetype is there. So, as a precursor to the Sabbath ceremony, the creation rest intimates that Eden is a special place of God's habitation and that the garden within Eden is a place of even greater intimacy with God.

Of course, Christians acknowledge the typology of God's presence in Eden as a foreshadowing of the incarnation of Jesus Christ, the penultimate tabernacle of God among men. In other words, the creation account foreshadows the eternal habitation of God with His people (Rev 21:3). On the seventh day, Adam and Eve dwelled where God dwelled; under His authority, they exercised dominion in that place; and from that designated location, they could expand their family into greater realms. Just as God sustained the universe on the seventh day and could be heard "walking in the garden in the cool of the day" (Gen 3:8), so the Jews acted out that kingly dominion in their home-garden by refraining from sweat-cursed labor and enjoying their peace and harmony with God. The Jews did not perceive their Sabbath work restriction as mere listlessness and inactivity, but allowed to themselves those sustaining activities such as caring for a baby, dressing, engaging in relationships, and moving about their domicile. Surely, their Sabbath domain was limited, but this reflected the boundaries of the garden compared to the larger geography of Eden in which it existed (Gen 2:8–10). The Lord describes His relationship to the created domains of heaven and earth in terms of ownership, inhabitancy, and rest.

> Thus says the *Lord*: "Heaven is My throne, And earth is My footstool. Where is the house that you will build Me? And where is the place of My rest? (Isa 66:1; quoted in Matt 5:35 and Act 7:49)

As Lord, He determined that the seventh day should be a day without creating, and in this sense He did not work on the seventh day and so rested from that kind of work, but this does not mean that He ceased every other kind of work in His own habitation. On His seventh day of rest, the Lord still sustained the universe to the minutest detail of every biological, geological, and astrological system, from His throne in heaven to the particular place of His presence in the garden of Eden, His private domain. From the freedom the Jews had to do some kinds of "work" on the Sabbath, Lincoln argues *a fortiori* that God has the same, if not more, freedom to do as He pleases.

> He rested from His work on the world but not from His work with humanity. He was not bound by the Sabbath, for if a person on the Sabbath may carry things around a private house, how much more may God work on the Sabbath since the whole world is His private domain.[22]

In Jesus' conflicts with the Pharisees about the Sabbath, He asserted His lordship over creation and therefore over the Sabbath, intimating the fulfillment of that which the seventh day and the Sabbath exemplified in terms of an expectation of an eternal state of rest that God maintains. To achieve that blessed state, God signified that He was willing to do the work of redemption on behalf of man, even on the Sabbath day, just as He took up the work of redemption for Adam and Eve in His garden-house on the seventh day of rest. As the Jews lived with the contradictions involving themes of work and rest, a few of them understood that the seventh-day rest, the Sabbath, the

22. Lincoln, "Sabbath, Rest, and Eschatology," 203.

sabbatic festivals, Canaan, and the temple were only temporary pictures of a more enduring eschatological rest when God and man coexist in fellowship.

Yet we have not exhausted the symbolic themes of the Sabbath requirement to remain in one's dwelling from the evening of the sixth day to the evening of the seventh day. As mentioned under the previous heading, the beginning and ending of the Sabbath underscored the theme of redemption through the substitution of one domicile for another. The redeemed Israelites first dwelt in tents, symbolic of their transiency, but these tents *were* the residences of the redeemed and therefore also symbolic of their community with God, who tented among them. Therefore, whether they lived in tents or in homes of stone, the most significant matter is that they were in the presence of God. No longer must they apply the blood to the doorposts of their home for they lived in the security and comfort of God's word. As a door is to a home, so a gate is to a city and a border to a country. They perform the function of separating those who are inside from those who are outside; and they convey the sense of identity, security, and protection. The home, the city, and the land of Canaan were types of a better land, a new Jerusalem, and a mansion prepared for us. It was the blood upon the doorposts that preserved the firstborn of Israel from the angel of death, so the Sabbath command to abide in their dwellings recalls the redemption of Israel just as surely as the Passover. Gates are also related to the theme of redemption. During the reign of King Asa, the kingdom of Judah prospered in the peace of God, which inspired Asa to fortify his cities with walls, towers, gates, and bars.

> And he built fortified cities in Judah, for the land had rest; he had no war in those years, because the Lord had given him rest.
>
> Therefore he said to Judah, "Let us build these cities and make walls around them, and towers, gates, and bars, while the land is yet before us, because we have sought the Lord our God; we have sought Him, and He has given us rest on every side." So they built and prospered. (2 Chr 14:6–7)

Only by the gates could one enter the city or depart it, but when they were closed they were veritable walls. Besides the possible ethical lessons of foresightedness and diligence on the part of Asa, the more important point to make is that redemptive peace is a heavily guarded and protected peace. Nothing is able to separate us from the love of God that is in Christ Jesus. Our spiritual peace and prosperity are secured by the unwavering power of God. Only in the security of this kind of relationship can the sheep go in and out and find pasture (John 10:9). The symbolic disfranchisement of an Israelite from the company of the redeemed could be found in their capital punishment outside the gates of the city (Deut 17:5). On a national scale, rebellious idolatry was recompensed by a breach of Israel's borders and the deportation of its citizens (2 Chr 36:15–21).

Because of the redemptive symbolism of gates, the Sabbath ceremonialized the culture of the redeemed by shutting the gates of the city and setting guards (Neh 13:19–22; Jer 17:24, 27). This contributed to the Jewish legislations about defining private and public domains, traveling within or between those domains, and carrying things from one domain to another; but, unfortunately, little rumination was devoted to the realm of redemption. With the advent of Christ and His all-sufficient death-payment for our sins, we have in reality that which the OT symbols and ceremonies looked forward to: an intimate and unshakable indwelling of the Lord (Rom 8:11; 1 Cor 3:16; Phil 3:17–19), a double-caress that binds us in fellowship with the Father and the Son (John 10:28–29), and a guarding peace that surpasses all comprehension (Phil 4:7), simply because our redemption is not based upon physical enclosures but spiritual declarations. There are no borders to patrol in Christendom, no city gates for us to monitor in some recurring seventh-day fashion, nor are we to remain in the security of our home on the Sabbath day (or any other day), for in Christ we are no longer of the world—just sojourners in it. These ceremonies of confinement defined the Sabbath institution and with their annulment Christians are released to greater freedoms in their Lord.

The Unbearable Sabbath (Trust)

The predominant character of Sabbath observance is cessation from labor and the avoidance of work. Without much amplification, the Pentateuch simply states that children, servants, and livestock "shall do no work" (Exod 20:10); and that the ox, ass, son of a servant or stranger "may rest" (Exod 23:12). On the basis of modern standards of legislation, this is certainly vague. What specific activities of man or beast, child or stranger, are regarded as work? Moses conveyed the words of the Lord, "Work shall be done for six days, but the seventh day shall be a holy day for you, a Sabbath of rest to the Lord. Whoever does any work on it shall be put to death" (Exod 35:2). That this one day is contrasted with the other six in which work may be done may imply that only occupational work is outlawed. However, the command to prepare on the sixth day what will be eaten on the seventh day (Exod 16:29) extended the scope of the work prohibition into the domestic realm. It is likely that the prohibition of lighting a fire meant that if one chose to eat on the Sabbath, the victuals could not even be warmed (Exod 35:3). The man who merely gathered sticks on the seventh day, presumably with the intention of building a fire (or to keep a fire going), was detained and later stoned to death for dishonoring the Sabbath through that form of domestic work (Num 15:32). Given such a broad definition of "work" and only two examples in case law, the Jews had to ask themselves, of all the things they could possibly do, either domestic and occupational, which of them, if done on the Sabbath, would be considered sinful—a profanation of the Sabbath, a violation of the covenant, and perhaps worthy of death?

Not until the days of impending judgment upon unfaithful Israel—nearly a thousand years later—was there any further description of what kinds of "work" activities were proscribed on the Sabbath. Jeremiah warned, "Take heed to yourselves, and bear no burden on the Sabbath day, nor bring it in by the gates of Jerusalem; nor carry a burden out of your houses on the Sabbath day, nor do any work, but hallow the Sabbath day, as I commanded your fathers" (Jer 17:21–22). Nehemiah amplified the list of prohibitions: "treading winepresses on the Sabbath, and bringing in sheaves, and loading donkeys with wine, grapes, figs, and all kinds of burdens, which they brought into Jerusalem on the Sabbath day . . . on which they were selling provisions" (Neh 13:15).

Additionally, the Jew could not buy things on the Sabbath (Neh 13:16), and from Nehemiah's actions, the gates to Jerusalem could not be opened or shut (Neh 13:19). Most of these prohibitions directly relate to activities intended to produce a living, but given the importance of the Sabbath and the apparent prohibition from working at all, would it not be wise to refrain from all manner of work on the seventh day, since the command also applies to children capable of work (Exod 20:9–10)? Is it work to repair a door, empty the trash, go swimming, carry an infant, or write a letter? The activities to consider are endless; some can easily be characterized as work, others cannot. In order to obey the command, "do no manner of work," the Jews were duty bound to inquire, regarding any conceivable activity, whether or not it constituted work.

Refusing to be baited in answering these questions, modern Sabbatarians take a different approach. Chantry warns his readers from seeking specific answers because their questions may be motivated by fear, or because their questions risk inflating the ego of the minister, and, finally, because an unhealthy relationship may develop between the church member and his leader—the member becoming overly dependent and the minister becoming overly authoritarian. A genuine Christian, Chantry maintains, is "delighted to keep the Sabbath holy," and with general principles alone, guided by the Holy Spirit, is able "to face every eventuality."[23]

> The Sabbath Day is to be kept in mind. It is to be devoted with joy to the worship and service of God. This day is special and is not to be cluttered with our work or with the employment of others, except so far as will serve in God's worship, in man's necessities, and in showing mercy to our fellow human beings.[24]

Unfortunately, these general principles are so vague that they beg questions anyway; and his definition fails to explain how cooking for one's family or gathering sticks for a fire is *not* a necessity or mercy for man. Chantry helpfully states that motivation and external obedience must go hand in hand, but the stick gatherer's motivation was never assessed as a mitigating factor to his outward profanation of the Sabbath. The question before Moses was whether or not the man gathered sticks, not *why* he gathered sticks or *how many* sticks he gathered. Yet Chantry muses "that the same Sabbath requirement be handled in various ways according to the motives of the ones who hear." This sounds as if it is up to the individual to decide for himself whether an activity is "work" or not, and up to the pastor to decide whether or not someone's motivation was honorable. As a pastor, Chantry would know that good intentions are not the final word when it comes to outward behavior.

Sabbatarian author Bruce Ray states that as we attempt to think out the implications of principles, "we will not always agree on how to apply them."[25] In fact, he disagrees with the ascetic interpretations of Pink and Pipa[26] with regard to the meaning

23. Chantry, *Call the Sabbath a Delight*, 79, 105.

24. Ibid., 105.

25. Ray, *Celebrating the Sabbath*, 111.

26. Pink, *The Lord's Day*, 18.

of Isaiah 58:13, which discourages the Jews from doing their own pleasure or speaking their own words. This phrase certainly includes all sorts of activities and varieties of work, but Ray focuses his attention on recreation alone and determines that "some moderate recreation may be admissible on the Sabbath."[27] This is as vague as the Scripture he hopes to interpret, and it begs many questions. Which moderate recreations may be admissible and which may not be admissible? Are all light recreations admissible and heavy recreations inadmissible? Who determines whether a recreation is light, moderate, or heavy? Ray wants to refrain from answering these kinds of questions because of the understandable risk of making oppressive traditions. The biblical and reasonable approach is not to flesh out what is and what is not a sinful work on the Sabbath, but "to think the best of those who may in good conscience reach different conclusions than we do."[28] While these sentiments from Chantry and Ray are worth mentioning, Sabbath-keepers need an objective standard to define what is or is not acceptable Sabbath behavior. Moral law is not defined subjectively. Seeking a definitive answer whether a particular activity is sinful is not something a Sabbath-keeper should avoid, for the answer helps erect a fence of safety to ensure a comfortable rest within the requirements of Sabbath law.

Noticing the juxtaposition of the Sabbath command (Exod 35:1–3) and the following description of the work involved in the construction of the tabernacle (Exod 35:4–29), the Jews developed such a "fence" by classifying prohibited work into thirty-nine categories.

sowing	plowing	reaping	binding sheaves	threshing
winnowing	sifting (selecting)	grinding	sifting in a sieve	kneading
baking	shearing the wool	washing it	beating it	dyeing it
spinning	putting it on the weaver's beam	making two thrum threads	weaving two threads	separating two threads
making a knot	undoing a knot	sewing two stitches	tearing in order to sew two stitches	catching deer
killing	skinning	salting it	preparing its skin	scraping off its hair
cutting it up	writing two letters	scraping in order to write two letters	building	pulling down
extinguishing fire	lighting fire	beating with the hammer	carrying a possession from one place to another	

27. Ray, *Celebrating the Sabbath*, 110.

28. Ibid., 111.

It was educed that every type of work that went into the construction of the tabernacle was the type of work that was forbidden on the Sabbath. The Hebrew word for "work" is the same in both passages, and the context provided a rational association. Kaplan explains that

> The prohibition is not against actual labor as much as against ritual work. We have also seen that in order to understand the Sabbath, we must define ritual work as any act in which man interferes with nature and shows his mastery over it.[29]

All of the principal categories above are "fathers" (*aboth*) to further categories called "descendants" (*toledoth*). Heschel elaborates:

> If you scatter two seeds, you have been sowing. In general, the principle is laid down, that anything by which the ground may be benefited is to be considered a 'work' or 'labour,' even it were to sweep away or to break up a clod of earth. Nay, to pluck a blade of grass was a sin. Similarly, it was sinful labour to do anything that would promote the ripening of fruits, such as to water, or even to remove a withered leaf. To pick fruit, or even to lift it from the ground, would be like reaping.[30]

Ironically, over the centuries through the process of inference and deduction, all intending to bring honor to the Sabbath day, a labyrinth of prohibited labors was constructed by religious leaders. Hertzberg presented this rabbinic impression from the Mishnah, which noted, even in those days, the extravagant development of rules concerning the Sabbath:

> The rules about the Sabbath, Festal offerings and sacrilege are like mountains hanging by a hair, for there is scanty teaching about them in Scripture while the rules are many.[31]

Present-day Sabbath-keepers are no different, asserts Gary North.

> Their claim rests on the fact that they are not employed for profit on Sundays, and they do not watch the Green Bay Packers play the Cleveland Browns on television. Some of them will not listen to a news broadcast or read the Monday morning issue either, knowing that it was printed on Sunday.
>
> Naturally, the Monday morning Sabbatarian quarterbacks who at least enjoy *reading* about the Packers-Browns game, even though it is immoral to watch it or play it, resent the rigor of their fellow Sabbatarians who refuse to read the Monday afternoon account of it (the morning edition, as I have already mentioned, goes unread). They think of the others as "legalists," while extremists who follow the implications of their position naturally view their weaker brethren as "latent antinomians." Such is the way of men: he who re-

29. Kaplan, *Sabbath*, 26. The Lord's prescription that altars be constructed with natural rocks indicates the possibility that man may inadvertently profane something holy by acting upon it, "for if you use your tool on it, you have profaned it" (Exod 20:25).

30. Edersheim, *Life and Times*, 1051.

31. Hertzberg, *Judaism*, 114.

> sents getting his toes stepped on calls his brother a legalist; he who delights in stepping resents all others' obvious inconsistency.[32]

Attempting to keep the Sabbath lends itself to this nitpicking. Richard Gaffin pines for the days when Reformed communities argued every week about the implications of Sabbath-keeping, revealing how seriously they revered the day.[33] While discord is not a Sabbath duty, discomfort is. First of all, resting on the seventh day from *all* work was extremely disruptive for the Jew. It affected the whole of his lifestyle on that day. What inconveniences are Sabbatarians enduring to honor the day? Modern Sabbatarians by comparison are only mildly inconvenienced by their attention to this command. The Jews of ages past were pressed to trust the Lord for their provisions, but that aspect of trust is entirely missing from the observance of modern-day Sabbatarians. Only a century ago, if Sabbatarians provided a service on an urgent basis, no payment was accepted—not on Sunday or any following day—trusting that the Lord would eventually provide for their means. But today, it is considered an "emergency" to employ workers to hook up unresting machine pumps to the udders of uncomfortably milk-laden cows on the Christian Sabbath, and to eventually get paid for that milk.

Secondly, partner to the definition of work is the matter of enforcement. The justice due to those who failed to keep the Sabbath in Israel was the same as to those who murdered, courted witchcraft, or practiced idolatry. Obviously, no Jew wanted the epithet "Sabbath-breaker," hence the face-saving and self-effacing adherence to the most rigorous rules. One does not have to speculate why the Jews observed, with painstaking precision, the traditional Sabbath regulations passed down from preceding generations. Likewise, many Christians will adhere to Sabbath observances, not because they understand and approve of the rationale and not because they have made this the topic of thorough study, but because they don't want to be judged by Sabbatarian zealots or face the displeasure of their elders.

Lastly, Sabbath law teaches that an activity can be acceptable to God six days of the week, but it is *sinful* on the seventh day—not merely inappropriate, or shortsighted, or even blundering and insensitive, but *sinful*. Even if one attends two services on Sunday and visits an aunt in the rest home, it remains a sin to vacuum the house, handle a business call, or make tomorrow's to-do list. Christians intuitively have a hard time observing the Sabbath because these restrictions seem so contradictory to liberty in Christ.

It takes work to keep the Sabbath.[34] Indeed, it is even work to remember it! This commandment, above the others, affirms that even while attempting to please God by rigorous attention to the details of the law, one cannot be sure enough has been done (or in this case, one cannot be sure enough has *not* been done). Like the Pharisees of Jesus' day, those who attempt to keep perfectly the Sabbath today will become slaves

32. North, "Economics of Sabbath-Keeping," 827–28.

33. Gaffin, "Westminster and the Sabbath," 125.

34. This is why the author of Hebrews could say paradoxically "Let us labor therefore to enter into that rest" (Heb 4:11), meaning the labor of faith, not of works. Legalism will make work out of resting.

to the day. Ironically, the part of the Ten Commandments that was meant to be a reminder of the hardship of past slavery and to ensure a day of commemorative rest became a severe taskmaster. However, in spite of the benefits of a weekly rest from work, the Jews found that they spent considerable energy trying to keep the Sabbath without tension and guilt.

Ceasing from labor was commonly defined in terms of refraining from carrying a burden (Jer 17:22). Therefore, the Mishnah opens with regulations designed to answer what constituted a burden; what is its weight, where a burden may or may not be carried, lifted, placed or thrown, and the matter of guilt for purposely, innocently, or accidentally breaking this part of the command.

> Similar difficulties were discussed as to the guilt in case an object were thrown from a private into a public place, or the reverse. Whether, if an object was thrown into the air with the left, and caught again in the right hand, this involved sin, was a nice question, though there could be no doubt a man incurred guilt if he caught it with the same hand with which it had been thrown, but he was not guilty if he caught it in his mouth, since, after being eaten, the object no longer existed, and hence catching with the mouth was as if it had been done by a second person.[35]

It was determined rather graciously to allow parents to carry their children, even if the child were holding in his hands that which the parent was otherwise disallowed from carrying for fear of breaking the Sabbath. But if a male child required circumcision on the Sabbath, a Gentile was asked to shoulder the load for the trek to the temple. A man with a wooden leg was permitted to make use of it on the Sabbath, but nary a child upon stilts. A man with false teeth left them out on the Sabbath day in the unlikely event that should they fall from his mouth he would be tempted to lift them back up; and likewise, a woman was to refrain from wearing ornaments that might inadvertently be carried. The restrictions are innumerable, with little redeeming spiritual value, full of casuistry and complicated outward rules. Jesus' indictment of the Pharisees for placing on men's backs burdens that were too cumbrous to bear applied to these very kinds of Sabbath restrictions (Luke 11:46). Kaplan explains that carrying an item is an expression of ownership, a right that must not be exercised on the Sabbath in recognition of the Lord's ultimate ownership of all things. Thus, it is impermissible to carry anything out of the house, such as a handkerchief, keys, a wallet or purse.[36] As ridiculous as these regulations are to the modern mind, they were born out of pious intentions to keep the Sabbath a sacred day. Yet the question remains: what constitutes the work of carrying a burden? What weight may a person uphold on the Sabbath? These questions are as important for modern-day Sabbath-keepers as they were for religious men of old.

The preoccupation with burden carrying is ironic in view of the other "burdens" people carry throughout their lives. Reflecting on the consequences of his iniquities,

35. Edersheim, *Life and Times*, 1048.

36. Kaplan, *Sabbath*, 33.

David characterized them as terrible weights oppressing his mortal frame, "Like a heavy burden they are too heavy for me" (Ps 38:4). The burden of unconfessed sin is oppressive on those whose hearts have been made tender toward the Lord, but those who are fools in the Lord's eyes ignore the damning freight. A "fig's weight" of sin is too much to carry on any day of the week, especially by those who know the Redeemer. Call upon the Lord any day of the week and He will carry your sins away! If you are oppressed by sin, He will break the yoke of your burden and bring you joy (Isa 9:4). The Jewish Sabbath day of rest discouraged carrying a burden because it looked forward to the day when the exemplar of rest would relieve us of such encumbrances of sin and misery as we daily run the race of faith (Heb 12:1–2).

Another matter to consider is the scope of the work prohibition as it applies to livestock. For the Jew, the temptation would be to rest himself but make his servants and animals, or even his own children, continue to work. They might reason that animals should continue to work daily, since they know nothing of God and derive no spiritual benefit by resting. But the word of the Lord commanded that beasts rest even as the freeman, his children, servants, sojourners, and slaves. Since the Sabbath is a type of redemption, let us explore the possible typical explanations for requiring the animals to rest. Since refraining from labor, especially in an agrarian economy, can pose a severe hardship, the Jew who rested from his labors expressed an abiding trust in God who promised to provide for him even when he suspended his normal activities for a day. However, if this same man continued to make his servants and animals work, then that man could not truly assert that he trusted the Lord to provide. For the Sabbath-type to fully represent salvation, not one iota of man's labor, or his will, or his good intentions must enter into it—"not of blood, nor of the will of the flesh, nor of the will of man, but of God" (John 1:13). If the Lord is to provide, He must do it entirely; and if the Lord is to be trusted, we must trust in Him exclusively.

> And therefore we cling to this foundation, which is firm forever, giving all glory to God, humbling ourselves, and recognizing ourselves as we are; not claiming a thing for ourselves or our merits, and leaning and resting on the sole obedience of Christ crucified, which is ours when we believe in Him.[37]

The extension of the work prohibition to other people and animals typifies the extent of work from the created realm required to merit salvation: absolutely none! As McGee warned his readers, "Don't you dare even 'pick up a little stick' and try to add to His work of redemption!"[38] Nothing else will save us, not our own works or the labors of others. Nothing else may be trusted to bring us into the eternal rest save Jesus and Him alone; not our church, not the prayers of others, not even our gentle ways with animals.

Calvin mused that since the animals cannot be truly sanctified (being like inanimate objects) they must derive no benefit from the rest—only that they benefit us and serve to remind us to be like them: humble in our station. His penchant for ethical lessons misses the point of the Sabbath type, which represents the salvation not only

37. *Ecumenical Creeds and Reformed Confessions*, 100. (Belgic Confession, Art. 23).

38. McGee, *The Sabbath Day or the Lord's Day*, 19.

of humanity, but of the whole world! It must be remembered that man's sin affected not only humanity, but the whole creation. That animals must share in our work is normative from creation, but since the fall, they too must gruel alongside us and suffer mortality with us (Ps 104:29–30; Eccl 3:19; Joel 1:18–20; Rom 8:19–22). Thus, it is fitting that the Sabbath previews not only the redemption of man but the deliverance of the whole cosmos (Hos 2:18)! Commenting on this verse, Matthew Henry believes the redeemed "shall enjoy perfect peace and tranquility, as if they were in a league of friendship with the whole creation."[39] For not only is the war between men indicative of the war between man and God, but also the "war" between man and beast. The safety described by Hosea is not only an actual place of security coupled with the emotional sense of trust, but freedom outside from the alarm of battle cries of both man and beast. Sabbath law typifies the comprehensive effects of Christ's salvation in restoring the earth and its inhabitants to its original state (Isa 11:6–10; 65:17–25).

Finally, there is the matter of applying the Sabbath work restriction to inanimate objects, even though Scripture gives no hint that there should be such an application. Edersheim explains that this concern was characteristic of the more stringent sects at the time of Christ.[40] Such strictness was surely aimed at those who devised ways to accomplish *something* over the course of the Sabbath or those who appeared to take advantage of the law. Modernity has introduced many new dilemmas for the Jews, some answered with strictness and some with grace. Kaplan elaborates on the numerous restrictions under the category of "burning," all of which allow man to extract energy from nature.

> Obviously, this category forbids such acts as striking a match or turning on a stove. It also prohibits smoking on the Sabbath. An automobile engine works by burning gasoline. Turning on the ignition and stepping on the accelerator causes it to burn. It is therefore forbidden to drive a car on the Sabbath. Heating a piece of metal so that it glows is also in the category of burning. When an electric light is turned on, its filament is heated white hot, producing light. This is therefore forbidden on the Sabbath. In general, any use of electricity violates the spirit of the Sabbath, since it involves extracting energy from nature. According to many authorities, electricity has the same status as fire with regard to the Sabbath. In any case, the practice of all observant Jews is to avoid turning any electrical appliance on or off. Since a telephone also works by electricity, it also should not be used.[41]

The grace comes in with the next category of work: extinguishing or putting out a fire. Therefore, the process of burning may continue if it was begun before the arrival of the Sabbath. Under this rubric, the Jews were able to have a hot Sabbath meal on Friday night. This rule also allows refrigerators and clocks to run incessantly.

Those Christians who want to keep the Sabbath alive must also ponder whether the work prohibition extends to inanimate objects. Robert Needham, a devout

39. Henry, *Commentary*, 4:890.

40. Edersheim, *Temple*, 121.

41. Kaplan, *Sabbath*, 35.

Sabbatarian, exulted over the scientific "finding" that an engine, if given a weekly rest, will last more than twice as long as an engine that works every day. Even a flat-edge razor, he asserted, if stropped every day will begin to lose its sharpness due to the parallel alignment of metallic molecules within the razor's matrix. It is as if God has hidden clues in the world of nature to remind us not to repeat a work every single day.[42] However, if we follow this line of thinking, it would appear to be holier to own two or three flat-edge razors so that one of them may rest from its work of being stropped (not to mention that the owner gets a cleaner, less painful shave). But what about men who own an electric razor? Should they forego their morning shave every Sabbath so the shaver can "rest as well as you?" Does it matter that the shaver works only five minutes every day compared to the eight hours a day worked by man? A Christian Sabbatarian deals with this topic differently from a Jew. The Jews analyze the problem in terms of ritual work and categories of work and apply it to a specific day of the week. The Sabbatarian on the other hand, views the matter as a creation ordinance, a principle of rest (non-work) that extends throughout created nature and is not particularized to a specific day of the week. So, the observant Jew will not shave on the Sabbath because shaving, as well as cutting hair and trimming finger-nails, is a member of the "shearing" category of work.[43] However, the Christian Sabbatarian will still shave on the Christian Sabbath provided he has duplicate devices so that one device may "rest" for a period of time while the other device works. The Jew treats shaving as his work, and the Sabbatarian treats shaving as the work of an inanimate object. For the Sabbatarian, it does not matter that his razor gets its rest on the wrong day of the week, or that its rest does not follow the creation pattern of six days of stropping and shaving and one day of rest.

The work restriction as part of Sabbath law was intended by the Lord to convey the redemptive theme of trust. Not working was a spiritual reminder that God Himself must do the work of salvation and that man's work may not in the least enter into it. The extension of the work prohibition to other classes of people and to working animals portrayed the exclusivity of saving faith—that it must be in God alone. Carrying a burden, one of the specifically proscribed categories of works, expressed the truth that no one was able to shoulder the burden of their own sin, a burden that the Messiah alone would bear. It is a sad state indeed that Christian Sabbatarians exchange all this spiritual capital—that in all things, Christ might have the preeminence—for their own legalistic "mountain on a thread." It is not doing, but done; it is not trying, but trust.

The Breakable Sabbath or Shabbat Fatale (Guilt)

The phrase "break the Sabbath" occurs in the gospels as an accusation against Jesus, usually for healing, but is absent in the OT.[44] This does not mean that the Jews

42. Needham, "Keep the Sabbath Holy," n.p.

43. Kaplan, *Sabbath*, 43.

44. Except for one "tongue in cheek" use of the phrase by Jesus, "breaking the Sabbath" was used primarily by the Pharisees. This perhaps reflects the heightened status of the Sabbath as somehow representative of the whole Mosaic law. In the OT, one may break a covenant, an oath, or an alliance, but not

perfectly kept the Sabbath; in fact, their unmindfulness of any of the demands of the Law brought the accusation from God of "breaking the covenant" (Lev 26:14–15; Isa 24:5). In fact, to ignore even the least of a ceremonial law was considered "breaking the covenant," such as bringing foreigners into the sanctuary (Ezek 44:7). Jeremiah, Isaiah, Ezekiel, and Nehemiah specifically depict the Lord's dissatisfaction with the manner in which Israel kept the Sabbath. Jeremiah stood at the gates of Jerusalem crying to unrepentant passers-by to discontinue carrying burdens and to stop working (Jer 17:21–22). With an allusion to ignored Sabbath law, Isaiah decried the emptiness of their temple rituals, sacrificial system, and calendar festivals (Isa 1:13–14). Ezekiel recounts how Israel was given the Sabbath after their deliverance from Egypt (Ezek 20:12–13). Despite the significance of the Sabbath, the wilderness Israelites displayed little esteem for the ceremony of their sanctification (Exod 16:27–28; Num 15:32). Israel continued to profane the Sabbath with the divided worship of their hearts and the depravity of human sacrifices (Ezek 22:8; 23:38–39). Unchanged after the seventy-year exile in Babylonia, the Jews in Jerusalem were chastised by Nehemiah for their disregard of the Sabbath by conducting commercial business (Neh 13:17).

As Murray has stated so well, the sanctity of Sabbath is that which is involved in sanctifying it.[45] And what better way to advance the *sanctity* of the Sabbath than enforcing the *sanction* for violation of it; that is, the *holy* penalty for violating Sabbath regulations. Failure to keep the Sabbath was a capital offense; therefore, it was critical to understand the details of its observance to avoid the supreme penalty. H. Freedman notes in his introduction to the Babylonian Talmud, "In actual practice this [the death penalty for Sabbath-breaking] was hedged about with so many restrictions as to make its application virtually impossible."[46] So, failure to effect the death penalty was just another way the Jews failed to sanctify the Sabbath.

The first recorded infraction, soon after the Sabbath was given in the wilderness, involved some Israelites who went out on the Sabbath day in search of manna (Exod 16:27–29). This simple search for manna on the Sabbath aroused the Lord's ire against Israel! They were admonished but not punished. If, as Sabbatarians insist, the Sabbath was already known to the Israelites, the Lord surely would have judged the offense more harshly. Instead, we see the Lord handle the infraction graciously since the legal ramifications of disobedience had not yet been declared. However, after the delivery of the Law at Mount Sinai, the Lord made plain the importance of this command.

> You shall keep the Sabbath, therefore, for it is holy to you. Everyone who profanes it shall surely be put to death; for whoever does any work on it, that person shall be cut off from among his people.
>
> Work shall be done for six days, but the seventh is the Sabbath of rest, holy to the Lord. Whoever does any work on the Sabbath day, he shall surely be put to death. (Exod 31:14–15)

break an individual commandment.

45. Murray, *Collected Writings*, 1:209.

46. Freedman, "Introduction," xxxiii.

So, when the children of Israel discovered a man who merely gathered sticks on the Sabbath, they presented Moses and Aaron with the task of adjudicating the *second* recorded infraction of the Sabbath. At the Lord's direction, the congregation stoned the man to death (Num 15:32–36). Having been given an example of case law, the Jews were now responsible for enforcing the Sabbath through their civil courts. Throughout the remainder of the OT, there is not one record of anyone else receiving the death penalty for profaning the Sabbath, even with the prophets repeatedly indicting the Jews for their stiff-necked heedlessness of the fourth commandment. Having abdicated their judicial responsibility, the Lord Himself, after years of long-suffering and warnings, administered punishment for their polluted Sabbaths. With scathing mockery, likely concerning their disobedience to the clear mandate to "kindle no fire" on the Sabbath (Exod 35:3), Jeremiah prophesied in the name of the Lord, "But if you will not heed Me to hallow the Sabbath day, such as not carrying a burden when entering the gates of Jerusalem on the Sabbath day, then I will kindle a fire in its gates, and it shall devour the palaces of Jerusalem, and it shall not be quenched" (Jer 17:27). Likewise, for their disobedience of the Sabbatic Year, particularly the commandment contained in God's covenant with Israel to release servants after seven years of service, Jeremiah spoke for the Lord:

> Therefore thus says the Lord: 'You have not obeyed Me in proclaiming liberty, every one to his brother and every one to his neighbor. Behold, I proclaim liberty to you,' says the Lord—'to the sword, to pestilence, and to famine! And I will deliver you to trouble among all the kingdoms of the earth.' (Jer 34:17)

Breaking the covenant was the basis for these judgments (Jer 34:13–14), as well as King Zedekiah's failure to honor his renewal of the covenant with the princes and people of Israel (Jer 34:8, 18–20). God's covenant with Israel, as recorded by Moses, discloses the repercussions for ignoring the Sabbatic Year.

> I will scatter you among the nations and draw out a sword after you; your land shall be desolate and your cities waste.
>
> Then the land shall enjoy its Sabbaths as long as it lies desolate and you are in your enemies' land; then the land shall rest and enjoy its Sabbaths.
>
> As long as it lies desolate it shall rest—for the time it did not rest on your Sabbaths when you dwelt in it. (Lev 26:33–35)

The Lord's judgment of seventy years dispersion to Babylonia ensured that the promised land recovered from all those years of unlawful use, providing an ongoing testimony of the Lord's zeal for every detail of the Law. The Jews learned through suffering, dispersion, and death that they did not have the option to selectively obey the details of the covenant. Returning to the land, the Jews decided to finally obey the Sabbath. So by the time of Christ's first advent, the fervor for honoring the Sabbath became especially legalistic in the Pharisaic and Essenic sects. Profaning or breaking the Sabbath was considered to be one of the most atrocious crimes.

How do Sabbatarians and Sabbath-keepers view the death penalty for Sabbath-breaking? Rushdoony asserts,

> None will argue that the old death penalty for violations of the Sabbath is still binding, or ever has been since Christ. The whole of the New Testament forbids such an interpretation. But, equally clearly, any law which at one time brought forth a death penalty for violation must involve a principle so basic to man and nature that obviously a hard central core remains in some sense binding in every age.[47]

He agrees that exacting the death penalty for breaking the Sabbath is antithetical to the new covenant ethic, yet asserts that the death penalty conferred some sort of sabbatical continuity during the new covenant. Somehow, the part that is left behind (the death penalty) is the same part that keeps the Sabbath relevant! So how can a fulfilled and declawed ceremonial law continue to exert power over Christians and, indeed, over the unregenerate? Was Christ's fulfillment of the Sabbath lacking in some regard that a "hard central core" withstood the power of His resurrection? The death penalty was accorded to violators of other ceremonial commandments, such as priests who failed to wash prior to eating holy food (Lev 22:9) or who drank wine in the tabernacle (Lev 10:9), and even the incorrigibly wicked child (Lev 20:9),[48] but we are hard-pressed to enlarge upon these as containing a "hard central core" that is crucial to Christian or civil law. And if the church believes that professing Christians who commit idolatry, witchcraft, adultery, rape, trafficking persons, etc., should be excommunicated, which were capital offenses under the old covenant, then why aren't Sabbath-breakers excommunicated? Sabbatarian John Murray skirts the question altogether.

> There were ordinances in Israel, regulating the observance of the Sabbath, which were peculiar to the circumstances of the people of Israel at that time, and we have no warrant to believe that they are of permanent obligation.[49]

If the death penalty proclaims the seriousness and enduring moral nature of this commandment and establishes its central position within the Decalogue, thus inferring its equality to the other nine, why is the penalty for breaking the Sabbath ignored by modern Sabbatarians but the penalty for murder and other crimes is sustained? With the lapidation of the stick gatherer of Numbers 15 in mind, Gary North notices the same inconsistency.

> This passage is crucial to the understanding of what the Sabbath ordinances demanded of God's covenant people. The violation of the Sabbath in so "small" a matter as the gathering of sticks involved the offender in a capital crime. Judicially, there was no distinction between this crime and murder. Both re-

47. Rushdoony, *Institutes of Biblical Law*, 133. In an earlier, theonomically oriented work, James Jordan mused that a civil death penalty is still warranted for pagan worship on the Lord's Day and failure of Christians to worship on the Lord's Day (*Christianity and the Calendar*, 45, 48).

48. This particular capital crime may have other symbolic intentions as it pertains to redemption. The Lord chastised Israel for being rebellious children (Isa 1:2) who deserved the sword if they failed to repent (v. 20). Indeed, all of the children of men have been rebels and are deserving of the most severe judgment of God. However, as Isaiah continues, it is through the forbearance of the Lord in mercy that any should have hope of righteousness if they are willing and obedient (vv. 18–19).

49. Murray, *Collected Writings*, 1:207.

> quired the death penalty. The modern Sabbatarian, by citing Old Testament references to the Sabbath in support of his position, inevitably involves his position with this passage. He is required to regard the tiniest violation of the Sabbath with the same horror as he would regard the murder of a member of his family. All offenses, from stick-gathering through playing professional football, have to be seen as capital crimes. There is no escape from this situation: if the standards of Hebrew practice are worth proclaiming, then the requirements of Hebrew jurisprudence are worth enforcing. While our contemporary civil codes do not presently impose the death penalty on Sabbath violators, consistent Sabbatarians should not rest on the other six days of the week until the civil government is persuaded to impose such a sanction against the violators. *If covenant law is binding, then covenant law's enforcement is equally binding.* The man who deviates from this principle is, Biblically, an antinomian.[50]

Murray attempts to answer his own inconsistency by drawing attention to the difference between the sanctity of the commandment and the level of enforcement between the old and new covenants.

> For example, in respect of the fifth commandment it was provided that the man who cursed father or mother was to be put to death (Exod. 21:17; Lev 20:9). In respect of the seventh it was provided that the adulterer and the adulteress were to be put to death (Lev 20:10). Now, however grievous these sins are, we do not believe that the sanction by which they were punished under the Mosaic law is applicable under the New Testament. Such provisions of the Mosaic law are so closely bound up with an economy which has passed away as to its observance that we could hold to the continuance of these provisions no more than we could hold to the continuance of the Mosaic economy itself.[51]

But all Murray has done is answer one inconsistency with another. Unanswered is why and how the new covenant, sealed with the blood of Jesus Christ, has affected the sanctions of the old covenant against both moral and ceremonial laws, especially capital punishment for adultery, Sabbath-breaking, and murder. Furthermore, his answer provides no justification for Sabbatarians to soften the seriousness of Sabbath-breaking compared to adultery and murder.

There is no difference between moral commandments and ceremonial commandments in this matter; the disobedient are sinners, and death is the inevitable fruit of sin. Not all sins required a civil death penalty, yet those that did were among the most detrimental to the purity and vitality of the nation. The first sin of humanity was against the ceremonial law "do not eat of the Tree of Knowledge," which resulted in the "death" of Adam and Eve.[52] The second recorded sin, the premeditated murder of Abel, was against the moral law not to take a human life, a right held by God alone. Homicide carried with it the sanction of capital punishment from the beginning (Gen

50. North, "Economics of Sabbath-Keeping," 829 (emphasis in the original).

51. Murray, *Collected Writings*, 1:211–12.

52. I call this "ceremonial" as opposed to moral, because the fruit of the tree did not really transfer "knowledge" to the one who ate the fruit. The tree was a test: symbolic of trust and obedience if left untouched, symbolic of distrust and disobedience if eaten.

4:10–11). Cain was graciously spared according to God's mysterious purposes for humanity—allowing the coexistence of dark and light—yet one possible purpose was to symbolically allow the blood of Abel to continually cry out for justice, a righteous claim unanswered until the shedding of the blood of Jesus Christ.[53]

> But you shall not eat flesh with its life, that is, its blood.
>
> Surely for your lifeblood I will demand a reckoning; from the hand of every beast I will require it, and from the hand of man. From the hand of every man's brother I will require the life of man.
>
> "Whoever sheds man's blood, By man his blood shall be shed; For in the image of God He made man. (Gen 9:4–6)

The punishment for murder through civil courts was confirmed with Noah on the basis that man was created in the image of God, making it a law applicable to all humanity. In general, even pagan nations have applied the principle that murderers be put to death. When the Lord gathered Israel to Himself, this principle was ratified in His Law (Exod 21:28; Num 35:16; Lev 24:17; Deut 21:1–9). Though the blood of Christ was shadowed by Abel's blood as well as the Mosaic sacrificial laws, His actual death has not removed the righteous sanction against homicide through existing civil laws (Rom 13:3; Matt 26:52), nor has His death altered the permissibility of having to

53. I disagree with Kaiser's theory that family law superseded homicidal law in the sparing of Cain's life. He says, "The family was barred from acting as prosecutor, jury, witness, judge, and executor. Since we assume that only the family was available at this early stage in the history of civilization, the principles institutionalized in the law of juvenile delinquents in Deuteronomy 21:18–21 must have been in vogue restraining the family by virtue of blood ties from assisting in the prosecution of their own child. Therefore, the family was so important, that it could not kill any part of itself." *Toward Old Testament Ethics*, 168. This theory loses virulence in view of his previous statements that murder is the most extreme and irremediable of crimes against man *and* God, and that the Mosaic law allowed ransom or substitution for all capital offenses except premeditated murder (Num 35:31). In the case of Cain, God did not need Adam and Eve to take Cain's life; He could have done it Himself, sparing them from that pain. Instead, He intervened with grace, and it was this grace that superseded human capital law. Furthermore, God allowed Cain to propagate in order that he symbolically would become the murderous father of all unregenerate souls, a murderer of man being the highest form of rebellion against God. Lastly, the example of family law to which Kaiser refers has the family as witnesses and accusers to the sin of rebellion for which their children may suffer capital punishment. Indeed, the situation in Exodus 32:25–29 has Levitical warriors slaying their own sons, brothers, friends, and neighbors due to idolatry. There is no reason to suppose that civil war for idolatry is cause to execute one's family member, but civil judgment for premeditated murder is not.

The settling place for James Montgomery Boice is also unsatisfactory. He surmises that we should be "extremely careful about imposing [the death penalty] and...make every possible effort to show mercy instead." *Genesis: An Expositional Commentary*, 1:258. Boice established that God gave man the right to enact the death penalty through Noah, but after reviewing the eighteen capital crimes under the Mosaic law, he asks which of them we would be willing to *reinstate*. This begs the question: When were these laws disestablished (or *disinstated*) in the first place? And when is our willingness to obey God's laws a measure of their validity? He also assumes that these capital crimes must be treated in an all-or-nothing fashion. With these assumptions clogging his thinking, he merely opts for erring on the safe side of mercy to all. This ends up portraying God as unmerciful from the days of Noah to the advent of Christ—as a time when God apparently commanded men to be unmerciful to one another. I propose that better solutions can be found by testing the eighteen capital crimes for ceremonial/typological meanings.

kill in war or in self-defense.[54] Abel's murder typified that Christ must *innocently* suffer and die at the hands of evil men (Isa 53:7–8; Dan 9:26; Matt 23:35; Heb 11:4, 12:24). Abel's abbreviated life and the Mosaic laws dealing with the conviction of crimes worthy of capital punishment were designed by God with Christ in mind. The safeguards of law meant that the death penalty should be sparingly employed. So not to confuse Christ's death with that of heinous criminals, a perversion of justice was necessary in order to effect the crucifixion of Jesus.

With the exception of murder, all other death penalties in the Mosaic law have to do with improprieties of the priesthood, sexual perversions of the populace, false worship, and actions disruptive of the community peace. One consideration in the interpretation of capital crimes that Christians need *not* entertain is to explain them as a cultural requirement or to magnify some secondary gain for Israel by enforcing capital punishment. For example, the International Standard Bible Encyclopedia adduces that "the nation consisted of newly emancipated slaves, and therefore required harsh measures to keep them in check."[55] This is hardly a Christocentric understanding of the Law. Though the capital case of the man gathering sticks had the secondary effect of restricting would-be Sabbath-breakers, this secondary effect cannot be its main, intended purpose. It is true that punishment has the general effect of coercing right behavior (Deut 17:11–13; 19:19–21; 21:21) and that enforcement of the death penalty tested the resolve of the Israelites to trust and obey God. However, if the Lord had wanted a more preventive oriented legal basis to induce compliance of the Jews, He could have instituted the death penalty for *all* infractions against His holy will. That would have instilled the fear of God and kept them in check! However, the Lord set apart only certain violations as worthy of death; therefore, it is our duty to discover why. A naturalistic approach to understanding the death penalty will negate any attempts to understand this from a ceremonial/redemptive perspective. The death penalty for Israelites could not be effected on the basis of only one witness, but by two or three (Deut 17:6–7; 19:15). The Lord Himself complied with this principle before meting out judgment against the Israelites (Deut 30:19), and it forecasted the testimony of false witnesses against the incarnate Lord Himself and perhaps even Peter's denials (Matt 26:34, 60).

> This will be the third time I am coming to you. "By the mouth of two or three witnesses every word shall be established."
>
> I have told you before, and foretell as if I were present the second time, and now being absent I write to those who have sinned before, and to all the rest, that if I come again I will not spare—
>
> since you seek a proof of Christ speaking in me, who is not weak toward you, but mighty in you. (2 Cor 13:1–3)

54. Therefore, when allowed, a Christian may exert his political right to enact the death penalty for murder. In our modern world, dominated by humanistic philosophy, the unregenerate think they are better than God by sparing the lives of murderers so they can be rehabilitated and reintroduced into society, or separated in prison for life.

55. ISBE, 4:2504–5. Do new believers, recently emancipated from their sin, also require harsh measures to check their freedoms in Christ?

Apostle Paul applied this Mosaic law while handling the affairs of the church, specifically divisive and sexual sins that were not properly dealt with by the local church leaders (2 Cor 13:1), the same sins that deserved the death penalty under the old covenant. After a period of some three to five long-suffering years, Paul purposed to effect discipline himself when he arrived, acting in Christ's stead. That is, Paul sees in old covenant law an application during the new covenant dispensation to apply ecclesiastical justice in the name of Christ. Church discipline emanates from a Christocentric understanding of old covenant law (Matt 18:15–17). Of note is Paul's choosing a law having to do with the repercussions of "cutting off" someone from the benefits of the national fellowship and his association of that application with the ministry of Christ to His church. The author of Hebrews quotes the same legal statute (Heb 10:28), but draws another conclusion from the perspective of the new covenant.

> For if we sin willfully after we have received the knowledge of the truth, there no longer remains a sacrifice for sins,
>
> but a certain fearful expectation of judgment, and fiery indignation which will devour the adversaries.
>
> Anyone who has rejected Moses' law dies without mercy on the testimony of two or three witnesses.
>
> Of how much worse punishment, do you suppose, will he be thought worthy who has trampled the Son of God underfoot, counted the blood of the covenant by which he was sanctified a common thing, and insulted the Spirit of grace?
>
> For we know Him who said, "Vengeance is Mine, I will repay," says the Lord. And again, "The *Lord* will judge His people."
>
> It is a fearful thing to fall into the hands of the living God. (Heb 10:26–31)

In this sternest of warnings against outright rejection of the truth of Jesus Christ as evidenced by a withdrawal from the Christian community, the guilt is magnified as a result of the existence of a better covenant. Yet the dispensing of judgment is left to the Lord Himself, as often happened during the old covenant era (Lev 18:29; 20:3–6; 23:30). The early church did not employ capital punishment but merely symbolized that severe outcome through excommunication (assuming there was no repentance and recompense to those offended). Paul maintained a serious concern about sexual sins and apostasy in the church, and he retained the principle of testimonial corroboration of those sins before rendering ecclesiastic judgment. Furthermore, willful rejection of Christ was considered even more offensive toward God in view of the advent of the better covenant. However, the literal application of capital punishment was forgone, and instead, the offender was to be "cut off" from the church community through excommunication. Sins that were punishable by death under the old covenant (sexual immorality and apostasy) are now punishable by excommunication under the new covenant.

Paul invokes the Mosaic law of two or three witnesses in another context: the discipline of an elder. He relates to Timothy the secondary effect—a congregational warning—in the public rebuke of an ordained minister.

> Do not receive an accusation against an elder except from two or three witnesses.

> Those who are sinning rebuke in the presence of all, that the rest also may fear.
>
> I charge you before God and the Lord Jesus Christ and the elect angels that you observe these things without prejudice, doing nothing with partiality.
>
> Do not lay hands on anyone hastily, nor share in other people's sins; keep yourself pure. (1 Tim 5:19–22)

Paul singles out sins within the episcopacy and relates this to a leavening effect on other elders and the flock of God. Following the standard of adjudication involved in capital offenses, two or three witnesses must be privy to these severe breaches against the vows of ordained ministers. Timothy is therefore enjoined, in the view of heavenly witnesses, to pass judgment on his peers without partiality, thus dissociating himself from their sins. Neither should a man be ordained "hastily," without a complete understanding of their life and doctrine in order to avoid this most challenging disciplinary dilemma.

Scripture endorses the idea that Christ's blood put an end to animal sacrifices based upon the redemptive themes in those ceremonies. Christ was the *telos*, or end point, of the sacrificial symbols; He was the antitype of these bloody old covenant types. But what about the symbols and types of the nation Israel? Do they not find their end and antitype in Christ's church? We may not have an explicit teaching about the effect Christ's death had on Israel's civil penalties; however, as documented above, we have examples of the application of Israel's civil law to the church; and in two cases, where capital punishment was indicated for Israel, only excommunication was administered in the church. It bears mentioning that we do not see Israel's civil laws directly correlated to the state.

It is not enough to simply assert that the death of Jesus Christ has done away with some or all death penalties without knowing why. We cannot wave Christ's death around as if it were a magic wand to eradicate any "severity" of the law we discover in the OT. Thus, the capital laws applying to the Levitical priesthood are either fulfilled in Christ or they have modified applicability to the antitype in the church. As a type, capital punishment for heinous sins in Israel foreshadowed excommunication for heinous sins in the church, which means that the discipline of excommunication "must needs be" an attribute of a healthy church. Sin was not necessarily redefined, but one punishment was supplanted by another through fulfillment. Therefore, the laws requiring capital punishment are not civil laws that must become secular laws, but ceremonial laws that foreshadowed the life of the church in the context of Jesus' death and resurrection. The literal death penalty in Israel for certain sins is replaced by the church's duty to excommunicate those who demonstrate a total disregard for the purity and life of the church: primarily abusers of their office, profane and sexually impure persons, and those whose profession of faith is supplanted by fundamental heterodoxy. The church must not be like Israel who was too timid to apply the death penalty when indicated, but should employ the sanctifying benefit of discipline, even excommunication, when called for.

The old covenant prescribed capital punishment for infractions against both moral and ceremonial commands. Therefore, under the old covenant, the association of the death penalty with a commandment, in and of itself, does not confer morality on that commandment. The morality of a command must stand on other grounds. However, the severity of punishment underscores the relative importance of those laws as they pertained to the life of Israel, and now to the life of the church. As members of the new covenant, we must first distinguish whether a law invoking capital punishment is moral or ceremonial, as this will affect its intent and application. Secondly, we must answer whether the sanction for violation of these moral laws is to be applied to the church in the form of excommunication. Thirdly, ceremonial laws carrying the death penalty need to be explained in terms of Christ's fulfillment of them; whether a NT ethic can be drawn from them and whether the application of that sanction can be made based on that symbolism. Lastly, of all capital crimes, the punishment for murder stands apart from Mosaic law, having been revealed prior to the giving of the Law and grounded on man being made in the image of God (Gen 4:10–11; 9:6; 42:22).

There are about 77 separate capital violations in the Mosaic law and they can be categorized under seven general headings.[56]

- Sins of the priesthood involving moral laws, such as offering to false gods or having a promiscuous daughter
- Sins of the priesthood involving ceremonial laws, such as failing to wash before temple service
- Sexual sins of the populace, such as sodomy, adultery, homosexuality, and incest; and sins against humanity, such as slave-trading
- Sins of the people involving ceremonial laws, such as failing to resolve uncleanness before approaching the temple and failing to keep the Passover or the Sabbath
- Blatant moral sins of unbelief, such as idolatry, witchcraft, and divination
- Sins disruptive of the community, such as cursing or striking parents, defrauding in marriage, gluttony, drunkenness, and rejection of priestly counsel
- Sin of murder, including concurrent accidental death of mother and fetus and accidental death by an animal known to be injurious to man

The capital offense for Sabbath-breaking does not necessarily mean that Sabbath-keeping is a moral command. If it is a moral command, then, as North reasoned, every Christian "is required to regard the tiniest violation of the Sabbath with the same horror as he would regard the murder of a member of his family." Yet, we must also

56. Some offenders were "cutoff" as opposed to being "put to death," "burned with fire," "stoned to death," or "to die." "Cut off" is from the Hebrew word, *karath*, which means to cut or to covenant. It invokes the idea of being cut to death as the form of punishment for breaking a covenant. Interestingly, there are no legal threats of death for murmuring, greed, and disbelief, though many Israelites were killed by the Lord for such offenses.

consider the possibility that the Sabbath was a ceremonial law with a capital sanction, just as was the case for transgressing the Feast of Weeks (Exod 12:15) or the Passover (Num 9:13). If the Sabbath was a ceremonial law, then the exterior performance of the Sabbath would be discontinued and the spiritual symbolism of the Sabbath would be realized in Christ and His redemption.

So, what is the spiritual symbolism conveyed by the death penalty as pertaining to these three festivals that every Israelite was to observe? Why did the Lord decree as a capital offense breaking the Sabbath, eating leavened bread during the Feast of Weeks, and refusing to keep the Passover when one is able? It is because of what the ceremony symbolizes that we come to understand what the death penalty symbolizes. Failure to keep the Sabbath incurred a death penalty because the Sabbath was a premier ceremonial sign of the covenant. To reject the Sabbath or to treat it casually was tantamount to standing against the Lord's covenant with Israel. More importantly, since the Sabbath is a symbol of redemption, the ceremonial effect for premeditated disobedience was separation of that person from the community of the redeemed through death, a symbol of eternal punishment. On the national level, disobedience to the several Sabbath institutions implied a pandemic rejection of God's kingdom, which made Israel susceptible to the judgment of God, as if they were a heathen nation (Jer 17:19–27). Jeremiah's vision of a properly kept Sabbath, as well as the offering of sacrifices of animals, grain, and incense, was symbolic of the arrival of the Messianic age. Those who kept ceremonial laws in faith were justified by God and made to partake in the realities that the ceremonies portrayed.

Those who kept the Sabbath in faith received the promise of eternal rest through Jesus Christ. Now that Christ has come and fulfilled the redemption portrayed in the Sabbath, we do not fear ever being cut off from God; for if we are in Christ, we shall remain forever. The Jews were made to fear a chastising death for disobeying a ceremonial command, but the true meaning was to engender fear of being cut off from the God of redemption (Phil 2:12; Heb 3:12; 10:31). Hence, from the perspective of the NT, the writer to the Hebrews could say, regarding the symbolic Canaan rest, "fear lest you come short of it" (Heb 4:1); that is, be sure that you are approaching God on the basis of resting faith and not on the basis of your works.

The Inflammable Sabbath (Security)

One specific prohibition given to the Jews at Sinai was to refrain from kindling a fire on the Sabbath (Exod 35:2–3). It seems plain enough to conclude, when coupled with the command to cook one's meals the day before, and to do one's work on the preceding days, that one may not start or "stoke up" a fire on the Sabbath for either occupational or domestic purposes. Fire was certainly used in the home for meal preparation, but it was also used to provide ambient light and heat. Did the prohibition mean that the Jews could not kindle a fire to keep a child warm on a cold day or to warm food and drink for the pleasure of the sick? Was it acceptable to continue to fuel a fire in your home that was started the day before? These questions are important because the death penalty and the Lord's judgment loom over the heads of the disobedient.

> But if you will not heed Me to hallow the Sabbath day, such as not carrying a burden when entering the gates of Jerusalem on the Sabbath day, then I will kindle (*yatsath*) a fire in its gates, and it shall devour the palaces of Jerusalem, and it shall not be quenched. (Jer 17:27).

How does the modern Jew interpret the prohibition against lighting a fire on the Sabbath? Heschel spiritualizes "kindle no fire" to mean avoiding on the Sabbath day any interpersonal controversy and anger.[57] Maimonides and Jordan[58] interpret the command to refrain from adjudicating conflicts on the Sabbath. This spiritualization of the text has some merit since the Lord used the same phrase metaphorically of a forthcoming judgment, however, it implies that "kindling the fire" of personal wrath is suitable on other days of the week, but not on the Sabbath. Trepp mentions that Jews, referring to the exact time of sunset recorded on their calendar, light two candles in the moments before sunset on Friday evening. He adds:

> Fire means any kind of flame. It includes the turning-on of electric light, of heat, or the use of the automobile, radio, or television; all are prohibited.[59]

With the arrival of new technology, it is logical and in keeping with the spirit of the law to refrain from using modern conveniences that perform the same function as did fire in ancient times. Notwithstanding the scrupulosity of conservative Jews and the clear commandment to "kindle no fire," Sabbatarians do not think of denying themselves the conveniences of fire and electricity. Without any NT defense, Murray asserts that the prohibitions and regulations of Sabbath observance, such as kindling a fire and applying capital punishment, were exclusive to the Mosaic economy.[60] Citing the failure of government to enforce God's sanction for adulterers and young rebels, and his "deeper understanding of the sanctity of the commandments," he asserts that the death penalty and the fire-starting prohibition were annulled. But Murray neglects two fundamental premises of Reformed hermeneutics, as stated by Greg Bahnsen.

> Scripture, then, is quite clear, in teaching that the requirement of full obedience to God's commands extends to the active promoting of obedience to those commands in others.[61]
>
> To summarize; we must assume continuity of moral duty between the Old Testament and New Testament. Accordingly, by operating upon this biblical assumption, the burden of Scriptural proof lies directly and heavily upon anyone

57. Heschel, *Sabbath*, 29. The context of Heschel's quote does not lend itself to an assumption that this is the whole of what he means.

58. Jordan, *Sabbath Breaking and the Death Penalty*, 67.

59. Trepp, *Book of Jewish Observance*, 73, 71.

60. Murray, *Collected Writings*, 1:211–12.

61. Bahnsen, *By This Standard*, 35.

> who would deny the validity or the relevant authority of some particular Old Testament stipulation for our day.[62]

First of all, Murray uses the failure of Christians to influence society and the failure of governments to recognize the authority of God in the administration of justice to defend his sense that the death penalty is an unsuitable punishment for Sabbath-breakers. Secondly, without so stating, he recognizes the impossibility of any government, however much aligned biblically, to agree to administer capital punishment for profaning Sunday. Perhaps too, he personally shudders at the thought of having to put millions of people to death, including members of his family or congregation, for the least infraction of the Sabbath. North again points out the hypocrisy of Sabbatarian sophistry when it comes to obeying the law of "no fire:"

> The very architecture of our churches is a standing testimony to the unwillingness of contemporary Christians to accept the implication of the Sabbath. We fill our buildings with all sorts of electrical appliances; we heat and cool the rooms to a comfortable 75 degrees, both winter and summer. We often pride ourselves on the efficiency of modern technology, forgetting that many men and women must go to work and operate the machines that provide the power—the fuel—for our gadgets. These workers are committing Sabbatarian capital crimes each Sunday, and every Christian Sabbatarian who uses these gadgets, apart from some legitimate emergency, sends people to hell every Sunday, morning and evening, as he sits in the comfort of his air-conditioned church. If the Sabbatarian creeds are correct, then Sabbatarians are weekly condemning others to the flames of eternal torment, just so that they can sit in 75-degree comfort.[63]

If Sabbath-breaking is as scandalous a sin as idolatry, murder, and sexual immorality, then, according to Bahnsen, we would expect that the new covenant authors would demonstrate the continuing morality of Sabbath-keeping by condemning Sabbath-breaking in general or mentioning any number of ways in which the Sabbath could be profaned (Rev 21:8). An Israelite was stoned to death for taking action in *preparation* for starting a fire (i.e., collecting wood), so if any Sabbath law stood out as most considerable, it was the prohibition from starting a fire.

Certainly, the command to "kindle no fire" only reinforced with austerity the command to do no manner of work on the Sabbath. It emphasized and defined just what God meant when He said to do no work, not even to build a fire for one's most basic needs. Yet, why did the Lord focus on "kindling a fire" when He could have mentioned a variety of other seeming necessary works, such as washing cooking utensils or repairing a broken wall? Given the Lord's figurative use of "kindle a fire" as his judgment against Israel, a fitting typological meaning is this: partakers of the Lord's rest will never experience the fire of His condemning wrath. That is, by refraining from kindling a fire, the Jews were enacting the freedom from God's fiery judgment that resulted when they abided in God's rest through faith. This recalls the Edenic paradise prior to the fall and the curse of God signified in the flaming sword of the

62. Ibid., 153.

63. North, "Economics of Sabbath-Keeping," 834.

angel. There was no fiery judgment before sin, and there will be no fiery judgment for sinners redeemed by the grace of God.

We must not confuse "kindle a fire" with lighting a candle, though both involve flames. And even though the prohibition against kindling a fire is often logically extended to candle-lighting, the Jews were never told *not* to light a candle on the Sabbath. Could it be that what is commended of the woman in Proverbs 31:18, that "her lamp does not go out by night," was prohibited on the Sabbath day? Indeed, the flames of oil-burning candles in the sanctuary burned continuously. As a metaphor, the *constrained* flame of a candle gives light to expose, to illuminate, and to beacon; however, the *unleashed* flames of burning wood are consuming, perilous, and radiating—something to be feared.

> They have provoked Me to jealousy by what is not God;
> They have moved Me to anger by their foolish idols.
> But I will provoke them to jealousy by those who are not a nation;
> I will move them to anger by a foolish nation.
> For a fire is kindled in My anger,
> And shall burn to the lowest hell;
> It shall consume the earth with her increase,
> And set on fire the foundations of the mountains.
> (Deut 32:21–22)

The unceasing candlelight in the sanctuary emitted by the combustion of pure olive oil (Exod 27:20) may typify the eternal radiance and effulgence of the Lord's glory in the heavenly estate, but the vision of a tempestuous and ravaging conflagration pictures the unquenchable wrath of God against the whole earth (Ps 50:3; Isa 47:14; 66:16; Jer 4:4, 15:14; Amos 5:6). The Sabbath day reflected not only attitudes of trust in God (no manner of work) and peace with God (rest and abide at home), but *security* with God (no fire kindled). Those of us engrafted as branches into the everlasting covenant take especial consolation in the promise that God's fiery wrath will never come upon us by virtue of the blood of Jesus Christ (Rom 5:9; 1 Thess 1:10).

If the typological meaning of the prohibition is not properly understood, then there is no basis for annulling it. It is illegitimate to simply brand it as one of those "severe" commands of the old covenant that we are no longer to obey because of the liberty granted in the new covenant. There is either a typological meaning that allows us to properly consider its fulfillment in Christ, with subsequent annulment, or it continues with the same (supposed) moral force as doing no work on the Sabbath. The type must be about Christ and His redemption, not about our feelings of devotion. Spiritualizing the command to "kindle no fire" may engender pious sympathies for anger management or increased spiritual zeal, but it focuses the ceremony on people's behavior rather than on redemption. For the Jews, the kindling of fires came to a stop on the Sabbath. By all prerogatives of divine righteousness, God's wrath would burn freely among the children of men, but typified in the Sabbath prohibition, no flames of His wrath will be ignited among the faithful. Toward those who revere Him, the indignation against sin has been quenched already and the passion of His jealousy has been abated through

Jesus Christ. We are secure from the wrath to come! This also explains why God was so severe to the man who gathered sticks on the Sabbath: it was as if, typologically speaking, he disregarded the sacrifice of Jesus Christ that made rest possible.

Consider the emphasis of fire in the Passover memorial:

> Then they shall eat the flesh on that night; roasted in fire, with unleavened bread and with bitter herbs they shall eat it. Do not eat it raw, nor boiled at all with water, but roasted in fire—its head with its legs and its entrails. You shall let none of it remain until morning, and what remains of it until morning you shall burn with fire. (Exod 12:8–10)

It was not enough that the lamb was slain and eaten raw, as was the pagans' food, but it had to be subjected to intense heat and flames. Not only was Christ's blood shed but he incurred the fiery wrath of God as our sin-bearer. The fire typified the severe and consuming judgment of God against sin (Lev 10:6; 1 Kgs 18). The lamb was subjected to fire in two ways: first, to make the lamb palatable and edible, and secondly, to carbonify and consume. The first fire typifies that the judgment against sin was acceptable, even desirable, to God. Having paid for sin, Christ is now able to save them to the uttermost as He is incorporated through the "eating of His flesh." The second fire typifies the severity of God's wrath against sin in that the remaining portion is utterly consumed, wherefore, no sin of ours remains to be dealt with. The Sabbath typifies the fellowship of man and God following the redemptive removal of sin, "Now where there is remission of these, there is no longer an offering for sin" (Heb 10:18). If the sacrifice is realized in Christ then the command to kindle no fire is realized in the result of His sacrifice: the judgment has already passed. As Isaiah considered our created and redeemed estates, he could assure the faithful in metaphorical terms, "Fear not, for I have redeemed you . . . When you walk through the fire, you shall not be burned, Nor shall the flame scorch you" (Isa 43:2). The Sabbath law prohibiting the kindling of fires has been fulfilled; therefore, Christians need not give any care for the keeping of that ceremony. We have good reason to exult in the redemption of Christ that keeps us free from the wrath to come.

The Bloody Sabbath (Sacrifice)

There is an inviolate association between the sacrifices and the Sabbath, as closely knit as bitter herbs and the Passover, or the shofar and the Feast of Trumpets; for without the former, the latter is meaningless. Indeed, the blood-spilling offerings, all of which pointed to the Messiah, were part of *all the feasts*, including the Sabbath and New Moon. Every Sabbath, two lambs were sacrificed in addition to the two lambs of the Continual Burnt Offering.

> And on the Sabbath day two lambs in their first year, without blemish, and two-tenths of an ephah of fine flour as a grain offering, mixed with oil, with its drink offering—
>
> this is the burnt offering for every Sabbath, besides the regular burnt offering with its drink offering. (Num 28:9–10)

Considering the effort involved in slaying—disembowling, dissecting, offering, and transporting the animal—that is a lot of work! Though the Lord commanded other festival sacrifices to continue in spite of coinciding with a Sabbath, the Jews, in deference to the Sabbath, attempted to reduce the amount of work these sacrifices demanded, thus ameliorating the tension they felt by working on the day of rest. Edersheim described some of these changes as related to the Passover, i.e., they would not wash away the blood on the Sabbath nor carry the slain animals upon their shoulders; but in spite of these concessions, the priesthood understood that all their religious services "made void the Sabbath."[64] They realized that they could not perform their sacerdotal duties without violating the prohibition from work. The Sabbath presented a paradox for the priesthood. Work was prohibited but work was demanded, hence the priest's maxim: "There is no Sabbath in the Sanctuary."[65] Even if the sheaf offering occurred on the Sabbath, the priests would proceed to the field carrying their sickle and "harvest" about seven gallons of barley, and carry it back in baskets to the temple to be prepared by fire and admixtures.[66]

The Continual Burnt Offering (Exod 29:38–42) finds its symbolic origin in the days of creation, the first indication of divine partition, i.e., the day from the night, the morning from the evening. This one offering devolves upon two yearling lambs, one offered in the morning and one in the evening (around 3 p.m.). It is a testimony of the Lord's ownership of each and every day, for, as in the days of creation, He involves Himself in this world successively, without interruption. As given to the Jews, it symbolized the everlasting presence of Yahweh within their community, the consecration of their relationship, and thus the continuity of the blood-covenant (Exod 29:42–46). The Sabbath offering, on the other hand, commemorates the first divine act of redemption for Adam and Eve. Two lambs, one offering. Two sinners, one race. God, after judging their sin with a curse upon every work of their hands and bringing toil and hardship to them and their succeeding generations, ushered them into a spiritual rest while yet in their mortality. Two lambs slain on the seventh day: a work initiated by God, completed by God, and presented by God. Two skins presented on the seventh day: needed by man, unearned by man, yet received by man. This is the paradigm for Levitical priests who "break the Sabbath" while slaying animals: 1) to imitate the Lord who broke His rest to redeem Adam and Eve, 2) to acknowledge that human efforts to atone for sin are completely worthless, 3) to remember God's mercy to a disobedient people, and 4) to engender hope for the promised seed that would inaugurate the *dénouement* at the end of the ages. This was the work of God accomplished on the seventh day, and it was the duty of the priests to search this out and instruct the people on this most basic of redemptive tenets.

64. Edersheim, *Temple*, 150–51.

65. Ibid., 123. This awareness parallels the teaching in Hebrews that Joshua never gave Israel a true rest even in the land of rest. This awareness was divinely inspired and leads us to the anticipation of an enduring rest, an enduring Sabbath, and an enduring sanctuary.

66. Ibid., 170–71.

For Adam and Eve, as well as their successive generations, the means of recapturing the lost rest was prefigured in the sacrifice of two animals. Sacrificing animals in the temple on the Sabbath emulated God's priestly work in providing skins for our first parents in the garden, and, of course, it prefigured the sacrifice of Jesus upon the cross, for "without shedding of blood, there is no remission" (Heb 9:22). In the tearing of the temple veil at the death of Christ, physically evincing the end of the Levitical priesthood and all those activities associated with it, no longer could the priests offer the requisite sacrifices as a national presentation of the Sabbath to the Lord. Without these sacrifices, the Israelites would be observing the Sabbath in vain. A Sabbath without sacrifices amounts to a presumptuous mockery of the symbolism inherent in its observance.

The inconsistency of Sabbatarianism is greatest at this juncture. Sabbatarians agree that Christ fulfilled the sacrificial duties of the Sabbath and that continuing to offer bloody sacrifices denigrates the sacrificial act of Jesus Christ upon the cross. Yet they state that His death did nothing to the remaining Sabbath laws. Like modern Jews without the temple, Sabbatarians think their "mitvahs" are enough to present the Sabbath to God. But the law is clear in this: without the required sacrifices, gifts, and oblations, the Sabbath is an empty observance, even if every Jew and every Sabbatarian perfectly avoided every prohibited work. Paradoxically, as Jesus observed, the Sabbath was profaned by the sacrifices! As O. Palmer Roberston described the nature of a divine covenant, "death stands at the beginning of a relationship between two parties, symbolizing the potential curse-factor in the covenant."[67] The death of animals atoned for the failure of faithful Israelites to keep the Sabbath, and the death of Israelites was the justice due those faithless souls who profaned the Sabbath. The Sabbath contained two elements of death that distinguished it as a sign of the Mosaic covenant. If Christ's death annulled the need to make those sacrifices and the civil duty to punish violators, then His death also removed the need to follow the other Sabbath duties that made the sacrifices necessary in the first place.

Now the offerings themselves on the Sabbath day were burnt offerings, signifying the exhaustion of heavenly wrath upon sin and pointing back to the first bloody sacrifices in the garden. The need for Sabbath sacrifices can only be traced to the defilement of the seventh day rest by Adam and Eve. As Bonar concluded his thoughts about the significance of the burnt offering within the temple, he too transports to the garden scene.

> Within the gate stood the *cherubim*, occupying the hallowed spot where the Tree of Life waved its branches. This resembled the *Holy of holies*; and the veil that prevented the approach of any from without was the *flaming sword*, flashing its sheets of fire on every side. But opposite to this sword, at some distance, we see an *altar*, where our first parents shed the blood of sacrifice—showing in type how the barred-up way of access to the Tree of Life was to be opened by the

67. Robertson, *Christ of the Covenants*, 11.

> blood of the Woman's bruised Seed. On this *altar* bloody and unbloodly offerings were appointed to be presented in their Season. [68]

The sacrifices, along with the other carnal Sabbath occupations, have Christocentric and redemptive meanings that link the beginnings of the human experience to the culmination of the Father's redemptive work. The Lord's acceptance of the burnt offering was connected to the symbolic gesture of the priest when he leaned his weight upon the head of the innocent animal. This signified that propitiation of sin was based on a resting faith in the object of the sacrifice (2 Cor 5:21). Therefore, the burnt sacrifices offered on the Sabbath pointed back to the faith of Adam and Eve. While we do not have detailed records of their conversation with God, we are informed that they accepted the skins presented by God and heard the promise that a Seed should come. That "Seed" must come from a godly line; therefore, by the Lord's seventh-day sacrifices, the faith of Adam and Eve was established. Finally, the perpetuity of these Sabbath sacrifices indicates the faithfulness of God to reserve for Himself a remnant, thus ensuring an unbroken continuity of a people of faith.

The burnt offerings were not the only presentations made on the Sabbath day. In addition, the priests were required to prepare and bake twelve loaves according to a cherished formula, and to arrange them on the table in the holy place at the commencement of the Sabbath (Exod 25:30; Lev 24:5–9; 1 Chr 9:32). These loaves collectively were called the "showbread" (literally "Bread of the Presence"), which was understood by the rabbis to represent the Messiah. Edersheim provides details of the Levitical duties as described in the Pentateuch and supplemented by the Mishnah.[69] The loaves were cooked to resemble the shape of the ark of the covenant and anointed with oil in the shape of a cross. Four priests entered the holy place to remove the old showbread and two incense bowls, and these were immediately replaced with fresh loaves and incense from the hands of another quartet of priests, thus insuring that the showbread was before the Lord continually. The new loaves were offered to God enveloped by the fragrance of sweet incense and illuminated by the flickering light of the golden lampstand. The old bread was then shared among the two shifts of priests and those who were in a state of Levitical purity.

The showbread ceremony was a Sabbath duty, and as such, invested the ceremonial Sabbath with additional Messianic and spiritual meaning. Commenting on Christ's proclamation that He is the bread of life (John 6:35), Wybren Oord comprehends a connection with the showbread.

> He was declaring Himself as the bread within the Holy Place—the Showbread! Jesus came to give us the true bread, the bread that will bring us into fellowship with the Father, and whoever eats of this bread will have life.[70]

68. Bonar, *Commentary on Leviticus*, 30–31. (emphasis in the original).

69. Edersheim, *Temple*, 123–26. First Samuel 21:6 verifies that the replacement loaves were fresh and hot, though it is not said whether the exchange took place Friday evening or Saturday morning. Jesus' mention of David's example, as it related to His own Sabbath conduct, indicates that the showbread was baked on the Sabbath.

70. Oord, "The Table of Showbread," 8.

Both the manna and the showbread, which define and memorialize the Sabbath, are fulfilled types of Christ. The table on which the bread was placed came into use every Sabbath day, and with all the fixtures and utensils, gave appearance that the Sabbath in the tabernacle was indeed God's home among the Israelites. We see at once that the "Bread of Faces" can represent the Lord Jesus who is ever before the Father, pleasing Him and delighting in Him, and at the same time recognize that the loaves are an honorary gift from Israel to God. With an understanding that the tripartite sanctuary followed the spiritual realm of the heavens, the "perpetual bread" represented a special manifestation of His Presence among the throng of worshipers that was mediatorial, communicable, and durable. Edersheim posits that, by virtue of its presence in the Holy Place, the covenant-people owned His Presence as their bread and their life, and as the priests ate the showbread as Israel's representatives, God accepted and ratified Israel's dependence upon Him. From later references, it appears that this offering was highly esteemed by Israel (1 Chr 23:29; 2 Chr 13:10; Neh 10:33). And perhaps because of its obvious relationship to the twelve tribes of Israel, it fostered a hope for an era when the concourse of worshippers at Jerusalem would be from a unified Israel. Also, each loaf was uniform in its size signifying that each tribe, despite its present population and treasure or its history and future, was before the Lord on equal terms. From the NT perspective, this speaks of the equality of all believers in Christ, regardless of their differing nationality, gender, or social standing (Gal 3:26–29).

> The numbered tribes are a clear picture of the numbered Church. Hence every child of faith is present in the Presence-bread. They all are members of the Lord. They all in Him appear before the Father's eye. Degrees of faith may vary. Some may but touch with trembling hand the very edge of Jesus' garment. Others may live with their enraptured head upon His very breast. But if there be vital faith, there is an oneness with the Lord which never, never can be parted. Christ holds each one within Himself. He shows Himself the compound of them all. They lived in Him. They died in Him. They rose in Him. They sit together in heavenly places in Him. God's look, which rests upon His Son, sees them. The love which smiles on Jesus smiles on them.[71]

The author of Hebrews was so determined to prove the perfections of Christ that his passing mention of the showbread (Heb 9:2) served only to adduce the limitations of tabernacle worship "symbolic for the present time in which both gifts and sacrifices are offered which cannot make him who performed the service perfect" (Heb 9:9). The showbread is an artifact of a bygone era, fulfilled in Christ and His redemption of a kingdom of priests. Yet it remains for us, as those who also understand that these ancient rituals symbolized eternal truths, to see that the Father delights in the unified worship of His saints. The twelve loaves were not brought into the sanctuary on separate days of the week, but they were brought in together on the Sabbath day. It is ironic and lamentable that the controversy over the Christian's day of worship (Sunday v. Saturday) has led to a disunified expression of Christian reverence. And it is particularly the failure of the church to fully relegate the Sabbath to the ceremonial

71. Law, *Gospel in Exodus*, 106.

past (as it has done with the Sabbath sacrifices and showbread) that this state of fragmentation exists.

The Unwinding Sabbath (Redemption)

It is directly stated in Scripture that the Sabbath commemorated the deliverance from slavery (Deut 5:15). Not that it is essential to have such a clear expression of the ceremonial nature of the Sabbath, for the primary means by which the Sabbath is observed—to rest—is an understandable benefit following years of slavish toil. Yet the command to rest on the Sabbath was not merely to provide the opportunity to cease labor and be released from the rigors of work. More importantly, it was an exercise to break from self-reliance and self-interest. This is illustrated by the circumstances associated with the inaugural Sabbath commandment: the miraculous and gracious double-portion of manna on the sixth day. The work that would have been required to gather and prepare the manna on the seventh day was not necessarily eliminated; it was merely offset to the previous day. And the manna that was eaten on the Sabbath was as much a testimony of God's gracious provision as on any other day. On the Sabbath they were released from the work of food preparation and from ordinary employments that conflicted with a particular devotion to God in remembrance of their release from Egypt. On the Sabbath, with all the work already completed, they could remember how on the day of their deliverance, the Lord did all the work while they stood still in wonderment and awe.

> Is this not the word that we told you in Egypt, saying, 'Let us alone that we may serve the Egyptians?' For it would have been better for us to serve the Egyptians than that we should die in the wilderness." And Moses said to the people, "Do not be afraid. Stand still, and see the salvation of the *Lord*, which He will accomplish for you today. (Exod 14:12–13)

The command to remember the Sabbath was a call to trust in God totally: resting in His unsurpassable salvation from troubles, relying upon His gracious provision for livelihood, hoping in His beneficent promises, and reposing in glorious communion with Him. Self-serving work was completed the day before so the attention of one's mind, and the affection of one's heart might be focused upon the Savior of Israel. *Trust* is the essential duty of the Sabbath; therefore, this weekly observance was an unmistakable foreshadowing of the salvation of Jesus Christ *through faith*. The Jews were to repose in the salvation of the Lord who delivered them from their bondage to sin.

Therefore, the back reference to creation cannot mean 1) that the Sabbath is some sort of "creation ordinance" about worship, 2) that we are to reflect on the sanctity of time, 3) that we are to weekly celebrate our work, 4) that we are to have some sort of rhythm to our life, or 5) that efficiency and relaxation are spiritual virtues for Christians. All of these claims miss the point of the redemptive themes of the Sabbath. If anything, the mention of the creation rest in Sabbath law should have engendered a heartfelt desire to return to the garden, as it were, to be in that blessed state of fellowship with God without the presence of sin. This is the spiritual intention of drawing a link between the Jewish Sabbath and the creation rest. All of the Sabbath rituals designed for Israel were bolstered by the creation episode to enlarge their redemptive typology. God's rest, as a thing or a place, is typological of redemption and foreshadows the instauration of the eternal rest. Man's rest, as a human determination, is typological of the means of redemption, which indicates the requisite trust, belief or faith in God's promises, without which no one will enter God's rest (Heb 4:3).

THE TWO WORKS OF THE WEEK'S REMAINDER

Preparing for the Sabbath

By NT times the day preceding the Sabbath came to be called the Day of Preparation or Sabbath-eve.

> Now when evening had come, because it was the Preparation Day (*paraskeue*), that is, the day before the Sabbath (*prosabbaton*) . . . (Mark 15:42)

The Day of Preparation could be considered part of the Sabbath ceremony as it commemorated the bestowal of the double-portion of manna to the Israelites in the wilderness. On the Day of Preparation, the Israelites received their bread for the day and the next, that they were required to prepare, according to their tastes, the day before the Sabbath (Exod 16:23). Failing to prepare the meal one day in advance could put them in the position of breaking the Sabbath. So, when Israel departed the wilderness and the manna stopped, were the Jews to cast away the Day of Preparation because they no longer received the double-portion? There is no indication that the command to prepare meals a day in advance was mitigated in any way when the manna stopped. Upon their arrival in Canaan, they were to gather the *old grain* on Sabbath-eve (Josh 5:11). The practice of meal preparation, an inseparable aspect of Sabbath-keeping, remained as a reminder of the historicity of forty years supply of manna in the wilderness.

Kaplan cites the wisdom of sages past regarding the command to prepare meals before the Sabbath: "He who prepares on Friday, will eat on Shabbos."[72] However, preparing for the Sabbath was not just about meal preparation. If the reward for adherence to the preparatory ritual were a mere meal, then the spiritual lesson would be missed altogether (Heb 13:10). Instead, the Spirit teaches that he whose heart is prepared to hear the Lord will dine with Him for eternity (Rev 3:20, 22). Though food preparations were commanded to be done the day preceding the Sabbath, the Jew really should have been preparing all week for the upcoming Sabbath, just as Heschel reminds his Jewish readers:

> [The Sabbath] needs the companionship of all other days. All days of the week must be spiritually consistent with the Day of Days. All our life should be a pilgrimage to the seventh day; the thought and appreciation of what this day may bring to us should be ever present in our minds.[73]

72. Kaplan, *Sabbath*, 48.
73. Heschel, *Sabbath*, 89.

The Jew practiced ceremonially the process of salvation as modeled by God in the creation account. The resulting rest was what the Lord's creative work was ultimately leading toward. That is, the individual days may stand out as completed days, but they really form a unity of preparation for the final day of the week. So, in a sense, the six days preceding the Sabbath were a picture of the Lord's work in their life leading them to their ultimate redemption. The Lord first prepared for His creation rest in thought; then, completing the planned six days of creation, hallowed the seventh day because everything that was prepared for it was "very good." Each day of creation was a day of preparation that made ready a cosmos, and especially a humanity, to share in His forthcoming rest. The concept and activity of *preparation* are divine in origin, modeled by our Creator who has prepared beforehand (*proetoimazo*) that we, His workmanship, should walk in good works (Eph 2:10) and ultimately experience the glory of His riches (Matt 25:34; Rom 9:23). By His Spirit we know that our Heavenly Father has prepared (*hetoimazo*) a great number of blessed things for us to enjoy (1 Cor 2:9–10) and by faith we know that the material world was prepared (*katartizo*) by the spoken word of God (Heb 11:3). The Lord's preparations actually began prior to the foundation of the world, and coupled with the six days of creation, to make ready the typological rest on the seventh day, which our first parents were meant to enjoy forever.

> Oh, how great is Your goodness, which You have laid up for those who fear You, which You have prepared (*pa'al*) for those who trust in You in the presence of the sons of men! (Ps 31:19)

Whether in His work with individuals or with the nation Israel, the Lord has in mind an intended end, and thus prepares according to His redemptive purposes. Thus, it was not unusual for the Lord to ask the Israelites to prepare themselves and their household for the upcoming Sabbath, to make themselves ready prior to the Sabbath rest. Obviously, preparation has its practical benefits, but the *ceremonial* ritual of preparation has a spiritual meaning. In other words, the Lord did not include preparatory rituals to teach his people how to better manage their lives, but to symbolize spiritual preparation for forthcoming spiritual realities (Exod 12:3–6; Deut 16:16–17; Lev 23:42). To be prepared is to be ready; and for the Jew, nothing was more important than to be prepared for the arrival of the Messiah.

> In those days John the Baptist came preaching in the wilderness of Judea, and saying, "Repent, for the kingdom of heaven is at hand!" For this is he who was spoken of by the prophet Isaiah, saying: "The voice of one crying in the wilderness: 'Prepare (*hetoimazo*) the way of the Lord; make His paths straight.'" (Matt 3:1–3)

The preparation of one's heart and life to meet the Messiah was of paramount importance to the Jews. John the Baptist proclaimed, as it were, on the sixth day—the day of preparation—the upcoming arrival of the Kingdom of Heaven (the seventh day). John frantically urged the last minute preparations of the heart: repentance before God. Though the Messiah has come, His demand for preparatory repentance has not changed and His daily offer of redemption has not changed. However, He has expanded His charge to all men everywhere, in ways not experienced with Israel (Acts

17:30–31). Neither in this day of grace is preparation to meet God a matter of waiting for an appropriate day, for "*Today*, if you will hear His voice, do not harden your hearts" (Heb 4:7).

All who repent and trust in Jesus Christ have their remaining days as a "day of preparation" for the second coming of the Lord and the complete fulfillment of the promise of the heavenly rest. The believer in the risen Jesus Christ has both entered into that rest (in partial fulfillment) and awaits that rest (of complete fulfillment). We are confident in a completed salvation, being found in Him and having received the seal of the Holy Spirit, yet we yearn for the finalization of our salvation when our soul is unshackled from this sin-encrusted body. This state of tension that occupies our brief lifespan is the framework for the work of God who daily prepares us through sanctification. We are saved, yet we are to work out our salvation with "fear and trembling" (Phil 2:12), presumably on a daily basis. Preparation is a matter of Christian obedience, a measure of the desire to please the Savior, a lifestyle of the soldier engaged in spiritual conflict (Luke 12:47).

Our work of preparation is wonderfully and graciously subjoined by the Lord's work of preparation in our lives through the gift of the Holy Spirit (2 Cor 5:5). God Himself is preparing now on a daily basis for the second re-creation rest of eternity by sanctifying His saints on a daily basis and preparing them as a bride for His beloved Son (Rev 21:1). Our Lord assured us in the tenderest way of His plan to prepare abodes for us in heaven (John 14:1–3). Dear Christian, we have our "day of preparation," which comprises our whole life: the sanctifying work of God in our lives and His preparation of a people for the endless rest of salvation.

Working Toward the Sabbath

The fourth commandment is not only about resting on the seventh day, but working the preceding six days: "six days you shall labor and do all your work" (Exod 20:9). The pattern of work and rest for Israel was dignified by the pattern followed by the Lord in the first week of creation. The dignity of their work was by virtue of their redemption, otherwise their work was valueless (Isa 64:6). Yet there were crucial differences between their recurring work-week and the Lord's week of creation. The Lord's daily work in creation was not a slavish work; therefore His rest was not a redemptive rest for Himself. The Lord worked legitimately and righteously for six days and possessed the authority to bless the seventh day. The Israelites, however, were rescued from slavish work and oppression (Deut 26:6–7). Their work was directed by taskmasters and benefited a kingdom that stood against the Lord. They were in no position to grant themselves any rest, so the Lord redeemed them and blessed their Sabbath and made it holy. The pattern of work and rest in creation symbolized the Lord's ongoing work in the lives of every Israelite intending to bring them to redemptive rest. No man could ever legitimately model God's rest as if he had earned that rest from a perfect work.

On the surface, their Sabbath rest appeared as a gift for having toiled as slaves; however, it was not physical rest and refreshment that the Lord intended to represent in their Sabbath, but freedom from enslaving sin. Only as they acknowledged their slavery to sin and their powerlessness to end its dominion over them (Deut 5:15; Rom 6:15–22; 1 Cor 6:9–11), could they cry out to the God of their fathers for deliverance. Superficially, the pattern of work and rest called man to outwardly imitate God and to physically rest after six days of labor, but this ignores the intended spiritual meaning to reflect on the fact that God's rest began in perfection and was ruined by sin. Their rest was a memorial of the Lord's sinless seventh-day rest and a token of the future eternal rest; it was a reminder that their inward state of sinfulness must be despised as a slave despised his mistreatment and that they must call out to God for redemption from their sins as a slave would call out for redemption from slavery. But those of us who have come to understand the spiritual meaning of redemptive rest have no reason to repeat the outward ceremony, for we possess in Christ the forgiveness of all our sins and the guarantee of an eternal habitation with God.

If the creation week and the Sabbath are viewed primarily as types of redemption, which have now been fulfilled, then we have increased freedom to order our work schedule within the constraints of God's word. We can relax and have non-functional time on a weekly basis, if that pleases us. We can be sick and take off work without guilt. We can take a vacation or eventually retire. We can even work seven days a week, but the Christian does not have the freedom to dismiss the obligation, clearly stated in the NT and modeled in the life of the early church, to attend a weekly congregational meeting for worship (Heb 10:24–25). A Christian can have any alternative work schedule, but there are no alternatives to the unified worship of Christ's church. Therefore, a Christian's first responsibility in deciding his whereabouts during the week is to the Lord, by joining with like-minded believers in their weekly worship. By so doing, he proclaims his belief in the risen Lord Jesus, who died to make men free indeed.

5

Sabbath and the Feasts

The Calendar Conundrum

One cannot properly address the Jewish feasts without an understanding of the complexities of accounting for the passage of time with the use of a calendar. A calendar should have two properties: 1) absoluteness, in order to affix specific dates to specific events and to correlate events to other cultures, and 2) perpetuity, in order to span the fluctuations of man's history, however long it has been and however long it will last. Unfortunately, these two divine qualities are of relatively recent concern as ancient cultures used their own calendar systems based upon a changing understanding of the measurement of time. Not until the ascendancy of the Roman Empire were there thoughts of an international calendar, and not until the rise and spread of Christianity has calendar accuracy taken on such significance.

Young adults soon learn that the Leap Year attempts to reconcile the earth's 365 day, near-six-hour transit around the sun by adding one day every four years. The need for calendar corrections has been understood for millennia. The Egyptians knew quite precisely the time it took for the earth to orbit the sun, yet were satisfied with a calendar year of 365 days.[1] But it was Julius Caesar in 46 BCE who authorized and mandated the universal addition of a second sixth-day, or bissextus, in February just before the new year began on the Calends of March. A leap year, or bissextile year, of 366 days every four years attempts to account for the five hours, forty-eight minutes, and forty-six seconds difference between the calendar year and the solar year.[2] However, even with that adjustment, an excess of seventy-four hours, fifty-three minutes, and twenty seconds accumulates over any 400 year period. The next major change in the calendar system came in the fourth century when Constantine, Emperor of Rome, adopted and protected the Christian religion by the Edict of Milan in 313 CE. As a result of his paternalistic favor, the seven-day week became standardized, Sunday was

1. Faulstich, *Bible Chronology*, 3–5.

2. Duncan, *Calendar*, 202. He says the most accurate tropical year is 365 days, 5 hours, 48 minutes, 46 seconds.

declared as a day of rest for all subjects to pursue their religious and personal interests, and the unified celebration of Easter became a matter of importance. As a result of Constantine's pro-Christian position, the Jewish community became stigmatized and Christians questioned how they could determine the date for Easter without having to resort to the announcement of Passover by the Jews. Emperor Constantine called for, and presided at, an ecumenical council to settle the matters and unify the beliefs and practices of the church. The Council of Nicaea convened in 325 CE and determined that Easter would be celebrated on the first Sunday after the first new moon following the spring equinox, and *not* based on the Jewish determination of the Passover. Duncan explains an oversight of the Nicene Council.

> Another blemish in the Nicaea solution was the failure of the council's bishops and time reckoners to correct the central flaw in Caesar's calendar: the annual error of 11 minutes. This meant that an Easter tethered to a fixed spring equinox would drift backward with the rest of the calendar, falling behind the true orbit of the earth by one full day every 128 or so years. By 325 the Julian calendar was already three days behind where it stood when Caesar introduced his reforms in 45 BCE, when the vernal equinox fell on March 25.[3]

This error stood for well over a millennium. In response to a better understanding of calendar drift, a new system was adopted in 1582 under Pope Gregory XIII (1502–1585) that corrected the excess of ten days and provided for additional adjustments three times every four hundred years.[4] The impetus for the eponymous Gregorian calendar was to ensure that religious holidays, especially Easter, were being celebrated annually on the proper date. However, some nations were hesitant to adopt the common-sense solution to the drift of some ten days that had accumulated since the Council of Nicaea—the United Kingdom did not adopt the Gregorian calendar until 1752. It is also critical to understand that when the Roman Catholic Church effected the calendar change in 1582, ten days were suppressed by counting October 5th as October 15th. Though the date was changed, the day of the week was not changed.

Attempts to rely upon the moon's twenty-nine day, twelve-hour orbit around the earth leads to the same difficulties for precisely accounting for time. The calendar of the Babylonians was based primarily on the moon, as evidence has shown that as early as 432 BCE they recognized that 235 lunations roughly approximates nineteen solar years.[5] The Jewish calendar is based both on the lunar month and the solar year, hence a lunisolar calendar.[6] The Jewish calendar in use today, developed over the centuries under the auspices of the religious leaders, was published for general knowledge in 359 CE by Hillel II.[7] Because the Romans prohibited the Jews from announcing the

3. Ibid., 53.

4. For a more detailed analysis of the accumulated excess of time see Zinberg, *Jewish Calendar*, 30.

5. 19 years = 6939.6018 days. 235 months = 6939.68865 days. This results in an error of about one day every 219 years.

6. Edersheim, *Temple*, 136; Finegan, *Biblical Chronology*, 31–32.

7. Zinberg, *Jewish Calendar*, 39. The Jewish calendar follows the Metonic Cycle, named after the Athenian Meton (432 BCE) who discovered that nineteen solar years (6935 days) very nearly equates

New Moon celebration, Hillel promulgated the calendar rules so the Diaspora could observe the feasts of the Lord in unison on the proper day. During its nineteen year cycle, the Jewish calendar employs six different types of years, varying in the number of days in two different months and occasionally adding a thirteenth whole month.

> Minor adjustments, such as alternating the length of the months between 29 and 30 days, took care of the remaining one-day difference and also provided for the elimination of other difficulties foreseen by Hillel. Yom Kippur, for instance, can never fall on a Friday or a Sunday; to have two consecutive days of work-cessation would create too much hardship.[8]

The Jews did not consider it important to maintain exactly 365 days each year; the goal was to keep feasts in their respective seasons. The Lord told Moses on the eve of the exodus regarding the Feast of Unleavened Bread, "You shall therefore keep this ordinance in its season from year to year" (Exod 13:10). Moses certainly used a calendar system (Exod 40:17), but how many days elapsed during their inaugural year is unknown (it was probably 354 days long, or twelve lunar months). The Egyptian calendar probably in use at that time accounted for the year with twelve thirty-day months with the intercalation of five days at the end of the year (365 days); however, the Lord required Israel to begin each month with the lunar appearance, thus forcing the Jews to separate their culture from that of their oppressors even in the accounting of time.

> The calendar we know as the Egyptian calendar has no link to the moon at all, although it kept the old hieroglyph. In the Egyptian calendar, there were 12 months of 30 days each. The months each had three "weeks" of 10 days each. Between the end of the 12th month and the beginning of the first month of the next year were five epagomenal (extra) days, resulting in a fixed year of 365 days every year. This calendar, almost a quarter of a day shorter than the tropical year, constantly shifted with respect to the seasons.[9]

There is no reason to believe that the newly liberated Jews simply duplicated the existing Egyptian calendar since it was based on Nile flooding and pagan gods; however, the Jews would have learned some of the "tricks of the trade" and applied them to their new national calendar, such as the knowledge that a solar year is slightly longer than 365 ¼ days, causing fixed dates to move forward (i.e., from the third to the second) one day every four years. However, the origination, development and employment of those calendar adjustments necessary to keep the celebration of required feasts in the proper season remains a mystery. Though there are few records of the Jewish calendar system prior to 359 CE, it must not be supposed that the nineteen-year cycle was adopted at that time. The names of the months of the Jewish calendar

---

235 lunar months: the sum (6936 days) of nineteen moon years (6726 days) and seven leap years of thirty days (210 days). The nineteen solar years assumes 365 days in every year, the nineteen moon years assumes 354 days in every year.

8. Trepp, *Book of Jewish Observance*, 83. Zinberg mentioned that Hillel determined that a Sabbatic Year could not be a leap year, because an extra month of land rest was considered intolerable.

9. Hagen, "The Egyptian Calendar," n.p.

are based on names of the Babylonian calendar that used a similar nineteen-year cycle, so its existence may be traced at least to the first captivity (680 BCE).[10]

On the eve of Israel's release from bondage, the Lord said, "This month shall be your beginning of months; it shall be the first month of the year to you" (Exod 12:2–3). God had placed the gold and silver orbs in the sky for the delight of earth's life and decreed their heavenly paths (Ps 104:19; Jer 31:35) to function as measuring rods of time: the day, month, and year (Gen 1:14). Since the sun, moon, and stars are themselves created entities under God's sovereign management (Josh 10:12–14), they should not be worshipped (Deut 4:19; 17:3). The predictability of the earth's rotation and solar orbit, the moon's orbit around the earth (Jer 31:36), and the stellar reference points, provide the basis for the construction of calendars in order to standardize the measurement of time and to furnish the framework into which all events can be set in order of succession. The orbiting paths, rotations, and speed of heavenly bodies within the solar system provide the apparent absolute reference points with which to measure time. The incomprehensible expanse of the universe provides the apparent perpetuity for measuring time compared to the life times of men and nations. For the Jewish nation, the Lord's calendar was not limited to its function of measuring time, but to further reveal Himself and the Messiah in subtle yet profound ways.

A calendar was necessary for the people of Israel in order to strictly observe the multitude of festal occasions. The Lord did not prescribe the names of the months of the year, so it is reasonable that the Jews simply numbered them or borrowed names from other cultures. The only month mentioned in Hebrew is Abib (Nisan), the month that Israel left Egypt (Exod 13:4; 23:15; 34:18; Deut 16:1), but Abib also has an Egyptian meaning of "sprout," indicating spring. Nehemiah mentions Nisan, Elul, and Kislew (Neh 2:1; 6:15; 1:1), each adopted Babylonian names. The end of the ceremonial year coincided with the Feast of Ingathering in the autumnal month of Tishri (Exod 23:14–16). However, present-day Jews celebrate their civil new year on Rosh Hashana, the Feast of Trumpets (Tishri 1), with the sanctification of the New Moon in autumn. Because the feasts were commandments of the Lord, integral to the covenant with Israel, the leaders of Israel were responsible for accounting for the passage of time and declaring the arrival of each feast day in its appropriate season. So, if the Jewish months alternated between thirty and twenty-nine days, there would be 354 days in the first year, eleven days short of a solar year. Obviously, a leap year of twenty-nine or thirty days every three years would keep the lunar cycle proximate to the solar cycle, but because of the accumulation of differences over the years and the difficulty managing the implications of the observance of a multitude of holy days, the computations became much more complicated.

> The Jewish Ordinary year is therefore 10 to 13 days shorter, and the Jewish Leap year is 17 to 20 days longer than its corresponding General year, thus causing

10. Duncan, *Calendar*, 14.

> Tishri 1 of the following year to occur 10 to 13 days earlier, or 17 to 20 days later, in the General year, than Tishri 1 of the current year.[11]

As well as could be understood at Moses' time with simple math and a knowledge of the length of a solar year, the Israelites had the tools necessary to reconcile their lunisolar calendar with the solar year. By today's standards, their system is complicated, but not impossible.

The Floating Sabbath Day

Reformed theologian R. J. Rushdoony gave credence to Curtis Clair Ewing's theory that the operating calendar in Moses' time was borrowed from the Egyptians and used twelve thirty-day months to account for the year's passage, to which three days were added to Ellul and two days were added to Adal in order to achieve 365 days.[12] Based on Ewing's proposal that Israel used a solar calendar and not a lunar calendar, Rushdoony asseverates that the "Hebrew sabbath and the modern Saturday cannot be equated," because the Sabbath supposedly shifted one day back each year to a different day of the week. The force of this understanding supposedly provides clear proof against the attempt of Christians "to treat Saturdays as the true sabbath" with an ulterior goal to promote Sunday as the new Sabbath. Unfortunately, the rationale employed is in error and the conclusion is misguided, so it is regretful that C. C. Ewing's legacy continues to be passed on.[13]

Curtis Clair Ewing's calendar research and thesis were based on the earlier writings of a Methodist minister, Samuel Walter Gamble (1852-?) who published "Sunday—The True Sabbath of God," in 1900 to counter the inroads of Seventh-day Adventists who undermined the restrictions of Sunday labor laws.[14] Writing in 1958, Ewing's pamphlet attempts to answer Seventh-day Adventists who question the Reformed understanding that Sunday is the Christian Sabbath.

> Why do you not keep Saturday as the Sabbath when you stress the necessity of returning to the principles of Divine law as a solution to our national problems?[15]

That is, the Adventist queries, if one claims that the Sabbath is a moral commandment, as are the other commandments in the Decalogue, then what scriptural basis can be mustered to defend a Sunday-Sabbath in preference for a Saturday-Sabbath? Ewing attempts to disarm the question by challenging the supposed assumption that

11. Zinberg, *Jewish Calendar*, 70.

12. Rushdoony, *Institutes of Biblical Law*, 134–36.

13. Ewing's work has been mentioned by Reformed authors familiar with Rushdoony (E. Calvin Beisner, PCA, Knox Theological Seminary, Bob Burridge, PCA, Genevan Institute for Reformed Studies, and James Bordwine, PCA, Westminster Presbyterian Church.) and by Anglo-Israelite authors directly succeeding Ewing (Pastor Mark Downey, Kinsman Redeemer Ministries). Apostle LeGrand Richards and Elder Bruce R. McConkie, both of the Church of Jesus Christ of the Latter Day Saints, quote Gamble.

14. Gamble, *Sunday: The True Sabbath of God*, 7–12.

15. Ewing and Ewing, "Israel's Calendar," 5.

the Sabbath of the old covenant always occurred on Saturday, so his simplistic answer is, "Israel never kept Saturday as the Sabbath, so why should I?" What he actually means is that Israel didn't keep the Sabbath on Saturday year after year on a fixed day of the week and that it only happened to fall on Saturday every seventh year. In fairness to Pastor Ewing, the main points to support his thesis are as follows:

1. The original Jewish calendar was borrowed from the Egyptians. It was oriented to the solar year and comprised twelve thirty-day months. The "law of necessity" required the addition of three days at the end of Elul (sixth month) and two days at the end of Adar (twelfth month) to keep the cycle of six days work and one (day) of rest. The present Jewish calendar, which is lunar based, did not arise until 359 CE.
2. In David's time, a year had twelve months (1 Kgs 4:7), and in Noah's day, Moses wrote of a five month period of 150 days (Gen 7:11; 8:3) which indicates a thirty-day month. In addition, Daniel's prophecy (Dan 7:25; 12:7) and John's Revelation (Rev 12:6; 11:2–3; 13:5) lead to the computation of thirty-day months. Therefore, Israel accounted for the year with twelve months of thirty days.
3. The New Moon celebration is really a New Month celebration and has nothing to do with the moon. The Hebrew word for month (*chodesh*) is different than the word for the moon (*yerach*). Therefore, the Jews did not base their months on lunations.
4. A year has 365 days in it. If divided by seven, it gives fifty-two weeks with one day left over. This extra day was absorbed in a forty-eight-hour Sabbath on the 4th and 5th of Sivan as shown by Leviticus 23:15, 16, and 21. This caused the Sabbath to shift to a different day of the week, yet also maintained the fixed Sabbaths.
5. God never commanded that the Sabbath be observed on the seventh day of the week. The command is to observe the Sabbath every seventh day, with six days of work intervening. Since a "rest" is a rest, a Sabbath can be two days long provided no work comes between.
6. The annual feasts that required Sabbath observance were synchronized to fall on the weekly Sabbaths, thus maintaining the six days of work and one day of rest cycle, except for one 48-hour Sabbath on Sivan 4 and 5 (Feast of Weeks/Pentecost) which resulted in the shifting of the Sabbath cycle to a different day of the week during that year.
7. The phrase "first day of the week" in the NT really means "first of the Sabbaths." Therefore, Sunday is called the Sabbath nine times in the NT. When Christ fulfilled the ceremonial law regarding the Sabbaths, He brought the old order of Sabbaths to an end, which occurred on variable days of the week, and established a new order of Sabbaths, which are fixed on Sunday.

8. Hebrews 4:9 says that there remains a Sabbath-keeping for God's people and the Pentecost Sabbath (Sivan 4–5) shifted from Saturday to Sunday, so the Sabbath has been on Sunday ever since.

To summarize, Ewing suggests that the Sabbath migrated from Saturday to Sunday because Christ's resurrection was on the second half of a forty-eight-hour Sabbath. His death and resurrection fulfilled the ceremonial calendar of the Jews, which had a shifting Sabbath, and at the same time fixed the Sabbath on Sunday for Christians. Therefore, what is essential to Sabbath-keeping is not the day of the week, but the sequence of seven days. His theory then is merely a technical justification for Christian worship on Sunday instead of Saturday; however, it is a total re-invention of Israel's calendar based on conjecture and spurious analysis. Rather than answer each of Ewing's arguments, it should be sufficient to demonstrate the error of his two major premises that originally Israel used the Egyptian solar calendar of twelve thirty-day months (which was not based on the moon) and that Israel's present calendar is a construct of the fourth century.

Ewing's thesis requires the month to be disassociated from the new moon, in spite of the fact that the Egyptians initially associated the month with the appearance of the new moon. The hieroglyph for "month" pictures a crescent moon above a star. Archeology has documented that the Egyptians initially used a lunar calendar, but later dynasties used a civil calendar of thirty day months. Furthermore, other Egyptologists, like Parker, document that the Egyptians used two calendars concurrently: 1) the civil calendar of 365 days, and 2) a religious lunar calendar of 354 days.

> The lunar calendar was by far the older system used to tell time in Ancient Egypt. Yet, even with the invention of the civil calendar, the lunar remained in use throughout Egypt's history as the primary system for determining the dates of the religious festivals.[16]

Like Israel, the primitive understanding of a "month" was that it was a lunar phenomenon. So when Israel departed Egypt and was given her new calendrical system, it would not have been unusual for the new moon and month to be contextual synonyms. Also of interest is that the Egyptian civil calendar divided the month into three 10-day sections, called decans, so it is possible that Israel had not even practiced the concept of a seven-day week prior to leaving Egypt.

> In the civil calendar each season is composed of four months, each month is made up of three weeks, and each week consisted of ten days. The total number of days in the civil year is 360. At the end of the last month of the civil year five days were added that were considered to be independent from the year. These were viewed as the days in the year on which several gods were born as these days were outside of the mundane civil calendar and thus of a spiritual nature. These were termed the Heriu-renpet or "the Days Upon the Year," however Egyptologists refer to them as the epagomenal days.[17]

16. Parker, *Calendars of Ancient Egypt*, 708.

17. Wisner, *Eye of the Sun*, 99; Finegan, *Biblical Chronology*, 19.

Luther offers proof of this by noting that Pharaoh commissioned Joseph to "teach his elders wisdom" (Ps 105:22), but the Egyptians "were not burdened with circumcision, much less with the law of Moses, which was not yet promulgated."[18] If the Lord approved the use of the Egyptian calendar, why did He tell Moses in the seventh Egyptian month that it was Israel's first month? Again, it is highly improbable that Israel borrowed a particularly pagan calendar based on Nile flooding and agriculture, which incorporated worship of their gods, the same gods mocked by the Lord through severe plagues. Furthermore, the Lord stated that a new era was beginning for Israel (Exod 12:2). Indeed, the Lord told Israel specifically, "According to the doings of the land of Egypt, where you dwelt, you shall not do" (Lev 18:3). The typology of redemption from Egypt meant separating from their former manner of life and establishing new spiritual norms. Regarding the ceremonial feature of the Feast of Unleavened Bread to purge the yeast from their homes, Bonar says the Lord "prepared a type of the truth, that a delivered, redeemed man must shake off his former connection with pollution."[19] Egypt was not only a severe taskmaster but a polluter of souls as well, born out by the number of souls that fell in the wilderness. The Egyptian calendar was an expression of Egyptian idolatry. The new set of festivals given to Israel at their deliverance was predicated on a new calendar to account for and order their days, and this included a variable-length month based on the appearance of the new moon, a week consisting of seven days culminating in the Sabbath, and variable length years in order to keep feasts in their respective seasons. Israel's Redeemer created and instituted not only a menagerie of feasts but the shelves of time on which to place them. The feasts produced practical benefits in ordering their lives and reminding them of their redemption, and the paradigm shift in time-accounting demonstrated the extent of His lordship. More significantly, the new feasts forecasted a more significant and enduring spiritual redemption, and the new calendar forecasted the totality of change necessary when becoming a child of God (2 Cor 5:17; 1 Pet 1:18–19). Time was not the jurisdiction of man, but of God.

In an attempt to corroborate the thirty-day month theory, Ewing cites biblical references that span the breadth of recorded history from Genesis to Revelation, assuming they all relate to the same calendar. As proof that Israel adopted Egypt's calendar, Ewing notes that Noah weathered the deluge for a five month period of 150 days (Gen 7:11; 8:3), which computes to five thirty-day months.[20] First of all, Noah predated the Egyptians, and there is no proof that the Egyptians accounted for calendar dates the same as Noah.[21] Secondly, 150 divided by five only gives the average number of days in a month, not the actual days in each month. For example, February 1 to June 30 is 150 days, but two months have thirty days, two months have thirty-one days,

18. Luther, "Against the Sabbatarians," *Luther's Works*, 47:85.

19. Bonar, *Leviticus*, 400.

20. Referencing Edward Mahler's Handbook, Finegan notes that the flood chronology presents two ways to account for the passage of the year: the lunar method and the solar method. Finegan, *Biblical Chronology*, 15–16.

21. Finegan, *Biblical Chronology*, 10–14.

and one month has twenty-eight days. Thirdly, Ewing's calendar has ten months with thirty days, one month with thirty-two days and one month with thirty-three days. He even suggests that Israel had a month of thirty-seven days once every twenty-nine years. Certainly, an average length month cannot be made the standard for every other month of any calendar year in any culture.

Ewing then claims that the Hebrew word *chodesh* means "month" and not "New Moon," despite the meaning of newness in the root word. This claim is contrary to all definitions.

> Although this word properly means "new moon," it is commonly used as an equivalent to our word "month" because the month began when the thin crescent of the new moon was first visible at sunset. It was used along with the more rare [yerach] meaning "moon" . . . the Hebrew calendar used a lunar month fitted into a solar year.[22]

That the calendar month and new moon are identical is supported by Josephus:

> But at the beginning of the second year, on the month Xanthicus, as the Macedonians call it, but on the month Nisan, as the Hebrews call it, on the new moon, they consecrated the tabernacle, and all its vessels.[23]

While *chodesh* may be translated "month," context guides the translation of words with multiple meanings. Psalm 81:3 is an interesting example where *chodesh* could be translated "month" rather than "new moon." "Blow the trumpet at the time of the New Moon, at the full moon, on our solemn feast day." Some authors believe this verse refers to the New Moon celebration on Tishri 1, the Feast of Trumpets, which begins the new year.[24] However, the verse specifically mentions a "full moon," and there are no full moon celebrations. Barnes states,

> It is not certain, however, that the word used here means new moon. Prof. Alexander renders it in the month; that is, in the month, by way of eminence, in which the Passover was celebrated. The word used—chodesh—means, indeed, commonly the new moon; the day of the new moon; the first day of the lunar month (Num 29:6; 1 Sam 20:5,18,24); but it also means a month; that is, a lunar month, beginning at the new moon, Gen 8:5; Exod 13:4; et al.[25]

Since there was no full moon celebration, the context of Psalm 81 is best understood as Israel's redemption from Egypt, highlighting the celebration of Passover. Since Passover occurs on the fourteenth/fifteenth of the month, the only way it could be a full moon is if the month began at the appearance of the new moon.[26] So, Asaph is simply drawing attention to the month in which the Passover took place.

22. Weber, "hōdesh," TWOT, 1:266.
23. Josephus, *Ant.* 3.8.4, 92.
24. Howard and Rosenthal, *Feasts*, 110; Edersheim, *Temple*, 190.
25. Barnes' *Notes*, 4:266.
26. Raphael, *Festivals*, 68.

Ewing goes on to accept the historical reference of Dion Cassius, a second-century Roman historian, who "says that Israel left Egypt on Saturday," thus agreeing that Israel's first year of redemption began with Saturday Sabbaths. He further accepts the traditional teaching that the Jews observed Saturday Sabbaths during the year of Christ's crucifixion, acknowledging that Christ rested in the grave over a Saturday Sabbath. Yet he maintains that fixed Saturday Sabbaths did not arise until 359 CE. So, Ewing mentions two historic examples of Sabbaths occurring on Saturday but offers no examples from history that demonstrate Sabbaths occurring on any other day of the week.

Finally, his unsupported theory begs the question why the Jews, in 359 CE, would adopt such a complicated lunisolar calendar system in favor of what Ewing calls a simple and orderly solar calendar? Raphael notes that after centuries of practicing the New Moon celebration, the customs for announcing the New Moon were recorded in the Mishnah with contributions by Gamaliel in the first century.[27] The New Moon was verified by two witnesses before a notification fire was kindled on the Mount of Olives and carried on to alert the Exile in Babylonia. Obviously, a month of thirty days does not need to be verified by two witnesses and announced to all Israel. Furthermore, this reference predates Ewing's claim that the lunisolar calendar didn't arise until the fourth century CE. Obviously, the Jews' use of a lunisolar calendar preceded the official publication of it in the fourth century by at least three hundred years. At every point, Ewing's theory suffers under examination.

The festival calendar and the Levitical priesthood were the two predominant brushes the Lord used to paint the chiaroscuro of redemption in the old covenant. While the temple, the priesthood, and the sacrifices seem to be the clearest types of redemption, the experience of them was largely confined to the Levite tribe and residents of Jerusalem. What involved the whole nation in redemptive themes, down to the children and homemakers, were the recurring feasts within the framework of a calendar system. While the feasts themselves portrayed the work and person of Jesus Christ, the framework for their observation was the calendar and the predictable movement of the earth, sun, and moon. Though the festival system has been rendered obsolete, including the lunisolar calendar, the heavens remain as expressions of the inestimable power of God and His unchangeable nature (1 Thess 5:8–10).

FORECASTING FREQUENCIES

In his introduction to Leviticus, Scottish preacher Andrew Bonar (1810–1892) contemplated the full measure of truth contained in that fascinating and divine book.

> The one great principle of interpretation which we keep before us is apostolic method and practice. This is the key we have used. We find the sacred writers adduce the likeness that exists between the thing that was typified and the type itself, and there they rest satisfied. So we lay down this as our great rule,—there must be obvious resemblance. And next, we search into these types, in the belief

27. Raphael, *Festivals*, 58–60.

> that Christ is the centre-truth of Revelation; and surely no principle is more obviously true? The body or substance of the law is Christ (Col 2:17), and types are a series of shadows projected from Christ, "the body." It is this Messiah that has been, from the beginning, the object to be unveiled to the view of men; and in the fact that New Testament light has risen lies our advantage in searching into what these things signify.[28]

The priesthood, the tabernacle services, and the system of recurring holy days and festivals, all work together to prefigure Jesus Christ and His Kingdom through the fascinatingly divine method of typology. The whole sacred system of private and public worship was designed by the Lord God with the specific purpose of telling forth the ministry of His Son and His Bride, so "there must be obvious resemblance." Hence, the feasts are the property of the Lord, times that He has appointed in wisdom for His lofty and holy purposes between Himself and His people (Lev 23:4).

Daily

Not a day was to elapse without the shedding of innocent blood; at the very least, two young lambs were slain, one in the morning and one in the evening (Num 28:1–4). The daily sacrifice, or Continual Burnt Offering, amounted to well over 700 lambs every year. Josephus explained that the evening sacrifice took place from the ninth hour to the eleventh hour,[29] that is, from 3:00 to 5:00 p.m. Josephus noted that upon their return from Babylonian exile and the re-erection of the temple and its altar, the complete sacrificial system was reinstated despite concerns of neighboring nations.[30] All the sacrificial observances required of the Jews were inextricably linked to each other as forward-pointers to the coming Messiah. Matthew, Mark, and Luke record that Jesus expired during the crucifixion at the ninth hour, the same time as the second (evening) daily sacrifice (Matt 27:46–50; Mark 15:34–37; Luke 23:45–46).[31] Referring to this connection, the author of Hebrews realized that because our Lord Jesus has offered the supreme sacrifice of His own perfect life, He need not *daily* to offer sacrifices as did the Levitical priests (Heb 7:27). What is true of the most frequent blood-letting sacrifices is true of the less frequent sacrifices: they are all done away. With the emphasis on the day, the Continual Burnt Offering looked back to the beginning of days, evening and morning, as each day was a special gift to humanity. The daily sacrifices continued regardless of the Sabbath, a horrible reminder that even with Sabbath observance the stain of sin still colored that day as much as any other day. Whatever spiritual benefit was derived from Sabbath-keeping, it was no salve or panacea for the origination of sin in the garden.

28. Bonar, *Leviticus*, 8.
29. Josephus, *J.W.* 6.9.3, 749
30. Josephus. *Antiq.* 11.4.1, 291.
31. Doig, *New Testament Chronology*, 272–73.

Weekly

A week is a period of seven days, a hebdomad. We use the word "week" to mean the passing of seven days regardless of what day begins the period. Unlike the day, month, and year, which were specifically given by the Lord for calendar use (Gen 1:14; 8:22; Ps 104:19), the week is atypically unrelated to any astral or planetary phenomena. Non-biblical records confirm that the concept of a week occurred primarily among Semitic populations, and indeed the first biblical instance was used by Laban, the Aramean (Gen 29:27–28). A seven-period indicates a divine stamp on time in terms of the Lord's involvement in human history. *Shabua* is restricted to the passing of seven days or periods (Gen 29:27, 28; Lev 12:5; Jer 5:24; Dan 10:2, 3), and for Israel, this was applied to 1) post-partum uncleanness (Lev 12:5), 2) the Feast of Weeks or Shavuot, (Exod 34:22; Num 28:26; Deut 16:9(2),10,16; 2 Chr 8:13), and 3) by Daniel in his prophecy of Israel's future (Dan 9:24, 25, 26, 27).

The Feast of Weeks derives its name from the fact that seven weeks (or seven seven-periods) must be counted before celebrating their fourth calendar festival. Howard and Rosenthal note that modern Jews celebrate Shavout on Sivan 6, but historically, "the celebration of Shavout was never tied to an actual calendar date."[32] The Feast of Weeks occurs fifty days after the Feast of First Fruits, marking the passage of seven weeks (*shabua*) plus one day. Greek speaking Jews called this festival Pentecost. Through this festival in particular the Lord gave the annual calendar a *prophetic* quality since the Jews were to *count* days until the expected feast. The commemorative reason for the feast is not specifically mentioned, however, it is generally related to the exodus (Deut 16:9–12). Tradition now associates the giving of the Law at Mount Sinai as the commemorative reason for Shavout. With the advent of Jesus Christ and His fulfillment of the Passover and the First Fruits, the disciples turned their attention to things yet future (Acts 1:4–8). Rather than entreat the disciples to count until the next event, He wisely advised them to wait. When the Feast of Weeks arrived, another fulfillment of Israel's calendar took place through the descent of the Holy Spirit from heaven (Acts 2:1–4). At this point, the prophetic nature of Israel's calendar was confirmed to Christians. It may appear that the apostles and disciples were commanded by the resurrected Lord to be in Jerusalem for that Pentecost. However, Jesus did not specifically advise attendance at that festival nor did He tell them to count the days until that festival, as required by law; He only counseled them to wait in Jerusalem. The gift of the Holy Spirit on that day was a fulfillment of the Feast of Weeks (Pentecost) and therefore, it was the end of Israel's counting.

The second most frequent cycle of time in the Hebrew calendar is the hebdomadal cycle that ended with the Sabbath. But the Jews did not refer to this cycle of Sabbaths as a week (*shabua*); the Sabbath was understood merely as the seventh day. Certainly, the Sabbath is precious for its uniqueness, but many of the other feasts duplicate the weekly Sabbath by calling for one or two convocational rests, the primary aspect of Sabbath

32. Howard and Rosenthal, *Feasts*, 90.

observance, which brings the Jew back to the exodus.[33] Rest, as has been demonstrated already, served to remind the Israelites that they were miraculously delivered from slavery. Besides the weekly Sabbaths, the Lord commanded the observance of seven additional Sabbaths during each calendar year. These annual Sabbaths are celebrated just the same as weekly Sabbaths, so the typology of rest is not dependent on a recurring cycle of seven days, but is comfortable even with sporadic annual appearances.

The Sabbath is unique among the feasts of Israel because it is unrelated to astronomical phenomena, it is associated with the first week of creation, and it is recorded in the Ten Commandments. It is the most frequently observed ceremonial law by the whole population of Israel, it is a sign of the covenant (indicating a weekly renewal), and it is the most highly regarded ritual. The Sabbath is similar to the other feasts because it is commemorative of the deliverance from Egypt, it is a unifying celebration in Israel's calendar, and it is a redemptive type fulfilled in the appearance of Jesus Christ. Finally, the Sabbath is unique in that it is replete with redemptive typology, unmatched by other ceremonial laws. Appendix 3 demonstrates the commemorative features of Sabbath law, how it prefigured Christ in His first advent, and the echoing grand fulfillment in the age to come.

Monthly

Just as the week was celebrated with a Sabbath, each month was celebrated with a Rosh Chodesh, or moon renewal. The Lord elevated the spiritual significance of the New Moon by referring to their redemption as the beginning of *months* (Exod 12:2). Thus, the New Moon evoked memories of redemption from Egypt. The reappearance of the thin lunar crescent in the evening sky is another creative token of renewal and restoration embodied in the deliverance of Israel. The arrival date of the new moon was common knowledge, especially to those tending herds, as exemplified by the young shepherd David (1 Sam 20:5), but as has been noted earlier, the ruling body officially declared the holiness of the day upon the observational testimony of two credible witnesses.

The Jewish experience of the New Moon led to the discovery that roughly one of seven months fell on the Sabbath. This posed a problem for witnesses of the New Moon, whether they should travel on the Sabbath to make credible testimony to the court. The court depended on these testimonies to officially proclaim the New Moon celebration, a duty detailed in the Law (Lev 23:4). As Maimonides explained, this duty took precedence over the Sabbath.

> If a witness who had observed the new moon on the night of the Sabbath was sick, he was allowed to ride an ass, or to be carried on a litter. If the witnesses were afraid of enemies who might be lurking for them on the road, they were

33. The Sabbath (Deut 5:5), the Passover (Exod 12:27; Deut 16:1), the Feast of Weeks (Exod 34:14: Deut 16:2), the Feast of Tabernacles (Lev 23:43), and the Jubilee (Lev 25:55) specifically refer to the Egyptian captivity.

allowed to take along weapons; and if it was a long journey, they were allowed to carry along food.[34]

Even if a witness rationalized, based upon the obvious brightness of the new moon, that others who lived closer to Jerusalem could testify of its arrival, they were still duty bound to violate the Sabbath.

The sacrifices of the New Moon continued regardless of what other feast day coincided with it. For example, the Feast of Trumpets was fixed on the first day of the seventh month (New Moon) and had its own prescribed order of sacrifices, yet the daily and monthly sacrifices were to be completed first (Num 29:1–6). The sacrifices of each New Moon were not insignificant, amounting to ten burnt offerings, ten meal offerings, ten drink offerings, and one sin offering (Num 28:11–15). Edersheim notes that it took well over 170 priests to manage the sacrifices of the New Moon alone.[35] The number of animal sacrifices (ten) probably refers back to the ten judgments against Egypt prior to their deliverance. Israel's redemption began in Egypt with ten episodes of plagues that specifically targeted ten deities of the Egyptian religion.

	Plague	God	Title and Function
1	Nile water turned to blood	Hapi	Father of the gods, The god of the Nile.
2	Frog infestation	Heka	The "Toad" goddess of resurrection and procreation
3	Gnat infestation	Geb	The god of earth and vegetation
4	Fly infestation	Kepfi	The god of insects
5	Livestock	Aphis	The "Bull" god
6	Boils	Thoth	The god of intelligence and health
7	Hail	Nut	The goddess of the sky
8	Locusts	Anubis	The god of the fields
9	Darkness	Ra	The Sun god
10	Death of firstborn	Pharaoh	Pharaoh was god incarnate, hence death of a god

The sound of trumpet blasts was characteristic of the feast of the seventh month (Feast of Trumpets), but was also a part of every New Moon celebration.

> Also in the day of your gladness, in your appointed feasts, and at the beginning of your months, you shall blow the trumpets over your burnt offerings and over the sacrifices of your peace offerings; and they shall be a memorial for you before your God: I am the Lord your God. (Num 10:10)

34. Maimonides, *Sanctification of the New Moon*, 11.

35. Edersheim, *Temple*, 192.

The trumpet makes its resounding noise by the controlled breaths of its master. The Jews call this trumpet a *shofar*, meaning "hollow," indicating the lifelessness of the object until the trumpeter chooses to make it sing. The use of the shofar on the New Moon commemorates the assembly of Israel at the base of Mount Sinai to hear the voice of their redeeming God; "the sound of the trumpet (*shofar*) was very loud, so that all the people who were in the camp trembled" (Exod 19:16, 19). The shofar is reminiscent of the redemption of Israel and, as an element of the New Moon celebration, it specifically portrays the revelation of God's will through the instrument Moses, His prophet. It also signifies that covenantal life must spring from the voice of God through a spiritually inclined heart (Isa 55:3). The written word, God-breathed in origin, is His trumpet call to all inhabitants of His earthly footstool. The tone of the New Moon celebration was a public proclamation of the kingship of the Lord as they confessed His presence and sought His remembrance of them, a remembrance that would cause Him to save Israel from all her enemies.

> The object of it [blowing trumpets] is expressly stated to have been "for a memorial," that they might "be remembered before Jehovah," it being specially added: "I am Jehovah your God." It was, so to speak, the host of God assembled, waiting for their Leader; the people of God united to proclaim their King.[36]

A work prohibition on the New Moon is disallowed by Trepp;[37] however, the prophet Amos intimates a New Moon work prohibition similar in scope to the Sabbath because the anger of the Lord was for an ongoing disregard for the New Moon and the Sabbath (Amos 8:5). Rushdoony and Kurtz believe that the work prohibition was a later customary addition to the Law (not at all commanded by the Lord) because there is no evidence that Moses made such a demand of Israel.[38] However, the postulate that the work prohibition is merely traditional is also unreasonable on two grounds. It begs the question why the Jews, given their distaste for keeping the Sabbath, would make their lives more difficult by making a tradition that they could not keep? And why would the Lord in judgment of Israel equate their failure to keep the Sabbath (that He commanded) with their failure to keep a tradition (that they invented)? Regardless of the origin, whether by addition or revelation, the Sabbath work limitations were duplicated by the Lord in a variety of other feasts. Therefore, the weekly Sabbath does not stand alone in the Hebrew calendar in foreshadowing an eschatological rest, but is allied with the New Moon and the annual feasts to resoundingly proclaim that salvation is the exclusive work of God to be received through the resting faith of men. For this reason, the New Moon and the Sabbath are often mentioned with the annual festivals as a summary of their calendar laws in both the Old and New Testaments (1 Chr 23:31; Neh 10:33; Isa 1:13–14; Hos 2:1; Col 3:16). The Sabbath and New Moon are mentioned together because they are year-through festivities as opposed to the annual feasts.

36. Ibid., 191.

37. Trepp, *Book of Jewish Observance*, 84.

38. Rushdoony, *Institutes of Biblical Law*, 150; Kurtz, *Offerings, Sacrifices and Worship*, 353.

The spiritual symbolism inherent in these sister celebrations merited mention by Isaiah in his prophetic descriptions of the future kingdom of God. Isaiah notes the important position and noble quality of the New Moon as an eschatological emblem of renewal to describe the ultimate re-creation of the universe (Isa 66:22–23). The earthly and temporal symbolism of these holy days is richly applied to the future kingdom of God, wherein the present universe is purged and renewed, and all believers worship the Lamb during the perpetual rest of salvation.[39] Yet there is more. The idea of renewal is a common theme among Christ's saints (Rom 12:2) and is evident in David's penitential prayer (Ps 51:10). With the temple sacrifices in mind, David longed for something more intimate with God; it was not enough for David to be renewed but once a month! David knew in his heart that the pitiful sacrifice of animals was insufficient to completely deal with sin (vv. 16–17). Likewise, a recurring ceremony of renewal is also inadequate to overcome the degeneration in the soul.

The common understanding of the ceremonial status of the New Moon is that it pictured redemption as a "renewing" event. Indeed, the moon had always been there in the sky, so each "new moon" is really a recycling of the same old moon. Crescent means "increasing," so that the New Moon celebration actually focuses upon the predictable and increasing disclosure of the moon until it reaches its full revelation. The New Moon typifies the kingdom of God in its overall progress through time and by way of increasing revelation. With regard to God's kingdom, it has already arrived in the advent of Christ (Mark 1:15; John 3:3), yet there remains a full disclosure of it (Luke 22:18; Acts 14:22). In terms of biblical revelation, the zenith was in the advent of Jesus Christ (Mark 1:15; Heb 1:1–3)—the express image of God, the Prophet greater than Moses, and the Word made flesh—yet it remains that a full disclosure is forthcoming (1 Cor 13:9–12; 1 John 3:2). It may be observed that from the birth of Christ, His life, and His ministry were also crescive, like the New Moon. As an infant and child, He was present among Israel, yet hidden from general knowledge, like the moon before its illumination. Then, at His baptism, the "thin crescent" of His Messianic appointment was heralded, so that John the Baptist could reflect, "He must increase" (John 3:30), indicating the expected and progressive unveiling of the person of Jesus Christ to the Jewish nation. The "fullness" of reflected light was revealed to the disciples at His resurrection (Heb 2:9), a light that will be surpassed at His second coming (2 Thess 2:8).

Annually

In addition to the triad of daily, weekly, and monthly observances, the Lord established seven annual feasts palpably bound to the work of an agrarian society. There is a symbolic intention to the use of agricultural terms in the annual feasts and the laws of the land, and there is an obvious association of these laws with Adam's duties as a divine husbandman on earth. Working the soil, sowing, tending, and reaping are not

39. If one is inclined to assert that the Sabbath will be kept during the unending rest, then an equal emphasis must be assigned to the New Moon. Just how will the Sabbath be kept in heaven? Shall the elect of God worship Him only once a week and every twenty-nine or thirty days? Shall sin and trespass offerings be made in heaven, as Ezekiel prophesies in Chapter 46?

humanly contrived metaphors of spiritual concepts, but divinely intended metaphors from the beginning of creation. For example, the garden of Eden itself represented the sanctuary of God to be iterated in the ark, the tabernacle, the land of Canaan, and eventually the new Jerusalem. Man is of the ground (Gen 2:7), and depending on his soul-status, he may be a good tree (Ps 1:3) or a prickly brier (Ezek 28:24); good wheat or tares (Matt 13:24–30). Man's inner being is likened to soil, and harvesting to winning souls. Gleaning is not just about the Lord's care for the poor, but also suggests reserving a remnant for salvation.

> Now, some have thought that this gleaning left to the poor, in corners of the fields and scattered up and down, may refer figuratively to the remnant to be gathered, during this dispensation of the Christian Church, from Israel. I should rather apply it to both dispensations. During Israel's dispensation (barley-harvest), there were to be handfuls left to the stranger. This may be the Gentile remnant brought to know Jehovah in that age, samples of whom were Rahab . . . Then, during the Christian dispensation, there have been gleanings left for Israel, now a stranger, and poor and needy; as at this day we see in the converted Jews of our own land.[40]

Thus, the number, arrangement, tenor, and legal details of Israel's feasts were primarily spiritual in essence; and any tangible benefits derived from obedience to them are really secondary to the spiritual substratum of these ceremonial laws.

Leviticus 23 lists the seven annual feasts to be kept "in their seasons" and the Sabbath leads the list as the heart and focal point of them all. The Sabbath is classified as a feast, and without the Sabbath, the annual feasts lose something of their character. The Sabbath is central to the feasts of the Lord because, 1) it is used to determine the date of the Feast of Weeks (Lev 23:15); 2) it is used to determine the date of the wave offering for the Feast of the First Fruits (Lev 23:11); 3) it is used as a core for the observance of the Feast of Unleavened Bread (Lev 23:7–8), the Feast of Weeks (Lev 23:21), the Feast of Trumpets (Lev 23:24–25), the Day of Atonement (Lev 23:28, 32), and the Feast of Tabernacles (Lev 23:35–36); and 4) it is the most regularly recurring feast, cycling every seventh day, as opposed to the remaining feasts that occur annually. Kurtz asserts that even the three yearly feasts of the land—Passover, Weeks (Shavout), and Tabernacles—"though moving in a different sphere from the sabbatical feasts . . . were closely related to them both in form and substance."[41] Thus, the unifying strands of the Jewish national worship are the Sabbaths and the sacrifices; and in the larger context, the festival calendar and the priesthood.

The summary of ceremonies (Lev 23:37–38) is reiterated in Hebrews in a discussion of the divine services and priestly functions of the tabernacle (Heb 9:8–10). Focusing on the Day of Atonement when the high priest entered the holy of holies before the presence of God, the author of Hebrews notes that actual blood was necessary to gain intimate access to God, yet the repetition of those sacrifices declared the temporality of that divine service. He then proclaims that the death of Jesus alone

40. Bonar, *Leviticus*, 411.

41. Kurtz, *Offerings, Sacrifices and Worship*, 344.

satisfied the daily, weekly, monthly and yearly sacrificial requirements for blood to appease our God, and to eternally open the way to the true holy of holies in heaven. What ecstasy to hear that a permanently effective and gloriously perfect sacrifice had put an end to the daily, weekly, monthly and annual "gifts and sacrifices," the "foods and drinks, and various washings, and carnal ordinances" that comprised the Jewish religious system! The end of the Day of Atonement, the Levitical priesthood, all the particulars of temple administration, personal gifts and offerings, meant they had been fulfilled in Jesus Christ. Spurgeon envisions encompassing implications in the meaning of the temple veil tear.

> No mean miracle was wrought in the rending of so strong and thick a veil; but it was not intended merely as a display of power—many lessons were herein taught us. The old law of ordinances was put away, and like a worn-out vesture, rent and laid aside . . . The annual ceremony of atonement was thus abolished. The atoning blood which was once every year sprinkled with the veil, was now offered once for all by the great High Priest, and therefore the ace of the symbolical rite was broken up.[42]

That is, the tear of the veil alone, that was passed only once per calendar year, symbolized the abolishment of *all* the temple sacrifices, the *whole* priesthood, and the *complete* calendar of festivals. Christ's one sacrifice fulfilled not only the sacrifices on the Day of Atonement but all of the sacrifices demanded in the Law. Christ's priestly service fulfilled not only the functions of the high priest but all of the functions of the whole priesthood. Christ's rending of the veil fulfilled not only the Day of Atonement, "the ace of the symbolical rite," but fulfilled the remaining calendar ordinances of the old covenant as well. The Day of Atonement was a Sabbath in the fullest sense of its meaning (Lev 23:28–32). Christ's sacrifice ended the Sabbath, the New Moon, and the yearly feasts, as well as the Sabbatic Year and Jubilee.

Passover. The Passover solemnizes the final plague responsible for the deliverance of Israel from years of arduous bondage. A spotless firstborn male lamb was selected and slain, and its blood placed on the two door posts and on the lintel. The participants, while dressed in garb fit for a hasty departure, cooked the meat of the lamb over fire, and consumed the prepared meat in its entirety (excess meat was to be burned) in the evening with unleavened bread and bitter herbs. When the plague advanced by dark of night, the Lord passed over those houses on which the family faithfully and obediently applied the lamb's blood. Commanded to observe this ordinance forever (Exod 12:14, 24), the Jews were reminded of the sober cost of life—the firstborn of man and animal—necessary for their freedom; that three strokes of blood alone separated their firstborn from the angel of death.

Based on the fulfillment of the Passover by Christ's sacrifice on the cross, Paul infers the fulfillment of the Feast of Unleavened Bread by making a spiritual application for the saints of God within the context of church discipline.

42. Spurgeon, *Morning and Evening*, April 19, morning.

> Your glorying is not good. Do you not know that a little leaven leavens the whole lump?
>
> Therefore purge out the old leaven, that you may be a new lump, since you truly are unleavened. For indeed Christ, our Passover, was sacrificed for us.
>
> Therefore let us keep the feast, not with old leaven, nor with the leaven of malice and wickedness, but with the unleavened bread of sincerity and truth. (1 Cor 5:6–8)

Referring to the licentious person that this body of believers had tolerated in their fellowship, Paul illustrates that such toleration of sin will affect the whole congregation. Because believers are now in Christ, they are spiritually "unleavened," that is, purged of their sins, and must now live a life of sincerity and truth. Yet there was one obvious morsel of leaven in their midst that they failed to address righteously, namely a man of immoral license. Thus, Paul admonished them to spiritually "keep the feast," that is, to ensure that sincerity and truth characterize their church by excommunicating the unrepentant man. Paul's reference to the Passover draws upon the typological relationship between the sacrificial lamb and the sacrifice of Christ, and his reference to the Feast of Unleavened Bread finds a typological relationship between leaven in the home and tolerated sin in the house of God. "Keeping the feast," then, is a metaphor of the redeemed life, one that has been cleansed from former ungodly behavior. Clearly, the man who should have been excommunicated was "old leaven." Paul did not urge an annual application of this ceremonial law, but a daily preoccupation with removing the unsanctifying effects of sin from the fellowship of the church so that sincerity and truth may prevail.

Apostle Peter's first letter to the church had the Jewish Diaspora in mind, the people of his commission (Gal 2:9). Yet among his audience were Gentiles, also "elect according to the foreknowledge of God," who joined the spiritual journey of their Jewish predecessors as scattered sojourners throughout the earth. The allusion to Jewish displacement from the promised land would be a bitter reminder of God's judgment against the Jews unless what was originally promised by God was symbolic of greater realities. The prospect of Christ, "By faith he [Abraham] lived as a foreigner in the country that God had promised him" (Heb 11:9) is favored over the literalism of Moses, "all that land you promised would be their possession forever" (Exod 32:13). From the fulfillment of the promised land in Christ, Peter alludes to the fulfillment of the Passover and gives it new meaning for Jewish converts to Christ.

> Therefore gird up the loins of your mind, be sober, and rest your hope fully upon the grace that is to be brought to you at the revelation of Jesus Christ. (1 Pet 1:13)

Mindful that the Passover had been fulfilled by the death of God's firstborn Son and Christ's own allusion to the spiritual preparedness intended in the Passover (Luke 12:35), Peter adverts to the ceremony of girding one's loins (Exod 12:3–11); again, not as a yearly ritual, but as a daily endeavor to disengage the mind from possible obstacles, to make fit one's reason for anticipated engagements, and to fortify the senses in preparation for hardships. "Girding the loins" is an allusion of the faithful Jews in Egypt who waited in fear, as pilgrims in the land of death and darkness, for the salvation of the Lord. It is plain that Peter understands the Passover meal at home to be about living life "ready to go" and "awaiting salvation," rather than worship and communion. Likewise, the outward rituals of Sabbath-keeping are not about physical rest and recuperation, but about a spiritual rest that prepares believers to set their hope fully on the grace of God that will be brought to them at the revelation of Jesus Christ.

These NT references to the Passover and Feast of Unleavened Bread probably do not fully exhaust the intended symbolism contained in them, yet the apostles made a spiritual application to the church based on the analogy of symbols and types. Though the apostles participated in the Passover after the resurrection (Acts 18:21), their *personal* desire to participate in Jewish festivals was not construed as a general duty for other saints. Neither does it appear that the apostles attempted to correlate or fuse the yearly Passover with the weekly Lord's Supper. While it is commonly asserted that the Passover was "replaced" by the Lord's Supper—that the Lord's Supper is the "Christian Passover"—Paul's discussion of the communion of the saints finds parallel in the privilege of Levite priests to partake of the residue of sacrifices and gifts (Lev 8:31; 24:9), and not the Passover.

> The cup of blessing which we bless, is it not the communion of the blood of Christ? The bread which we break, is it not the communion of the body of Christ?
>
> For we, though many, are one bread and one body; for we all partake of that one bread.
>
> Observe Israel after the flesh: Are not those who eat of the sacrifices partakers of the altar? (1 Cor 10:16–18)

His mention of the altar of Israel and its sacrifices is not intended to promote the countenance of these ceremonies, for that is "Israel after the flesh," but to teach that the laws regarding the altar and sacrifices translate to ecclesiastic laws of spiritual association and profession. Thus, our participation in the church's "meal" demonstrates our allegiance to, and communion with, the parties of that meal. Christians take communion to demonstrate their personal and corporate allegiance to and fellowship with God through Jesus Christ (Heb 9:26–28). Therefore, Paul urged the Corinthians to avoid participating in outwardly pagan rituals because that contradicted their Christian profession. The corollary is that if a professing Christian chooses not to regularly share the new covenant meal (communion) he is denying his very profession of Christ. Furthermore, a church that infrequently observes the Lord's Supper removes a preeminent opportunity for Christians to fellowship with God, to proclaim allegiance to Christ with other saints, and to renew their personal profession of faith. Finally, Paul associates the Lord's Table with the sacrificial altar (1 Cor 11:21)—not the Passover meal in the home.

> Paul's reference . . . suggests that the celebration of Christ's sacrifice now serves as the centerpiece for Christian worship as did the altar—the Lord's table in the

> OT—where the people of Israel went to worship by bringing their sacrifices to the Lord.[43]

When Jesus lifted the wine as symbolic of the "blood of the covenant" he related His Supper to the sealing of the old covenant atop Mount Sinai (Exod 24:8).[44] This meeting of Moses, Aaron, Nadab, and Abihu, along with seventy elders, to eat and drink before the Lord seems to restrict the inaugural covenant meal to notable and privileged leaders in a representative manner. This finds fulfillment in the participation of the Twelve at the institution of the Lord's Supper. However, Christ's command to "Do this in remembrance of Me," was understood to be a new ceremony for Christ's disciples, reminding them, through the symbolism of the bread and wine, of Christ's death for them (1 Cor 11:23–26). As such, the apostles, in Christ's stead, ensured the continuance of this ceremony through the leadership of the local church and emphasized the serious spiritual essence of this observance to the congregation. Christ desired to complete the Passover in anticipation of His forthcoming suffering and to formally inaugurate the new covenant for its incorporating effect on believers.[45] When Paul addressed the Corinthians about the importance of the Lord's Supper in terms of their association with the world, he established a connection between the Lord's Supper and the priestly meal laws, not the Passover.

> There is no single Old Testament precedent for the sacrament of the Lord's Supper, not even the Feast of the Passover, which might superficially appear to be the most obvious candidate for this status.[46]

Therefore, the idea that the Passover itself requires ceremonial replacement is too comprehensive and specific with regards to its supposed analogue in the Lord's Supper. At best, the similarities between the Passover and Lord's Supper are superficial and few, as summarized in Appendix 4.

Those who maintain a direct analogy between the Passover and Lord's Supper (replacement) eventually struggle with the question of "admission requirements" to the Lord's Supper. Calvin accepted a substitutive correspondence between the Lord's Supper and Passover, inclining him to at least allow children, who were unlikely to be able to make a credible profession of faith, to partake of the Supper.

> Circumcision, which, as is well known, corresponds to our baptism, was intended for infants, but the Passover, for which the Supper is substituted, did not admit all kinds of guests promiscuously, but was duly eaten only by those who were of an age sufficient to ask the meaning of it (Exod. 12:26). Had these men

43. Ciampa and Rosner, "1 Corinthians," 729.

44. Letham, *Lord's Supper*, 53–54.

45. Based on the differences between the Synoptics and John 18:28 and 19:14, as well as earlier variants in the Greek text, Meier proposed that the Lord's Supper was not at all associated with the Passover meal. Finegan, *Biblical Chronology*, 357–58.

46. Venema, "Evidence Regarding the Participation of Children," 23.

> the least particle of soundness in their brain, would they be thus blind as to a matter so very clear and obvious?[47]

However, even with this text (Exod 12:26), the duty to instruct the young inquirers is not so clear and obvious that it can be construed as the definitive "admission ticket" to the Passover, as there was simply no need for Moses to describe how four-year-olds were to be fed at the Passover. The Jewish understanding though was to include children of all ages in the Passover meal.

> The Rabbis taught: Everyone is obligated to drink the four cups of wine—men, women, and children . . . It is a man's duty to make his children and his household happy on the Festival, for it was said: *(Deuteronomy 16:14) And thou shalt rejoice in thy feast, thou and thy son, and thy daughter, and thy manservant, and thy maidservant, and the Levite, the stranger, the fatherless, and the widow that are within thy gates.* With what does he make them happy? With wine.[48]

The example of the Corinthian church allowing their observance to degenerate into a common meal would have been more likely if whole families were allowed to participate in the Lord's Supper. But their practice (agape feast) does not confirm that the Passover was the basis for their family communion or that the Lord even desired children to partake of the emblems. The problem at the Corinthian church was that they treated the Lord's Supper as a common meal instead of a sober ritual, symbolic of the union of believers in Christ. Paul's warning to adult believers at the Lord's Supper (1 Cor 11:27–34) echoes the warnings made to functioning priests of the temple (Lev 24:1–16) that they approach their communal privileges with reverence. Leithart wisely distinguishes between the warning made to priests and the privilege of family members to partake of sacrificial meals.

> Exhortations concerning right use do not in themselves establish any criteria concerning *who* may use it. Right use and authorized use are two different questions.[49]

While this distinction is valid, it does not follow, as Liethart concludes, that the admission requirements to the Lord's Supper are identical to the admission requirements of the Passover. Given the minor correspondence between the Lord's Supper and 1) the Passover, 2) the priestly meals laws, 3) the instauration meal of the Mosaic covenant, and 4) the consumption of the showbread, the church is hard pressed to be dogmatic about directly applying particular OT laws or popular traditions to the Lord's Supper.[50] NT references to the Passover give no reason to consider it as a predecessor of the Lord's Supper. As Edersheim summarized, "The Institution of the Lord's Supper is recorded by the Synoptists, although without reference to those parts of the Paschal

47. Calvin, *Institutes*, 550 (4.16.30).

48. Auerbach, *Babylonian Talmud*, 100–101. See also, Edersheim, *Life and Times*, 826. Wine was usually watered down for children.

49. Leithart, "A Response," 301.

50. Venema, "Evidence Regarding the Participation of Children," 22–27.

Supper and its Services with which one or another of its acts must be connected."[51] The NT treatment of the Lord's Supper gives no reason to look for antecedents in OT law; it is a new ritual for members of the new covenant.

The historic position of Reformed churches is to admit to the Lord's Supper only those who have made a public profession of faith.[52] Interestingly, this position avoids altogether the question of whether to draw an analogy between the Lord's Supper and the Passover. Instead, it relies on the teaching of the new covenant alone, as it should. O. Palmer Robertson concluded, "The entire manner of worship must be changed when the priestly order changes."[53] If the Supper portrays the unity of Christ's body through the participation of those professing to be redeemed and walking in godliness, then a public profession of Christ appears to be a rational requirement for participation. This sacrament is not a common meal but a corporate spiritual meal to be taken in faith. It was not instituted to provide physical sustenance for the believer and his children, for as Paul said, "What! Do you not have houses to eat and drink in?" (1 Cor 11:22). The OT meal laws were secondarily designed to provide for the daily nourishment of the priesthood and their families, and as such, they are irrelevant to the question concerning participation in the Lord's Supper by those too young to make a credible profession of faith. The symbolism of the Lord's Supper has to do with the unity of those whose faith has made them partakers of Christ's resurrected life. It is not a meal for children. As long as the Lord's Supper is called the "Christian Passover," church members will be compelled to consider the admission of children based on a direct analogy to the Jewish ritual.

Firstborn Laws. In the darkest hour of the night, the Angel of Death sought out the firstborn in judgment, both man and beast; of man, whether they were old or young, of noble or common birth; and of animals, whether clean or unclean. None escaped death save those concealed behind the blood-covered doors of their homes. By all rights, every firstborn son should have tasted death, but by God's grace many were spared of that judgment. As a result of the judgments against Egypt, the Lord instituted the law of the firstborn (Exod 12–13): a law that was not tied to the calendar, as was the Passover, but commemorated redemption and forecasted Christ nevertheless. The Lord commanded that all firstborn were to be consecrated to the Lord, signifying, by the representative birth, that all Israel was required to attend to the Lord in priestly service (Num 8:15–18). Therefore, the parents were required to redeem, or buy back from the Lord, every firstborn male for five shekels of silver (Num 3:47). As if this symbolism were not enough, the Lord added sabbatic symbolism to the law of the firstborn; first, in a work prohibition for animals and secondly, by incorporating eighth-day laws.

51. Edersheim, *Life and Times*, 826.

52. Hyde, "Table Manners," 141–42; Knight, "The Lord's Supper," 282–96; Letham, *The Lord's Supper*, 56; Keddie, *The Lord's Supper is a Celebration of Grace*, 11–12.

53. Robertson, *Israel of God*, 68.

> The firstborn of your sons you shall give to Me. Likewise you shall do with your oxen and your sheep. It shall be with its mother seven days; on the eighth day you shall give it to Me. (Exod 22:29–30)

Like all Hebrew males awaiting circumcision, the firstborn of all clean animals were to be presented to the priests for their support and sacrificial use on the eighth day (Exod 22:29) or thereafter (Lev 22:27). The root word of "eight" is *shamen*, meaning "fat" or "superabundance," which aptly describes the plenteous stores set apart for the priestly clan. The significance of eighth-day laws is that they portray a recurring theme in Scripture of histories coming to a point of completion and yet beginning again in unquantifiable abundance and seamless eternity.

> So that as a numeral [the number eight] it is the super-abundant number. As *seven* was so called because the seventh day was the day of completion and rest, so *eight*, as the eighth day, was over and above this perfect completion, and was indeed the *first* of a new series, as well as being the *eighth*. Thus it already represents two numbers in one, the *first* and *eighth*.[54]

The sabbatic link with firstborn laws is the prohibition of labor for those firstborn animals, as if labor makes the animal unfit to be sanctified to the Lord (Deut 15:19). This preferential treatment of retained firstborn animals speaks of the divine favor of God on those who are His firstborn, declared "clean" by His chosenness (Exod 4:21–23; Num 3:11–13; Heb 1:6), and, of course, to Christ, His only begotten Son. As the Lord was resurrected on the eighth day, the shadows of eighth day laws and historical types are more fully understood (discussed in greater detail in chapter 12). The eighth-day laws supersede the perfection of seventh-day Sabbath laws, so both the Sabbath and eighth-day ceremonies shadowed forth the ministerial work, rest of death, and resurrection of Christ to a new and everlasting life. As such, Christian worship on the first day of the week is more thoughtfully attributed to the typology of eighth-day ceremonies.

First Fruits. When Israel first entered the land of Canaan, it was the first time that the First Fruits offering could be presented to the Lord. They observed the Passover and enjoyed the first fruits of Canaan, then the manna ceased (Josh 5:10–12). Thereby, Israel rehearsed the death, burial, and resurrection of Jesus Christ. The initializing feasts in the land of rest were eight days long and they anticipated the completion of redemption and the resurrection beyond a sabbatic rest. Just as the firstborn held a preeminent place in the Lord's economy of Israel, so did the first fruits of crops, baked goods, oil, and wine. And as would be expected, there is eighth-day symbolism with this third festival of Israel.

> And on the fifteenth day of the same month is the Feast of Unleavened Bread to the *Lord*; seven days you must eat unleavened bread.
>
> On the first day you shall have a holy convocation [Nisan 15]; you shall do no customary work on it.

54. Bullinger, *Number in Scripture*, 196 (emphasis in the original).

> But you shall offer an offering made by fire to the *Lord* for seven days. The seventh day shall be a holy convocation [Nisan 21]; you shall do no customary work on it.'"
>
> And the *Lord* spoke to Moses, saying,
>
> Speak to the children of Israel, and say to them: When you come into the land which I give to you, and reap its harvest, then you shall bring a sheaf of the first fruits of your harvest to the priest.
>
> He shall wave the sheaf before the *Lord*, to be accepted on your behalf; on the day after the Sabbath [Nisan 16? 22? other?] the priest shall wave it. (Lev 23:6–11)

The Feast of First Fruits was primarily an offering of the first sheaf of barley harvested in the spring shortly after the Passover, "the day after the Sabbath" (Lev 23:11), implying the eighth day. Because the text is not explicit, and because a feast day convocation may be called a Sabbath (Lev 23:24–25, 28, 32, 36, 39), and feast day Sabbaths could occur on any day of the week, several schools of interpretation developed about this verse.

Syntactically, the phrase "on the day after the Sabbath" would seem to refer to the nearest contextual Sabbath, which is the second holy convocation of the Feast of Unleavened Bread (Nisan 22). Yet, it could also refer to the unnamed weekly Sabbath or the first convocation Sabbath (Nisan 16). Howard and Edersheim explain that the traditional understanding, as documented by Josephus, was that the Sabbath in question was the *first* day of the Feast of Unleavened Bread;[55] while the Sadducees and Samaritans understood this to be the first weekly Sabbath of the Passover season.[56] Both schools understood that the reaping required for the First Fruits could not occur on a Sabbath and that the actual date was of some importance because the Feast of Weeks expressly occurs fifty days after this Sabbath. The traditional view seems to be favored on the practical ground that reaping the first field of grain after a long winter should begin as soon as allowed by law: the day after the first sabbatic holy convocation. If they waited until after the nearest weekly Sabbath, the harvest could be delayed as many as six days later.

However, there is good reason to consider that the traditional practice was in error based on the eighth-day symbolism of firsts (firstborn, first sons, first fruits)—the *eighth* day being the *first* day of a new week. This means that the Sabbath in question was either the nearest weekly Sabbath of the Passover season (as the Sadducees conjectured) or the *second* convocation of the Feast of Unleavened Bread. In either case, this would allow a "week" to go to completion and "on the day after the Sabbath" (the eighth day) they could celebrate the Feast of First Fruits. Since the Feast of Weeks is an eighth-day ceremony [(7x7 Sabbaths)+1] and the Jubilee [(7x7 Sabbatic Years)+1], the initializing Feast of First Fruits should incorporate eighth-day symbolism (and indeed it does), so that a "week" comes to completion first [7 days+1]. The eighth-day symbolism is lost in the traditional view that the Sabbath in question is the first

55. Howard and Rosenthal, *Feasts*, 76; Edersheim, *Temple*, 170; Raphael, *Festivals*, 69.

56. Rordorf, *Sunday*, 187; Doig, *New Testament Chronology*, 274–75.

day of the Feast of Unleavened Bread. However, the question is moot since the Lord sent His Holy Spirit on a Pentecost that satisfied both the traditional practice and the alternative view, since the weekly Sabbath coincided with the first day of the Feast of Unleavened Bread (John 19:31). The Lord decreed that the resurrection should occur on a first-day Feast of First Fruits, for the sheaf that was lifted up and accepted before the Lord on our behalf was Christ (Lev 23:11; John 12:24).

Sun/1st day	Mon	Tue	Wed	Thu	Fri	Sat/Sabbat
				13 14	14 15	15 16
				Preparation for Passover Lord's Supper	Prosabbatom Passover Crucified and buried	Sabbath 1st Conv. of Unleavened Bread
16 17	17 18	18 19	19 20	20 21	21 22	22 23
First Fruits Resurrection					2nd Convocation	

From the NT perspective, the Feast of First Fruits was a shadow law from which a variety of applications were derived. First of all, Christ is called the first fruits of the resurrection (1 Cor 15:20) intimating that the resurrection of the bodies of the faithful would come in successive stages of God's harvesting plan of redemption; and that resurrection immediately follows the completion (symbolized in the number seven) of these successive stages. With the knowledge of the "first" comes an expectation of a "second." Secondly, the Holy Spirit being given to the saints of the new covenant is a sort of first fruits that evokes anticipation of a greater measure of the Holy Spirit required to completely redeem our bodies in the resurrection (Rom 8:23). James, the Apostle, refers to believers as the "first fruits of his creatures," making the redemption of man the prelude to the redemption of all created things (Jas 1:18). John, the Revelator, notes the consecration and favor of the first fruits as applicable to the 144,000 souls redeemed from among men (Rev 14:4). These references underscore the fulfilled status of first fruit shadow laws and the realized spiritual application of redemption and resurrection within a structure of time.

Like other first fruit offerings that represented the whole of a crop, a select portion of dough was offered to God as a "heave offering" in thankfulness for the whole. Paul's allusion to this type of first fruit offering (Num 15:20) draws upon the principle that God has indeed separated to Himself those who will be joined together as a whole "lump" of redeemed people, both Jew and Gentile (Rom 11:16). The fulfillment of firsts is the fulfillment of eighths, which in turn means the precursory fulfillment of sevenths. While we may anticipate the ongoing structuring of time as the Lord works out the redemption of all things (Rom 8:18–25), the Christian church is under no obligation to observe any of the calendar feasts of Israel, the Sabbath included.

Feast of Trumpets. As with every seventh day and every seventh year, so the Feast of Trumpets shares in the septimal division of time on the seventh month of the year and additionally displays its sabbatic character with a concurrent Sabbath observance (Lev 23:24). Yet it was not merely another New Moon celebration, but an annual feast, and was thereby distinguished by the set of ten sacrifices made that day: seven lambs, one young bull, one ram, and a sin offering of a kid goat (Num 29:1–6). Compared to the usual New Moon celebrations, the Jews further distinguished the Feast of Trumpets by blowing longer blasts of the shofar. This feast is the foremost of the New Moon celebrations because it also heralds the beginning of a new civil year and carries with it eschatological hopes. Jewish tradition also holds that the seventh month is the time period of the creation and probably marks the day of man's creation. Tishri also is the month that calls the Jews to begin anew, "starting a new year by acknowledging God as King, Judge, and Redeemer."[57]

As noted before, this is the only annual feast that occurs when the night is dark,[58] indicating that the coming of the glory of the Lord does, and will, occur when the expression of the fall of man is at its nadir, i.e., the brutal murder of her young (Exod 1:13–16; Matt 2:16). It initiates the remaining three feasts in the seventh month of the calendar. The next feast, the Day of Atonement, occurs ten days later. Scripture does not explicitly link the Feast of Trumpets to any particular event related to their deliverance from Egypt; however, the blowing of shofars provides a link with two passages that record the blowing of a shofar by the Lord God Himself. The first occurrence is when the Israelites were assembled at Mount Sinai to witness the descent of the glory of God in fire and smoke, announced by long, hard blasts of the shofar (Exod 19:18–20). The second occurrence is a prophetic passage describing a second revelation of the glory of God from above, at the end of time (Zech 9:14). Howard notes that "the ancient rabbis repeatedly quoted this verse in connection with the coming of the Messiah."[59] The New Moon celebrations are minor in comparison with the grandeur of the annual Feast of Trumpets, indicating a significant escalation in the display of glory (2 Cor 3:7–11) and a dramatic increase in the future revelation of God's glory and majesty, when there is "no need of the sun or of the moon" (Rev 21:23).

There are sufficient overtones to link the Feast of Trumpets with the exodus and there are also eschatological intimations of the future age. In the latter case, the timing of the feasts suggests a two-stage fulfillment of Scripture as a former-latter expression. The first set of annual feasts (four) occurred in the spring and the last set of feasts (three) occurred in the fall. The association with harvests and the closing of times intimates two stages of the call of redemption: 1) of Israel and the revelation of His glory at Mount Sinai and the tabernacle, and 2) the expansion of the gospel to the Gentiles accompanied by the revelation of His glory through the incarnate Son (John 1:14: 6:38, Luke 2:9, 2 Pet 1:17). The fulfillment of the Feast of Trumpets also comes in

57. Trepp, *Book of Jewish Observance*, 87.

58. Howard and Rosenthal, *Feasts*, 105.

59. Ibid., 114.

two stages: 1) Christ's initial trumpet call to the Jews and Gentiles and 2) His remaining trumpet call to the world to gather the elect (Matt 24:31; 1 Cor 15:52). Though the Feast of Trumpets remains as a metaphor for the Lord's evangelistic call to the lost, the Christian church is under no obligation to observe the externalities of that feast. Likewise, though a "rest" remains, in no way are the present saints of God pledged to observe a Sabbath.

Day of Atonement. Though no reason is given for the celebration of the Day of Atonement (Exod 30:10; Lev 23:26–32), it probably refers back to the days of Israel's affliction under Egypt, however now, they must afflict their own souls (Lev 16:29) and yearn for personal salvation as opposed to the mere termination of the hardship of slavery. Another contributing theme could be the first altar built by Moses at the foot of Mount Sinai to establish the covenant between God and Israel (Exod 24:1–8). The yearly consecration of the national altar refreshed them about the absolute holiness of God, their corporate sinfulness, their need for an intermediary, and of their vows to live in obedience to Him. As the place where the Lord meets with Israel and the four corners of the altar are anointed with blood, the Day of Atonement finds its archetypes in the presence of God in the garden of Eden with its four rivers emanating from its fertile land. It is the most solemn of all Israel's feasts because only on this day of the year, the high priest alone would enter once into the holy of holies to make atonement for repentant Israel. It is a calendar fast, a calendar Sabbath, and a calendar sacrifice, for a calendar-year of sin that contaminated the priesthood, the people, and the temple—all of which needed to be expiated by blood. Kurtz points out the sabbatic character of the Day of Atonement.

> But for all that, just because expiation was the basis of all worship, the fundamental condition of all fellowship with God, it also required a distinct, culminating manifestation, or a festal day set apart exclusively for that purpose; and this was precisely the object and meaning of the yearly day of atonement, which had also a sabbatical character on account of this its great importance.[60]

Fixed on the tenth day, it was imbued with the sabbatic character of the seventh month. The Sabbath of the Day of Atonement described in Leviticus 16:31 is a "Sabbath of rest," which literally means a "Sabbath of Sabbaths." It is *the* Sabbath of the year, the most holy day of the year (Exod 30:10). This surpassing quality of holiness is attributed to many tangible ceremonies and artifacts of the temple and priesthood, as well as here, a ceremonial day of the year. The altar was most holy (Exod 29:37), as were the table, lampstand, utensils (Exod 30:26–29), and incense (Exod 30:36). Of the sacrifices, the burnt offering is the most holy of all sacrifices made by fire (Lev 2:3). Most holy are the sin offering (Lev 6:25), the trespass offering (Lev 7:1), the grain offering (Lev 10:12), the showbread (Lev 21:22; 24:9), and devoted things (Lev 27:28–29).

The declaration of the utmost holiness of those ceremonies and circumstances was meant to symbolically declare the exceeding measure and transcendent quality of the holiness of the triune God. Though the character of holiness has been removed

60. Kurtz, *Offerings, Sacrifices and Worship*, 346.

from such earthly and carnal things, God has in no way fluctuated (Jas 1:10) in His severe holiness. Hebrews 9 lists thirty or so holy things that have been fulfilled in Christ. They are described in terms of their 1) *meaning* ["signification" (v. 8), "figure" (v. 9, 23, 24) and "things to come" (v. 11)], 2) *effect* ["cannot make him . . . perfect" (v. 9)], and 3) *duration* ["until the time"(v. 10)], as opposed to having an essential attribute of holiness. Which of these is not abrogated with the daybreak of the new covenant? Which of these did not lose the quality of holiness? The author of Hebrews, contemplating the Day of Atonement (Heb 9), realized that the perfection symbolized in its seventh-day attributes (Sabbath of Sabbaths, seventh month) was merely shadowed in these sacrificial laws, and therefore, could *never* really be the means to *complete* sanctification: "the law . . . can never with these same sacrifices . . . make those who approach *perfect*" (Heb 10:1). The yearly requirement for this most holy day, "a statute forever" (Lev 16:29), implied the continual need to provide a covering of blood for individual and collective, and confessed and unconfessed sin. Hebrews mentions many things that symbolized and foreshadowed the new covenant; so many that the author was unable to elaborate the full details of their fulfillment (Heb 9:5). The author of Hebrews does not specifically mention any calendar impositions; however, his description of the one day of the year when the high priest entered the holiest of all can only be understood as the Day of Atonement. By extrapolation, the other feast days and seasons are to be understood as symbolic of new covenant realities, just as the one goat and one bull sacrificed on the Day Atonement encompassed all the bloody sacrifices of Israel's divine service. In contrast to the repetition of a calendar event, the author of Hebrews includes two single historical events: 1) the inauguration of the first covenant by Moses with the sprinkling of blood upon the people and the "book" (cp. Exod 24:1–8), signifying that without the blood of Christ, neither can sin be purged from our being nor can the law be utterly fulfilled through our obedience, and 2) the consecration of the tabernacle with blood (cp. Exod 30:25–30; 40:9–10; Lev 8:10, 15), signifying that true worship is ultimately acceptable only through the blood of Jesus Christ. As expected, both history and calendar ceremonies were allies in forecasting the coming realities of the redemption of the Jesus Christ.

We must not underestimate the significance of the command to "afflict your souls" as an integral part of the ceremonial law on the Day of Atonement. The Jews understood this to mean fasting and prayer, because the sins of that year were under review by the Lord, so confession, repentance, and redress (if anything was owed) preoccupied one's mind for the day.

> To take these steps within the setting of an immensely long fast celebrated publicly in common with fellow Jews promotes the corrective action called for with a force that is never likely to be reached in short episodes of private contemplation. The mystique of *Kippur*, with a variety of ceremonies that have been generated over the centuries, offers a theatre of collective emotion that has no parallel.[61]

61. Raphael, *Festivals*, 81.

Whatever practical benefits a fast may hold for Christians today, it may not supplant the spiritual meaning of it in terms of its fulfillment in Christ. There is no yearly covering for sins, therefore, no need to engage in a calendar ritual of fasting and prayer for sins that have already been thoroughly cleansed from our souls. For a brief period and for a specific people, the Day of Atonement was the holiest day of the year, but with the coming of Christ it has been *promoted* to an ordinary day; stripped of its holy sacrifices, the holy Sabbath, the holy convocation, and its fast. It is a better day without these shadows of the past. As an ordinary day it is now showered with glory in greater measure than ever it was as the Day of Atonement! The implication of a fulfilled Day of Atonement, itself a "Sabbath of Sabbaths," is that the holiest of all calendar days is emptied of that title, for the day of Christ's death and resurrection is of infinitely greater significance.

Feast of Tabernacles. We come to the seventh annual feast, the most joyous one of the year, which spans a period of seven-eight days. Seven, eight. Unlike the seven-day Feast of Unleavened Bread, this feast calls for a Sabbath on the first and *eighth* day.

> Speak to the children of Israel, saying: 'The fifteenth day of this seventh month shall be the Feast of Tabernacles for seven days to the *Lord.*
>
> On the first day there shall be a holy convocation. You shall do no customary work on it.
>
> For seven days you shall offer an offering made by fire to the *Lord.* On the eighth day you shall have a holy convocation, and you shall offer an offering made by fire to the *Lord.* It is a sacred assembly, and you shall do no customary work on it.' (Lev 23:34–36)

This autumn feast commemorated the pastoral care of the Lord during the forty years of wilderness journeying as well as an annual acknowledgment of the gracious blessings and provisions of the Lord during the year. The Lord's provision for the past year is matched by an equally impressive number of sacrifices, along with their meal and drink offerings (Num 29:12–38), that required all twenty-four divisions of the priesthood to administer![62]

Sacrificial Requirements of the Feast of Tabernacles									
Day	15	16	17	18	19	20	21	Total	22
Bull	13	12	11	10	9	8	7	70	1
Ram	2	2	2	2	2	2	2	14	1
Lamb	14	14	14	14	14	14	14	98	7
Goat	1	1	1	1	1	1	1	7	1

The septenary and sabbatic symbolism is overwhelming, but is certainly not limited to the frequency of the number seven as a symbol of completeness and perfection. One lamb alone speaks of the blood of Jesus Christ, but we have in this feast a myriad of animals slaughtered, indicating not only the severe need of propitiation but the extreme

62. Howard and Rosenthal, *Feasts*, 136.

cost of sacrifice to God. Whatever future these sacrifices foretold, the faithful Israelite could expect that it would be a work of God of inestimable worth and perfection.

The design of this feast holds more meaning. This is repeatedly identified as a seven-day feast since the Israelites were to dwell in booths for seven days, but the "marching orders" include sacrifices and a Sabbath on the eighth day (Tishri 22). Since the eighth-day sacrifices are different than the preceding seven days, and by calling the feast a seven-day feast, it draws attention to the sacrifices of days one through seven. The descending number of bulls sacrificed ends with the number seven, rather than with the number one. Any sequence such as this will automatically be divisible by seven, but the Lord selected a sequence that ended on seven and totaled seventy. This speaks of the Lord's work of redemption over a period of time that will culminate in a specific work of distinction and excellence (7), and it represents a culminating disposition of the world of "Egypt," the old covenant's symbol of Satan's kingdom (10x7).[63] The final Sabbath of the year, the eighth-day Sabbath, was contrasted with the previous seven days of rejoicing as a "solemn assembly" (Lev 23:36; Num 29:35; Neh 8:18), from a peculiar word (*atsarah*) denoting "restraint" and "closing up." The sacrifices made on that day did not connect numerically to the preceding sacrifices, so this final Sabbath was an appendix to the cycle of feasts each year. Likely causing Israelites to look ahead to the next year with expectation, this symbolically represents the closing up of all time as the Lord opens up an eternity to be shared with His beloved in Christ. As Bonar states,

> And some suppose the final state, after the days of Christ's kingdom, may be hinted at here—"the ages to come"—the undescribed, unknown, but unutterably blessed eternity after the Thousand Years.[64]

As the festival system is reviewed in Leviticus 23, the Sabbath begins and ends the ceremonial cycle of time. This represents the rest of God at the beginning of creation and the final state of rest for God's people, but it also signifies the overarching presence and activity of the Lord of the Sabbath who will guarantee that redemptive rest to those who trust Him. With the recollection of God's enduring care solidly on the nation's mind, and the hopes of similar blessings for the upcoming year, this season of joy brought the expectation of the life-giving rainy season, from September to March and the satisfaction that the cycle of life would continue under the Lord's sovereign care.

> Because the Feast of Tabernacles is observed at this important juncture when the anticipation of rain is at its highest, the two have become inseparably connected. Even today, the prayers for rain remain an important part of Tabernacles' observance.[65]

63. Edersheim, *Life and Times*, 577. Also part of the Feast of Tabernacles was a ceremony of Illumination. It was after this, that another ceremony took place, a "solemn testimony made before Jehovah against heathenism."

64. Bonar, *Leviticus*, 425.

65. Howard and Rosenthal, *Feasts*, 137.

Though not called for in Scripture, a distinct ceremony involving water arose about a hundred years before Christ in conjunction with the sacrifices of the week, which symbolized the season of rain. Each morning, while the sacrifices were being prepared, the high priest, accompanied by a procession of musicians and worshippers, went to the Pool of Siloam to fetch a "quart" of water. The high priest returned to the temple area through the Water Gate, so named for this ceremony, while the people shouted, "Therefore with joy you will draw water from the wells of salvation" (Isa 12:3). As the water was poured upon the holy altar, the Levite choir sang from the Messianic psalms (113–18), and the people waved their palm branches, shouting "Hosanna," which means "Save now!" So, during the Feast of Tabernacles, the anticipation of rain gave way to the expectation of the Messiah who would save Israel from their oppressors. As the number of bull sacrifices decreased over seven days, the excitement about Messiah increased, such that on the seventh day of the feast, the high priest marched around the altar seven times instead of once, and the trumpeters sounded off three sets of seven blasts instead of the usual three. This seventh day was called the "Great Hosanna," and beside the anticipation of rain, the ceremony enlivened the hope that God would pour out His Holy Spirit upon Israel. It is probably on this day that John records the following teaching of Jesus.[66]

> On the last day, that great day of the feast, Jesus stood and cried out, saying, "If anyone thirsts, let him come to Me and drink.
>
> He who believes in Me, as the Scripture has said, out of his heart will flow rivers of living water."
>
> But this He spoke concerning the Spirit, whom those believing in Him would receive; for the Holy Spirit was not yet given, because Jesus was not yet glorified. (John 7:37–39)

Regardless of the actual day, Christ's assuring words are taken as a fulfillment of the Feast of Tabernacles. The worshippers anticipated the Messiah and the pouring out of the Holy Spirit, and Jesus claimed to be the personal expectation of these promises. "Come to me" is His gentle command to those aware of their spiritual thirst. The Feast of Tabernacles is fulfilled as dry souls turn to Christ for rivers of living water. And "Come to me" is His gentle command to those aware of their spiritual weariness. The Sabbath is fulfilled as burdened souls turn to Christ for comforting rest. In these words, "Come to me," there is no less obvious a fulfillment of the Sabbath than of the Feast of Tabernacles.

So, at the close of Israel's annual calendar—a ceremonial timetable of the Lord's work of redemption—is an eighth-day Sabbath. This indicated and foreshadowed first-day significance when Israel's calendar would have completely served its purpose in forecasting the advent of Jesus Christ. The Sabbath is not held over into the new covenant because it defined the beginning and the end of the ceremonial calendar. However, the weekly importance of the Sabbath was re-visioned in the weekly importance of the first-day worship of the new covenant. Thus, first-day worship

66. Matthew Henry, Jamieson, Faucet and Brown, and Adam Clark suppose this took place on the eighth day, while Kevin Howard suggests the seventh day.

acknowledges the fulfillment of the Sabbath, yet gives tribute to the central place of the Sabbath in Israel's history by repeating on a weekly basis.

Periodically

Besides sharing redemptive features with the New Moon and annual feasts, the Sabbath has two other long-range ceremonial relatives: the Sabbatic Year and the Jubilee. The Sabbatic Year occurred every seven years and the Jubilee occurred every fiftieth year (the year following seven Sabbatic Years), and like the Sabbath, both commemorated the exodus from Egypt (Lev 25:1–2; 38, 42), specifically the cessation of slavery, the liberation from the past, and the prospects of a new beginning. Because these two holy times require a rest for the land, they are unmistakably logarithmic enlargements of the sabbatic theme. Just as seven Sabbaths plus one day ([7*7]+1=50 days) was a measuring rod to determine the Feast of Weeks, seven Sabbatic Years plus one year ([7*7]+1=50 years) measured to the Jubilee, so both are eighth-day ceremonies. There are records of rabbinic discussions whether the Jubilee was concurrent with the seventh Sabbatic Year, but the general consensus, as well as the plain sense of Pentateuchal law, confirms that the Jubilee occurred the year following the forty-ninth Sabbatic year, so that the land lay fallow two successive years. Still disputed though, is whether the Jubilee was the first year of a new cycle of Sabbatic Years (so that forty-eight years followed each Jubilee) or the year preceding a new cycle of forty-nine Sabbatic years (so that forty-nine years followed each Jubilee). Howard and Rosenthal choose the latter,[67] but this causes the Sabbatic Year to shift forward in the "week" of years. Like the shifting Sabbath proposed by Ewing, this creates problems with time accounting, particularly the Lord's reckoning of how many Sabbath Years were neglected during a 490 year period of Israel's history. That is, if the Land Sabbath shifted forward every fifty years, during any 490 year period only sixty-eight Sabbatic Years and nine Jubilees

Jubilee as Preceding a New Cycle of Sabbatic Years						
1	2	3	4	5	6	7
						Sabbatic
						Sabbatic
						Sabbatic
						Sabbatic
						Sabbatic
						Sabbatic
						Sabbatic
Jubilee	1	2	3	4	5	6
Sabbatic						
Sabbatic						

67. Howard and Rosenthal, *Feasts*, 196.

would occur. This would make the Lord's judgment of seventy years captivity at least suspect if not a trifle spiteful.

In spite of the spiritual benefits and redemptive overtones, the Jews failed to keep the Sabbath of the Land for 490 consecutive years, and suffered the judgment of deportation for a "pay-back" of seventy years, "until the land had enjoyed her Sabbaths" (2 Chr 36:21). This judgment makes sense only if the Sabbatic Year occurred every seventh year without shifting. Failure to keep the Sabbath of the Land was an implicit rejection of the truth that they were "gifted" the land from the Lord; therefore, the Lord made them captives again in a foreign land. The Lord specifically intercepted their folly at 490 (10x7x7) years because of the symbolic meaning of His seventy-year (7x10) judgment. He allowed their worldliness (symbolized by the number 10) to develop to "perfection" (7x7) and then meted out the "ideal" (7) punishment under the rule of Babylonia (10). The symbolism was based on the Sabbath of the Land and not the Jubilee, though they had failed to observe *that* law nine times during that 490 year period. In other words, if the Lord was keeping a strict account of the number of times the land missed its Sabbath rest, then Israel really owed seventy-nine years.

Jubilee as First Year in a New Cycle of Sabbatic Years						
1	2	3	4	5	6	7
(Jubilee)						Sabbatic
						Sabbatic
						Sabbatic
						Sabbatic
						Sabbatic
						Sabbatic
						Sabbatic
Jubilee						Sabbatic
						Sabbatic
						Sabbatic

Israel was given these sabbatic laws in the wilderness where they neither had to till the soil nor reap the harvests, but they knew they were responsible to obey these laws upon entrance into the promised land. Under the Lord's direction, they crossed the Jordan River, designedly on the anniversary of the exodus—on the tenth day of the first month—and were fed manna up to the day after their first Passover (Nisan 15).

> Now the children of Israel camped in Gilgal, and kept the Passover on the fourteenth day of the month at twilight on the plains of Jericho.
>
> And they ate of the produce of the land on the day after the Passover, unleavened bread and parched grain, on the very same day.

> Then the manna ceased on the day after they had eaten the produce of the land; and the children of Israel no longer had manna, but they ate the food of the land of Canaan that year. (Josh 5:10–12)

They entered Canaan and ate of crops, vineyards and groves that they had not planted, dressed, or cultivated. There were no servants to manumit, debts to settle, boundaries to re-measure, or inheritances to reclaim. With the exception of some agricultural obligations, their first year in Canaan was for the most part a Jubilee Year. Based upon the fact that the Lord had purchased Israel with a price, they were His bond-servants; therefore, He did not want them to oppress each other or sanction permanent slavery (Lev 25:42–43, 55). Furthermore, even though the Lord granted and allotted land to the Israelites, His true abode was in heaven, the place He eventually desired them to be; therefore, He wanted them to consider themselves to be strangers and pilgrims in the land with Him (Lev 25:23). These laws were first and foremost about the reality of their redemption and their position of favor with the Lord. Therefore, these times were especially poignant for those who had temporarily lost their inheritance or freedom.

Sabbatic Year. Every seventh year following their entrance into Canaan, the land was to lay fallow, so it achieved its own "rest" (Exod 23:10–11). Because the Israelites were to refrain from "working the land," all debt payments were released for that year (Deut 15:1–4). For this reason, the Sabbath of the Land was also called the Year of Release (Deut 15:9). This law applied only to the land of Israel and the Israelites (Lev 25:2), so foreigners were not released from debt payment (Deut 15:3). Lastly, the Law was read in public, to every man, woman, and child, to those who came to Jerusalem for the festival of Tabernacles (Deut 31:10–13) when the holy year began, commemorative of the giving of the Law and of the reading of the Law by Joshua (Josh 8:30–35).

Jubilee. Following the Day of Atonement of the seventh Sabbatic year (49 years), the fiftieth-year Jubilee was announced by the great blasts of ram horns. The grandest of all Jewish festivals was marked by its rare appearance on the calendar, but virtually ensured that every Israelite, assuming God's grant of seventy years, would live to see at least one Jubilee in their lifetime. The land received a supernumerary sabbatic rest so that two such years fell side by side. Property that was previously leased to negotiate debts was unconditionally restored to the original owner, and lives given in bond service were categorically released. As its name implies, this was a most joyous time, as it followed the Day of Atonement when Israel acknowledged the Lord's forgiveness of the previous year's sin.

As previously noted, the Sabbatic Year did not forgive debts, but merely postponed debt service because the Israelites were unable to farm the land. "However, foreign debtors were not released from debt payment to Israelites during a Sabbatic Year (Deut 15:3) since foreigners were able to farm their lands."[68] The implication is that the Jews did not consider the law of the Sabbatic Year as constraining the Gentile nations. Even though it was rooted in the pattern of the Sabbath (and ultimately in

68. Ibid., 195.

the pattern of creation) it was *not* binding upon the nations. If the premise for global application of the weekly Sabbath is rooted in the creation week then the Sabbath of the Land must also be a universal command because it was similarly patterned after the creation week. Many Reformed authors, past and present, have consistently drawn this conclusion.

> Clearly, the renewal of the earth is a basic aspect of the Sabbath. The renewal of all things is basic to the Sabbath, and the earth is central to this renewal. Men can ignore the Sabbath requirements of the earth only at the peril of judgment and death. Clearly, the death penalty is operative in history, and nations which mine the earth and use its resources abusively are doomed to die. The logical assumption then is this: if contempt of the Sabbath is so serious with respect to the earth, is it not equally serious with respect to man and beast?[69]

Rushdoony correctly recognizes the association of the weekly Sabbath with both the Sabbatic Year and Jubilee, and therefore points out the oversight of many Sabbatarians whose single mantra is weekly worship and rest rather than logically extending their concern to the land. For Rushdoony, this means at least leaving the weeds to grow, not pruning the grape vine or the fruit tree, and allowing fruit to drop and rot. Presumably, this is done once every seven years. But shouldn't Christian Sabbatarians be synchronized in their observance of these natural laws in order to be a testimony to the world? As laudatory as it is to care for the soil, the Sabbatic Year is not about environmentalism, crop rotation, ecosystem development, soil conservation, water management, or protection of endangered species.

What basic, natural principle in the creation demands a land rest every seventh year? And what scientific evidence is there that the sixth year crop produces a double-portion over the crops of the first through fifth years? If the Israelites observed these laws, it was the Lord Himself who ensured the *miraculous* produce necessary to provide for their sustenance while the land lay fallow. The pattern is merely symbolic of redemptive themes and is not meant to be an enduring environmental commandment. Also, the Jews were unable to obey either of these laws until they actually came into possession of the land. These institutions derived meaning only in relationship to the promised land, and thus they enlarged the redemptive theme of Canaan rest. From Egypt and through the desert, the Israelites entered a land of milk and honey. It was not virgin territory—they reaped what they had not sown and gathered what they had not tended. They entered without debts, without cares, without conscription, but these blessed circumstances were merely a shadow of the heavenly bliss of eternity; so the Lord through these shadow laws commemorated the new beginning of Israel and planted the prospect for a more glorious and enduring new beginning. That final and fulfilled Jubilee occurred during the first advent of Jesus Christ and every person who puts their trust in Him has entered the real Jubilee.

Rushdoony goes on to state that the Sabbath cannot be reduced to either humanitarianism or soil conservation because it is a spiritual matter, but he only means that

69. Rushdoony, *Institutes of Biblical Law*, 142.

man cannot rely on Sabbatic regulations as a *quid pro quo* for blessings and prosperity without the requisite faith. So Sabbatarians are still left with a duty to apply Sabbath principles to the land, or perish. It is true that the Sabbath of the Land (Lev 25:4, 6; 26:34, 43) occurred every seventh year in the same pattern as the creation week. Just as man and beast cycled in their work from one week to another, the land cycled in its work from one season to another. Likewise, the Jubilee allowed the cycles of land ownership to revert to the original. Together, taking into consideration the association of these laws with the Sabbath and the creation, it becomes apparent that not only must man and beast be redeemed and restored to their original estate, but the earth and property as well. This is something that the Lord will accomplish according to His divine redemptive plan. Even if the whole world obeyed these laws man could not reclaim the original garden state.

But commentators are prone to enlarge upon the commercial and economic benefits of these laws making claim that they remedied all sorts of social evils. Apparently, these laws shunned avarice, abolished poverty, mitigated against slavery, prevented inequities, and equalized the distribution of wealth. Thus, had Israel truly kept these laws to the letter, she would have reaped untold riches; therefore, present nations would do well to mimic these legislations. However, the Lord gave no promise that poverty would be a byword in Israel (Deut 15:9–11; Matt 26:11); rather, the continual existence of poverty represents the scarcity of hearing God's word (Prov 29:18; Amos 8:11).

At the same time, the Lord's tenderness toward the indigent reflected His sentiment for those who were poor in spirit (Matt 5:3), thus the Lord required merciful treatment of the poor, giving without usury, just as He had given the land to Israel (Deut 25:35–38). Likewise, the Lord required fair and gracious treatment of those less fortunate because Israel was once afflicted in Egypt (Exod 21–24). However, oppression would continue unabated, indicating the utter depravity of man and his habituation to sin. The oppressed knew only too well their need of a Savior (Jas 2:5). The Lord looked among the children of Israel for someone who could stand in His place as a heavenly representative of justice, but found no one (Ezek 22:29–31).

Finally, debts will always accumulate, indicating our spiritual indebtedness to God (Jer 5:4). As Jesus questioned about the resultant gratitude of two debtors, forgiven of their respective debts, "Which of [the debtors] will love [the creditor] more?" The answer, of course, given correctly by the disciple Peter, was that the man who had much forgiven would be more sympathetic to the creditor (Luke 7:42). It should be clear that these civil laws were intended to be spiritually arousing and related by meditation to the Lord's work of salvation, the expectation of the Messiah, and to a deeper understanding of the moral law of God. Our Jesus made Himself poor, that through His poverty, we may be made rich (2 Cor 8:9). While it is laudable to raise the standard of living of the poor and to remove unfair and oppressive practices in government and industry, there is still a danger lurking for those in a land of bounty (Prov 30:8–9; Rev 3:17). Establishing a world without slavery and poverty may give us a false sense of freedom (John 8:33). "Jesus was the high priest who blew the jubilee trumpet throughout all the land of Israel, when He proclaimed, 'The kingdom of heaven is at hand!'"[70] Bonar acknowledges the partial fulfillment of the Jubilee in the first advent of Christ and pronounces the forthcoming fulfillment of the Jubilee in full measure as the redeemed people of God enter paradise.

The Sabbatic Year and the Jubilee draw out an aspect of the Sabbath that is often overlooked, but was present when the Sabbath was first given in the wilderness: trust. During the Sabbatic Year and Jubilee, the Israelites were to refrain from the industry of agriculture and instead find their nourishment like a sparrow, which neither sows nor reaps (Matt 6:26). This was predicated on the fact that the land was God's land (Lev 25:23) and that He was sojourning with them. Anticipating their reaction to the command to observe these statutes two years in succession (the seventh Sabbath of the Land followed by a Jubilee), the Lord clarified for them what He expected, and how He would bless their trust in Him.

> So you shall observe My statutes and keep My judgments, and perform them; and you will dwell in the land in safety.
>
> Then the land will yield its fruit, and you will eat your fill, and dwell there in safety.
>
> And if you say, "What shall we eat in the seventh year, since we shall not sow nor gather in our produce?"
>
> Then I will command My blessing on you in the sixth year, and it will bring forth produce enough for three years.
>
> And you shall sow in the eighth year, and eat old produce until the ninth year; until its produce comes in, you shall eat of the old harvest.
>
> (Lev 25:18–22)

Just as the Israelites in the wilderness received the double-portion of manna prior to the Sabbath, the Lord ensured, while they resided in Canaan, sufficient stock and provisions for each Sabbath, Sabbatic Year, and Jubilee. The object lesson is clear: trust the Lord for your needs because He will work unfailingly on your behalf. Without the Lord's *miraculous* involvement in crop output this agricultural strategy would fail.

This idea of miraculous production came to King Hezekiah following a devastating siege by Sennacherib on the land of Canaan just prior to the Sabbath of the Land. If there was a time to despair, a time to question whether to obey the Lord or not, that was it. But the Lord assured Hezekiah that He would protect Israel from further onslaughts and bless the fields and streams so they would provide ample produce to sustain his countrymen. The sign of this miraculous yield from unsown and uncultivated fields was defined by the Lord as applying to His supernatural protection of Israel and His raising them again as from the dead.

> This shall be a sign to you: You shall eat this year such as grows of itself, And in the second year what springs from the same; Also in the third year sow and reap, Plant vineyards and eat the fruit of them.
>
> And the remnant who have escaped of the house of Judah Shall again take root downward, And bear fruit upward.

70. Bonar, *Leviticus*, 449.

> For out of Jerusalem shall go a remnant, And those who escape from Mount Zion. The zeal of the *Lord* of hosts will do this. (2 Kgs 19:29–31)

Again, the metaphor is one of new beginnings, likening the remnant of Israel to a new garden in fertile soil, the increase of which is the Lord's doing. The protection of a remnant of Israel and the provision for those who are weak and helpless, are benefits to those who rest from their own feeble works and repose in the God who has shown Himself to be completely dependable to work on their behalf. As beautiful as the type is, the reality is incomprehensibly more so.

In spite of the ceremonial status of the Sabbatic Year and Jubilee, the Christian church has attempted to apply it externally in some fanciful ways. It is reported that Pope Boniface VIII in 1300 was the first to enact a "Christian Jubilee." During the following two centuries, the Jubilee was redefined as a period of one hundred, thirty-three, and twenty-five years! Rather than having anything to do with the returning of land to original owners and the forgiveness of debts, the Roman Catholic Church emphasized whether doors to their basilicas should be open or shut. The Protestant church has made more significant applications in civil law through bankruptcy laws (illegal to declare bankruptcy more than once in seven years) and tort law (claims of injury must be made within seven years). The most notable application of the Jubilee was made during the abolitionist movement in England and America by carrying forward the idea of manumission of slaves. But again, the application was strained because the Jubilee proclaimed unconditional liberty only for those brought out of Egypt (i.e., the Jews), not slaves of other nations, who could be permanent slaves and passed like property from one generation to another (Lev 25:44–46). Furthermore, following the Jubilee, Jews could encounter conditions that forced their return to the status of a bond servant or to lose possession of their inheritance. However, the institution of slavery in America was "forever" ended by federal law on January 1, 1863. Lastly, neither in the Americas nor the United Kingdom was there any application of the Sabbatic Year to the soil or the return of land-property to those who had been dispossessed of it. Though the Jubilee inspired many religious people to favor emancipation, it was a biblical concept taken out of context. If anything, the Jubilee, through its repetitious requirement, typified that true freedom could never be achieved on earth. Instead, a Christianized nation would better abolish slavery on the basis of gospel freedom in Jesus Christ, an evangelical love for the lost, and a humility in knowing that all men—our neighbors—stand equal before God (Luke 10:27–37). A glimpse of this is seen in Paul's endearing letter to Philemon on behalf of his slave and property, Onesimus, to receive him not as a servant, but as a brother in Christ, and to put to Paul's account whatever was owed in the matter (Phlm 1:16–19). If the Messiah had not come, Paul might have reminded Philemon to ensure Onesimus gets his weekly rest from labors, but Paul envisions a more radical effect on their relationship in view of the work of redemption by Jesus Christ. Though in chains, Paul was living out the fulfilled Jubilee. The countries of the earth can free all who are oppressed, apportion land to every family, develop systems to eliminate debt, and give the land a Sabbath rest, but they can never duplicate the reality that is forthcoming for the saints of God in Christ (Isa 64:4; 1 Cor 2:9–10).

Convocationally

Besides the weekly Sabbath, the Lord ordained seven annual Sabbaths. All of these Sabbaths were chosen times during the year that belonged to the Lord, which required certain actions and attitudes from the people as they came to Him in holy communion.

> "Speak to the children of Israel, and say to them: 'The feasts [*mo'ed*] of the *Lord*, which you shall proclaim to be holy convocations, these are My feasts [*mo'ed*]. 'Six days shall work be done, but the seventh day is a Sabbath of solemn rest, a holy convocation. You shall do no work on it; it is the Sabbath of the *Lord* in all your dwellings." (Lev 23:2–3).

As the Sabbath heads the forthcoming list of feasts, its association with the annual holy days is further deepened by sharing the dignity as a "holy convocation." Before we get too comfortable calling the Sabbath and the other holy days "feasts," it is best to come to an understanding about the Hebrew words in use.

> Unfortunately, to most English readers that word "feast" is misleading, as here used, because . . . the one word "feast" is used to translate two Hebrew words of different meaning from each other. There is the Hebrew word *chag* (plural *chaggim*), which rightly enough is translated by our English word "feast'" and there is the other Hebrew word, *mo'ed* (plural *mo'adim*), which means simply an appointed time or season.[71]

So, the weekly Sabbath and the seven annual holy days with their respective Sabbaths are all "appointed times," from a root word meaning "to determine or fix."[72] Of this group, three of the "appointed times" are also called "feasts" (*chag*) in the sense of joyous times of festivity, "you shall rejoice in your feast (*chag*)" (Deut 16:14). First, the Feast (*chag*) of Unleavened Bread; second, the Feast (*chag*) of Weeks; and third, the Feast (*chag*) of Tabernacles (Deut 16:16). What held these three appointed times together was the obligation of all adult males to personally appear before the temple in Jerusalem, not "empty-handed," and make offerings to God (Deut 16:16).

> The intention of these festal gatherings three times a year was not primarily a politico-national one . . . but first and chiefly a religious one. Israel was to be brought thereby three times a year to the renewed consciousness that it belonged to the sanctuary, to be reminded of its covenant and feudal obligations towards Jehovah, the God and King of the land, to appear before Him and do homage to Him, and present its tribute as vassal in the first-fruits and tenths of its harvest-produce.[73]

71. Baxter, *Explore the Book*, 1:136.

72. Kurtz, *Offerings, Sacrifices, and Worship*, 341–42. Those who view the Sabbath as a mo'ed: Kurtz, 342; Bonar, *Leviticus*, 396; Edersheim, *Temple*, 134;

73. Kurtz, *Offerings, Sacrifices, and Worship*, 345.

The three feasts emphasized the Trinitarian nature of the God who three-times redeemed Israel from bondage. Through the "loins" of the patriarchs, He saved them three times. First, He delivered father Abraham from Pharaoh in Egypt (Gen 12:10–20); secondly, He relieved Isaac from starvation (Gen 26:1–4); and thirdly, he rescued Jacob from his devious and pursuing uncle Laban (Gen: 31:1–3). In each case the Lord tied their safety to His covenantal promises of the land. As a nation, He delivered them from the grasp of Pharaoh in Egypt (Num 1), then he relieved them from starvation in the wilderness (Num 11), and finally, He preserved them from the treachery of their own brothers (Num 14). Again, in each case the Lord reminded Israel of the promised land. As such, a part of the religious obligations of worship included representative migrations to the place God had determined to place His Name. The priesthood resided in Jerusalem and represented all Israel every day through the work of the sacrificial system, and the males dispersed throughout the land appeared before Jerusalem three times a year as representatives of their families back home. Concerning the designation of these "appointed times" as "holy convocations," Kurtz informs us that

> No precise account is to be found in the law, but which cannot be regarded in any other light than as a meeting of those members of the community who were near the sanctuary, for the sake of edification by means of sacrifice and prayer . . . No doubt this included the blessing of the people by the priest in the words prescribed in Num 4:24–26.

The phrase "holy convocation(s)" is used nineteen times and is applied generally to the *mo'adim* (Lev 23:2, 4, 37; Isa 1:13), to the weekly Sabbaths (Lev 23:3), and to the annual Sabbaths of the Feast of Unleavened Bread (Lev 23:7–8), Feast of Weeks (Lev 23:21), Feast of Trumpets (Lev 23:24), Day of Atonement (Lev 23:27), and the Feast of Tabernacles (Lev 23:35–36). From the Hebrew word *miqra*, the convocation is a "calling together" to attend a public meeting, but as Kurtz mentioned above, this applied primarily to those in Jerusalem since the Israelites resided in an 8,500 square mile country. Aware that the Sabbath is defined as a holy convocation, Sabbatarians have reasoned that this required *local* public meetings throughout the land of Israel. Thus, if the Sabbath lingers with moral force for the church, then the congregational prescription remains as well.

> If the Sabbath was an "appointed time," it was a time for worship. Similarly, "holy convocation" always means a public assembly for worship. From the time of Moses, Israelites worshiped every Sabbath. Leviticus 23:2–3 thus requires participation in Sabbath convocation, and nothing has changed this in the New Covenant. If we don't assemble at the appointed time, we sin—and we insult the Lord who has made the appointment.[74]

Though a "holy convocation" seems to intimate a large public meeting open to all Israelites, it was nothing of the sort. Only three of the annual feasts required a pilgrimage of all *healthy* males to Jerusalem, so only these three feasts came close to a calling together of Israel. On the Day of Atonement, also designated as a "holy convocation,"

74. Leithart, "Worship First and Last," 16.

those residing outside Jerusalem remained at home and worshipped by keeping the day as prescribed. Scripture advances the principle that individual Israelites were to be present when bringing their sacrifices to the temple (Lev 1:1–4), but what about the appointed sacrifices for Israel made on the appointed days that had been purchased with public funds?

> It followed that, as the morning and evening sacrifices, and those on feast-days were purchased with money contributed by all, and offered on behalf of the whole congregation, all Israel should have attended these services. This was manifestly impossible, but to represent the people twenty-four courses of lay attendants were appointed, corresponding to those of the priests and the Levites. These were the "stationary men," or "men of the station," or "standing men," from "their standing there in the Temple as Israel's representatives" . . . Their duty was twofold: to represent all Israel in the services of the sanctuary, and to act as a sort of guide to those who had business in the Temple.[75]

According to Edersheim, this tradition developed as early as David's time, well before the development of a synagogal form of worship. Of course, the Sabbath and all appointed times were times of worship, but it was worship as defined by God. On the seventh day of the week the general population remained at home to rest, as it is written, "it is the Sabbath of the *Lord* in all your dwellings" (Lev 23:3). However, in Jerusalem a representative "holy convocation" (Lev 23:3) took place as the priesthood offered two additional lambs, the accompanying grain and drink offerings, and the showbread on behalf of the whole congregation of Israel. With this understanding, it is difficult to envision, as Leithart suggests above, how nothing of this has changed in the new covenant! Indeed, none of the weekly or annual Sabbaths called for local congregational worship meetings wherever the Israelites felt inclined to meet. The designation "holy convocation" describes only the representative worship in Jerusalem by the Levitical priesthood.

Summarily

Israel, as a nation, relived significant historical events and rehearsed spiritual realities through commemorative holy days, seasons, and years. These celebrations or feasts were not adopted through tradition, assimilated from foreign lands, mandated by counsels, or chosen by leaders, but given by special revelation as a cohesive group by their heavenly King. More than this, the ceremonies linked to the passage of time, from the Sabbath to the Jubilee, were meant to engender hope that, in time, the Lord would fulfill his promises and manifest His presence through the Messiah in a spectacular way. Linking these ceremonies to time meant that they would only be observed for a time, and the very nature of their observance forecasted what would be accomplished, thus bringing the very observances to an end. The arrangement and patterns contained in the twelve cyclical feasts is put forth in Appendix 5. Commentators have devised various ways to categorize the sabbatic festivals given to Israel by the Lord—"I

75. Edersheim, *Temple*, 135–36.

also gave them My Sabbaths" (Ezek 20:12). Rushdoony identifies seven Sabbaths[76] and Baxter more accurately identifies ten sabbatic institutions.[77] Other authors have whimsically determined that there are creation Sabbaths, Mosaic Sabbaths, Christian Sabbaths, and even eternal Sabbaths. However, there are actually three major groupings of Sabbaths given to Israel: 1) the weekly Sabbath, 2) the seven, individual, annual Sabbaths associated with the *mo'adim* of Israel, and 3) two periodic sabbatic years for the land. Regardless of their sequential and symbolic differences, all of the sabbatic institutions are ceremonial.

Most theologians admit to the ceremonial nature of all these feasts and holy days, with the occasional exception of the Sabbath. Despite clear statements that these laws were to continue forever, the NT makes equally clear their temporary nature. The whole calendar system was a type of Jesus Christ, His work, and ministry; therefore, we have every reason to dismiss it by virtue of the surpassing realities it forecasted. This is the historic position of the church, as here argued by Origen:

> If it be objected to us on this subject that we ourselves are accustomed to observe certain days, as for example the Lord's day, the Preparation, the Passover, or Pentecost, I have to answer, that to the perfect Christian, who is ever in his thoughts, words, and deeds serving his natural Lord, God the Word, all his days are the Lord's, and he is always keeping the Lord's day. He also who is unceasingly preparing himself for the true life, and abstaining from the pleasures of this life which lead astray so many,—who is not indulging the lust of the flesh, but "keeping under his body, and bringing it into subjection,"—such a one is always keeping Preparation-day. Again, he who considers that "Christ our Passover was sacrificed for us," and that it is his duty to keep the feast by eating of the flesh of the Word, never ceases to keep the paschal feast; for the pascha means a "passover," and he is ever striving in all his thoughts, words, and deeds, to pass over from the things of this life to God, and is hastening towards the city of God. And, finally, he who can truly say, "We are risen with Christ," and "He hath exalted us, and made us to sit with Him in heavenly places in Christ," is always living in the season of Pentecost . . .[78]

Origen did not "keep" festivals exteriorly; however, he did worship on the Lord's Day. As he lived the Christian life in maturity, he realized the fulfillment of all the shadow feasts every day. Even his weekly participation in weekly worship was counted as a daily reality. The fact that the festivals have spiritual meaning does not obligate Christians to continue the outward observance of them, for Christ's fulfillment of the feasts of time advances to us the reality in everyday fashion. We possess a quotidian token of the culmination of their fulfillment that will endure for an eternity (Isa 66:22–23). Our Lord chastised the Pharisees that "the day" has arrived, and it is *Him* (Luke 12:54–56). The whole Jewish calendar pointed to the glories of Jesus Christ, so that Isaiah could

76. Rushdoony, *Institutes of Biblical Law*, 150. He mistakenly lists the Passover in place of the Day of Atonement. He joins the Sabbath of the Land and the Jubilee in one category and combines the pairs of Sabbaths during the Feast of Unleavened Bread and Tabernacles.

77. Baxter, *Explore the Book*, 1:139.

78. Origen, *Cels.* 8:22 (*ANF* 4:647).

roar, "Lift up your eyes on high, and see *who* has created these things (Isa 40:26). It is not the heavenly bodies controlling our calendar that holds the Christian's spiritual interest but the Lord Himself.

6

Sabbath and the Canaan Rest

CANAAN AND CANAAN

Canaan, the Cursed One

CANAAN WAS THE SON of Ham, the grandson of Noah, and the brother to Cush, Mizraim, and Put (Gen 10:6). As a result of Ham's presumptive rebellion against Noah, Ham's son Canaan was cursed to be a slave—"a servant of servants he shall be"—a pronouncement that sounded more ominous and sobering than the curse given to Adam (Gen 9:25–27). On the surface, the curse seems to be directed at the wrong individual; however, the gist of the curse is this: "As Ham has been a shame to me, so shall Canaan be a shame to Ham." Ham shamed his father in two ways: 1) exposing his father's nakedness, that is, finding fault with Noah to undermine his authority, and 2) failing to be a godly son, not only through his own rebellion but by his attempt to entice his brothers. Ham, the youngest son of Noah, attempted to assume the authority of his father, and even beguiled his older brothers to be partner to his machinations. He had neither the training nor experience, neither the leading of God nor the confirmation by godly men to assume the position of leadership in that community. Through Ham's four sons, the ungodly "sons of men" resumed their march to the four corners of the earth; and whatever "rest" Noah enjoyed in the new world was quickly disturbed. This saga of unrealized rest anticipates a more enduring rest. Noah was not the one to restore true rest to a fallen world, nor was he meant to be, for Noah had neither the power nor the authority to undo the treachery of sin. Yet Noah's life foreshadowed that when the true messenger of rest would enter the world, He too would be beguiled by someone very close to Him. However, the forecasted one would have the power and authority to provide true rest in spite of the treasonous actions of his brethren.

Noah's curse was directed at Ham's youngest son, and perhaps related to his moniker "to stoop." As for Canaan, scant is known about his following years, yet his descendants came to possess a plenteous and verdant land (Gen 10:15–19). On the surface, it appears that Canaan was blessed instead of cursed. Ironically, the faithful remnant through Shem were the ones who suffered the curse of slavery, enduring the humiliation and rigors for about 490 years in a foreign land, yet promised to be given the very land occupied by Canaan's descendants. God ordained this to display a common redemptive theme. The wicked seem to prosper, the faithful seem to suffer, but in the end God will ensure that the faithful are rewarded with eternal life while the wicked are rejected and punished. The faithful should not fret about the status, progress, and wealth of the heathen nations (Jer 12:1–2).

These events are real history, but they are not recorded simply as historical records. Instead, the Lord foreshadows details about a future redemptive event that He will bring to pass. Noah's calling to bring rest to the world was anticipated in his birthname and his father's hope, and though Noah proved inadequate for the task, his life foreshadowed one who would restore rest perfectly and completely. Genesis history moves from Noah's death to Abram's relocation into Canaan. The true rest was not realized through Noah, but the promise of rest remained as symbolized in the land of Canaan. The patriarchs of faith grasped that the earthly model of rest—for them, the promised land of Canaan—represented a heavenly spiritual reality as the eventual reward for the faithful. This is how Abraham understood the promise (Heb 11:13).[1]

Canaan, the Land of Promise

Our interest in the land of Canaan develops during the life of Abraham, who moved with his relatives from Ur, the place of his nativity, to Haran, just outside the land of the Canaanites. As O. Palmer Robertson reminds us, the land was not chosen to indulge Abraham with blessings but to be the avenue for His blessings to branch out to the nations.[2] While in Haran, around 2003 BCE, Abraham was commanded to leave his relatives and travel farther west to Canaan (Gen 12:5–7).[3] Though Abraham lived among the Canaanites, even forming a confederacy (Gen 13:14) and doing business with them (Gen 23:1ff), he would not allow his son Isaac to marry from the daughters of the Canaanites (Gen 24:3) because of their idolatry (Gen 15:16) and because the promise of the land was to Isaac (Gen 17:19, 28:12–15). Isaac understood the promise of God and gave to his son Jacob the same charge to marry in the family (Gen 28:1–5). Through the providence of God, Jacob and his twelve sons dwelt in Egypt, and upon his death Jacob was buried in Canaan (Gen 50:12–13) where his father Isaac (Gen 35:27–29) and his grandfather Abraham (Gen 25:8–9) were buried. The book of Genesis ends in Egypt with the reassuring words of Joseph that God would revisit them and bring them to the land He swore to give Abraham, Isaac, and Jacob.

Exodus tells of the growth of the Israelites in Egypt and the ascendancy of a Pharaoh who grew to mistrust them and forced them into slavery. Moses was forced to flee from Egypt for murdering an Egyptian, and at Mount Sinai the Lord spoke to him from the burning bush, assuring him that He would deliver Israel from oppression and bring them to the land of Canaan (Exod 3:7–8). After the Lord delivered the Israelites from Egypt and brought them to Mount Sinai, they lapsed into idolatry; however, the Lord was still ready to lead them into Canaan (Exod 33:1–3). Moses commissioned

1. Robertson, *Israel of God*, 5–6.

2. Ibid., 11.

3. This promise is repeated in Gen 13:14–18; 15:7–8, 18–21; 17:6–8; 18:9; 24:7; 26:1–5; 28:12–15.

twelve men to survey the quality of the land and to assess the strength of its inhabitants (Num 13:1ff), but after reconnoitering the land for forty days, the majority returned discouraged. This caused the Israelites to weep in fear and murmur in disbelief (Num 14:1–2). This failure to trust in God's ability to perform what He promised was dis-consonant both with their miraculous deliverance from Egypt only months earlier and the Lord's promise while they were at Mount Sinai to do even greater things with them in Canaan (Exod 34:10–11). In spite of the confidence of Joshua and Caleb, the Israelites determined to stone them, elect a new captain and return to Egypt (Num 13:4, 10). This offended and angered the Lord (Num 14:11) who determined to keep them as wanderers in the desert for forty years until He prepared the next generation to conquer the land of Canaan. In response to the Lord's chastisement, some men acknowledged their sin, but presumptuously decided to move ahead on the basis of God's earlier promise to enter the land, only to be badly defeated in battle against the Amalakites and Canaanites because they were not entering the land under the direct guidance of God (Num 14:40–45).

Clearly at issue is the unbelief of the overwhelming majority of the Israelites toward the God of their deliverance and the God of their future inheritance. It is almost incomprehensible how they could have failed to take God at His word, having seen His compassion at their plight in Egypt and having been eyewitnesses to the display of His power in their deliverance. The egregious faithlessness of Israel was such a nadir in their history that King David warned his own and successive generations about the severe consequences of such unbelief: "They shall not enter My rest [*menuchah*]" (Ps 95:8–11). Despite the declarative reiteration of the promise to the evacuees through Moses and the heartening demonstration of belief in Caleb and Joshua, the sin of unbelief pervaded the camp. In response to this unbelief, the Lord withheld their entrance into Canaan, a year for each day the spies surveyed the land (Num 14:34).

Since entering Canaan was predicated on the faith of the Israelites, it serves as a type of salvation, that the way into heaven is through faith. Furthermore, the pitiful attempts of some Israelites to take Canaan in their own strength signifies that the promised rest of redemption will not be realized by "works of righteousness " on our part, but only through the means chosen by God. With the Canaan-type fulfilled in the first advent of Jesus Christ, the quest for a Canaan habitation no longer exists as a spiritual goal of new covenant believers. Freed from the bondage of sin, we enter by faith into the restful territory of Jesus Christ who reigns from His heavenly throne, triumphant over our spiritual enemies. Our Zion is the kingdom of Christ, a borderless and unconquerable land of rest, prepared by the obedient Son of David for the saints (Ps 132). The church of Jesus Christ is not to be preoccupied with inhabiting a land when its citizenship is already in the heavenlies (Eph 1:3; 2:6). Canaan may speak, by metaphor, of our future transference into the presence of God, even as our present state of spiritual rest in Christ, but we would confuse matters to refer to the land in which we now live as a "Christian Canaan." As O. Palmer Robertson summarized,

> In this age of fulfillment, a retrogression to the limited forms of the old covenant must be neither expected nor promoted. Reality must not give way to shadow.[4]

The Canaan rest has been fulfilled in Christ. The land of milk and honey is a portrayal of the glorious celestial land inhabited by those who rested in the promises of God made to the saints of old. This fulfillment encompasses the complete landscape of biblical rests that the Lord portrayed in the old covenant: the seventh day rest in Eden, the renewed earth following the flood, and the land of Canaan amplified with its sabbatic land rest.

Canaan, the Land of Rest and War

In the first month of the fortieth year in the desert, the new generation of Israelites encamped in the wilderness of Zin only to be faced with a paucity of water (Num 20:1–2). In the anniversary month of Israel's release from bondage and the experience of the Lord's care for them in their peregrination, the people erupted in bitterness against Moses and Aaron, not only about the shortage of water, but the inability to cultivate figs, vines, and pomegranates. Repeating the grievances of their fathers—as though the wilderness years taught them nothing—this new community yearned to be dead rather than free. They yearned to be back in Egypt rather than with the Lord. Moses and Aaron despaired and immediately approached the tabernacle to seek the Lord's advice. The glory of the Lord appeared to them and, rather than condemning Israel, the Lord responded graciously by instructing Moses to take the rod, assemble the congregation before a chosen rock, and speak to the rock that it might produce the desired flow of water. This was to demonstrate to the Israelites the power of God's word alone. So Moses assembled the congregation as he was commanded, but rather than speaking to the rock, he scolded the Israelites saying, "Hear now, you rebels! Must we bring water for you out of this rock?" (Num 20:10). Clearly, Moses was exasperated with the people because they were repeating the sins of the previous generation, but as the emissary of the Lord, he misrepresented the forbearance that the Lord had earlier demonstrated. Moses acted as if he himself were the provider of life-giving water. He angrily struck the rock two times, but the Lord took the two blows as coming from Moses *and* from Aaron, for He chastised them both in return, "Because you did not believe Me, to hallow Me in the eyes of the children of Israel, therefore you shall not bring this assembly into the land which I have given them" (Num 20:12). Now it was not Israel in their disbelief who was restricted from the Canaan rest, but Moses and Aaron. Aaron died shortly after this incident and was disapproved specifically with regard to his failing at Meribah-Kadesh (Num 20:24). If anyone was poised to bring Israel into the promised land, it was Moses, but his actions invalidated any possibility of his bringing many sons to glory. The severity with which the Lord treated Moses and Aaron was to emphasize, by way of typology, those superior qualities of character necessary to escort God's chosen people into redemptive rest. This account of the faltering of Moses and Aaron was not so much an object lesson about the repercussions

4. Robertson. *Israel of God*, 31.

of lapses in faith as it was to proclaim that there would be another to bring God's people into everlasting rest—a man who was more than a man, who could love the unlovable, give aid to the seed of Abraham, and release them from the fears that hold them in bondage; a man who could listen to the voice of God and accurately represent Him before His beloved people. Such a one we have in Jesus, who is not ashamed to call us brethren; for He who sanctifies and those whom He sanctifies are one! (Heb 2:10–18). Jesus exemplified in His earthly ministry a full and unwavering confidence in the Father and He identified Himself with God's children despite their weaknesses. So, in contrast to Moses, Jesus properly represented the grace of God toward sinners without resentment, He endured the tribulations laid upon him with meekness, and He possessed a resolute love for the people of God.

Though Moses could not enter the land himself (Deut 32:4–52), he was the spokesman for the Lord to the nation as they stood ready to enter the land.

> For as yet you have not come to the rest (*menuchah*) and the inheritance which the Lord your God is giving you.
>
> But when you cross over the Jordan and dwell in the land which the Lord your God is giving you to inherit, and He gives you rest (*nuach*) from all your enemies round about, so that you dwell in safety,
>
> then there will be the place where the Lord your God chooses to make His name abide. (Deut 12:9–11)

After the Israelites crossed over the Jordan River on dry land, they were circumcised as a sign of their partnership in the covenant with Abraham and of their freedom from the reproach of having lived as slaves in Egypt (Josh 5:9). This signifies that a person must be born again through faith (circumcision made without hands) to enter into the promised land of rest. Furthermore, as has been noted by many a commentator, Israel entered Canaan under the command of Joshua, foretelling the day when our valiant Captain leads His people in victory into the true promised land. To Joshua alone, the Lord's theophanic appearance as "Commander of the Lord's Army" reminded him of the Lord's sovereign presence and rule during the upcoming conquest of Canaan so that no soldier, sergeant, or general could boast about their military achievements (Josh 5:13–15). Though Joshua led Israel into the land, he was reminded that he was merely a man, for if the people of God are to enjoy rest, God Himself must lead them! The first and most critical battle at Jericho demonstrated that the Lord must do what man cannot do in order to secure the promised land of rest. Accompanied by the ark of the Lord, surrounded by seven priests, each with their own trumpet sounding, the Israelites were instructed about the ubiquitous presence of God, His desire to be the central theme of their walk, and His demand that His word is proclaimed in the congregation within earshot of the enemy. The presence of the seven priests on the first six days underscores the assurance of complete victory on the seventh day, a triumph so sure that each infantryman had no reason to doubt the Lord, only to behold His salvation. The analogy to the seventh day of creation—God's rest of completion—is unmistakable as Israel prepares to enter their Canaan rest. However, the seventh day was not a day of rest entirely, for the Lord brought down the stronghold of the enemy, triumphing over them in it. The redemptive work of God on behalf of the Israelites was necessary on the seventh day. Furthermore, the preservation of Rahab and her family indicated that the Lord would be the redeemer of all who trust in Him, including those who were once at war with Him (Rom 5:10; Col 1:21). The necessity of trust in the saving work of God on the seventh day was a recurring theme for Israel.

After five years of conquest in the land, defeating no fewer than thirty-one kings (Josh 12:1ff), the Israelites apportioned the land by lot for an inheritance to future generations.

> So Joshua took the whole land, according to all that the Lord had said to Moses; and Joshua gave it as an inheritance to Israel according to their divisions by their tribes. Then the land rested (*shaqat*) from war. (Josh 11:23)

Indeed, the land of Canaan was now a land of rest, for the Lord finally made good upon His promise.

> The Lord gave them rest (*nuach*) all around, according to all that He had sworn to their fathers. And not a man of all their enemies stood against them; the Lord delivered all their enemies into their hand. (Josh 21:44)

At this point, what is typified is the ability of the Lord to complete what He set out to do, that eternal salvation will surely come to pass no matter what obstacles seem to be in the way. As the Israelites entered the land of Canaan "they ate the food of the land of Canaan that year" (Josh 5:12), indicating that God's redeemed people immediately experience the benefits of God's redeeming love and care for them. Centuries later, as King David mused within his palace walls of cedar how "the Lord had given him rest (*nuach*) from all his enemies all around" (2 Sam 7:1), he thought it would be appropriate that the ark of the covenant, reminiscent of the deliverance of Israel from Egypt and the eventual possession of Canaan, should have its own place of rest. The Lord replied to David through Nathan that it was never His desire to have a permanent place for the tabernacle (2 Sam 7:6–7) but that He would honor the request during the lifetime of his future son. Furthermore, David was informed that there were enemies yet to conquer. After this, in the strength of the Lord (2 Sam 8:6), David zealously resumed the campaign against all the inhabitants of Canaan as predicated by the promise (2 Sam 7:10–11). At the end of his life, before commissioning his son Solomon to build a house for the Lord, David spoke to the assembly of the valiant men of Israel:

> Then King David rose to his feet and said, Hear me, my brethren and my people: I had it in my heart to build a house of rest (*menuchah*) for the ark of the covenant of the Lord, and for the footstool of our God, and had made preparations to build it.
>
> But God said to me, You shall not build a house for My name, because you have been a man of war and have shed blood. (1 Chr 28:2–3)

It was rest from enemies that inspired David to consider building a place of rest for the ark of the covenant. But David misapprehended the level of peace that his nation enjoyed. First of all, the peace and rest was really incomplete for there were enemies still lingering in the land; and secondly, and of greater importance, David erringly focused upon national peace instead of spiritual peace and rest through redemption. So, David was a typological iteration of Moses, a man after God's own heart who could conceivably prepare a place of rest for the ark of God, thereby symbolizing true national rest. However, he was disapproved for the task. David's concept of true rest was short of the perfections of rest that God intended. Perhaps it was at this juncture in David's life that he realized there was a rest beyond the rest of Canaan (Ps 95), for even though Israel possessed the land of rest, she did not thoroughly enjoy it. By postponing the completion of the temple to Solomon's reign, the Lord typified that one should come after David who desired the peace of Israel through the indwelling presence of God. Furthermore, the Lord desired a provider of rest who would paradoxically conquer the true enemies of God without being a man of bloodshed.

Canaan, the Work of God

The Israelites had to wait forty years before they were ushered into the land of promise because Canaan was the Lord's to give, not theirs to take. To take Canaan on their own terms and by their own strength and strategy, or any other land would be the work of an imperialistic nation. By waiting for the Lord to accomplish His will through them, according to His own majestic purposes, Israel was assured of the source and righteousness of what they received. Abraham had to wait during his season in Egypt before returning to Canaan (Gen 21:34; 20:1). Jacob had to wait in Egypt as well, dying without personally returning, but maintaining the hope of returning through the lives of his children (Gen 49:25, 29). Though seated in heavenly places with Jesus Christ (Eph 2:6), Christians have to wait in the earthly wilderness before being brought to their heavenly residence in resurrected bodies. Like the patriarchs, we put our hope in the God whose promises are sure, "eagerly waiting for the adoption, the redemption of our body" (Rom 8:23). When these promises are ultimately fulfilled, we will have had nothing to do with their accomplishment, therefore, we will be roused to give all praise and glory to God.

It was He who delivered the Israelites from bondage, who nurtured them in the wilderness, who fought the battles in Canaan, who built the temple, who gave them peace and prosperity in the land of promise. The land of Canaan was indeed a land of rest and it represented the blessings of eternal life. Should Israel not trust in the Lord exclusively, often demonstrated by obedience to His law, then they would be judged by separation from the land. That is, in the flesh, Israel would experience life apart from a trusting relationship with God, and "find no rest," not even a resting place for their wandering feet! (Deut 28:65).

In all respects, Canaan, like the Sabbath, represents salvation as the final result of God's work on behalf of sinful men who put their trust in Him. As the Israelites prepared to enter Canaan, a type of salvation, Moses clarified that it was not for any righteousness on the part of the new generation that they were being allowed to enter the land, for they were a "stiff-necked people" (Deut 9:6). The blessings of Canaan were certainly undeserved, for if Adam and Eve were banished from Eden, who were the Israelites that they should dwell in Canaan? It is only by God's grace that anyone should ever experience temporal blessings, and it is only by faith that anyone could ever understand that God does so to foreshadow even greater realities. As the writer of Hebrews conveys, it was by faith that Abraham remained in Canaan (Heb 11:9), that the Israelites crossed the Red Sea (Heb 11:28), and that the battle of Jericho was won (Heb 11:30). Promises were received (Heb 10:33), but only as down-payments for the fulfillment of greater, better, and more enduring promises. For Abraham "waited for the city which has foundations, whose builder and maker is God" (Heb 11:10); the patriarchs desired "a better, that is, a heavenly country" (Heb 11:16); and others who feared not death, looked for a "better resurrection" by the hand of God (Heb 11:35). The writer of Hebrews understood that the land of Canaan was a type of salvation rest, both in its present and ultimate aspects. Therefore, it is the people of faith who enter the rest of God (Heb 4:3), typified in the rest of Canaan (Heb 4:3, 5), the rest of creation (Heb 4:4), and the rest of the Sabbath (Heb 4:9); and who know in themselves that they have in heaven a better and a more enduring substance (Heb 10:34). We no longer look for a physical land of rest and its temple of rest; neither do we look for a weekly day of rest or the Edenic rest, for the promised rest is a present possession of every believer in Jesus Christ (Heb 4:3). It is no wonder that the promise of rest in Canaan became a springboard for the writer of Hebrews to proclaim that the rest of God in salvation is still open today to those who respond to God in faith (Heb 4:7–8); and that the recurring Sabbath observance became a metaphor to encourage believers, with the promise of heaven's rest, to remain faithful to God through the diligent application of righteous living (Heb 4:9–11). Canaan was a type of the heavenly rest, not the realization of that promise. In Canaan the Israelites were to observe three commemorative ordinances of rest involving the land (Lev 26:2, 34–35), two of which—the Sabbatic year (Lev 25:1) and the Jubilee (Lev 25:28, 38)—were impossible to obey until they were actually in possession of the land. The very mention of a Sabbath *for the land* intimates the truth that even the land requires redemptive rest. Though Canaan was called the "land of rest," it could never serve as the source of their rest.

During the period of the Judges, the idea of rest (*menuchah*) in the land continued as a source of hope for the faithful. The story of Ruth revolves around the restoration of land through a kinsmen redeemer, but it begins with the loss of hope as Elimilech and Naomi forsook Israel in search of a better life in Egypt. The land of Israel had its barren years, but more alarming was the want of faith in the household of Elimilech. Their comfort and security shifted from the land of promise to taking wives in Moab. Only after the Lord took Elimilech and his three sons did the idea of returning to Israel come to mind. Regrettably, Naomi did not envision Israel to be the source of hope for her daughters-in-law, for she urged them to remain in Moab to find their rest there (Ruth 1:9). However, Ruth was unsatisfied with Moab as a guarantor of blessing and instead sought the God of Israel and His people. Once Naomi became enlightened to the possibility of land redemption through Boaz, she encouraged Ruth's faith by saying, "My daughter, shall I not seek security (*manoach*, rest) for you, that it may be well with you?" (Ruth 3:1). They were both helpless as widows—and Ruth more so as a foreigner—but through a kinsman redeemer the hope of regaining the inheritance of Elimilech could be realized. Elimilech failed by selling his birthright, but Boaz acted in faith by purchasing the land for Naomi and Ruth. And if this were not enough, Ruth became betrothed to Boaz, the giver of rest. Regaining her faith, Naomi inspired her daughter in faith, saying "sit still," for Boaz must do the work necessary to "perpetuate the name of the dead" (Ruth 3:18; 4:10). There could be no rest (*manoach*) until Boaz completed the work of redemption. From the Hebrew words *menuchah* and *manoach*, rest means "all is well with the world." Heschel meditates on the richness of the Sabbath and sees pictured in its rest the hope of eternal life.

> To the biblical mind *menuha* is the same as happiness and stillness, as peace and harmony. The word with which Job described the state after life he was longing for is derived from the same root as *menuha*. It is the state wherein man lies still, wherein the wicked cease from troubling and the weary are at rest. It is the state in which there is no strife and no fighting, no fear and no distrust. The essence of good life is *menuha* . . . In later times *menuha* became a synonym for the life in the world to come, for eternal life.[5]

The rich typology of the OT and the consecrated meditations of ancient men lend deeper meaning to the Revelation of Jesus Christ to Apostle John.

> Then I, John, saw the holy city, New Jerusalem, coming down out of heaven from God, prepared as a bride adorned for her husband.
>
> And I heard a loud voice from heaven saying, Behold, the tabernacle of God is with men, and He will dwell with them, and they shall be His people. God Himself will be with them and be their God.
>
> And God will wipe away every tear from their eyes; there shall be no more death, nor sorrow, nor crying. There shall be no more pain, for the former things have passed away. (Rev 21:2–4)

This describes the complete and final fulfillment of all of God's promises to His people throughout history. It takes us out of time into eternity, from the temporal observance of times to the eternal rest found in God's presence. Though the word rest is not specifically used by John in this passage,[6] the description of the promised rest is evident. It shares with the prophets, the disciples of Jesus, and spiritual men throughout the centuries, both Jewish and Christian, the sacred hopes for peace from insurmountable enemies, for the absence of bitter tears, for the removal of shackles severe, for the calm of unencumbered relationships, and for the elimination of the constant pursuit of self interests.

5. Heschel, *Sabbath*, 23 (referring to Job 3:13, 17).

6. John does say earlier that the wicked have "no rest day nor night" (Rev 14:11).

THE TABERNACLE AND THE TEMPLE

The Tabernacle of Rest

Before the temple was conceived in David's mind, there was the tabernacle, itself the original, tangible figure of rest, which God Himself designed to display the riches of His grace and the beauties of His salvation. Before the tabernacle, the patriarchs constructed only makeshift altars to the God of heaven and earth, but now there was a place to call the house of God, a place for God's very presence among men. The symbolism of the tabernacle is vast and varied, alluded to in typological fashion in the NT writings of 1) the incarnation of Jesus Christ (John 1:14), 2) the collective and individual indwelling of God in church members (1 Cor 6:19; 2 Cor 6:16), and 3) the arrangement of heaven and earth (Heb 9:2–8). As Apostle John witnessed in an ecstatic vision the culmination and rectitude of all things in the creation of a new heaven and earth, the symbolism of the tabernacle was presented to him as a new Eden, cosmic and irrefrangible. A heavenly voice proclaims with assurance and wonder that the effects of the Adamic curse will finally be undone, placing a redeemed humanity in a better garden—heaven itself (Rev 21:3–4). The presence of God in the shekinah glory in the midst of Israel and the incarnation of God in the midst of history are antitypical enlargements of God's presence in the midst of the garden (Gen 3:8; Lev 19:30; 26:2). Yet it is the new heaven and earth that is the antitype of them all, for no more shall man run away from God in fear, but enjoy Him forever in blessed harmony and rest. The theme of rest is essentially about holy communion with God, but for there to be communion, God must descend from His lofty and magnificent abode and dwell among us, His people. The Lord sets off the splendor and majesty of this type by completing the revelation of Exodus with a record of the completion of the construction of the tabernacle (Exod 40). In stark contrast to the opening pages of Exodus, where Israel is "tabernacled" in a foreign land, far from the land promised to Abraham, and far from the God who called them, the final chapter of Exodus describes the desired result of fellowship with the God who condescended to be with man, "in the sight of all the house of Israel" (Exod 40:38).

The earthly tabernacle was designed and constructed for a nomadic people—of posts and canopies, pillars and draperies, precious metals and favored woods—that allowed for disassembly and reassembly at another location (Exod 40:34–38). Though the tabernacle moved from place to place, it still represented the distinct presence of God within the community. Though the architectural intent of the tabernacle featured its temporariness, each time it was set up, it came to its place of *rest*, assuring the Israelites that they too would eventually come to their place of rest in Canaan. Yet the tabernacle also represented the tension within man's soul: that God is there yet out-of-reach. The truth of God's reality and ubiquity, yet man's separation from Him, is confirmed by God's provision of a means to approach Him. Let God Himself reveal the way back to Eden, to the seventh day of rest. Let God fulfill the promises to Adam and Abraham and confirm with His people that He is pleased with them.

> And let them make Me a sanctuary, that I may dwell among them. According to all that I show you, that is, the pattern of the tabernacle and the pattern of all its furnishings, just so you shall make it. (Exod 25:8–9)

While in the wilderness, the people of Israel encamped around the tabernacle, but they could not by themselves enter into the presence of God, so the priest performed representative functions for the people. After Israel entered Canaan and assumed their territorial inheritance, the distance from the tabernacle accentuated the need for representative ministrations before the presence of God. So, every Sabbath day the work of the priests in the tabernacle constituted the "holy convocation" demanded in the Law (Lev 23:3). Faithful Jews throughout the land who observed the Sabbath in their community were counted by the Lord as appearing before the tabernacle through the representation of the priesthood. These holy convocations of representative worship have been bettered by the direct worship of the church, who, through the Holy Spirit, are assured of Christ's presence wherever they meet and of His overwhelming acceptance of them (Matt 18:20; Acts 10:35; Heb 4:16). Yet, even this does not compare to the glory we will experience at the final revelation when we will see Him as He is (1 John 3:2; Rev 22:3).

Chapters 25–31 of Exodus describe the details for the construction of the tabernacle, and chapters 35–40 relate its completion. The work of the tabernacle is preceded by six formulae of divine address to Moses (Exod 25:1; 30:11, 17, 22, 34; 31:1) reminiscent of the six days of creation, and the Sabbath institution marks the end of the first section and the beginning of the second section (Exod 31:12–17; 35:1–3) further associating the symbolism of sabbatic rest with the tabernacle. Not only that, the number fifty is the integral unit of measurement for the tabernacle boundaries, relating it to the Feast of Weeks (Pentecost) and Jubilee, both based upon the completion of sabbatic intervals (7x7+1). The tabernacle's north and south sides were one hundred cubits, the west and east sides fifty cubits, the perimeter of wholeness comprising six increments of fifty, displaying the symmetry and unity of the Godhead (Exod 26:6, 11; 36:13, 18). Hearkening back to Edenic geography, the sole opening to the tabernacle was on the east (Gen 3:23–4; Exod 27:13–19; 38:13) and the holy of holies containing the ark of the covenant was to the west (Exod 26:33), giving hope that undefiled access to God could somehow be regained by retracing the steps toward the Edenic gate where the cherubim stood guard and ultimately into the presence of God. Of the ten five-cubit increments of the eastern wall, four made up the "gate" composed of fine linen sheets of blue, red, and purple threads through which the worshippers passed. Worshippers could come *near* the presence of God, but the way into His effulgence, signified by the Holiest of Holies, was revealed only in types or copies (Heb 9:6–10).

> But Christ came as High Priest of the good things to come, with the greater and more perfect tabernacle not made with hands, that is, not of this creation. Not with the blood of goats and calves, but with His own blood He entered the Most Holy Place once for all, having obtained eternal redemption. (Heb 9:11–12)

That which the tabernacle typified has now been completed by the work of Jesus Christ upon the cross. He has entered heaven itself, the essence of rest with God, the climax of communion with God, affording us while on earth the confidence to approach God as a fully sanctified and redeemed people.

> For Christ has not entered the holy places made with hands, which are copies of the true, but into heaven itself, now to appear in the presence of God for us . . . (Heb 9:24)

The tabernacle, with its physical structure and attendant duties, is an artifact of a bygone era. The reality it promised remains for the children of God through the ministry of Jesus Christ, and it still foreshadows the ultimate fellowship with God in His very presence.

The Temple of Blood

The Lord affirmed that He would be the builder of the temple (1 Chr 17:10), indicating that it would continue to serve His purposes in proclaiming the glories of the coming Messiah and His kingdom of peace. At the temple dedication, Solomon, reflecting upon the words of Joshua when Canaan came into full possession of Israel, said, "Blessed be the Lord, who has given rest (*menuchah*) to His people Israel, according to all that He promised"(1 Kgs 8:56). Thus, the temple is a type of rest for the people of God as they fellowship with Him free from the distractions of external conflicts.

The temple was to Israel a monument and symbol of the completed rest that God had promised them centuries earlier during the exodus. In the center of the promised land was the city of David, and in the midst of that privileged city was the sanctuary of God, and within the depths of the temple was the glory of God. In its tripartite architectural form, the temple spoke of all that rest in God is: its splendor, its strength, its solace, its unity, its continuity, and its focus. There is unmitigated boasting about the place where God chose to inhabit, for the temple intimates an idyllic age when Jerusalem is the preferred nativity of all peoples (Ps 87). This borrows the archetypical images of Eden with its original inhabitants as the progenitors of a unified population and the four rivers flowing out from the garden as an unstoppable, all-encompassing blessing to the whole world. The temple planned and constructed by David and Solomon followed the general three-section design of the tabernacle, except that its perimeter was twice as long and the walls of stone three times as high. The doubling of the dimensions for the second "permanent" temple forecasts a temple yet to come that should exceed in every aspect and quality, and in duration. Like the tabernacle, the temple signified rest with God, causing the Lord to delay the actual construction of the temple to Solomon's reign to separate it from the bloodshed characterizing David's reign (1 Kgs 5:3, 5). However, the experience of peace and rest would eventually be polluted by man's blood.

First, the temple was destroyed during the invasion of the Babylonians circa 586 BCE due to Israel's violation of the Sabbath of the Land (2 Kgs 25:8–17; Jer 52:12–23). The temple and the land stood for rest, but Israel failed to honor the significance of that rest (2 Chr 36:21). David's concept of rest and his ability to provide an ongoing rest were wanting. Some seventy years later, a second temple was constructed upon the return of the Jews from exile (Ezra 1:1–11; 4:3). Similar in dimensions to the Solomonic temple, the Zerubbabel temple was notably lacking the ark of the covenant, the Urim and Thummin, and the shekinah glory. The absence of the ark was especially disconcerting since David planned the temple to be a place of rest for the ark (1 Chr 28:2). After construction of this second temple resumed, a ceremony of praise interrupted the progress after the foundations were laid (Ezra 3:11–13). The new temple aroused inward tension among the participants as some wept as they remembered what they lost and others rejoiced in what was being accomplished. Although some of the grandeur was diminished, His promises remained in full force and the mimesis of heavenly things continued to function until the appointed time. This signified again that the temple could never bring peace to the land.

It was this second temple that Herod rebuilt and refurbished in 20 BCE that awaited the birth of Christ, and though it bore Herod's name, it came to be the place where the Lord's name was glorified. The angel Gabriel appeared to Zaccharias, a Levite priest, in the holy place of the temple to announce the forerunner, John, while scores of worshippers were outside offering prayers of praise and petitions. As Edersheim astutely recognized, this particular moment of solemn, earthly worship at the temple parallels a scene revealed later in the Apocalypse (Rev 8:1–4). This earthy model of worship simulated heavenly worship in subdued fashion: for as great as Herod's temple was, a greater-than-the-temple would soon arrive (Matt 12:6). In spite of the reverence the temple inspired throughout Judea as an emblem of its spiritual heritage and splendor, it would eventually be burned and dismantled to its very foundation just as Christ had predicted (Matt 24:1–2; Luke 21:5–6).

Flavius Josephus related, as an eyewitness and emissary, the destruction of Jerusalem and the holy temple by Titus, Vespasian's son.[7] There were several factional groups within the city walls, and even while Roman legions staged themselves in the bucolic outskirts of Jerusalem, a group led by Simon, son of Giora, took control of the temple area and slaughtered many of their kinsmen. Four Roman legions encamped around Jerusalem, and over the course of months thousands of men were slaughtered in skirmishes and hundreds succumbed to famine and disease within the city walls. In and around the City of Peace, dead bodies of its inhabitants were hurled over walls without burial, mothers witnessed the starvation and murder of their young, and Roman soldiers eviscerated would-be escapees suspected of swallowing money. Eventually the battering rams pummeled the walls until a breach could be made, and the Roman army advanced incrementally, showing little mercy to the obstinate Jewish rebels who resisted them.

> Yet was the misery itself more terrible than this disorder; for one would have thought that the hill itself, on which the temple stood, was seething hot, as full of fire on every part of it, that the blood was larger in quantity than the fire, and

7. Fortuitous delays of the Roman siege allowed Christians to escape Jerusalem as they heeded Jesus' warnings of the impending judgment of that city and its temple.

> those that were slain more in number than those that slew them; for the ground did nowhere appear visible, for the dead bodies that lay on it; but the soldiers went over heaps of these bodies, as they ran upon such as fled from them.[8]

Ironically, the place God chose to dwell became a place of indescribable human carnage and misery. The city that promised to be the birthplace of nations became a mortuary, and the temple grounds dedicated to peace became the site of fratricide. Every internal war revealed a hidden conflict with Jehovah, and each breach of the covenant written on stone invited a breach of the city walls. All hopes for a return to Eden faded in view of such brutality and decimation, as all expectations of true worship languished without a temple. Despite the desire of Titus to preserve the temple for future Roman use, the actions of Jewish rebels and inflamed soldiers led to the inevitable razing of the temple. So, as Josephus calculated, the destruction of Herod's temple was decreed by God, because its fall, in 70 CE, came on the same month and day when Solomon's temple was destroyed by the Babylonians.

> "Behold, the eyes of the Lord *God* are on the sinful kingdom, And I will destroy it from the face of the earth; Yet I will not utterly destroy the house of Jacob," says the *Lord*.
>
> "For surely I will command, And will sift the house of Israel among all nations, As grain is sifted in a sieve; Yet not the smallest grain shall fall to the ground.
>
> All the sinners of My people shall die by the sword, Who say, 'The calamity shall not overtake nor confront us.'
>
> "On that day I will raise up The tabernacle of David, which has fallen down, And repair its damages; I will raise up its ruins, And rebuild it as in the days of old;
>
> That they may possess the remnant of Edom, And all the Gentiles who are called by My name," Says the *Lord* who does this thing. (Amos 9:8–12)

The imagery of Amos' prophecy in chapter 9 has an uncanny similarity to Josephus' record of doom of Jerusalem and is repeated here for two reasons. First of all, the judgment of the Lord *begins at the altar* that stands before the temple in the court of priests, the very altar upon which thousands of lambs were slain. Secondly, Amos *ends with the gospel* of God's kingdom that calls out to the Gentiles for salvation. Only years before its destruction, the Apostle James referred to this prophecy at the Christian council in Jerusalem as applying to the issue of subjecting Gentile believers to Jewish laws.

This prophecy does not apply alone to the first destruction of Jerusalem by the Babylonians because the carnage was not as great, the rebuilt city and temple did not match the previous exaltation, nor did salvation reach out to the remnant of Edom. However, James' understanding of Amos, as he quotes from the Septuagint, is that the conversion of Gentiles by Barnabas and Paul is a sign of the Messianic Kingdom, and hence the Lord's coming. There were other ancient texts that James could have cited to defend the evangelization of the Gentiles; however, this one was understood

8. Josephus, *J.W.* 6.5.1, 741.

to be a Messianic passage.[9] However, in the order presented by Amos, before rebuilding, restoration, or renewal can begin, there must first be a judgment of cataclysmic proportions, otherwise, to what is the Lord "returning"? This may account for James' paraphrase at just this point, as if he were putting together in his mind Jesus' prophecy of impending judgment on Jerusalem and a worldwide outreach. The restoration of the "tabernacle" of David refers not to the temple or sanctuary of God, but to David's fallen dynasty, now likened to the simple hut (*succoth*) built for the Feast of Tabernacles, which recalled when Israel was judged unworthy to enter the land of rest. Amos envisions the rebuilding of cities, the reestablishment of agriculture, the regathering of Israel, but *not* the reconstruction of the temple—not in the gospel age! There will be no need of a monument commemorating the blessing of rest, for it will be personified in Jesus Christ, in whom those chosen from every nation will be named.

9. Clarke, *Commentary*, 5:802 (Acts 15:16).

7

The Sabbath in the Gospels

TEACHING ON THE SABBATH

Jesus at the Synagogue

CHRIST BEGAN HIS MINISTRY in Galilee, preaching on the Sabbath and healing the infirmed, and upon his return to Nazareth, He was invited by synagogue leaders to teach the congregation (Luke 4:16). On this particular Sabbath, He expounded a messianic passage from Isaiah, which described His ministerial functions of preaching and healing (Isa 66:1–2; cf. Isa 58:5–7). It is no wonder that the Lord Jesus chose this messianic passage to announce His mission statement, for it condenses the gospel portraits of teaching and healing within the context of a sabbatical and eschatological motif. His teaching and healing aroused controversy on this Sabbath day because His work of redemption was thematically sabbatic. That is, the failure to properly understand the Sabbath predisposed the Jews to misunderstand Jesus. The significance of this passage should not be underestimated, because it "sets the agenda for the entire Gospel of Luke."[1]

Though there are no direct commandments in the OT supporting the practice of synagogue meetings and Scripture readings on the seventh day of the week (cf. Deut 31:9–13), Jesus' participation in this activity lends credibility to the divine development and heavenly approval of this tradition. History supports the thesis that the foundations for first-century synagogal worship were laid after the deportation of Israel to Babylonia following the destruction of the Solomonic temple in 587–598 BCE. It is proposed that without a temple the people could not meet with God, but with a local template of what was lost in the form of the temple in Jerusalem, it was hoped that the religious duties of the Jews toward God could be satisfied.[2] Jewish interpretations of Ezekial 11:16, in which the Lord promises to "be a little sanctuary for them in the countries where they have gone," hope to defend this shift from temple worship to synagogue worship. This interpretation misses the point of the metaphor, but even if taken literally, the context of Ezekiel further promises a return of scattered Israelites back to Jerusalem for a united form of worship, so synagogal worship should

1. Porter, *Hearing the Old Testament*, 111.

2. Weilerstein, *Jewish Heroes*, 2:114.

have ended once the Zerubbabel temple was completed. As such, the origin of the synagogue has been a topic of contemporary interest.[3]

Runneson notes that two Greek words were used to describe these public gatherings: *sunagoge* (assembly) and *proseuche* (house of prayer), conveying perhaps disparate origins of the synagogue; the former serving as a socio-political means to establish and maintain control of the community by the Persians, and the latter serving the religious goal of instruction and revitalization of its members. Runneson suggests that during the repopulation of Israel, assemblies occurred first at the city gates and then progressed to meeting rooms and eventually edifices specifically designed for these purposes. Nehemiah records, upon the return of the Israelites to Jerusalem, such an instance of public gathering at the city gates for the purposes of hearing the Law of God, not only its rehearsal, but its expository teaching for the understanding of the men and women assembled together "as one man" (Neh 8:1). If this is indeed a portrayal of the rudiments of synagogal practice as well as the authority to establish that tradition, then we must take note, too, that the occasion for this tradition was not the Sabbath, but the New Moon, specifically Rosh Hashana. Indeed, the men returned to Ezra to hear more from the word of the Lord on the next day (Neh 8:2) and throughout that festive month, concluding in a sacred assembly on the eighth day, the day after the Sabbath (Neh 8:18). The themes of this passage anticipate the mission of Christ's church based on His resurrection.

Edersheim proposes that upon Jesus' return to Nazareth, He was selected by one of the rulers to read from the prophets and deliver a sermon on the upcoming Sabbath. With the confidence and understanding of one having divine authority, Jesus expounded the word of God written by Isaiah, "so all bore witness to Him, and marveled at the gracious words which proceeded out of his mouth" (Luke 4:22). A full sermon was delivered, however, Luke records only the most memorable, perhaps the most significant, remark: "Today this Scripture is fulfilled in your hearing" (Luke 4:21). The sermon was followed by a question and answer period during which the doubters and skeptics prevailed, to whom Jesus retorted that God was not willing to bless the inhabitants of Nazareth with healing because of their lack of faith. His response insulted and infuriated the whole congregation (Luke 4:28). This exchange of words presaged Christ's upcoming years of gospel ministry among the Jews: He would be scorned instead of worshipped, and their national unfaithfulness would be rejected in favor of the humility and faith of the Gentiles.

Returning to the passage of Isaiah (Isa 66:1–2), it is crucial to address some particulars. First of all, since this passage refers to the work of the Holy Spirit—the anointing and commissioning to perform this heavenly ministry—ancient Rabbinic writings recognized the messianic emphasis of this passage.[4] Several themes dominate this passage: the work of the Holy Spirit in redemption, the duties of the Messiah in preaching and healing, the liberation of captive Israel, and the announcement of the

3. Runneson, *Ancient Synagogue*, 16–19; Orlinski, *Synagogue*, 3–72; Edersheim, *Life and Times*, 171, 298–312.

4. Edersheim, *The Life and Times*, 1000; Porter, *Hearing the Old Testament*, 113–14.

Jubilee year. These themes are reminiscent of the deliverance from Egyptian bondage and invoke the anticipation of the Prophet-Messiah, miraculous and powerful phenomena, freedom from oppression, and closer fellowship with God. Secondly, it would seem that the day of this announcement held particular importance in Jesus' mind: "*Today* this Scripture is fulfilled in your hearing" (Luke 4:21). This was not a matter of Jesus continuing in the anticipatory history of Israel, but of fulfilling what was previously recorded in Scripture. He is the end to which the Law and the Prophets pointed (Matt 5:17). He turns prophecy into history, and shadows into reality. Christ's ministry was predicted and foreshadowed, thus allowing confirmation of His office through the fulfillment of Scripture. Therefore, Jesus affirmed to those attending the synagogue on that Sabbath that His life and His work were the fulfillment of messianic Scripture (Luke 7:22).

His reference to the fulfillment of the year of Jubilee—a special Sabbath for the land and the people of God, following a sequence of seven sabbatic years—highlights His assertion that the sabbatic structure of time was completely fulfilled by His glorious presence. The Jubilee was now at hand; it was made complete in the living presence of the Son of God. The blare of silver trumpets to announce the onset of the Jubilee was now fulfilled in the proclamation of Jesus Christ—that the joy of salvation and the gladness of release could be experienced now through faith. Jesus' claim that the Jubilee was fulfilled implies that the Sabbatic Year and the Sabbath are likewise fulfilled in Himself.[5] By announcing the fulfillment of the Jubilee, when in fact the Jubilee had not yet arrived, Jesus declared that His Jubilee is an ongoing reality and no longer a semicentennial event. What was illustrated in the rarest of their national ceremonies would become the daily experience of those who turn to him brokenhearted, that they may be healed; as prisoners, that they might be released; and as spiritually blind, that they may be illuminated. Christ's Jubilee mission was to set men free from the tyranny of their sin, a far greater need than the temporary economic freedom of the national Jubilee. Jesus did not come to teach about the Jubilee, but to fulfill it.

HEALING ON THE SABBATH

The Conflict Begins

Some suppose that Christ came to teach the proper way to keep the Sabbath, but His instructions about the Sabbath are best understood in relationship to His messianic duty to proclaim the Acceptable Year. The violent reaction to His Sabbath conduct was primarily because of unbelief in His messianic claims as opposed to differing interpretations of Sabbath law. It must be reemphasized that the rabbinic traditions concerning the Sabbath arose during preceding centuries from the zealous desire to keep the Sabbath holy. They reasoned, with all intentions of honoring the Lord and properly interpreting Scripture, that it was better to err on the safe side of debatable issues (legalism) than risk standing in liberty. Whatever earthly discomfort was incurred by keeping these pious traditions paled in comparison to the judgment of God for

5. Bonar, *Leviticus*, 451.

failing to keep holy the Sabbath day. The unfortunate consequence was that these additions to the law became a stumbling block to the recognition of the Messiah when He came. That is, when Jesus healed on the Sabbath, instead of witnessing the fulfillment of messianic prophecy, the Sanhedrin saw only a rebellious Sabbath-breaker. While they deemed that no godly prophet, and certainly not the Messiah, would controvert the law of God (John 9:16), their hypocrisy as spiritual shepherds was exposed (John 10:9–11; Ezek 34:4). As leaders of Israel, they failed the people by blinding them to the true typological nature of the Sabbath, which was to urge men everywhere to cease from their own works and rest in the salvation of the Lord.

Oral Teachings

Various oral traditions existed at the time of Christ, some of which can be discerned in the Talmud, which was redacted around 200 CE. Christians assume that the various sects of Judaism observed the same rules of conduct on the Sabbath; however, there were various interpretations about what was permissible and what was not. For example, the House of Shammai discouraged comforting mourners and visiting the sick on the Sabbath, while the house of Hillel permitted it.[6] Yet the Pharisees held a position of power and influence, so they felt compelled to challenge the lifestyle and doctrines of this new and popular teacher. Edersheim relates some of the rules and regulations that may have concerned the matter of effecting a cure on the Sabbath; for example, ear packings were allowed to remain in the ear if placed prior to the Sabbath but could not be replaced if they fell out on the Sabbath day. A dressing for a wound may be applied on the Sabbath only to prevent an injury from worsening, but not for the purpose of healing. Crutches may be used but false teeth may not, for if the latter inadvertently fell from the mouth, the owner would be tempted to pick up the burden. "Bones might not be set, nor emetics given, nor any medical or surgical operation performed."[7] Indeed, only those remedies believed to prevent the actual loss of life were allowed, such as a medicine that kept the airway patent. However, if a remedy would simply improve a situation or cure a non-life-threatening ailment, it was not allowed. Luke documents this pious yet unmerciful interpretation of God's law in which six days are allowed for the purposes of healing, but the seventh is reserved for those devotional activities marked by unconcern for the interests of the flesh (Luke 13:16). But is this what was intended by God in the Sabbath commandment?

Call the Sabbath a Delight

The OT parameters of acceptable Sabbath behavior consisted mainly of prohibitive commands with one rare exception found in Isaiah.

> If you turn away your foot from the Sabbath, From doing your pleasure on My holy day, And call the Sabbath a delight, The holy day of the Lord honorable,

6. Auerbach, *Babylonian Talmud*, 60.

7. Edersheim, *Life and Times*, 1050–54.

> And shall honor Him, not doing your own ways, Nor finding your own pleasure, Nor speaking your own words. (Isa 58:13)

To call the Sabbath a delight was to distinguish it as a day to honor the Lord in ways not possible on other days. Isaiah was correcting the pervading attitude that the Sabbath was an inconvenient, difficult, and monotonous commandment. The Israelites at that time favored the mundane as opposed to the heavenly, but God ordered their week to establish a difference between the mundane and the heavenly through a ceremonial calendar that spoke of better things. It was not that God undervalued the first six days of the week, but those days found meaning through the significance of the Sabbath. The Sabbath, by completing the week, intimated that all of life was to be directed toward the spiritual.

Yet the dichotomy between the lifestyle of ordinary days and those acceptable behaviors enjoined by Sabbath observance can lend itself to hyperpiety, especially if the spiritual foreshadowing is not discerned. The Sabbath prohibited doing your own things, seeking your own pleasures, and speaking your own words, but not to the exclusion of such enjoyments and necessities that one becomes, as it were, a prisoner shackled to the Sabbath (Mark 2:27). Yet those who attempt to keep the Sabbath must develop a system of applications, both tolerable and rigorous, otherwise the Sabbath becomes indistinguishable from any other day. And those who adhere to their system eventually must ascribe a special holiness or merited grace to what they choose to do or not to do, or a special insight to understanding the Scriptures in ways less obvious to others. Heschel eulogizes the decision of the following Sabbath-keeper as capturing the essential attitude of heart and mind:

> A pious man once took a stroll in his vineyard on the Sabbath. He saw a breach in the fence, and then determined to mend it when the Sabbath would be over. At the expiration of the Sabbath, he decided: since the thought of repairing the fence occurred to me on the Sabbath I shall never repair it.[8]

Heschel litters his essay with examples of the pious dichotomizing that germinates from Sabbath observance, such as, "Six days a week we seek to dominate the world, on the seventh day we try to dominate the self,"[9] as if mastery over self is not a daily concern. Even the Christian, who regards the Sabbath commandment on equal footing with the other nine, is prone to the development of hyperpiety. Christian Sabbatarians often promote the Sabbath as the means to save western civilization.

> Nothing but a weekly day of worship will begin to touch the ignorance which has gripped humanity. This alone, under God, can save families, churches, schools and governments from total moral collapse. Only as God's people return to the habit of engaging in systematic spiritual exercises for an entire day each week, then will the moral fabric of our age begin to be strengthened.[10]

8. Heschel, *Sabbath*, 32.

9. Ibid., 13, 30.

10. Chantry, *Call the Sabbath a Delight*, 11, 12; Dawn, *Keeping the Sabbath*, 43.

Hopkins asserted at the National Sabbath Convention of 1863 that the "religious observance of the Sabbath will insure the permanence of free institutions, because it promotes health and wealth, a spirit of enterprise, and those forms of material prosperity which will result in the contentment of some people."[11] This is similar to the Jewish hope that if they "would observe the Sabbath properly even once, the son of David [the Messiah] would come."[12] But proper Sabbath-keeping was not intended to be the catalyst for the arrival of the Messiah, nor is sabbatizing the Lord's Day the means to transform our fallen world.

The Sabbath was intended to encourage the weekly preeminence of the Lord in the mind of the Jewish people: His sovereign intendance of the nation and each individual, His provision for their daily needs and His readiness to answer their cries for help, His forbearance of their sin and His merciful cleansing of their conscience. Yet the Sabbath was merely the ceremonial means to encourage the very activities and attitudes now inspired by the Holy Spirit in the heart and mind of each believer in Jesus Christ (Rom 5:5; 8:13; 9:1; 14:17; 15:13). The Sabbath could only speak of Christ in subdued form, but the mission of the Holy Spirit is to proclaim Christ fully (John 15:26)

> Then you shall delight yourself in the Lord; And I will cause you to ride on the high hills of the earth, And feed you with the heritage of Jacob your father. The mouth of the Lord has spoken. (Isa 58:14)

Isaiah places the Lord above the day; delighting in the Sabbath should have led to delighting in the Lord. Those who delighted in the Lord were pledged a heavenly habitation glistening from the vantage point of earth's spectacular heights and promised salvation gleaming in the shared blessings of Jacob. Victory over surrounding enemies and full possession of the land promised to Abraham were symbolic promises of the benefits of salvation that the Sabbath also portrayed in symbolic form.[13] To delight in the Lord was to possess and prize those things in which the Lord Himself delights, such as mercy (Micah 7:8), integrity and honesty (Prov 11:1; 12:22), uprightness and purity (Prov 11:20), and prayers of faith (Prov 15:8). The Jew was asked to call the Sabbath a delight, whereas the Christian calls the Lord his delight. The Jew had one day in seven to devote to the Lord, whereas every day is full of spirituality for the Christian. To the Jew, each day of the week is viewed as a pilgrimage toward the Sabbath, but for the believer in Jesus Christ, each day of his earthly life is a pilgrimage toward his eternal rest with Jesus. To the Jew, the Sabbath is a bride and queen, cherished and prized; to the Christian, Jesus Christ is the beloved groom and exalted King, adored and worshipped. For the faithful Israelites of old, to call the Sabbath a delight was to see Christ pictured therein.

11. Hopkins, "The Sabbath and Free Institutions," n.p.

12. Hertzberg, *Judaism*, 117.

13. Pipa admits the symbolism of the former, but denies the symbolism of the latter. Pipa, *Lord's Day*, 12–24.

ACCUSED OF BREAKING THE SABBATH

There are six gospel portrayals of Jesus healing on the Sabbath: 1) the man with the paralyzed hand (Matt 12:9–14; Mark 3:1–6; Luke 6:6–11), 2) various sick persons in Nazareth (Mark 6:1–6), 3) an infirmed woman (Luke 13:10–17), 4) a certain man with dropsy (Luke 14:1–6), 5) the infirmed man at the pool of Bethesda (John 5:1–14; 7:19–24), and 6) the blind man (John 9:1–34). The various reactions of the pious elite were as follows: to persecute Jesus and plot to kill him (John 5:16); anger (John 9:23); to be filled with fury and connive to do harm (Luke 6:11); to indignantly correct Jesus (Luke 13:14); silence (Luke 14:4); and unbelief (Mark 6:5). No matter what day of the week Jesus chose to heal, it was a raw demonstration of His heavenly authority and power, but when He healed on the Sabbath, the context shifted to that of typological fulfillment, His messianic credentials, and redemption. These Sabbath confrontations were less an opportunity for teaching observers godly Sabbath manners than they were for identifying just how far Israel had drifted from knowing the Lord.

However, from the standpoint of teaching proper Sabbath conduct, Jesus stated that it was fitting to give water to one's animals and to rescue an animal in danger; that is, to do good even to animals on the Sabbath (Matt 12:11, 12; Luke 13:15; 14:5); that it was ethical to do good and to save a life (Luke 6:9) and to circumcise a man (John 7:22). These statements do not provide much additional information concerning the liberty with which to balance the restrictions in the Torah. Furthermore, His citations that it was proper on the Sabbath to circumcise and to save a life were allowances already understood by the Pharisees.

Aryeh Kaplan believes there is a sabbatic connection between the manna and creation, noting that the Lord worked miracles on six days, but refrained from the miraculous on the Sabbath.[14] This may help explain the origin of the Pharisee's objection to Christ miraculously healing on the Sabbath. When Jesus was challenged about healing on the Sabbath, His answer—that healing was in the same category of "works" as religious duties and acts of mercy—was intended to remove the religiously imposed stumbling block to their acceptance of the signs of His messiahship and not merely to set the record straight about the legitimacy of miraculously healing on the Sabbath. Who else was healing the infirmed by a spoken word, let alone on a Sabbath day? Obviously, when Jesus healed a person on the Sabbath, He was entirely within the scope of Sabbath observance for He neither lifted a burden nor accepted wages.

> And therefore the Lord reproved those who unjustly blamed Him for having healed upon the Sabbath-days. For He did not make void, but fulfilled the law, by performing the offices of the High Priest, propitiating God for men, and cleansing the lepers, healing the sick, and Himself suffering death, that exiled man might go forth from condemnation, and might return without fear to his own inheritance.[15]

14. Kaplan, *Sabbath*, 15.
15. Irenaeus, *Haer.* 4.8.2 (*ANF* 1:471).

The Pharisees were guilty of hypocrisy for disallowing healing while allowing other good deeds and they were guilty of disbelief when the miracles were performed. Even if the rabbis were convinced that healing on the Sabbath was proper to do, it would settle only an intellectual matter and not the issues of their heart.

There are two perplexing situations recorded in the Gospels that brought the accusation against Jesus of disregarding the grandeur of the seventh day: 1) healing an impotent man and commanding him to carry his bedding, and 2) allowing his disciples to pluck and eat corn, and then defending them. Both of these accounts also deal with the authority of Jesus to command others what they could do on the Sabbath. If Jesus wanted to dispute halachic law, He could have done so diplomatically by quoting the learned rabbis of the past and providing His analysis of Scripture before inflaming His audience by fractious actions. Thus, the design of these Sabbath conflicts was to accomplish something more profound than merely correcting legal misunderstandings.

The Case of the Bed-carrying Man

Only Apostle John records this miracle and he does so as the first instance of a Sabbath conflict in his gospel (John 5). The prelude to the conflict records how Jesus, while visiting Jerusalem for a feast, went by the Pool of Bethesda ("House of Mercy") where a multitude of blind, lame, and paralyzed people gathered hoping for a miraculous cure by the stirring of those waters. Jesus presented Himself to the one man who could not help himself into the waters.[16]

> Jesus said to him, "Rise, take up your bed and walk."
>
> And immediately the man was made well, took up his bed, and walked. And that day was the Sabbath.
>
> The Jews therefore said to him who was cured, "It is the Sabbath; it is not lawful for you to carry your bed."
>
> He answered them, "He who made me well said to me, 'Take up your bed and walk.'" (John 5:8–11)

John carries us from the expectation of healing by a pool to healing by a person in order to demonstrate that the glory of the Lord had appeared to Israel as prophesied by Isaiah (Isa 35:5–7). Christ eventually related the man's healing to sin (John 5:14), so this passage reflects John's intent to relate this account to a redemptive theme. The physical state of those hoping for a cure parallels the spiritual affliction of the lost: those too weak to lift themselves from their sinful ways, those blinded in their hearts to the saving words of the gospel, and those paralyzed in their soul from ever seeking God.

Sabbath-Breaker. The initial concern of the Jewish leaders was twofold: first, that Jesus healed on the Sabbath, and second, that the man carried his bedding at Jesus' behest. The escalation of anger implies that carrying a burden on the Sabbath was more serious a breach than healing on the Sabbath. Certainly, Jesus did not break the Sabbath by healing the man, because His act of healing was consistent with the Torah

16. If the man had been healed at the pool on the Sabbath, would the Pharisees have accused God of breaking the Sabbath?

(John 7:19–24). Holding Jesus to the example of God in the wilderness—performing miracles only on the first six days of the week—proved to be a detrimental misconception of the prerogatives of God. As Ironside noted, "they should have expected God to work," because God has been working every day for the redemption of sinful men.[17] The Pharisees did not perceive the work of God in redeeming the life of a helpless man and focused only on the work of that man in carrying his bedding on the Sabbath, an activity seemingly in opposition to the declared will of God. The Pharisees were well acquainted with the prophecy of Jeremiah and its fulfillment in history.

> Thus says the *Lord*: "Take heed to yourselves, and bear no burden on the Sabbath day, nor bring it in by the gates of Jerusalem;
> nor carry a burden out of your houses on the Sabbath day, nor do any work, but hallow the Sabbath day, as I commanded your fathers." (Jer 17:21–22)

Jeremiah's admonition was weighty, for if the Jews carried burdens in disregard to the holiness of the day, the Lord threatened to carry them *and their possessions* away to foreign lands as a consequence of inflaming His wrath (Jer 17:27; 20:4–5). The Jews had reason to believe that a burden included their wealth, produce, and possessions, and was not necessarily limited to the work of one's occupation. Of the thirty-nine principle categories of forbidden acts in the Talmud, the thirty-ninth applied to carrying burdens: taking an object from the private domain to the public, or transporting an object in the public domain.[18] The leaders were obliged to ascertain the nature of the infraction and to prescribe a punishment in order to forestall any further judgment from God. Certainly, carrying one's bedding could be compared to the Numbers 15 incident of gathering sticks, which *did* incur the death penalty.

The Sabbath tractate advances the idea that carrying a thing is related to both work and rest. Rest is a state that people and things enjoy, but that state can be disturbed by work, through use or performance, by action upon or change, and by transportation. In the case of the man carrying his bedding, the man acted upon the bedding by rolling it, picking it up, and then transporting it from its place of rest while in a public area. Though there are no case examples specific to this matter, it could be inferred that carrying bedding was similar to carrying other burdens: "The same is the case with mats of which tents were made, whereby the ground enclosed by the mats becomes private; and if many such tents were made, carrying from one tent into another is permitted, provided an Erubh is made. If the mats were rolled up, however, such carrying is not permitted."[19] The man's bedding was his domain, so he was not allowed to move his domain by rolling it up and carrying it elsewhere. Given this backdrop, the Jews had reason to believe that the man, and Jesus who intentionally gave the command, profaned the Sabbath.

Commentators have proposed a variety of explanations for this controversial command, and it is not always clear whether the healed man violated the Mosaic

17. Ironside, *John*, 186.
18. *b. Shabbat* 73a–73b.
19. *b. Shabbat* 101b, trans. Rodkinson.

law or a man-made tradition. The answer to this question affects the conclusions one makes regarding Christ's motive and justification for provoking the dispute. Some commentators, despite the evidence above, believe that Jesus' command breached no clear proscription in the Torah. Those less sure about the clarity of the command to carry no burden suggest that since Jesus gave the law, He would not break it. Therefore His command must have been within the scope of proper Sabbath-keeping. This is not an unreasonable view considering the minutia-minded rabbinical traditions that earned Jesus' criticism (Matt 23:1–4).

As legalistic as the Pharisees were, Jesus' answer does not address their concern with halacha; His studied advice to the Pharisees after observing their reaction was, "do not judge according to appearance, but judge with righteous judgment" (John 7:24), indicating that His defense comes strictly from the Torah. It was not enough that Jesus merely expose the Pharisees' obvious sin of hypocrisy, but He wanted to reveal the truth about who He is. Already in the Mosaic law are laws that allow the breaking of the Sabbath with impunity, and these laws justified Jesus in the performance of a work of redemption on the Sabbath. Likewise, Jesus' command to the healed man exerted his lordship of the Sabbath in two significant ways.

First of all, just as God commanded Israelite parents to break the Sabbath by carrying their eight-day old baby to the priests to be circumcised, so could Jesus command the healed man to carry his bedding in view of his healing and redemption. The former portrayed the faith of the parents in the Lord's ability to circumcise the wicked heart of men and the latter portrayed the faith of the healed man in Jesus to forgive his sins. If Jesus had merely corrected the Pharisees about a tradition, he would not have demonstrated His lordship over the Sabbath. The demonstration of His authority must parallel the authority of divine law. "If the Sabbath is nullified by this insignificant ritual [circumcision]," as Goppelt recognizes, "how much more is it nullified by the great thing Jesus did—the healing of an entire person."[20] That the Sabbath law was to be abolished is apparent in the OT, for the priests, who by command worked on the Sabbath, "disobeyed" the Sabbath. The priests were allowed to break the Sabbath because they simulated the God of all mercies by offering sacrifices and oblations on the seventh day on behalf of the nation. Ironically, the Pharisees attempted to deny to others what they allowed for themselves—God working on their behalf.

Secondly, the Sabbath law restricting carrying a burden was specifically chosen by Jesus to speak of its typological fulfillment in Christ. Quoting again Goppelt, "Jesus justifies this breach of the Sabbath by declaring that his work is identical with God's work" (John 5:17).[21] Of course, once the healed man was seen by the Pharisees and confronted for his disobedience to the law of Moses, he identified Jesus as the person who both healed him and told him to carry his bed. Jesus' answer is instructive.

> But Jesus answered them, "My Father has been working until now, and I have been working."

20. Goppelt, *Typos*, 192.

21. Ibid., 192.

> Therefore the Jews sought all the more to kill Him, because He not only broke the Sabbath, but also said that God was His Father, making Himself equal with God.
>
> Then Jesus answered and said to them, "Most assuredly, I say to you, the Son can do nothing of Himself, but what He sees the Father do; for whatever He does, the Son also does in like manner. (John 5:17–19)

Jesus' answer on that Sabbath day appears to be a tacit admission that the healed man *was* working by carrying his bedding. The lame man, now healed, worked; Jesus, who healed, worked, just as the Father in heaven has worked ever since the creation to redeem broken men. Just as Jesus did what He saw the Father do, so the man did what he saw the Son do; thus, the man's work was God's work (John 14:9–11). The accusation that Jesus was breaking the Sabbath by commanding the man to carry his bed was tantamount to accusing God of breaking the Sabbath by commanding the priests to offer up sacrifices on the Sabbath. It was proper to do the work of God on the Sabbath and Jesus equated Himself with God who works redemptively everyday for His people. Only as an extension of the divine will of Christ could the man be justified in carrying a burden on the Sabbath.

Why were the Israelites prohibited from carrying a burden in the first place? It was to demonstrate that during the true rest of redemption, their burden of sin no longer had to be carried by them. The lame man's healing displayed that very redemptive rest and so the Lord released him from the Mosaic law that foreshadowed the newness of life realized in Christ. What kind of authority must a person have to defy a Mosaic law as opposed to a tradition?

We would be remiss to think that Christ's object-lesson was to cause the Pharisees to rethink their definition of a burden; for example, you can carry a beach towel but not an ice cooler. His command to the man was intended to create an opportunity to proclaim His nature and authority, which if rightly understood would have bearing on Sabbath law (John 7:21–24). The debatable nature of these Sabbath conflicts was to both obscure and proclaim the gospel message intended in them (Luke 10:21–24), so that those with eyes to see may see Jesus, their Savior, and those without eyes to see will see only a lawbreaker and blasphemer. John develops this obvious theme by relating the account of the healing of the blind man (John 9), again on the Sabbath, to His power to redeem men to whom it was given to believe and be healed (John 12:37–41). The second aspect of engendering these Sabbath conflicts was to subtly claim the fulfillment of the Sabbath by His advent. If Jesus has the power to heal the lame and the authority to contravene the law, then He has the right to proclaim His gospel message: "He who hears My word and believes in Him who sent Me has everlasting life, and shall not come into judgment, but has passed from death into life" (John 5:24).

Forty Less One. Christ wasn't merely claiming similarity with God, but equality. Likening His healing and command to the man to carry his bedding to the continuous work of God upholding the universe and caring for Israel was claiming to Himself the exceptional privileges of deity. That is, Christ was stating that He superseded Sabbath law in His person. The Pharisees considered Jesus to be destroying the law, but Christ objected that there is a difference between destroying and fulfilling: "I did not come to destroy but to fulfill" (Matt 5:17).

The prohibition from work on the Sabbath meant that our work, no matter what it is, is insufficient to effect redemption. The Sabbath envisioned the day that all those of faith enter into God's presence on the basis of some extraordinarily divine work that no mere man could do. Everything that Jesus did was what the Father prescribed for Him to do and was in alignment with His calling, His vocation, and His life's work; but the Jews had to suspend their God-given work on the Sabbath in deference to the work of the forthcoming Messiah. Christ's calling and occupation were to heal, to proclaim liberty, and to redeem a people to Himself—a work that was only foreshadowed in the occupations of Moses and Aaron. Moses whined, "I am not able to bear all these people alone, because the burden is too heavy for me" (Num 11:14), but our Lord Jesus is able to single-handedly provide rest for every weary soul that comes to Him. Aaron was expected to bear the names of Israel upon his shoulders when he entered the holy place (Exod 28:12), but soon failed in his calling to care for Israel by fabricating a false idol of gold (Exod 32:3–6). But Jesus, our Lord, is able to uphold the government upon His shoulders and to assume as rightful heir the Davidic kingdom (Isa 9:6–7).

As discussed in chapter 4, the Jews reasoned that the prohibited works were those involved in the construction of the tabernacle, the building of the place of worship and sacrifice.[22] As a result of this initial supposition, the Jews compiled an inventory of thirty-nine principle categories of work, which they referred to as "forty, less one."[23] But why say, "Forty, less one" instead of thirty-nine? This implies the existence of one more unspoken work.

> See, I have called by name Bezalel the son of Uri, the son of Hur, of the tribe of Judah.
>
> And I have filled him with the Spirit of God, in wisdom, in understanding, in knowledge, and in all manner of workmanship,
>
> to design artistic works, to work in gold, in silver, in bronze,
>
> in cutting jewels for setting, in carving wood, and to work in all manner of workmanship. (Exod 31:2–5)

Our occupation is a calling from God, and it begins with Him calling us by name (Matt 1:21). Our work is intended to *earn us a living*; it is the means by which we provide for ourselves, our families, and even the destitute, and which ultimately brings inner satisfaction and freedom from a multitude of cares. This is especially true if we acknowledge the Lord as an integral part of our occupation (Eph 6:5–8; Col 3:23). Our general calling in life is to work by manual labor and intellect, "to take dominion," whether it is in the home or the field, and by so doing, ultimately work for the advancement of the kingdom of God. But if our work has so much dignity and is guided by such holy purposes, why was a whole nation asked to cease from their works, from the activities that earned them a living and defined their calling in life? The prohibition

22. Kaplan, *Sabbath*, 26–44.

23. *b. Shabbat* 69a, 73b.

from work on the Sabbath was not so much a declaration that man's work was sinful, but that man's work was for a different purpose than to effect redemption. The work of redemption is not a calling that God has given to any man, so working on the Sabbath was tantamount to declaring that man is able to redeem himself. Only Jesus the Messiah, the fusion of divine and human natures, was assigned that work, the "less one" work.

By referring to the categories as "forty, less one" the Jews mysteriously drew attention to a final, legal work that completed the count to forty. To further typify the work of redemption of Jesus Christ, the Lord exempted the priesthood from Sabbath work prohibitions because their typical redemptive work was required every day. Of the thirty-nine classes of prohibited works, the priests violated at least seven of them as they accepted gifts from the people (an exchange of money), restrained animals for sacrifice (trapping), slit an animal's throat (slaughtering), removed its skin (skinning), transported its carcass to the altar (carrying a burden), submitted it to be burned (burning), and washed their hands and clothes (washing). But these "violations" were legitimatized by the Lord because they were symbolic of the work of Jesus Christ in redemption. The priests were called to this work as Jesus was called to His work: "My Father has been working until now, and I have been working" (John 5:17). The Father's work is seen in the Son's work. The Son's work is seen in the work of the priests and of the healed man. When confronted for working, the healed man justified his action by the authority of Jesus Christ, just as Jesus claimed the authority of the Father for His supposed violations and as the priests justified their infractions on the basis of God's word. Jesus chose this particular man to heal and to command in order to symbolize the redemption of Israel around sabbatic themes.

The Sabbath of the Lord looks back to the first week of creation when Adam sinned on the seventh day requiring the Lord to interrupt His rest to redeem Adam. Adam renounced his pitiful attempt at self-redemption, suspended his dominion work, and then waited for the Lord to clothe his nakedness. The Lord carried the burden of Adam's sin, just as He has carried the burden of Israel's sin. Acting in Christ's stead, the healed man modeled the Lord who carries the burden of Israel, implying that the Messiah has come to bear our griefs and carry our sorrows (Isa 53:4). In this way, Christ proclaimed that He is the Messiah, the Redeemer of Israel, thus fulfilling the Sabbath and demystifying the meaning of the work prohibition.

> In short, although it is remotely possible that Jesus is here presented as provoking a clash over rabbinical legalism about the Sabbath, there is no compelling reason to suppose He is precipitating a crisis over the Torah.[24]

In other words, John's retelling of this incident was not intended to dismantle the whole law of God or to specifically correct a misapplication of Sabbath law. However, besides proclaiming His power, authority, and unity with the Father, this passage involves the soteriological meaning of the Sabbath, the work prohibition, and burden-carrying, which later fueled the understanding that fulfilled ceremonial laws were no

24. Carson, "Jesus and the Sabbath," 81.

longer necessary under the new covenant. The Pharisees weren't responsible for the development of Sabbath traditions generations before them, nor were they obligated to correct all the legal misinterpretations of the law, but they were responsible for hearing and believing the claims of Jesus Christ and bending their knees to Him. If they believed, Jesus would have saved their souls as easily as He had healed the lame man. This was their disgraceful hypocrisy. It was more important for them to enforce obedience to Sabbath rules than to lead the people to Jesus in the obedience of faith. Just as their focus on carrying the bedding overshadowed the miraculous healing, so did their works-orientation overshadow the offer of salvation.

The Case of the Ear-plucking Disciples

The second situation that brought about the accusation of Sabbath-breaking is recorded synoptically in Matthew 12:1–8, Mark 2:23–28, and Luke 6:1–5, where the disciples and Jesus, on a Sabbath walk through grainfields between towns, were caught plucking and eating ears of corn. Matthew's account gives the most detail, save for Mark's quote that the Sabbath was made for man and not vice versa, and follows:

> At that time Jesus went through the grainfields on the Sabbath. And His disciples were hungry, and began to pluck heads of grain and to eat.
>
> And when the Pharisees saw it, they said to Him, "Look, Your disciples are doing what is not lawful to do on the Sabbath!"
>
> But He said to them, "Have you not read what David did when he was hungry, he and those who were with him:
>
> how he entered the house of God and ate the showbread which was not lawful for him to eat, nor for those who were with him, but only for the priests?
>
> Or have you not read in the law that on the Sabbath the priests in the temple profane the Sabbath, and are blameless?
>
> Yet I say to you that in this place there is One greater than the temple.
>
> But if you had known what this means, 'I desire mercy and not sacrifice,' you would not have condemned the guiltless.
>
> For the Son of Man is Lord even of the Sabbath." (Matt 12:1–8)

It is likely that Jesus was aware of the presence of the Pharisees who followed close at hand, looking for an opportunity to accuse Him, in this case, of Sabbath-breaking by harvesting and threshing grain. It appears that Jesus did not take of the grain Himself. It can be assumed that the disciples were aware of the oral teachings on the Sabbath, but they did what was either customary to themselves or what was permitted by Jesus. As in the preceding case, Jesus assumed responsibility for the actions of His disciples whom He commanded. His final assessment, though, in verse seven, was that their conduct was *guiltless*. The reason for this, according to many commentators, is that the Law did not prohibit the satisfying of thirst or the alleviating of hunger on the Sabbath. For example, Rushdoony asserts:

> Since hunger alleviated is a part of redemption, it is proper for one who is hungry to "pluck and eat corn" on the Sabbath (Matt 12:1–8; Mark 2:23–28; Luke

> 6:1–5), and the same is true of thirst, so that a thirsty animal can be taken to water in fulfillment of the Sabbath (Luke 13:15).[25]

But this conflict is not merely to assert that hunger may be satisfied whenever one chooses.[26] To be without food on the Sabbath is to admit, in nearly every case, that one failed to make provision for the Sabbath beforehand as required by law. It is inconceivable that Jesus would have forgotten to obey the letter of the law to prepare his meal on Friday (Prosabbaton) and then claim some "emergency" exemption on the Sabbath simply because He was hungry (cf. Matt 26:17; Mark 14:12; Luke 22:8–9). There is no indication in the text that their need to eat on the Sabbath was related to any previous predicament or any special circumstances. The Sabbath law prohibited all manner of work, including meal preparation. The Lord trained Israel in the desert not to go looking for food on the Sabbath by supplying a double portion of manna the day prior. If the design of manna was merely to satisfy hunger, then the Lord could have showered down manna on the Sabbath, just like any other day and all hungry Israelites could pick up manna *in situ* and eat. However, the Israelites were instructed to gather on Friday sufficient food for two days, and if one failed to do that there was no recourse to address one's hunger on the Sabbath day, for as Moses said, "you will not find it in the field" (Exod 16:25). So, for forty years in the wilderness, hunger on the Sabbath did not exempt careless Israelites from the demands of the law to take what the Lord provided at the time He directed. The justification for plucking the ears of corn must be along other lines.

Once in the land of Canaan, the Lord made provision for the poor with gleaning laws that allowed those impoverished Israelites to go through fields and pick what was left behind. So the question arises, did the gleaning laws allow the poor to gather grain on the Sabbath? Or were the poor, like the rich, required to lay up on the sixth day what they would eat on the seventh?

> When you reap the harvest of your land, you shall not wholly reap the corners of your field, nor shall you gather the gleanings of your harvest.
>
> And you shall not glean your vineyard, nor shall you gather every grape of your vineyard; you shall leave them for the poor and the stranger: I am the Lord your God. (Lev 19:9–10)

> And you shall proclaim on the same day [the Feast of Weeks, the fiftieth day, a day following a weekly Sabbath] that it is a holy convocation to you. You shall do no customary work on it. It shall be a statute forever in all your dwellings throughout your generations.
>
> When you reap the harvest of your land, you shall not wholly reap the corners of your field when you reap, nor shall you gather any gleaning from your harvest. You shall leave them for the poor and for the stranger: I am the Lord your God. (Lev 23:21–22)

25. Rushdoony, *Institutes of Biblical Law*, 131.

26. Yang, *Jesus and the Sabbath*, 171–75.

> When you [a gleaner] come into your neighbor's vineyard, you may eat your fill of grapes at your pleasure, but you shall not put any in your container.
>
> When you come into your neighbor's standing grain, you may pluck the heads with your hand, but you shall not use a sickle on your neighbor's standing grain. (Deut 23:24–25)

It is clear that those who owned fields were allowed to harvest only upon the first six days of the week, because harvesting *with a sickle* was considered work and *carrying the harvest back* to one's home in a vessel was considered bearing a burden. With the Deuteronomic law restricting gleaners from ever using a sickle to gather grain or carrying away fruit from the fields—privileges of those who actually owned the fields—the poor were unable to comply with the commandment to prepare their meals the day before the Sabbath. Gleaning, therefore, was not considered a work in the same sense as harvesting, for the food so gathered was eaten immediately without cooking or preparation, and was not taken away for storage or sale. Since the commandment requiring pre-Sabbath meal preparation commemorated the double-portion of manna—God's provision for the Israelites in the wilderness—it is understandable that gleaners in the promised land were exempt from that commandment because God provided for their sustenance by another means. Those who reaped and stored and sold the fruit of their harvest were experiencing a blessing from God, similar to the double portion of manna, and were therefore expected to lay in store for the Sabbath as did their forefathers in the wilderness. The gleaners, on the other hand, lived like the creatures of the earth that are *daily* fed by God. Sustained in this fashion by the God who watches over the sparrow, the gleaners experienced daily the providence of God in a different way than the average Israelite. Those who owned fields and stored food were perhaps more likely to look upon their wealth and forget the Lord (Deut 8:11–14, 17–18), but the poor faced their own temptations (Prov 30:8–9). So, it is not that their faith was greater, nor were their temptations greater, but gleaners were simply released from the particular demand of the law to prepare their meals the day before the Sabbath. That is, the Lord allowed a select group to feed themselves on the Sabbath without the compulsion to prepare meals beforehand. Gleaning laws were typological of the coming redemption in Christ, and these laws were fulfilled in the corn fields when Christ and his disciples went through them and ate. Those who keep company with Jesus, who are poor in spirit and hunger after righteousness, will be fed by Him in a daily fashion, freed from the technicalities of Jewish ceremonies.

We need not attempt to justify His actions on any other basis than Scripture. The simplest and most satisfying explanation for their actions is that because "the Son of man has nowhere to lay his head" (Matt 8:20), he most certainly was qualified to glean on the Sabbath. In this light, Jesus and His disciples were within the bounds of Mosaic law. The Pharisees, however, disallowed what God allowed; they obstructed the *legal* mercy of God from touching the lives of the poor. In their quest to keep the Sabbath day holy, to safely protect the day from careless impiety, they elevated obedience to the minutest technicality to such an extent that it overshadowed the merciful exemption already contained in God's law. That the merciful nature of God was being despised by the Pharisees is obvious from Jesus' quotation of Hosea, "For I desire mercy and not sacrifice, and the knowledge of God more than burnt offerings" (Hos 6:6).

By quoting Hosea, Jesus addressed the failure of the Pharisees to recognize and practice the mercy of God above punctilious obedience to sacrifices and burnt offerings. The Hosea passage equates the secondary importance of the sacrificial system with either the Sabbath in general or the Pharisee's legal encrustations to the Sabbath. That the former bears the relationship is evident in that both David and Hosea wrote that even when done properly according to the law, ceremonial sacrifices meant nothing if moral law was forgotten. Likewise, any obedience to Sabbath law meant nothing if mercy was trodden down. This could never be said of the other nine commandments, e.g. "For I desired mercy and not the detestation of idols, and the knowledge of God more than honoring my name," or "For I desired mercy and not the honest treatment of other's property, and the knowledge of God more than sexual purity." In this sense, none of the moral dictums can be said to be lesser or greater than another. Yet, through Hosea, He distinguished between the absolutely necessary law of mercy and the temporary ceremonial law of sacrifices; and through this midday meal in the field, the Lord distinguished between the legal mercy of gleaning laws (though they were ceremonial) and the less important ceremonies of Sabbath laws. The Hosea passage predicts the annulment of sacrifices in the same fashion as Psalm 40:6 (Heb 10:5–10), but as Christ relates this to the Sabbath, there is an intimation that the Sabbath must also be done away. As Matthew Henry concluded, "In healing on the sabbath day . . . the sabbath-rest must give way."[27]

Instead of justifying His actions on the basis of gleaning laws, Jesus confounded the Pharisees by way of other Scriptures: a narrative from the life of David and the duties of priests on the Sabbath. His citation of the temple service deals directly with the question of Sabbath observance, whereas the conduct of David and his troops does not.

> The original argument—from David's conduct—was of a spontaneous, popular kind, but it was anything but conclusive from the scholarly, legal point of view. For one thing, in the case of David, it had not been a question of the Sabbath at all. David, when hungry, had eaten of the showbread; which was no proof, technically, that you might, in a similar situation, break the Sabbath. But an even more serious objection was that what Jesus adduced was the conduct of a historical figure, instead of a law. He quoted a narrative saying that David had acted in a certain way, but not a provision allowing you to act in this way.[28]

Sabbath-Breaking King. Following the death of Goliath, David became more prominent in the eyes of his countrymen, thus stirring passions in Saul, who jealously conspired for his death. David escaped multiple attempts to take his life and while in hiding, approached the priest, Ahimelech, and asked for bread.

27. Henry, *Commentary*, 4:907 (on Hos 6:6).

28. Daube, *New Testament and Rabbinic Judaism*, 68. The case of David did involve the Sabbath indirectly, since he ate on the Sabbath the showbread that was reserved for the priests. Though not capitalized on by Jesus, David also traveled a distance likely farther than a Sabbath day's journey.

> So the priest gave him holy bread; for there was no bread there but the showbread which had been taken from before the LORD, in order to put hot bread in its place on the day when it was taken away. (1 Sam 21:6)

Saul was eventually informed that the priests assisted David by giving him bread and the sword of Goliath. Saul ordered Ahimelech to appear before him and subsequently ordered his death and the massacre of eighty-five priests and unnumbered other men and women and their young (1 Sam 22:9–19). The fact that David and his troops ate the week-old showbread is a minor detail in the larger tale of intrigue and malfeasance surrounding the desperation of Saul to retain his kingdom.

Ahimelech would surely have known that the most holy food could only be eaten by the priests (Lev 24:9), and possibly by their families and purchased servants (Lev 22:10–15). Jesus confirmed this was the case, that David ate the showbread unlawfully (Matt 12:4). There is only one reason why Ahimelech would give David the expired "bread of the presence" and that is because David was the anointed King. Ahimelech skirted about the law because he was faced with the real presence of the King-awaiting. The young men were also allowed to partake of the showbread by virtue of their direct association with King David, provided they had complied with the rules that normally applied to priests—that they were ritually clean. Had any other person approached Ahimelech begging for bread, the most holy showbread would never have been considered.

To be satisfied with the superficial comparison that Jesus and His disciples were hungry like David and his troops ignores the fact that Jesus and His disciples were already justified as gleaners. Jesus' citation of David's improper conduct provided more profound similarities between David and the Messiah than mere hunger. Jesus' use of this historical incident was not to provide a legal justification for His actions, but to claim typological fulfillment.[29] David clearly broke the covenantal law of God, but was not condemned *because of who he was*. Jesus' use of this Scripture likens His own behavior with the lawbreaking behavior of David, and reasons that He too should not be condemned *because of who He is*. The compelling call of David to assume the throne took precedence over the ceremonial law that reserved the showbread for the priests. Ahimelech realized the subservience of the Levitical priesthood to the Lord's anointed king.

Yet the similarities go even deeper. Like David, Jesus was a hunted and persecuted man, not for any wrong that He had done, but because the Lord was working mightily through Him. David was the one "who kept My commandments and who followed Me with all his heart, to do only what was right in My eyes" (1 Kgs 14:8). Likewise, our Lord, as described prophetically by David, was completely obedient to the will of God (Ps 40:6–8). David was not interested in merely satisfying his own hunger, but was caring for the troops who were exhausted and famished. Likewise, the Captain of our Faith feeds the hungry soul and gives the weary rest, eliciting greater devotion and thankfulness from His soldiers. David's troops were ritually clean and Christ's elect

29. Yang, *Jesus and the Sabbath*, 176.

are spiritually clean by His word (John 15:3). Those who demonstrated allegiance to David put their lives at risk, and so Jesus warned His disciples that they too would pay the ultimate price for their commitment to Him (John 15:20).

If David represents Jesus, then surely the Pharisees are to be likened to the jealous, power-grabbing Saul, who had the potential to have a long-lasting kingdom, but was rejected by God for his disobedience and lack of faith (1 Sam 13:13–14; 15:35; 16:1). David's history provides more than a simulacrum with the hounding accusers in the corn field. Saul was rejected and David was chosen. God took away the first that He may establish the second. Saul, after becoming wounded in a battle with the Philistines, secured his own death by falling upon his sword. The Pharisees, by rejecting the Messiah, secured the judgment of God in spiritual suicide. What Saul stood for came quickly to an end, but David prevailed and was established. The showbread, the Sabbath, and all the ceremonial ephemeralities must give way to the everlasting kingship of Christ. David eventually became king (2 Sam 5:1–5), but it is significant that he was regarded as the rightful king before his coronation (1 Sam 16:12–13). Likewise, Jesus, though not yet crowned by His Father in Heaven, was the King-awaiting while in His earthly habitation. As King, Jesus could do as He pleased in concert with the Father, even skirting around the technicalities of ceremonial law. What a joy it is to be in the company of King Jesus and share in His anointed role (2 Cor 1:21)!

Sabbath-Breaking Priest. The second line of reasoning in Jesus' argument, involving temple worship on the Sabbath, was directly applicable to the case at hand and rests on a direct precept of law (Num 28:9), hence, Jesus' scathing remark, "Have you not read in the law?" The crucial point underlined by Jesus is that the Sabbath takes a second position to the sacrificial duties of the priests. God required offerings to be dedicated at the temple, even on the Sabbath, establishing the rule that Sabbath observance, specifically the prohibition of work, must yield to temple service. This applied not only to official sacrifices, but to the rite of circumcision.

> From what we have learned above, we see that for the circumcision itself and all its necessary accessories the Sabbath may be violated, according to the dictum of R. Eliezer. Whence does he deduce this? This is the reasoning of R. Eliezer: It is written [Leviticus 12:3]: "And on the eighth day shall the flesh of his foreskin be circumcised." Thus, as it says distinctly the eighth day, it makes no difference what day the eighth falls on, whether it be Sabbath or not.[30]

So the Pharisees already knew the principle that the Sabbath could be "violated" through obedience to other commands. However, care was exercised to limit the possibility of real violations during the performance of legitimate "violations." For example, in the matter of circumcision, questions arose regarding carrying the knife to the temple, using water to wash blood from the wound, dressing the wound, and carrying the child to and from the temple. Yet reason tells us that if the priest was duty-bound to circumcise a child on the eighth day, then the parents were allowed by law to carry their child to the priest on the eighth day, even if it was a Sabbath. Yet the Talmud

30. *b. Shabbath* 131b–32a, trans. Rodkinson.

placed restrictions on godly obedience by requiring the parents to have a Gentile carry the baby to the priests. On the other hand, if the baby was sick on the eighth day, they postponed the circumcision until the baby was well.

Though it is true that the Sabbath was sometimes legitimately violated, especially by priests, there is no obvious connection between the services of the temple and the disciples plucking ears of corn from another man's field. Jesus recasts the analogy between David and Himself to an analogy between the priesthood and Himself, such that His supposed violation of the Sabbath was legitimate because He is a priest in the performance of His duties. It is not that Jesus draws an analogy between priestly Sabbath work and picking corn, but between the exemption of Levitical priests from Sabbath law and His personal exemption from Sabbath law. In other words, assuming that Jesus broke the Sabbath—which He did not—He had every right to do so because as a priest He is making ready the work of redemption. He first claims kingship and now the priesthood, advancing a mystery of the Messiah, who not only is the progeny of David but appointed by God as high priest. In one of Christianity's earliest apologetics, Justin Martyr questions his Jewish inquirer.

> For, tell me, did God wish the priests to sin when they offer the sacrifices on the Sabbaths? or those to sin, who are circumcised and do circumcise on the Sabbaths; since He commands that on the eighth day—even though it happens to be a Sabbath—those who are born shall be always circumcised? or could not the infants be operated upon one day previous or one day subsequent to the Sabbath, if He knew that it is a sinful act upon the Sabbaths? Or why did He not teach those—who are called righteous and pleasing to Him, who lived before Moses and Abraham, who were not circumcised in their foreskin, and observed no Sabbaths—to keep these institutions?"[31]

It is preposterous to assume that God contradicted Himself when He decreed that priests should work on the Sabbath. We hesitate to claim that the priest's work on the Sabbath is actually sinful, yet their labors appear to be of the same categories of work that are sinful for everyone else on the Sabbath. How is it that the Lord permitted this to happen? God purposed through these shadow laws to proclaim the reality that the Lord was compelled to provide redemption on His seventh-day rest for fallen man. During the reign of the Mosaic law, this priestly work of God in the garden of Eden was recounted and reenacted as the priests worked redemptively for Israel on the Sabbath. During the first advent of Christ, "God in the flesh" worked on the Sabbath by healing and forgiving sins in fulfillment of this legal paradox. The design of these ceremonial laws was to foreshadow the redemptive work of Christ that could not be limited to only six days of the week, but was necessary every day since the fall of Adam.

All Sabbaths Fulfilled. The foundation of His argument has been laid. By the example of David, which by no means was unjustified, He demonstrated that Sabbath law was subservient to the demands of God's chosen king, and, by the precept of law, the Sabbath was subservient to the duties of the appointed priesthood. What unifies these two scriptural citations is the principle of order. Therefore, Jesus concluded, "Yet

31. Justin, *Dial.* 27 (*ANF* 1:208).

I say to you that in this place there is One greater than the temple" (Matt 12:6; 41–42). If David, as King of Israel, could circumvent the lesser of God's laws (ceremonial law), then Jesus, as King of Kings, could do likewise. Also, if the priests could work on the Sabbath in the performance of their duties, then Jesus, because He is the high priest of heaven, could do likewise. Underlying His argument is the unspoken assertion of who He is: the high priest of an everlasting order and the reigning king of an invisible kingdom. He is greater than King David and superior to the high priest; more so, He is greater than the temple and the Sabbath. He is the chosen Son of David, whom David called "Lord"; He is the high priest after the order of Melchizedek, which never ends; and He is the Lord of the Sabbath, to do with it as He pleases in pursuit of mercy, goodness, and justice (Matt 12:8; Mark 2:28; Luke 6:5). David is dead, the priesthood is over, the temple is destroyed, and the Sabbath is annulled; but Jesus entirely fulfills what the person, the office, the place, and the time foreshadowed (Matt 11:28).

No Sabbaths Harmed. Sabbatarian author Bruce Ray dismisses the themes of redemptive and messianic fulfillment and proposes that Christ battled the Pharisees to assert His prerogative to remove only the unnecessary and stifling traditions that had been added to the Sabbath and to restore the Sabbath to its original intention.

> Jesus blasted the Pharisaic Sabbath, but in doing so he did not harm the biblical Sabbath at all. Indeed, he liberated it, restored it, and filled it full of meaning once again.
>
> The conflict was not so much a personal matter between Jesus and the Pharisees as it was a conflict between the holy Sabbath of God and the painfully distorted Pharisaic Sabbath. It was part of Jesus' mission to liberate, heal, and redeem the Sabbath from captivity. [32]

In Ray's thinking, Christ removed the Talmudic tarnish so the Sabbath could shine once again and be truly appreciated and enjoyed as the means by which He blesses men with life. The meaning of the Sabbath that was apparently lost by the Jews is that "not only works of worship and piety, but also works of necessity and mercy, are appropriate Sabbath activities" and that keeping the Sabbath will "refresh, heal, and restore breath and strength to the body."[33] But the so-called Christian Sabbath is not a restored Jewish Sabbath, freed from the legalisms of the Pharisees and the resultant dread; rather, it is an impressionistic rendering of the Sabbath, complete with its own rules and threats.

> The rejection of the Sabbath rest today still carries a death penalty, though not by civil authorities. Those who reject God's rest and insist on their full ability to labor without ceasing bring death upon themselves in the form of unrelieved stress, hypertension, heart attacks, strokes, and a multitude of diseases. Sabbath breaking still brings death physically. And it brings death spiritually.[34]

32. Ray, *Celebrating the Sabbath*, 73, 83.

33. Ibid., 83.

34. Ibid., 85–86.

Building on this superficial view of the Sabbath conflicts, Sabbatarians devise their own customs when the Sabbath may be guiltlessly broken: works of necessity and works of mercy. Based upon their own definition of Sabbath-keeping, Sabbatarians subjectively decide what mercy or necessity they may allow themselves. They presume they have the authority to make exceptions when it seems right in their own eyes, but the Lord was very specific about the measure of mercy for gleaners with regard to Sabbath law. *Ad hoc* exceptions of mercy and necessity taken by Sabbatarians serve only their own sense of piety. They are not poor and destitute, unable to reap the rewards of their labor, unable to store for a harder times, unable to sell one possession to buy another; yet modern Sabbatarians make a mockery of God's mercy to the poor by claiming a mercy anytime they have to drive to the shopping center in their Town Car to buy cream for their Sunday cup of java.

The point is that by law (the exemption for gleaning), God pronounced an exemption to the law (no manner of work on the Sabbath). If the goal of Sabbatarians is to rejuvenate the biblical Sabbath, then their only source for law is what has been given in the law. In the wilderness, there were no gleaners, but once Israel arrived in the land of Canaan, God declared a legal proviso specifically for gleaners. Why? It was a matter of practical mercy for sure, but the spiritual significance of that mercy was to point to a profound detail about redemption: that Sabbath gleaners are a type of Christ's redeemed who are given exception to the ceremonial laws of Israel. The apostles may have appeared to be Sabbath-breakers, but in reality they signified that the redeemed of Christ would be sustained by Christ. Even though the redeemed of Christ may be accused of Sabbath-breaking, they are guiltless in His presence.

JESUS AND THE SABBATH

The Example of Jesus

For Jesus to "fulfill all righteousness" He must have kept the ceremonial law perfectly, even up to the point of His death. To that end, His circumcision was accomplished on the eighth day according to the faithfulness of his parents (Luke 2:21–24). As a child, He accompanied His parents to the festivals, such as the Feast of Passover (Luke 2:41–50). During His ministry, Jesus urged obedience to and participated in numerous old covenant laws—laws that would later be annulled by His work on the cross—such as the law of the leper (Lev 14:1–32; Matt 8:1–4; Mark 1:40–45); and, only days prior to crucifixion, the Feast of Unleavened Bread and Passover (Matt 26:17–19). Like a true son of David, His heart was stirred with passion to protect the interests and propriety of temple worship, causing Him to rebuke those who made business of the temple arena (John 2:13–17; Ps 69:9)—a temple that would later be destroyed. Having dispensed with the "faulty" old covenant (Heb 8:7–8) and having ushered in the superior new covenant (Heb 8:6), His earthly example of obedience to carnal ordinances of the old covenant (Heb 9:1–15) can no longer be considered an endorsement of the same for new covenant believers.

Matthew relates an occasion when Jesus paid the redemption tax (Matt 17:24–27; Exod 30:11–16), a tax that every male over the age of twenty paid for the general support of the temple. Whether rich or poor, each man paid the half shekel. When questioned by the tax collector whether Jesus paid this tax, Peter answered in the affirmative because it had been the Master's habit to pay this tax. He submitted to this tax, not to diminish His sovereignty, but to proclaim a great truth about His deity. Arguing from the general concept of taxation as practiced by the Gentiles—kings extracting taxes only from those who are strangers (i.e. non-relatives)—the redemption tax must be a tax from God, the King, upon his subjects, the Jews. Jesus claims exemption from this tax because He is the king's son. Yet while He lived, He must obey the law to fulfill all righteousness, so He miraculously provided the amount due for both Himself and Peter. Jesus could have claimed exemption because of His sinless perfection, for the tax was atonement for the soul.

So, after Christ's death and resurrection, were Jewish Christians required to continue to pay this tax? How would the apostles apply this truth to themselves and fellow believers upon the realization that the disciples of Christ are no longer subjects but adopted sons of God and co-heirs with Christ? Furthermore, were Gentile converts required to pay the temple tax?

> It was no ordinary tribute, therefore, which Israel was to pay to Jehovah as its King, but an act demanded by the holiness of the theocratic covenant. As an expiation for souls, it pointed to the unholiness of Israel's nature, and reminded the people continually, that by nature it was alienated from God, and could only remain in covenant with the Lord and live in His kingdom on the ground of His grace, which covered its sin. It was not till this sinful nature had been sanctified by a perfect atonement, and servitude under the law had been glorified and fully transformed into that sonship to which Israel was called as the first-born son of Jehovah, that as children of the kingdom they had no longer to pay this atonement-money for their souls.[35]

This pericope immediately declared the deity of Christ, but after His resurrection it takes on new significance regarding the structure of the law. Because He is the Son of the Father, He is exempt from this tribute (though He pays it), while Peter, a subject of the King, must rightfully pay his half-shekel as atonement. In a nutshell, Christ proclaims His deity and demonstrates His submission to the Father by an act of humility. Jesus declared that Peter was a *subject* of this kingdom even though the Lord God had already called the nation Israel His *firstborn* (Exod 4:22; Jer 31:9). At this point, His teaching is anticipatory of His death on the cross; that the final and eternally efficacious sacrifice for sin must be made by the Son of God, a person who is in a class all by Himself. Jesus said, "Destroy this temple, and in three days I will raise it up" (John 2:19). While He spoke of His body in death and resurrection, He more subtly predicted the destruction of the temple and its transcendent reconstruction in the heavenly kingdom. In time, the temple tax would no longer be required, not simply because the temple was destroyed, but because Christ fulfilled that ceremonial

35. Keil and Delitzsch, *Commentary*, 1:459 (Exod 30:16).

law. How was the temple tax fulfilled by Christ? First of all, this tax was not an earthly payment to a sovereign, but a covenantal obligation with eyes toward the temple, the centerpiece of their redemption and continued fellowship with God. It was a memorial that each person (a male of age as a representative), whether rich or poor, was equal before God in his unredeemed nature and that it was by God's grace that they maintained their fellowship with Him. The price paid—a "split" shekel—was a pittance, a share that any man could make, indicative of the necessity of faith by all who render tribute to the Lord for the redemption of their soul. Returning to Christ's lesson for Peter, once viewed from the perspective of the resurrection and that our half-shekel has been paid by faith, there is another level for understanding the scope of Christ's exemption from the temple tax. It is only required of subjects, but we have become actual family members of our sovereign God. For this reason, Christ said, "Then are the sons free," indicating not only His own exemption but the exemption of all the sons of God in Christ. The remaining subjects of God's earthly rule will pay equal tribute to the Lord in recognition of their own fallen nature by bending their knee at the final judgment.

Christ's example of obedience to Jewish ceremonial laws was not neccessarily to model proper behavior for Christians. It was expected that the Messiah would indeed be obedient to the law of God and though the Pharisees thought Jesus was a Sabbath-breaker, in reality, He never dishonored the Sabbath in any fashion. Yet in these conflicts He demonstrated that He had every right to be exempt from those laws that forecasted His Messianic rank and work. Now that they are fulfilled, Christians are exempted from those same laws by virtue of their union with Christ. This spiritual reality lays down the foundation for understanding the difference between moral and ceremonial laws. The Christian relates to ceremonial law not as an exacting outward duty, but as a sublime enlightenment of God's eternal design for redemption and of His Christ who brought it to completion.

While Jesus lived, the new covenant remained a powerless document, a prophecy yet to be fulfilled, "For a testament is in force after men are dead, since it has no power at all while the testator lives" (Heb 9:17). As symbolized in the refulgent face of Moses, the old covenant had its days of glory, but passed away, giving way to the exceeding glory of the risen Lord (2 Cor 3:7–8). Jesus was the Lord of the old covenant, therefore, He was Lord of something that passes away. It does no dishonor to the lordship of Jesus Christ that the old covenant endured for but a season. The ceremonies and memorials had to give way to the exceeding glory of Jesus Christ, through whom these laws were fulfilled. The gospel record of Sabbath conflicts was not to present Jesus as a provocateur, a revolutionary, or a catalyst for covenant renewal. Jesus did what it was in His nature to do: to speak the truth about Himself, to redeem men from their sin, and to call a people to Himself, and in all this He fulfilled the Sabbath.

Sabbath Made for Man

While clothed in humanity, Jesus claimed to be Lord of the Sabbath. He not only made a claim of authority over the Sabbath as a prerogative of His deity, but of His humanity. As the federal head of the redeemed race, He has authority over the Sabbath. His lordship over the Sabbath is the logical precursor to the statement that *man* is above the Sabbath. The statement "The Sabbath was made for man, not man for the Sabbath," appeals to the principle of order. As Sabbatarian author Chantry asserts:

> From the order in which man and Sabbath were created, our Lord determines which was intended to serve the interest of the other. Since man was created before the Sabbath was made we must conclude that the Sabbath was made to serve man's well-being. Man was not made to be subordinated to the interests of the Sabbath. The Sabbath was intended for man's help and welfare.[36]

Both Sabbatarians and non-Sabbatarians agree that the institution of the Sabbath succeeded the creation of man, therefore holding an inferior position to the interests of man. Jesus' statement seems simple enough, but it raises two questions: When was it made (or instituted), and for whom was it made?

First of all, the Sabbath was not made on the seventh day of creation. It was given as a precept to Israel, which is a type of the redeemed people of God. The Sabbath was uniquely Jewish; it was not for any other nation. The seventh day of creation, on the other hand, was merely a prototype of the later ceremonial Sabbath and a pattern for other seventh-day types, therefore, the seventh-day pattern is for the redeemed. The seventh day of the creation week was God's first day of rest, a rest that was only briefly experienced by sinless Adam. Since Adam was of the elect lineage of Christ (Luke 3:38), the seventh-day rest is better understood as applicable only for the redeemed of mankind. The seventh-day rest symbolized the heavenly abode of the redeemed—not unbelievers (Heb 4:3–4). The context for Christ's statement, "the Sabbath was made for man," involved Jewish leaders, Jewish law, and Jewish citizens. There is nothing in the context that relates this Sabbath controversy to Gentiles. The Sabbath was made for *redeemed* man.

Secondly, Jesus' maxim employs a rhetorical device called antimetabole, in which the elements of the thesis are transposed; i.e., Eat to live, but do not live to eat. The veracity of the thesis is strengthened by its contrast with the playful antithesis. The antithesis does not necessarily have to be true or achievable; in fact, what makes these sayings work is the utter foolishness of the antithesis. With rare exceptions, nobody lives to eat. Thus, the antithesis "(made) not man for the Sabbath" is primarily to highlight the truth of the thesis: "The Sabbath was made for man," and is not to propose a real possibility that man was made for the Sabbath. It would be a rare exception to find someone who was specifically made by God to be a Sabbath-keeping machine. So it is not necessary to think in terms of the creation week when man was "made," as

36. Chantry, *Call the Sabbath a Delight*, 57. One could quibble about the origin of the Sabbath, whether or not it was "created," and the intention of the Sabbath, whether or not its function was primarily to "help" mankind with physical rest and welfare.

Chantry feels compelled to think.[37] Jesus only states that the ultimate purpose of man is not found in obedience to the Sabbath.

Chantry notes a grammatical similarity between two sayings of Christ: "the Sabbath was made (*ginomai*) for man, and not man for the Sabbath," and "nor was man created (*ktizo*) for the woman, but woman for the man," and concludes that since the latter refers to creation, so does the former. However, the similarity is only in that they use the same figure of speech. The latter saying by Paul (1 Cor 11:9) *does* refer to the creation since the Greek word *ktizo* consistently describes the creative acts of God. However, Jesus' saying about the Sabbath is not referring to the creation since He used the word *ginomai* instead of *ktizo*; otherwise, the antithesis would be "man was not created (*ktizo*) for the Sabbath." Jesus is not establishing that the Sabbath was made at creation or that the Sabbath itself was created, only that when the Sabbath was made (given to Israel), it was not made to rule them in such a way that His redemptive work should be obscured by law. Chantry offers no convincing reason why these two disparate sayings of Jesus should be synthesized to force a conclusion that is not supported by the creation account.

Thirdly, the Jewish mind would understand this maxim as speaking only to the Jews even though put in the general terms of mankind. Barnhouse assures his readers that in the OT, "the word 'man' frequently was the equivalent of the Jewish man," and this understanding is replicated in the NT.[38] For example, Malachi prophesied to Israel as though they were the sum of all that God created and would have fellowship with, a sort of universality of Israel. All humanity is created in God's image; does this make God the Father of all men?

> Have we not all one Father? Has not one God created us?
> Why do we deal treacherously with one another
> By profaning the covenant of the fathers? (Mal 2:10)

Matthew Henry, commenting on the above verse, says,

> But here it seems to refer to the Jewish nation: Have we not all one father, Abraham, or Jacob? This they prided themselves in, We have Abraham to our father; but here it is turned upon them as an aggravation of their sin in betraying the honour of their nation by intermarrying with heathens: "Has not one God created us, that is, formed us into a people, made us a nation by ourselves, and put a life into us, distinct from that of other nations? And should not this oblige us to maintain the dignity of our character?" [39]

Sabbatarians believe Christ's statement ("Sabbath made for man") refers to mankind in general. However, Jesus' remark was directed to the Pharisees who forced Jews to obey traditional Sabbath rules. The Sabbath-keeping system was so burdensome for *Israel* that it appeared that "man" (meaning the Jewish person) was made for the Sabbath. To this, the Lord Jesus offered a profound truth that should have resulted

37. Ibid., 54, 55.
38. Barnhouse, *Expositions of Bible Doctrines*, 4:183.
39. Henry, *Commentary*, 4:1172–73.

in repentance and a new outlook on Sabbath law: that the Sabbath, as designed for the Jews, was to be in a supportive and subordinate relationship to them in order to prepare them to recognize the Messiah when He came. Sabbath-keeping was designed to engender a hope for a rest beyond the Sabbath, just as they hoped for a Prophet beyond Moses, a cure for sin beyond sacrifices, and the presence of God beyond the temple. Such faith would recognize the Messiah when He came, for these outward laws concurrently projected a better, more enduring, reality (John 5:39; Col 2:17).

Ceremonial laws have a dual application: first, toward Israel, and second, toward the redeemed. The outward performance of ceremonial laws was a temporary duty of the Jews, but the spiritual reality is for whosoever to possess and enjoy in faith. Thus, Jesus' statement "the Sabbath was made for man" had two levels of meaning. As the outward rite, Sabbath-keeping was for the Jews. As a spiritual reality, the rest of God is for whoever has ears to hear and eyes to see the mysteries of God in faith—that His seventh-day rest after the creation could be recaptured in Christ. Interpretively, if one wants to discuss the Sabbath in its outward manifestation and legal duties, then at once the context requires limiting its scope to the Jews. However, if the spiritual reality is the focus, then the context requires expanding the scope of its spiritual benefits to include all mankind, should they believe. The Sabbath, as law, was made for Israel to prepare her heart through obedience to receive by faith the redemptive work of Christ. However, the Sabbath, as a type, was symbolic of redemption and was made for all mankind to see the gospel of Christ contained therein, that they may be saved.

8

Sabbath and the Resurrection

Turning Point

THE RESURRECTION OF JESUS Christ from the dead is a crucial and paramount doctrine for the Christian, not only as a guarantee of the complete justification of sinners, but also as the basis for abrogating the old covenant and establishing the new covenant.[1] Moreover, the hope of the elect has changed from possessing a land to possessing Christ, from seeking Eden to seeking a heavenly abode in God's eternal kingdom. As the apostles intersected the Jewish and pagan cultures, the basis of their preaching was the fact of the resurrection of Jesus Christ, and not, as was with Israel, the history of the exodus by Moses (Acts 2:22–24; 3:14–15; 4:10, 33; Rom 10:9). The title of a future resurrection to glory replaced the claims of historical rights to establish a kingdom in the land of Canaan. When Jesus died on the cross, was buried, and rose again from the dead, the means and manner of God's rule of righteousness on earth changed emphasis. The clearest examples of this change, and perhaps the most significant, are the discarding of temple sacrifices and the discontinuation of the Aaronic priesthood.[2] Based on the implications of the resurrection, Acts and the Epistles paint an even more glorious picture of Jesus Christ than what was presented in the Gospels. It is not in the Gospels but in the Epistles that we clearly learn of the annulment of ceremonial laws.

CEREMONIAL LAWS

Those regulations of the former covenant that Christians are no longer to obey in particular are now called *ceremonial laws*. Says Turretin:

> The ceremonial law is the system of God's positive precepts concerning the external worship in sacred things, prescribed to the ancient church, either for the sake of order or of signification.[3]

1. Abrogate means to abolish, do away with, make void or invalid, nullify, or annul. These words will be used interchangeably. The basis for abrogation of an old covenant law is in the fulfillment of what it foreshadowed.

2. Bahnsen, *By This Standard*, 162; Bahsnen, *Five Views on Law and Gospel*, 98–99.

3. Turretin, *Elenctic Theology*, 2:146. Though I prefer not to refer to Israel as the church, the definition is correct.

The Belgic Confession of Faith, a sixteenth-century document of the Christian Reformed Church in the Netherlands, defined the believer's relationship to ceremonial law.

> We believe that the ceremonies and figures of the law ceased at the coming of Christ, and that all the shadows are accomplished; so that the use of them must be abolished among Christians: yet the truth and substance of them remain with us in Jesus Christ, in whom they have their completion. In the mean time we still use the testimonies taken out of the law and the prophets, to confirm us in the doctrine of the gospel, and to regulate our life in all honesty to the glory of God, according to His will.[4]

With the advent of Jesus Christ, various histories, laws, and systems of the former covenant were fulfilled by His life and work, His incarnation and glorification, and His offices and character. The principle that the former is replaced by the better leads to an unavoidable conclusion: the Christian has no obligation to observe the ceremonial laws of the former covenant. What "truth and substance" remain are to be seen in the person and work of Jesus Christ and to be admired by His saints, but not repeated in carnal ordinances as though the Messiah is yet to come.

The Jews expected that upon the arrival of the Messiah, based upon the prophecy of Jeremiah (Jer 31:31), certain legal mandates and civil functions would be reformed or altered. Edersheim, refraining from listing numerous supporting examples of rabbinic speculation, offered this preeminent notion:

> But the Talmud goes even further, and lays down the two principles, that in the "age to come" the whole ceremonial Law and all the feasts were to cease. And although this may be regarded as merely a general statement, it is definitely applied to the effect, that all sacrifices except the thank-offering, and all fasts and feasts except the Day of Atonement, or else the Feast of Esther, were to come to an end—nay, that what had formerly been "bound" or forbidden would be "loosed" or allowed, notably that the distinctions between clean and unclean animals would be removed.[5]

With this prospect before the apostles, the Lord progressively revealed to the church that certain Mosaic laws were "shadow laws," unfit for common Christian practice. As the early church identified Jesus Christ as the Passover Lamb who was slain for the sins of the world, they realized that His death fulfilled and supplanted the sacrificial system. Concurrent with this understanding, the apostles proclaimed that Jesus was the Prophet, Priest, and King foretold centuries before. Jesus superseded Moses and all the prophets as the final and express spokesman for God (Heb 1:1–2), He replaced the Aaronic and Levitical priesthood with an enduring and heavenly order (Heb 5:4–6), and He was enthroned as the irreplaceable Regent of the kingdom of God (Heb 7:1–2; 1 Tim 6:15–16). Apostle John admits that even though the disciples fetched the donkey for Jesus' kingly entrance into Jerusalem only days before His crucifixion, they

4. Schaff, *Creeds of Christendom*, 3:412–13 (Belgic Confession, Art. 25).

5. Edersheim, *The Life and Times*, 1034.

were unconscious that their actions were participatory in the fulfillment of prophecy (John 12:16; Zech 9:9). Not until the glorification of our Lord and perhaps the giving of the Holy Spirit at Pentecost did the apostles begin to fully comprehend the scope of prophecies and redemptive laws that were fulfilled at the first advent of Christ. The outward performance of Jewish ceremonies became a matter of relative insignificance compared to the realization that they were designed and commanded to prepare the Jewish nation for the arrival of the Messiah (Gal 3:24–25).

Dietary Laws

As the apostles proclaimed the saving gospel of Christ, Gentiles began to respond in faith. This initiated a vexing problem: should converted Gentiles live as Jews, or should believing Jews and Gentiles live as Christians? Shortly after Paul's conversion, Peter had a vision of a blanket spread with sundry animals descending from heaven (Acts 10:9–16). Based on Peter's recoiling at the command to kill and eat, he was obviously continuing to observe Jewish dietary laws some *twenty years* after the resurrection of Christ! This highlights the difficulty that even the apostles experienced in releasing themselves from the compulsion to obey ceremonial laws. Yet this vision was not given to simply release Hebrew Christians from trivial ceremonies. Rather, it was primarily intended for the leadership of the church to establish that God's plan of redemption was not exclusive to Israel alone. This was not a new idea at the time of Peter's vision, for Apostle Matthew already substantiated the realization that Jesus' advent fulfilled the Messianic prophecy of Isaiah to reach the Gentiles large-scale (Matt 12:18, 21). Therefore, Peter's vision reemphasized what the apostles should have already known and practiced: that the Lord commanded them to go out and make disciples of all the nations (Matt 28:19) and to take the saving message of the glorification of Jesus Christ to the uttermost parts of the earth (Acts 1:8). That is, the Lord had already declared the Gentiles clean for the purposes of evangelism through His death and resurrection, "that the blessing of Abraham might come upon the Gentiles in Christ Jesus" (Gal 3:13–14).

In one sense, the vision should not have been necessary. However, Peter's persistence in nullified ceremonies impeded the work of the church in reaching and discipling Gentiles, and it created strife and division among the saints (Gal 2:14). Through this vivid, watershed lesson, the Lord released the Jewish contingent from the application of dietary laws of separation so they would be free to preach the gospel to the Gentiles. Peter's vision was not so much about enlarging the selection of foods available to Christians as it was about freeing believing Jews from ceremonial laws in order to broaden their ministry to the Gentiles (Acts 15:7). This vision also served to answer the question whether Gentiles should live as Jews. In those matters of law that were fulfilled with the coming of the Lord, Gentiles have no obligation to adhere to them. Indeed, neither do Jewish believers!

Circumcision

Of particular concern to Jewish converts to Christianity was whether or not to circumcise their young or to require the same of pagan converts. Circumcision stood alone as the sign of God's covenant with Abraham, which *was* a covenant of faith; thus circumcision seemed as much a sign for Christians as it was for Jews. But Apostle Paul clearly teaches that circumcision has no spiritual, moral, sanctifying, or salvific efficacy for the believer (1 Cor 7:17–20; Rom 2:25–29; Gal 5:2–6). At the Jerusalem Council addressing this very issue, Apostle Peter considered the rite to be an unbearable burden to pagan converts and James asserted it was a trouble to require it in the church (Acts 15:5–21). While this was a response to those who taught circumcision was necessary for salvation, are we to suppose that requiring circumcision as a matter of righteous conduct would not also be a burden? No, to require or promote circumcision at all was a burden. Even though the substance remains through the fulfillment of circumcision in the death of Jesus Christ and the spiritual realization of circumcision in the believer's heart, there remains no substantive morality with regard to the outward performance of that rite (Rom 2:25–29).

A few centuries later, Justin Martyr debated with Trypho about the topic of circumcision. Trypho wondered how such a vital and enduring sign for the Jew could be so quickly dismissed by Christians and rendered inoperative. Justin replied,

> The command of circumcision, again, bidding [them] always circumcise the children on the eighth day, was a type of the true circumcision, by which we are circumcised from deceit and iniquity through Him who rose from the dead on the first day after the Sabbath, [namely through] our Lord Jesus Christ. For the first day after the Sabbath, remaining the first of all the days, is called, however, the eighth, according to the number of all the days of the cycle, and [yet] remains the first . . .
>
> As, then, circumcision began with Abraham, and the Sabbath and sacrifices and offerings and feasts with Moses, and it has been proved they were enjoined on account of the hardness of your people's heart, so it was necessary, in accordance with the Father's will, that they should have an end in Him who was born of a virgin, of the family of Abraham and tribe of Judah, and of David; in Christ the Son of God, who was proclaimed as about to come to all the world, to be the everlasting law and the everlasting covenant, even as the forementioned prophecies show.[6]

Justin argues for the end of circumcision based on the symbolism of the day on which circumcision was commanded to be performed: the eighth day. A week of life is completed and the organ of life is purified on the beginning of a new week, symbolizing a new birth. While circumcision certainly identified the infant with the culture of Judaism, it is the fulfillment of what it foreshadowed that rendered it obsolete (Jer 9:23–26). Apostle Paul links the concept of circumcision with the death, burial, and resurrection of Jesus Christ (Col 2:11–14). The circumcision of Christ's death relates to the body of sin removed and the circumcision of Christ's resurrection relates to the

6. Justin, *Dial.* 41 and 43 (*ANF* 1:215–16).

natural body giving way to the spiritual body (1 Cor 15:44). Therefore, believers, by virtue of their union with Christ, share in a completed salvation (the passage of seven days) and the promise of resurrection (eighth day). So, the fulfillment of circumcision relates to that newness of life that identifies with His resurrection day (Rom 6:1–10).

Though Jews under persecution have attempted, through mutilation, to reverse circumcision in order to hide their identity, for the most part, circumcision is an irreversible act. Thus, Justin argues that our spiritual circumcision launches us into a new life that cannot be undone by human will. Secondly, since circumcision is no longer required, neither are the typological ceremonies that commenced centuries later under Moses, the Sabbath included. Lastly, the event that changed everything was the resurrection of Jesus Christ from the dead on the eighth day. Commenting on the eighth-day resurrection, Henry correctly understands the signification and fulfillment of the Sabbath as Jesus rested in His Sabbath grave. He then correctly links that fulfillment to Paul's warning to the Colossians about the Sabbath day, and he associates that fulfillment with the end of all Jewish feasts.[7] Other Jewish festivals have their own particular fulfillment in other aspects of Jesus' ministry; yet fulfillment alone of the Sabbath gives added force to the conclusion that His resurrection on the eighth day encompasses them all. Those ceremonies of the former covenants found their end in the Messiah, for what they forecasted in shadow found fulfillment in the incarnate Son of God, who is our Righteousness, our Amen, and our Everlasting Rest.

THE WEAKENED SABBATH

Sabbatarians laud and esteem the Sabbath to the extent that it becomes personified and in need of salvation itself. Bruce Ray presumes that the "Sabbath with its ceremonies and sacrifices, died with Christ and rose again" to become the Lord's Day.[8] Somehow the ceremonies and sacrifices that defined the Sabbath and the man-made traditions that bound the Sabbath remained underground while some essential aspect of this Sabbath-being was resurrected. "When God the eternal Son took upon himself the nature of a man and visited his people, he came to set the captives free, including the captive Sabbath."[9] The Sabbath does not require redemption any more than any other ceremonial law, perverted by legalism or not. It is not men who weakened the Sabbath, but Christ Himself. In a similar vein, Barcellos admits that "Hosea 2:11 clearly prophecies the abrogation of Old Covenant Israel's Sabbaths, 'along with all her appointed feasts'" and relates this to Colossians 2:16.[10] Indifferent to this truth, Barcellos also claims that the OT forecasted a continuing Sabbath in Isaiah 56:1–8, that there is some creational and decalogically moral Sabbath essence that "transcends covenantal bounds."[11] But if Isaiah is prophesying an ongoing Sabbath, then Isaiah is

7. Henry, *Commentary*, 5:355 (on Matt 28:1).

8. Ray, *Celebrating the Sabbath*, 94.

9. Ibid., 73.

10. Barcellos, "Old Testament Theology of the Sabbath," 41.

11. Ibid., 45.

also prophesying the continuity of the temple, with its walls and altar, offerings and sacrifices, and the laws of the eunuch under the old covenant. Certainly, Isaiah looks forward to the advent of Christ and the revelation of His salvation and righteousness (Isa 56:1), but the references to these ceremonial structures and laws by which Israel keeps justice and does righteousness, are merely symbolic of the requisite faith in what they foreshadowed. Indeed, this passage is more about the engrafting of faithful Gentiles, as pictured in the rewards given even to faithful outcasts (Isa 56: 5–6, 8), than about the observance of the Sabbath by Jews and Gentiles in the interadvental period. Unfortunately, what Christ has abrogated by His resurrection, Sabbatarians are trying to resurrect and promote as a panacea for many ills harming the church and society. I could not agree more with Chantry that the Western church has become so worldly that it trivializes the Lord's Day, but it does no service to the church to infuse and confuse the Lord's Day with the Sabbath.

The Epistles were written from the Spirit-informed perspective of the resurrection of Christ and should be the hermeneutical starting place for developing an understanding of the Sabbath and Lord's Day. McCartney advances two hermeneutic principles that are well-known among Christians.

> First, obscure passages of Scripture should be interpreted in the light of clear passages. Second, whenever a NT writer explicitly interprets an OT text, this interpretation is true.
>
> In general, any interpretation begins life as a hypothesis that accepts some things which appear to be clear, and then proceeds to build on that base. There is a little bit of danger, however, because one text may be "obscure" only because an ostensibly "clear" text has been misunderstood, but if the interpreter is aware of this danger and maintains humility with respect to the interpretation, he or she can make progress up the hermeneutical spiral by using the clear to look at the obscure.[12]

Sabbatarians have entered this danger zone by treating Apostle Paul's clear texts as unclear simply because they have determined to give more weight to their assumptions and to their misunderstanding of obscure passages. What is a more lucid starting place for understanding the character of the old covenant, including the Sabbath, than the Pauline doctrine of the resurrection?

> The Resurrection is the accomplishment of the work of salvation that outranks and replaces the literal Sabbath. Its celebration on the first day is therefore in terms of salvation rather than of the literal rest that was a sign of the finished work of God in Christ. In other words, in the fulfillment, though the consummation of that fulfillment is still outstanding, the concept of literal rest has been transformed.[13]

12. McCartney, *Let The Reader Understand*, 170.

13. Lincoln, "Sabbath, Rest, and Eschatology," 205.

ROMANS 14:1–7

> Receive one who is weak in the faith, but not to disputes over doubtful things. For one believes he may eat all things, but he who is weak eats only vegetables. Let not him who eats despise him who does not eat, and let not him who does not eat judge him who eats; for God has received him. Who are you to judge another's servant? To his own master he stands or falls. Indeed, he will be made to stand, for God is able to make him stand. One person esteems one day above another; another esteems every day alike. Let each be fully convinced in his own mind. He who observes the day, observes it to the Lord; and he who does not observe the day, to the Lord he does not observe it. He who eats, eats to the Lord, for he gives God thanks; and he who does not eat, to the Lord he does not eat, and gives God thanks. For none of us lives to himself, and no one dies to himself.

Attaching holiness or spirituality to the particulars of a diet, or attributing a special honor or significance to a day is a matter of little, if any, spiritual benefit (1 Cor 8:1). Paul's heartfelt teaching is for mutual reception in Christian love in spite of minor differences about diet and days, knowing that the Lord has received us all (Rom 14:1; 1 Cor 8:1). It is certain in Paul's mind that the Lord's Day has been set apart for congregational worship to symbolize the unity of Christ's body and that the first day of the week reaffirms the historicity of the resurrection, but this significance is different from the holiness that God attributed to specific days of the Jewish calendar. As Stott surmised, "No day *in itself* has any special sanctity."[14] There is no controversy about the proper understanding and decorum of Christian first-day worship, but with regard to the particular controversies between saints, Paul does reduce matters of diet and days to that of insignificance. There is room for a Gentile to maintain a vegetarian diet without being scolded, and there is room for a Jew, like Paul, to eat any manner of meat without offending God. There is room for an ungrounded Jewish convert to observe holy days of the bygone economy without fear of judgment and concomitantly, a Gentile believer is free to disregard these once-significant ceremonies, including the Sabbath.

Eat All Things

On the subject of eating, Paul introduces two consumers, both of whom count their diet a matter of spirituality: one who in faith eats only herbs, presumably a vegetarian, and the other who in faith eats all things. While there are Jewish vegetarians today, Jews living in Paul's time consumed meat. Jewish communities residing in other nations were well-equipped for raising and selling livestock, so it is unlikely that a Jew in Rome would have had difficulty finding kosher meats (Deut 12:15–21). The vegetarian was likely a Gentile who restricted his diet as a result of a worldly philosophy and is characterized by Paul as being weak in faith, because he denies himself, for whatever reason, that "which God created to be received with thanksgiving by those who believe and know the truth" (1 Tim 4:3–4).

14. Stott, "Sabbath, Lord's Day," *NIDNTT*, 3:410.

Paul could have argued that the Lord removed all distinctions between meats (food) on the basis of Christ's own teaching (Matt 15:11) and plainly identify the error of the herb eaters. However, just because there is no distinction of meats, it does not follow that every Christian *must* eat some or all types of meats. Paul understands that if all edible meats are within the liberty of Christian behavior, it would be as wrong to compel an herb eater to consume meats as it would be to compel a meat eater to abstain. Therefore, our diet is a matter of personal conscience. Of greater import is how Christian brethren relate to each other over such issues. Paul allows the weaker brother to retain his restrictive diet, if he eats in faith and does not judge his brother who eats anything put before him. And the brother who understands the truth may not glory in his understanding and challenge his weaker brother; for the weaker brother is not harmed by his abstemious diet and perhaps in time, the Lord will bring the weaker brother to a fuller understanding of the truth. The tension in the Roman church is similar to the controversy at Corinth where some Christians were offended at the thought of eating meat offered to idols (1 Cor 8:1–13). Paul's conclusion there, that what we eat under the new covenant does not commend us to God, is in harmony with his conclusion to the Roman Christians. Lastly, while Paul invokes the principle of love with regard to these controversies when it involves individual believers and negatively affects their relationship, he is altogether more adamant in condemning those who teach the congregation of God to abstain from certain foods (Col 2:16; 1 Tim 4:1–3).[15] Leaders of the church are responsible to the flock of God to lead by example and teach correct doctrine, even regarding minor issues of diet.

Esteem All Days

Paul is concerned that these minor matters have occasioned disputes that erode the unity that should characterize Christ's church (Rom 13:13–14). Commentators generally refer to three possible causes for offense: 1) a Gentile convert who desires to celebrate a national anniversary or pagan festival, 2) a Jewish convert who continues to observe Jewish ceremonies, such as the Passover or the Sabbath, or 3) someone impassioned with assigning to the Lord's Day the attributes of the Sabbath. Now, the Greeks had their special days, and history records the resistance of Christians to syncretize worldly philosophies with the Judeo-Christian worldview. However, Craig Blomberg dismisses the thesis that Paul is addressing primarily Gentile festivals or syncretisms involving the Sabbath.[16] While the congregation in Rome was predominantly Gentile, there were Jewish converts in the area (Acts 28:24); so the influence of Judaism was active, even as a minority. Jewish believers understood the importance of their history as the foundation for the new covenant and understandably transferred their religious notions to church practices. Therefore, when Paul speaks of those who give regard to certain days, he likely means those who observe traditional Jewish ceremonies. Henry assigns the controversy to inadequately discipled Jews who "were not well instructed

15. Still, *Expositor's Bible Commentary*, 12:317.

16. Blomberg, "The Sabbath as Fulfilled in Christ," 127.

touching the cancelling of the ceremonial law by the death of Christ."[17] It must be remembered that the Sabbath was more important than any other Jewish holy day and venerated for its special holiness and elevated status. If there was a day to esteem, a day that required keeping, then the Sabbath is it. In all likelihood, Paul wrote to those Jews who continued to meet on feast days and the Sabbath in addition to the Lord's Day.[18] Paul attempted to diffuse the differences by making allowances for both positions, not necessarily because one position is right and the other wrong, but because the Lord who saves is the same Lord who sanctifies, and with mutual understanding, the law of love may prevail (Rom 13:8–10). While Paul was not specifically addressing any errors concerning the manner of worship and decorum on the Lord's Day, his letter to the Romans provides no defense for sabbatizing the Lord's Day. And, we must be careful not to project on Gentile converts the same attitude toward the Lord's Day that the Jews had toward the Sabbath. D. A. Carson concludes,

> At the stage for which we have evidence in Acts, however, there is no suggestion of a day of rest, nor even that Sunday has as yet an exclusive place in church worship compared to the other days of the week. It may well have been *primus inter pares*, ("the first among equals," cf. Acts 2:46) because it commemorated the day of the Resurrection, but we have no evidence that it was more than this.[19]

Two Greek verbs are used by Paul to describe a person's sentiment toward days: *krino* (esteem) in verse five and *phroneo* (regard) in verse six. *Krino* is used mildly to describe ratiocinating about the proper decorum and duty indicated for a particular day, and in this very chapter, it is used negatively of those who sit in judgment of their brother when no real sin has been committed (Rom 14:3, 4, 10, 13). Whether or not Paul intended the paronomasia, one may *krino* (esteem) the day but may not *krino* (judge) his brother who has a different opinion. *Phroneo* is also a function of the mind, meaning to think about or to set one's mind on something. *Phroneo* is variously translated "regard," "value," "respect," "observe," and "keep," indicating not only the attitude but the action or duty commensurate with the day in question.

Interestingly, Paul does not contrast esteeming (particular) days with *not* esteeming *any* days, but with esteeming *all* days alike. A Christian who does not esteem any day has not fully grasped the sovereignty of the Lord over all the earth, including the measured days of his life. With all the holy days of the Mosaic covenant fulfilled in the Lord Jesus Christ, the church would understandably conclude that each and every day is the day that the Lord has made (Ps 118:24), including Sunday.

> The new religion [Christianity] is too free and exuberant to be trained down to 'times and seasons' like its tame and rudimental predecessor [Judaism]. Its feast is daily, for every day is holy; its moon never wanes, and its serene tranquility is an unbroken Sabbath.[20]

17. Henry, *Commentary*, 6:381.
18. Rordorf, *Sunday*, 137.
19. Turner, "Sabbath, Sunday, and the Law," 137.
20. Eadie, *Commentary on Colossians*, 173.

Consequently, every day is filled with glory, honor, blessings, and meaning. The text nowhere admits that the mature believer does not esteem the Lord's Day, only that he esteems all days alike. Also, the text nowhere admits that the mature believer esteems the Lord's Day more than he esteems all other days. The text nowhere admits that the ungrounded believer esteems the Lord's Day more than he esteems other days. Lastly, the text nowhere admits an exception of the Lord's Day to the days esteemed by a day-esteemer or an all-days-esteemer. Paul's statement merely assures us that day-esteemers have a sincere attitude, that when they observe or keep a special day, they do so to the Lord. Obviously, both the day-esteemer and the all-days-esteemer esteem the Lord's Day to some extent, so the Lord's Day is *included* in both schemes rather than excluded.[21] While it is probable that no controversy existed between the day-esteemers and the all-days-esteemers with regard to the decorum of the Lord's Day, it is possible that the day-esteemers expected more piety on the Lord's Day than given by the all-days-esteemers. But the early church manifested the idea that esteeming all days included esteeming the Lord's Day.

> If it be objected to us on this subject that we ourselves are accustomed to observe certain days, as for example the Lord's day, the Preparation, the Passover, or Pentecost, I have to answer, that to the perfect Christian, who is ever in his thoughts, words, and deeds serving his natural Lord, God the Word, all his days are the Lord's, and he is always keeping the Lord's day.[22]

Even in this later example from Origen, the Christian church viewed their observation of days in a different way than the Jews. While Christians observed the Lord's Day on the first day of the week, they were at the same time always "keeping" the Lord's Day. The Lord's Day was not a holy day, so it was included in the "all days" that were esteemed by mature Christians.

While it may appear that Paul takes a laissez-faire approach to diet and days with the Romans, he has actually provided a Christian ethic about these matters in other epistles. While our diet does not commend us to God (1 Cor 8:8), some may depart the faith as a result of following man-made commandments to abstain from various foods (1 Tim 4:1–3). A weak brother could be offended, and even perish, through the callous exercise of true liberty (1 Cor 8:9–11). While the Jewish holy days were symbolic of greater things, they could never positively affect the conscience (Heb 9:9). Should a Jew return to the practice of ceremonial laws after learning and receiving the truth, he was sure to incur God's displeasure (Heb 10:25–27). Christians could be cheated of their reward and succumb to bondage by observing festivals, New Moons, and Sabbaths (Col 2:16–18; Gal 4:9–11). These matters are more serious to Paul under other contexts, but here Paul is addressing the topic in its earliest form where innocent differences, because of a lack of knowledge, are assuaged by love to maintain an edifying fellowship in a heterogeneous congregation. Paul's main advice to the Romans is

21. Turretin, *Elenctic Theology*, 2:96; Henry, *Commentary*, 6:381–82; Jamieson, Faucet, and Brown, *Bible Commentary*, 3.2:273; and *Barnes' Notes*, 10:299–300.

22. Origen, *Cels* 8.22 (*ANF* 4:647).

directed to the mature believer who must receive one who is weak in the faith. This means avoiding heated discussions and making judgments about the weaker brother because of his misconceptions about adiaphora. In the process of time, and with love, the day esteemer will grow in his understanding and discover a fearless and proper way to honor the Lord.

GALATIANS 4:8–11

> But then, indeed, when you did not know God, you served those which by nature are not gods. But now after you have known God, or rather are known by God, how is it that you turn again to the weak and beggarly elements, to which you desire again to be in bondage? You observe days and months and seasons and years. I am afraid for you, lest I have labored for you in vain.

Weak and Beggarly Elements

One could attempt to explain away the mention of days, months, times, and years to some pagan rituals to which the Galatians were returning, but this cannot be the case. Paul begins his warning to the Galatians, both Jewish and Gentile, with his recollection of his disagreement with the Apostle Peter while in Jerusalem about the relationship of Gentile believers to Jewish customs and law.

> But when I saw that they were not straightforward about the truth of the gospel, I said to Peter before them all, "If you, being a Jew, live in the manner of Gentiles and not as the Jews, why do you compel Gentiles to live as Jews?" (Gal 2:14)

It must be resolved at once that Peter, when compelling Gentiles to live as Jews, was not advocating salvation by works. He did not lose his salvation over this matter, nor was his own salvation even questioned at this point. His hypocrisy in refusing to dine with Gentiles was a step backward in the Christian faith, an example to the Galatians of the ease with which Jewish influence can upset the purity of a believer's character and actions. In Christ, Peter was set free from the former distinctions of nationality and from the painstaking regulations that courted his mind at every turn, so he could engage in unrestricted fellowship without fear or remorse. Not only did Peter's behavior affect Barnabas (Gal 2:13), but to the extent that Peter avoided any Gentile, he, in effect, compelled Gentiles to engage in Jewish separatism. Through that episode of separatism, Peter and the others were declaring themselves clean and the Gentiles unclean. Whatever benefit he felt in separating himself from his brethren was an illusion of his mind, for God had made Jew and Gentile one in Christ.

The emphasis of Christian worship is unity in Christ, so in Christ all nationalities are holy, separated to Him. God removed the former distinctions based on natural birth, language, and geography, and declared a holiness based upon the new birth (Gal 3:1–3). The matter that occupies the mind of Paul in regards to the Galatian congregation is that some Jews were requiring the Gentiles to receive the Abrahamic covenantal sign of circumcision. Insofar that anyone would teach that circumcision was necessary for salvation, Paul condemned it as a false gospel. And insofar that anyone required circumcision, or any other Jewish custom, as a matter of Christian obedience (sanctification) to the law, Paul condemned it as a return to bondage. Regardless of the rationale for demanding circumcision of the Gentile, Paul declares it to be a work of the flesh, unnecessary and ineffectual for imparting any spiritual blessing. He is not questioning the saving faith of those who disagree, but reminds them that the Holy Spirit was imparted to them on the basis of faith and not of works.

Abraham's circumcision was a testimony of his faith. Amazingly, the covenant sign of God's promise to Abraham, the father of faith, came to be regarded as bondage under the new covenant economy if performed as a means of gaining God's favor for salvation or as a means of God's grace in sanctification. If the Abrahamic covenant sign of faith is no longer required, then *a fortiori* the signs of the Mosaic covenant are also illegitimate for new covenant believers. If the foremost personal sign of chosenness—which had its roots prior to the Mosaic law—was inactivated by the death of Jesus Christ, then certainly the succeeding generation of covenantal signs (ceremonial laws) are "old and faded away." Paul's answer to the Judaizers was not that circumcision is required, yet not for salvation, but that circumcision is no longer required at all, especially not for Gentile converts. It is a step backward toward Judaism and essentially denies the sin-removing death of Christ (Col 2:11).

Paul not only attacks compulsory or obligatory circumcision, but the observance of times as well. It may be understood in Paul's mention of "days, months, seasons, and years" that the indigenous Galatians were engaging in the Jewish observances of time, either by compulsion for salvation, or with the false belief that they were simply obeying God. Because these were signs of the old covenant, Paul expresses his shame in them that they should observe them, for if the greater sign of circumcision is annulled, so are the lesser signs of the Sabbath, New Moon, festivals, and feast days.

> It hurt him to the quick after his own merciful deliverance to see these Gentile Christians drawn into this spider-web of Judaizing Christians, once set free, now enslaved again. Paul does not itemize the "days" (Sabbaths, fast-days, feast-days, new moons) nor the "months" (Isa 66:23) which were particularly observed in the exile nor the "seasons" (passover, pentecost, tabernacle, etc.) nor the "years" (sabbatical years every seventh year and the Year of Jubilee). Paul does not object to these observances for he kept them himself as a Jew. He objected to Gentiles taking to them as a means of salvation.[23]

23. Robertson, *Word Pictures*, 4:303. It is my opinion that his reference to Isa 66:23 under the category "months" and his statement about a particular exilic observance do not accurately represent what Paul had in mind. He should have placed the monthly New Moon observances under the category "months" rather than under "days," for these were commanded to be observed in the Law. Furthermore, it is *not* obvious from Scripture that the Galatians observed "times and months" as a means to salvation, as opposed to a means of sanctification. Certainly, if Paul could observe such rituals without clouding his conscience, then so could a Gentile. The bottom line is that these ceremonies were never intended for the Gentiles. Paul was not interested in changing the culture of Judaism, but as Jews became Christians, they would see the futility of continuing to observe rituals that forecasted Christ's work of redemption.

Contrary to Robertson's concluding remark, Gentiles were not basing their salvation on these laws, because Paul previously appealed to their understanding that they received the Holy Spirit by faith. The Galatian Gentiles were like Peter, who received the Spirit by faith but felt compelled to observe ceremonial laws that profit nothing. Nowhere does Paul condemn the Galatians for their obedience to moral law as a means of salvation; he only mentions observance of ceremonial laws. So, when Paul speaks of the "works of the law," he is speaking of the performance of ceremonial laws as a duty of the normal Christian life. Since the ceremonial laws of the Mosaic covenant presaged the Messiah and His work, obedience to them before Christ came was an evidence of faith in what they pointed to. The way of salvation is faith—the same faith that Abraham exemplified prior to receiving the ceremonial law of circumcision. But now that the reality has come, it is illegitimate, even risky, to observe shadow laws.

Days, Months, Times, and Years

There is no reason to question the meaning of these terms as Jewish observances of time, notwithstanding the predominant Gentile population.[24] The Galatians did not know God and served other gods, but the Jews were not unlike their pagan counterparts—souls who did not know God and served other gods (Isa 42:16–17; Jer 2:11; John 8:19). While the phrase is not specific to Jewish ceremonies, it does not follow that they are specifically excluded by the use of general terms. Paul continues his pleading, not willing to let the significance of their error to continue and directly relates the observance of times to Jewish law: "Tell me, you who desire to be under the law, do you not hear the law?" (Gal 4:21). The law that Paul directs his readers to heed is not the Ten Commandments, but an account from the life of Abraham, now revealed as a type of the two covenants that sprung from Abraham. The ceremonial laws of time that Judaizers observed and compelled others to observe, says Paul, are to be likened to the sons of Hagar, to be thrown out, so as to terminate any hope of continued friendship. These laws of time, now likened to bad seed, capture and bind adherents, but those of faith are joined to the "one Seed," Christ, in true freedom. Even before the Jews were given these ceremonial laws, the Lord provided a type in the life of Abraham that spoke of their eventual disposal.[25] There is no biblical rationale to sustain the

24. McGee, *Thru the Bible*, 5:178. Hendrickson, *New Testament Commentary*, "Galatians," 165–66; Jamieson, Faucet and Brown, *Bible Commentary*, 3.2:388. Jervis' suggestion of Celtic observances as opposed to Jewish is not convincing (*Galatians*, New International Bible Commentary on the New Testament, 9:115).

25. Paul uses the word "allegory," and some authors capitalize on this as if a typological interpretation gives it a different meaning. Carson encourages more research on fallacies as pertaining to literary genre: "Our modern definitions of 'parable' or 'allegory' may not be quite what ancient writers meant by these terms," *Exegetical Fallacies*, 137. Goppelt states that allegorical interpretations ignore the historicity and literal meaning of the text in search of a deeper meaning, *Typos*, 18. Galatians 4:21–31 fulfills the criteria of a typological interpretation of biblical history. Paul depends on the facts and sees a foreshadowing and heightening of that history in the present predicament of the Galatians. Though Ishmael was a child of Abraham, Ishmael's birth was a work of the flesh—Abraham's unbelieving attempt to obtain the promise of God. This foreshadowed the well-intentioned, but faithless, pursuit of the promise by Jews through obedience to ceremonial laws. Thus, the work of the flesh by Abraham is heightened in the work of the

argument that the weekly Sabbath was somehow spared from disfellowship—that God would allow one child of the flesh (pursuing righteousness through Sabbath-keeping) to intermingle with the children of promise (those who believe enter into rest). Any benefit seemed to be derived from the makeshift application of Jewish Sabbath law to the Lord's Day is both an illusion and a manacle.

Many Reformed scholars view Paul's list in Galatians as encompassing all Jewish feasts, both legal and man-made, excepting the Sabbath. For example, Barnes excludes the Sabbath from Paul's list because it is in the Decalogue and was observed by Jesus and the apostles during their lifetime.

> The days here referred to are doubtless the days of the Jewish festivals. They had numerous days of such observances, and in addition to those specified in the Old Testament, the Jews had added many others as days commemorative of the destruction and rebuilding of the temple, and of other important events in their history. It is not a fair interpretation of this to suppose that the apostle refers to the Sabbath, properly so called, for this was a part of the Decalogue; and was observed by the Saviour himself, and by the apostles also.[26]

Of course, the Sabbath "properly so called" is the weekly observance of the Jews on the seventh day of the week. While the Sabbath is in the Decalogue, the Lord's Day is not. Contrary to the conclusion of Barnes, it *is* a fair interpretation to include the Sabbath in Paul's list of days, months, seasons, and years because the Sabbath is a functional and basic unit of the whole Jewish calendar system and ceremonially foreshadows Christ as does every other calendar law. This is why Paul did not want Gentile Christians compelled to observe *any* Jewish holy days (though there may have been occasion for some level of participation for specific purposes). The issues before Paul are the protection of Christian liberty and the freedom from being compelled to obey man's traditions or abolished ceremonial laws. In the end, Barnes limits liberty and compels believers to observe a lightweight Sabbath on the Lord's Day, just the opposite of what Paul is teaching.

> Religious festivals formed a noted and splendid part of the ritual of that [Mosaic] law; but they were only designed to be temporary; and having served their end in commemorating certain great events connected with the Jewish commonwealth, and in typifying certain mysteries now clearly revealed by the gospel, they ceased, and, along with other figures, vanished away. To retain these, or to return to them after the promulgation of the Christian law, or to imitate them by instituting festivals of a similar kind, is to doat on shadows—to choose weak

flesh of the Pharisees because the true child of promise, Jesus, has arrived (Gal 3:15–16). Abraham's actions foreshadowed Jewish rejection of Christ in favor of a man-centered, works-oriented pursuit of the promises of God. The end of Ishmael foreshadowed the end of the Jews who do not hold to Jesus in faith—they lose their favored status with God and become, as it were, non-Jews (Isa 29:13; Jer 7:11; cp. Matt 12:41). With regard to the covenants, Jesus is the covenant of faith and His covenant is the terminus of the Mosaic covenant. Paul's identification of the Mosaic law with Ishmael is not as much to pit the new covenant against the old covenant as it is to condemn the pursuit of the promises of God through a faithless use of the old covenant.

26. *Barnes' Notes*, 11:363–64.

> and beggarly elements—to bring ourselves under a yoke of bondage which the Jews were unable to bear, and interpretatively to fall from grace and the truth of the gospel.[27]

COLOSSIANS 2:14–17

> Having wiped out the handwriting of requirements that was against us, which was contrary to us. And He has taken it out of the way, having nailed it to the cross. Having disarmed principalities and powers, He made a public spectacle of them, triumphing over them in it. So let no one judge you in food or in drink, or regarding a festival or a new moon or sabbaths, which are a shadow of things to come, but the substance is of Christ.

Handwriting of Ordinances

Paul was a missionary to the Gentiles, but his evangelistic approach was piloted by the principle "for the Jew first and also for the Greek" (Rom 1:16). Though the Gentiles did not assent to be covenanted with God through the Mosaic law, he includes both Jews and Gentiles as indebted servants or guilty parties to "the handwriting of ordinances that was against us." Sabbatarian commentators who draw a distinction between ceremonial Sabbaths and the weekly Sabbaths seem to restrict the handwriting of ordinances to ceremonial laws.[28] Other authors are less specific and use ambivalent terminology, but seem to gravitate toward moral law.[29] J. Vernon McGee posits, "What did God write on that cross? He wrote the ordinances—He wrote the Ten Commandments. He wrote a law which I cannot keep, ordinances of which I am guilty of breaking."[30] John MacArthur explains that the decrees against us refer to the "Mosaic Law," or, "His law," that Jew and Gentile have violated.[31] Calvin summarily rejects the theory that only moral laws are in view and at the same time believes that it is insufficient to limit the phrase to ceremonial laws alone.[32] Elsewhere in the *Institutes*, when Calvin discusses the redemption of Jesus Christ upon the cross, he refers to the

27. Thomas M'Crie, Lectures on the Book of Esther (1838), as quoted by Schwertley, *Regulative Principle*, 58.

28. "Jewish ceremonial law is here represented" Barnes, *Notes*, 12:265; "Most evidently means the ceremonial law," Clarke, *Commentaries*, 6:523; "must be understood of the ceremonial law," Henry, *Commentary*, 6:611. Barthe and Blanke think the Mosaic law is improbable, and relate *cheirographon* to the "demands" in v. 20–21 (AB 34B, 328–31)—though it seems strange that these man-made petty demands required the death of Jesus on the cross to wipe them away.

29. Alluding to or mentioning specifically the Ten Commandments or the Law: Bruce, NICNT, 10:106; Eadie, *Commentary on Colossians*, 159; Geisler, *Bible Knowledge Commentary*, 2:678; Hendricksen, *New Testament Commentary*, 12:121; Jamieson, Fausset, Brown, *Bible Commentary*, 3:448; Wright, *TNTC*, 12, 18:111.

30. McGee, *Thru the Bible*, 351.

31. MacArthur, *Commentary on Colossians*, 112.

32. Calvin, *Institutes*, 311–13 (2.7.16–17); *Commentaries*, 21:188–90 (Col 2:14).

handwriting of ordinances as directly related to those sins of ours that were imputed to Christ,[33] from which our guilt is acquitted.[34]

So, what is the handwriting of ordinances that was against us, that was blotted out and taken out of the way, having been figuratively nailed to the cross of Jesus at the time of His crucifixion? How does this action and Christ's triumph over unholy spirits provide the rationale for Paul's statement, "So let no one judge you" about specifically mentioned and well-understood practices? Whatever was nailed to the cross was unmistakably nailed there by God the Father Himself and is related to that divine grace that made us alive in Christ and provided forgiveness for all our trespasses (Col 2:13). The handwriting of ordinances against us was nailed to the tree just as surely as the Son was nailed to the tree, so Paul's illustration represents what Christ accomplished on the cross.

The word picture presented by Paul also informs us that we have a certificate or bond of indebtedness to God that we must pay, yet the death of Jesus satisfied that bond, so the Father could cancel the debt by overwriting it with an "X," never to present the indebtedness to us again. This illustration supplements Paul's assertion that we have been forgiven all our transgressions (2:13). Figuratively, God prepared a list of those ordinances that we have all disobeyed and then nailed it to the cross to depict the complete payment of an imposing debt. The forgiveness of our trespasses and sins has no meaning without reference to the holiness of God as revealed in His law. Thus, the handwriting of ordinances solidly suggests the Ten Commandments written by the hand of God, but soon broken by the idolatry and license of the people. Still too, the Pentateuch, a compilation of God's law written by Moses, may be in view as the expert witness against us of our obstinacy and rebellion (Deut 31:21). The ordinances against us are also like the iron-carved record of our deeply imbedded wrongdoings, the justification for the Lord's rage and judgment against us (Jer 17:1–4). This list of ordinances that was against us must be comprised of 1) ceremonial ordinances, 2) moral ordinances, or 3) a combination of the two. If they were singularly ceremonial commandments, then why would God judge the Lord Jesus only for our disobedience to these lesser commandments—commandments that were required exclusively of the Jews and nullified upon the enactment of the new covenant? If they were only moral ordinances that were nailed to the cross, then how does the substitutionary death of Jesus release us from the obligation to keep inconsequential ceremonial ordinances? However, if the handwriting of ordinances against us comprised both moral and ceremonial legislations, then both the substitutionary death of Christ and the abolishment of ceremonial law are justified. The necessity of Christ's death for real sins against a holy God and the necessity for the discontinuation of ceremonial law finds its logical and imperative justification only if the handwriting of ordinances represents (sins against and fulfillment of) both moral and ceremonial law. Whether the handwriting of ordinances refers to the Pentateuch or the Ten Commandments is

33. Ibid., 440 (2.16.6).

34. Ibid., 457 (2.17.5).

moot, for *both* contain moral and ceremonial law. Cross-referencing Paul's mention of written ordinances and the death of Christ in other passages demonstrates that both moral and ceremonial laws are to be understood (Rom 7:4; Gal 3:10; Eph 2:14–16. See also Gal 3:13–14; Heb 7:18; 8:13; 9:9, 10; 10:7–10). If the Gentiles were commanded to obey the ceremonial law after their conversion, then Christ would merely be grafting Gentiles into Judaism, rather than making in Himself one new organism from the two. Christ died for the infractions of all mankind against God's enduring moral law and He died also for the disobedience of the Jews to the provisional ceremonial laws. By the cross on which Jesus died, Paul unites Jew and Gentile. As the centerpiece of our great salvation, the cross establishes the guiltiness of all mankind and so unifies those who come to it through faith. So, Paul apprehends simultaneously that the cross provides real atonement for the sins of the world and fulfills laws symbolic of that culminating event. Thus, as Paul comprehends the cross and the death of Jesus Christ, the handwriting of ordinances against us has a broad and deep reference to sins against both moral and ceremonial law.

Having already reminded the Colossians about the true doctrine of circumcision in verse eleven, it is fair to say that when Paul mentions meat and drink, feast days, New Moons, and Sabbaths, he is alerting the Gentile majority to stand in their liberty against Jewish legalism, or the "idol of human tradition."[35] Since the kingdom of heaven is not concerned necessarily with matters of diet and days—though historically these were matters of piety with the Jews—the converts to Christ need not focus their lifestyle on laws that have been nullified by the death of Jesus. Paul could not have been clearer in relegating the Sabbath, properly so called, to the realm of annulled ceremonies. Relating this passage to the fourth commandment, Calvin resolved,

> With [God commanding the Jews to keep the shadowy Sabbath until the Lord's coming] in view, we can understand what Saint Paul says: that now we are no longer subject to this ancient servitude of observing the Sabbath day, for it is necessary for us to render this honor to Jesus Christ, to content ourselves with what he himself has brought us without any longer having what was exterior under the law.[36]

While Calvin attempted to avoid self-contradiction between his belief in the ceremonial Sabbath and his belief in the applicability of the fourth commandment—by refraining from legislating Sunday behaviors (Judaizing the Lord's Day)—contemporary Sabbatarian authors seem to magnify the inevitable confusion. For example, J. Douma agrees emphatically that the weekly Sabbath is under consideration by Paul.

> There is no reason for excluding reference to the weekly Sabbath here. Just as in Galatians 4:10, there can be no doubt that Paul is here rejecting the demand

35. Wright, "Colossians," TNTC, 118–99; Beale, "Colossians," *Commentary on the New Testament Use*, 860.

36. Farley, *Calvin's Sermons*, 101.

> for observing the Sabbath. The Sabbath is included when he describes fasts and feasts as "a shadow of things to come," whereas Christ is the "substance."[37]

So, if Paul rejects Sabbatarianism because of the shadow-substance paradigm, then how can Reformed believers justify their Sabbatarianism with a clear conscience? Douma answers that Calvin spiritualized the Sabbath too much and offers his own interpretation that the Sabbath is all about liberation. He then questions whether the term "ceremonial" has a precise meaning, preferring instead the term "provisional." Furthermore, he questions whether the term "shadow" describes a "differentiated messianic typology," that is, whether there is a direct relationship between the external duty of an OT command and its fulfillment in Christ. Finally, he asserts that there were shadows of things to come for Judaism and shadows of things that had come for the church. So he concludes,

> Christ is the fulfillment of the Sabbath. That shadow too has disappeared, but in its place something else could arise which, just like the Sabbath, commemorates liberation. Anybody wanting to maintain the fourth commandment without keeping time with the clock of redemptive history, must stick with the *Jewish* Sabbath. But then such a person will catch no glimpse of the true, liberating intention of the fourth commandment. For that liberation presupposes a different Sabbath after Christ than before Christ.[38]

In other words, the clock of redemptive history has "liberated" the church from the Jewish Sabbath on Saturday and put in its place a Christian Sabbath on Sunday. Douma is not really clear on how Christ fulfilled the Sabbath, and even though he admits the Sabbath is fulfilled, he claims that it has been replaced by another shadow law. However, Paul makes no distinction between feast days, New Moons and Sabbaths with regard to the shadow-substance paradigm. That is, what basis does Douma have to single out the Sabbath for special treatment so it could be replaced by a postshadowing Lord's Day? Paul asserts that they are all shadows and that they all have their substance in Christ. Now that Jesus Christ has been raised from the dead, the shadow has been removed—signifying that the ceremonial regulations fulfilled their purpose in pointing to Christ and are now supplanted by the living Jesus Christ (Col 2:17).

A Sabbath or The Sabbath?

While Calvin and Douma admit that the text refers to the weekly Sabbath, other Sabbatarians propose that the word *sabbaton* as used in this text means "lesser" Sabbaths because it is not preceded by a definite article. For example, Barnes attempts to distinguish between the feast-day Sabbaths (*a* Sabbath or *Jewish* Sabbaths) and the weekly Sabbaths (*the* Sabbath).

> Greek, "of the Sabbaths." The word Sabbath in the Old Testament is applied not only to the seventh day, but to all the days of holy rest that were observed by the Hebrews, and particularly to the beginning and close of their great festivals.

37. Douma, *Ten Commandments*, 136. Also, Barcellos, "Old Testament Theology of the Sabbath," 41.
38. Ibid., 137.

> There is, doubtless, reference to those days in this place, since the word is used in the plural number, and the apostle does not refer particularly to the Sabbath properly so called. There is no evidence from this passage that he would teach that there was no obligation to observe any holy time, for there is not the slightest reason to believe that he meant to teach that one of the Ten Commandments had ceased to be binding on mankind. If he had used the word in the singular number—"*The* Sabbath," it would then, of course, have been clear that he meant to teach that that commandment had ceased to be binding, and that a Sabbath was no longer to be observed. But the use of the term in the plural number, and the connection, show that he had his eye on the great number of days which were observed by the Hebrews as festivals, as a part of their ceremonial and typical law, and not to the moral law, or the Ten Commandments.[39]

First of all, the Greek *plural* form *sabbata* reflects only the innocent effort to transliterate the Aramaic *singular* noun *sabbathah.* In other words, the Aramaic singular noun for Sabbath is homophonic to the Greek plural noun. Because of this, the Greeks constructed the singular form *sabbaton*, commonly used in NT times to speak either of a Sabbath day or Sabbath days. Actually, no syntactical patterns exist in the NT involving the noun *sabbaton* and any preceding articles, so Barnes' statement is defenseless. In fact, according to Vincent, the plural form is used only once in the NT of more than a single day (Acts 17:2), thus all the other twenty uses of the plural form are with a single Sabbath day in mind.[40] In the LXX, "there does not seem to be any difference in meaning between the singular and plural forms of the Greek equivalent."[41] Not only this, all other occurrences of the word "Sabbath" in the NT refer only to the weekly Sabbath (where not translated "week" based upon the context). Besides, all festival Sabbaths are already included under the heading of feast days, so Paul is unmistakably referring to weekly Sabbaths.[42] And if we take into account the sabbatic quality of the New Moon celebration (Amos 8:5), it is as if Paul is asserting that the yearly, monthly, and weekly Sabbaths have met their antitype in Christ Jesus.

Earlier Sabbatarians, such as Owen (1616–1683), attempted to distinguish between the weekly Sabbath, epitomized in the fourth commandment, and the "Jewish Sabbaths" of the festival calendar, hoping to sequester the former from Paul's theology of Sabbath fulfillment.[43] However, Turretin (1623–1687) anticipated the groping argument that Paul is referring to something other than weekly Sabbaths.

> In vain is the reply that weekly Sabbaths are not meant, but the various others prevailing among the Jews (which were typical). [1] What ought to be proved is taken for granted. The words of the apostle do not admit it because, since they are general and treat of Sabbaths in the plural without any limitation, they ought also to be extended to all; nor does it become us to restrict what the apostle has not

39. *Barnes' Notes*, 12:267. Barnes admits that if Paul truly meant the weekly Sabbath, then surely it is abrogated, notwithstanding its mention in the Ten Commandments.

40. Vincent, *Word Studies*, 909.

41. Stott, "Sabbath, Lord's Day," *NIDNTT*, 3:405.

42. Torrey, *Ought Christians to Keep the Sabbath?* 29–31.

43. Owen, "Excercitations," *Exposition on the Epistle to the Hebrews*, 690–91.

> restricted. [2] Festivals are here distinguished from Sabbaths. [3] The Sabbaths are specially meant (which were sanctioned by the fourth commandment) which frequently recurred and whose observance the Jews and Sabbatarians among the primitive Christians insisted upon.[44]

The truth of the matter is that Paul *is* referring to *the* Sabbath or the weekly Sabbath, so Barnes' and Owen's fearful conclusions must follow: the fourth commandment "had ceased to be binding."

Not Really the Sabbath

Faced with differences of opinion among ordained officers of the Orthodox Presbyterian Church (OPC), a Committee on Sabbath Matters was organized in 1973, "to study the extent to which the Westminster Confession of Faith and Catechisms faithfully reflect the Scripture teaching in regard to the Fourth Commandment."[45] Based upon the findings, the OPC would have the tools to determine whether a doctrinal offense had been committed and whether church discipline was an appropriate action against those who held variant views of the fourth commandment and secondary standards. Since the Sabbath is specifically mentioned by Paul in Colossians, along with other ceremonial commands, this verse was the kingpin of their study and required a fresh interpretation. First, their conclusion:

> The Sabbath was not abrogated for the New Testament dispensation. Colossians 2:16, 17 refers to the loosing of the bonds of the Mosaic requirements in respect to ceremonial and sacrificial elements of the Old Testament holy days in the light of Christ's perfect sacrifice; but it does not remove the obligation of the Fourth Commandment itself. Such passages as Romans 14:5, 6 and Galatians 4:10 do not nullify all distinctions between days, since the New Testament itself distinguishes the first day of the week from other days, as in 1 Corinthians 16:2; Acts 20:7, and designates that day as the Lord's Day or Christian Sabbath as in Revelation 1:10.[46]

Through this report, the OPC provided a novel way to exclude the Sabbath *per se* from the category of OT shadows mentioned in Paul's letter to the Colossians. With the proper knowledge that Paul is relating these items to the shadows of Christ's sacrifice, they make the assumption that ceremonial laws are restricted to those involving sacrifice. They first limit Paul's reference to meat and drink to the "system of official sacrifices to be made for all Israel" presented at the temple, *and* by extension, the reference to a feast day, New Moon, or Sabbath is limited to the *sacrifices* made on those respective days. If only sacrifices and offerings are to be counted as shadows, then the committee could conclude that "meat and drink" does not refer to actual edibles and drinkables.

44. Turretin, *Elenctic Theology*, 2:85.

45. Orthodox Presbyterian Church, Fortieth General Assembly, "Report of the Committee on Sabbath Matters," 92.

46. Ibid., 104. For the most part, this argument was restated thirty-five years later by Adventist Ron du Preez in *Judging the Sabbath*.

> [Meat and drink] cannot refer to the Mosaic dietary laws (contrary to many commentators), since there were no such laws on matters of drink. (The only rules about drink apply to priests on duty and to Nazarites—Leviticus 10:9; Numbers 6:3—and were not applicable to the ordinary believers to whom Paul writes.) Much less can they refer to some hyper-pious additions to the law made by overzealous Jews.
>
> There is no other meaning for these two words in Colossians 2:16 that fits the meaning of the "shadow," and is thus drawn from the Old Testament, except that which understands them as referring to meat- and drink-offerings.[47]

Their only objection to the prevalent understanding that "meat and drink" refer to common food and drink is that the OT discusses drink only in relationship to the Aaronic priests and Nazarites. This is hardly an objection, but their preconceptions prevented them from mentioning several other regulations concerning kosher food and drink for the common Jew contained in the Scriptures[48] and the traditions concerning food and drink in extra-biblical documents.

The Greek words employed by Paul in Colossians 2:16, *brosis* and *posis*, mean eating and drinking. This is comparable to Paul's use of these words in Romans 14:17, where what one eats and drinks is understood.[49] Even though the majority of Jewish dietary laws involved eating, there were a few that applied to drinking, so it is not unlikely that the Colossian believers were being seduced into dietary rules that involved drink. The committee referenced only Leviticus 10:9 and Numbers 6:3, to which could be added Leviticus 11:34, 36 and Daniel 1:8.[50] Though insignificant in number, these are still unquestionably drink regulations for ordinary Jews, in contradistinction to the committee's contention that "there were no such laws on matters of drink." Paul himself took the Nazarite vow as a Christian Jew (Acts 18:18), so it is certainly plausible that Jews urged Gentiles in Colossae to take such vows that involved abstention from wine (perhaps even holding up Paul as an example). Luke also records that when Paul returned to Jerusalem in order to make peace regarding rumors of his teaching, he was urged by the apostles to participate in the sacrificial cleansing of four Jewish believers who took such vows (Acts 21:15–25; Num 6). While it is possible that Gentiles questioned Jews about the merits of these vows, it is more likely that Jews urged Gentiles to perform these vows for themselves; therefore, the apostles protected the Gentiles from those ceremonial laws (Acts 21:25). Regardless, these drink laws prefigure Christ as surely as laws concerning eating, and all dietary laws are as ceremonial in essence as sacrificial laws.

The committee also maintained that "meat and drink" cannot refer to "some hyper-pious additions to the law made by overzealous Jews," because Paul relates meat and drink to shadows; and shadows cannot be man-made traditions. I have already

47. Ibid., 100.

48. Wright, "Colossians," TNTC, 119.

49. Barth and Blanke, "Colossians,"AB 34B, 337–38.

50. Old Testament laws also prohibited the drinking the blood (Lev 3:17; 7:26,27; 17:11–14; 19:26; Deut 12:16, 23, 24; 15:23; Ezek 33:25). This prohibition is upheld in the New Testament (Acts 15:20, 29; 21:25) because it endorses a respect for the blood of Jesus Christ.

demonstrated that "meat and drink" can refer to proper Mosaic laws and thus serve as shadows of redemption, but there is no reason to exclude the possibility that Paul envisions Jewish traditions as well. Suggesting that the Essenes were influencing the Colossians, Vincent stated that "the Essenes abjured both wine and animal food,"[51] and were set against the Greek and Roman customs of enforced conviviality (i.e., the obligation to drink all of the wine that is set before you).[52] However tempting it might be to package Paul's thoughts into discrete modules, there is convergence of several themes within this syncope. Paul's warning to the Colossians addressed Jewish law (2:16–17), pagan mysticism (2:18–19), and Gnostic asceticism (2:20–23); all of which militate against the liberty Christians have in a supremely sufficient Jesus Christ (Gal 2:4). Paul's mention of Christ's victory over principalities and powers (v. 15) is antithetical to the forthcoming warning against the pagan worship of angelic beings (v. 18). Likewise, Paul uses the phrase "commandments of men" in relation to Gnostic traditions, a phrase that the Lord used (Mark 7:7) and Paul used (Titus 1:14) to describe Jewish additions to the law. So, contrary to the conclusion of this committee, there is no reason to exclude from the context Jewish additions to the law. Regardless of the specific origin of legalisms concerning food and drink, Paul instructed the Colossians in unity with Jesus' teaching that it is not what enters the mouth that defiles a man (Matt 15:11) and that "the kingdom of God is not eating and drinking, but righteousness and peace and joy in the Holy Spirit" (Rom 14:17).

As the OPC acknowledged, many commentators hold the opinion that Paul is speaking of the ceremonial nature of dietary laws to the Colossians. The implication of this, which makes Sabbatarians shudder, is that Paul must also be speaking of the ceremonial nature of calendar laws, the weekly Sabbath included. Again, the OPC attempts to reduce the scope of the mention of the Sabbath as ceremonial law by limiting the definition to the sacrifices made on that day.[53] The committee sells short Christ's work on the cross to think that only the official sacrifices are fulfilled in Christ. With this artificial division in place, they may safely abolish the sacrifices made on a Sabbath day, yet retain all other Sabbath laws that affected "personal worship." They propose the actual controversy involved Colossian Gentiles criticizing Jews for supporting the temple sacrifices as opposed to Jews urging Gentiles to participate in dietary and calendar customs! Paul doesn't even mention the temple or the sacrifices or tithing to keep that system running, so this proposal is pure presumption. If this was indeed the historical background for Paul's advice, the implication is that Paul actually encourages the support of temple sacrifices by Gentile Christians!

Next, the committee connects Colossians 2:16 to the list of sacrifices in Numbers 28–29 and Ezekiel 45:17, and concludes,

> The subject is not the individual worshipper's offerings, nor his personal acts of worship on those days, but the system of official sacrifices to be made for all

51. Vincent, *Word Studies*, 2:909.

52. Freeman, *Manners and Customs*, 202.

53. This view is (was) also held by James Jordan, *The Christian and the Calendar*, 18, 25.

> Israel . . . Wherever it occurs in the Old Testament, the phrase "sabbaths, new moons, and feasts" always has reference to the official sacrifices to be offered on those days in behalf of the covenant nation, and never refers to individual observance of those days.[54]

While it is true that temple sacrifices are within the context of each use of "Sabbaths, New Moons, and feast days"[55] in the OT (1 Chr 23:31; 2 Chr 2:4; 8:13; 31:3; Ezra 3:5; Neh 10:33; Isa 1:13, 14; Ezek 45:17; 46:3; Hos 2:11), the committee certainly makes more of this than needs be. It is only reasonable, when narrating the momentous history of temple worship, that temple sacrifices are the focus. Indeed, the association of the temple and its sacrifices with the festival calendar, including the weekly Sabbath, demonstrates the comprehensive scope of ceremonial law in the life of Israel. Besides, contrary to the committee's findings, the context in several passages does mention some individual contributions indicative of personal worship: tithe and first fruits (2 Chr 31:3), tithing and keeping Tabernacles (Ezra 3:5), tithing (Neh 10:33), abstention from work on feast day Sabbaths (Num 28:17–18; 28:26; 29:1; 29:7; 29:12), and the provision of animals and harvest according to precise measures and proportions (Ezek 45:17). So the committee's distinction between corporate, official, sacrificial worship and individual or personal worship is invalid because the former derives from and is supported by the latter. The revenue that fueled temple worship was the responsibility of the eleven tribes, met variously by free gifts in the form of vows or property to be sold, and compulsory taxes.

> Besides . . . votive offerings, and the sale of the surplusage of incense, flour, etc., the people were wont on the Sabbaths and feast-days to bring voluntary contributions "in their hand" to the Temple. Another and very large source of revenue was from the profit made by the meat-offerings, which were prepared by the Levites, and sold every day to the offerers. But by far the largest sum was derived from the half-shekel of Temple tribute, which was incumbent on every male Israelite of age, including proselytes and even manumitted slaves.[56]

In all of these references, the phrase "feast days, New Moons, and Sabbaths" presents a summary of Israel's form of worship, to which the writers add other adjunctive forms such as daily sacrifices, incense, gifts, tithes, showbread, grain offerings, festivity, tribute money, wood offerings, and the like. Obviously, Paul does not use this stock phrase to defend the support of the temple and the priesthood by the Colossian church, a congregation that resided some 800 miles away from Jerusalem.

Sacrifices are an integral and defining aspect of calendar feasts and holy days—so much so that a failure to properly offer the sacrifices makes the holy day a sham, despised by the Lord despite the festive attitude of its adherents (Hos 2:11). Without the sacrifices, all other attempts to observe the day are futile exercises. As Lange poignantly

54. Orthodox Presbyterian Church, Fortieth General Assembly "Report of the Committee on Sabbath Matters," 101.

55. Paul reverses the order of the stock phrase from "Sabbaths, New Moons, and feast days" to "feast day, New Moon, or Sabbath," which finds similarity only to Ezek 45:17; Hos 2:11; and *War Scroll* 2:4.

56. Edersheim, *Temple*, 55.

stated, "The enjoyment of the sabbath by the people depended on the regular functions of the sacred priesthood on that day."[57] If Christ's death removed the sacrifices of these holy days and seasons, then there is nothing remaining for us to observe. Paul may have allowed Jewish Christians to involve themselves in temple worship, but he never expected it of Gentile believers. Paul's quest for a unity of faith (Col 3:10–14) could ultimately never allow for a divided worship, so it was inevitable that Jewish Christians follow the new form of worship expected of Gentiles (Col 1:25–27).[58] The Gentiles did not need to circumcise their young or themselves (Col 2:11). They were free from dietary restrictions and distinctions of clean and unclean (Col 2:21). Gone were the obligations of calendar, representative, and place worship (Col 2:16), for Christ indwells the Gentile on the basis of faith and has fulfilled what all the Jewish ceremonies foretold. This was the direction the Lord was bringing His one new man, the church, for as Peter concluded, the Jews shall be saved in the same manner as the Gentiles (Acts 15:11).

Another problem with its analysis is the failure to appreciate the fact that when someone has a liberty to enjoy, they almost never occupy themselves with thoughts of ways to restrict that liberty. Paul's emphasis in Colossians 2:13–14 is the canceling of our personal spiritual debt—this doctrine is *the* foundation for Christian liberty. Thus, Paul logically moves from the canceling of personal sins against God and the resultant freedom from condemnation to the fulfillment of ceremonial laws and the resultant freedom from being judged by other Christians. Paul's command, "Let no one judge you . . ." is primarily for those whose liberty is being menaced by advocates of rules about meat and drink, feast days, New Moons, and Sabbaths. The OPC committee turns this passage upside down and makes the Gentile Christians the curtailers of Jewish liberty to practice invalidated ceremonies.

Thankfully, the single dissenter to the majority report, Richard M. Lewis,[59] understood the Colossians passage correctly, and stands as an example of letting the text speak unequivocally while dismissing all contrary presuppositions.

> When Paul places the Sabbath among the shadows, his meaning can hardly be misunderstood: he is placing the Sabbath commandment within the ceremonial law which has been fulfilled in Christ. But it is absolutely impossible to evade the force of his words: "Let no man therefore judge you . . . in respect of . . . the Sabbath day." These words can only mean that the keeping of the Sabbath cannot be made the criterion for testing one's piety. A statement such as this could never have been uttered by an inspired speaker of the Old Testament times. That Christians are no longer under the obligation of keeping the Sabbath could hardly have been stated in clearer terms than the words of Colossians 2:16, 17.[60]

57. Lange, *Commentary*, 8:217 (Matt 12:5).

58. Rordorf, *Sunday*, 138–39.

59. Pastor Lewis passed away in November 2007 at the age of 83. Five years before he died, and thirty years after his dissenting opinion, the Northern California Presbytery of the OPC entertained charges against Rev. Lewis for failing to retract his former position in favor of the findings of the 40th General Assembly. To their credit, the charges, brought by five of their pastors, were dropped.

60. Lewis, "Minority Report (I)," 107.

What could be clearer? The Sabbath is in the same category of commandments as the feast days, New Moons, diet regulations, and circumcision. They are all cancelled in their totality because they have all been completely fulfilled in Christ. If it is a denial of Christ's death to continue offering sacrifices according to the law, why is it not a denial of what Christ provided by that death (i.e., spiritual rest) to continue in the outward rest according to the law? If His death nullified the forward-looking ceremonies of His death, then certainly His life nullifies the forward-looking ceremonies of His life. Because Christ fulfilled the Sabbath—both the ceremonies that envisioned his death and the ceremonies that guaranteed His resurrected life—those in Him need not make sacrifices, engage in ritual rest, or forgo preparing a fire. The continuation of Sabbath-like observances in Christian churches represents reluctance to fully rest in Christ as the conclusive fulfillment of the Sabbath type, and it further evinces that the Colossian heresy is as much a contemporary problem as a historical one. The regrettable outcome of this committee's work is that its membership may face church discipline based on this distressing level of scholarship.

HEBREWS 4:1–11

> Therefore, since a promise remains of entering His rest, let us fear lest any of you seem to have come short of it.
>
> For indeed the gospel was preached to us as well as to them; but the word which they heard did not profit them, not being mixed with faith in those who heard it.
>
> For we who have believed do enter that rest, as He has said: "So I swore in My wrath, 'They shall not enter My rest,'" although the works were finished from the foundation of the world.
>
> For He has spoken in a certain place of the seventh day in this way: "And God rested on the seventh day from all His works";
>
> and again in this place: "They shall not enter My rest."
>
> Since therefore it remains that some must enter it, and those to whom it was first preached did not enter because of disobedience,
>
> again He designates a certain day, saying in David, "Today," after such a long time, as it has been said: "Today, if you will hear His voice, Do not harden your hearts."
>
> For if Joshua had given them rest, then He would not afterward have spoken of another day.
>
> There remains therefore a rest for the people of God.
>
> For he who has entered His rest has himself also ceased from his works as God did from His.
>
> Let us therefore be diligent to enter that rest, lest anyone fall according to the same example of disobedience.

Contextual Rest

The writer of Hebrews addresses the tendency of Jewish believers to return to Jewish customs and laws by advancing the superiority of Jesus over Moses (3:1–6) with the admonition to fully place their confidence in Jesus (3:8–14), and then relevantly cites the ninety-fifth Psalm of David. Beginning with the word "Today," the author of Hebrews focuses upon the fact that each day of every week, month, and year may be called "Today." The overarching emphasis in this letter to Jewish Christians is to evade any temptation to return to Judaism while undergoing persecutions (Heb 3:12), "to take them off from the ceremonies of the law, to which they were so wedded."[61] Reconsidering Judaism would be an act of unbelief, a trampling underfoot the Lord Jesus, who is the Testator of the new covenant, the Apostle and High Priest of the new nation, the chosen Son of the new house. The author is not pleading simply that Christianity is better than Judaism, but that God Himself was leading and directing all of Jewish history to culminate in this day. The Canaan experience was metaphor enough to inspire serious thought about the consequences of unbelief. The author begins in chapter 3, verse 7, with the testimony of the Holy Spirit to King David recounting the bitterness of Israel's unbelief (Ps 95). Regarding the choice facing some of his readership—whether they withdraw from Christ in unbelief—the author of Hebrews envisions them, as it were, standing on the shore of the Jordan River with promised Canaan before them. Shall they emulate faithful Joshua and believe the Lord in anticipation of receiving a fruitful land, or shall they regret ever leaving Egypt and long for the days of leeks and onions? With Israel's history in the wilderness, and eventually in Canaan, drawn on the board as an illustration, the author ignores the actual timeline to present the idea that one is either going to enter Canaan in belief (at the end of forty years) or not enter Canaan due to unbelief (right after the exodus). The Hebrew Christian who pulls away from Christ is no different from the Israelites of the past who were taken by the deceitfulness of sin and unbelief and incurred the Lord's displeasure and judgment (3:12–13). Yet the surpassing reality, presented metaphorically in the remaining Canaan rest, is their salvation through Jesus Christ. So the author takes care to encourage those who have *already* entered into rest through faith, and at the same time to warn those who are deceived about their status in the church. The Canaan rest is not merely an illustration, but a foreshadowing type of entering into the Lord's salvation, living the Christian life, and possessing a future blessedness. The Holy Spirit made this plain to David when He said "today," meaning that the borders of salvation land are open every day to those who would believe. It is not a hebdomadal rest, taken every seventh day, but a hodiernal one, approachable on any given day through the diligence of faith (4:11). In Hebrews 4, the author conjoins the Canaan theme with two other prefigurements of rest—the creation rest and the sabbatic rest—that anticipated the day when the lost enter the kingdom of God through faith in Jesus Christ.

Soteriological Rest

Hebrews 4 commences with a grim warning: tremble readers, because some Israelites did not enter the land of Canaan—they came short of it. They experienced the redemption of the Lord from Egypt and witnessed the power and glory of God, but they

61. Henry, *Commentary*, 6:715.

did not believe the gospel that was preached to them. The reality that unites those he forewarns with the history of their fathers is the preaching of the gospel and the want of a faithful response. It fell on deaf ears then; it can fall on deaf ears now. Since the gospel is still being preached today, the land of Canaan, as a symbol of salvation, is still being presented as the reward to those who believe. The author introduces the Canaan rest as a promise in Hebrews 4:1 and pleads that they would believe (2 Cor 4:3–4, 5:20). Verse 2 reminds the reader that the issue is unbelief, a deficit of faith, a failure to trust. But what about those who already believe? Verse 3 assures them, "For we who have believed do enter that rest." The promised rest is to those who believe the gospel of Jesus Christ. Clearly, this is the proclamatory and invitational call of the gospel, "For indeed the gospel was preached to us as well as to them" (Heb 4:2).

The supporting scriptural quote, "I swore in My wrath," provides a stark contrast to the positive statement just made. Just as surely as unbelief will incur the wrath of God and cause Him to swear that you will not enter, more so will belief secure the blessings of God and the fulfillment of His promise to bring you into the Canaan rest, to save you from your sins (Heb 6:13–18). Clarke concurs that entering into that rest means a present possession.

> The meaning appears to be this: We Jews, who have believed in Christ, do actually possess that rest-state of happiness in God, produced by peace of conscience and joy in the Holy Spirit—which was typified by the happiness and comfort to be enjoyed by the believing Hebrews, in the possession of the Promised Land.[62]

The gospel of Jesus Christ is now being preached in the world, and those who hear it are likened to two groups of Israelites: those who do not believe and those who believe. Underscored by the author's later emphasis on "today," salvation rest becomes the present possession of the believer. A. T. Lincoln reminds his readers that the present tense is used, which "is to be taken as a true present and not simply as having a future force."[63]

Having noted the typical meaning of the promised rest in Canaan, the author proceeds to inform us about another typic rest: the rest of God on the seventh day, "although the works were finished from the foundation of the world." The meaning of the seventh-day rest augments the meaning of the Canaan rest. With respect to the Canaan rest, those who desire to enter therein must believe, but, with respect to the creation rest, they must also cease from works as a means of entering in. Ceasing from works and believing God are congruous descriptions of what it means to fully trust in Jesus Christ for salvation. Just as the Canaan rest was a type of salvation, so is the seventh-day rest of God. With the advent of Jesus Christ, the creation account can now be understood as a redemptive type. This is how the gospel was preached even from the foundation of the world, that those who believe should have eternal life (Rom 1:16; 2:16; 2 Thess 1:8). The seventh day was His rest and Canaan was His rest. The whole idea of entering into salvation rest with God is predicated upon a work being

62. Clarke, *Commentary*, 6:710 (Heb 4:3).

63. Lincoln, "Sabbath, Rest, and Eschatology," 212.

accomplished by God on behalf of man, who, if he would have it, must cease from his own works and believe. The echoing of Psalm 95, "they shall not enter *My* rest," emphasizes, along with Genesis 2:2, "and *God rested* on the seventh day from all His works," that salvation rest is *God's* rest—His by decree, His by right of work, and His to freely give by grace. Salvation is a present possession that those of faith receive and enjoy today, and its fullness will be realized according to the divine will by both His promise and oath.

Eschatological Rest

The author resumes in verse 6 with two thoughts that supplement verses 1 and 2: there is a rest that remains, and a life of disobedience bars entrance into that rest. Drawing a second draught from Psalm 95, in verse seven he underscores that David was not merely recounting history but that Israel's history had an incredible future application. David saw that the Canaan rest was beyond the actual borders of Canaan and available in a spiritual way to those of faith any day of the week. "Today" is not restricted to the single nychthemeron during which David wrote the Psalm. "Today" means daily, not only the day in which we live but all days yet future as they arrive. David hoped that he, too, would eventually live in the presence of God Almighty in a resurrected body, "My flesh also will rest in hope" (Ps 16:9–11). Knowing that the promise of God is as sure as the day in which we live gives great consolation (Luke 23:43). Likewise, the author's warning is applicable daily from now on, as it has been since the days of David and even from the beginning of creation. This understanding should not be a surprise for Christians who know that the promises of God are both a present reality and a future eventuality. As McCartney explains, "The tension between 'already' and 'not yet' is even greater now that Jesus has ascended and sent the Holy Spirit."[64] After forty years, Israel eventually entered Canaan under the leadership of Joshua, so the Holy Spirit revealed to David that there is another Canaan, another rest, into which believers may enter. While king of Israel, David yearned for the Lord's promise of rest in Canaan to be fully realized by its inhabitants, and he worked vigorously, both militarily and spiritually, to effect that promise. In David's meditations, the Holy Spirit revealed to him that it was not his work but the Lord's, and that it was not this land but a better land that he was hoping to possess. For David, the promised rest was certainly eschatological, as it is for those whom God has yet to add to His church.

The author draws to a close regarding the symbolic rest, repeating for the third time that it remains for some to enter in, only this time, the word *sabbatismos* is used (verse 9). It should be obvious at this point that the *sabbatismos* rest is the same as the Canaan rest and is the same as the creation rest; each of which is typological of the redemptive rest provided to believers in Jesus the Messiah. The *sabbatismos* rest is presented as yet another figure of rest that believers may enter. Morrison understands the following as the plain sense of this passage.

64. McCartney and Clayton, *Let The Reader Understand*, 204; Irons, "Entering God's Rest," n.p.

> The writer is using a different word for rest, but he is not referring to a different rest. Both *katapuasin* and *sabbatismos* are being used as metaphors for salvation. As can be seen by the word "then" or "therefore," it is the same rest that is mentioned in verse 8.[65]

By presenting Sabbath-keeping as a type, the author is concurrently claiming that the Sabbath is as ineffective in providing a true rest to the people of God as was Canaan. It was already plain to the Jews that they were not experiencing the creation rest of God. The Holy Spirit Himself informed David that Canaan was not the ultimate rest of God. Now, through the author of Hebrews, the Holy Spirit informs us that Joshua did not bring Israel into true rest, nor did their Sabbath-keeping. The rest that Christians possess now by faith is the same rest that Jesus Christ will provide in the days ahead for the future faithful. He has accomplished the work necessary to bring in the eschatological rest. These thoughts are summarized in Appendix 6.

The author links the Sabbath-keeping rest with the creation rest and the Canaan rest simply because they all involve ceasing from works. In verse 10, God exemplified for man at the creation that true rest is a ceasing from works (Heb 4:3–4). The thwarted plans of Israel to take Canaan by force demonstrated that true rest must be achieved through the Lord's work. Finally, the Lord instructed the Jews through Sabbath-keeping to cease from works in order to enjoy rest. The impact of this connection is that religious works are an unnecessary component of entering the true rest of God. One must believe the gospel of Christ, and believe alone, not counting on one's obedience to bring about the salvation rest of God. While the general emphasis of rest in Hebrews 4 is a present possession, the writer intimates, through the unfulfilled rests of creation, Canaan, and Sabbath-keeping, that there is an eschatological rest yet to be fulfilled. To complete the presentation of historic, geographic, and ceremonial rests as types of salvation, the author makes his final allusion to the sanctifying aspect of salvation.

Sanctifying Rest

In verse 11, the author draws a connection between receiving salvation by faith and working out your own salvation with fear and trembling. In the face of persecution, true faith rises above punishing obstacles. Relinquishing one's stated faith is a sure sign of inner disbelief in the promises of God. While presenting the eschatological rest, the author encourages believers to buckle down and get serious. With this thought, Dwight L. Moody exhorted his flock about preparing for heaven,

> Our rest is to be in heaven. In Hebrews 4:9, we read, "There remaineth therefore a rest to the people of God." That is another treasure we are to have in heaven. Let us not talk of rest down here, we have all eternity to rest in. What we want is to be faithful in the few months or years that we are here, and then we shall rest as eternal ages roll on. This is the place for *work*.[66]

65. Morrison, *Sabbath, Circumcision, and Tithing*, 157.

66. Moody, "Heaven, Part 2," *Twelve Select Sermons*, 142.

The final encouragement of this passage in Hebrews has to do with the necessity of daily vigilance in the Christian life. Just as the rest in Jesus is available every day, those who are in Jesus labor daily and experience assurance in their own hearts of their secured position in Christ.

Sabbath Remains

Having already explained the typology of the creation rest and the Canaan rest, the author of Hebrews completes the grand theme of redemptive rest with the Sabbath, the Jew's most prized and exalted ceremony. It is unlikely that within a stiff warning against returning to Judaism and works-oriented living—the very antithesis to simply trusting God—that the author would interject a command to keep the Sabbath. The *sabbatismos* remaining is another metaphor proclaiming that salvation rest is available by faith now, a rest that, like eternal life, begins now and continues forever in the future. Early Reformers, such as Turretin, have argued this understanding of the rest remaining.

> The eternal and heavenly is that by which, being received into heaven most perfectly freed both from sin and from the labors and troubles of this life, we rest eternally in God: "There remaineth a rest for the people of God" (Heb 4:9), viz., a heavenly rest under which eternal happiness is usually shadowed forth.[67]

John Calvin's brief comment about verse 9 corroborates this: "He draws the conclusion, that there is a sabbatizing reserved for God's people, that is, a spiritual rest; to which God daily invites us."[68] This rest is further described by Calvin as the ultimate happiness that those of faith will enjoy with the Father "when there will be a likeness between men and God." He agrees that *sabbatismos* is an allusion to the Sabbath, and is so mentioned to underscore its ceremonial nature and annulment with the advent of Jesus Christ.

> But I doubt not but that the Apostle designedly alluded to the Sabbath in order to reclaim the Jews from its external observances; for in no other way could its abrogation be understood, except by the knowledge of its spiritual design. He then treats of two things together; for by extolling the excellency of grace, he stimulates us to receive it by faith, and in the meantime he shows us in passing what is the true design of the Sabbath, lest the Jews should be foolishly attached to the outward rite. Of its abrogation indeed he does expressly speak, for this is not his subject, but by teaching them that the rite had a reference to something else, he gradually withdraws them from their superstitious notions. For he who understands that the main object of the precept was not external rest or earthly worship, immediately perceives, by looking on Christ, that the external rite was abolished by his coming; for when the body appears, the shadows immediately vanish away. Then our first business always is, to teach that Christ is the end of the Law.[69]

67. Turretin, *Elenctic Theology*, 2:78.
68. Calvin, *Commentaries*, 22:98 (Heb 4:9).
69. Calvin, *Commentaries*, 22:99 (Heb 4:10).

The allusion to the Sabbath is based upon its typological similarity to the creation rest and the Canaan rest. Taking Hebrew 4:9 as a starting point for devotional thoughts, Charles Spurgeon elaborates on the beauties of the heavenly rest:

> Heaven will be much different than earth. Here we are weary of toil and suffering. There, in the land of the immortal, fatigue is unknown . . . Ah, toilworn laborer, just think: you will rest forever. Can you imagine it? It is rest that remains an eternal rest.[70]

The sabbatism cannot mean the keeping of earthly Sabbaths, for this beckons the believer to provide the rest for himself. No other earthly reality or institution can provide in full measure the eternal character and substance of the rest which remains.

But Sabbatarians have deviated from the teachings of early Reformers by suggesting that the Sabbath as a type must remain to assure us of the eschatological rest.[71] Ray quotes several authors (John Pipa and Arthur Pink) who believe that *sabbatismos* refers to Sabbath-keeping proper. He even intimates that one cannot achieve the final rest of God without faithfully keeping an external Sabbath down here.

> That final rest will only be obtained by those who persevere in their faith and obedience to the living Christ . . . Continuing to be faithful to Jesus in this life requires, among other things, obeying God's commandments—including the command to remember the Sabbath day by keeping it holy. Although the day of the week and some aspects of the manner of celebrating the day have been changed by the Lord of the Sabbath, the New Testament does not abrogate Sabbath keeping as such. In fact, it requires it.[72]

Ray asserts that the old covenant Sabbath wasn't abrogated; it was given a face lift and reappears as the Christian Sabbath, yet he admits that "there is no one text that explicitly says this." The *sabbatismos* that remains is not about physical rest or congregational worship, but about redemption in Christ in its "already and not yet" phases. To reiterate Calvin, "For he who understands that the main object of the precept [Sabbath-keeping] was not external rest or earthly worship, immediately perceives, by looking on Christ, that the external rite was abolished by his coming."[73] If one comprehends the fullness and adequacy of resting in Christ by faith, then it should be explicitly clear that the old covenant Sabbath has been abolished. What remains is the gospel of the risen Christ for the unbelieving world, not a new call to the old covenant. McGee delightfully and simply explained his daily appreciation for the fact that he is at rest in the One who is resting.

> Well, the way I understand the Epistle to Hebrews, the Sabbath day is now this day of grace in which we live, and Christ, after He died on the cross and came back to life, went back to the right hand of the Father and sat down. He sat down, not because He was tired, but because He had finished your redemption and

70. Spurgeon, *Morning and Evening* (January 18, Morning).
71. Gaffin, "Westminster and the Sabbath," 132–39; Jewett, *Lord's Day*, 84.
72. Ray, *Celebrating the Sabbath*, 50–51.
73. Calvin, *Commentaries*, 22:99 (Heb 4:10).

> mine. So now He tells me, 'You rest in Me.' I have a Sabbath day everyday—I rest in Christ.[74]

John Murray responds that this attitude may seem pious, having a sort of truth about it, but that it fails to distinguish the Lord's Day, Sunday, from all the others.

> To obliterate this difference may appear pious. But it is piosity, not piety. It is not piety to be wiser than God; it is impiety of the darkest hue. The Sabbath day is different from every other day and to obliterate this distinction either in thought or practice is to destroy what is of the essence of the institution.[75]

Murray supposes that belief in a fulfilled Sabbath militates against Christian congregational worship. His fear is not unlike those who think salvation by grace through faith alone encourages the neglect of good works. But true knowledge leads to true worship. The author of Hebrews was concerned that persecution, love of the praise of men, and failure to see in Jesus the fulfillment of all that was written by Moses and the Prophets would keep professing believers away from the assembly. However, he did not utter, "Do not forget to keep the Sabbath as the manner of some is," for his interest was not to introduce and reinforce an obligation to ceremonial law, but to exhort them in the performance of a higher, more nobler obligation to meet with fellow believers for mutual edification and for worship. The author understood the ceremonial essence of the Sabbath yet still encouraged weekly assembly of Christians on the Lord's Day. Murray, Ray and others chastise those who hold the very doctrine advanced by the author of Hebrews!

The new covenant introduced a paradigm shift in worship, not a Sabbath shift. Christ's rest is not church attendance on Sunday. Christ's rest is not like the ephemeral day of God's creation rest; nor is His rest like the transient occupancy of Canaan. Neither is the rest of Jesus to be compared to the cyclical rest of the Sabbath that consumed but one-seventh of the week, and which, like the sacrifices of the priests, by its repetitive nature demonstrated its inadequacy (Heb 7:27; 9:25; 10:11). We no more need to observe the Sabbath to keep the reality of the heavenly rest before us than to live in the land of Canaan to assure ourselves that there is a better land. No, the rest found in Jesus is a present possession, indestructible and everlasting.

74. McGee, *Thru the Bible*, 5:532.

75. Murray, *Collected Writings*, 1:209.

9

Sabbath or Lord's Day?

FROM LORD'S DAY TO CHRISTIAN SABBATH

The Lord's Day

As Apostle John began to relate the glorious revelation of Jesus Christ, received by the hand of angelic messengers while an outcast at the Isle of Patmos, he stated "I was in the Spirit on the Lord's Day, and heard behind me a great voice, as of a trumpet" (Rev 1:10). This solitary NT appearance of the phrase *κυρακὴ ἡμέρα*, or "Lord's Day," has puzzled theologians for centuries. It seems distinguishable from the future cataclysmic "Day of the Lord" within the revelation (Rev 6:17; 16:14) and elsewhere in other epistles (2 Thess 2:2; 2 Pet 3:10), yet John himself does not use the phrase "the Day of the Lord." Some propose that if John wanted to mention that the vision took place on Sunday, he could have used the phrase *ἡ μία τῶν σαββάτων*, or "first day of the week," which occurs in his own gospel to describe the day of the resurrection (John 20:1, 19) or in Luke's history of the early church to describe the weekly fellowship of believers (Acts 20:7). However, if the phrase "Lord's Day" was already understood to mean Sunday, then Apostle John had no reason to state the fact any differently. This has been the popular view.

Of course, without the benefit of solid historical, literary evidence, we are left with conjecture. However, a more current analysis by Bauckham on the historic use of the word *kuriakos* (Lord's) in secular Greek literature and early Christian writings finds that Christians indeed validated the use of the phrase "Lord's Day" as synonymous with Sunday and that by the time John wrote the Revelation, the phrase was already common.

> The term [*κυρακὴ ἡμέρα*] is not simply interchangeable with *ἡμέρα* (*τοῦ*) *κυριου*, since by long established usage the latter referred to the eschatological Day of the Lord. Thus if early Christians wished to call the first day of the week after their *κύριος*, they could not use the term *ἡμέρα* (*τοῦ*) *κυριου* without ambiguity and confusion. This, it would seem, is the reason why *κυρακὴ ἡμέρα* early established itself as the common Christian name for Sunday.[1]

1. Bauckham, "The Lord's Day," 225.

Besides distinguishing the weekly day of worship from the future Day of the Lord, the adoption of the phrase "the Lord's Day" was also necessary to distinguish the weekly Christian day of worship from that of the Jews, the Sabbath. This is confirmed in the writings of the early church fathers.

> On the day of the preparation, then, at the third hour, He received the sentence from Pilate, the Father permitting that to happen; at the sixth hour He was crucified; at the ninth hour He gave up the ghost; and before sunset He was buried. During the Sabbath He continued under the earth in the tomb in which Joseph of Arimathaea had laid Him. At the dawning of the Lord's Day He arose from the dead, according to what was spoken by Himself, "As Jonah was three days and three nights in the whale's belly, so shall the Son of man also be three days and three nights in the heart of the earth." The day of the preparation, then, comprises the passion; the Sabbath embraces the burial; the Lord's Day contains the resurrection.[2]

The early church did not call Sunday the "Christian Sabbath;" it was the Lord's Day. What mainline Christians have accepted for centuries through tradition has been verified through exacting historical research. But what have been misunderstood are the rationale for adopting the first day of the week for recurring Christian worship and the authority by which such a change took place. While John validated the phrase "Lord's Day" as the first day of the week, more importantly, the Lord chose the first day of the week for its significance to communicate the closing vision of the NT canon. John Wesley expresses the commonly held view that the vision was unified in its delivery and that the day upon which the vision was received was none other than our weekly Sunday.

> *On the Lord's day*—On this our Lord rose from the dead: on this the ancients believed he will come to judgment. It was, therefore, with the utmost propriety that St. John on this day both saw and described his coming.[3]

The authority and empowerment of the church came in a cluster of first-day occurrences. The descent of the Holy Spirit on the first day of the week at Pentecost was the beginning of a particular and especial development of apostolic authority. Its boundary of completion came with a second descent of the Spirit, as it were, to visit John, the last of the apostles, on the first day of the week, to "wrap up" the Lord's written message to the church. First-day significance for the church was not chosen by man, but by God. The first day of the week was decreed by the Lord to supplant the ceremonial calendar filled with its Sabbaths, so that its institution was a divine necessity rather than the pragmatic tradition of the early church.

2. Ignatius, "Epistle to the Trallians" (*ANF* 1:70). This quote comes from the long version, which is considered by most to be a later interpolation of Ignatius' shorter epistle. Just how much later is difficult to tell, but the longer version was constructed near the time of Ignatius. Given the fact that he was an apostle of John, this reference to the Lord's Day is certainly not out of step historically since John used the phrase himself.

3. Wesley, *Explanatory Notes*, 938–39.

During the second century, Apostle John's phrase "the Lord's Day" conclusively became synonymous with Sunday, the day of Christian worship.

> And on the day called Sunday, all who live in cities or in the country gather together to one place, and the memoirs of the apostles or the writings of the prophets are read . . . But Sunday is the day on which we all hold our common assembly, because it is the first day on which God, having wrought a change in the darkness and matter, made the world; and Jesus Christ our Savior on the same day rose from the dead.[4]

Interestingly, Justin relates Christian worship to the first day of creation as opposed to the seventh, indicating that the early church conceptualized Christ's resurrection as a new beginning, that is, what happens *after* the Sabbath is over. Indeed, the resurrection signified the first day of a kind of re-creation of mankind (1 Pet 1:3). Jesus was the forerunner of the bodily resurrection of the dead (1 Cor 15:23) and the guarantor that all new creations (2 Cor 5:17) will surely be resurrected to the sinless glories of God's eternal kingdom (Rom 6:5; 2 Cor 5:1). Christ's death was our death and is past, signifying the completion of the work of salvation and the fulfillment of all seventh-day types. Paul inveighs against those who teach that there is no resurrection (1 Cor 15:13–14) or those who teach that it is past already (2 Tim 2:18), thus solidifying the resurrection (and first-day themes) as a fundamental doctrine of the church (Heb 6:2). As a core teaching, the fact of the resurrection went hand-in-hand with the preaching of the gospel of Jesus Christ (Acts 1:22; 4:33) and was instrumental in the shift from Jewish synagogal meetings on the seventh day to Christian church meetings on the first day of the week.

> Our study of the origins of the Lord's Day has given no hint of properly sabbatical associations; for the earliest Christians it was not a substitute for the Sabbath nor a day of rest nor related in any way to the fourth commandment. It was simply, by the normative custom of the apostolic church, the day on which Christians met to worship, and, for us, the use of its title, the Lord's Day, in Revelation 1:10 gives that custom the stamp of canonical authority.[5]

The Replaceable Sabbath

By the thirteenth century the theology of the Lord's Day changed. Thomas Aquinas regarded the Sabbath and the Lord's Day as two separate days; however, he viewed the latter as the NT *replacement* for the former. From the idea that the new covenant introduced Christian traditions for Jewish ceremonies based on similarity, such as circumcision giving way to baptism and the Lord's Supper approximating the Passover, came the forced and fanciful system of religious holidays common in the Roman Catholic Church.

4. Justin, *1 Apol.* 67 (*ANF* 1:186).
5. Bauckham, "The Lord's Day," 240.

> As to the sabbath, which was a sign recalling the first creation, its place is taken by the "Lord's Day," which recalls the beginning of the new creature in the Resurrection of Christ. In like manner other solemnities of the Old Law are supplanted by new solemnities: because the blessings vouchsafed to that people, foreshadowed the favors granted us by Christ. Hence the feast of the Passover gave place to the feast of Christ's Passion and Resurrection: the feast of Pentecost when the Old Law was given, to the feast of Pentecost on which was given the Law of the living spirit: the feast of the New Moon, to Lady Day, when appeared the first rays of the sun, i.e. Christ, by the fulness of grace: the feast of Trumpets, to the feasts of the Apostles: the feast of Expiation, to the feasts of Martyrs and Confessors: the feast of Tabernacles, to the feast of the Church Dedication: the feast of the Assembly and Collection, to feast of the Angels, or else to the feast of All Hallows.[6]

This teaching blurred the differences between the old and new covenants and paved the way for works orientation. The old covenant was replete with foreshadowing symbols of the work of Christ that the Lord determined to bring to an end (Heb 9:9–10). In contrast, the new covenant has only several ordinances that look back on the accomplished salvation of the Lord. It was fitting for a *better* covenant to have *fewer* ordinances: one, performed only once that identifies the child of God as an heir to the kingdom, and the second, a recurring and sustaining ordinance of remembrance of the life and work of Jesus Christ. Again, similarity does not connote identity. Baptism is *not* a Christian circumcision, and communion is *not* a Christian Passover,[7] neither is the Lord's Day a Christian Sabbath. This is as absurd as calling the new covenant the "Christian old covenant."

But the thinking of Thomas Aquinas continues to this day in Reformation churches.

> The faith of Abraham was commended in that he believed in God's promise concerning his seed to come, in which all nations were to be blessed. Wherefore, as long as this seed was yet to come, it was necessary to make profession of Abraham's faith by means of circumcision. But now that it is consummated, the same thing needs to be declared by means of another sign, viz. Baptism, which, in this respect, took the place of circumcision, according to the saying of the Apostle (Col 2:11, 12).[8]

It is conjecture on the part of Aquinas to state that it was *necessary* that the act of physical circumcision be replaced with a new physical sign to signify the *same thing*. Paul does not speak of physical baptism: "you were also circumcised with the circumcision made without hands" (Col 2:11–13). It is plain that the circumcision of the Christian is spiritual and not ritual, and that it is actually the death of Christ, which

6. Aquinas, *Summa*, 2:1085 (Q. 103, Art. 3).

7. Letham, "Given For You," 12. "The Last Supper is often thought to be the Passover meal, with a direct connection following between the Passover and the Lord's Supper. However, this is not entirely clear . . . Paul's reference to Jesus as "our Passover" (1 Cor 5:7) is to his death, not the meal the previous night. The connection with the Passover is the cross, not the Supper as such."

8. Aquinas, *Summa*, 2:1085 (Q. 103, Art. 3).

was *His* circumcision, into which we were spiritually baptized. The proximity of the word "baptism" to "circumcision" in this text does not mean that the old covenant sign was replaced with the new covenant sign. It is a statement that the ceremonial law of circumcision was fulfilled by Christ in His death and that we are now immersed in the benefits of that death. The idea of replacing ceremonies is a puzzling position given the fact that Aquinas did correctly teach that the ceremonial laws of the old covenant ceased with the fulfillment of that which they foreshadowed: "Consequently the prescriptions of the Law must have ceased then altogether through their reality being fulfilled."[9] With the reality being fulfilled, there is absolutely no need to replace the former laws with new ceremonies that signify the same thing! Referring to circumcision and the Sabbath, Goppelt asserted, "None of these institutions from past redemptive history are replaced by better ones. All are replaced by the one new institution, Christ, and by the new creation that is found in him."[10] The Lord's Day is not meant to refresh the themes of the Sabbath, such as not working or resting or abiding at home. Referring to the Lord's Day as the Christian Sabbath is an Aquinian idea, and it behooves Christ's church to distance itself from this line of reasoning.

The Christian Sabbath

During the seventeenth century, when Protestants flourished across Europe and established their identity through confessional standards and catechetical instruction, the term "the Christian Sabbath" was popularized and became synonymous with Sunday. The following chapter will discuss the factors leading to this designation in greater detail, but at this point it is sufficient to point out that the church existed for 1,500 years without such a terminology. In other words, a doctrinal change brought about the concept of a "Christian Sabbath." This term has generated confusion between the apostolic traditions of Christian worship and the Jewish traditions of Sabbath observance. While Protestants correctly rejected eleven of the invented holy days as Judaizing, they retained the concept that the Lord's Day replaced the Sabbath, thus ensuring confusion throughout Reformation churches. The implication of sabbatizing the Lord's Day is that Sabbath law is still binding on Christians. Francis Turretin, an early Reformer, saw the unfortunate implications of holding to this view.

> If this precept is in all its parts moral and perpetual, then we are still at this time (under the New Testament) bound to the particular observance of the seventh day, nor could a transference of it have been made to the Lord's Day.[11]

As mentioned previously, early Jewish Christians could not have guiltlessly worshipped on Sunday unless they understood the Sabbath to be a ceremonial command. Anyone who worships on Sunday implicitly accepts the ceremonial status of the fourth commandment.

9. Ibid., 2:1085 (Q. 103, Art. 3).
10. Goppelt, *Typos*, 192.
11. Turretin, *Elenctic Theology*, 2:85.

> Some contemporary writers, however, wish to go further than this, in claiming that Sunday *is* the Christian Sabbath, and that its observance is therefore a fulfillment of the fourth commandment. We have already seen enough to realize what short shrift this approach would have received from Paul. Not only is he opposed to the reestablishment of the Decalogue as a law for the Christian life, but he is also quite happy to allow the seventh-day Sabbath to be observed—a position quite incompatible with any identification of Sunday as the Christian Sabbath.[12]

Why do Christians continue to invoke the Sabbath as the basis for the Lord's Day? It is because they fear Christian worship will come to a standstill without it and they need a legal hammer at hand to enforce attendance. But there is no need for this. If Christ can raise up rocks to sing His praises (Matt 3:9), why would it be so difficult for Him to raise up His beloved, who are indwelt by the Holy Spirit, to worship at the appointed time (Ps 116:18–19; 122:1–2)?

FROM APOSTOLIC AUTHORITY TO THE REGULATIVE PRINCIPLE

Tradition ☺, Tradition ☹

There is a place for the continuance of traditions within the church of Jesus Christ, whether they were spoken by the apostles, demonstrated by them, or written in a letter through the power of the Holy Spirit. Apostolic traditions carry the same force as commandments from God: "stand fast and hold the traditions (*paradosis*) which you were taught, whether by word or our epistle" (2 Thess 2:15). *Paradosis* is variously translated as tradition or ordinance, and means to concretely transmit a precept. Paul uses this word five times in his letters to convey both apostolic commandments (1 Cor 11:2; 2 Thess 2:15; 3:6) and Jewish traditional law (Gal 1:14; Col 2:8). Judaism has a long history of concern with the accurate and faithful transmission of legally binding laws, so Paul, trained as a Pharisee, could speak with understanding of the authority and significance of establishing new traditions for the church, as reasoned from the Torah and the teachings of Christ, or given to him by the Holy Spirit. Paul was given the authority by the Lord Jesus Christ to command the nascent church in new protocols that were consistent with the moral law of God and with the developing identity of the church. What traditions are in Paul's mind as he addressed his second letter to the Thessalonians? The immediate context gives the sense that the traditions of the church are opposed to lawlessness, deception, the pursuit of unrighteousness, and apostasy. The traditions to which Paul refers are theological and of such character and importance that they influence and guide Christian behavior in righteousness. They are the moorings that allow the believer to stand fast against legalism, syncretism, worldliness, and apostasy. Whether or not your weekly worship opens with a benediction is hardly the kind of tradition to awaken someone from luke-warmness or to stabilize a congregation against pharisaism; however, failing to assemble together in weekly congregational worship (Heb 10:25) is a sure sign of worldliness and apostasy. Whether or not your pastor was trained at a seminary, he is still susceptible to

12. De Lacey, "The Sabbath/Sunday Question," 185.

worldliness and predation, but a church that allows its leaders exclusive control without a presbyterian government (1 Pet 5:1–3), or places into leadership those who are theologically untested and immature in the faith (1 Tim 3:6–7) is opening the doors to unrighteousness and deception. The traditions which Paul refers to are essential to the safety, growth, and maturation of the Christian in the larger context of his or her fellowship with the saints. With the closure of the written canon, these apostolic traditions must now be supported directly from Scripture, yet they may find corroboration in the history of the early church.

> Therefore, by tradition, we are constrained to cast off all tradition not in, or provable by, Scripture. The fathers are valuable witnesses to historical facts, which give force to the intimations of Scripture—such as the Christian Lord's day, the baptism of infants, and the genuineness of the canon. Tradition (in the sense human testimony) cannot establish a doctrine, but can authenticate a fact, such as those mentioned.[13]

Jameison, Faucet and Brown's commentary comprehends Paul's favorable use of the word *paradosis*, but there are other traditions that are likely to affront believers and subvert the mission of the church, such as those that developed in the Roman Catholic Church. Standing against such unbiblical traditions and abuses of Scripture, Martin Luther emphasized the centrality of God's word in determining what is to be done by the Christian and what is to be avoided.

> We ought first to know that there are no good works except those which God has commanded, even as there is no sin except that which God has forbidden. Therefore whoever wishes to know and to do good works needs nothing else than to know God's commandments.[14]

Luther objected to the mass, the papacy, and the doctrine of purgatory; to pilgrimages, fraternities, and relics; and to the invocation of saints and the system of indulgences simply because there was no proof of them in Scripture. Thus, the most fundamental doctrine of the Reformation, which recaptured the tenor of the early church, is the supreme authority of Scripture in all matters of faith and practice. Since Luther's charge, the Protestant church made scriptural authority a core doctrine in church confessions and catechisms, yet she has grappled with the implications of this ethos when itemizing the moral law of God that a believer must obey. The Heidelberg Catechism (1563) attempts to answer the question about what things a Christian may do.

> [Question 91] What do we do that is good?
>
> [Answer] Only that which arises out of true faith, conforms to God's law, and is done for his glory; and not that which is based on what we think is right or on established human tradition.[15]

13. Jamieson, Faucet, and Brown, *Commentary*, 3.3:477 (2 Thess 2:15).
14. Luther, "Treatise On Good Works," *Works*, 187.
15. Heidelberg Catechism, *Ecumenical Creeds and Reformed Confessions*, 54.

In his commentary on the Catechism, Ursinus elaborated on this question only in general terms with an eye to countering Roman Catholic misunderstandings. The only specific human tradition that he spoke against was the doctrine of supererogation, "by which they understand such works as are done over and above what God and the law require of them."[16] Ursinus also introduces the idea that there is a difference between good works in general and good works in worship (which is more restrictive).

> It is not sufficient for the worship of God, that a work be not evil, or not prohibited: it must also be commanded by God, according to what the Scriptures declare, "To obey is better than sacrifice."[17]

It is not the best scriptural proof text, and, unfortunately, he provides no specific examples, but the historical context of this catechism viewed the introduction of human traditions in the Roman Catholic Church as the gateway to the development of will worship. However, Ursinus appears to contradict himself when he answers in the affirmative the question, "Is it lawful for the Church to institute ceremonies?" He proposed four qualifications: 1) they must not be unholy, but agreeable to the word of God, 2) they must not be based in superstition, 3) they must not be too numerous lest their sheer number creates a burden, and 4) they must not be empty or unprofitable.[18] Unfortunately, neither does he provide specific examples of authorized ceremonies in worship. So, on the one hand, worship activities must be specifically commanded by God, and on the other hand, the church may institute human traditions in worship that generally agree with God's word and are empirically beneficial. But who is to say that a tradition has sufficient biblical warrant or whether it is ultimately edifying for those who practice it? The Heidelberg Catechism and Commentary address the topic of worship and church meetings in general terms, but leave the church to work out the specifics.

The Westminster Confession (1646) begins its teaching with the doctrine of the word of God.

> The whole counsel of God concerning all things necessary for His own glory, man's salvation, faith, and life, is either expressly set down in Scripture, or by good and necessary consequence may be deduced from Scripture: unto which nothing at any time is to be added, whether by new revelations of the Spirit, or traditions of men.[19]

The purity and wholesomeness of God's word answers the propensity of man to do what is pleasing in his own sight. This is a noble doctrine, however, the consequence of man's deduction from Scripture can be seriously flawed leading to the inadvertent opposite of this doctrine: men deriving dogmas that go beyond the plain, normative, and manifest sense of Scripture. The Westminster Confession then applies

16. Ursinus, *Commentary on the Heidelberg Catechism*, 481.

17. Ibid., 477.

18. Ibid., 574.

19. *Westminster Confession of Faith*, 22 (chap. 1, par. 6).

this doctrine of *sola Scriptura* specifically to matters of worship, which serves to reinforce a dichotomy between life at church and life at home or in the world.

> But the acceptable way of worshipping the true God is instituted by Himself, and so limited by His own revealed will, that He may not be worshipped according to the imaginations and devices of men, or the suggestions of Satan, under any visible representation, or any other way not prescribed in the holy Scripture.[20]

This emphasis of adhering to the word of God during worship is certainly understandable since it was especially important that a gathering of the saints was marked by a unity of the faith (Eph 4:11–14) and peaceable relations (1 Cor 14:33). The orderly conduct of worship services (1 Cor 14:40; Col 2:5) requires conformity in doctrine (1 Cor 15:1–2; Col 2:7) and uniformity in practice (1 Cor 14:26–39; Eph 4:3). This WCF tenet was further refined by the Puritans and came to be called the "regulative principle of worship," summarized as follows:

> Whatever is not commanded by Scripture in the worship of God is forbidden. Anything that the church does in worship must have warrant from an explicit command of God, be deduced by good and necessary consequence, or be derived from approved historical example (e.g., the change of day from seventh to first for Lord's Day corporate worship).[21]

While the desire for proper worship is commendable and the discussion of specific applications is necessary, the fruit of this principle has not necessarily achieved what it hoped to produce. John Frame has ventured to offer some criticisms of what the regulative principle has become, though he agrees with it for the most part.[22] Regarding the narrow application of the regulative principle to official church worship rather than all worship, he asserts that *that* distinction is clearly unscriptural. Regarding the development of rules about elements and parts of worship, he maintains that there is no scriptural warrant for it. Indeed, he asseverates that Scripture does not provide a "systematic or exhaustive list of the events that were authorized" for worship services, thus the church must make sense of both the generalities and specifics applicable to worship within the principles of God's word. Frame reminds his readers that the regulative principle was developed to countercheck the power of the church-state to impose on worshippers such doctrines, practices, and ceremonies that were clearly unscriptural.

For Luther, the Roman Catholic Church traditionalized certain doctrines and practices that were egregiously opposed to the word of God—and to be rejected outright—such as the mass, the rosary, monastic vows, and brotherhoods. However, there were some traditions that he believed the church had the power to enact for the sake of order or spiritual edification, such as fasts and holy days. As explained in the Augsburg Confession, Luther objected that these traditions become equated with the word of

20. *Westminster Confession of Faith*, 89–90 (chap. 21, par. 1).

21. Schwertley, *Regulative Principle*, 4; See also Williamson, "The Scriptural Regulative Principle of Worship."

22. Frame, *Worship in Spirit and Truth*, 37–62.

God, by claiming 1) that by the observance of them, God was pleased, and 2) that by failure to comply with them, sin was assigned.[23]

Unfortunately, the regulative principle has been turned around to produce the very thing that it was meant to correct: elevating the traditions of men (formulated through deduction) to the unequivocal level of God's precepts. For example, one contemporary author wrote an article to persuade Reformed readers to attend the traditional second service on the Lord's Day.[24] He begins with an acknowledgment that "Scripture does not specifically state that we should attend [church services] twice" and deduces from Hebrews 10:25 that it is a sin to have poor church attendance. Certainly, the idea of "forsaking" begs definition, but it is unfathomable to claim that someone who worships every Sunday morning is forsaking the assembling together because they do not attend a second service. Kleyn capsulizes his argument with the statement: "Failure to attend church twice on Sunday is a serious sin." Thus, the end point of his deduction is assumed to be equivalent to the declarative word of God, and therefore he has created a sin where there was none before. There is nothing wrong with his piety and personal interest in hearing the word of God as much as possible, but to make his own determinations or the preferences of a denomination a standard for all Christians is certainly presumptuous.

Lawrence Eyres, writing for the *Ordained Servant*, echoes the same concern about churches dropping the second service for lack of attendance.[25] He too cites Hebrews 10:25 as presenting an ideal standard for church worship that should make Christians think twice about meeting in homes on Sunday evening. Of course, Hebrews 10:25 says nothing about where meetings should be held, how many meetings must take place, how long the service should be, what time services should commence, and the like. He then declares, "An obvious advantage of evening congregational worship is found in the fact that it is much easier to keep the whole day sacred if it is begun and ended with corporate worship."[26] This assertion is not an exegesis of Scripture but an appeal to his sense of piety based on the assumption of a sabbatic Lord's Day. He certainly has not established as fact that the Lord's Day is more *easily* kept sacred by requiring attendance at two worship services as opposed to one. The easy road is evidenced by the number of empty pews at the evening service. He really means that keeping the sacredness of the Lord's Day, as he defines it, is difficult, and that Christians must dig deep within themselves to attend this second mandatory meeting. Now, once he establishes the second service as scripturally defensible in his mind, he reasons that those who do not attend the second service are "mistaken and misguided" and headed for disaster. Of course, we would never say these things to believers who exercise true Christian liberty, so Eyres has made non-attendance at the second service a sin.

Another example of the elevation of man's traditions to the word of God is prohibiting musical instruments in church and restricting musical content to the Psalms.

23. *Creeds of the Churches*, 101 (art. 28).

24. Kleyn, "Is Once Enough?," 18–20.

25. Eyres, "The Evening Worship Service," 84.

26. Ibid., 84.

This hotly contested topic finds most of its compelling evidence in history rather than Scripture, as there are only rare examples of the use of instruments and newly composed songs during the early church centuries and only a few mentions of music in the NT.[27] Yet the practice of exclusive psalmody is defended and proclaimed as an undeniable conclusion of the regulative principle. Reg Barrow explains,

> Most Reformed folk agree that every element of worship must be divinely instituted by the word of God, (which is commonly called the regulative principle or scriptural law of worship), thus any time that we raise our voices to God in public worship without a clear mandate from God as to the content of the songs we are singing, we are offering "strange fire." Now, all but the most ignorant are aware that there can be no neutrality in the things of the Gospel; either you are obeying Christ or you are not. So, for those that adhere to a Reformed view of the regulative principle, you either must sing Psalms exclusively and confront your brother in Christ that they are sinning by including man-made compositions in their worship-song (doing something that is forbidden—sinning by commission) or, they must sing their man-made compositions (thinking that God has instituted such) and admonish you that you are sinning by singing only Psalms, because you exclude (sinning by omission) the divinely instituted man-made compositions in your public worship.[28]

The regulative principle is wielded as if it were the Eleventh Commandment to force Christians to accept the proposition that Paul's reference to "psalms, hymns, and spiritual songs" (Eph 5:19; Col 3:16) was meant as a mandate from God to sing only the Psalms in church worship without instrumental accompaniment. Some early Reformers, such as Calvin, justified the proscription of musical instrumentation by claiming that the instruments of the old covenant were ceremonies to be discarded, that their use was nothing less than Judaism.

> The intention of [musical instruments] was to stimulate the worshippers, and stir them up more actively to the celebration of the praise of God with the heart. We are to remember that the worship of God was never understood to consist in such outward services, which were only necessary to help forward a people, as yet weak and rude in knowledge, in the spiritual worship of God. A difference is to be observed in this respect between his people under the Old and under the New Testament; for now that Christ has appeared, and the Church has reached full age, it were only to bury the light of the Gospel, should we introduce the shadows of a departed dispensation. From this, it appears that the Papists, as I shall have occasion to show elsewhere, in employing instrumental music, cannot be said so much to imitate the practice of God's ancient people, as to ape it in a senseless and absurd manner, exhibiting a silly delight in that worship of the Old Testament which was figurative, and terminated with the Gospel.[29]

Notwithstanding the erudition of Calvin, he has not demonstrated how musical instrumentation is a shadow of Christ in His work and office or how the historical

27. Martin, *Worship in the Early Church*, 39–52.

28. Barrow, Review of *Psalms*, 1.

29. Calvin, *Commentaries*, 5:495 (Ps 92:1–4).

examples of song and instrumentation were divinely appointed by God. The only instruments that were commanded in the Law were: 1) the shofar (Lev 25:9) used in connection with calendar celebrations, and 2) silver trumpets (Num 10:1–10) used to summon the congregation. In Clark's comments about the New Moon celebration (Ps 81:3) and the use of the shofar, which *is* ceremonial, he intones,

> In a representative system of religion, such as the Jewish, there must have been much outside work, all emblematical of better things: no proof that such things should be continued under the Gospel dispensation, where outsides have disappeared, shadows flown away, and the substance alone is presented to the hearts of mankind. He must be ill off for proofs in favour of instrumental music in the church of Christ, who has recourse to practices under the Jewish ritual.[30]

While Clark correctly identifies the emblematic (typological) use of the shofar, he has not identified how or in what way the shofar was emblematic: only a vague statement of its foreshadowing better things. So, what better things has Clark offered to the church in terms of congregational worship? He argues from a particular instrument (shofar) the general prohibition of *all* musical instruments under the new covenant. This would be like prohibiting curtains, swags, and valances in a church building because of the emblematic meaning of the torn temple veil.

David's use of the harp and psaltery was not ceremonially mandated by God, but was chosen by David because he was gifted by God with musical skills; they were instruments culturally available to him, and it added beauty and richness to his compositions for personal worship and pleasure. Though not specifically commanded, the divine approbation of David's opus has resonated in the hearts of the faithful, inspiring them to magnify the name of the Lord in concert (Ps 34:3). David praised the Lord with his whole heart (Ps 9:1), his lips (Ps 119:171), his mouth (Ps 51:15), and also in song (Ps 69:30), with the lute (Ps 71:22) and harp (Ps 33:2). The accompaniment of voice with instruments displays a unity and fullness of worship with which God is exceptionally pleased (2 Chr 5:12–14). After his appointment as king, David purposed to bring the ark of the covenant to Jerusalem in joyous celebration. While Uzzah's death (1 Chr 13) interrupted that procession and reminded David that the law of God required the Levites to carry the ark (1 Chr 15:15), he nonetheless reorganized the Levites into a choir and orchestra without arousing the anger of the Lord (1 Chr 15:16–29).

Only the scorn of Michal detracts from the magnitude of David's unrestricted worship. Moses' custom on the Sabbath day involved the integration of voice and stringed instruments in praise to the Lord (Ps 92:1–3). So, it is not Judaizing to play a stringed instrument (Ps 150:4) or to form a choir (Ps 68:25), and it is not idolatry to play drums or cymbals (Exod 15:20; Job 21:12; Ps 68:25). Though there is a paucity of historical evidence for music in the early church, there is no hint that this was based on an apostolic prohibition.

30. Clarke, *Commentary*, 3:477 (Ps 81:3).

The alternative, called the liberal or permissive principle, common in Lutheran and Evangelical churches, is to allow anything in worship that is not specifically prohibited by Scripture. Even this principle has its flaws. The church of Jesus Christ struggles to obey its Lord: half tend toward austerity, the other half toward liberality. King Solomon resolved that heavenly wisdom ultimately provides the balance between these extremes (Eccl 7:16–17). Truly, neither the regulative principle nor the liberal principle is the schema *ne plus ultra* to determine how to conduct a worship service or how to order your private life. The quest for order and propriety in church worship is not necessarily achieved through the *administrative* rule of the pastor and elders, but through their *ministerial* roles (2 Cor 6:3). It is especially important for leaders to ensure that worship is consistent with God's word; and the corollary is to assure their sheep that nothing has been added to worship in the form of will worship and idolatry, and nothing taken away from worship in the form of legitimate liberties. The day of the week (first day, Sunday) and the frequency (weekly) have been determined by God in His Word, whereas the place and time of day, even the number of meetings, have been left to the church to decide. The purpose and elements of worship have been prescribed by our Lord to include the fellowship of the saints, attention to the apostles' doctrine, prayer, and communion. While this may not be an exhaustive list, the purpose of worship must not be subverted by novelties, entertainment, superstitions, syncretism, showmanship, or egocentrism.

The transition from the Jewish calendar to a weekly Christian Lord's Day is evident in Acts and the Epistles and enjoys an exceptionally strong historic tradition. The association of first-day worship with the resurrection of Jesus Christ is a reasonable explanation for this apostolic tradition. We have both biblical and early church history in addition to a scriptural rationale to support the claim that first-day worship came through apostolic decree. However, the tradition of calling Sunday the Sabbath or the Christian Sabbath has no scriptural support whatsoever, and its traditional use is only four centuries old. During that time, it has caused confusion, inspired controversy, and led to church schisms. This Reformed tradition, though born out of good intentions by godly men, has not been profitable for members of Christ's body.

The first-century church was given a new paradigm for congregational meetings and worship, loosely modeled after the synagogue service, but in the wisdom of God, specific methodologies and particular details were omitted from Scripture.

> The New Testament tells us a little more about the Christian meeting (which was more like the synagogue than like the sacrificial worship of the temple), but it gives us no systematic or exhaustive list of the events that were authorized for such services. Certainly it gives us no list of elements in the technical sense of Puritan theology—actions requiring specific scriptural authorization as opposed to circumstances or applications that do not.[31]

The Lord has never relaxed His demand for a holy people, yet despite our frequent sin, He has not resorted to micromanaging our assemblies. We have every reason to

31. Frame, *Worship in Spirit and Truth*, 54.

make our life a continuous praise of His name, and He has sent us into the world to proclaim His gospel. In order to achieve this, He calls us into His presence weekly for congregational worship and edification.

FROM SCRIPTURE TO REASONABLE TRADITIONS

The Priesthood and Pastorate

The authoritative will of God was delivered to the apostles and their corpus of Scripture concluded this special revelation to His people, the church. Yet God's authority continues in the pastorate within the bounds of Scripture. As such, various church doctrines and traditions have developed having to do with the calling and training of our pastors, their function, and organization. Just as the priests of the old covenant were a gift to Israel and were responsible for the reliable communication of God's word to the people of Israel (Exod 32:26, Num 18:7) the ministers of Christ's church possess the same status and are responsible for the same calling (Eph 4:7–13). The similarity of the pastoral minister to the Jewish priest is worth noting, but the matter of extrapolating and applying sundry old covenant priestly duties to pastors and teachers is not a simple one, especially considering the fact that the priestly title is conferred upon all believers in the church, both male and female, and that many of the priestly duties were ceremonial (i.e., typological) in nature.

One must first take into account that the Lord Jesus fulfilled the hereditary qualifications of the Levitical priesthood, not so much by His lineage as by His surpassing greatness and uniqueness; therefore, He displaced the Mosaic priesthood with the better Melchizedekian priesthood (Heb 7). This fact has led to the inconsequentiality of lineage as a criterion for attaining the superior priesthood. Hence, the new covenant priesthood is conferred upon all true believers, regardless of nationality, race, social standing, or gender. It may be supposed, therefore, that women may now aspire to ministerial offices of the church, but neither the old nor new covenants provide for this. The universal priesthood of believers was foreshadowed not only in the Levitical priesthood but in the prophetic decree of God, "You shall be to Me a kingdom of priests and a holy nation" (Exod 19:6), which was intended for all people of Israel. Despite this decree, the Lord maintained a distinction between men and women with regards to the ministerial offices in Israel, based on the creation. This distinction existed before the giving of the law and continued through it into the new covenant age (1 Pet 3:5–6). Therefore, apostle Paul appealed to the pre-Mosaic distinction of men and women at the creation (1 Cor 11:7–10) with regards to the offices of the church and draws application for the authoritative and leadership roles of the church (1 Tim 2:11–14ff). Thus, the strand of male leadership runs from creation to the consummation, because it anticipates when Christ, as Head above all, leads His bride to an everlasting kingdom and home. The fulfillment of the Mosaic priesthood does nothing to dismantle the chain of authority that God has ordained for His church through the leadership of men under Christ. The priesthood of the Mosaic covenant foreshadowed three levels of the priesthood of the church: 1) the general priesthood of all believers,

2) the leadership priesthood of all men, and 3) the official priesthood of select men. All of these are under the authority of Jesus Christ, our solitary and indefatigable High Priest and Head, even as He was foreshadowed prior to and within the law of Moses.

Though not commanded in the Pentateuch, the traditions of Israel demanded that the priests complete a course of instruction followed by examination prior to performing in their official capacities. This Jewish consuetude is given apostolic warrant for those who would be elders or deacons of a new covenant church, though neither the method and duration of instruction, nor the format and comprehensiveness of examination are inscripturated.[32]

> Likewise deacons must be reverent, not double-tongued, not given to much wine, not greedy for money, holding the mystery of the faith with a pure conscience. But let these also first be tested; then let them serve as deacons, being found blameless. (1 Tim 3:8–10)

By law, all Levitical men were expected to serve God in the duties and maintenance of temple worship and the spiritual leadership of their communities. Likewise, Christian men should aspire to those qualities that make them fit for serving the church. Too many men sit on the sidelines unaware that Christ has given them this priestly ministry of leadership. The intimation of Paul is that one's character and doctrine are made evident (tested) over time through the circumstances of life and their interactions within and without the context of the church. Thus, young men should aspire to develop qualities of heart, such as righteousness, godliness, faith, love, patience, and gentleness (1 Tim 6:11), just as Levitical men studied and prepared for their various roles associated with the temple, such as music, helping, prayers, administration, sacrifices, cleanup, and ministering to people. The Aaronic priests had higher official capacities compared to the Levitical priests, and this corresponds to the special calling of our ministers: pastor-teachers, elders, and deacons. Though the functions of Aaronic and Levitical priests differed, the moral requirements were the same.

Church Membership

> It is the duty of all believers, according to God's word, to separate themselves from those who do not belong to the church, in order to join this assembly wherever God has established it, even if civil authorities and royal decrees forbid and death and physical punishment result.[33]

As early as 1561, when the Belgic Confession was authored by Guido DeBrès, church membership was an issue, and it has remained so ever since. The Reformed Church in the Netherlands was under intense persecution by the Roman Catholic

32. Scriptural examples of the instruction of priests and elders include personal mentoring (Prov 2:1–5; Gal 6:6; 2 Tim 2:2), mass education (Deut 5:1; 2 Chr 17:7; Neh 8:7–8; Matt 5:1–2) and formal schools (Phil 3:4–6). Those who teach were taught themselves (Titus 1:9). Regardless of the style of training, leaders are expected to be mature, wise, and spiritually directed (Exod 18:21, 22; 2 Chr 19:5–11; Rom 12:8; 1 Cor 6:5; 12:28; 2 Tim 2:24; Jas 3:1)

33. *Ecumenical Creeds and Reformed Confessions*, 107 (Belgic Confession, art. 28).

Church, and many Reformed believers avoided joining themselves to the Reformed Church for fear of losing their life, a scenario not unlike that facing Jewish converts in the first century (Acts 7:54–60; Heb 10:32ff). Six years later, DeBrès was martyred for his faith because of his unyielding resolution to join himself to the Reformed Church. With this backdrop, many Christian leaders wonder why so many professing Christians fail to join themselves to a local church, especially since the fear of persecution has been removed. Obviously, there are other factors at work.

While many view church membership as a formal, public avowal of commitment to a particular church or denomination, this is only a one-dimensional view of church membership. Therefore, we distinguish between 1) the minimum requirements to belong to Christ's universal church—faith alone, in particular soteriological doctrines through confession (Rom 10:10), 2) formal minimum requirements that identify membership in Christ's church—baptism and communion (Acts 2:41–42), and 3) the evidential minimum requirements of a plausible faith—an appetite for God's word, acceptance of sound doctrine, a desire to fellowship, a hatred of sin, and love for the saints and the lost (John 8:31–32; 1 John 4:1–6; Jas 2:17–18). These are historically recognized criteria for admission to the Lord's Supper, which characterizes the unity of believers in Christ, i.e., those who are members of the true body of Christ.[34]

DeBrès wrote the Belgic Confession with two particular persons in mind: one who was fearful to associate with a legitimate local church in the first place and one who would depart that church under duress. Today, the landscape is notably different. There are those who profess Christ and refuse to join a church at all or attend several churches with competing theologies; those who attend a single church erratically; and those who leave a church for the slightest of personal reasons. Underlying this phenomenon is a profound ignorance of the necessity to be involved on a personal level in the body of Christ. However, if you profess Christ, you are commanded by the Lord to go to the house of God (Heb: 10:21), draw near to Him in faith (Heb 10:22), and not waver in your confession (Heb 10:23), give consideration to those assembled with you (Heb 10:24), resolve to assemble with like-minded believers (Heb 10:25), and actively build up your neighbor who sits by you (Heb.10:25).

Most articles on this topic dwell upon the shortcomings of the sheep, since most articles are written by pastors and other trained ministers in the church, but it is not only the sheep who are flaky (Heb 7:28). We have church leaders who are intolerant of any deviation in secondary doctrines and others that promote a "casual, come-as-you-are attitude."[35] Underlying this phenomenon is a pastorate that underestimates the power of the Holy Spirit to lead and guide the saints into truth through Christ-like leadership and the power of their own example. There is no question that at the level of the local church, leaders are responsible to God for the manner in which they lead those under their charge (Heb 13:17). The corollary is that church members are responsible before God how they submit to church leadership. Pastors and elders have a

34. Hyde, "Table Manners," 135–43.

35. Sande, "Taking Church Membership Seriously," n.p.

legitimate and biblical interest to know who should be under their care, and are free to make a roster of those who are committed to that congregation. This intimate knowledge of those under the rule of a local church is evident in Paul's direction to Timothy to compile a list of particular widows to be cared for through the church (1 Tim 5:9).

Making a list is the first step of an administrative action with regard to church membership. The second step is for the leaders to define the nature of the relationship. The elders at the Jerusalem church did such a thing by composing an authoritative letter, based on Scripture, that protected Gentiles from Judaizing, commended missionaries in their service, and commanded specific behaviors expected of Christians (Acts 15:22–29). The council's letter presumes that Christians will heed their authority. The third administrative step belongs to the prospective church member: to read, understand, and agree with the definition of the relationship, often contained in confessions (Acts 17:11; 2 Cor 13:5; 1 John 4:1). Martin summarized the early biblical evidence of what made the Christian community so cohesive.

> Only on the ground of the possession of a clearly defined body of Gospel truth can we account for the believers' organizing themselves into communities with a definite cultus (that is, a practiced religious devotion which draws men into a society of worshippers or devotees), a standard of belief and a precise membership from which defaulters and heretics could be, and in fact were actually, excommunicated and in which disciplinary measures were exercised.[36]

This is Christ's church, and it is the duty of all to commend those who build it up and censure those who disturb its peace and doctrine. While many church leaders realize the importance of membership, it is not so readily apparent to a large body of professing Christians. While most pastors assume that it is because these mavericks resist submitting to authority, it is also because these sheep have legitimate fears that their membership vows will be turned against them in illegitimate ways. Therefore, the real issue is church authority, whether it is employed faithfully in Christ's stead or abused (1 Tim 5:19–20; 1 Pet 5:2–3).

Christ considered it essential to humble Himself by taking on human flesh and experiencing the fallout of the fall in order to help those, through identification with them, who suffer the consequences of sin (Heb 2:17–18). Christ's humility qualified Him for the priesthood. The author of Hebrews elevates the empathetic leadership of Moses who was sorely grieved over Israel's sin, and even though Moses demonstrated episodes of faithlessness he "was faithful in all his house as a servant," (Heb 3:1–5) as a type of Christ. While Christ is the ultimate Head over His holy, catholic church, He has ordained men (Heb: 5:1; Exod 28:1) to function as His representatives in a unique fashion, which they must do in all faithfulness, humility, and empathy. John Calvin notes that by virtue of the incarnation, Christ extends, as it were, His hands to us, so we should have no fear or dread of His majesty, since He is also our brother, in demonstration of His inclination to succor us and His ability to provide for our needs.[37]

36. Martin, *Worship in the Early Church*, 55.

37. Calvin, *Commentaries*, 22:107–8 (Heb 4:15).

Likewise, our ministers and elders, who are brothers in Christ, must be approachable, swayed to effect our benefit, and equipped to render godly counsel (2 Cor 6:3). Church membership is directly related to the manner in which the minister and elders of a church exercise their authority and promote the concept of church unity.

In view of their formidable ministry, members of the church are expected to bring joy to them through obedience and submission to the word of God preached by them (Heb 13:17). Paul urges the same: "Recognize those who labor among you, and are over you in the Lord and admonish you, and to esteem them very highly in love for their work's sake" (1 Thess 5:12–13). Unless you are attending a church faithfully, you cannot obey this command from the Lord. Once in obedience to administrative church membership, you must be willing to risk, and not be surprised at, having a church leader who is wanton, controlling, unteachable, or prideful. Perhaps God has placed you there to bring to light these very problems. If Christ, in humility, took on human flesh to identify Himself with mankind, but specifically His own, then we are certainly bound, by His example, to take on the challenges of church membership to identify ourselves with Him through membership in His church.

The Lord's Supper

Practices among Christian denominations display tremendous variety with regards to the frequency and timing of this observance as well as the purpose, efficacy, and protocol. The variegated traditionalization of the Lord's Supper is the result of a wide range of circumstances, biases, and lackluster hermeneutics.[38] As indicated by Luke, the Lord's Supper was a principal reason for gathering together each week in congregational worship.[39]

> Now on the first day of the week, when the disciples came together to break bread, Paul, ready to depart the next day, spoke to them and continued his message until midnight. (Acts 20:7)

Most commentators agree that this was a Sunday evening meeting, at a recurring gathering of Christians on the first day of the week following their normal day of activities and work.[40] They came together in order to break bread. This does not mean that preaching was secondary, but when they came together, they purposed to commune in the symbolism of the covenant meal as the Lord had commanded and as the apostles had established by tradition. They came together to break bread, on the first day of the week—the day commemorating His resurrection and the outpouring of the Holy Spirit. This particular gathering was especially poignant for the congregation: Paul and his companions were departing the next day, so precious few hours remained

38. Trice, "'Drink of It, All of You,'" 21–28.

39. Letham, *Lord's Supper*, 57–60.

40. Barnes, *Notes*, 10:288; Henry, *Commentary*, 6:208; Jamieson, Fausset, Brown, *Commentary*, 3:146; Kistemaker, "Exposition of the Acts of the Apostles," *New Testament Commentary*, 716; Pipa, *The Lord's Day*, 126–27; Robertson, *Word Pictures*, 3:339; Rordorf, *Sunday*, 200–215; Turner, "Sabbath, Sunday, and the Law," 128–30; Yang, *Jesus and the Sabbath*, 260.

to be exhorted and instructed by such spiritual men. However, if Paul had departed a few days prior, these saints at Troas would have still gathered together on the first day of the week to break bread.

What is the biblical basis for preaching the word of God weekly on Sunday? This is not a question about the importance of preaching God's word—but why do we assemble to hear preaching every Sunday? Frame, Godfrey, Greidanus, Long, Wiersby, Horton, and Dever have all written books about preaching or worship, but none of them cite a biblical mandate for preaching on Sunday.[41] It is merely taken for granted that preaching is a paramount function of the weekly assembly of professing Christians. Is it just a tradition of men that individual saints have the freedom to comply with or not, or is it by the command of the Lord? If any proof of an answer is sought from the history of the apostles, then the example of Paul preaching at the church in Troas describes the normative practice of the early church. And if weekly preaching was the norm, established by apostolic tradition, then the Lord's Supper more so, because the disciples of Christ primarily came together to break bread.

When Jesus commanded the apostles to so remember Him, He did not specify the frequency of the feast, whether the commemorative meal be consumed before or after a common meal, who should dispense the elements, or whether to do it in the evening or morning. With limited initial information, the apostles were left with a decision how to implement the Lord's command. Luke emphasized that the early Hebrew Christians lived out the implications of their faith on a daily basis (Acts 2:46–47; 5:42), engaging in those functions of the church commensurate with growth. This was a transitional period for the church, and eventually, with the addition of Gentiles to her ranks and the separation from Judaism, the apostles were faced with providing a structure and routine to preserve and protect the flock of Christ. Daily congregational meetings were impractical and monthly assemblies were inadequate to maintain the unity of the faith. Familiarity with the practical benefits of weekly synagogal meetings may have factored in the development of an apostolic tradition, but it would not have been simply an empirical decision of the apostles. The Lord Jesus Christ ruled from heaven through the apostles and was bringing about the creation in Himself of one new man (Eph 2:15) composed of both Jews and Gentiles by removing the barrier of ceremonies that formerly separated them. With the Sabbath fulfilled, the weekly cycle took on new meaning. The concept of the week recalls the creation, but now the emphasis is on a spiritual re-creation. The church emphasized the relationship between the new beginning of the resurrection and the light of the gospel to the first day of creation and its supernatural light. First-day worship connotes a fresh beginning, not a sabbatical termination. The Sabbath *per se* was not driving the apostolic tradition of Lord's Day assembly, yet the synagogal emphasis on studying the Scripture, prayer, and fellowship were adapted to form a distinctive new covenant liturgy for the growing community of believers.

41. Dever, *Nine Marks*; Frame, *Worship in Spirit and Truth*; Godfrey, *Pleasing God*; Greidanus, *Preaching Christ*; Horton, *A Better Way*; Long, *Witness of Preaching*; Wiersbe, *Real Worship*.

> There can be no doubt that, at the time of Christ, public prayer occupied a very prominent place in the ordinary daily services of the Temple. Yet the original institution in the law of Moses contains no mention of it; and such later instances as the prayer of Hannah, or that of Solomon at the dedication of the Temple, afford neither indication nor precedent as regards the ordinary public services.[42]

The Sabbath traditions of prayer and Scripture study were free to remain, to become incorporated into the worship of the Christian church, but Sabbath law itself was fulfilled and no longer obligatory.

With regard to the frequency of the Lord's Supper, neither the Belgic Confession nor the Heidelberg Catechism makes direct comment. However, in the latter, the Lord's Supper is compared to the Popish Mass (LD #30), which would give every indication that the early Reformers observed the Lord's Supper every Sunday. Christ promised, with a view to congregational worship, that when the saints gather together, they can count on His mystical presence (Matt 18:20). The Lord's Supper uses symbols of His presence: the bread of His life and the wine of His blood. While the Reformers rejected the fanciful Roman error of transubstantiation, they did properly understand the figurative language of signs. Thus, the signs name the things signified. "The rule which the pious ought always to observe is," notes Calvin, "whenever they see the symbols instituted by the Lord, to think and feel surely persuaded that the truth of the thing signified is also present."[43] Thus, at congregational meetings we know Christ is present with us, so it behooves us to recognize it tangibly through the use of the symbols of the Lord's Supper. The association between the reality and the symbols of that reality is broken if we observe the Supper only on occasion. That is, if Christ is present in a special way during congregational worship, then the symbol of His presence—the Eucharist—should be present as well.[44] Thus, Calvin concludes, based on his knowledge of the ancient apostolic canons and his reference to Acts 2:42:

> Thus we ought always to provide that no meeting of the Church is held without the word, prayer, the dispensation of the Supper, and alms.[45]

Francis Turretin, also observing the quadripartite marks of the true church in Acts 2:42, proclaimed, "As therefore the apostolic church was discerned by these signs, by the same it ought to be known at this day."[46] Zacharius Ursinus (1534–1583), the author of the Heidelberg Catechism, said the Supper is to be frequently celebrated,[47] a phrase repeated in the Westminster Directory of Public Worship (1645)—hardly synonymous with annually, quarterly, or even monthly. Puritan Thomas Goodwin argued that Acts 2:42 states the minimal requirements of church services are weekly preaching, praying, fellowship, and communion. Charles Spurgeon chastised, "Shame on the

42. Edersheim, *Temple*, 105.
43. Calvin, *Institutes*, 564 (4.17.10).
44. Keddie, *The Lord's Supper*, 35–45.
45. Calvin, *Institutes*, 601 (4.17.44).
46. Turretin, *Elenctic Theology*, 3:89.
47. Ursinus, *Commentary on the Heidelberg Catechism*, 381.

Christian Church that she should put it off to once a month, and mar the first day the week by depriving it of its glory in the meeting together for fellowship and breaking of bread, and showing forth the death of Christ til He come." Jonathan Edwards remarked, "It seems plain by the Scripture, that the primitive Christians were wont to celebrate this memorial of the sufferings of their dear Redeemer every Lord's Day." Finally, Calvin opined against the annual remembrance and said, "Each week, at least, the table of the Lord ought to have been spread for the company of Christians."[48] Hart and Muether admit that their frequency for observing the Lord's Supper was inherited from American Presbyterianism rather than deduced from the Scriptures.[49] Wilson argues that there is no scriptural basis for observing the Supper less frequently than weekly.[50] The scriptural burden of proof is on those who desire *infrequent* observance of the Lord's Supper. A weekly observance of the Lord's Supper has been a traditional practice through the centuries and is reasonably supported by the Bible.[51]

FROM SABBATH TO LORD'S DAY

A. T. Lincoln summarizes the scholarly research presented in *From Sabbath to Lord's Day*. The deliberative and thorough analysis of the contributors provides the biblical evidence for the institution of the Sabbath in the wilderness shortly after the exodus, versus the creation. The Sabbath and other rests are eschatological and redemptive themes that find fulfillment in the Lord Jesus Christ and present both a reality now and a future culminating fulfillment in the eschaton. The Ten Commandments are unique but they are inseparable from the old covenant, being a summary of it, but are not necessarily comprised of moral laws alone. Regarding the gospel accounts, it is clear that Jesus places Himself above Sabbath law and gives reason for His followers to view the Sabbath from the perspective of His lordship and messiahship. Finally, the epistles and Acts provide the framework for the transition to first-day worship because the Sabbath is a shadow of a bygone era and is ultimately opposed to the reality of fulfillment in Jesus Christ. His resurrection and ascension are evidences of His lordship over life and the springboard for designating the first day of the week as the Lord's Day. Thus inscripturated through the apostles, saints of the new covenant have canonical, divine authority for first-day assembly and body life. Early patristic literature demonstrates the tradition of first-day worship without the incorporation of a 24-hour rest, and only after centuries did the notion arise that the Sabbath had any functional application on the Lord's Day. With all these commendable findings and Lincoln's criticisms of Sabbatarian transference theology, he seems to backtrack when it comes to making final conclusions.

48. Calvin, *Institutes*, 602 (4.17.46). See also Godfrey, "Calvin on the Eucharist," 129–34; and Horton, *A Better Way*, 157–59.

49. Hart and Muether, "The Lord's Supper: How Often?" 97–98.

50. Wilson, "On Weekly Communion," 15–20.

51. Mathison, *Given For You*, 292–97.

> [There is] no justification from the New Testament or from the early church's writings for any continuity that would include the necessity of abstinence from work and of physical rest on the Lord's Day. We do, however, need to insist on some sort of continuity of force for the fourth commandment, since this commandment is not simply left in abeyance.[52]

From his following discussion, the matter of abeyance is related to the fact that the Sabbath still prefigures a future rest. However, other Jewish feasts have ongoing eschatological intentions but the church does not look for some sort of continuity of force in them for this dispensation. The Sabbath and the Jubilee and the Feast of Tabernacles may be incompletely fulfilled, but this does not necessitate a present *forceful* application. We may use them as metaphors, but they carry no moral force. Lincoln goes on to quote fourth-century writer Epiphanius.

> Therefore, that sabbath prescribed by the law has retained its validity until his arrival; but after it has been abolished, he (God) has given (us) the great sabbath, which is the Lord himself; he is our rest and our sabbath observance.[53]

The validity of the Sabbath as a moral force was temporary; abolished laws have no continuity of force. Epiphanius uses the Sabbath as a metaphor for what it fulfilled and in whom it was fulfilled. This is not the language of continuity of force, but of fulfillment.

Then in a section that deals with the similarities and differences between the Lord's Day and the Sabbath, Lincoln's conciliatory emphasis leads to some other contradictions.

> Even if it is agreed that Sunday is the new Christian day for worship and that the Sabbath commandment is not to be applied to it, there remains an analogy between the two institutions of the Old Testament Sabbath and the New Testament Lord's Day.[54]

As a fulfilled ceremonial law Lincoln restates that the Sabbath has no application force ("not to be applied") but somehow paves the way for force based on analogy. He goes on to list five analogies, each of which he highly qualifies: 1) weekly, one day in seven, 2) celebration of redemption, 3) prefigured future rest of consummation, 4) the notion of worship, and 5) the concept of lordship. The only unique analogy between the Lord's Day and the Sabbath is the frequency, but as Lincoln acknowledges, the Sabbath is about the whole of the seventh day from Friday evening to Saturday evening, whereas the Lord's Day is about the first day of the week, Sunday, from morning to evening. The Lord's bodily resurrection was sufficient reason to elevate the first day of the week as a symbol of the Christian life and to provide a new perspective on time that transcended the Jewish calendar. Christ's reappearance to the disciples a sennight

52. Lincoln, "From Sabbath to Lord's Day," 394.

53. Ibid., 396.

54. Ibid., 398.

later (John 20:26) betokened the weekly cycle of gathering saints in the presence of the Lord.

Sabbatarians assume that the continuing cycle of seven days (though seemingly shifted to Sunday) proves that the Sabbath lives on; therefore, the position maintained in this book is a self-contradiction.

> Many regard this sabbath institution as a shadow of things that were to come and, therefore, as an ordinance to be observed, it has passed away, because that of which it was a shadow had been realized in the full light of the new and better covenant. At this point suffice it to ask the question: Has the pattern of God's work and rest in creation ceased to be relevant? Is this pattern a shadow in the sense of those who espouse this position?[55]

To rephrase the first question: If the *weekly* Sabbath is not to be observed, how can one advocate the *weekly* observance of the Lord's Day (without appealing to the creation)? In answer to this question, the relevancy of the first week of creation is in the redemption that it foreshadowed and in the symbolism of the number seven. The creation week was not an ordinance—it was a historical type—and, as such, may be fulfilled. The creation week symbolism did not cease because of the resurrection, so the number seven continues to proclaim the perfections of God's work in and through the church. Therefore, the current practice of the church to meet weekly is not directly based on the creation week or the Sabbath as a model of work and rest or as an example of recurring weeks, yet the weekly practice honors the historicity of the creation week and continues to symbolize the perfections of God's work through the church.

To rephrase the second question: If the weekliness of the Sabbath is a shadow, why does the church continue to meet in a weekly pattern? Again, the week bears the stamp of the divine. After all, the week is an artifact of the divine mind that purposed to reveal its perfection through the number seven. While the Sabbath and the Lord's Day follow a weekly sequence, there is no biblical or historical evidence that the weekliness of the Lord's Day was directly based on the former. The whole ceremonial calendar, which included the Sabbath, was rendered obsolete for Christians, yet the Lord, in His wisdom, decreed that His saints meet on Sunday, based on the resurrection, and weekly, based on the recurring appearances of Jesus and the Holy Spirit. The Lord's Day is primarily a celebration of what took place on the eighth day and to this the weekliness of Lord's Day gatherings is secondary. And while the number seven may remind the church of the creation and God's perfection, these are still secondary to the eighth day/first day reminders of the resurrection, the gift of the Holy Spirit, the new creation, and the new covenant.

First-day assembly and worship is a biblical warrant from God, unmodifiable by the supposed belief that Christians may gather for worship on just any day of the week. The Lord purposed that His beloved saints gather together in unity on the first day of the week in commemoration of His bodily resurrection and the baptism of the Holy Spirit. First-day worship confirms the significance and authority of the new

55. Murray, *Collected Writings*, 1:219; Owen, "Excercitations," 676–77.

covenant and the surety that what remains yet to come will be accomplished according to God's will. The canonical letters of Luke (Acts 20:7), Paul (1 Cor 16:2), the unknown author (Heb 10:25), and John (John 20:26; Rev 1:10) carry the same moral force as if God Himself had descended with smoke and fire and thunderings to give us the command. The Christian has no more authority to alter this mandated day of worship than the Jews had to move the Sabbath. Sabbatarians have sought the *jure divino* from the Fourth Commandment and Evangelicals have denied it altogether,[56] however, to the dismay of both camps, the preponderance of evidence demonstrates that the Sabbath is fulfilled and the Lord's Day is decreed.

Regrettably, history demonstrates the wiles of the devil to confuse and dismantle what should be a defining and unifying charter of the church. Christians by apostolic tradition worship on Sunday in memory of the risen Lord, and are commanded never to forsake assembling together. The early church grew exponentially amid turmoils and persecutions without an appeal to the continuing force of the Sabbath commandment. Christians meet together to worship under the new covenant force of divine goodness, not because of the threats of the old covenant Sabbath. Christians may well consider the works of God in creation on Sunday, as they do on any other day of the week, but on Sunday, in particular, they must hear the word of the Lord in preaching, remember Him in the Lord's Supper, pray to Him in fervency, and fellowship with the members of His body in the love of the Holy Spirit. Any Christian who understands this will stop what he's doing and go worship the Lord in corporate assembly.

56. Dennison, "The Perpetuity and Change of the Sabbath," 147.

10

The Sabbath in Church History

Apostolic Teaching

THE PERSECUTION OF STEPHEN was based upon the belief that Christianity was radically different from Judaism. The Jewish leaders painfully observed the effects of Jesus' teaching on His disciples, taking issue with the predictions of change.

> They also set up false witnesses who said, "This man does not cease to speak blasphemous words against this holy place and the law;
> for we have heard him say that this Jesus of Nazareth will destroy this place and change the customs which Moses delivered to us." (Acts 6:13–14)

There are three crucial distinctions between Christianity and its roots in Judaism: holy things, the law, and the customs. The vitriolic reaction of these so-called protectors of the temple against the apostles was based upon their observation that a new system of theology and practice was being advocated. Let us not likewise react that these three—holy things, the law, and the customs—should be changed, "for if that first covenant had been faultless, then should no place have been sought for the second" (Heb 8:7). Though some of the laws of the former covenant were inferior in relation to the superior realities of Christ, the old laws cannot be said to be anything less than good (Gal 3:19–25). Yet these ceremonial laws isolated the Jews from their pagan neighbors, became the point of contention and ridicule, and represented a wall of separation between the two peoples. This was meant by God to display the isolation between sinners and Himself—the Jew included—so when Christ abolished the ceremonies of Judaism, the gospel of peace and the law of moral commandments would become the unifying theology and practice for Jew and Gentile alike (Eph 2:14–16). The Christian church had no central temple or holy place—not Jerusalem and not the Pantheon—for they were themselves the temple of God, made holy by the indwelling Holy Spirit. At the beginning of the Christian church, it was a stumbling block to require Gentile believers to observe Jewish rituals: "to whom we gave no such commandment" (Acts 15:24). This chapter presents a brief look at some of the more significant historical documents that give evidence of the changing attitudes about the relationship of the church to the Sabbath ceremony of the old covenant.

CHURCH FATHERS

The Didache (50–120 CE)

The Didache, one of the earliest writings of church morality and order, begins with the first command, "Thou shalt love the God that made thee [and] thy neighbor as thyself," and then continues:

> And this is the second commandment of the teaching. Thou shalt do no murder, thou shalt not commit adultery, thou shalt not corrupt boys, thou shalt not commit fornication, thou shalt not steal, thou shalt not deal in magic, thou shalt do no sorcery, thou shalt not murder a child by abortion nor kill them when born, thou shalt not covet thy neighbor's goods, thou shalt not perjure thyself, thou shalt not bear false witness, thou shalt not speak evil, thou shalt not cherish a grudge, thou shalt not be double-minded nor double-tongued . . . My child, thou shalt remember him that speaketh unto thee the word of God night and day, and shalt honour him as the Lord . . . Thou shalt not withhold thy hand from thy son or from thy daughter, but from their youth thou shalt teach them the fear of God.[1]

There is an obvious acknowledgment of the moral perpetuity of decalogic commands save one: the fourth commandment. This is similar to the Pauline lists of sins where Sabbath-breaking is not even mentioned. Indeed, this document mentions the Lord's Day but not the Sabbath.

> And on the Lord's own day gather yourselves together and break bread and give thanks, first confessing your transgressions, that your sacrifice [of praise] may be pure. And let no man, having his dispute with his fellow, join your assembly until they have been reconciled, that your sacrifice may not be defiled.[2]

Various researchers have proposed fanciful alternatives to the more common understanding that Sunday, the Lord's Day, is in view. While Bauckham admits the context supports this understanding, he cautions that this single reference does not lead, in and of itself, to an undeniable conclusion (κατὰ κυριακὴυ δὲ κυρίου = "on the Lord's own day" = Sunday) unless supported by other evidence.[3] However, this early reference and John's use of the phrase κυριακὴ ἡμέρα in Revelation 1:10 does provide evidence that this phrase developed within the first century and carried a meaning peculiar to the Christian mind. Rordorf believes "the context points unambiguously to the weekly act of worship on Sunday."[4]

The Epistle of Barnabas (100 CE)

The Epistle of Barnabas, purported to have been written by the apostle Barnabas by early church fathers who quoted this work (such as Clement of Alexandria and

1. Lightfoot, *Apostolic Fathers*, 123–25 (*Didache*, chaps. 1, 2, 4).
2. Ibid., 128 (*Didache*, chap. 14).
3. Bauckham, "The Lord's Day," 228.
4. Rordorf, *Sunday*, 209–10.

Origen), was considered to be canonical as late as the fifth century. However, the preponderance of research dates this anonymous letter from 70–132 CE. Reminiscent of the letter to the Hebrews, this document quotes heavily from the OT in developing the premise that the gospel of Jesus Christ is discernable throughout the Law and the Prophets in the form of types, which, because they have been fulfilled, are no longer intended to be practiced. Beginning with the sacrificial system, he quotes Isaiah 1:11–13 (which mentions sacrifices, burnt offerings, rams, lambs, bulls, goats, oblations, fine flour, incense, New Moons, and Sabbaths) and concludes, "These things therefore He annulled, that the new law of our Lord Jesus Christ, being free from the yoke of constraint, might have its oblation not made by human hands."[5] He continues to explain that the promise of the land of Canaan and the promise of a new spirit (Ezek 11:19) were fulfilled in present-day believers: "We therefore are they whom He brought into the good land."[6] Quoting Jeremiah 4:4, he purports that the practice of circumcision, even though commanded to father Abraham and repeated in the law of Moses, is typological of our salvation.

> Therefore He circumcised our ears, that hearing the word we might believe. But moreover the circumcision, in which [the Jews] have confidence, is abolished; for He hath said that a circumcision not of the flesh should be practiced.[7]

Finally, he discusses the Sabbath as a type of the eternal rest and as a prophetic type of God's timetable for the human race.

> Moreover concerning the sabbath likewise it is written in the Ten Words, in which He spake to Moses face to face on Mount Sinai; *And ye shall hallow the sabbath of the Lord with pure hands and with a pure heart.* And in another place He saith; *If My sons observe the sabbath, then I will bestow My mercy upon them.* Of the sabbath He speaketh in the beginning of the creation; *And God made the works of His hands in six days, and He ended on the seventh day, and rested on it, and He hallowed it.* Give heed, children, what this meaneth; *He ended in six days.* He meaneth this, that in six thousand years the Lord shall bring all things to an end; for the day with Him signifieth a thousand years; and this He himself beareth me witness, saying; *Behold the day of the Lord shall be as a thousand years.* Therefore, children, in six days, that is in six thousand years, everything shall come to an end. *And He rested on the seventh day.* This He meaneth; when His Son shall come, and shall abolish the time of the Lawless One, and shall judge the ungodly, and shall change the sun and the moon and the stars, then shall He truly rest on the seventh day. Yea and furthermore He saith; *Thou shalt hallow it with pure hands and with a pure heart.* If therefore a man is able now to hallow the day which God hallowed, though he be pure in heart, we have gone utterly astray. But if after all then and not till then shall we truly rest and hallow it, when we shall ourselves be able to do so after being justified and receiving the promise, when iniquity is no more and all things have been made new by the Lord, we shall be able to hallow it then, because we ourselves shall have been

5. Lightfoot, *Apostolic Fathers*, 138 (*Epistle of Barnabas*, chap. 2).
6. Ibid., 142–43 (*Epistle of Barnabas*, chap. 6).
7. Ibid., 145 *(Epistle of Barnabas*, chap. 9).

> hallowed first. Finally He saith to them; *Your new moons and your sabbaths I cannot away with.* Ye see what is His meaning; it is not your present sabbaths that are acceptable [unto Me], but the sabbath which I have made, in the which, when I have set all things at rest, I will make the beginning of the eighth day which is the beginning of another world. Wherefore also we keep the eighth day for rejoicing, in which also Jesus rose from the dead, and having been manifested ascended into the heavens.[8]

Barnabas demonstrates an uncanny appreciation for the eschatologic application of the creation scenario. It is not just that the Lord created in six days and rested the seventh, but that God did so as a type of something yet to come. For Barnabas, the church is living in the seventh day (though an incomplete rest), awaiting the final outcome of the Lord's sovereign plan on the eighth day (a perpetual and complete rest). Barnabas is emphatic in relegating the Sabbath, along with the New Moon and sacrifices, to those ceremonial laws that are no longer required of followers of Jesus. He does not mitigate the abolishment of the Sabbath, as if some adverse effect would befall the church without some sort of Sabbath, but he dismisses it in its entirety.

Furthermore, Barnabas understood that even though the fourth word commanded Sabbath obedience, it was meant only as a type in conjunction with the example of God in creation. He therefore could urge his readers to "never forsake the commandments of the Lord," specifically decrying such sins as idolatry of carved images, taking the Lord's name in vain, disobedience to parents, murder (even of the preborn or infants), adultery, lying and slander, and covetousness and greed, yet failing to mention profaning the Sabbath in any of his long lists of transgressions.

Ignatius, Bishop of Antioch (30–107 CE)

Ignatius was the bishop of Antioch in the beginning of the second century. Both he and Polycarp were disciples of Apostle John, as affirmed by Origen, Irenaeus, and the historian Eusebius. Condemned for his Christian beliefs, he wrote various letters in the Pauline spirit during his final months awaiting martyrdom in 107 CE. In his letter to the Magnesians, he clearly distinguishes between Jewish conduct on the Sabbath and Christian conduct on the Lord's Day to indicate the superiority of being a disciple of Christ.[9]

> If, therefore, those who were brought up in the ancient order of things have come to the possession of a new hope, no longer observing the Sabbath, but living in the observance of the Lord's Day, on which also our life has sprung up again by Him and by His death—whom some deny, by which mystery we have obtained faith, and therefore endure, that we may be found the disciples of Jesus Christ, our only Master—how shall we be able to live apart from Him, whose disciples the prophets themselves in the Spirit did wait for Him as their Teacher?[10]

8. Ibid., 151–52 (emphasis and brackets in original; *Epistle of Barnabas*, chap. 15).
9. Bauckham, "The Lord's Day," 229.
10. *Epistle of Ignatius to the Magnesians*, chap. 9 (*ANF* 1:62–63).

The significance of the Lord's Day ascended to the rank previously held by the Sabbath. The Lord's Day is a celebration of the resurrection of Jesus Christ, the focal point of our redeemed life, without which we could not walk in newness of life. The Jew, by observing the Sabbath, lived only in anticipation of this hope.

The Epistle of Mathetes (130 CE)

This personal letter from an unknown disciple of the apostles was written to Diognetus, an inquirer into the Christian religion. It appears that Diognetus is still an idol worshipper but wonders which religion is correct: Greek pantheism, Jewish monotheism, or this novel religion called Christianity. The letter is both sincere and intelligent, representing one of the earliest expressions of Christian apologetics. Having explained the pagan error of worshipping images of stone and metal, Mathetes continues.

> And next, I imagine that you are most desirous of hearing something on this point, that the Christians do not observe the same forms of divine worship as do the Jews. The Jews, then, if they abstain from the kind of service above described, and deem it proper to worship one God as being Lord of all, [are right]; but if they offer Him worship in the way which we have described, they greatly err . . .
>
> But as to their scrupulosity concerning meats, and their superstition as respects the Sabbaths, and their boasting about circumcision, and their fancies about fasting and the new moons, which are utterly ridiculous and unworthy of notice,—I do not think that you require to learn anything from me. For, to accept some of those things which have been formed by God for the use of men as properly formed, and to reject others as useless and redundant,—how can this be lawful? And to speak falsely of God, as if He forbade us to do what is good on the Sabbath-days,—how is not this impious? And to glory in the circumcision of the flesh as a proof of election, and as if, on account of it, they were specially beloved by God—how is it not a subject of ridicule? And as to their observing months and days, as if waiting upon the stars and the moon, and their distributing, according to their own tendencies, the appointments of God, and the vicissitudes of the seasons, some for festivities, and others for mourning,—who would deem this a part of divine worship, and not much rather a manifestation of folly? I suppose, then, you are sufficiently convinced that the Christians properly abstain from the vanity and error common [to both Jews and Gentiles], and from the busy-body spirit and vain boasting of the Jews; but you must not hope to learn the mystery of their peculiar mode of worshipping God from any mortal.[11]

The traditions and hypocrisies of the Jews that were condemned by Christ are now scorned as worthless duties of a dying religion (Luke 13:10–17). Mathetes may seem less than gracious in maligning the ceremonies that God instituted, but he understands the ceremonies to have been symbolic of better realities, so continuation of them is utter foolishness. Mathetes does not fret that the annulment of the Sabbath will in any way hinder Diognetus from engaging in meaningful fellowship and worship on the Lord's Day.

11. *Epistle of Mathetes to Diognetus*, chaps. 3–4 (*ANF* 1:26).

Justin Martyr (114–165 CE)

Formerly a philosopher, Justin converted to Christianity and believed that the truths of the Bible provided a most comprehensive and satisfying worldview that deserved a hearing among all peoples. Writing during the middle of the second century, Justin has been called the father of Christian philosophy. He was also impressed with the humble and resolute lifestyle of the Christian, even in the face of death, a fate he eventually shared under the hands of Marcus Aurelius. Of the many works attributed to him, only the two Apologies (to the Greeks) and a letter to Trypho are unquestionably his. It is in the latter work that we find an exposition of the Christian mindset with regard to the old covenant. The letter to Trypho is the lengthy record of an amiable dialogue between Justin and a Jew named Trypho. At one point, Trypho apprises Justin of what he must do in order to obtain God's favor.

> If, then, you are willing to listen to me (for I have already considered you a friend), first be circumcised, then observe what ordinances have been enacted with respect to the Sabbath, and the feasts, and the new moons of God; and, in a word, do all things which have been written in the law: and then perhaps you shall obtain mercy from God.[12]

Justin replied,

> Is there any other matter, my friends, in which we are blamed, than this, that we live not after the law, and are not circumcised in the flesh as your forefathers were, and do not observe sabbaths as you do? Are our lives and customs also slandered among you?[13]

Christians in the early centuries were not Sabbath-keepers, and this was upsetting to Trypho who continued to argue the perpetuity of this old covenant law. The festivals, the Sabbath, and New Moon celebrations distinguished the Jews from the surrounding cultures, manifesting their obedience to God, but Christians appeared to be like those among whom they lived—those who despised God's law. Justin continued,

> The Lawgiver is present, yet you do not see Him; to the poor the Gospel is preached, the blind see, yet you do not understand. You have now need of a second circumcision, though you glory greatly in the flesh. The new law requires you to keep perpetual sabbath, and you, because you are idle for one day, suppose you are pious, not discerning why this has been commanded you: and if you eat unleavened bread, you say the will of God has been fulfilled. The Lord our God does not take pleasure in such observances: if there is any perjured person or a thief among you, let him cease to be so; if any adulterer, let him repent; then he has kept the sweet and true sabbaths of God. If any one has impure hands, let him wash and be pure.[14]

Perhaps Justin's most notable rumination is that he urges Trypho to consider the reason the Lord required so many ceremonies of the Jews. Why does God command

12. Justin, *Dial.*, 8 (*ANF* 1:198–99).
13. Ibid., 10 (*ANF* 1:199).
14. Ibid., 12 (*ANF* 1:200).

circumcision? Why does He require you to sweep out leaven and to be idle weekly? The Jewish ceremonies appear overly peculiar and superstitious because the Jews perform them without understanding the real reason for doing them. The Christian understands now why these ceremonies were required of the Jews—because they foreshadowed Christ and His redemption—therefore participation in these ceremonies would be a futility beyond reason. Justin does not regard the Sabbath as a moral commandment since he sets it against the moral commandments of honesty and fidelity. Spiritually understood, unleavened bread speaks of a pure life and the Sabbath speaks of our perpetual redemption in Christ. Justin continued his argument against Sabbath-keeping by noting that none of the patriarchs ever kept the Sabbath, yet they were fully justified by God through faith. Therefore, Sabbath-keeping is totally unnecessary for a Christian. Before moving onto other subjects with Trypho, Justin summarizes his argument that circumcision and the festivals are not binding on true worshippers of God.

> Wherefore, Trypho, I will proclaim to you, and to those who wish to become proselytes, the divine message which I heard from that man. Do you see that the elements are not idle, and keep no Sabbaths? Remain as you were born. For if there was no need of circumcision before Abraham, or of the observance of Sabbaths, of feasts and sacrifices, before Moses; no more need is there of them now, after that, according to the will of God, Jesus Christ the Son of God has been born without sin, of a virgin sprung from the stock of Abraham. For when Abraham himself was in uncircumcision, he was justified and blessed by reason of the faith which he reposed in God, as the Scripture tells.[15]

Justin understands that Christ's appearance has fulfilled the ceremonial laws so that they may be spiritually understood and spiritually kept. Thus the Sabbath rest is experienced on a daily basis in Christ. Furthermore, repentance from sin is analogous to resting from the outworking of sin, so that in repentance a Christian keeps "the sweet and true Sabbaths of God." The church of Jesus Christ is an institution that disregards the Jewish Sabbath in favor of the new covenant ritual of the Lord's Supper on the eighth day of the week that honors the resurrection of Christ (Ch. 41). His confidence in the passing nature of ceremonial law causes him to consider the implications of continuing in those laws, that depending on these laws as the avenue of salvation is to separate oneself from the Lord's salvation. However, Justin shares his opinion that it is possible for a Jew to trust fully in Christ, yet continue in Jewish ceremonies by reason of culture or ignorance, and still be saved. He advises only that these Jewish Christians do not compel Gentiles to observe the same (Ch. 47), a mindset consistent with apostolic doctrine (Gal 2:14).

Irenaeus, Bishop of Lyons (120–202 CE)

Irenaeus wrote of his vivid childhood recollection of Polycarp: "The discourses which he delivered to the people; also how he would speak of his familiar intercourse with John, and with the rest of those who had seen the Lord; and how he would call their

15. Ibid., 23 (*ANF* 1:206).

words to remembrance."[16] As Bishop of Lyons, a position he assumed in 180 CE, he wrote a five-volume polemic, *Against Heresies*, which condemned Gnosticism and its advocates, Valentinian and Marcion. Because the focus of his treatise was the false teachings of the Gnostics, there was little need to discuss the relationship of the Christian to the Sabbath; however, what few references there are demonstrate agreement with the elders who went before him.

> Moreover, we learn from the Scripture itself, that God gave circumcision, not as the completer of righteousness, but as a sign, that the race of Abraham might continue recognizable. For it declares: "God said unto Abraham, Every male among you shall be circumcised; and ye shall circumcise the flesh of your foreskins, as a token of the covenant between Me and you." This same does Ezekiel the prophet say with regard to the Sabbaths.[17]

Irenaeus distinguishes circumcision from those commands that display righteousness—for example, honoring parents, guarding one's tongue, and protecting life—because circumcision was essentially a signal command of the former covenant. Like driving down a road, once the sign is recognized and obeyed, you find yourself moving beyond the power of that sign. The Sabbath, declares Ezekiel, is also a sign of the former covenant (Ezek 20:12, 20) and has no directing power over those of the new covenant. Furthermore, the patriarchs were justified before the Lord on the basis of faith without the ceremonies of the Mosaic covenant.

> And that man was not justified by these things, but that they were given as a sign to the people, this fact shows,—that Abraham himself, without circumcision and without observance of Sabbaths, "believed God, and it was imputed unto him for righteousness; and he was called the friend of God."[18]

Not only that, the patriarchs were exempt from the demands of the Mosaic covenant, not just because they anteceded it, but because they were the objects of a preceding covenant, "The Lord did not make this covenant with our fathers, but with us" (Deut 5:2–3).

In the end, Irenaeus concludes that obedience to the ceremonies of the Mosaic covenant avails nothing toward righteousness, nor does it add to one's obedience to moral law. Obedience to the moral law alone is pleasing to the Lord and is all that He requires.

> This same declaration does Esaias make: "To what purpose is the multitude of your sacrifices unto Me? saith the Lord. I am full." And when He had repudiated holocausts, and sacrifices, and oblations, as likewise the new moons, and the sabbaths, and the festivals, and all the rest of the services accompanying these, He continues, exhorting them to what pertained to salvation: "Wash you, make you clean, take away wickedness from your hearts from before mine eyes: cease from your evil ways, learn to do well, seek judgment, relieve the

16. Irenaeus, *Fragments of Lost Writings* 2 (*ANF* 1:568).
17. Irenaeus, *Haer.* 4.16.1 (*ANF* 1:480).
18. Ibid., 4.16.2 (*ANF* 1:481).

> oppressed, judge the fatherless, plead for the widow; and come, let us reason together, saith the *Lord*."[19]

Those who have been justified by faith keep the Sabbath daily by finding rest in the kingdom of God.

> But the Sabbaths taught that we should continue day by day in God's service. "For we have been counted," says the Apostle Paul, "all the day long as sheep for the slaughter;" that is, consecrated [to God], and ministering continually to our faith, and persevering in it, and abstaining from all avarice, and not acquiring or possessing treasures upon earth. Moreover, the Sabbath of God (*requietio Dei*), that is, the kingdom, was, as it were, indicated by created things; in which [kingdom], the man who shall have persevered in serving God (*Deo assistere*) shall, in a state of rest, partake of God's table.[20]

Tertullian (160–225 CE)

Tertullian, an ante-Nicene church father of the second and third centuries, was in agreement with Justin, Irenaeus, and Barnabas regarding the past disposition of the Sabbath and the adoption of the Lord's Day (Sunday). Indeed, the common practice of Christian Sunday worship was so entrenched that his rebuttals to Sabbath advocates are laced with mockery. With extensive training in law, literature, and Greek and Roman languages, he was well-equipped to become a prolific writer and apologist for the Christian faith. Tertullian notes specifically that the patriarchs were free of circumcision and Sabbath-keeping, and lived lives of faith that commended them to God in much the same manner as Christians.

> [L]et him who contends that the Sabbath is still to be observed as a balm of salvation, and circumcision on the eighth day . . . teach us that, for the time past, righteous men kept the Sabbath, or practiced circumcision, and were thus rendered "friends of God." For if circumcision purges a man since God made Adam uncircumcised, why did he not circumcise him, even after his sinning, if circumcision purges? . . . Therefore, since God originated Adam uncircumcised and inobservant of the Sabbath, consequently his offspring also, Abel, offering him sacrifices, uncircumcised and inobservant of the Sabbath, was by Him [God] commended [Gen. 4:1–7, Heb 11:4] . . . Noah also, uncircumcised—yes, and inobservant of the Sabbath—God freed from the deluge. For Enoch too, most righteous man, uncircumcised and inobservant of the Sabbath, He translated from this world, who did not first taste death, in order that, being a candidate for eternal life, he might this time show us that we also may, without the burden of the law of Moses, please God.[21]

As Tertullian continues his rebuttal, he devotes a chapter to the Sabbath, noting its temporary institution from Moses until Christ.

19. Ibid., 4.17.1 (*ANF* 1:483).
20. Ibid., 4.16.1 (*ANF* 1:481).
21. Tertullian, *Adv. Jud.* 2 (*ANF* 3:153).

> It follows, accordingly, that, in so far as the abolition of carnal circumcision and of the old law is demonstrated as having been consummated at its specific times, so also the observance of the Sabbath is demonstrated to have been temporary.[22]

Consequently, he distinguishes two Sabbaths: 1) the temporary, carnal ordinance of the Jews characterized by cyclical rest and abstention from work, and 2) the eternal, spiritual Sabbath that is fulfilled in Christ and kept by the faithful through daily abstention from the "servile work" of sin. The spiritual Sabbath is both the present experience and the future hope of believers. The Lord never gave the Sabbath to Israel to be observed perpetually.

Origen (185–254 CE)

Origen was a pupil of Clement of Alexandria and a successor at the School of Alexandria. He was a prolific writer, so much so that Jerome regarded Origen as the next greatest Christian author after Apostle Paul. At the urging of his friend Ambrosius (not the Bishop of Rome), one of Origen's first works was a response to an atheistic criticism of Christianity by Celsus, written some seventy years before. Origen was an apologist, a pastor, and a theologian, yet at the same time, he was influenced by Greek Neoplatonism and developed an allegorical method of scriptural interpretation, a shortcoming that has drawn criticism, as pointed out by Greidanus.

> In looking for the real message at this "deeper" level, allegorical interpretation violates the historical nature of the biblical narrative and ultimately denies the value of redemptive history.[23]

For example, in one of his surviving works, a *Commentary on the Gospel of John* [229 CE], he discerns that the narrative describing Jesus riding on a donkey and the foal of an ass into Jerusalem, describes the word of God (Jesus) coming into the soul of man (Jerusalem), first with the old covenant (donkey) and then with the new covenant (foal).[24] Though he does have a tendency to look for hidden spiritual meaning to various texts of Scripture, this is not to say that his entire yield is so affected. He properly understands that the Passover lamb is a type of the propitiatory death of Christ and he provides other reasonable typological interpretations of historical narratives. From the succession of Moses by Joshua, Origen discerns that Joshua is a type of Jesus Christ "who succeeds the dispensation through the law, and replaces it by the preaching of the Gospel."[25] From the introductions to the Gospels, "the *beginning* of the Gospel of Christ, the Son of God," he advances the idea that John the Baptist is a type of the OT that must give way to the new.[26] Origen glories in the new covenant dispensation as a time when truth and grace prevail, providing freedom to attain true

22. Ibid., 4 (*ANF* 3:155).
23. Greidanus, *Preaching Christ*, 88.
24. Origen, *Comm. Jo.*, 10:18 (*ANF* 9:396).
25. Ibid., 6:26 (*ANF* 9:372).
26. Ibid., 1:14 (*ANF* 9:304).

spirituality. He quotes Isaiah (Isa 1:13) and Paul (Col 2:16) as proof texts for the carnal and typological essence of the Jewish sacrifices, holy days, New Moons, and Sabbaths. Introducing the Gospel of John, Origen points his readers to the narrative about the birth and naming of John the Baptist, noting that Zacharias (meaning "memory") and Elizabeth (meaning "oath of God") gave the herald of Christ the name "Joannes" (meaning "gracious"), thus indicating that the promises of God were not forgotten, but at the appointed season, God brought in the grace of the gospel that He promised.

> Thus was he born to make ready for the Lord a people fit for Him, at the end of the Covenant now grown old, which is the end of the Sabbatic period. Hence it is not possible that the rest after the Sabbath should have come into existence from the seventh of our God; on the contrary, it is our Saviour who, after the pattern of His own rest, caused us to be made in the likeness of His death, and hence also of His resurrection.[27]

The end of the old covenant is the end of the Sabbath. Yet the Christian now enjoys the rest of salvation, not because of the seventh-day Sabbath but because of the first-day resurrection. Christ's death over the Sabbath was our death, therefore, we live in the likeness of His resurrection life on the first day.

Eusebius of Cæsarea (265–340 CE)

Writing in the fourth century, Eusebius of Cæsarea was both a historian of the Christian religion and a proponent of the faith. He was a participant in two of the most significant events affecting the Christian religion: the Edict of Milan in 313 CE, by which Constantine allowed a relative freedom of religion, and the Council of Nicea in 325 CE, which affirmed the deity of Jesus Christ. In his scholarly work, *Ecclesiastical History*, he documented the first three centuries of Christianity, making use of the library and archives in Cæsarea. He turned his comments to some Jewish converts to the gospel, called the Ebionites, who rejected the canon of Scripture and the deity of Christ:

> These men, moreover, thought that it was necessary to reject all the epistles of the apostle, whom they called an apostate from the law; and they use only the so-called Gospel according to the Hebrews and made small account of the rest [of the Scriptures]. The Sabbath and the rest of the discipline of the Jews they observed just like them, but at the same time, like us, they celebrated the Lord's days as a memorial of the resurrection of the Savior.[28]

It is interesting to note that both the Sabbath and the Lord's Day were observed by the Ebionites. Of course, they would have kept the Sabbath with a work prohibition, but their observance of the Lord's Day did not involve a work prohibition, otherwise they would have celebrated two Sabbaths in sequence.[29] This would have been an unmanageable burden to say the least.

27. Ibid., 2:27 (*ANF* 9:342).
28. Eusebius, *Hist. eccl.*, 3.27.4–5 (*NPNF*2 1:159–60).
29. Skarsaune, "The Ebionites," 446.

Eusebius also notes the relationship between the rejection of the Pauline, Johanine, and Petrine Epistles to the practical error of keeping the Sabbath. Had the Ebionites been fully taught the doctrines of the church as contained in these epistles, they would have understood the reason why Christians dismissed the Sabbath and celebrated instead the first day in honor of their figurehead's resurrection.

> The day of [Christ's] light . . . was the day of his resurrection from the dead, which they say, as being the one and only truly holy day and the Lord's day, is better than any number of days as we ordinarily understand them, and better than the days set apart by the Mosaic law for feasts, new moons, and Sabbaths, which the apostle [Paul] teaches are the shadow of days and not days in reality.[30]

The Jews criticized the practices of the Christian as aberrant from the Law; however, Eusebius argues that Christians are no different from the patriarchs who did not observe calendar laws.

> [The early saints of the Old Testament] did not care about circumcision of the body, neither do we [Christians]. They did not care about observing Sabbaths, nor do we. They did not avoid certain kinds of food, neither did they regard the other distinctions which Moses first delivered to their posterity to be observed as symbols; nor do Christians of the present day do such things.[31]

Eusebius lived through the Diocletian Persecution (303–311 CE) to witness the Edict of Galerius (311 CE), which paved the way for tolerance of the Christian religion.

The Edict of Milan (313 CE)

Eusebius provides the text of the Edict of Milan, which he made from extant copies of the Latin text, along with numerous other letters from Constantine Augustus (306–337 CE) regarding the relationship of the church to the state.[32] The Edict of Milan begins with a statement that the basis of the decree was rooted in the past understanding that religious toleration subserves the "common weal and prosperity" of a nation. The Christian religion is mentioned throughout the document, without mention of any other, to ensure that Christians are left free to engage in their religious exercises, that property once seized is restored, and that inequalities against Christians be amended. The benefit expected by Constantine was that through equal protection of the law, the State would enjoy social tranquility and not incur the displeasure of any god(s). Seven years later (321 CE), Constantine promulgated a civil rest on the first day of the week, Sunday, again reasoning that religious freedom would ensure the blessings of "heavenly providence."

> All judges and city people and craftsmen shall rest upon the venerable day of the sun. Country people, however, may freely attend to the cultivation of the fields, because it frequently happens that no other days are better adapted for planting

30. Eusebius, *Dem. ev.*, 4.16.
31. Eusebius, *Hist. eccl.*, 1.4.8 (*NPNF2* 1:87).
32. Ibid., 10.5.2–14 (*NPNF2* 1:379–80).

> the grain in the furrows or the vines in the trenches. So that the advantage given by heavenly providence may not of a short time perish.[33]

While historians and theologians may speculate about the motive and meaning behind the Edict, the theory espoused by Seventh-day Adventism is particularly out of line:

> It was the emperor's policy to unite the conflicting interests of heathenism and Christianity. He was urged to do this by the bishops of the church, who, inspired by ambition and thirst for power, perceived that if the same day was observed by both Christians and heathen, it would promote the nominal acceptance of Christianity by pagans and thus advance the power and glory of the church. But while many God-fearing Christians were gradually led to regard Sunday as possessing a degree of sacredness, they still held the true Sabbath as the holy of the Lord and observed it in obedience to the fourth commandment.[34]

The Emperor's concept of rest was anything but a reference to a Jewish sabbatism since farmers were allowed to work on the day of rest. The Edict does not mention the Sabbath or the Lord's Day, only the "venerable Day of the Sun," so it is difficult to support the thesis that Constantine was attempting to establish a Christian sabbatism. As Bauckham concluded, "While it is probable that at least some Christians desired the status of an official holiday for Sunday, there was scant theological justification for this, [because] in Christian thought the ideas of Sabbath rest had been so consistently reinterpreted that physical rest from work was precisely what it no longer meant."[35]

While we may lament the repercussions of decisions made by men in history, we cannot undo what God has decreed to take place. If Apostle Paul could look beyond the injustice done to him through imprisonment and see the realization of the divine plan to further the gospel (Phil 1:12, 27–30), then our cynosure, when evaluating the Edict of Milan, should be the sovereign outworking of God's will on earth. Constantine's edict was primarily pragmatic: a day free of commerce provided freedom for many of his subjects to attend pagan festivities and Christian meetings so his kingdom could enjoy the natural prosperity that follows a contented people. But with regard to the gospel, it allowed not only the upper class, but more importantly, the common man and his children who served others daily, to hear the gospel preached. Without this edict, Christians would have continued their meetings on the first day of the week before or after work. This new practice seemed similar to the Jewish sabbatic model and because of this association, church leaders began to call for physical rest on the Lord's Day. There are scant references to this, balanced by objections to sabbatizing the Lord's Day,[36] but the Edict of Milan, rather than shifting the Sabbath to the first day of

33. *Codex Justinianus* 3:12:2.

34. White, *Great Controversy*, 53. This includes Bacchiocchi's claim that anti-Semitism and protectionism were responsible for the disuse of the Sabbath and its replacement with Sunday observance; Bacchiocchi, *From Sabbath to Sunday*, 197–98.

35. Bauckham, "Sabbath and Sunday in the Post-Apostolic Church," 281; Nelson, *Biblical Study*, 103–15.

36. Jewett, *Lord's Day*, 128–33.

the week, as proposed by Seventh-day Adventists, actually initialized the association of the Lord's Day with physical rest.

Sylvester, Bishop of Rome (314–335 CE)

Sylvester, the Bishop of Rome, was not present at the Council of Bishops in Nicea, but is believed to have communicated with Constantine about the Arian controversy prior to the synod. Many Seventh-day Adventists cite Sylvester I as the pope who transferred the Sabbath rest to the first day of the week and the one who urged that Sunday be called the Lord's Day. This claim is sometimes made by Roman Catholics as well. The only source for this information appears to have been made by Rabanus Maurus (776–856 CE), an abbot of Fulda and later archbishop of Mainz, Germany, who claimed that the holy doctors of the church insisted that Sabbath laws be transferred to the Lord's Day. However, Maurus' claim is a prochronism, an intrusion of post-Augustinian theology into the third century. As Bauckham's research has shown, Augustine's theology of the Sabbath, which "never treated Christian obedience to the Sabbath commandment as the observation of a day," dominated medieval interpretations of the Sabbath.[37]

Since Sylvester and Eusebius were contemporaries, Adventist Scheifler quotes Eusebius' commentary on Psalm 91 (Psalm 92 in English versions) as proof of the Catholic transference of the Sabbath to the Lord's Day.

> And all things whatsoever that it was duty to do on the Sabbath, these we have transferred to the Lord's day, as more appropriately belonging to it, because it has precedence, and is first in rank, and more honorable than the Jewish Sabbath.[38]

It should be patently obvious that Scheifler's interpretation of Eusebius does not substantiate the claim that the Sabbath was transferred to the Lord's Day, for the Jewish Sabbath remains secondary in any week occupied by the Lord's Day. Without the context, Scheifler's minimalistic quote misleads the reader. Bauckham quotes extensively from this commentary to provide the necessary context for understanding what Eusebius meant by "all things . . . transferred," and concludes,

> The care with which Eusebius avoids the idea of inactivity on the Sabbath is notable. The Sabbath was devoted to the service of God and works pleasing to God. The activity of Christians on the Lord's Day is analogous to the activity of the priests on the Mosaic Sabbath; it is the service of God in worship. It is this *priestly* activity of worship that has been transferred from the Sabbath to Sunday.[39]

That is, the Christian, by analogy, performs priestly works of worship, but does not concern himself with a carnal rest, for it was the Levitical priests who broke the Sabbath through their priestly work. Eusebius regarded the saints of the NT era to be daily worshipping God, yet on a weekly basis they honored the Lord by a separate

37. Bauckham, "Sabbath and Sunday in the Medieval Church," 300.

38. Scheifler, "Which Pope Changed the Sabbath?" n.p.

39. Bauckham, "Sabbath and Sunday in the Post-Apostolic Church," 284.

gathering with spiritual service and communion. The continuing controversy from Judaizing sects eventually forced the bishops of all the Eastern churches to assemble again to determine a common Christian ethic regarding the Sabbath and Lord's Day.

Council of Laodicea (364 CE)

The Synod of Laodicea was a local council of some thirty bishops, convened to settle issues, among them the relationship of the Christian to the Sabbath. Of the fifty-nine Canons of this Council, the sixteenth and twenty-ninth canons mention the Sabbath. Later, the Council of Chalcedon (451 CE) confirmed these canons, imbuing them with ecumenical force. Canon 16 curiously enjoins that "The Gospels are to be read on the Sabbath [i.e. Saturday], with the other Scriptures." Canon 29 specifically condemns the practice of Sabbatarianism on the seventh day of the week, but commends a spiritual rest on the Lord's Day.

> Christians must not Judaize by resting on the Sabbath, but must work on that day, rather, honoring the Lord's Day; and, if they can, resting then as Christians. But if any shall be found to be Judaizers, let them be anathema from Christ.[40]

A physical rest on the Sabbath or the Lord's Day was condemned as Judaizing. The Jewish Sabbath appeared to promote laziness, so Christians were advised to work on the Sabbath. And to bring honor to the Lord's Day, Christians were encouraged to spiritually rest. The Christian rest was not inactivity or refrainment from ordinary labor, but spiritual service to God in worship by virtue of the spiritual significance of the fulfilled Sabbath. Daily resting from the burden of sin and worldliness was "resting then as Christians." While Christians spiritually rested in Christ every day, when Sunday was freed from commerce, Christians began to perceive rest as a weekly, physical experience. The fact that Christians had to stop work in order to congregate together introduced a mild analogy to the Jewish Sabbath.

Furthermore, the promulgation of a weekly civil holiday removed any roadblocks to attending weekly worship on the Lord's Day, thus introducing the expectation that all professing Christians faithfully attend worship services. It must not be forgotten that many professing Christians lapsed under the persecution of Licinius (Constantine's brother-in-law), so presbyters (elders) were burdened with training repentant Christians to remain committed to church attendance in spite of persecution, and convincing new converts to do the same. In time, the Sabbath/Lord's Day analogy would prove helpful in discipleship. However, this shift in thinking could not happen quickly because the church had condemned the sabbatic practice of physical rest for three centuries. Sabbath-keeping and sabbatizing the Lord's Day were still fringe heresies.

40. Council of Laodicea, canon 29 (*NPNF*2 14:148).

Augustine of Hippo (354–430 CE)

Augustine was a worldly man until his conversion and in short order he arose to the office of Bishop of Hippo in 396 CE. Augustine was a prolific writer, and his understanding of the Sabbath is evident in his letter *The Spirit and the Letter* (412 CE), which addressed the claim of some Christians that it is possible to live a sinless life. He seems not to consider this a substantial error since the Scriptures state emphatically that no man can be justified in His sight, but of more concern to Augustine was the heresy that a man can perfect himself through the exercise of his own will. His conclusion was that the letter of the law kills without the work of the Holy Spirit in a person's life. While he acknowledged that the letter of the law may refer to ceremonial laws, it is actually moral law that kills because it aggravates sin through its knowledge. Augustine equated the error of the Jews in Paul's day with the error of the Pelagians who gloried in their self-justifying ability to keep the law. Augustine then distinguished between the law of works that commands "Thou shalt not covet," and the law of faith that seeks to obey the same command.

> Accordingly, by the law of works, God says to us, Do what I command you; but by the law of faith we say to God, Give me what Thou commandest. Now this is the reason why the law gives its command,—to admonish us what faith ought to do, that is, that he to whom the command is given, if he is as yet unable to perform it, may know what to ask for; but if he has at once the ability, and complies with the command, he ought also to be aware from whose gift the ability comes. "For we have received not the spirit of this world," says again that most constant preacher of grace, "but the Spirit which is of God, that we might know the things that are freely given to us of God."[41]

This distinction is necessary, for, when Paul admonishes those Jews who seek justification through circumcision, we tend to limit the phrase, "works of the law," to Jewish ceremonies and not to moral laws. Immediately, he directs the reader to consider the Ten Commandments that summarize the law of God.

> Well, now, I should like to be told what there is in these Ten Commandments, except the observance of the Sabbath, which ought not to be kept by a Christian . . . Which of these commandments [adultery, stealing, murder, coveting] would any one say that the Christian ought not to keep? Is it possible to contend that it is not the law which was written on those two tables that the apostle describes as "the letter that kills" [2 Cor 3:6], but the law of circumcision and the other sacred rites which are now abolished? But then how can we think so, when in the law occurs this precept, "Thou shall not covet," by which very commandment, notwithstanding its being holy, just, and good, "sin," says the apostle, "deceived me, and by it slew me?" What else can this be than "the letter" that "killeth"?[42]

Paul's phrase "the letter that kills" is unmistakably referring to the Decalogue (2 Cor 3:3), so it is not merely the letter of ceremonial law that kills but moral law also.

41. Augustine, *Spir. Et Litt.*, par. 22 (*NPNF*1 5:92).

42. Ibid., par. 23 (*NPNF*1 5:93).

> Well, then, is it owing to the one precept about the Sabbath-day, which is included in it, that the Decalogue is called "the letter that kills?" Because, forsooth, every man that still observes that day in its literal appointment is carnally wise, but to be carnally wise is nothing else than death? And must the other nine commandments, which are rightly observed in their literal form, not be regarded as belonging to the law of works by which none is justified, but to the law of faith whereby the just man lives? Who can possibly entertain so absurd an opinion as to suppose that "the ministration of death, written and engraven in stones," is not said equally of all the Ten Commandments, but only of the solitary one touching the Sabbath-day?[43]

Augustine concludes that the letter of the moral law is a killer if approached in a servile manner, rather than under the motivation of love and grace. It is not that love, hope, and faith appeared suddenly at the advent of Christ, for the old covenant proclaimed the same, but in shadow form. Even within the Ten Commandments is hidden a shadow of the grace to come in the Sabbath commandment.

> It was not for nothing that the nation was commanded on that day to abstain from all servile work, by which sin is signified; but because not to commit sin belongs to sanctification, that is, to God's gift through the Holy Spirit. And this precept alone among the others, was placed in the law, which was written on the two tables of stone, in a prefiguring shadow, under which the Jews observe the Sabbath, that by this very circumstance it might be signified that it was then the time for concealing the grace, which had to be revealed in the New Testament by the death of Christ[44]

Augustine concludes that the law written on our hearts includes only nine of the ten commandments, assigning the Sabbath and other observances of days, circumcision, the ceremonies of certain meats, and the complicated rituals of sacrifices and sacred things to that group of ceremonies described as a "slavish yoke" and a prefigurement of the grace of our Lord. With the exception of the Sabbath, the Ten Commandments comprehend the moral law of God, a law that pre-existed Israel and continues for the church.

Now, Bauckham reminds his readers that Augustine was faced with correcting the errors of the Manicheans, an especially widespread religion at the time and from which Augustine converted, so he was well-suited to defend the cohesiveness of old and new covenant moral law.

> In the first place, he established definitively the central place of the Decalogue in Christian moral theology. Against the Manichean dualist rejection of Old Testament law, he defended the Decalogue as the sum of the law of love; the first three precepts expound the love of God, the last seven the love of neighbor.[45]

43. Ibid., par. 24 (*NPNF*1 5:94).

44. Ibid., par. 27 (*NPNF*1 5:95).

45. Bauckham, "Sabbath and Sunday in the Medieval Church," 300. The third precept is the Sabbath commandment under Augustine's enumeration of the Ten Commandments, an accounting followed by the Roman and Lutheran churches.

Augustine unmistakably categorizes the Sabbath as a temporary ceremony of the Mosaic economy, and because of its ceremonial significance, he attributes to it the shadow of grace to come. Augustine views the Ten Commandments from several perspectives. From the perspective of the letter of the law, all of the Ten Commandments are spiritually lethal to those who think they can achieve righteousness thereby. From the perspective of the NT, the Decalogue may be divided into nine moral commandments and one ceremonial commandment. From the perspective of God's intention with the Decalogue—including the foreshadowing Sabbath—Augustine envisions a cohesive statement of the moral law of God, which is the law of love. It is from this last perspective that Augustine divides the commandments by their orientation: the first three commandments are toward God (this includes the Sabbath) and the remaining seven toward man.[46] Based on his method of dividing the commandments, it seemed especially satisfying to him that three commandments belong to God and the remaining seven to man. Furthermore, it was the spiritual significance and intent of the Sabbath—the imparting of grace to live in faith to God—that allowed Augustine to categorize it as a godward commandment. While Augustine's general belief is correct—that the Sabbath is a ceremonial law—I believe he is incorrect on two minor points. First, the spiritual significance of the work prohibition is not about refraining from sin, but refraining from works-righteousness. Secondly, the division of the Ten Commandments is better understood from a redemptive perspective than a perspective based on love-orientation.

ROMAN CATHOLICISM

Gregory (I) the Great (540–604 CE)

By the year 461 CE, the Bishop of Rome was recognized as a superior officer to other bishops in the Western church. Traditions now common to Roman Catholicism were already taking root, such as a liturgical mass, a monastic life, symbolic outfits, ecclesiastical hierarchy, and declaration of days to honor saints. As Cairne reviews this period of history, specifically the importance of Gregory the Great, he says,

> He stood, as Augustine did in this day, at the divide between the two worlds of classicism and medieval Christianity and became the symbol of the new medieval world in which culture was institutionalized with the church dominated by the bishop of Rome.[47]

Gregory I was the first bishop of Rome to be given the papal title, a term he did not favor, but a position that he protected and strengthened. He stands between Augustine and Aquinas as one of the greatest theologians in church history, though he never learned Hebrew or Greek. In the interpretative tradition of Augustine, Gregory

46. The Roman Catholic Church adopted the division of Augustine, which combined the first and second commandments, putting the Sabbath in the third position; and separating the tenth commandment into two separate commandments. See the section on Aquinas for a discussion of the different ways the early church divided the Ten Commandments and how the structure carried symbolic overtones.

47. Cairns, *Christianity Through the Centuries*, 166.

I, in a letter to Roman citizens, corrects the doctrine of those who attempt to enforce a literal physical rest for Christians.

> It has come to my ears that certain men of perverse spirit have sown among you some things that are wrong and opposed to the holy faith, so as to forbid any work being done on the Sabbath day. What else can I call these [men] but preachers of Antichrist, who when he comes will cause the Sabbath day as well as the Lord's day to be kept free from all work. For because [the Antichrist] pretends to die and rise again, he wishes the Lord's day to be held in reverence; and because he compels the people to Judaize that he may bring back the outward rite of the law, and subject the perfidy of the Jews to himself, he wishes the Sabbath to be observed. For this which is said by the prophet, 'You shall bring in no burden through your gates on the Sabbath day' [Jer 17:24] could be held to as long as it was lawful for the law to be observed according to the letter. But after that the grace of almighty God, our Lord Jesus Christ, has appeared, the commandments of the law which were spoken figuratively cannot be kept according to the letter. For if anyone says that this about the Sabbath is to be kept, he must needs say that carnal sacrifices are to be offered. He must say too that the commandment about the circumcision of the body is still to be retained. But let him hear the apostle Paul saying in opposition to him: 'If you be circumcised, Christ will profit you nothing' [Gal 5:2].
>
> We therefore accept spiritually, and hold spiritually, this which is written about the Sabbath. For the Sabbath means rest. But we have the true Sabbath in our Redeemer Himself, the Lord Jesus Christ. And whoso acknowledges the light of faith in Him, if he draws the sins of concupiscence through his eyes into his soul, he introduces burdens through the gates on the Sabbath day. We introduce, then, no burden through the gates on the Sabbath day if we draw no weights of sin through the bodily senses to the soul. For we read that the same our Lord and Redeemer did many works on the Sabbath day, so that he reproved the Jews, saying, Which of you does not loose his ox or his ass on the Sabbath day, and lead him away to watering ? If, then, the very Truth in person commanded that the Sabbath should not be kept according to the letter, whoso keeps the rest of the Sabbath according to the letter of the law, whom else does he contradict but the Truth himself?[48]

Gregory's core understanding is that the Sabbath is a fulfilled ceremonial law that should no longer be literally applied. You might as well bring back to life *all* the ceremonies if you are going to bring back any one of them! (That would be a false resurrection, so to speak). Only the spirit of antichrist would draw us away from the revealed mysteries of Christ; therefore, commanding a Sabbath rest is against Christ Himself. In effect, the resurgence of ceremonial law is a denial of the work of Christ *in the flesh*, a trademark doctrine of the antichrist (1 John 4:3). His allegorical interpretation of Jeremiah's orders does not diminish his position that the Sabbath is a Jewish ceremonial law.[49]

48. Gregory the Great, Selected Epistles 13:1 (*NPNF2* 13:92).

49. The gates are better interpreted as the entrance to the true city of God, the division between the world and heaven, much like the gates separating Eden from the fallen world. It is a reminder that sin and wickedness cannot enter the presence of God (Gen 4:7; Ps 5:4; Rev 14:20) and that we, in our sin,

The views of Augustine and Gregory the Great predominated through the end of the first millennium, though examples of Judaizing Sunday can be found.[50] Bauckham cites Peter Comester as the "first exegete to apply the Sabbath commandment literally to Christian observance of the first day" during the twelfth century.[51] During the following century, "Sunday rest became a general law of the church when it was incorporated in the Dectretals of Gregory IX."[52] H. R. Gamble noted various examples of localized English and European laws from the seventh to eleventh centuries that defined the timing of the Lord's Day (commencing at 3:00 p.m., Saturday), restricted work and travel, warned citizens of divine judgments for carelessness, and dissuaded hiring a cook for holy days (although a cook hired by the month could cook on a holy day). But Gamble is quick to note, "It must not, however, be supposed that even in the Middle Ages there were no voices to protest against this casuistry. There were those who saw and denounced the renaissance of Judaism."[53]

While it is helpful to acknowledge the scattered, yet progressive, acceptance of a physical rest on Sunday, it is more important to understand the bases for these practices in empiricism and religious authoritarianism. Obviously, since work restrictions benefited the laboring class, there was a popular acceptance of a weekly period of rest. Furthermore, church leaders affirmed a righteous care for the hardships faced by those subjects, and for that reason allowed recreations to be done on Sunday. However, the clergy were remiss that the populace squandered their time in sloth or irreligious activities. Their expectation that all citizens attend Mass in this church-state led to the need to force compliance through the appeal to Sabbath law.[54]

Eventually the Roman Catholic Church based its justification of Sunday rest on the supposed transference of the Sabbath to the Lord's Day by the custom and consent of Christian people. On the other hand, in the Orthodox Church, the liturgical calendar held a preeminent place, so the Sabbath and Lord's Day remained as separate feast days. Religious services were held on both days and fasting was forbidden on both days. The Sabbath commemorated the creation of the world and Christ's rest of death, encouraging Christians to reflect upon the eternal Sabbath. Yet the Lord's Day, commemorating the resurrection of Christ through the Eucharist, remained the most important day of the week. The Orthodox Church retained the Jewish concept of the day beginning in the evening and the timing of the Passover, values which contributed to the growing differences between the Western and Eastern churches.

---

cannot approach God (Exod 19:10–12; Lev 20:7). It also implies that there must be a means to leave the burden of sin behind before entering His presence (Lev 16:2; Ps 140:13) and that the sacrifices, Sabbaths, and New Moons are ultimately inadequate to serve that purpose (Isa 1:10–14; Hos 2:11). Were it not for God's sovereign grace, we would have no hope of enjoying His presence within the gates of His kingdom.

50. Laband and Heinbuch, *Blue Laws*, 10–14; Rordorf, *Sunday*, 171–173.

51. Bauckham, "Sabbath and Sunday in the Medieval Church," 304.

52. Ibid., 303.

53. Gamble, *Sunday and the Sabbath*, 96.

54. Rordorf, *Sunday*, 167–68.

Thomas Aquinas (1234–1274)

Leading up to Thomas Aquinas was the development of Scholasticism in the high Middle Ages, a period when the faith of the Bible was integrated with the intellectual pursuit of truth. It was a virtue to question and examine what had long been held to determine its rationality, yet the truth of the Bible still hedged in the extent and order of man's reason. Laws for the church abounded, defining every ecclesiastic system and reaching into the private lives of all citizens as well as the political decisions of nations, with the epitome of law resting in the pope. Because of the excesses of the church, the Dominican and Franciscan orders—committed to poverty—took root, but anyone who denied the authority of the pope was declared a heretic and subjected to the punishing rule of the Inquisition. Men were free to pursue liberal (freemen) studies, yet not all subjects were oriented toward Christianity. The works of Aristotle, the contributions of Maimonides, and the rise of Mohammedanism were competing worldviews that Aquinas answered in his *Summa Theologica*. His system of theology was comprehensive and endorsed topics that now characterize the Roman Catholic Church, such as the treasury of merit, indulgences, the seven sacraments, purgatory, the mass, transubstantiation, and the authority of the pope.

His views on the Sabbath may be found predominantly under the general topics of law, the law of the old covenant, and the ceremonies of the old covenant (First Part of the Second Part, Questions 90–108, and the Second Part of the Second Part, Question 122).

> As Augustine proves (*De Spiritu et Litera* xiv), even the letter of the law is said to be the occasion of death, as to the moral precepts; in so far as, to wit, it prescribes what is good, without furnishing the aid of grace for its fulfillment.[55]

Quoting from Augustine's *The Spirit and the Letter* (q.v.), Aquinas answers affirmatively that the Decalogue contains moral law—those laws that kill without the grace of God. However, he veered from Augustine who excepted the Sabbath commandment *in its entirety* as a moral law.

Let us begin with his answer to the question, "Whether all men were bound to observe the Old Law?" Aquinas answers that all men were bound only to observe that part of the old law that contained precepts of the natural law (a reflection of eternal law). However, their obligation was not to the old law *per se*, but to the transcendent natural law. Those parts of the old law that were peculiar to the Jews were not obligatory on non-Jews. Aquinas continues his dialectic by asserting that the old law contains moral (emanating from natural law), judicial (laws regarding justice among men), and ceremonial (laws touching on worship, holiness, and sanctification) precepts; and that these three can be distinguished in the Decalogue as well.

Though Augustine is quoted throughout this section, Aquinas broke from Augustine in his answer to the question "Whether all the moral precepts of the Old Law are reducible to the 10 precepts of the Decalogue?" Known to Aquinas were those who viewed the Sabbath commandment as strictly ceremonial, as did Augustine, and who

55. Aquinas, *Summa*, 2:1033 (Q. 99, Art. 2).

argued that higher moral laws could not be reduced to lesser ceremonial commands. That is, we could not derive from any natural law (or moral law) that it was fitting to cut the skin from the male organ on the eighth day following his birth or that a person was unclean for seven days after touching a dead body, requiring ablution on the third and seventh days. Nor could one determine from natural law that worship must take place on the seventh day of the week, encompassing a twenty-four hour period when no burdens are lifted, no business is conducted, and no cooking is performed. These sorts of laws must be directly revealed by the Lord. However, Aquinas states,

> The precept of the Sabbath observance is moral in one respect, in so far as it commands man to give some time to the things of God, according to Ps 45:11: "Be still and see that I am God." In this respect it is placed among the precepts of the decalogue: but not as to the fixing of the time, in which respect it is a ceremonial precept.[56]

At this juncture, Aquinas took the first step toward Sabbatarianism by moralizing a ceremonial command (to derive from a ceremonial command a moral obligation). He seems to think he understands *why* God placed this ceremonial command within the midst of the Decalogue: to assert the moral necessity to give some time to the things of God. Had circumcision been in the Decalogue, Aquinas would assert that the moral component is that the faithful must identify themselves with the covenant; or if the law of uncleanness, that all Christian men must keep themselves unspotted from worldly ways. Indeed, there is a reason for the Sabbath in the Decalogue, but it is not about giving God some of your time. At this point, Aquinas has not postulated an adequate explanation. Aquinas continues his analysis of the Ten Commandments by addressing the number of commandments, their order, the range of virtues and vices, their formulation as to negative or positive, and their continuity and immutability. For the most part, his respect for the word of God is evident as he shows no inclination to question the rationality of God who assembled the Ten Commandments. However, concerning the reason for including the Sabbath commandment in the Decalogue, Aquinas provides only conjecture.

> Hence the precept about hallowing the Sabbath is placed among the precepts of the decalogue, as a moral, but not as a ceremonial precept.[57]

How much of our time is God's time (Ps 27:4; 32:6; Eccl 3:1–11; Isa 59:21), and how much of what we do pertains to the things of God (Ps 4:8; 1 Cor 10:31)? The first three commandments already address our relationship to God based on the understanding that He alone is God, supreme and incorporeal, the sovereign God who saves and judges; who transcends time, ruling from one generation to the next; and who demands from all the inhabitants of the world their obedience, love, and reverence. Without appealing to the Sabbath, we could derive a moral obligation to worship God

56. Ibid., 2:1039 (Q. 100, Art. 3).

57. Ibid., 3:1695 (Q. 122, Art. 4).

continuously. And if we properly understood the spirituality of the Sabbath, we could derive a duty for daily worship, as Calvin noted.

> [The Sabbath] is a perpetual rest which God commands: one without any interval . . . It is necessary for the faithful throughout their life to keep the sabbath day, and to desist from their own wills and actions, and to endeavor to dedicate themselves to God in all humility in order to align themselves with him and to find peace in his obedience.[58]

However, the laws of Sabbath worship—two sacrifices and twelve loaves—were only a minor part of the Sabbath ethic for Israel. There are plenty of other ceremonial laws that better entail giving time to God in worship. While Aquinas fished for a rational explanation for the presence of the Sabbath in the Decalogue, his answer is not satisfying because he ignored the overwhelming ceremoniality of the Sabbath.

Another reason Aquinas sought a moral obligation from the Sabbath commandment is the structure of the Decalogue as he understood it. The oldest system for enumerating the Ten Commandments comes from Philo Judaeus of Alexander. Called the *Philonic division*, common to Reformed and Evangelical churches, it places the Sabbath in the fourth position. Since the Ten Commandments are not specifically numbered in Scripture, Aquinas used the *Augustinian division* that combined the first two commandments (no other gods, no idols) into one commandment, thus shifting the Sabbath into the third position. This seemed to satisfy the numerical association of the number three with the homage and service owed to God.

> The three precepts that direct man in his behavior towards God may also be differentiated in this same way. For the first refers to deeds; wherefore it is said, "Thou shalt not make . . . a graven thing": the second, to words; wherefore it is said, "Thou shalt not take the name of the Lord thy God in vain": the third, to thoughts; because the sanctification of the Sabbath, as the subject of a moral precept, requires repose of the heart in God.[59]

For Roman Catholics and Lutherans, the fourth commandment (obey parents) has to do with authority, occupying an intermediate position in a sequence of duties to God (1–3), to parents (4), and to our fellow man (5–10).

> The precepts of the decalogue are directed to the love of God and of our neighbor. Now to our parents, of all our neighbors, we are under the greatest obligation. Hence, immediately after the precepts directing us to God, a place is given to the precept directing us to our parents, who are the particular principle of our being, just as God is the universal principle: so that this precept has a certain affinity to the precepts of the First Table.[60]

Aquinas continues to asseverate that the ceremonial laws of the old covenant did not precede the giving of the Law but were specifically designed for that epoch. He acknowledges four objections that might contradict this conclusion: 1) that circumcision

58. Farley, *Calvin's Sermons*, 106.

59. Aquinas, *Summa*, 2:1041 (Q. 100, Art. 5).

60. Ibid., 3:1696–97 (Q. 122, Art. 5).

was given to Abraham, 2) that clean and unclean animals were described by Noah, 3) that a priesthood existed before in Melchizedek, and 4) that various patriarchs erected altars and prepared sacrifices; and Aquinas adequately answers them all. No mention is made of a Sabbath commandment prior to the Mosaic law. Had the Scriptures indicated a pre-Mosaic Sabbath institution, surely Aquinas would have mentioned this along with the four other supposed examples of pre-Mosaic ceremonial law. Aquinas recaps that the ceremonies of the old covenant ceased with the coming of Christ, leading to his conclusion that continuance in their observance was a mortal sin.

However, Aquinas blurs the foreshadowing features of Jewish ceremonies and analogous spiritual realities of the church; hence, the figurative sense in which a ceremonial command was fulfilled becomes a new figure for the church. For example, in the OT there was a single tabernacle or a single temple, the figure of which is said by Aquinas to portray the unity of worship. This same figure (unity of worship) is realized in the congregations of Christians, so "our church takes the place of both temple and synagogue: since the very sacrifice of the church is spiritual."[61] Likewise, the vestments of the Aaronic priesthood signified their office and virtues; therefore, these should be replaced with symbolic garb, such as the alb, which denotes purity. The continual burnt offering, speaking of the eternity of Jesus Christ, requires the church to convey the same truth by performing a daily mass.

> Baptism, which is the sacrament of Faith, corresponds to circumcision . . . In the New Law the sacrament of the Eucharist corresponds to the banquet of the paschal lamb. The sacrament of Penance in the New Law corresponds to all the purifications of the Old Law. The sacrament of Orders corresponds to the consecration of the pontiff and of the priests. To the sacrament of Confirmation, which is the sacrament of the fulness of grace, there would be no corresponding sacrament of the Old Law, because the time of fulness had not yet come . . . The same applies to the sacrament of Extreme Unction, which is an immediate preparation for entrance into glory, to which the way was not yet opened out in the Old Law, since the price had not yet been paid. Matrimony did indeed exist under the Old Law, as a function of nature, but not as the sacrament of the union of Christ with the Church, for that union was not as yet brought about.[62]

The correspondence or analogy between Israel and the church led to the transference of the figure contained in the old ceremonies to the new covenant, and where there was no new covenant counterpart, one was invented.

> As to the sabbath, which was a sign recalling the first creation, its place is taken by the "Lord's Day," which recalls the beginning of the new creature in the Resurrection of Christ. In like manner other solemnities of the Old Law are supplanted by new solemnities: because the blessings vouchsafed to that people, foreshadowed the favors granted us by Christ. Hence the feast of the Passover gave place to the feast of Christ's Passion and Resurrection: the feast of Pentecost when the Old Law was given, to the feast of Pentecost on which was given the

61. Ibid., 2:1063 (Q. 102, Art. 4).

62. Ibid., 2:1070 (Q. 102, Art. 5).

> Law of the living spirit: the feast of the New Moon, to Lady Day, when appeared the first rays of the sun, i.e. Christ, by the fulness of grace: the feast of Trumpets, to the feasts of the Apostles: the feast of Expiation, to the feasts of Martyrs and Confessors: the feast of Tabernacles, to the feast of the Church Dedication: the feast of the Assembly and Collection, to feast of the Angels, or else to the feast of All Hallows.[63]

So, the second step toward Sabbatarianism was the uncritical acceptance of figurative explanations for ceremonies of the old covenant coupled with a disproportionate interest in the analogy between Israel and the church, leading to the replacement method supposed to have occurred with circumcision and the Passover. As noted in chapter 8, Aquinas believed it was *necessary* to replace the former signs because they rendered grace to the recipients, thus ensuring that the church receives like grace. Christians were not called upon to observe the letter of the old covenant but were now commanded to observe a man-made invention that carried forward some spiritual theme and supposedly conferred some grace in its observance. The justification of replacement was eventually attributed to the authority of the church because there appeared to be no scriptural ground for it: "In the New Law the observance of the Lord's day took the place of the observance of the Sabbath, not by virtue of the precept but by the institution of the Church and the custom of Christian people."[64]

With the Sabbath in the decalogic spotlight, it became necessary to find *spiritual* ways to observe it without *literally* observing it (which would be a mortal sin). Transferring the Sabbath to Sunday seemed to assuage any fear of sinning by Judaizing, and to ensure that Judaizing did not occur, Aquinas continued to state that the physical rest was not to be practiced literally, so the necessity of attending mass was not equated with or based upon the figure of rest. However, from the literal rest, which Aquinas viewed as a judicial command, he derived the moral principle that servants be treated fairly and not burdened with excessive labor.[65] Though Aquinas derives from the Sabbath a general moral duty to set aside time for God, he correctly guards against the implication that the Sabbath should fix the time of worship with regard to frequency and duration. However, contradiction was inevitable. We gather together on Sunday "not by virtue of the precept [of the Decalogue]," yet that same precept contains a moral law to set aside some time for the worship of God. The Sabbath rest is figurative and ceremonial, but that same rest is interpreted literally to assert a moral obligation to suspend work for worship. The ceremonies of the old covenant find their fulfillment in Christ, but they are replaced by ceremonies in the new covenant that vouchsafe the same graces and relay the same message.

As Augustine noted, it is the moral law that kills without the life-giving Spirit, and as Aquinas agreed, moral laws kill without the grace of God. Death is proclaimed in nine commandments, but the hope of eternal life is contained in one. As a shadow of the gospel of grace within the Decalogue, the Sabbath speaks of Christ and His

63. Ibid., 2:1085 (Q. 103, Art. 3).

64. Ibid., 3:1696 (Q. 122, Art. 4).

65. Ibid., 2:1102 (Q. 105, Art. 4).

redemption. The hunt for a moral precept within the Sabbath command gives us only one more way to realize sin, but we need a Savior. Christ is the end of the law and the sum of the law (John 5:39, 2 Tim 3:15; Luke 24:27). And if this is so, which of the Ten makes us wise to salvation through faith in Jesus Christ? Which of the Ten preaches Jesus Christ and Him crucified? Which of the Ten expounds to us the things concerning Himself? It is the ceremonial, signal, and redemptive Sabbath command.

The Catechism of Trent (1566)

Though the Roman Catholic Church had a historical interest in catechesis, they never developed a uniform or systematic method for the instruction of converts or its lay members until the Reformers designed catechisms to raise biblical knowledge of their converts. Following the catechetical formula of Protestant churches,[66] the Roman Catholic Church, in its counter-Reformational Council of Trent (1566), devised a catechism inculcating the Apostles' Creed, the Sacraments of the church, the Ten Commandments, and the Lord's Prayer. This format constrained all authors to address the Sabbath commandment and exploit its legislation as applicable to the Lord's Day. As the catechism begins, the Sabbath commandment prescribes the external worship which we owe to God, and obligates the pastor to exhort and instruct the faithful so that that those who carefully comply with it are more easily induced to keep all the other Commandments. In keeping with Aquinas' teaching, the Catechism of Trent quickly contradicts itself attempting to explain how the Sabbath commandment prescribes weekly worship but not actually on the Sabbath and not actually with Sabbath-keeping.

> Neither is it a principle of the natural law; we are not instructed by nature to give external worship to God on that day, rather than on any other. And in fact the Sabbath was kept holy only from the time of the liberation of the people of Israel from the bondage of Pharaoh. The observance of the Sabbath was to be abrogated at the same time as the other Hebrew rites and ceremonies, that is, at the death of Christ. Having been, as it were, images which foreshadowed the light and the truth, these ceremonies were to disappear at the coming of that light and truth, which is Jesus Christ.[67]

It correctly affirms that the Sabbath is not a moral command, but ceremonial. However, it erroneously concludes that because it is ceremonial, it is then *subject to change.*

> But the Church of God has in her wisdom ordained that the celebration of the Sabbath should be transferred to "the Lord's Day."[68]

This is a far cry from abrogation; for changing, altering, or manipulating something requires one to work with the same materials, but abrogation is the death of a law,

66. Luther's Small Catechism (1526); Calvin's Catechism (1560); Heidelberg Catechism (1563)

67. *Catechism of the Council of Trent*, 264.

68. Ibid., 267.

the stripping away of any authority of that law, and the ceasing of all its effects. Moving the Sabbath to another day is merely an amendment of the former law. Augustine once taught that resting the whole day was nothing more than sloth, but now the Roman Catholic Church determined to keep Sunday just as a Jew kept the Sabbath, that no servile work was deferred to the Lord's Day.

Even though the Sabbath commandment is classified as ceremonial, no effort is made to explain its fulfillment, only that it was a sign that man should dedicate himself to God. And since the Sabbath has been moved to the Lord's Day, the Lord's Day must carry on the signal work of the Sabbath.

> [The Lord's Day] is also a sign of a spiritual and celestial Sabbath. The spiritual Sabbath consists in a holy and mystical rest, wherein the old man being buried with Christ, is renewed to life, and studies to act in accordance with the spirit of Christian piety . . . The celestial sabbath . . . is that life which we shall enjoy with Christ, in the fruition of all good, when sin shall be no more.[69]

There is no mention of the typological fulfillment of the Sabbath, only that it is now symbolic of the daily mystical rest of an ongoing sanctification and of the final heavenly rest at the end of the ages. If the Sabbath was fulfilled, it must be fulfilled in Christ, completely and perfectly. However, according to this catechism, the Sabbath is at one moment ceremonial and abrogated, then moral and incumbent upon all mankind to obey. The Sabbath commandment cannot come to its fulfillment-rest because it has been transferred to another day to continue in its work of convicting sinners.

The Sabbath whispered in Aquinas' writings that natural law requires only some time to be devoted to the things of God; this catechism clamored of a literal duty to sanctify the whole day in the works of piety and to physically rest from menial work. Augustine excepted the Sabbath from the Decalogue as a moral force, but the Council of Trent made it a kingpin for obeying the other nine. The doctrine of the Sabbath and the Lord's Day became blurred and the Sabbath ascended to greater importance as a strong arm to enforce attendance at mass and expose the hoi polloi to sermons. While early Reformers questioned some of the doctrines of the Roman Catholic Church regarding the Sabbath commandment, only minor corrections were made, as they had more serious matters with which to concern themselves.

Pope John Paul II (1998)

With pastoral concerns for the episcopacy and faithful citizens of the Roman Catholic Church regarding worldly cultural influences that diminish attendance at Sunday Mass and the forthcoming celebration of the Jubilee in the year 2000, Pope John Paul II delivered a letter titled *Dies Domini*, or "The Lord's Day," on Pentecost, 1998. This refreshing and uplifting document extols the virtues of Christ and His resurrection as the primary cause for first-day worship.

69. Ibid.

> The fundamental importance of Sunday has been recognized through two thousand years of history and was emphatically restated by the Second Vatican Council: "Every seven days, the Church celebrates the Easter mystery. This is a tradition going back to the Apostles, taking its origin from the actual day of Christ's Resurrection—a day thus appropriately designated 'the Lord's Day.'"[70]

Not once did he claim that by the authority of the church the Sabbath was moved or transferred to the Lord's Day. Interestingly, he states that Sunday is "more than a 'replacement' for the Sabbath (contrary to Aquinas), therefore, Sunday is its fulfillment" (par. 59). However, the Sabbath did not foreshadow the Lord's Day as he implies. John Paul II acknowledges that Sunday worship is a tradition of the church that dates back to apostolic times, and that there was a transition from seventh- to eighth-day worship as the gospel spread among the Gentiles (par. 19–26). Tradition, without citing its source, seems to carry enough authority to obligate Christians to Sunday worship, but in the end, this is really inadequate. Rather, Sunday worship must rest on nothing other than the commandment of the risen Lord, which it has through the tradition (i.e., commandment) of the apostles.

While he makes good use of Scripture and history, confusion remains about the relationship of the Sabbath to the Lord's Day. He sees in the creation story a Sabbath principle and reasons that rejoicing in the creation was not abrogated with the fulfillment of the Sabbath. In the section "The Fulfillment of the Sabbath," he provides no examples of how the Sabbath was actually fulfilled in Christ; however, he quotes Saint Gregory the Great as declaring, "For us, the true Sabbath is the person of our Redeemer, our Lord Jesus Christ." This attitude pervades John Paul's letter as he structures it around the manifestation of Christ's glory with respect to His involvement in creation, His first advent and resurrection, His Bride's remembrance in the Eucharist, His benefits to mankind, and His centrality over time. As such, the tenor of his letter is encouraging and full of joy, with little emphasis on micromanaging the affairs of the faithful in terms of how to externally keep Sunday holy.

THE REFORMATION

Martin Luther (1483–1546)

Among many disputes with the established Roman Catholic Church was Martin Luther's observation that works-righteousness was fostered and cultivated by a host of holy days. What began as an expression of piety and provided opportunities for the church to engage in worship developed into a system of burdensome and worthless activities. Luther rightly emphasized salvation by faith alone and not by works, but his detractors accused him of doing away with good works entirely. This, along with a request from Spalatin, the preacher for the Elector of Saxony, for a sermon on good works, provided the impetus for his booklet, *On Good Works*. Published several years after the incident in Wittenberg in 1517, Luther employed the Ten Commandments, as

70. John Paul II, "Dies Domini," par. 3.

did Aquinas, to advance the outward manifestation of the Christian religion. Referring to the Sabbath commandment, he said,

> Spiritually understood, this Commandment has a yet far higher work, which embraces the whole nature of man. Here it must be known that in Hebrew "Sabbath" means "rest," because on the seventh day God rested and ceased from all His works, which He had made (Gen 2:3). Therefore He commanded also that the seventh day should be kept holy and that we cease from our works which we do the other six days. This Sabbath has now for us been changed into the Sunday, and the other days are called work-days; the Sunday is called rest-day or holiday or holy day. And would to God that in Christendom there were no holiday except the Sunday; that the festivals of Our Lady and of the Saints were all transferred to Sunday; then would many evil vices be done away with through the labor of the work-days, and lands would not be so drained and impoverished. But now we are plagued with many holidays, to the destruction of souls, bodies and goods; of which matter much might be said.[71]

Luther appears to retain the Roman Catholic teaching that the Jewish Sabbath was transferred to the Christian Lord's Day, yet grumbles that there are far too many special days in which work is ceased and the cycle of six days work and one day rest is interrupted. However, he quickly moves to the meaning and intention of the Sabbath for saints of the new covenant: that the working man must pause from his labors and go hear God's word preached, yet this cessation from work in order to worship is *not* to be equated with the Sabbath command to rest.

> The bodily rest is that of which we have spoken above, namely, that we omit our business and work, in order that we may gather in the church, see mass, hear God's word and make common prayer. This rest is indeed bodily and in Christendom no longer commanded by God, as the Apostle says, Colossians 2:16, "Let no man obligate you to any holiday whatever"—for they were of old a figure, but now the truth has been fulfilled, so that all days are holy days, as Isaiah says, chapter 66:23, "One holy day shall follow the other"; on the other hand, all days are work-days. . . . For a day of rest is at present not necessary nor commanded except only for the teaching of God's word and prayer.[72]

More importantly, Luther sees in the nullified Sabbath command the necessity of daily refraining from works of self-righteousness, works done in our own strength, and works of the flesh, and instead rest in faith so God alone may work through us. The Sabbath commandment was fulfilled, but its place in the Decalogue affords us a new meaning. Every day is for us is a Sabbath of resting from selfishness and resting in the Lord; every day is a work day in that God is working out His holy will in our lives. He supports six days of work and one day for worship, but this is not based on the authority of the abrogated Sabbath commandment. Yet he still considers Sunday to be a holy day to hear God's holy word. His one-line explanation of the Sabbath commandment in his Small Catechism (1529) is, "We should so fear and love God as not

71. Luther, "Treatise On Good Works," *Works*, 1:240–41.

72. Ibid., 1:241.

to despise preaching and his word, but deem it holy, and willingly hear and learn it."[73] While the Sabbath made no demands on Israel to hear the preaching of the holy word on a weekly basis, this is what the Sabbath meant to Luther.

Luther's confrere and friend, Philip Melanchton, was familiar with Luther's writings and furthered Reformation thought with the preparation of the Augsburg Confession for the Diet of Augsburg in 1530 under the reign of Charles V. This document endeavored to support the ancient creeds of the church and to reform the existing church with an amplification of certain topics, such as the cardinal Christian doctrines, faith and good works, and the nature of the church of Christ. Under the heading "Matters of Dispute," Melanchthon begins correcting the false teachings of the Roman Catholic Church on the Mass, marriage of priests, the sacraments, and confession (made to priests). Melanchthon carefully notes that those who burden the conscience of saints with human traditions do so by one of two ways: 1) as if such regulations earned God's grace or imparted special holiness and, 2) as if such regulations were necessary for salvation. He notes that teachers in the past constantly invented new traditions involving foods and days and clothing, "as if these were a necessary service of God by means of which grace could be earned if they were observed and a great sin committed if they were omitted."[74]

> Besides, there is dispute as to whether bishops have the power to introduce ceremonies in the church or establish regulations concerning foods, holy days, and the different orders of the clergy . . . Besides, they appeal to the fact that the Sabbath was changed to Sunday—contrary, as they say, to the Ten Commandments. No case is appealed to and urged so insistently as the change of the Sabbath, for thereby they wish to maintain that the power of the church is indeed great because the church has dispensed from and altered part of the Ten Commandments.[75]

The Roman Catholic Church maintained that it had the power to effect changes and to decree innovative regulations for its members. If the church has that much power, enough power to change the Ten Commandments, its authority may confidently stand side by side with Scripture. However, this idea was untenable to the Reformation mind. Melanchthon continues,

> Again, those who institute human ordinances also act contrary to God's command when they attach sin to foods, days, and similar things and burden Christendom with the bondage of the law, as if in order to earn God's grace there had to be a service of God among Christians like the Levitical service.[76]

The abuse of spiritual authority and the doctrine of replacement theology matured into a number of false practices that the Reformers attempted to correct. Witnessing the seemingly daily addition of new ceremonies and holy days, of saints to venerate

73. Luther, "Small Catechism," *Creeds of Christendom*, 3:74–75.

74. *Creeds of the Churches*, 88 (Augsburg Confession, Art. 26).

75. Ibid., 100–101 (Art. 28).

76. Ibid., 101.

and fasts to keep, Melanchthon asserts, "There are clear passages of divine Scripture which forbid the establishment of such regulations for the purpose of earning God's grace or as if they were necessary for salvation."[77]

> Of like character is the observance of Sunday, Easter, Pentecost, and similar holy days and usages. Those who consider the appointment of Sunday in place of the Sabbath as a necessary institution are very much mistaken, for the Holy Scriptures have abrogated the Sabbath and teach that after the revelation of the Gospel all ceremonies of the old law may be omitted. Nevertheless, because it was necessary to appoint a certain day so that the people might know when they ought to assemble, the Christian church appointed Sunday for this purpose, and it was the more inclined and pleased to do this in order that the people might have an example of Christian liberty and might know that the keeping neither of the Sabbath nor of any other day is necessary.[78]

Melanchthon is correct in asserting that the Lord's Day is not a replacement for the Sabbath. Indeed, the Sabbath is dead to the Christian, just like every other signal ordinance of the old law. But he is imprecise to attribute the Lord's Day to the appointment of the church. Instead, the Lord's Day was appointed on the authority of Jesus Christ, who 1) fulfilled the shadows of the Jewish ceremonial calendar, 2) foreordained His resurrection on the first day of the week and the gift of the Holy Spirit on Pentecost, 3) inspired the apostles to record these historical events in canonical literature, and 4) directed the apostles to establish the Lord's Day tradition for His church.

Melanchthon also understood the relationship between the introduction of legalism into the church and the concurrent failure to teach the righteousness of faith with clarity and purity. When the doctrine of sanctification is poorly understood by God's people and when ministers of the gospel use fear to control the congregation, all sorts of regulations, rules, and ceremonies are imagined with hopes to provide increased order and regimentation in the churches.

> Some argue that although Sunday must not be kept as of divine obligation, it must nevertheless be kept as almost of divine obligation, and they prescribe the kind and amount of work that may be done on the day of rest. What are such discussions but snares of conscience? For although they undertake to lighten and mitigate human regulations, yet there can be no moderation or mitigation as long as the opinion remains and prevails that their observance is necessary. And this opinion will remain as long as there is no understanding of the righteousness of faith and Christian liberty.[79]

Prior to the Augsburg Confession, the church in Switzerland instituted changes in its religious calendar reflecting the growing discontent with the plethora of holy days. In 1527, only Christmas, Easter, and All Saints Day, in addition to Sunday were considered holy days in which work was prohibited, except for harvesting, which was

77. Ibid., 102. He cites Col 2:16, 20–23; Acts 15:10; 2 Cor 10:8; and Titus 1:14.

78. Ibid., 103–104.

79. Ibid., 104.

considered a necessary work.[80] These reforms were partial and conciliatory, whereas other reforms, such as banning the Mass, were decisive and divisive. Swiss Reformer Zwingli agreed with the Augsburg Confession except for the presence of the Lord in the Sacrament. In the years following the confession, under various circumstances, Reformation divines such as Beza, Farel, and Calvin each signed the document.

Luther authored a second catechism (the Large) in 1530 conforming to the format of his earlier catechism (the Small). He used the Ten Commandments to teach Christian morality; the Apostles' Creed to inculcate Christian beliefs, the Lord's Prayer to instruct Christian piety, and finally, a section on the sacraments of the church. This catechetical format was duplicated in various catechisms over the next several centuries. Regarding the fourth commandment, Luther begins with a confusing array of statements about the meaning of the Sabbath and the creation rest, the imposition of the Sabbath on the Jews and their misapplication of it, and its external use and its proper use, but concludes that it is a ceremonial law of the old covenant.

> Therefore, according to its literal, outward sense, this commandment does not concern us Christians. It is an entirely external matter, like the other ordinances of the Old Testament connected with particular customs, persons, times, and places, from all of which we are now set free though Christ. To offer ordinary people a Christian interpretation of what God requires in this commandment, we point out that we keep holy days not for the sake of intelligent and well informed Christians, for these have no need of them. We keep them, first, for the sake of bodily need. Nature teaches and demands that the common people—man-servants and maid-servants who have attended to their work and trades the whole week long—should retire for a day to rest and be refreshed. Secondly and most especially, we keep holy days so that people may have time and opportunity, which otherwise would not be available, to participate in public worship, that is, that they may assemble to hear and discuss God's Word and then praise God with song and prayer.[81]

Mirroring the views of Aquinas, Luther attaches two natural obligations by virtue of the Sabbath commandment. First of all, as manual laborers and servile employees have duties that could easily occupy their whole life, it is a matter of benevolence to afford them respite from their toils one day per week. Those who lead a cloistered life and those whose wealth frees them from such labors have little need for this kind of physical rest. According to Luther, to sanctify the Lord's Day is "nothing else than to devote it to holy words, holy works, holy life." [82] However, he blurs any previous distinction between the Lord's Day and other days by declaring, "Indeed, we Christians should make every day a holy day and give ourselves only to holy activities—that is, occupy ourselves daily with God's Word and carry it in our hearts and on our lips." [83] The holiness of the day is really about our personal holiness derived from obedience

80. Bromiley, *Zwingli and Bullinger*, 27.

81. Luther, *The Large Catechism*, 20. See also "Against the Sabbatarians," *Luther's Works*, 4:91–93.

82. Ibid.

83. Ibid., 21.

to God's word. The centrality of the word of God determined Luther's insistence to attend church to hear God's word preached, learned, memorized, and meditated upon. To Luther, this is the "strict observance of this commandment [the Sabbath]" [84] and since a day has been set aside for such purposes it behooves those who profess Christ to attend themselves to His word.

Thus, Luther vacillates between his definition of the Sabbath as a ceremonial law bearing no external application for Christians and a binding law incurring God's judgment if disobeyed. It is a commandment that must be fulfilled on the appointed day of public worship, but it is also a commandment that is fulfilled whenever God's word is heard or read and then practiced in faith. This confusion arises because Luther has not extracted himself from the presuppositional trap that the weekly similarity between the Sabbath and the Lord's Day implies moral equivalence in other respects. As careful as he is to classify the Sabbath as a ceremonial law, he continues to retreat to it as a paradigm for Christian worship.

It is perhaps worth mentioning at this time that a contemporary of Luther, Andreus Rudolf Carlstadt, is claimed by Seventh-day Adventists to have been a Sabbatarian, in their understanding of the term, because of "his observance of the seventh day".[85] Andrews devotes a chapter of his book to the controversies and kinship between these two early Reformers, all to come to this quote of Luther's criticism of Carlstadt's views of the relationship of the old covenant laws and the present-day church.

> Indeed, if Carlstadt were to write further about the Sabbath, Sunday would have to give way, and the Sabbath—that is to say, Saturday—must be kept holy; he would truly make us Jews in all things, and we should come to be circumcised: for that is true, and cannot be denied, that he who deems it necessary to keep one law of Moses, and keeps it as the law of Moses, must deem all necessary, and keep them all.[86]

Andrews would have us believe from this quote that Carlstadt worshipped on Saturday like a Seventh-day Adventist. Nothing could be further from the truth. Various histories affirm that Carlstadt was employed as a fellow professor of theology at Wittenberg University with Luther in 1519 and banished from preaching and publishing in 1524 for adopting the view that Scriptures alone were not necessary for revelation and for inciting people to destroy statues that were present in the churches. Luther wrote a pamphlet in the end of that year entitled *Against the Celestial Prophets*, a venomous rebuttal to the Zwickau prophets who believed that they could receive direct revelation from God outside Scripture. Carlstadt was included in this censure because he had adopted these views and demonstrated an inability to discern several conceptual differences between the old and new covenants (Heb 5:12–15). While he held many proper views and was an ally with Luther against Eck (a Roman Catholic theologian), he seemed easily persuaded and ruled by passion. Carlstadt agitated for

84. Ibid., 22.

85. Andrews, *History of the Sabbath*, 447.

86. Ibid., 457.

the destruction of idols on the basis of God's command to Moses (Deut 7:5), thus Luther chastised him for going back in time for ethical examples without having any new covenant principles to guide and hedge in his understanding and application.

> If Carlstadt, like Moses, was right in teaching people to break down images, and in calling in for this purpose the aid of the disorderly rabble, instead of the proper authorities, then the mob had the power and right to execute in like manner all the commands of God. And the consequence and sequel of this would be, what was soon shown by Munzer. 'It will come to this length,' says Luther, 'that they will have to put all ungodly people to death; for so Moses (Deut 7), when he told the people to break down the images, commanded them also to kill without mercy all those who had made them in the land of Canaan.' [Referring to Deut 7:5][87]

Because Carlstadt confused the theocracy of Israel with the church, he decided that *Sunday* should have a physical rest comparable to the Sabbath of Israel.

> Acting on this idea, he demanded that Sunday should be observed with rest in all the Mosaic rigour of the term; this rest he identified with that 'inaction,' which formed his idea of true union with God.[88]

So Carlstadt's lapse from *sola scriptura* and his unbridled, yet selective, mimicry of the old covenant summoned Luther's mocking reply that if one was going to invoke the Sabbath commandment, why not observe it as laid out in the OT—on Saturday where it belongs. And if the Law is still binding, then bring back circumcision as well. Luther was confident that the physical rest that defined the Sabbath was ceremonial, therefore any attempt to enforce it on the saints was a sin. This view was adopted by Heinrich Bullinger who wrote the Second Helvetic Confession in 1566. After describing the Lord's Day as a time "consecrated to religious exercises and to a holy rest," he cautions that,

> We give no place unto the Jewish observation of the day, or to any superstitions. For we do not account one day to be holier than another, nor think that mere rest is of itself acceptable to God. Besides, we do celebrate and keep the Lord's Day, and not the Jewish Sabbath, and that with a free observation.[89]

So, Carlstadt was not a seventh-day Sabbatarian but a Lord's Day Judaizer, well ahead of his time, but well off-target.

John Calvin (1509–1564)

Regarded as the greatest theologian of the Reformation, Calvin had a penchant for encouraging the faithful application of God's law for the glory of God, especially in view of the vices of men's hearts. Like many Reformers, Calvin's teachings about the Sabbath and the Lord's Day are nestled within his exegesis of the Ten Commandments.

87. Koestlin, *Life of Luther*, 311–12.

88. Ibid.

89. *Creeds of the Churches*, 179–80 (Second Helvetic Confession, Ch. 24).

Like Aquinas, Calvin believed that the Sabbath was a *ceremonial* law, but its placement within the Decalogue provided the *moral* impetus for congregational worship and personal devotion. He considered the Sabbath to be the crucial ceremonial law, that if a Jew failed to understand and observe it properly, it affected his whole attitude toward God's law.

> For whosoever has defied the Sabbath day has insofar as possible put under his feet the whole service of God. And if the Sabbath day is not observed, all the other days lose their significance.[90]

Calvin naturally reflected that this proper kind of piety be likened to the Christian's disposition toward the Lord's Day without it appearing like Judaism. He desired believers to come together faithfully and humbly on the Lord's Day to hear the sermon and to receive the sacraments, just as the Lord desired the Jews to keep the Sabbath, but without all the formalities. While Calvin's sentiment is spiritually and pastorally motivated, and while he attempts to keep the Sabbath and the Lord's Day separate, the very conjuring of the Sabbath in the context of an exposition of moral law introduces a beguiling temptation to call Christians to observe the Sabbath. In his quest to fill the pews with pious Christians and to uphold the highest standards for Christian conduct, Calvin attempts to balance the typological Sabbath, the fulfilled and ceremonial Sabbath, with an apodictic Sabbath, a resourceful and applicable Sabbath.

> But as this commandment stands in peculiar circumstances apart from the others, the mode of exposition must be somewhat different. Early Christian writers are wont to call it typical, as containing the external observance of a day which was abolished with the other types on the advent of Christ. This is indeed true; but it leaves the half of the matter untouched.[91]

This other half was better untouched. He agrees with the historic understanding of the Sabbath type and views the Sabbath command in the Decalogue as distinct from the other nine commands. He even concludes his exposition with opprobrious remarks for those who attribute sanctity to the Lord's Day as a Jew does the Sabbath and for those who allege the cycle of seven days to be the moral aspect of the Sabbath that remains, but his tinkering with Sabbath applications actually infused the Sabbath with new life. Calvin is comfortable with retaining and adopting the Sabbath for Christian purposes, even claiming that Apostle Paul did so, but his persuasion is essentially Aquinian. As such, there are inconsistencies in Calvin's treatment of the ceremonial Sabbath as a moral guide for Christians. As Richard Gaffin observed, "[Calvin] plainly has difficulty in accepting the fourth commandment, without qualification, as binding for all times and places."[92] Calvin's view of the fourth commandment is accurately summarized in three points.

90. Farley, *Calvin's Sermons*, 100.

91. Calvin, *Institutes*, 339 (2.8.28).

92. Gaffin, *Calvin and the Sabbath*, 150.

> The design of the Fourth Commandment is, that, being dead to our own affections and works, we may meditate on the kingdom of God. Now there are three things here to be considered:
>
> 1. A spiritual rest, when believers abstain from their own works, that God may work in them;
> 2. That there may be a stated day for calling on the name of God, for hearing his word, and for performing religious rites;
> 3. That servants may have some remission from labor.[93]

His first point states that the Sabbath is fulfilled in a person when they live in faith, both in their salvation and sanctification, thus every day is an experience of the fulfilled Sabbath.

> Now it is possible to ask: why were the Jews commanded to rest solely on the seventh day? For we must not interpret this to mean that only one day a week we should renounce our thoughts and affections; rather we must continue in this attitude throughout our life. In brief, it is a perpetual rest which God commands: one without any interval.[94]

Calvin is not interested in promoting an outward performance of the Jewish Sabbath, but he advances the spiritual understanding of the typical Sabbath rest. That is, we spiritually obey the Sabbath rest by daily placing "ourselves before God to the end that he alone may work in us, that he alone may guide and govern us by his Holy Spirit."[95] Therefore, God's work in us must not be restricted to one day in seven, so God must ever be working, without rest, for the spiritual profit of His beloved who are ever resting in Him. The Sabbath was fulfilled in Christ's redemption of us, and it is fulfilled daily by God's work in us and our continuing faith in Him. This is a fair understanding of the Sabbath type as alluded to in Hebrews. This constant need to live in faith requires contrition and humility.

> It serves, accordingly, as a way of humbling us, seeing that God will always find so much more to command in us with respect to his service and the fact that we are nowhere near [fulfilling] the requirements of this spiritual rest.[96]

But Calvin falters over the implications of such terms as "figure," "type," "ceremony," and "shadow" with regard to the Sabbath while he is more lucid and unambiguous elsewhere in his Institutes. A suitable definition of ceremonial law, according to Calvin, embraces specificity (to the Jews), purpose (to foreshadow Christ and His redemption), means (external, typological rituals), and temporality (until Christ comes).

> The ceremonial law of the Jews was a tutelage by which the Lord was pleased to exercise, as it were, the childhood of that people, until the fulness of the time

93. Pringle, "One Hundred Aphorisms," *Institutes of the Christian Religion*, 680.
94. Farley, *Calvin's Sermons*, 106.
95. Ibid., 101.
96. Ibid., 107 (brackets in the original).

> should come when he was fully to manifest his wisdom to the world, and exhibit the reality of those things which were then adumbrated by figures.[97]

As Calvin compares the old and new covenants, ceremonial laws were obscure and temporal whereas the new covenant manifests the realities as eternal.

> The Old Testament is literal, because promulgated without the efficacy of the Spirit: the New spiritual, because the Lord has engraven it on the heart. The second antithesis is a kind of exposition of the first. The Old is deadly, because it can do nothing but involve the whole human race in a curse; the New is the instrument of life, because those who are freed from the curse it restores to favour with God. The former is the ministry of condemnation, because it charges the whole sons of Adam with transgression; the latter the ministry of righteousness, because it unfolds the mercy of God, by which we are justified. The last antithesis must be referred to the Ceremonial Law. Being a shadow of things to come, it behoved in time to perish and vanish away; whereas the Gospel, inasmuch as it exhibits the very body, is firmly established for ever.[98]

Any other ceremonial law of the old covenant is free from the groping and dissection of its parts in search of moral legislation. It is enough for every other ceremonial law to speak of Christ and Him alone. Concerning the typic Aaronic high priest, Calvin claims Christ alone holds the office without vicar or successor, and does not resign the honor to any other. He does not imagine a moral law that establishes a supreme priestly office for the church. When Calvin ponders the figure of the temple, it is Christ who constantly appears as our advocate and intercessor in the presence of the Father. He searches no further for some moral dictum to engage priests to speak to God for us. As Calvin considers the innumerable shadow sacrifices at the altar, it is Christ, by the sacrifice of His life, who wiped away our guilt and made satisfaction for sin. He would not impoverish the glory of Christ in fulfilling these types by calling for a replication of these sacrifices at the Christian altar. With regard to the Sabbath, Calvin rightly elevates the Lord as "the truth, at whose presence all the emblems vanish; the body, at the sight of which the shadows disappear. He, I say, is the true completion of the Sabbath."[99] But Calvin is compelled to dwell not so much on what Christ has done, but on what we must do, because he adopted and retained the suppositions of Aquinas. In fairness to Calvin, he defends himself against Judaizing by distinguishing between 1) the need to stop work to attend church services and the ritualistic day-long Sabbath rest, 2) the compliance with apostolic tradition to gather on Sunday and the assignment of sanctity to the Sabbath day, and 3) the weekly sermon and a continuing symbology of the number seven. But what pains he must take to distinguish the Lord's Day from the Sabbath when he invokes the Sabbath to inculcate the church about the Lord's Day!

Calvin's second point understands the Sabbath as a time when Israel engaged in congregational worship and stands as a model for weekly church worship.

97. Calvin, *Institutes*, 663–64 (4.20.15).

98. Ibid., 393 (2.11.8).

99. Ibid., 341 (2.8.31).

> Hence also it is evident, what was the true and lawful method of keeping *the Sabbath*. When God commanded his people to abstain from working on that day, it was not that they might give themselves up to indolent repose, but, on the contrary, that they might exercise themselves in meditating on his works. Now, the minds of men are naturally blind to the consideration of his works, and must therefore be guided by the rule of Scripture. Though Paul includes the *Sabbath* in an enumeration of the shadows of the law, (Colossians 2:16) yet, in this respect, our manner of observing it is the same with that of the Jews: the people must assemble to hear the word, to public prayers, and to the other exercises of religion. It was for this purpose that the Jewish Sabbath was succeeded by the Lord's Day.[100]

Calvin admits, unfortunately, in one breath that the Sabbath is a shadow of the law and that Christians should continue to observe it. However careful Calvin is to note the similarity is only in respects of having some time to assemble for public worship and that the exacting observance of the ceremonial Sabbath is no longer binding on Christians, his ascertainment presents a contradiction. To assert that the Sabbath *was* ceremonial and *is* moral leaves us open to problems concerning the nature of its existence—it is both abrogated and legally binding.

This was further complicated by the church-state relationship that sought to mimic a theocratic Israel and by Calvin's misconception that the biblical Sabbath required all Israelites to assemble at the synagogue. Calvin's blood was deeply pastoral and pious, and he would that all pursue the glory of God as demanded by Scripture. His preaching on the Sabbath was influenced by his observations about mankind and his knowledge of the depravity of man.

> Now let us consider whether those who call themselves Christians require of themselves what they should. There is a large group which thinks that Sunday exists for the purpose of enabling them to attend to their own affairs and who reserve this day for that [purpose] as if there were no others throughout the week for deliberating their business. For though the bell tolls the sermon, they seem only to have time for their own affairs and for one thing and another. The rest glut themselves and are shut up in their houses because they do not dare display a manifest scorn on the streets; in any case, Sunday is nothing more than a retreat for them in which they stand aloof from the church of God.[101]

Calvin also noted the bleak spiritual condition of those who attended the sermon sporadically.

> It is true that they will come five or six times a year to the sermon. And to do what? To make fun of God and of all his doctrine. It is true that they are the swine who come to foul the temple of God and who deserve instead to be in stables. It would be better if they would remain in their stinking holes; in short, it would be better if such rabble and disgusting people were completely cut off from the temple of God rather than permitted to mingle with the company of

100. Calvin, *Commentaries*, 16:227 (Luke 4:16; emphasis in the original).

101. Farley, *Calvin's Sermons*, 109.

> the faithful. But still, how often they come! If the bell tolls long enough, you will see them take their seats.[102]

Based on the theocratic application of the Sabbath, Calvin expected all the citizens of the land to attend the sermon and listen with grateful ears, but based on the Christian Lord's Day he preferred that believers alone apply themselves to the call to worship. This tension is inevitable when a Jewish ceremonial law is used to compel non-Christians to attend church meetings.

Calvin's final point enjoins believers with servants to afford them a time of rest from their ordinary labors, so as not to be cruel to them. Calvin does not explain why he thinks this particular Sabbath law is not a shadow law but must be "adapted to every age."[103] However, in his sermons on the Ten Commandments, he ventures to explain how it is morally binding, not so much that servants benefit from that rest, but that the owner gains spiritual understanding and enlightenment.

> Now insofar as this is the case, that the commandment concerning the Sabbath day is contained in the first table, it follows that it belongs to the spiritual service of God and that it is pointedly not a question about the charity which we owe our neighbors.[104]

Because the Sabbath commandment was a duty toward God, according to Aquinas, Calvin did not think the respite given to servants should be understood simply as a benefit for people or for society. As he attempts to explain how kindness to those inferior to us (a duty to man) is in fact a duty to God, he continues to draw out duties to man and then retracts what he says. God gave the Israelites rest, but alas, this "was not his [God's] principle aim for there to be one day a week in which people ceased to work in order to catch their breath and be spared total exhaustion," because this is a commandment on the first table of stone, and should tell us a duty to God. As close as Calvin comes to making this a duty to God, he seems to say that when you come to worship God, by allowing your servants rest from labor, you are cultivating in yourself an attitude of single-minded devotion to the Lord, by forgoing whatever gain your servants may add to your treasures. Yet he does not require servants to be given a full day of rest as the commandment actually states, nor the rich, because they do not labor like a servant.

Calvin looks at the respite for animals differently.

> Thus when God willed for cattle and asses to be rested on the seventh day, it wasn't because he had made them participants in that spiritual rest which we discussed earlier, but it was in order that the Jews, seeing their stables closed, might understand. And what were they to understand? [That] God sets in our midst before our eyes even dumb animals as a sign and visible sacrament. And their purpose is that, for our part, we might be that much more retained for God's service, knowing that we would be violating the entire law if we did not

102. Ibid., 112.

103. Calvin, *Institutes*, 341 (2.8.32).

104. Farley, *Calvin's Sermons*, 122.

> think of that which forms the principal point of all our life, which is, that we learn to denounce ourselves and no longer follow our [own] appetites, or reason or wisdom. For our God should govern us. And we should become like dead creatures in order that he might live in us and we no longer pursue our own course which is so utterly corrupt. Accordingly, that is how God meant for the Jews to regard dumb brutes: as a visible sign which he had given them to the end that they might be that much more restrained and thereby admonished to keep the Sabbath day in complete reverence.[105]

Calvin assures us just what God meant by commanding the Jews to give the animals rest: animals are a sign to His people to practice self-denunciation and self-denial. He seems to include both the Jew and Christian as pupils of that sign, but avoids urging Christians to obey the external law of making working animals rest one day in seven. He spiritualizes, if not allegorizes, the rest for livestock in Aquinian style.

Better understood, the Lord forced the Israelites to trust Him by suspending all manner of work in and around the home, and this was indeed a difficult matter for them, as it should have been, that the more difficult it was to obey the greater the faith was required. This is why the Lord required working animals to rest, so all means to production and self-service would come to a halt, sustaining the theme of full-hearted trust in the Lord's ability to provide an everlasting rest.

The Jews were given external commands to portray spiritual realities, and now that the rest in Jesus Christ has come and the saving faith that He engenders, the specific external command to afford servants, strangers, and animals rest on the Sabbath is abrogated. Surely we must be kind with respect to them, but that kindness is not necessarily comprehended in reposing from all labor once a week. To be consistent, if we are morally required to provide an external rest to servants and strangers, then we must give it to working animals as well. Or, if we are no longer required to give animals rest, then we are no longer required to give servants rest. Calvin's struggle was that the Sabbath appears on the first table of the law; therefore, all applications must be with respect to the worship owed to God. The practical principle—that we cannot be in two places at the same time—could be used to promote worship to God, clearly a first-table item; but he found it difficult to force the square peg of relationships between Jews and their servants and cattle into the round hole of worship toward God. While this interpretive guideline was a consideration for Calvin and served to limit the extent of his application of Sabbath law, succeeding Reformers did not feel constrained to adopt it and found new avenues to Judaize the Lord's Day.

Not infrequently, Calvin reminds his hearers that the Sabbath is a shadow, yet he determines to draw out applications for the church. Because of this ambivalence, Calvin was not without detractors who objected to him using the Sabbath as a means to compel weekly worship and a weekly rest for servants. In other words, his critics believed there was no "other half" to the Sabbath commandment besides its ceremoniality, as was taught for the first millennium of church history. These men were not against weekly church attendance, nor were they defending a right to mistreat servants

105. Ibid., 120 (brackets in the original).

and animals, however, they objected to Calvin's intimation that the Sabbath was the basis for the Lord's Day, a point of departure that would inevitably lead to the transference of Sabbath law and its holiness to the practice of the church.

> They complain that Christian people are trained in Judaism, because some observance of days is retained. My reply is, That those days [the Lord's day] are observed by us without Judaism, because in this matter we differ widely from the Jews. We do not celebrate it with most minute formality, as a ceremony by which we imagine that a spiritual mystery is typified, but we adopt it as a necessary remedy for preserving order in the Church . . . They [the Jews] did not desist from manual labour on the ground of its interfering with sacred study and meditation, but as a kind of religious observance; because they dreamed that by their cessation from labour, they were cultivating the mysteries which had of old been committed to them. It was, I say, against this preposterous observance of days that the Apostle inveighs, and not against that legitimate selection [of a day for assembly] which is subservient to the peace of Christian society. For in the churches established by him, this was the use for which that Sabbath was retained.[106]

But the question remains: Why retain an abrogated Sabbath? And why make use of it if the Sabbath typified realities now present in Christ? And if Christians continue the particulars of Sabbath law in order to remind themselves of these realities, then what makes the practice of the Christian any different than the custom of the Jew? But Calvin asks,

> Religious meetings are enjoined us by the word of God; their necessity, experience itself sufficiently demonstrates. But unless these meetings are stated, and have fixed days allotted to them, how can they be held?[107]

The NT answers Calvin's question, by stating 1) the reason for gathering together (a risen Lord), 2) the agenda of the meeting (apostles' doctrine, fellowship, breaking of bread, and prayer), and 3) the day on which it should occur (weekly, on the first day of the week). Is not the teaching of the NT sufficient to enlighten Christians in their duty to assemble together, without the invocation of a nullified ceremony? Common sense teaches us that we cannot be in two places at the same time and that meetings have to be announced if attendance is desired. If, as Calvin proposed, the Sabbath was included in the Decalogue to teach us these obvious things, then he has magnified a trifle and opened the door to Judaism, rather than proclaiming the sovereignty of God through typology, the fulfillment of ceremonies through Christ's redemption, and the introduction of a new covenant through the power of the Holy Spirit. Oh, that Calvin made use of the Sabbath to better preach Christ and Him alone!

Calvin eventually asked himself why the Sabbath is included in the Decalogue and concluded that physical rest, weekly worship, and kindness to servants are not its main purpose. There must be some deeper and richer purpose for the inclusion of a ceremonial command in the Decalogue, as he admits, "There is something here of an

106. Calvin, *Institutes*, 342–43 (2.8.33, emphasis added).

107. Ibid., 342 (2.8.32).

unexpected nature."[108] Calvin concludes that the uniqueness of this commandment speaks of the superabundance to be enjoyed by the faithful as they rest from their personal inclinations and allow God alone to work in them.[109] Calvin was near to understanding this completely, but he inherited the framework of Aquinas that sought to draw out moral obligations from the fourth word rather than the mysteries of Christ and His work of redemption.

The Belgic Confession (1561)

The influence of Calvin among European communities accelerated even amidst serious persecution by Roman Catholics. In the Netherlands, Guido de Brès composed a confession of faith for Belgians that was adopted by the Synod of Dordt in 1574. This confession and the Heidelberg Catechism became the secondary standards of the Reformed Church of Holland. Protestants approached the dogma and traditions of the Roman Catholic Church with skepticism, especially its superstitions and mysticisms, but certain doctrines were adopted uncritically. For example, the Roman Catholic Church believed it possessed the right to punish heretics by taking their lives. Calvin adopted this view to the chagrin of other Reformers. With wars and persecutions abounding, the Reformers also began to question the relationship of the church to the state, and the powers rightly conferred to them.

As touching the Sabbath, the Belgic Confession makes no mention of it, not even of the Lord's Day, but does advert to the need of believers to separate from the world and join with the true church in order to maintain unity, to submit to its doctrine and discipline, and to serve one another, even if magistrates prohibit it with threats of bodily harm and death. It was not necessary, in discussing the nature and organization of the visible and invisible church, to rely upon a Jewish ceremonial law as a starting point. The Belgic Confession does contain a statement (Article 25) about the relationship of the Christian to the ceremonial laws of the past.

> We believe that the ceremonies and figures of the law ceased at the coming of Christ, and that all the shadows are accomplished; so that the use of them must be abolished among Christians: yet the truth and substance of them remain with us in Jesus Christ, in whom they have their completion. In the mean time we still use the testimonies taken out of the law and the prophets, to confirm us in the doctrine of the gospel, and to regulate our life in all honesty to the glory of God, according to his will.

Here it is noted that the truth and substance of past ceremonies and figures remain in Jesus Christ. They do not remain in us, nor do they remain as continuing figures and ceremonies for the church. What truths they portrayed are to be found in the redemption of Jesus Christ. To ensure that Christians did not discard the OT as a whole, the Belgic Confession supported its relevance and continuance in the new

108. Farley, *Calvin's Sermons*, 123.

109. Ibid., 122–23.

covenant epoch provided it confirmed the gospel of Jesus Christ and supported the pursuit of righteousness for the glory of God.

The Heidelberg Catechism (1563)

The Heidelberg Catechism was composed by Zacharias Ursinus and Caspar Olevianus by the request of Elector Frederick III, a provincial ruler in Germany, and it was subsequently adopted by a Synod in Heidelberg. Ursinus was a pupil of Melancthon, and Olevianus was a student of Calvin. It follows the format of Luther's Smaller Catechism and Calvin's Catechism, progressing through the Apostles' Creed, the Ten Commandments, and the Lord's Prayer with some modification. The framework for this structure duplicated a tradition of the Roman Catholic Church that ensured the order of worship followed the pattern of the gospel: our conviction as sinners, our redemption in Jesus Christ, and our expression of gratitude through obedience. The scope of Christian doctrine, though broad and well-formulated, is somewhat limited by the format. At the pinnacle of advancing the grace of God through the incarnation of Jesus Christ, Ursinus posits in Question 19, "How do you come to know this?"

> The holy gospel tells me. God himself began to reveal the gospel already in Paradise; later, he proclaimed it by the holy patriarchs and prophets, and portrayed it by the sacrifices and other ceremonies of the law; finally, he fulfilled it through his own dear Son.[110]

In truth, the ceremonies of the old covenant are christocentric. The course of history from the creation of Adam and Eve to the prophecies of Malachi is a record of God's sovereignty and a revelation of the mystery of the gospel intended to culminate in the advent of Jesus Christ. His incarnation, death, and resurrection are the complete fulfillment of that record, for even though the consummation of the ages has not yet come, in Christ, God calls the things that are not as though they are, because His word is sure. The catechism cites Colossians 2:17, which admits that food and drink, festivals, New Moons, and Sabbaths were but shadows, and Christ is the fulfillment and substance of them.

However, in the latter half of the Heidelberg, question 103 readdresses the Sabbath commandment under the postulate of our thankful response of obedience to God, clearly at odds with its ceremonial designation and its substance in Christ.

110. *Ecumenical Creeds and Reformed Confessions*, 18.

Q. What is God's will for you in the fourth commandment?

A. First,
that the gospel ministry and education for it be maintained,
and that, especially on the festive day of rest,
I regularly attend the assembly of God's people
to learn what God's word teaches,
to participate in the sacraments,
to pray to God publicly,
and to bring Christian offerings for the poor.
Second,
that every day of my life
I rest from my evil ways,
let the Lord work in me through his Spirit,
and so begin already in this life
the eternal Sabbath.[111]

However, the question they answer is: What is God's will for the church on the Lord's Day. None of the six obligations of weekly Christian worship are based on actual Sabbath injunctions. One would think the correct answer to the question is:

A. First, to rest at home as God rested on the seventh day
From all manner of work
Such as the gathering of sticks, the lifting of
burdens, the kindling of fires, the cooking of meals,
and the conducting of business transactions;
Which all in Israel must observe: men, women, children, servants, and beasts,
From eventide on the sixth day until eventide on the seventh day
Second, to meditate upon the works of God in creation and in redemption
For all the world belongs to God
And we especially, whom He has redeemed from Egypt.
Thus shall we remember the Sabbath day and keep it holy,
That we may please God and avoid His displeasure through divine or civil judgment.

This is to say that their notion of the fourth commandment is radically different than its biblical portrayal in the OT. Of the sixty verses cited for this answer, only two mention the Sabbath. In the second half of his answer, Ursinus repeats the correct historic understanding of the fulfilled Sabbath: Christians realize the substance of it 1) on a daily basis as they rest from their evil ways and allow the Lord to work righteousness through them, and 2) for eternity, as they have experienced the finality of their salvation that the Sabbath adumbrated. It would have been better for Ursinus to discuss the true marks of the church along with the sacraments and church discipline, rather than under the rubric of the Sabbath. Instead of proclaiming the gospel by Christ's fulfillment of the biblical Sabbath, the fourth commandment came to be extolled as the central expression of Christian gratitude, service, ministry, and worship. While

111. Ibid., 61.

previous Reformers guarded themselves from making this ultimate connection, there were a number of exegetical failures that made this inevitable.

- Failure to familiarize themselves with the teachings of the early church fathers regarding the Sabbath.
- Failure to expand the understanding of how the Lord's advent fulfilled each specific Sabbath command beyond "resting from one's sins."
- Failure to be consistent in the treatment of ceremonial laws and types.
- Failure to satisfactorily explain why the ceremonial Sabbath was placed within the body of the Ten Commandments.
- Failure to recognize the limitations of the Ten Commandments as a means to inculcate Christian ethics.
- Failure to differentiate the biblical Sabbath from the tradition of the synagogue.
- Failure to emphasize the authority of the apostles under the inspiration of the Holy Spirit to institute a new order of congregational worship.
- Failure to distinguish the Sabbath from the Lord's Day.

While all this may not be apparent from the answer to question 103, Ursinus provided a more comprehensive view of his thinking in his *Commentary on the Heidelberg Catechism*. Published posthumously in 1584, it comprises his prepared and edited lectures on the Heidelberg Catechism. His theological training is apparent in his systematic approach, the comprehensive treatment of the topic, and his attempts to properly divide the word of God. A preliminary question about the position of the Sabbath command within the body of the Ten Commandments was important to previous theologians, and on this question Ursinus reviews the various divisions and adopts the Philonic method. This fixes the Sabbath as the fourth commandment on the first table and characterizes it as pertaining to those things of the *immediate* worship of God. The *mediate* worship of God is how we relate to fellow man. Then, Ursinus happily states the obvious.

> That we may form a correct judgment, or come to a proper understanding of every commandment, it is above all things necessary that we consider the design, or end of each precept of the Decalogue; for the end of the law shows its meaning, and from the object which God intends, and wills to accomplish by each commandment, we may easily and correctly judge concerning the means which lead to the attainment of this end.[112]

Hallelujah! There is a design to the Decalogue, an end of the law, and a proclamation of the means to that end. Ursinus merely takes the face-value of each commandment and provides a structure for better understanding how each command relates to the other. Obedience is the means to righteousness. However, Paul reminds us that

112. Ursinus, *Commentary on the Heidelberg*, 503 (Q. 93, General Rules, #4).

the Jews were fervent in their affections toward God and formulated systems for expounding and applying the law to their lives, but in one thing they were ignorant: they saw the law as the means to attaining righteousness on the basis of their obedience. But isn't that what the Ten Commandments are all about: How to love God and our fellow man? Not really, for "Christ is the end of the law for righteousness to everyone who believes" (Rom 10:4). If God designed a summary of the law that establishes *His righteousness*, then where in that summary is *His Christ*, who is its end, and the means to that end, which is *His redemption*? It is in the fourth commandment.

The prelude to the Decalogue establishes the parties to the covenant, God and Israel (redeemed man), yet the Lord chose Moses to mediate the covenant with Israel who awaited Him at the base of Mount Sinai. Moses, as a type of Christ, descended the resplendent heights of Mount Sinai in the presence of God, his face shining with the glory of his former estate, to visit his people. He came to present Israel with a two-table, stony document that summarized the forthcoming law of God. Moses acted as a mediator between the Lord God and Israel. The separation of two parties begs the existence of a mediator. So, the Ten Commandments are not merely a delineation of the top ten moral dictates for mankind. Their arrangement, order, and specificity are about Christ as mediator and what is required to reconcile God and man. Though God is in three Persons, His essence is a unity; therefore, if the law merely reflected His moral essence then it should have been written on a single tablet. However, the Decalogue is divided in two, representing the existence of separation. The law separates man from God with regards to absolute righteousness. The first three commandments clearly represent God and the last six represent man. The fourth commandment symbolically stands between God and man as Mediator, just as Moses stood between God and Israel with the law.

The Mediator is on the first table because, unlike Moses, Christ truly comes from God and is fully God. Yet Christ, by becoming fully man, joins with man to make him complete. Man cannot become complete simply by keeping the law, but he must experience through faith a life-altering union with Christ. The ceremonial Sabbath is the evangelion within the Ten Commandments that addresses the redemption of man. It is Christ Himself who takes the place of the Sabbath in the Decalogue. The Lord's Day is not a continuum of the Sabbath or its replacement; it is a fresh ordinance for the church of God based upon the completion of redemption that was twice sealed by the Lord, first by His resurrection and second by the descent of the Holy Spirit.

As Ursinus expounds the Sabbath commandment, it is obvious that he is really teaching about the Lord's Day. What were regarded as two distinct days in the past by the church fathers, Ursinus has practically made synonymous. He proposes that the Sabbath was fulfilled in respect of the seventh day and now Christians have the liberty to select any day of the week on which to worship.

> But although the ceremonial Sabbath has been abolished in the New Testament, yet the moral still continues, and pertains to us as well as to others; for there is now just as much necessity for a certain time to be set apart in the Christian church for the preaching of God's word, and for the public administration of the

> sacraments, as there was formerly in the Jewish church. Yet we must not suppose that we are restricted or tied down either to Saturday, Wednesday, or any other day.[113]

But he has not explained what the seventh day typified, that it may find its fulfillment in Christ; and even though he states the seventh day is ceremonial, he still proposes that Christians could have continued to worship on the Sabbath (Saturday). Yet he acknowledges that early Christians worshipped on Sunday and theorizes that the Saturday Sabbath was moved to Sunday, not so much by divine command but by the empirical decision of the apostles to further distinguish themselves from the Jews. This undermines the authority of the apostles.

The second major break with the teachings of the church fathers is the idea that the Sabbath commandment was enjoined prior to Sinai (i.e., the exodus of Israel), that it was practiced by the patriarchs from the beginning of creation.

> The Sabbath of the seventh day was appointed of God from the very beginning of the world, to declare that men, after his example, should rest from their labors, and especially from sin. This commandment was subsequently repeated in the law as given by Moses, at which time the ceremony which had respect to the observance of the seventh day, as a day of rest was made a sacrament of sanctification . . .
>
> The reason why the ceremonial Sabbath of the seventh day is now abolished, is because it was typical, signifying the benefits of the Messiah, and admonishing the people of God of their duty.[114]

Ursinus may have adopted the theory of the Reformed Englishman John Hooper, who, in his widely published book, *Declaration of the Ten Holy Commandments* (1548), claimed that God instituted the Sabbath from creation. So not only is the Sabbath confused with the Lord's Day, it is also confused with any pre-Mosaic form of worship. So, only 300 years after Aquinas and fifty years after Luther, the admixture of the Sabbath and Lord's Day developed into a general concept that the Lord's Day is the Sabbath, fostering the idea that the Sabbath remains a viable force in Christian living. The introduction of Sabbatarianism is evident in his Commentary, for the Sabbath-Lord's Day requires 1) bodily rest for man and beasts, 2) faithful attendance at the weekly public assembly, and 3) the obligation of magistrates to enforce Sabbath-keeping on nonbelievers to prevent offending the church. But if there is anything to obey in the Sabbath commandment, it is the gospel contained therein (John 6:29; 2 Thess 1:8; 1 Pet 4:17).

The Westminster Confession of Faith (1647)

The Westminster Confession of Faith (WCF) is considered by many Reformed adherents to be the greatest single statement of Reformed Christian doctrine. Hammered out by a commission of 151 Puritans for the English Parliament only a generation after the publication of the King James Version, this document provided the creed of the

113. Ibid., 563.

114. Ibid.

national church amidst ongoing religious civil war. In this document, the Lord's Day and the Sabbath are fused together, making a whole day of physical rest and spiritual exercises obligatory upon all the subjects under the rule of England. Twelve years later, the English people tired of the strict way of life of the Puritans and persecuted them throughout England.

In spite of the thoroughness of this seventeenth-century document, important truths are omitted concerning the Sabbath and the Lord's Day. The Fortieth General Assembly of the Orthodox Presbyterian Church was faced with this discovery, which was reported to them by a committee they had appointed years earlier to study the relationship of the WCF to the fourth commandment.

> The weekly Sabbath is an eschatological sign. This truth, central to the teaching of Hebrews 3:7—4:13 as well as fundamental to the entire biblical revelation concerning the Sabbath, does not find expression in the Westminster Confession of Faith and Catechisms. The reason for this would appear to be that the Standards mention the Sabbath commandment primarily in terms of its bearing on the more specific matter of public and private worship.[115]

The Committee further reasoned that this omission has "contributed to the uncertainty over the Sabbath in our own and other Reformed churches." But this is not merely an omission; it is the consequence of accepting faulty suppositions and extrapolating them to unbiblical proportions. In this document, and in the affiliate Larger and Smaller Catechisms, there is absolutely no mention that any part of the Sabbath commandment is ceremonial. If the Sabbath is not ceremonial or typological, it is not eschatological. Chapter 19 asserts that the moral law given to Adam was the same law summarized in the Ten Commandments, implying that the Decalogue is comprised completely of moral legislation. The English Puritan, Thomas Watson (1620–1686), who expounded the Westminster Shorter Catechism in his book, *A Body of Practical Divinity*, takes that implication and claims propositional truth.

> The thing I would have you now observe is, that the commandment of keeping the Sabbath was not abrogated with the ceremonial law, but is purely moral, and the observation of it is to be continued to the end of the world. Where can it be shown that God has given us a discharge from keeping one day in seven?[116]

But where can it be shown that the Ten Commandments summarize the moral law given to Adam? Where can it be demonstrated that the Sabbath commandment is purely moral? Yet, when answering why Christians worship on Sunday, Watson states that the seventh day was a ceremonial aspect of the Sabbath.

> The old seventh-day Sabbath, which was the Jewish Sabbath, is abrogated, and in the room of it the first day of the week, which is the Christian Sabbath, succeeds. The morality or substance of the fourth commandment does not lie in

115. "Report of the Committee on Sabbath Matters," Fortieth General Assembly of the Orthodox Presbyterian Church, 1973, 104.

116. Watson, *Ten Commandments*, 94.

> keeping the seventh day precisely, but keeping one day in seven is what God has appointed.[117]

Was the fourth commandment, as God gave it to Israel, about the Christian Sabbath or the Jewish Sabbath? Was there anything else in the fourth commandment that was abrogated than merely the day of the week on which it fell? More importantly, where can it be shown that God abrogated the Jewish Sabbath and installed a Christian Sabbath in its place? And how did Christ's death provide the basis for moving the whole Sabbath backward thirty-two hours, disturbing the moral pattern of worship supposedly set from creation? So, besides omitting fundamental truths about the Sabbath, the Westminster codified interpretive errors that budded with Aquinas and blossomed with early Reformers. This explains the "uncertainty" that interferes with a proper understanding of the Sabbath, its presence in the Decalogue, and its relationship to the Lord's Day.

Chapter 21 of the WCF covers the topic, "Of Religious Worship and the Sabbath-day," of which the concluding paragraphs discuss the Lord's Day.

> As it is the law of nature, that, in general, a due proportion of time be set apart for the worship of God; so, in his Word, by a positive, moral, and perpetual commandment binding all men in all ages, he hath particularly appointed one day in seven, for a Sabbath, to be kept holy unto Him: which, from the beginning of the world to the resurrection of Christ, was the last day of the week; and, from the resurrection of Christ, was changed into the first day of the week, which, in Scripture, is called the Lord's day, and is to be continued to the end of the world, as the Christian Sabbath.
>
> This Sabbath is then kept holy unto the Lord, when men, after a due preparing of their hearts, and ordering of their common affairs beforehand, do not only observe an holy rest all the day from their own works, words and thoughts, about their worldly employments and recreation; but also are taken up the whole time in the public and private exercises of His worship, and in the duties of necessity and mercy.[118]

The chapter title itself belies the preference for calling the first day of the week the Sabbath, instead of the new covenant designation, the Lord's Day. Indeed, the neologism, "Christian Sabbath," merely whitewashes the Judaizing of the Lord's Day. Calvin was accused of Judaizing, and he was much more restrained in his search for moral granite in the Sabbath, finding only that heavenly citizens set apart some time to attend church services. The WCF decrees that the whole world set apart "the whole time in the public and private exercises of his worship." So, once the idea was accepted that the Lord fixed the Sabbath in the Ten Commandments to promote a system of worship, the *ceremonial* Sabbath transformed into the *moral* Sabbath. The exclusive emphasis on the Sabbath as moral legislature eclipsed any consideration of its fulfillment in Christ.

117. Ibid., 95.

118. *Westminster Confession of Faith*, 94–95.

If the Sabbath needs be the basis for Lord's Day worship, what prevents the literal application of other Jewish ceremonies for their supposed spiritual enrichment of the church? Huey, a Sabbatarian and Messianic Christian, reflects on the spiritual benefits of keeping the 40-day period associated with Yom Kippur (Day of Atonement) and continues,

> When coupled with the eight days of Passover and the Feast of Unleavened Bread in the Spring, the eight days of the Feast of Tabernacles in the Fall, and the eight days of *Chanukah* in the Winter, it is almost like God is setting apart four special extended times throughout the year when He wants to get the absolute attention of His people. In His omniscient way, the Lord knows that the human propensity to wander needs frequent correction and fine tuning. Perhaps the week celebration of *Shabbat* is not enough to keep people directed toward proper worship and obedience to the Creator.[119]

Huey's mention of four seasons (40+8+8+8) totals sixty-four other religious days that God-fearing people can participate in to renew their sense of spirituality and to involve themselves in the public and private forms of worship. But given our propensity to wander, why not add even more religious meetings, retreats, seminars, seasons, holy days, and anniversaries? If any part of a negative answer is that those other seasons are fulfilled and no longer are binding on Christians, or, that they are not specifically commanded in the new covenant, then the same answer applies to the Sabbath. If the hope of the Reformers was to instill religion with a call to the Sabbath, let me assert here that *Shabbat* is not enough. Whether you are a Saturday or Sunday Sabbath-keeper, it is not enough. But He who fulfilled the religious festivals and system of worship commanded under the Law *is* enough through the means He ordained under the new covenant: a daily personal worship and a weekly corporate worship on the day of His resurrection.

Not only was there a fusion of the Sabbath and Lord's Day, there was a deeply admixed church and state that tended toward the theocratic model of Israel. Beginning with the Roman Catholic Church during the Middle Ages, the papacy held such control that national kings considered their office as derived from the church. The "trump card" was the pope's power to open or close the door to heaven. While excommunication was applied to individuals—stripping them of the right to be a judge, an attorney, a guardian, or party to any contracts, or to obtain a Christian funeral—the pope also had the power to interdict whole nations, suspending all religious services until the ruler yielded to the pope's charge. This authority of the church over all the citizens of a nation accents Aquinas' teaching that the Sabbath commands man to give some time to the things of God.

Shortly after the publication of the Augsburg Confession (1530), the pope reacted to the establishment of Lutheranism by persuading Charles V, then the Spanish Emperor of most of Europe, to squelch the heretics by way of force. However, German princes formed the Schmalkaldic Treaty, a commitment to defend militarily the faith of their region. Though they broke from the Holy Roman Empire, the religion of these

119. Huey, "Reflections on Returning," 5.

Germanic peoples (Saxony) was still chosen by the regional princes. Personal conscience meant little during this time, so the church-state paradigm was adopted by the early Reformers who also used the power of the state to enforce their particular beliefs.

> In spite of Luther's stress on personal religion, Lutheran churches were "established" churches. They retained an ordained clergy who considered the whole population of a given territory members of their church. The churches looked to the state for salary and support. Official Protestantism seemed to differ little from official Catholicism.[120]

But not all Protestants believed in a church-state union. In 1525, Grebel and Manz, students of Zwingli, took the battle of the Reformation in Zurich to greater lengths. They believed the Bible taught believer's baptism and rejected the practice of forced infant baptism that made all people members of the established church. Since baptism was the means by which a newborn became a subject of the state and a member of that region's religion, they decided to re-baptize each other and prevent the baptism of their young. Manz, a founder of Anabaptism, was martyred by drowning at the hands of fellow Reformers. Even Calvin, within the city-state of Geneva, was faced with the unhappy business of executing the heretic Servetus, who was neither Catholic nor Protestant, in 1553. While great effort was made to convince Servetus of the truth of the Trinity, his obstinacy forced the Genevan Council to order his death by burning at the stake in compliance with Leviticus 24:16.

It was the responsibility of the state to promote the true religion, so heresy was not only a sin before God but a destabilizing force within society. Calvin would later write in his Institutes, "The duty of magistrates . . . extends to both tables of the Law,"[121] therefore, the Sabbath commandment was counted upon to inculcate the masses in the doctrines of the state's religion. The pews were not always well-filled, which convinced pastors of the established church that the peasants' hearts were not inclined toward spiritual matters. However, Sunday observance was the best means to indoctrinate the common man with the things of God.

> In the late 15th and early 16th centuries, large segments of the English people ignored worship services. Contemporary reports complain how those who did attend would come and go as they pleased, interrupting the service as they did so. Entertainments, such as the blood sport of bearbaiting, athletic competitions, dancing, gambling, church-ales and fairs were more widely attended than worship services. Often, those who did attend services could not wait for them to be over so they could participate in some form of secular entertainment. This is not surprising, since the English working person labored long hours for six days each week, with little chance for diversion. Sunday was their only time off.
>
> Many churchmen, not just Puritans, expressed concern for the general disregard of Sunday sanctity. Kenneth Parker has amply shown in his exhaustive work *The English Sabbath* that English Christians had long supported the custom of Sunday services by appealing to the Fourth Commandment. On this basis

120. Shelley, *Church History*, 249.
121. Calvin, *Institutes*, 657 (4.20.9).

> Parker argues that Sabbatarianism did not originate with Puritans, but had been a well-established belief in the English church.[122]

As mentioned earlier, the development of Sabbatarianism was several centuries in the making, so the WCF did not invent, but rather legislated Sabbatarianism for the state church. This is why the Westminster Larger Catechism asks (Question 118): Why is the charge of keeping the Sabbath more specially directed to governors of families, and other superiors?

> A. The charge of keeping the sabbath is more specially directed to governors of families, and other superiors, because they are bound not only to keep it themselves, but to see that it be observed by all those that are under their charge; and because they are prone ofttimes to hinder them by employments of their own. [Exod 20:10; Josh 24:15; Neh 13: 15, 17; Jer 27:20–22; Exod 23:12][123]

Just as rulers of nations were obliged to promote religion, so the lesser leaders were to promote religion at their level. All business owners and estate managers were required to ensure that those laboring for them were to desist from work in order to attend church. This is consistent with the WCF statement about Christian Liberty in chapter 20, paragraph 4, and the Civil Magistrate in chapter 23, paragraph 3.

> 20:4. And because the powers which God hath ordained, and the liberty which Christ hath purchased, are not intended by God to destroy, but mutually to uphold and preserve one another; they who, upon pretense of Christian liberty, shall oppose any lawful power, or the lawful exercise of it, whether it be civil or ecclesiastical, resist the ordinance of God. And for their publishing of such opinions, or maintaining of such practices, as are contrary to the light of nature, or to the known principles of Christianity, whether concerning faith, worship, or conversation; or to the power of godliness; or such erroneous opinions or practices as, either in their own nature, or in the manner of publishing or maintaining them, are destructive to the external peace and order which Christ hath established in the Church: they may be lawfully called to account, and proceeded against by the censures of the Church, *and by the power of the civil magistrate.*[124]

> 23:3. The civil magistrate may not assume to himself the administration of the Word and sacraments, or the power of the keys of the kingdom of heaven: yet he hath authority, and it is his duty, to take order, that unity and peace be preserved in the Church, that the truth of God be kept pure and entire, that all blasphemies and heresies be suppressed, all corruptions and abuses of worship and discipline prevented or reformed, and all the ordinances of God duly settled, administered, and observed. For the better effecting whereof, he hath power to call synods, to be present at them, and to provide that whatsoever is transacted in them be according to the mind of God.[125]

122. Orr, "From Sunday to Sabbath," n.p.
123. *Westminster Confession of Faith*, 206.
124. Ibid., 87–88 (emphasis added).
125. Ibid., 100–101.

Under the freedom of Christ's rule on earth, national leaders to workforce superiors had a duty to enforce the principles of Christianity for the benefit of religion and society, involving, if necessary, the arm of civil justice. Coerced Sabbath-keeping eventually led to the same Judaizing focus on outward behavior rather than inner spiritual realities. While the Confession was adopted wholeheartedly by Scotland, the English Parliament accepted it with some revision, such as the deletion of chapter 20, paragraph 4. By 1658, Congregationalists adapted the WCF to their liking by replacing chapter 23, paragraph 3 with the following text.

> Although the magistrate is bound to encourage, promote, and protect the professors and profession of the gospel, and to manage and order civil administrations in a due subserviency to the interests of Christ in the world, and to that end to take care that men of corrupt minds and conversations do not licentiously publish and divulge blasphemy and errors, in their own nature subverting the faith and inevitably destroying the souls of them that receive them; yet in such differences about the doctrines of the gospel, or ways of the worship of God, as may befall men exercising a good conscience, manifesting it in their conversation, and holding the foundation, not disturbing others in their ways or worship that differ from them, there is no warrant for the magistrate under the gospel to abridge them of their liberty.[126]

When the WCF migrated to the Americas with the founding of the American Presbyterian Church, it underwent revision in 1788, again rewriting chapter 23, paragraph 3.

> Civil magistrates may not assume to themselves the administration of the Word and Sacraments; or the power of the keys of the kingdom of heaven; or, in the least, interfere in matters of faith. Yet, as nursing fathers, it is the duty of civil magistrates to protect the church of our common Lord, without giving the preference to any denomination of Christians above the rest, in such a manner that all ecclesiastical persons whatever shall enjoy the full, free, and unquestioned liberty of discharging every part of their sacred functions, without violence or danger. And, as Jesus Christ hath appointed a regular government and discipline in his church, no law of any commonwealth should interfere with, let, or hinder, the due exercise thereof, among the voluntary members of any denomination of Christians, according to their own profession and belief. It is the duty of civil magistrates to protect the person and good name of all their people, in such an effectual manner as that no person be suffered, either upon pretense of religion or of infidelity, to offer any indignity, violence, abuse, or injury to any other person whatsoever: and to take order, that all religious and ecclesiastical assemblies be held without molestation or disturbance.[127]

The revision also changed the Larger Catechism, answer 109, by removing as a sin against the second commandment, the *toleration* of false religion, so as not to involve the civil government in every matter that distinguished a church from the state church. Since those times, the idyllic concept of a separation of church and state, as envisioned

126. Schaff, *Creeds of Christendom*, 3:720 (Savoy Declaration, Ch. 24).

127. Ibid., 720–21.

by early Anabaptists, has become the accepted norm in Protestant churches; however, the related catechism question 118 has not been amended by several Reformed denominations to reflect that change (that superiors enforce Sabbath attendance).

William Barker noted the fact that American Presbyterians modified the WCF because of the realization that the involvement of the civil magistrate in religion could bring more harm than good.

> The area of church and state relations is the outstanding example of this principle [that synods and councils of the church may err] as American Presbyterianism has found it necessary—primarily because of new historical circumstances—to amend the Westminster Confession in three places that referred to the civil magistrate.[128]

The unfortunate admission here is not that the WCF was altered to more accurately reflect the teachings of Scripture, but that the Confession was only true under a specific set of circumstances, i.e., when the state could be counted upon to enforce Christian beliefs and behaviors on all its citizens.

Not only were civil law and the magistrate called upon to encourage Sabbath-keeping (though not enforced), Reformers also invoked the wrath of God. "The law of the land lets sabbath-breakers alone, but God will not," threatened Thomas Watson.[129] He taught that a Christian sanctifies the Sabbath by preparing himself the night before, arising early and calling the Sabbath a delight, and spending the whole day in meditation, prayer, singing psalms, and hearing the word. Sins to be avoided are any manner of secular work, selling meat, working in your business behind closed doors, visits, or "dressing great feasts," long walks in the field or lengthy journeys, engaging in sports or pastimes or dancing, sitting idly at home, discussing worldly affairs, and other "carnal pleasures." He also considered as corrupt the habits of Jews to wear their best apparel and to enjoy the most appetizing meal of the week on their Sabbath. All but the most ardent Sabbatarians might consider this burgeoning list somewhat legalistic, but it is based squarely on the Aquinian teaching that the fourth commandment has a cardinal morality attached to it. As long as the Sabbath is afforded a dram's weight of moral gold, these conclusions are inescapable. Failure to keep the Sabbath strictly, Watson warns, makes you vulnerable to "sudden visible judgments," such as fire from heaven for carrying a burden, dropping dead when dancing, bearing deformed children for hunting, and ultimately, damnation for your ensuing life of sin.

While the Reformed churches made strides in redefining the relationship of church and state, their Sabbatarianism continued unabated, challenged only occasionally by the lack of interest in spiritual worship and the eventual development of seventh-day Sabbatarianism through the Baptists. The Baptists trace their origins to the Puritans of England as a group of Christians that questioned the biblicity of infant baptism and the overbearing relationship of the church and state. Both the General Baptists and the Particular Baptists had their beginnings in England in the early 1600s,

128. Barker, "Lord of Lords," 413.

129. Watson, *Ten Commandments*, 120; elsewhere 93–122.

through the leadership of John Smyth and Henry Jacob respectively. The Particular Baptists, thus called because of their acceptance of the Calvinistic doctrine of salvation, published the London Confession of Faith in 1644. Church ministers were paid by the congregation and not by civil government. Later, in 1677, the Particular Baptists rewrote entirely their confession following the format of the Westminster Confession, solidifying their spiritual camaraderie with the Calvinistic branch of the Reformation. This is known as the Second London Confession in England and was adopted in the Americas in 1742 as the Philadelphia Confession. Like the Church of England, it deleted chapter 20, paragraph 4, and chapter 23, paragraphs 3 and 4, about the relationship of the civil magistrate to individual conscience and the church. Its statement on public worship (chapter 22) repeats with few changes the entire WCF chapter 21 "Of Religious Worship, and the Sabbath Day."

CIVIL SABBATARIANISM

One of the Scottish commissioners at the Westminster Assembly was Samuel Rutherford (1600–1661), the author of *Lex Rex: the Law and the Prince*, which advanced political theories based on biblical teachings. He posited that rulers did not necessarily have a divine right of rule, but there must be a constitution that rules both the ruler and the people, which is based on the biblical view of a covenant (which was eventually secularized as a "social contract"). Furthermore, grounded on the universal sinfulness of man, there must be equality under law for all citizens and the power of the state must be separated into different spheres to prevent absolute power of the majority as well as the monarch. Furthermore, the people possessed a natural right to rebel against the tyrannical expression of government. These theories were adopted by John Witherspoon, the only minister to sign the Declaration of Independence, and John Locke, whose writings also influenced the formulation of the American Constitution.

The religious base for American government in Reformed Christianity is undeniable. At the heart of constitutional rule are those laws of nature that are self-evident among all men, placed in men's hearts by an omniscient God. With the concurrent teaching that Lord's Day worship was a creation ordinance and an expression of the law of nature, it was only reasonable to enact laws that endorsed this apparently self-evident concept that time needed to be set aside for the worship of God. It was also the experience of European immigrants to the American continent that Sunday was generally free since the days of Emperor Constantine. So, it was only natural that laws were written ensuring a day of civil rest on Sunday.

The laws applying to businesses and recreation on Sunday came to be called "blue laws."[130] According to Snopes, the origin of the term refers to "Reverend Samuel Peters' 1781 book, General History of Connecticut, [which] described onerous colonial laws in the following manner: Blue Laws; i.e., bloody Laws; for they were all sanctified with whipping, cutting off the ears, burning the tongue, and death."[131] As can be expected,

130. Laband and Heinbuch, *Blue Laws*, 8.

131. Mikkelson, "Blue Laws," n.p.

concepts of independence, the effect of the Enlightenment, the rise of industrialism, the acceptance of evolution, and the introduction of competing worldviews would gnaw at the Christian consensus in England, Canada, and the United States, and make civil Sabbatarianism one of many battlegrounds. Nietzche cynically remarked, "It was a master stroke of English instinct to hallow and begloom Sunday to such an extent that the Englishman unconsciously hankers for his week- and work-day again."[132]

This resistance to civil Sabbatarianism was countered with even more strident preaching on the topic and the formation of lobbying groups to ensure that all citizens benefited from the Christian understanding of weekly rest and recuperation. That is, all men have a natural entitlement to liberty, but that liberty must be in the pursuit of moral obligations, such as the Puritanical concept of a Sabbath rest. As such, certain states and localities enacted laws to ensure compliance with their form of Sabbath-keeping. For example, in Missouri, "Every person who shall be convicted of horse racing, cock fighting, or playing at cards or games of any kind, on the first day of the week, commonly called Sunday, shall be deemed guilty of a misdemeanor, and fined not exceeding fifty dollars."[133] The Lord's Day Observance Society was established in England in 1831 to lobby for legislation that prevented businesses from operating on Sunday. Saratoga, New York, was the site for the "National Sabbath Convention" in 1863. Philip Schaff, author of *Creeds of Christendom*, was secretary of the New York Sabbath Committee beginning in 1864, whose stated goal was not to protect the religious observation of the Sabbath, but to protect the civil institution of a day of rest.

Forced compliance made many enemies of the Christian religion, and some of the stoutest and most strident came from within the church, for as John B. Dykes said, "No foreign foe provokes alarm, but enemies within."[134] For example, Robert Ingersol (1833–1899), son of an abolitionist preacher, sought to rid the United States of the Bible and the Sabbath. Among the agenda of the Liberal League (1878), which Ingersoll founded, were such goals as,

- That the exemption from taxation of all church property be halted
- That education be secularized, federalized, and compulsory
- That religious oaths in official settings be prohibited
- That all Sabbath laws be repealed
- That no state or federal law endorse any religious view
- That the government not apportion funds for religious use, including the chaplaincy
- That atheism be afforded freedom of speech and press

Southern Presbyterian minister Robert Lewis Dabney (1820–1898) countered with the publication of *The Sabbath and the State* (1880). Dabney realized, as a

132. Nietzsche, *Beyond Good and Evil*, 99.

133. Blakely, *American State Papers*, 298.

134. Dykes, "Jehovah, to My Prayer Give Ear," (1868) *Psalter Hymnal*, 115.

Protestant, that he would not want to be compelled to quit business on a Catholic holy day simply because he lived in a land with a majority of Catholics who demanded that non-Catholics give some measure of respect for their religion. So Dabney approached the matter not by claiming the right of majority or the tradition of ages, but by appealing to the nature of man, government, and theism. He argued that, "The right of the State to exist must imply its right to preserve the essential conditions of its own existence."[135] So Dabney focused his arguments on the nature of man to set aside time for worship regardless of their creed, and that theism is essential to the maintenance of civil government, so that Sunday laws are not necessarily an expression of Christianity but empirically good for the well-being of man and society. Neither of these arguments would persuade an atheist today, for he would no sooner argue that our weekly day of rest be moved to Wednesday, or, to make things interesting, favor the Christians one year and the seventh-day worshipers another year, or to opt for a rest cycle every sixth day or tenth day. The truth of the matter is this: the day of the week and the frequency of our gathering to worship *are* religiously significant for Christians. But to the profane person, Sunday is just a free day to pursue his or her own dreams, obligations, and enjoyments without religious oriented restrictions.

Many years would pass before blue laws were overturned. In the United States, the Supreme Court, in *McGowan v. Maryland*, 366 U.S. 420 (1961), acknowledged the religious orientation of blue laws but believed there was a secular purpose promoted, thus upholding Maryland's law that prohibited commercial sales, excepting items such as drugs, tobacco, newspapers, and some foodstuffs. Since then, many states that had Sunday Closing Laws repealed them. In Canada, the first Supreme Court battle occurred with *Robertson and Rosetanni v. The Queen* (1962), which upheld the Lord's Day Act, preventing the operation of certain businesses, in this case, a bowling alley. Then in 1985 another challenge, *R. v. Big M Drug Mart Ltd.*, [1985] (1 S.C.R. 295), was brought against the Lord's Day Act, putting the century-old law to rest, ruling that no legitimate secular purpose was served by a religious-based closing law.

Sabbatarians tried in vain to turn the tide of secularism. The Massachusetts Council of Churches remains opposed to the repeal of Sunday laws and claims that it is not attempting to force Christian behaviors on everyone else, only that it desires to preserve the benefits of a uniform time for rest and renewal. But how can the state realize these benefits without forcing all citizens to remain at home to physically rest and renew themselves on Sunday? Enforcing civil Sabbatarianism will not effect the salvation of pagans or prevent the decline in church attendance, as documented by Craig Harline.[136] In a country that is multicultural and espouses the freedom of religion, Christian practices relative to their religious worship cannot be forced on pagans; that is, we cannot compel them to put aside their agendas while we attend church. This is *not* what the Lord's Day requires.

135. Dabney, "Sabbath of the State," 2:606.

136. Harline, *Sunday*, 285.

Our Christian elders bemoan the days of old when all of society seemed to stop for the Christian Sabbath, but really, what good came of it? Are the Western States more spiritual for having forced the pagans to sit around home while Christians went to church? Has our country been drawn closer to our Maker because of the "natural" need for a weekly rest? Indeed not! The leisure time has made them feel self-sufficient and has given them an acnestis of self-gratification that cannot be relieved. In America most people have two days off, and unless they are already committed church-goers, the thought never crosses their mind to give some time to God. Rushdoony considered the nineteenth-century efforts in Scotland to give better working hours to railroad workers who worked ten hours a day, seven days a week, every day of the year. Claiming that the working conditions then were criminal and anti-biblical, he countered himself by admitting,

> And yet, clearly, the shorter working hours, the paid vacations, five eight-hour-day working weeks have failed to give men true rest. The increase of heart-attacks, ulcers, and other stress-induced ailments and diseases makes clear that the change in working conditions has not been any help to man.[137]

Jews who keep the Sabbath and Christians who keep the Lord's Day, both of whom also benefit from a five-day workweek, still have heart attacks and ulcers. Neither the Sabbath nor the Lord's Day is meant to make our lives stress-free and decades longer, serving as if it were "the calendrical equivalent to the health spa."[138]

The early church grew the first few centuries under multiple godless governments without the blessings of blue laws, but things changed under the providence of God. Emperor Constantine, because he was a monarch, had the authority to unilaterally declare a weekly day of rest on Sunday regardless of the sensitivities of the Jews. The Scottish Parliament, under the control of Covenanters, had the unmitigated authority to declare a weekly Sabbath rest for all inhabitants regardless of their creed, and gave ministers the duty to turn in those who did not attend church to face pecuniary penalties.[139] And Sunday Closing Laws existed while there was a Protestant consensus in the United States.

As regrettable as it is, times have changed. But the repeal of civil Sabbatarianism has not hurt the church of Jesus Christ. Christians should be content and praise God that pagans enjoy some time off from work and are happily obliged to take it on Sunday because it affords us the freedom to gather unimpeded for worship. However, this state of freedom may not last for long since there is an ongoing war against Christ. So, in this political environment it behooves Christians to employ their right of citizenship to freely practice their religion without impediment from the state and to pray that God would continue to afford us this freedom to worship (1 Tim 2:1–3).

Not all the fears of proponents of Sunday Closing Laws were realized; however, because of a lack of understanding of the importance of worship on the first day of the

137. Rushdoony, *Institutes of Biblical Law*, 157.

138. MacDonald, "Response," 58.

139. Gilfillan, *Sabbath in Light of Reason*, 438.

week, some Christians hold a diminished view of Sunday worship, and take jobs that require work on Sunday. Rather than pursuing their right to worship on Sunday—a right that previous Christians worked for—these Christians unwisely give up Sunday worship. Instead, if their employer is unaccommodating with regard to their religious conviction, they should consider using the legal system to ensure that they are not discriminated against in the workplace for their religious convictions. Of course, there are some occupations that require seasonal or occasional work on Sunday, so churches that provide multiple services on Sunday are better suited to uphold the significance of first-day worship and to exercise pastoral care for the flock. Churches that hold Saturday night services to accommodate the consumerist and recreational inclinations of their members are also diminishing the importance of first-day worship that the Lord ordained for His church. In the end, surrendering first-day worship in order to work divides and weakens the church.

SEVENTH-DAY SECTS

Seventh-day Baptists

Under the leadership of Dr. Peter Chamberlen (1601–1683), a physician and Puritan, the first Seventh-day Baptist Church was formed in London in 1653. Due to intense persecution under Charles II, many non-conformists were imprisoned and forced to recant while others fled to the Colonies to enjoy more religious freedom. The first Seventh-day Baptist Church was established in Rhode Island in 1671. It was not until 1687 that King James II enacted the Declaration of Indulgence that afforded freedom of conscience respecting the right of individuals to attend the church of their choice, or no church at all, without fear of penalty or reprisal.

Because Puritans de-emphasized the ceremonial nature of the fourth commandment, Seventh-day Baptists hold that the seventh-day Sabbath was not abolished by the death of Christ and that it is the only biblical day for Christian worship. Because Reformed churches accepted the idea that the Sabbath was moved to Sunday, this historical error was rightly denied by Seventh-day Baptists, which only strengthened their position. However, Seventh-day Baptists wrongly assume 1) that the apostles did not have the authority to establish weekly worship on Sunday in recognition of the resurrection of Jesus Christ and 2) that Sunday worship was not practiced by the early church until legislated by Emperor Constantine. These general views were adopted by the Seventh-day Adventists and eventually by Anglo-Israel churches.

British Israelism

It is perhaps misleading to use the title "British Israelism," but it conveys the origin of this movement early in the nineteenth century rather than its manifestation in the Anglo-Israelism of the World Wide Church of God, the Christian Identity Movement, and the Church of God Outreach Ministries. It is generally agreed that the father of British Israelism was John Wilson (c. 1800–1871), who suggested in 1840 that the peoples of the United Kingdom and surrounding vicinities were biologic descendants of the ten lost tribes of Israel and therefore blessed with "Scepter power," alluding to the blessing of Judah (Gen. 49:10). This teaching was embraced by William Miller (1782–1849), who in turn influenced Ellen White (1827–1915) of Seventh-day Adventism, Herbert Armstrong (1892–1986) of the World Wide Church of God, Howard Rand (1889–1991) of the Christian Identity Movement, and Joseph Jeffers (1898–1988) of the Kingdom of Yahweh. With supposed roots in Israel, these groups made a general adaptation of seventh-day Sabbatarianism to their way of life. Yet, not all advocates of Anglo-Israelism are seventh-day Sabbatarians. For example, Curtis Clair Ewing, cited in chapter 5, is a Sunday-Sabbatarian who identified himself as an Anglo-Israel believer.[140] His theory is reiterated somewhat by Charles Weisman, who proposes that the Saturday Sabbath is a false Sabbath because it was previously adulterated during the Babylonian captivity, and that the original Sabbath was on the first day of the week, which God reestablished as the Lord's Day through the white Christian peoples of northern Europe.[141]

Seventh-day Adventism

According to the Seventh-day Adventists, pockets of Christians have observed the seventh-day Sabbath since the first century. But as Ralph Orr concluded, "It is reasonable to believe that English seventh-day Sabbatarianism arose from Puritan Sunday Sabbatarianism—the one naturally and historically following the other."[142] The proper understanding and observance of the seventh-day Sabbath is a hallmark doctrine of this denomination, and, as their name denotes, they believe that the Christian Sabbath is rightly observed on the seventh day of the week (Saturday). They claim this teaching marks them as God's true church.[143]

This Bible-based cult[144] traces its 1863 foundation to the voluminous writings and visions of Ellen G. White (1827–1915), the continuation of the Adventist movement of the first half of the nineteenth century, and the Sabbatarian teachings of the Seventh-day Baptists. At the age of twelve, White, then Ellen Harmon, was baptized in the Methodist Church, and two years later her family began attending Adventist groups following the apocalyptic teachings of William Miller (1782–1849), who expected the physical return of Jesus Christ on October 22, 1844.

The Adventist movement suffered the Great Disappointment when Jesus did not arrive for His church as predicted, but Harmon garnered much support, along with other Adventist theoreticians, by recasting the Second Advent as a mystical occurrence when Jesus moved within the sanctuary of heaven into the holy of holies to commence the investigative judgment. Harmon eventually married a young Adventist preacher,

140. Ewing, "Excellent," n.p.

141. Weisman, "Sabbath and the Lord's Day."

142. Orr, "From Sunday to Sabbath," n.p.

143. Pinkosi, *Truth about the Sabbath*, 53.

144. Seventh-day Adventism is variously described as a partner of the gospel or as an apostate cult. Please see the defining and frank editorial from SDA Pastor Larry Kirkpatrick: http://www.greatcontroversy.org/editorial/ed37-sdamainstream-not.html.

James White, in 1846, and together they adopted the seventh-day Sabbath views of Joseph Bates (1792–1872), a minister who also questioned the doctrine of the Trinity.

> An interest in the seventh-day Sabbath among Adventists had originated before the October disappointment. J. A. Begg, a student of prophecy in Scotland, had first called their attention to it. But the real push for the Sabbath came from the Seventh Day Baptists. The first known attempt by that group to influence the Millerites took place in early 1842, but the Signs of the Times refused to publish the material. [145]

As the disheartened Adventists pondered over the following years their theology and presuppositions, and their identity and future, a particular group organized in 1863 in Michigan as the Seventh-day Adventist (SDA) Church. In 1898, Ellen G. White authored *The Desire of Ages*, a loose retelling of and commentary on the life of Christ. A chapter from this book, entitled "The Sabbath," for the most part mimics the Reformed teaching that permeated America at that time—that the Sabbath is a memorial of the creation of God, that it was practiced by the patriarchs well before the Israelites, that the Sabbath is a moral commandment for all mankind, that Jesus kept the Sabbath as an example for us to follow, and that the Sabbath and the Lord's Day are synonymous. Displaying the same confusion about the ceremonial essence of the Sabbath, her summary is characteristic of the Sabbatarianism of her times.[146]

Seventh-day Adventism teaches that Satan was so bent on destroying the church of Jesus Christ that he deceived the early church leaders to move the day of worship from Saturday to Sunday, which resulted in the Dark Ages. In particular, they teach that this apostasy, distinguished by the changing of times and seasons, was foretold by Daniel (the "little horn" of Daniel 7:8) and fulfilled by the Roman Catholic Church. As mentioned earlier, the Roman Catholic Church presumed to possess the authority to change the Decalogue for cultural and empirical reasons. Therefore, according to Adventists, Sunday worshippers are sinners of ignorance at best and apostates at worst. Only those who worship on the seventh day, as did the Savior when He was on earth, are considered members of the remnant church.

In addition, the SDA also defend their teaching and practice by claiming that seventh-day worship has been practiced by NT believers throughout church history and that they are merely reclaiming what has been lost through the entrenchment of Sunday worship by the apostate Roman Catholic and Protestant churches. SDA literature offers quotations from historians and church fathers supposedly demonstrating seventh-day Sabbatarianism of the early Christian church. The context is usually omitted, which allows the author to use a quote to defend his thesis when in fact the quote has no weight at all. For example, in Finley's book, *The Almost Forgotten Day*, starting with his section of quotes for the first-century church, he lists three references to prove his thesis that existing historical documents reveal a deep interest in Sabbath worship.

145. Knight, *Search for Identity*, 66.

146. White, *Desire of Ages*, 120–23.

> *Josephus*. "There is not any city of the Grecians, nor any of the barbarians, nor any nation whatsoever, whither our custom of resting on the seventh day hath not come!" (M'Clatchie, *Notes and Queries on China and Japan*, edited by Dennys, Vol. 4, Nos. 7, 8, p. 100.)
>
> *First Century Christians*. "Then the spiritual seed of Abraham fled to Pella, on the other side of Jordan, where they found a safe place of refuge, and could serve their Master and keep his Sabbath." (Eusebius's *Ecclesiastical History*, b,3, chapter 5.
>
> *Philo*. Declares the seventh day to be a festival, not of this or of that city, but of the universe. (M'Clatchie, *Notes and Queries*, Vol. 4, 99.)[147]

First of all, since Josephus and Philo were Jewish, it is reasonable to expect that they speak highly of the Jewish Sabbath. Concerning the quotation from Josephus, I used this quote earlier to demonstrate that the Sabbath is uniquely a Jewish phenomenon, and, if it is to be seen in any culture, it is because of Jewish influence. The context of this ethnocentric quote, in a work defending the Jews against the lies and misrepresentations of detractors, can be found in the closing remarks of Josephus to Epaphroditus lauding the law of God given to the Jews.

> We have already demonstrated that our laws have been such as have always inspired admiration and imitation into all other men; nay, the earliest Grecian philosophers, though in appearance they observed the laws of their own countries, yet did they, in their actions and their philosophic doctrines, follow our legislator, and instructed men to live sparingly, and to have friendly communication one with another. Nay, farther, the multitude of mankind itself have had a great inclination of a long time to follow our religious observances; for there is not any city of the Grecians, nor any of the barbarians, nor any nation whatsoever, whither our custom of resting on the seventh day hath not come, and by which our fasts and lighting up lamps, and many of our prohibitions as to our food, are not observed; they also endeavor to imitate our mutual concord with one another, and the charitable distribution of our goods, and our diligence in our trades, and our fortitude in undergoing the distresses we are in, on account of our laws; and, what is here matter of the greatest admiration, our law hath no bait of pleasure to allure men to it, but it prevails by its own force; and as God himself pervades all the worlds, so hath our law passed through all the world also. So that if anyone will but reflect on his own country, and his own family, he will have reason to give credit to what I say.[148]

His argument is this: Jewish laws are superior because the pagans will give up their endemic laws in favor of those of Jewish sojourners. As for the Sabbath, Josephus calls it "our custom," that is, it is peculiar to the Jews and does not enjoy cosmopolitan observance, but when pagans are introduced to it, they are inclined to mimic it. Josephus adds that the Jewish fasts, food prohibitions, and lamp lightings were also adopted by pagan nations into which they had been scattered, besides the general virtues encouraged by the law of God.

147. Finley, *Almost Forgotten Day*, 60–61.

148. Josephus, *Ag. Ap.* 2:40, 811.

Next, Finley's quote of Eusebius seems to allude to a group, the "spiritual seed of Abraham," who observed the Sabbath during persecution. Finley cites book 3, chapter 5, which follows:

> But the people of the church in Jerusalem had been commanded by a revelation, vouchsafed to approved men there before the war, to leave the city and to dwell in a certain town of Perea called Pella. And when those that believed in Christ had come thither from Jerusalem, then, as if the royal city of the Jews and the whole land of Judea were entirely destitute of holy men, the judgment of God at length overtook those who had committed such outrages against Christ and his apostles, and totally destroyed that generation of impious men.[149]

It will at once be obvious that the quotations are not identical, but contain sufficient similarities to confirm the reference, to whit: Christians sought safety in Pella from the persecution of the Jews and the judgment of God against Jerusalem. It is ironic that Finley quotes Eusebius, a fourth-century Christian historian who worshipped on Sunday, the Lord's Day. True Christians observed the Lord's Day "as a memorial of the resurrection of the Savior" and shunned the Jewish Sabbath as well as other ceremonial laws of the quondam covenant. True Christians assented to the doctrine of the virgin birth of Christ and His deity, while heretics denied both.[150]

Lastly, Finley attributes to Philo, an Alexandrian Jew whose lifetime overlapped the birth and death of Jesus Christ, some historical proof that Christians observed the Sabbath.

> But after the whole world had been completed according to the perfect nature of the number six, the Father hallowed the day following, the seventh, praising it, and calling it holy. For that day is the festival, not of one city or one country, but of all the earth; a day which alone it is right to call the day of festival for all people, and the birthday of the world.[151]

A review of Philo's works shows his concentration on the Jewish religion streaked with Platonic and allegorical thought, but nothing of early Christianity. It is reasonable, then, to expect Philo to write exaltingly about the Sabbath from a Jewish perspective as a memorial of the creation for mankind and also from a Greek perspective as the divine source of the repetitious number seven in nature. The pagans give homage to the Sabbath indirectly by their fixation on the number seven. Philo also exalts two seasonal Jewish feasts, the Feast of First Fruits and the Feast of Trumpets, which men are expressly commanded by law to celebrate because of their association with the number seven.

The uncritical use of historical evidence by SDA apologists is poor scholarship at best and deceptive at worst. Seventh-day Sabbatarianism is more than the sincere effort to precisely obey the Ten Commandments or to have the freedom to choose their own day of worship. Their legalistic preoccupation with a Saturday Sabbath has caused

149. Eusebius, *Hist. eccl.*, 3:5 (*NPNF2* 1: 215–16).

150. Ibid., 3:27 (*NPNF2* 1:239) and 4:18–20, (*NPNF2* 1:784–85).

151. Philo, *On the Creation*, 13.

them to separate from Christ's church on the very ground of the church's existence—the resurrection of Jesus Christ on Sunday.

Worldwide Church of God

This cultic sect was founded by Herbert W. Armstrong in 1932 during the heyday of radio broadcasting, when, allegedly, the gospel of Jesus Christ could be preached throughout the world according to Jesus' prophecy found in Matthew 24. Notable diversions from historic Christianity include the rejection of the Trinity and everlasting punishment, the belief in the attainment of godhood by good works, and Sabbatarianism. Borrowing further from the Jewish culture, Armstrong relied on the Jewish nineteen-year cycle in making predictions about the return of Christ.

The controversy about seventh-day worship was instrumental in the origins of this cult. Early in his marriage, Armstrong had disputes with his wife about what day should properly be set aside to worship God. Familiar with religion, but not previously faithful in church attendance, Armstrong began studying the Scriptures on his own and came to agree with his wife and the Seventh-day Adventists about the true Sabbath. Borrowing from Seventh-day Adventism, this cult taught that Sunday worship is the mark of the beast. Miraculously, the Worldwide Church of God recently endeavored to align itself with the Bible alone, as documented by Feazell.[152] Dale Ratzlaff's book, previously entitled *Sabbath in Crisis*, was a significant factor in this group's rejection of its seventh-day Sabbatarianism.[153]

Messianic Congregations

Emboldened by the lack of consensus within the Christian community of faith, converted Jews have felt out of place in a church dominated by Gentiles, often turning to their cultural heritage for a sense of belonging. They are joined by Westerners who desire traditionalism, asceticism, and novelty in their religion. Historically, the Jews distinguished themselves from pagan cultures by keeping the Sabbath, but Messianic congregations are returning to *Shabbat* from Friday evening to Saturday evening to become a beacon to the world. The movement is young and understandably diverse in its understanding and application of traditions bearing on the Sabbath, so I have relied on a single publication of Outreach Israel Ministries, based in Florida.

McKee attempts to motivate members of the Messianic movement by emphasizing that Sabbath-keeping within their congregations is a means to provoke unbelieving Jews (and Gentiles) to jealousy. Apostle Paul discussed this concept in his letter to the Romans, but it is the Lord who provokes Jews to jealousy through the widespread salvation of Gentiles (Rom 11:11; Amos 9:11–12), not the compulsion of Gentiles to live as Jews (Gal 2:14; Acts 15). Messianic Jews promote observation of the feasts of Leviticus 23 and a kosher diet, and ignore Paul's teaching that these things are shadows of Christ's ministry of salvation (Col 2:16). They interpret James' statement, "For

152. Feazell, *Liberation of the Worldwide Church of God.*

153. Bacchiocchi, *Sabbath Under Crossfire*, 12.

Moses has had throughout many generations those who preach him in every city, being read in the synagogues every Sabbath" (Acts 15:21), as a command for Gentiles to observe the Sabbath instead of a statement of fact about the unbelieving Jewish observation of the Sabbath. Indeed, Gentiles did not observe the Sabbath but were coming to faith in Christ without it.

Unfortunately, the Messianic movement blurs the line between moral law, ceremonial law, and Jewish tradition, resulting in a lack of consensus within its ranks. McKee teaches that "there is no such distinction [between ceremonial and moral laws] in the Scripture itself" and that the restoration of all things (Acts 3:21) means returning to the practice of male circumcision, distinctions in meat, appointed times, and the seventh-day Sabbath.[154] Worse, the movement compels Gentiles to live as Jews, so in the end, it is all about Jewishness and traditions and not about the new covenant ethic and doctrine.

SABBATICALS AND VACATIONS

Then there is that curious application of the Sabbatic Year, called a "sabbatical," a break from the rigors of educating college students, contrived in 1880 at Harvard University (so named for Puritan pastor John Harvard).[155] The Sabbatic year, which required the land of Israel to remain untilled and debtors and Jewish slaves to be released, was inventively applied to seminary professors, on a septenary basis, who "plows and tills himself, but is not expected to produce a crop of students that year."[156]

Sabbaticals nowadays, lasting months to years, are awarded after varying periods of extended service to teachers at universities to conduct research, to ministers of the gospel to renew their spirituality, and to business employees as an incentive for retention. Some mainline Protestant churches are adopting this innovation as a solution to the contemporary problem of clergy burnout.[157] Somehow, this obtuse application of the sabbatic principle loses its biblical virility for homemakers, bricklayers, and accountants. It is good for us that Apostle Paul did not take a sabbatical, but endured tribulations, needs, distresses, imprisonments, tumults, labors, and sleeplessness for the sake of the gospel (2 Cor 6:3–7). Yet anyone, after completing a period of service for the Lord, may withdraw for the sake of leisure and personal sanity and health without having to appeal to the Sabbath (Mk 6:30–31).

The original Sabbatic Year was determined absolutely, based upon Israel's initial occupancy of Canaan, and it applied to the whole land and nation. If morally applicable today, one would think that the first year of its application would have been for all Christians in the seventh year of the resurrection. However, sabbaticals invoked today are determined relative to the date of hire or empirically to suit the needs of the individual or institution. Sabbatarians must examine the Scriptures to determine

154. McKee, "Work of the Spirit: Heart," 12.

155. Eells, "Origin of Sabbatical Leave," 253.

156. Kang and Miller, "Overview of Sabbatical Leave," 7.

157. Bullock and Bruesehoff, "Clergy Renewal;" Sevier, "Journeying Toward Renewal."

whether they possess the freedom to take vacations for extended periods of time, for if the seventh day of rest is moral, then the remaining six days of work are also moral. If the seventh day cannot be relaxed, who are we to idle away our time during the remaining workdays?

> The Hebrew verb *ta'avod* appears in the Qal imperfect tense, meaning that an absolute literal translation would appear as "You work." Whether we realize it or not, the Bible tells us that we should be working, *at least in some capacity, for six days of the week*. (Note: I do not think that the Bible is against us having a vacation from time to time.) In Jewish theology, work is viewed as a command from God, because the one who does not work has the propensity to sin.[158]

McKee, who is a Messianic seventh-day Sabbatarian, cannot live with the implications of Sabbath law because he desires vacations even though the OT doesn't specifically authorize them. Seventh-day Sabbatarians do not really have a theological basis for taking vacations. Despite the emphatic quality of the command "You work," McKee is quick to sidestep its force to tell us that we can stop working and take a vacation from time to time. But if the fourth commandment moralizes the example of God for man to obey, then it is as much a sin to work on the day of rest as it is to rest on the days of work. Douma, who also likes vacations, asserts that the fourth commandment does *not* enjoin us to work six days, only that our work must be accomplished within the space of six days.[159] So, if someone completes their work in three days and does nothing for three more days, what exactly are they ceasing from on the seventh day? Can someone who is slothful for six days take a Sabbath rest on the seventh day? And if we can cram work into fewer days, can attendance at a second worship service this week fulfill the obligation to worship the following week?

Secondly, McKee informs us that God commands us to work that we may avoid sin. While Scripture endorses this view to an extent (Prov 21:25–26a), we must not conceptualize work merely as a deterrent from sin. If that were the case, we must work continuously in order to keep ourselves free from sin. Likewise, if work is what keeps us from sin, then God seems to especially invite the temptation to sin on the seventh day when no manner of work may be done. However, we know well enough that we sin in our mundane work (1 Chr 21:1–8; Rev 3:1–2) as well as in works of piety (Isa 1:11–13; Acts 5:1–4). Furthermore, if we regard work or busyness as the countermeasure against sin, we are not far from regarding our works as the measure of our righteousness (Isa 64:6). Scripture plainly teaches that righteousness must be imputed apart from works (Rom 4:1–4). This is why the creation week, which describes God's work and rest and prescribes man's work, must be viewed as a type of redemption.

There are two rests: 1) God's rest signifies the promise of eternal life, and 2) Israel's rest signified her faith in God alone. God's work is redemptive, so man's work is meaningless apart from that redemption. Solomon observed that without faith (rest), the benefits and blessings of our labor and skill lead only to envy, loneliness, and sorrow

158. McKee, "Work of the Spirit: Mind," 9 (emphasis in the original).

159. Douma, *Ten Commandments*, 156–57.

(Eccl 4:5–8). It is God's work that ushers in the peacefulness of redemption—God's rest. Man's work is not redemptive, but, if done in faith, is an extension of God's work in the world, which brings glory to God and brings reward to the faithful. The creation week was typological of God's sovereignty in action, culminating in the satisfaction of redemption, thus the pattern cannot be taken as a rigid example of some cycle of work and rest for humanity. Only in the fulfillment of the Sabbath in Christ is there a resultant freedom to take guiltless vacations in faith, even sabbaticals if you prefer.

THE FUTURE

As Voltaire said, "If you want to kill Christianity, you must abolish Sunday." Satan knows that to divide Christians on this topic is to divide and debilitate the church. The thesis of this book is to preserve and promote Christian worship on Sunday and to protect the church from seventh-day Sabbatarianism and Sunday sabbatizing. First-day worship is the clarion call of Christians to live in the comfort, strength, and hope of their Savior's resurrection. The early church correctly believed that the Sabbath was a ceremonial command and welcomed the ordination of the Lord's Day as a commemoration of the Lord's resurrection. However, the ascension of church power through the state and the influence of rationalism allowed the medieval church to begin to associate the fourth commandment with the Lord's Day. The Reformed church, by perpetuating the error of Aquinas, eventually expanded the scope of applications of Sabbath law and increased its moral muscle, forcing the church to practice Sunday Sabbatarianism.

Though the quest for holy worship was sincere, the teaching on the fourth commandment became less coherent and more strident, which led to conflict between the church and the secular world, and a riven church through the development of seventh-day Sabbatarianism. Seventh-day sects logically extended the implications of Sabbatarianism to include adherence to dietary and other calendar laws. While modern Evangelicals, in general, believe the Sabbath was a ceremonial command, their focus has been on their freedom to worship any day of the week, whether or not in church. Their lack of scholarship on the topic has led to a diminished view and practice of the Lord's Day and a feeble, unconvincing voice in the debate. Others, like Chafer, explain that "no command is given to keep the first day," yet he vilifies those who stay home as abnormal, ill-instructed, unwilling, and carnal.[160] But if there is no command, then there is no obligation to meet with like-minded believers, and no guilt or shame for avoiding the congregation of God.

The first day of the week signifies something central to the Christian core of beliefs: a complete redemption to the satisfaction of God, by His grace through faith; a true bodily resurrection of Jesus Christ on the first day of the week; the mediation of the new covenant secured by the indwelling of the Holy Spirit; and the promise of a resurrection to life of all believers at the end of the ages. Unity on this topic is essential. The following conclusions are supported by Scripture and history. They are

160. Chafer, *Major Bible Themes*, 295.

Christocentric and God-honoring, and have the potential of being spiritually unifying for the church.

- The creation account is not about the Sabbath. It is about the primal peace with God that was lost through sin because of a lack of faith. Before the fall occurred, the Lord foreknew how He would reconcile the world to Himself through the incarnation of Jesus Christ. The pattern of creation—six days of God's work and the ensuing rest—reverberates through Scripture to demonstrate God's sovereignty in effecting the work of redemption by grace, through the faith of man. The creation pattern and the sacrifices for Adam and Eve are archetypical visions of redemption, while the seventh-day rest and the promised seed are the first types of Christ.
- When Israel left Egypt they were given the Feast of Passover; a few weeks later in the wilderness they were given the Sabbath. At Mount Sinai, Israel received her full calendar of feasts. The Lord devised this new system of shadow laws to prefigure the person and work of the Messiah.
- The Ten Commandments are a summary of the Mosaic law and therefore contain both moral and ceremonial laws. The Decalogue itself was a figure, and the fourth commandment contains the gospel in shadow form.
- Christ in His earthly ministry was born under the law and obeyed the ceremonial laws as well as the moral laws. His obedience to ceremonial laws in no way endorses their continuity under the new covenant.
- Christ is the end of the law for righteousness. His perfect obedience to moral laws is the source of imputed righteousness to believers. His work of redemption—His incarnation, death, burial, and resurrection—is the fulfillment of all shadow laws, even though some of them are yet to be manifested in their entirety. He calls the things that are not as though they are. When Christ completed the work of redemption, all the calendar festivals of Israel, including the Sabbath, were fulfilled.
- The redemption of Jesus Christ initiated the new covenant. It is a continuance of the former covenants of promise, yet it is the fulfillment of what the former covenants forecasted.
- The apostles had divine warrant to establish first-day worship, and there was widespread acceptance of it. Scripture unfolds the transitional shift from things Jewish to things Christian as Gentiles were added to the ranks of the church. First-day weekly worship was the normative practice of the early church because it was the decretive will of God. The church did not move the Sabbath to Sunday.
- While there is no explicit scriptural mandate or justification for this tradition, we have scriptural foreshadowing and history of first-day significance, as well as the confirmation of early church writings to help us understand the

rationale for Sunday worship by Christians. First of all, Christ's resurrection and the inaugural descent of the Holy Spirit—the most important events of the church age—occurred on the first day of the week in fulfillment of Israel's shadowy calendar laws. These events fulfilled eighth-day calendar laws that spoke of an age after the seventh-day rest. First-day worship was the ineluctable fulfillment of the OT; it was pre-ordained that the New Testament church associate its historical existence with the first day of the week.

Any Christian group that hopes to recapture the era of the early church must practice first-day worship. As the church faces increasing persecution, our solidarity in Sunday worship will provide the avenue to refocus on the unifying effect of Christ's resurrection and the gift of the Holy Spirit. The leaders of seventh-day groups should consider this material soberly and guide their congregations back to first-day worship. Any accepted creed that formalizes Sabbatarianism should be amended. As noted earlier in this chapter dealing with the Westminster Larger Catechism, I recommend that various questions be deleted (98 and 118) or entirely rewritten (115–121). The Westminster Confession of Faith, chapter 21, paragraphs 7 and 8 could be amended as follows:

> As ordained by the Lord and established by apostolic tradition, members of Christ's body are commanded to assemble together on Sunday, the Lord's Day, in especial honor of Christ's resurrected life and the impartation of the Holy Spirit at Pentecost. Though maligned, persecuted, and tempted to do otherwise, all Christians are bound by their indissoluble union with Christ to assemble with like-minded believers in holy fellowship as testimony before the angels and the world of their allegiance to their Savior and Lord.
>
> At a minimum, Christians should assemble in love and faith to hear the apostles' doctrine, to fellowship with the saints, to remember the Lord as He commanded, and to offer prayers. Meetings should be orderly, the congregation should be edified, the rebellious should be warned, the poor should be cared for, the lost should be entreated to believe, and Christ should be magnified, all to the glory of God.

If denominations could modify the Westminster Confession in the seventeenth and eighteenth centuries due to changing political circumstances, then certainly the Westminster should be changed to bring it into harmony with the full teachings of Scripture. The Heidelberg Catechism question/answer 103 is better answered as follows:

> Q. What was God's intention with the Fourth Commandment?
>
> A. First, by the inclusion of this particular ceremonial law within the Decalogue,
> God reminds me that in the beginning, peace with God was lost through sin [Gen 3:6–7; Heb 4:4],
> and so proclaims to me and the whole world [Heb 4:7]
> the gospel in shadow form [Gen 3:15] and His Christ, who mediates both God and Man [Heb 9:15];

> that my own works are insufficient to merit salvation [Heb 4:10], and that by faith, I must rest in the saving work of Christ [Heb 4:2].
>
> Second, though His redemption is complete, I await the consummation of it, comforted by the truth that my rest in Christ is sure [Heb 4:3], both now and forever.
>
> Therefore, the ceremonies that once typified Him and His redemption are now abrogated and no longer required of the church [Isa 66:23; Col 2:16; Heb 4:9–11], for we live in the power of His resurrection on the first day [Matt 28:1; Acts 2:1–4; 42–47; 20:7; Heb 10:23–25; Rev 1:10].

Expository treatment of the Sabbath in the Ten Commandments should focus on the gospel of Christ through shadow forms and should be distinguished from the apostolic tradition of Lord's Day worship. Evangelical and Roman Catholic leaders should not succumb to the materialism of the age in order to accommodate the lay Christian's desire to have the best of both worlds: to squeeze in a little worship on Saturday night so they can go to a Saints v. Cardinals game on Sunday. If an alternative to Sunday morning worship is necessary for working church members, then hold a second service in the evening.

Moreover, a primary function of community worship on the Lord's Day is to remember the Lord through the communion of the Lord's Supper. Churches need to explore ways to keep this ritual fresh, accessible, frequent, and honoring to the Lord. True believers will faithfully worship the God of their salvation on the first day of the week, demonstrating the unity of their voice in praising God alone for the resurrection of Jesus Christ (Rom 10:9).

11

The Sabbath of Death

LIFE, WORK, DEATH, AND REST

"May he rest in peace," is the common epitaph for those who lie buried under the cold, sullen weight of earth's dark soil or in the wooden tombs of ships under the cover of an agitated sea. Death is often spoken of euphemistically as sleep or rest, for the body lies silent and still, uncommunicative and inactive. The cares of the world, the difficulties in relationships, the opportunities for sin, and the turmoil of the soul come to an end, impressing the bereaved onlookers that the person, whose body remains, is now at peace.

Jesus was mournful at the death of His beloved Lazarus and spoke of his death as though it were merely sleep (John 11:11–14). The metaphors are so common that in the above narrative the disciples had to be told in unadorned terms that Lazarus was dead. What also eluded their comprehension was that for the Lord, it is no more difficult to give life to the body that has died than it is for us to awaken a sleeping person. Jesus Christ truly is the Lord of both the living and the dead (Rom 14:9), and it was through His own death and resurrection that His lordship over these realms is manifested. Jesus is life and full of life, but He tasted death for every man (Heb 2:9). He was stung by death, but death was swallowed up by the victory of His unconquerable life.

In both life and death, Jesus is our only comfort and joy. In life we are assured by His promise of eternal life, and in our dark hour of death we are reminded of His suffering death in our stead. For the believer in Jesus Christ, the call of death is not to be feared, but to be earnestly hoped for (2 Cor 5:8–10). The knowledge that our heavenly rest awaits us beyond the grave and that we are beloved of the Lord in full acceptance, motivates us to work all the more diligently for the advancement of God's kingdom here on earth. Only in death is our obligation to work lifted, that our works may come under the review of our Master; and only in death is the summary of our life written. We labor daily because the hope of eternal rest is with us daily.

> Then I heard a voice from heaven saying to me, "Write: 'Blessed are the dead who die in the Lord from now on.'" "Yes," says the Spirit, "that they may rest from their labors, and their works follow them." (Rev 14:13)

The works that follow us are those directed by the Spirit of holiness. When we walk in obedience to God's moral law we experience a quiescent fellowship with Him, a soul's rest even while abiding in this tumultuous world. But at death, all our work, all labor and drudgery cease. No amount of rest on earth could ever reduce the appeal of ending our labors here on earth. Adam's curse prevails in spite of sabbatic or civil rests.

The Sabbath was about eternal life for those Jews who obeyed it in faith. When they carried no burden, they appropriated by faith the freedom from the burden of their sin through the foreshadowed vicarious death of Christ.

> Thus says the Lord: "Stand in the ways and see, And ask for the old paths, where the good way is, And walk in it; Then you will find rest for your souls. But they said, 'We will not walk in it.'" (Jer 6:16)

The Sabbath was also about the curse of eternal death for those who rejected the prefiguring details of the law and refused to walk in the way of the Lord. Jeremiah graphically portrayed the end of these wicked, stiff-necked Israelites who dared to flout the grace of God by carrying burdens on the Sabbath as they pleased: an unquenchable fire (Jer 17:27). When the Israelites received the Law they were warned that disobedience would bring them unrest, signifying their eternal state if they died in their sin. The Lord pronounced that His curse will just as soon come upon the Israelites as His blessing if they failed to hearken to the voice of the Lord in all His commandments and statutes (Deut 28:15). Scattered among the nations, they shall find no ease, neither shall the soles of their feet have rest; their lives shall hang in doubt with absolutely no assurance of continuation. Fear will fill their day that both the evening and the morning are despised, and finally, as they are displayed to be sold as slaves, they will find that even their enemies do not want them (Deut 28:63–68)! This is the curse the Lord Jesus gladly bore for us as "the chastisement for our peace was upon Him" (Isa 53:5).

The grave is not a place of true rest for every habitant. The temporal effects of God's curse upon the disobedient were but a token of the eternal consequences to be suffered in the tormenting regret of hell's fire. Peace with God is not obtained in one's death, but during one's life, through the supernatural preparation of the soul. In one sense, every man is born a dead man—"Let the dead bury their own dead" (Matt 8:22)—until made alive by the Spirit of God at conversion. In the mind of God, every soul comes into the world cursed with the living death of Adam, dead to God in our own trespasses and fallen nature (Col 2:13). Without the salvation of the Lord Jesus, not only would we be dead in our sins, we would die again in our sins sealing them to us (John 8:24; Rev 20:6). It is precisely because of the importance of the state of the soul, whether it is a dead man working to death or a living man resting in life, that the Sabbath type is a recurring theme in Scripture. The customs throughout the world that involve the adorning of the corpse are a reflection of man's intuition that the rotting flesh is unpresentable as a gift to its Maker. A dead body is not a thing of beauty, but the Lord assures the redeemed that though time render it to dust, God Himself will revive their mortal coil to be both alive and beautiful in His sight (Hos 14:5–7). This was the exaltation of David and the hope of all who trust in Christ, "God will redeem my soul from the power of the grave, for He shall receive me" (Ps 49:15). Through Christ's rest of death on the Sabbath and His rising to new life on the first day, we too are ushered from our former Sabbath-death into the true rest of eternal life. Jesus is the resurrection and the life; we share in His resurrection now (Rev 20:6), the resurrection that followed the Sabbath.

As mentioned earlier, the Hebrew word *shabath* can mean that something ceases to exist; hence, when we rest in death we cease. But cease from what? In death our essence does not cease, only the works done in our body, whether good or evil (Isa 14:3–4). Thus, it is proper to speak of death in terms of the meaning of our life's work as opposed to our quiddity. The Bible speaks of death as that time when works may no longer be added to or taken away from the record of our life on earth. By analogy to sleep, our rest in death implies a continuation of our soul but an end to our labors and cares. This was how Job understood the soul's nature in death.

> Or why was I not hidden like a stillborn child,
> Like infants who never saw light?
> There the wicked cease from troubling,
> And there the weary are at rest [*nuach*].
> There the prisoners rest together;
> They do not hear the voice of the oppressor.
> The small and great are there,
> And the servant is free from his master. (Job 3:16–19)

All those who died are there; whether great or small they are restricted from the activities that characterized their wicked life, or freed from those who would trouble them. Job did not fully understand the world inhabited by the dead, but he knew their conscious life would continue. They fell asleep in this world only to awake incorporeal in the next. We know now that in Christ we will arise from this sleep of death to a new day, putting on the glorious garments of our heavenly resurrection, evermore to bless and be blessed.

PREPARATION FOR DEATH

As signified by His placement in an earthen manger—a chiseled-out depression in ground stone—Jesus the Messiah was born into this world in order to die (Luke 2:12). As typified in Adam, even before the communication of the protevangelium, a bride was prepared through his deep sleep of death (Gen 2:21). We don't often think of this as our purpose in life, but for Jesus, each year that expired, each passing month, each departing week, and each closing day were bringing Him closer to His appointed death (Heb 2:9). As a child, when His family made their yearly trek to Jerusalem for the Feast of Passover, Jesus no doubt reflected on the business He was sent to do (Luke 2:41–50). He no doubt reflected every Sabbath how His beloved would benefit from His death-rest on the Sabbath, freeing them from the wrath to come. Ignatius understood the relationship of the ceremonial calendar to Christ's suffering and death, "The day of the preparation, then, comprises the passion; the Sabbath embraces the burial; the Lord's Day contains the resurrection."[1]

Indeed, Jesus' whole life, from conception to crucifixion, was a prosabbaton—a preparation for His Sabbath rest of death. It was not enough to just die; His death needed to be confirmed by burial (Matt 27:64). In His death-rest, the Sabbath was fulfilled. As typified in Adam's pre-ordained sleep, Jesus could not be presented His bride until He awoke from His sleep. Now that we live with Jesus in the power of His resurrection, the Sabbath represents a bygone era. We are dead to it now (Rom 7:4), but most alive in the One who conquered death and fulfilled the Sabbath ceremony completely. Not only was Jesus' earthly life a preparation for His work on the cross, it was a vindication of the creation of mankind.

Adam began his life and calling in the idyllic garden; created in sweet fellowship with God. Adam was given Eve to assist him in his duties and to remind him of his calling, but as our representative head, Adam failed. And Eve failed as a helper. Adam seemed powerless against the temptation to disobey God, and so fell, bringing all of humanity with him outside the garden. Where is the record of his battle with the Tempter, his struggle with the forces of evil, his sweat like great drops of blood? While Adam was created to live, Jesus was incarnated to die. Jesus began His physical life outside heaven, engaged in an epic battle with Satan, and incurred the curse of Adam, finally to return, as it were, to the paradisiacal garden with God. At the end of Jesus' earthly life, He went to the Garden of Gethsemane as the representative of a new humanity to struggle against the temptation to depart from His calling from God. Choosing a garden so named for the work of pressing oil from olives, Christ was pressed arduously to render that oil *ne plus ultra*, obedience to the will of God, anticipating the culmination of His work on the cross.

We too must live in preparation for death. As Daniel considered the close of the ages, it was not given to him to know end times in full disclosure, but the angel asked him to prepare for death, the time to rest from all the concerns about worldly commotion and war. "But you, go your way till the end; for you shall rest, and will arise to your inheritance at the end of the days" (Dan 12:13). While you live, go where I tell you to go, do what I tell you to do, and say what I want you to say, and so be faithful to the Lord's management of your life, for it is no mean thing for the Lord to so favor you. Be diligent to the end, for even in your death, the Lord will be there, so you may be assured of His continuing presence with you in your midnight sleep. The figurative language here encompasses all of life and beyond, with certainty and compassion. Dying in the Lord is unlike death without Him, "For if we believe that Jesus died and rose again, even so God will bring with Him those who sleep in Jesus" (1 Thess 4:13–14). We shall rest and arise to a resurrected life. For Daniel, resurrection was but an idea, but with the resurrection of Jesus Christ from the dead, resurrection is a reality and the cornerstone of the gospel (Acts 2:32–33).

1. Ignatius, *Epistle to the Trallians* 9 (*ANF* 1:70).

The first-day light of life is an eternal balm for the momentary Sabbath rest. In our resurrection to life, we rise justified before God, who sees fit to reward our former toil with an inheritance in His kingdom, the inheritance of His saints in the light (Col 1:12). Knowing that the corruptible must put on incorruption and the sting of death is vanquished through the victory of Christ's resurrection, we remain steadfast and unmovable in our works, for His resurrection imputes value and meaning to our life (1 Cor 15:58). For the elect of God, chosen in Christ: we live, we die, we live again, we never die. Our future is in the eternal kingdom of God where the glorious light of His presence, and that of the Lamb, makes inessential the physical powers of the sun and moon (Rev 22:5). Before the glory-light of creation's first day there was darkness. This is a type of Christ's first advent to Israel, a light that shines in darkness (Isa 9:2; Matt 4:16) and a light to the Gentiles (Isa 42:6–7; Luke 2:30–32).

The first-day light of creation was purposely decreed to shine upon the world before the actual creation of the sun, stars, and planets in order to typify that divine and transcendent light that illuminates the souls of men through belief in Jesus Christ (2 Cor 4:3–6). Christ Himself is our Covenant, a light for the nations (Isa 42:6). If God has indeed shone the light of the gospel in your heart, then there is really no alternative to first-day worship—the illuminating Lord's Day. The Lord's Day is the chief reminder that we live in the light of Christ's resurrection. It is no longer suitable to live in the darkness of buried ceremonies or the darkness of idolatry and revelry, for we "are all sons of light and sons of the day" (1 Thess 5:5). No longer is sleep (the rest of death) the emblem of our redemption, for we have been awakened to the illumination that the Lord's Day beams on every day of our week.

DEATH OF THE SABBATH

The concept that Jesus is the Passover Lamb has led some to theorize that His death was coincident with that of the paschal lamb. However, this is not a necessary construct, because by Jesus' one death on the cross, *all* the sacrificial deaths of the old covenant were fulfilled. The sacrificial ceremonies were fulfilled by the reality that they portrayed, not necessarily by the timing, number, or frequency. Christ fulfilled the Passover feast in His death, even if His death did not specifically coincide with the Passover sacrifice.

Adventist Samuele Bacchiocchi states that on the day before the Sabbath, Christ said "It Is finished," implying that redemption occurred on *that* day, a Friday. Thus, reasons Bacchiocchi, Christ's Sabbath rest of death was a real Sabbath-keeping, so it does not contribute to the typological redemption shared by other ceremonial feasts. Therefore, Sunday cannot be invested with the sense of eschatological rest that belongs to the Sabbath.[2] This spurious line of reasoning begins and ends with quasi-truthful statements, both of which require clarification.

It Is Finished. Bacchiocchi asks why Sunday should be chosen to celebrate the atoning sacrifice of Christ when His redemptive mission was completed on a Friday

2. Bacchiocchi, *Sabbath Under Crossfire*, 33.

afternoon when the Savior exclaimed, "It is finished." However, Jesus' concluding statement was made before He died, so are we to suppose that His death was unnecessary to effect salvation? "It is finished," applies to the full work of redemption that He would assuredly accomplish as He had up to that point (John 19:28). The full work of redemption includes His incarnation, His ordinary life, His ministry, the suffering, rejection, and betrayal, and then His ignominious death and burial, His resurrection, and His ascension (Lk 22:37; Gal 4:4–5). All of this was His work, a work from which He never rested (John 5:17) until it was complete; so His death and burial were a fulfillment of the Sabbath ceremony taken as the rest of death. He fulfilled the Sabbath in numerous other ways, as outlined in chapter 4, but as a symbol of death, Christ fulfilled the Sabbath by resting through it in the grave. This was not a Sabbath-keeping on the Lord's part because He was dead! Yet even His death was a continuation of His *work* of redemption. It is precisely because Jesus fulfilled the Sabbath that the eschatological meaning of rest remains for the saints of God.

Sunday Rest. Bacchiocchi was responding to Pope John Paul II's thesis *Dies Domini*, in which it is said that the Sunday rest continues the task of reminding us of the eschatological rest. The point well made by Bacchiocchi is that Sunday cannot be infused with Sabbath symbolism because the Sabbath did a fine job already pointing to the eschatological rest. The assumption of the Roman Catholic Church is the same assumption of the Adventist and Sunday Sabbatarians who reason that the reality of a forthcoming rest requires the practice of an external weekly rest during the new covenant. What is misunderstood by both Bacchiocchi and Pope John Paul II is that the eschatological rest is *daily* with the believer because Christ's redemption is available daily to the world and Christians are daily in hope of it simply because of the *fulfillment* of the Sabbath type through Christ's work of redemption. No weekly Sabbath rest is required to authenticate the hope of a bodily resurrection at the end of the ages because God has demonstrated the reality of resurrection already through Christ. Indeed, the hope of resurrection is a first-day event. It is not the function of the church to oblige an external rest in order to keep in mind the future hope of the resurrection. The very day on which we worship *is* our weekly reminder of the glorious resurrection of the Lord Jesus Christ that guaranteed our eternal rest.

Bacchiocchi is correct in asserting that the Sabbath was not moved to Sunday. There is no sense in moving an abolished command to another day because it has no more force on Sunday than it had on Saturday. McGee recalled a conversation with a man who challenged him to demonstrate scripturally where the Sabbath was changed to Sunday.

> "Saturday is Saturday, it is the seventh day of the week, and it is the Sabbath Day . . . The seventh day is still Saturday and is still the Sabbath day." He got a gleam in his eye and said, "Then why don't you keep the Sabbath day if it hasn't been changed?" I answered, "The *day* hasn't been changed, but I have been changed. I've been given a new creation. We celebrate the first day because that is the day

> He rose from the grave." That is what it means when he says that the ordinances which were against us have been nailed to His cross.[3]

This is the power of the resurrection! It has made the Lord Jesus Christ a gain to whoever calls upon Him for salvation; to be found in Him and share of His perfect righteousness through faith rather than glory in our own achievements and standing (Phil 3:8–10). The life of a saint of God has been redefined by the resurrection of Jesus Christ and the gifting of the Holy Spirit, events that occurred on the first day of the week. The shadows that once concealed Christ in the old covenant have been unveiled to expose the resplendent glories of the salvation of God through His Son (Luke 24:25–27).

For Jesus, His whole life was a preparation for His Sabbath death. All of history is a preparation for the death of death itself (Rev 20:14). And as Irenaeus said of Christ-followers: "The business of the Christian is nothing else than to be ever preparing for death"[4] (Phil 3:10). But of more importance is the reality beyond death. This was also the theme of ceremonial laws; and ceremonial laws fulfilled are ceremonial laws abolished. The Sabbath foretold His death and burial and so the Sabbath is not only merely dead, it's really most sincerely dead.

> He arose after the Jewish sabbath, and it was the passover-sabbath; all that day he lay in the grave, to signify the abolishing of the Jewish feasts and the other parts of the ceremonial law, and that his people must be dead to such observances, and take no more notice of them than he did when he lay in the grave. Christ on the sixth day finished his work; he said, It is finished; on the seventh day he rested, and then on the first day of the next week did as it were begin a new world, and enter upon new work. Let no man therefore judge us now in respect of the new moons, or of the Jewish sabbaths, which were indeed a shadow of good things to come, but the substance is of Christ. We may further observe, that the time of the saints' lying in the grave, is a sabbath to them (such as the Jewish sabbath was, which consisted chiefly in bodily rest), for there they rest from their labours (Job 3:17); and it is owing to Christ.[5]

Christ resurrected on the first day, not the Sabbath. We died and rose again in Christ (Rom 6:8; 2 Tim 2:11), so we are really living beyond the Sabbath. Yet we shall be like Him in His death, so that we too will die and sleep and have the comfort of knowing that our bodies will be resurrected at the last day. Our lot in Canaan will be granted for an everlasting possession (Dan 12:13), our abode in Jerusalem will be secured by an irrevocable contract (Jer 32:11–17), the rest in heaven will remain secure for the people of God (Heb 4:9), for the Lord Himself will descend from heaven and raise the dead to ever more be with Him (1 Thess 4:16–17).

3. McGee, *Thru the Bible*, 5:351–52.
4. Irenaeus, *Fragments of Lost Writings* 11 (*ANF* 1:570).
5. Henry, *Commentary*, 5:355 (Matt 28:1–10).

12

Sabbath Redemption

Complete Redemption

A DILATIVE MEANING OF Sabbath is *completion*. The sister words, *shabath*, *shabua*, and *shiba*—meaning rest, week, and seven, respectively—also convey the same sense of completion. Etymologically, Sabbath (*shabbat*) is derived from rest (*shabath*). Ceasing occurred at the end of the first five days of creation, but the sixth day marked the completion of God's work, giving significance to God's rest (*shabath*). *Shabbath* appears later in history in conjunction with Israel's redemption from Egypt and signifies the completion of their rigors in Egypt (Gen 15:13; Exod 12:40–41; Gal 3:17). Likewise, week (*shabua*) is derived from seven (*shiba*). The concept of a seven-period, or "week," came after the record of the seven days of creation. Frequently throughout Scripture, the semeiotic intent of the number seven is completion, fulfillment, and perfection.[1] The number seven is especially prominent in Revelation and, like every other word of Scripture, is there by God's pleasure and design.

> There is a sacred arithmetic, as well as sacred persons, places, and times. Numbers in the Scriptures are as significant as words. They are as much a part of the Apocalypse as anything else. And there is as much resting upon them, as upon any other class of particulars contained in this book.[2]

Likewise, a week is the passing or measure of seven days and is used in apocalyptic writings to symbolize the completion of various stages of redemptive history (Dan 9:24–27).[3] Of course, the number seven is used throughout Scripture to symbolize the perfection or completion of God's work. This symbolism is carried over into the biblical themes of rest[4] and Sabbath.[5] Yet even the sense of completion inherent in these words may divert the inquirer from the more profound and divine meaning of these words—redemption—for this is the ultimate and reboant theme of Scripture, the primary work of God to complete.

1. Gunner, "Number," *NBD3*, 834
2. Seiss, *Apocalypse*, 52.
3. Cohen, "shābûa`," TWOT, 2:899.
4. Vine, *Expository Dictionary*, 529.
5. Heschel, *Sabbath*, 106.

It was the ubiquitous appearance of the number seven in Genesis that lured Sabbatarians such as Dabney to suppose that the Sabbath was practiced during patriarchal times. However, while the number seven does not *mean* the Sabbath, it does mean redemption, so the frequency of the number seven in Genesis is a prelude of redemptive themes, not a historical indication of Sabbath-keeping. Redemption must take place in human history; therefore, in type and prophecy the Lord of salvation displays His intention, ability, and sovereignty over redemption with the number seven. (Appendix 7 depicts the seven historical covenants that span the redemptive plans of God.) Upon fulfillment of His redemptive plan, all His holy will and the perfections of His work will be the eternal theme of heaven's choir. If one seven means completion or redemption, then seven times seven means complete redemption.

SE7EN SE7ENS

First Sevens

Following the creation account, the next appearance of the number seven has to do with the protective mark on Cain, whereby the Lord would avenge sevenfold anyone who killed Cain. In this passage, the number seven is associated with both the mercy of God, in preserving even a murderer in hope of repentance, and His justice, in that the Lord will deal with the matter of sin in His own way and in His own time. Man's vengeance would be less than perfect or incomplete. Cain was the firstborn of Adam who reaffirmed the sinfulness of mankind, as like begets like. Likewise, Israel was likened to Cain, guilty of the blood of the prophets and ultimately of the Messiah (Matt 23:33–36; Luke 23:19; Acts 7:52–53), yet preserved in mercy and for justice by the omnipotent hand of God (Ps 59:11).

The "mark" upon Cain is the same Hebrew word (*owt*) used to denote the rainbow given to Noah (Gen 9:12) and circumcision given to Abraham (Gen 17:11), both redemptive and covenantal *signs*. The Lord is a God of promise and what He says is sure. From His first words to Adam, that one of his seed should arise as victor over the devil, to Malachi's prophecy that the Sun of righteousness shall arise with healing in His wings, the end is known from the beginning. In a general sense, God covenanted by the mark of Cain that He would deal with the matter of sin Himself and ensure the forthcoming Seed would fulfill His redemptive role.

The seventh generation from Adam in the line of murderous Cain leads us to Lamech, the second murderer, who presumed the Lord would grant him seventy times the seven-fold protection afforded Cain. Though we would hope that the Lord would instantly punish Lamech for his hubris and homicide, Scripture records that the Lord's long-suffering mercy was perfected through 777 years of Lamech's life. The record of Adam's sin answers for us the question why our world is both magnificent and cruel, why man is both noble and degenerate. We observe too that blood was shed to atone for sin in order to reestablish a friendly and harmonious relationship with the Lord. Next, the record of two apparently unrepentant sinners answers the question how God addresses the sin of the stubborn and rebellious. Christians who know God's holiness and hatred of sin wonder how He tolerates the most egregious perfidy and wickedness; however, in God's wisdom, the lives of Cain and Lamech were extended mercifully peradventure they repented and sought God's face (2 Pet 3:9).

Seven in Ten

The liturgical reading of the law of God in Reformed churches invariably leads to the Decalogue. The Ten Commandments are identified as the law of God that points out the sinfulness of men and leaves them hopeless of being reconciled with God. The Heidelberg Catechism correctly instructs its readers that the law of God establishes our misery because we are unable to perfectly obey it and therefore fall under its curse. As a summary of God's covenant, must it only convey curses and death? Yet with a growing familiarity with Scripture, students discover that curses are often answered with blessings, and judgments with hope. For example, Adam's curse was followed by the promise of the Messiah and the prophet Isaiah reminded Israel that there was yet a glorious future on the other side of profound judgment. But where is the hope in the Ten Commandments? Why did Paul refer to the covenant as a covenant of promise (Eph 2:12)? One could point out the promise associated with the fifth commandment (Eph 6:2) or the generational blessing for obedience found in the second commandment, but these are not obvious *redemptive* hopes. It is the figure of rest in the fourth commandment that portrays the completion of redemption and answers the curse of the law with a true and abiding promise of God.

The catechisms teach that the Ten Commandments are divided in such a way that the first four commandments pertain to our duties toward God, and the remaining six are our duties toward man. However, the pattern of four plus six is doubtful as a symbol of redemption. The first three commandments are unquestionably duties toward God and the last six commandments deal with man, but the fourth command occupies an intermediary position.[6] Jewish authors recognize the unique presence of this ritual command as a bridge between God and man.

> The Ten Commandments open with the words *your God*, and end with *your neighbor*. The first three concern reverence for God, the last six concern reverence for human life. Fourth in line, the Sabbath command deals with both our relations to God and our relations to one another. In that sense it spans the ideals of all the others; like Jacob's ladder, it spans heaven and earth.[7]

The Sabbath rests between the first three and the last six as if it belongs to both worlds. Rather than place the Sabbath commandment at the end of the Decalogue, it is poignantly placed between God (3) and man (6). This is because the Sabbath is not merely about the seventh day of the week but about the Mediator who stands between God and man (1 Tim 2:5). The Sabbath, typological of the Lord Jesus Christ, is positioned between the holiness of God and the sinfulness of man. The Sabbath recalls that in the beginning was God and that His work ended in the blessed state of rest. The first

6. Kline, "The Two Tables of the Covenant," 138.

7. Klagsbrun, *Fourth Commandment*, 22.

three commandments and the last six commandments impugn the heritage of man while on earth, but it is the fourth commandment that presents the gospel in shadow form. The redemptive type is positioned within the law to bind God and man together, thus offering hope even within the Decalogue that man and God could be reconciled.

Seven Sums

The number seven is also the compound of two representative numbers, wherein three, the number identifying the Godhead, and four, the number associated with the world, are in harmony. Both numbers signify completeness,[8] as do their sum.

> The peculiar character of the Mosaic festivals was expressed *formally* in their being regulated as much as possible by the number seven, as the stamp of the covenant of God with Israel (seven being compounded of 3, the divine number, and 4, the world number), and *materially* by their being separated from the labours, toils, and cares of everyday life for the sanctification and consecration of the whole man to purposes of religion and the worship of God. The common starting point for the entire legislation with regard to the feasts, was the seventh day, or closing day of the week, which was called for that reason the Sabbath, and as such infolded prototypically within itself the fundamental idea of festal celebration.[9]

This thought is echoed by Seiss as he reviews the significance of numbers in Scripture.

> Four is the worldly number. It proceeds from three, and includes three. And as three represents the Trinity—the highest, and the perfect—four designates that which proceeds from the Trinity, and is dependent thereon: the creation, the universe. Hence, the world resolves itself into four elements: fire, air, earth, and water. The points of the compass are four: north, east, south, west. There are four seasons, four winds, four grand divisions of the earth. The great world-powers of history and prophecy are four. The living beings, supposed to represent the forces of providence, are four. Ezekiel's vision of God's providence in the world revealed four cherubim, four wheels with four sides, four faces, and four wings. The waters in Eden were four . . . There is therefore no mistaking of this number.[10]

The passing of each week represents the principle of order in the universe, first the Godhead and then the created world. Each Sabbath cycle acknowledged the God of Israel as the Creator of the universe, and, therefore, the Lord over all and the only true God. He is Lord not only of man, but of beast and field, which is why the Mosaic sabbatic seasons extended to the land (Sabbatic Year) and commerce (Jubilee).

Redemption is also closely associated with the sum of six and one. The most obvious example is the combination of six ordinary days of the week followed by the redemptive Sabbath. To this may be added the Sabbath of the Land and the creation week. The story of Ruth opens with six characters and a dilemma, which anticipates a redemptive solution in the seventh character: Boaz. Even in the details of temple

8. Gunner, "Number," *NBD3*, 834.

9. Kurtz, *Offerings, Sacrifices and Worship*, 342 (emphasis in original).

10. Seiss, *Apocalypse*, 60.

artifacts, such as the golden lampstand (Exod 25:31), the redemptive thoughts of God in number can be appreciated. Made of pure gold and intended to light the sanctuary every evening, the sacred candelabrum was designed with six superior stems supported by one vertical shaft—seven total—each of which was adorned with representations of almond flowers, likened to a blossoming tree.

> The seven-fold branches support seven-fold lamps. Each summit is a coronet of fire. Little would be the profit of the costly frame, unless light sparkled from it. But it burns brightly. This is its especial purpose. The mystic number and the constant blaze show Christ a perfect and unfailing light.[11]

Simple in its beauty, regal in its purpose, the golden stand typified the coming Redeemer who would enlighten the world of the glories of God the Father. Specifically, as Barrett observed, "the predominantly higher center shaft points to Christ, who as the Ideal Prophet reveals God and truth."[12] And if Christ is the central shaft, then His elect are represented by the remaining six stems, which are inseparably joined to Him. All together the union manifests the complete disclosure of the gospel to mankind (2 Cor 4:4–6) and acknowledges the source of heavenly light to be the work of the Holy Spirit (John 15:26–27).

Sevens Multiplied

The signal and symbolic intention of the number seven is of divine design and is evident throughout the cycle of ceremonial feast days.

> Unquestionably, the number *seven* marks in Scripture the sacred measurement of time. The Sabbath is the seventh of days; seven weeks after the commencement of the ecclesiastical year is the Feast of Pentecost; the seventh month is more sacred than the rest, its "firstborn" or "New Moon" being not only devoted to the Lord like those of the other months, but specially celebrated as the "Feast of Trumpets," while three other festivals occur within its course—the Day of Atonement, the Feast of Tabernacles, and its Octave. Similarly, each seventh year is Sabbatical, and after seven times seven years comes that of Jubilee. Nor is this all. *Seven* days in the year may be designated as the most festive, since in them alone "no servile work" was to be done, while on the so-called minor festivals (*Moed Katon*), that is, on the days following the first of the Passover week and of that of Tabernacles, the diminution of festive observances and of restrictions on labor marks their less sacred character.[13]

The number seven unifies the ceremonial feasts of Israel because the ceremonies portray redemptive themes. Interestingly, there were seven annual Sabbaths given to Israel when work was suspended. Kurtz outlines the septupal feature even within the three convocational feasts of Israel, when adult males were required to appear in Jerusalem: Easter (Feast of Firstfruits), Pentecost (Feast of Weeks), and the Feast of Tabernacles.

11. Law, *Gospel in Exodus*, 112.
12. Barrett, *Beginning at Moses*, 281.
13. Edersheim, *Temple*, 134

> These three feasts were all, from their nature, festivals of rejoicing, and were called so. But though moving in a different sphere from the sabbatical feasts, they were closely related to them both in form and substance. Preservation is only a continuance of creation. Hence they also bear on every side the stamp of the number seven. The two most important of these feasts—Easter and the feast of Tabernacles—commenced on the 15th of the first and seventh months respectively, that is to say, 2 x 7 days from the commencement of the month. And Pentecost was kept on the fiftieth day from the commencement of the Easter feast, *i.e.*, at the end of seven times seven days. But as the Hebrews had only lunar months, the 15th day of the month was the time of full moon. And this represented the culminating height and fulness of time.[14]

Of course, the advent of Jesus Christ was neither tardy nor premature, but in the fullness of time. As God determined, sufficient events were completed in order to usher in the new covenant and its commemorative feast. Israel's complex system of historical recall decreed in the observation of days, months, and years gave way to the remembrance feast of the sacrifice of Jesus Christ. Pentecost (Shavout, Feast of Weeks) followed seven seven-periods after the Feast of First Fruits, and included in its ceremony the first fruit offerings of the summer wheat harvest. Just as the resurrection of Christ is represented in the Feast of First Fruits, so in Pentecost the second harvest represents the second and final stage of the resurrection of the redeemed. The first Pentecost after the resurrection of Christ was chosen by God to pour out the Holy Spirit upon the disciples, sealing them for the day of resurrection through the instauration of the new covenant. Redemption is frequently associated with the number seven as the concluding or ultimate event in time.

Messianic Sevens

Under the inspiration of the Holy Spirit, David wrote in the Psalms of the forthcoming miseries of the incarnate Messiah. There are seven "I am" statements of the humility and woe that He endured for our sakes (Ps 22:6; 40:17; 69:8; 69:20; 69:29; 102:7; 102:11). Scripture also records seven instances in which Christ speaks audibly during His crucifixion (Luke 23:34; 23:43; John 19:26–27; Matt 27:46; John 19:28; 19:30; Luke 23:46). The sixth and seventh of these sayings—"It is finished," and "Into Your hands I commit My spirit,"—find Christ asserting the full accomplishment of all the great designs of God as proclaimed by His prophets and subsequently resting in spiritual union with the Father, the blessed fruit of redemption.

> The work long contemplated, long promised, long expected by prophets and saints, is done. The toils in the ministry, the persecutions and mockeries, and the pangs of the garden and the cross, are ended, and man is redeemed. What a wonderful declaration was this! How full of consolation to man![15]

14. Kurtz, *Offerings, Sacrifices and Worship*, 344–45.
15. *Barnes' Notes*, 9:372 (John 19:30).

In our final book of the Bible, Jesus makes seven "I am" statements iterating these very thoughts: that in Him and through Him, redemption from this world has been completed and eternal life imbued by the One who inhabits eternity (Rev 1:8, 11, 17, 18; 21:6; 22:13, 16). These patterns of seven demonstrate a sense of completion through divine acts. Regarding the seven epistles to the early churches, Seiss notes that "Seven is the number of completeness. It here designates the whole Christian body, of all times and all places."[16]

There are occasions when David employs the number six to engender a sense of incompleteness, which cause the reader to anticipate the finality or completeness at some other time. For example, in a despairing Psalm, David asks six questions that almost demand a negative answer.

> Will You work wonders for the dead? Shall the dead arise and praise You? Selah
> Shall Your loving-kindness be declared in the grave? Or Your faithfulness in the place of destruction?
> Shall Your wonders be known in the dark? And Your righteousness in the land of forgetfulness? (Ps 88:10–12)

Since David already acknowledges the Lord as his Savior, the questions are better answered affirmatively. The Lord indeed will do wonders for those who are spiritually dead, and when He gives us life, we will rise to praise Him forever. His loving-kindness was made known to the world—the land of graves and destruction—through the preaching of the gospel. While the minds of men are darkened, and even the saints are prone to forget their God, yet the Lord continues to demonstrate His righteousness and power. This interrogative sextuplet looks for One who is both Light and Life and provides the sublime positive answer to these difficult questions.

Formal Sevens

> The Lord is my rock and my fortress and my deliverer; My God, my strength, in whom I will trust; My shield and the horn of my salvation, my stronghold. (Ps 18:2)

Scripture is replete with sevens, not only in word, but in form. From a simple verse to whole books (seven visions of John), patterns of seven may be found. In Psalm 18:2 there are seven metaphors or agnomens of the Lord, which are presented in a symmetrical pattern. He is called the Rock, Fortress, Deliverer, Strength (also trans. fountain, source, origin), Shield (also trans. buckler, defender), Horn of Salvation, and Stronghold. The first three names and the last three names are listed as triads, and the remaining metaphor is embraced by the words, God and trust. These are all expressions of salvation linked to the name of God and the need to trust him. In poetic form, David tells us that God is not just once our Savior, but seven times our Savior, and that our trust does not begin the process or finish it, but He is the Alpha and Omega of our trust. The seven names indicate the enoughness of our Lord, that His salvation is sure,

16. Seiss, *Apocalypse*, 37.

complete, and perfect. We need no other. The central metaphor "strength" is amplified for us by Clarke.

> When applied to God, [it] signifies fountain, source, origin, etc. God is not only the source whence my being was derived, but he is the fountain whence I derive all my good; in whom, says David, I will trust. And why? Because he knew him to be an eternal and inexhaustible fountain of goodness.[17]

The beauty of this verse is composed not merely in words, but in symmetry and number, so that every form of communication resounds with the thesis: God is my all in all, in whom I will trust. To me, He is completely and fully God—a seven God.

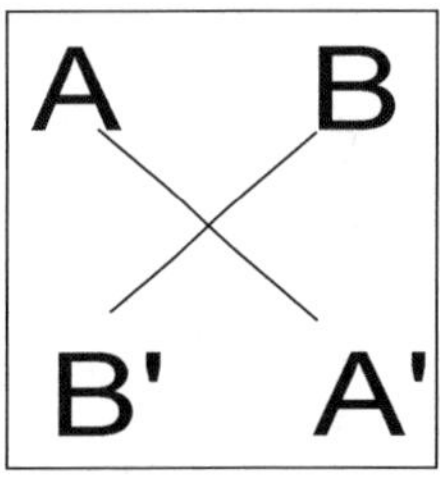

There is also a literary style called "chiasmus" that follows the pattern A B B' A' or A B C B' A'. The Greek cognate means intersection or crossing, indicating the intersection of two lines, as in the letter "X" or chi. It is not a pattern of rhyming words but of matching concepts, where the order of words (or concepts) in the first clause is repeated in inverse order in the second clause. The even-numbered chiasmus focuses on the repetition of a clause and amplifies its meaning and understanding. This was a common literary form among Semitic literature and is present throughout the Bible.

Structurally, the thought process goes to a place and returns the way it went. A tighter form of chiasmus, called an antimetabole, was used by Jesus to teach about the Sabbath (Mark 2:27).

A	The Sabbath	
B		was made for man
B'		Not man (was made)
A'	For the Sabbath	

Of interest to the symbolic meaning of seven and its relationship to the Sabbath is that a septenary chiastic structure indicates fullness or completion whereas a sextuple anticipates something to complete it. "These six things the Lord hates, Yes, seven are an abomination to Him" (Prov 6:16) demonstrates that six is insufficient a number to represent the full gamut of sins reprehensible to the character of God. Many of our translations miss the literary chiasmus in Genesis 9:6 composed of three conceptual pairs.

A	Whoever sheds		
B		The blood	
C			Of man
C'			By man
B'		His blood	
A'	Shall be shed		

17. Clarke, *Commentary*, 3:272 (Ps 18:2).

This structure lacks a central concept (between "Of man" and "By man") that would serve as a unifying theme or climax. The absence of the climatic statement shadows forth the propitiatory blood of Christ, whom God, in forbearance, passing over sins previously committed, set forth to demonstrate His righteousness (Rom 3:25–26).

When Isaiah considered the return of the dispossessed to Israel, he prophetically announced that in latter days, even Gentiles shall figuratively descend upon the holy land for the glory of its light and Lord. Of course, the missing climax to make full this chiasmus is the person of Jesus Christ, the true light of heaven, the bright and morning star, the first fruits of the resurrection.

Isaiah 60:1–3				
A	Arise, shine For your light has come!			
B		And the glory of the Lord is risen upon you.		
C			For behold, the darkness shall cover the earth,	
D				?
C'			And deep darkness the people	
B'		But the Lord will arise over you, And His glory will be seen upon you.		
A'	The Gentiles shall come to your light, And kings to the brightness of your rising.			

Proverbs 26:22–28 describes the fullness of sin characteristic of the talebearer. The central climatic verse, "Do not believe him," actually uses the number seven in this septenary chiasmus. Not only does wickedness attain its fullness and completion (Gen 5:31; 6:5), so does the righteousness imputed to believers in Christ.

Christ, in human form, is the fullness of God, so those in Christ are fully human, complete in Him (Col 2:9–10). As Paul considered the new covenant theme of complete redemption in the death, burial, and resurrection of Christ, he demonstrates that a complete Savior (v. 9) is able to accomplish the complete work involved in paying for sin (v. 11). In Him, we find our completeness as human beings (v. 10). We were fully dead, but He has made us fully alive (v. 13) having forgiven completely all our trespasses (v. 13). Through faith in the God who worked for our salvation and obtained complete victory over Satan (v. 12, 15), we possess a complete salvation and a complete Savior. Man's resting faith in a working God (v. 12) who provides a complete redemption through first-day resurrection serves as the springboard for Paul's conclusion: "Let no one judge you in food or in drink, or regarding a festival, a new moon, or sabbaths, which are a shadow of things to come, but the substance is of Christ" (Col 2:16, 17). Let the shadowy seventh-day Sabbath go. It is complete and made full in Christ. The number seven inherent in the Sabbath symbolizes the completeness and fullness of the work of Christ that ends with a redeemed people and a satisfied God.

Seven, Eight

From another angle, redemption is also the beginning. Hence, the redeemed are free on the eighth day, that is, the first day of the new week. The new week designates a new period of time, a better epoch, and a new generation. It is built upon that which preceded but brings us closer to that which is anticipated; it reaps the blessings earned or bestowed in previous days, and hopes for fulfillment of greater promises.

> Eight is the number of new beginning and resurrection. The eighth day is the beginning of a new week. The Jewish child was circumcised the eighth day, which was its birth into covenant relations. Noah was "the eighth person," and his family consisted of eight, and they started the new world after the flood. Christ rose from the dead on the eighth day. David was the eighth son of Jesse, and he established a new order for Israel. In the eighth year, the Jews were to sow the ground again as the fresh beginning of a new septenary. The eighth head of the beast was the revival of the seventh. Our Sunday, which celebrates the new creation which began in the Saviour's resurrection, is the eighth day, the first of the new week. And the eternal order of blessedness is to begin with the eighth thousand years from Adam.[18]

The superiority of eighth-day circumcision over the seventh-day Sabbath forecasted the church's sacramental practice of convening on the eighth day. The eight souls "saved through water" (1 Pet 3:20) were types of the eighth-day community of God's people baptized in the death of Christ, a people that Christ will convey safely to God. With the resurrection on the first day of the week, early Christians recognized that the number eight represented the new beginning after the perfect number seven had been accomplished. With Adam and Eve sinning on the seventh day, and having their sin atoned for and receiving God's pledge of a righteous seed, they began their new lives on the eighth day looking forward to Christ. Christ's resurrection early on the first day takes us back as if no time had transpired. For Adam and Eve, the eighth day began with the hope of the Messiah, but for the church, the eighth day exults in the fulfillment of that hope.

Based on the root word for fatness or abundance, the first mention of the number eight occurs in Genesis 5, of the number of hundreds of years that Adam lived after his son Seth was born, years marked by the prodigious growth of his family. Interestingly, in Genesis, the number eight occurs seven times, six of which describe the eight hundred-plus years that the first six patriarchs lived after the birth of their firstborn sons. Concurrent with this growth, the wicked multiplied in numbers and depravity. The righteous man of the seventh generation, Enoch, was translated, or taken away from the material world, to be with God a few decades after Adam had naturally expired. Seven other generations were alive at the time of Enoch's translation, some or all of whom were likely witnesses of this incomparable event, as were the disciples of the ascension of Jesus. Enoch's seventh-generation position suggests the completion of generations, much as Matthew and Luke identify Jesus as the culmination of godly generations. With the impending flood in view (the first of two earthly destructions) the first-second pattern of Adam's death and Enoch's translation affirmed to their antediluvian contemporaries the hope of an ongoing existence beyond this earthly vale. This hope of immortality was symbolized in the near-millennial life of Methuselah, the

18. Seiss, *Apocalypse*, 61.

firstborn of the eighth generation. Enoch and his great-grandson, Noah, understood the declination of morality in the world. So, another obvious first-second pattern is in the prophetic office shared by Enoch (Jude 14) and Noah (2 Pet 2:5) who warned the ungodly of impending judgment. Noah in a sense was "translated" to the new world as a family of eight on the eighth day, signifying again the association of eight with the resurrection to immortality in a new day. The sequence of events has the animals guided into the ark during the first seven days of rain and then all were shut in by the Lord. The forty-day downpour began, the first day of which (the eighth day) the ark rose with the waters above the earth (Gen 7:10–17). This links the first day (or eighth day) with the resurrection concept in redemption.

David was the second king of Israel; however, his coronation followed a pattern established from the beginning: the Lord takes away the first (Saul) that He may establish the second (David). Though Saul was the first king of Israel, he was not really the king of God's choice, for the matter of making a king was the desire of the people, which the Lord took as a rejection of his own kingship (1 Sam 8:1). Saul's reign was discounted, regional, and parenthetical, for the Lord already had in mind a man of superior character who would better represent Him as king of a united Israel. That man was David, and he served as the paradigm for all successive kings. More importantly, David foreshadowed the incarnation of Jesus Christ, the true and everlasting king of God's people. In this sense, David was the primary king of Israel, the first chosen and appointed by God. Yet David was merely a man, who, along with all the kings of Israel, was pictured in Saul, to be rejected in favor of the Christ, whose royalty was of a divine nature. Interestingly, David was the eighth son of Jesse (1 Sam 12–14). Since the root of Jesse (Isa 11:1; Rom 15:12), by primogeniture, belonged to Eliab, it is as if the seven sons had already served as king before David was chosen. As the eighth son, David was the superabundance of kingship having risen above his seven brothers. When David's eighth-position antitype arrives (Jesus Christ), said Isaiah, His kingship and kingdom will be unlike anything that preceded it (Isa 9:6–7).

A variety of eighth-day occurrences in the Mosaic law establishes the notion that its significance is a new beginning, a post-redemption theme. Leviticus 23 lists the feasts of the Lord: seven annual feasts, the number of completion, but begins with the weekly Sabbath as the eighth feast.

> Also on the fifteenth day of the seventh month, when you have gathered in the fruit of the land, you shall keep the feast of the *Lord* for seven days; on the first day there shall be a sabbath-rest, and on the eighth day a sabbath-rest. (Lev 23:39)

The association of the Sabbath with the eighth day is especially poignant in the Feast of Tabernacles that marks the completion of the festive calendar for the year. Thus, instead of ending on the seventh day, the final Sabbath is an eighth-day Sabbath. Recognizing this intriguing play on numbers (an eight-seven: that is, a first-day-last-day concept), Hugh Downie determined that it symbolized the "day of eternity . . . when the whole redeemed universe enjoys eternal rest."[19] It appears that Leviticus 23

19. Downie, *Harvest Festivals*, 153–54.

portrays a superabundance of sabbatic rest as the calendar comes to completion or fulfillment.

The Mosaic cleansing of the leper (Lev 14:9–32) connects the first-second pattern and the eighth-day theme to beginning anew and resurrection.

> And [the priest] shall sprinkle [the blood of one of two clean birds] seven times on him who is to be cleansed from the leprosy, and shall pronounce him clean, and shall let the living bird loose in the open field.
>
> He who is to be cleansed shall wash his clothes, shave off all his hair, and wash himself in water, that he may be clean. After that he shall come into the camp, and shall stay outside his tent seven days.
>
> But on the seventh day he shall shave all the hair off his head and his beard and his eyebrows—all his hair he shall shave off. He shall wash his clothes and wash his body in water, and he shall be clean.
>
> And on the eighth day he shall take two male lambs without blemish, one ewe lamb of the first year without blemish, three-tenths of an ephah of fine flour mixed with oil as a grain offering, and one log of oil. (Lev 14:7–10)

One bird must die, sacrificed in an earthen vessel over running water, and the other wings free. The two birds symbolize the cleansing of one person's life: dead in sin and earthy fleshiness yet revived by the living water to rise again above the earth as intended by the Lord in creation. The necessity, efficacy, and power of redemption are summarized in that our sin calls for a vicarious death, that God must enliven our soul, and that we have the hope of resurrection to a new life. Sprinkled seven times with the blood signifies the completeness of salvation. The liberated bird, first dipped in the blood of the other and in the running water, assures the restored man of a future resurrection on the basis of the blood of Christ and the water of the Spirit. Yet this healed man must continue on in the life of the congregation.

> After seven days of preparation, during which he was allowed to remain in the camp but still outside his tent or home, and after a renewed washing, bathing, and shaving of the whole body, in order that none of the old uncleanness might be carried over into the new sphere of life, the true consecration commenced on the eighth day.[20]

On the first and seventh day he ritually cleansed his body and his clothes and shaved off his hair to symbolize the purification of his life in real-time, yet as Bonar intimates, this refers also to the purification of the church, on the seventh day, that is, the end of all appointed time.[21] Either way, upon completion of the seventh day, there is yet another day, the eighth day, which signifies that which is beyond what has already been completed. Regarding the redemption of mankind, the eighth day is properly understood as 1) the church age when God establishes the faithful according to the gospel of Christ and the "revelation of the mystery kept secret since the world began" (Rom 16:25), and 2) the embracement of eternity with a new heavens and earth for all the saints of God following the second death.

20. Kurtz, *Offerings, Sacrifices, and Worship*, 435.

21. Bonar, *Leviticus*, 272.

Eighth-day shadow laws are also fulfilled by the first advent of Christ. He has surely completed the work of redemption, though there are things still future that He must settle, and only for the surety of their accomplishment can it be said that He has provided a complete salvation. Redemption is complete, so eighth-day newness is the byword of the church and the significance of eighth-day ceremonies is in their portrayal of the new covenant era. Circumcision, when first given to Abraham, was a sign of what went before it (Gen 17:10–14). It represented the fact that Abraham completely believed God's promise to make of him a great new nation and that through his bloodline, the Messiah would appear (Gen 15:6; Gal 3:16). For Abraham, circumcision was a seal of the righteousness that he had while uncircumcised (Rom 4:11). When given to Abraham, circumcision was an eighth-day ceremony, indicating that faith in Christ meant newness of life through the gift of the Holy Spirit, "that the blessing of Abraham might come upon the Gentiles in Jesus Christ, that we might receive the promise of the Spirit through faith" (Gal 3:14). The ceremony was continued through the Mosaic covenant, but lest the Jews misunderstand the significance of circumcision, Moses assured them that "He will prosper you and multiply you more than your fathers. And the Lord your God will circumcise your heart and the heart of your descendants, to love the Lord your God with all your heart and with all your soul, that you may live" (Deut 30:5–6; cf. Jer 4:4).

Meaningful life is an eighth-day life of trust in and love of God, as represented by Abraham, the father of faith. This eighth-day sign existed prior to the giving of the Law and was incorporated into Law, so that the Law confirmed that salvation was by faith apart from the works of the law (Gal 3:17). The circumcision ceremony was expanded as a shadow law to accent the implications of its significance by including laws of uncleanness and purification for women who give birth (Lev 12). Whether a woman gave birth to a male or female, she was ritually unclean, and through the elements of this law acknowledged her partnership with Eve in bringing sin into the world. Birth is bloody and painful, like circumcision, but that is the result of the curse. The requirement for a burnt offering and a sin offering indicates that God requires a different and vicarious blood, a young and tender blood in her place. Eve also received the promise that through a woman, a man would be born to avenge the work of the serpent. The eighth-day presentation of her son to the temple anticipated that day when all would be restored, hence, a new beginning. The initial days of uncleanness, seven total, indicates the completion of time before the Messiah comes.

Leviticus 12:1–8		
	Male	Female
Unclean	7 days	14 days
Circumcision	8th day	N/A
Purification	33 days	66 days
Total Uncleanness	40 days	80 days
Burnt Offering	First year lamb Or, if poor, a young pigeon or turtledove	
Sin Offering	Young pigeon or turtledove	

Circumcision for Abraham and following generations was also a sign of purification and separation for God's purposes of the organ of procreation in anticipation of the promised Seed. To a lesser extent, circumcision was a sign of identification with the commonwealth of Israel; however, the abrogation of the law of circumcision was not based on some fulfillment of the concept of identification. Jesus Christ was born of the seed of woman (Gal 4:4), "the son of David, the son of Abraham" (Matt 1:1), a true King and a true Patriarch, therefore, the ceremony that anticipated his arrival need no longer be performed because He actually came at the appointed time, took on flesh and lived among us, and was crucified for us (Rom 1:1–6). Requiring circumcision after the gift of the Holy Spirit was tantamount to declaring that Jesus was not the promised Seed of Abraham. This is not the exclusive view of circumcision, as Paul also conceived circumcision as the removal of the body of sin through the sacrificial death of Jesus (Col 2:11). Furthermore, Christ's circumcision of death becomes ours through the circumcision of faith, so Paul argues for its cancellation on the basis of faith in Christ's death (Rom 4:12). Christ reminded the Jews of the priority of circumcision over the Sabbath (John 7:21–24) and though both foreshadow redemption, it is the eighth-day ceremony that trumps the seventh.

Related to the uncleanness following parturition and the circumcision of males, is the law of the firstborn, the beginning of a new generation. Though enacted as a ceremonial reminder of Israel's purchase price from Egypt at the cost of Egypt's firstborn sons and livestock (Exod 13:14–15; Num 3:13), it foreshadowed the birth order, divinity, and privileges of Jesus Christ, the only begotten Son of God (Gen 49:3; Ps 89:27; Luke 2:22–23). Because Christ is the firstborn of God, we through adoption may call Jesus our Brother (Rom 8:28). Because He is the firstborn from the dead, He has assumed headship of the church (Col 1:8; Heb 12:23). These are mysteries that have attained significance under the new covenant and only foreshadowed in the old, hence firstborn fulfillment indicates a new beginning for the redeemed people of God. The firstborn of clean animals were consecrated to God through the priesthood, and the firstborn of man and beast (unclean animals) were required to be redeemed (Exod 13:2; 34:19–20; Num 18:15). The consecration of firstling calves, lambs, and kids were made on the eighth day: "Likewise you shall do with your oxen and your sheep. It shall be with its mother seven days; on the eighth day you shall give it to Me" (Exod 22:30; Lev 22:27). Jesus, the clean firstling of God, is commended back to God on the eighth day through the resurrection, having completely and perfectly fulfilled, as signified by the seven days of life, all that God had required of Him (Zech 12:10; John 19:26–27). It is not, as some commentators suppose, a lesson in animal science, that the young animal is supremely able to provide for its own needs by day eight, or to be a help to its mother's health by its seven-day presence, for firstborn laws are foreshadowing ceremonies of the qualifications of Jesus, the Son of God.

By distinction, firstborn males of unclean animals were to be sold, the price given to the priests, or killed by the family themselves by the breaking of their necks (Exod 13:13, 34:20). Should a family desire to keep a particular unclean animal, then the Lord approved the decision, but at a cost: in its stead a lamb was given or a redemption fee of five shekels was paid by the family. It was a particular grace that even unclean animals could be redeemed, signifying that the gospel of grace calls those who are not His people to be His people (Hos 2:23). Yet the Israelites were never allowed to forget the horrifying payment for their redemption from Egypt through the laws of the firstborn.

What the redemption of firstling unclean animals and firstborn male Israelites have in common is the timing of their consecration to the Lord. The clean firstborn animals were consecrated on the eighth day, but both unclean and Israelites were consecrated about two to three weeks later (Num 18:16). With the resurrection of Jesus Christ taken as the firstborn from the dead (Col 1:18; Rev 1:5), the redeemed of Israel and of the Gentiles must follow concurrently in the resurrection some period afterward, for "in Christ all shall be made alive. But each one in his own order: Christ the firstfruits, afterward those who are Christ's at His coming" (1 Cor 15:22–23). The Lord anticipated the inquiries of the young why firstborn ceremonies exist, so parents were instructed to reply, "By strength of hand the Lord brought us out of Egypt, out of the house of bondage" (Exod 13:14). The laws of the firstborn were about redemption. Though the resurrection is yet future for us, we are redeemed now in the present, fully belonging to God and fully accepted in the Beloved (Eph 1:6), for we have been bought with the inestimable price of Christ's blood (1 Cor 6:20).

> "Every day for seven days you shall prepare a goat for a sin offering; they shall also prepare a young bull and a ram from the flock, both without blemish.
>
> Seven days they shall make atonement for the altar and purify it, and so consecrate it.
>
> When these days are over it shall be, on the eighth day and thereafter, that the priests shall offer your burnt offerings and your peace offerings on the altar; and I will accept you," says the Lord *God.* (Ezek 43:25–27)

Ezekiel's vision came in the midst of Israel's deportation to Babylon, when hopes of returning to Jerusalem were at a low. In spite of her exile, Ezekiel prophesied reassuringly of the revival and restoration of national Israel. Among the detailed account of a revived temple worship is this dedication ceremony of seven days. Then on the eighth day *and thereafter*, Israel will be accepted in her worship. Again, the eighth day is a symbol of new beginnings, restoration, and resurrection, and here it is associated with the Lord's acceptance of our worship. As Christ was both the sacrifice and the priest, so we too, by the mercies of God, present our bodies a living sacrifice, holy, acceptable to God, which is our reasonable service (Rom 12:1). Having been consecrated to God we are now able to approach God directly for the forgiveness of sin and the restoration of fellowship as signified by the burnt and peace offerings.

The presence of eighth-day ceremonies should not be overlooked or underrated by the church, for they foretold the glories of Christ and His redeemed. Christ's resurrection on the eighth day, the day after the Sabbath (Lev 23:11), was "plainly prophesied" in Scripture.[22] The eighth-day ceremonies of the old covenant are fulfilled in the establishment of the new covenant; hence, the worship of the church is celebrated on the first day of the week by God's design and decree.

THE SABBATH COMPLETE

The Fulfilled Sabbath

One passage of Christ's superiority over the Sabbath that was not considered earlier is the healing of the blind man in John's gospel. John begins the account by noting Christ's interest in a blind man, known to those in Jerusalem to have been blind from birth. The disciples inquired as to the origin of the man's blindness, to which Jesus replied, "Neither this man nor his parents sinned, but that the works of God should be revealed in him" (John 9:3). John omits in the first part of his narrative the fact that this healing took place on the Sabbath day in order to contrast the symbolism of rest with the work of Christ. Jesus continued, "I must work the works of Him who sent Me while it is day; the night is coming when no one can work. As long as I am in the world, I am the light of the world" (John 9:4–5). The unmistakable imagery is the first day of creation, so Christ makes claim of being that first-day light that illuminates the whole of creation every single day. He can be none other than who He is: the Light of the world. Then coming to the blind man, a sixth-day man who lives in darkness, He fashions from some dust of the earth in His hands—new eyes as it were, a re-creation of man so he may be whole again and see God with eyes of understanding—and anoints his eyes to see. Anointing represents the chosenness of this blind man to become a sighted man, "not for price, nor reward" (Isa 45:13). Then the Lord confirmed the new creation of this man by urging him to wash in the pool of Siloam, meaning "Sent." Formerly blind, the enlightened saints begin a new life in the service of God. The gospel of Christ was set before the apostles in living color, and they would eventually come to realize that that Sabbath day was fulfilled when a blind man was made completely sighted.

Man is a six. Some say that people are zeros, nobodies, entities of insignificance, and there is some truth to this; but man is a six, not a zero. Man was created on the sixth day because God was developing the symbolism of redemption in the opening week of creation. Though what God had created on the sixth day was very good, man was not complete until he was joined with the Godhead in rest on the seventh day. In

22. Halverson, *Study of the Types*, 32.

order to be complete and perfectly whole, man needed to be with God in the garden on the seventh day—not the Sabbath, but God's rest on the seventh day. The seventh day represented the Lord Jesus Christ, who was already considered slain for the sins of the world, and who stood as the mediator between God the Father and man. Adam sinned on the seventh day, sacrifices were made on the seventh day, Adam believed God and was reconciled to Him on the seventh day. In spite of that reconciliation, Adam was still sent out of the garden. Why was Adam cast out if he was redeemed? It is because the seventh day and the garden were merely types of a more glorious unity between God and redeemed man. The seventh day of creation and the garden of Eden were not the ultimate realities. It is not the garden that saves, not the seventh day, not the Sabbath or the temple, but Jesus, the Lamb of God.

The Sabbath merely provided rest for the body—"Do no work therein"—but the rest provided by Jesus is for the whole of man—"You shall find rest for your soul." This is the true rest to which the former Sabbath pointed. That for which our hearts should seek and that which impels us more than the brightness of the sun is Jesus Christ. Nothing, not even the Sabbath, can be more glorious than He.

> And in that day there shall be a Root of Jesse, Who shall stand as a banner to the people; For the Gentiles shall seek Him, And His resting place shall be glorious. (Isa 11:10)

Now that Christ has actually arrived in history and satisfied the justice of God, fulfilling all the shadows of redemption, Christians celebrate their redemption by focusing on Christ's resurrection, the gift of the Holy Spirit, and the acceptability of their worship on the eighth day (first day) while retaining the seven-day sequence as a reminder of a completed and perfect redemption.

Against Apostle Paul's clear relegation of the Sabbath to the class of ceremonial laws, joined by the multitude of other commands involving the observance of time (Col 2:16), the arguments for its continuation are pretentious and unmerited. The example of God's rest in creation, while not insignificant by itself, does not obligate the sea of humanity to observe a recurrent hebdomadal rest and religious day of worship. The Sabbath was a ceremony for the Jews, a spiritual shadow of the greatest redemptive theme portrayed in God's holy word: salvation by the working grace of God through the resting faith of man (Col 2:17).

A new pattern of worship is demanded for the new covenant. Our new obligation is not to remember the Sabbath, but to remember Jesus Christ who took the bread and the wine and shared them with His disciples, emblems that now symbolize the new covenant (1 Cor 11:24–25). Our symbols of worship emphasize a completed redemption by Jesus Christ through His sacrifice and the unity all believers share by virtue of their position in Him (1 Cor 10:16–17). The monumental importance of first-day worship cannot be overemphasized, as it proclaims to the world the unity of faith in the resurrected Lord. Torrey summarized the first-day events associated with the resurrection—Christ's appearance to Mary and Peter (John 20:1, 14; Luke 24:34); to the Emmaeus disciples (Luke 24:1, 13–35); to the ten disciples (John 20:19–23); to the eleven disciples (John 20:26–29); to John on Patmos (Rev 1:10); and the giving of the Holy Spirit on Pentecost (Acts 2:20)—and exclaimed, "God, in every tangible way, in those New Testament times set His seal on the first day of the week."[23]

Deviations from this first-day precedent, exemplified by the separatism of seventh-day (Saturday) worship and the sabbatizing of the Lord's Day (Sunday), have only allowed Satan to sift us as wheat. Though the weekly pattern persists, it is secondary to the significance of the eighth day. The obligation to worship is not diminished or removed by the abrogation of any of the twelve ceremonies of time within the Jewish economy. For the redeemed, weekly worship is both a duty and a privilege. It will carry us through our insincerities and schisms now, and it will lead us to that pure and unadulterated thanksgiving and praise that will characterize our worship throughout eternity.

No Rest

Believers under the new covenant are not commanded to rest as a form of worship, yet the cry for such inactivity arises from time to time as authors sense the frustration of attempting to accomplish too much with too little time. Rather than find solace in the simple, yet profound command to redeem the time (Rom 13:11; 1 Cor 7:29; Eph 5:16; Col 4:5; Rev 1:3), many find appealing the practice of a sabbatic rest. But the rest they want is not the rest demanded by Sabbath law; it is merely a rest they find convenient to themselves. Margie Haack's concept of Sabbath-keeping is commonplace: "Entering into empty, nonfunctional time,"[24] inspiring those such as Marva Dawn to remove their wristwatch on Sunday, the "Christian Sabbath." This is not the Sabbath of old, but the traditions of men. As David Novak observed, Sunday Sabbatarians "have pretended—as far as Jews are concerned—that Sunday can have the sanctity Saturday has had for Jews, including the sanctity it had for Jews like Jesus and his disciples."[25]

But what about those Christians who struggle to even appear at church on Sunday because of the busyness of their lives? For American Christians, the temptation to forgo worship is due to the demands of employers, the quest for financial security, the pleasure of recreational and entertainment activities, and the draw of domestic duties. The Christian who has trouble stopping work or play in order to worship does not need a Sabbath; he needs to bring order to his life and exercise dominion over the expenditure of his time. This requires common sense and self-control, not a Sabbath whip. Regrettably, churches have accommodated these Christians by holding brief Saturday night services. They opt out of Sunday worship, which is based on the resurrection of their Lord, so they can be elsewhere, anywhere other than with the saints in worldwide worship. These Christians want both their religion and the world, and, unfortunately, pastors and priests are all too willing to minimize the distinctiveness and meaning of Sunday worship to accommodate them.

23. Torrey, *Ought Christians to Keep the Sabbath?*, 37.

24. Haack, "Sabbath Master," 29 (quoting Eugene Peterson in an unreferenced work).

25. Novak, "The Sabbath Day," 69–70.

The concerns of those who advocate sabbatic practices for modern-day Christians are real. They witness a church that has lost its salt because it so willingly ignores the duty to worship, the very thing that marks Christ's people from the world and provides them the environment in which to obey a host of interactive commands. The Christian who routinely abandons congregational worship is choosing to *un-identify* himself from the congregation of the redeemed. He may think that he is one with Christ and one with all other members of the church, but he avoids the sign of that unity by being elsewhere. Regularly missing Sunday worship isolates a person from the primary means of making a public profession of Christ: "Whosoever, therefore, shall confess me before men, him will I confess also before my Father" (Matt 10:32–33). Those who willingly give up their worship are exposing their lack of understanding of the gospel, and the possibility exists that these folks do *not* have a spiritual understanding of the gospel. Reader, if you neglect congregational worship for various reasons known to yourself, then let this paraenetic passage speak to your heart.

> And let us consider one another in order to stir up love and good works,
>
> not forsaking the assembling of ourselves together, as is the manner of some, but exhorting one another, and so much the more as you see the Day approaching.
>
> For if we sin willfully after we have received the knowledge of the truth, there no longer remains a sacrifice for sins,
>
> but a certain fearful expectation of judgment, and fiery indignation which will devour the adversaries.
>
> Anyone who has rejected Moses' law dies without mercy on the testimony of two or three witnesses.
>
> Of how much worse punishment, do you suppose, will he be thought worthy who has trampled the Son of God underfoot, counted the blood of the covenant by which he was sanctified a common thing, and insulted the Spirit of grace? (Heb 10:24–29)

What is the "willful sinning" but forsaking the assembly of believers? We forsake the means by which our life in Christ is sustained, and this is insulting to the Spirit of God. There is nothing to be gained by the church in browbeating people into attendance, especially with a nullified ceremonial commandment. Preach the gospel, teach its meaning, and the thankful soul will choose to kiss the Son (Ps 2:12) and join with those under His lordship (Rom 16:16) at the appointed meeting. Forcing regular church attendance by appealing to the Sabbath command is no better than enticing church attendance with entertainment and humor, gimmicks, and pageantry.

The pagans obviously enjoy a day off during the week to pursue their own interests, so it is inconceivable that God would want to force a Sabbath rest on all mankind to enable them to recuperate their bodies, invigorate their minds, and otherwise strengthen themselves in their rebellion against Him. Let the Egyptians stay behind to work, but let God's people go and worship Him! Instead, the church should be a haven of emotional and spiritual rest that entices, in Christ's stead, the weary and heavy laden. How shall people of the world become weary and heavy laden if we force a civil rest on them? Instead, they need to work and worry, sweat and toil, become slaves to their ambitions and the quests of others—"He brought down their heart with labor"—so that God perchance would expose their folly and cause their feet to hasten to the nearest city of refuge: the church (Ps 107:10–14).

Know Rest

The Christian life is likened to that of a soldier engaged in daily battles; there is no time for rest. He is always on call for service to the Lord. The Maccabeans discovered freedom when they fought against their enemies on the Sabbath day. The Christian should not have to struggle with this Jewish question. Leithart has noted well that even our worship is essentially militant as we acknowledge the lordship of Jesus Christ over the nations of the earth, review the promises of the covenant, and sing the praises of the God of our salvation.

> Worship is not a retreat to a safe haven where we can offer praise to God in blissful forgetfulness of the challenges before us. Worship is part of the Church's engagement with the world, one of the chief strategies in our combat.[26]

As such, a Christian who considers weekly worship an option excuses himself as a potential grunt in spiritual warfare and diminishes his ability to withstand the enemy as Christ's kingdom marches forward.

Lord's Day worship is commemorative and packed with meaning. The very fact that the Lord's Day is on the eighth day is a confirmation of the fulfillment of the Jewish calendar laws. The Sabbath is past and we now live in a new, enduring eighth day that awaits only the consummation of all things. The Lord's Day is a tribute to Christ who lived under the law and died under the law, therefore fulfilling all that the law said of Him. He is both the Sabbath complete and the complete Sabbath. The Lord's Day is a tribute to Christ, who, by virtue of His work and resurrection, offers Himself as the source of everlasting life to all who trust in Him alone for salvation. We still live with a recurring week and all the redemptive intonations that come packaged with it, but truly, each day is a day of work as God works in us, and each day is a day of rest as we rest in Jesus Christ. Only in the Lord can we experience the rest that was foreshadowed in the Sabbath, just as Moses was plainly told, "My Presence will go with you, and I will give you rest" (Exod 33:14).

> And, besides all this, thy soul should keep its constant Sabbath, since thy work is all ended by thy risen Lord.[27]

The kingdom of God remains outside the confinement of space and time and endures forever, so in Christ we find the Sabbath complete.

26. Leithart, "Worship is Warfare," 17.

27. Bonar, *Leviticus*, 398

Closing
Havdalah

THE SABBATH BELONGS TO the Jews and the Jews to the Sabbath. They have a special ceremony on the closing of the Sabbath called Havdalah, which means separation.[1] Customs developed within the Jewish culture to mark the transition from holy days to ordinary days, from the sacred to the secular. The prayers of Havdalah recognize the Lord as the One who calls for separation. Havdalah is bolstered by symbolic rituals involving wine, aromatics, and candlelight aimed at the human senses and the mind. It is mythical, mystical, and spiritual.

> Blessed are You, Lord, our God, King of the Universe, who creates the fruit of the vine. (Amen).
>
> Blessed are You, Lord, our God, King of the Universe, who creates varieties of spices. (Amen)
>
> Blessed are You, Lord, our God, King of the Universe, who creates the light of the fire. (Amen)
>
> Blessed are You, Lord, our God, King of the Universe, who distinguishes between the sacred and the secular, between light and dark, between Israel and the nations, between the seventh day and the six days of labor.
>
> Blessed are You, Lord, who distinguishes between the sacred and the secular. (Ah-main)

The mood is partially melancholy, as the delights of the Sabbath day come to an end and there is a desire to carry that experience into the days following. There may also be a sense of relief that the Sabbath is over as the lighting of a twisted pair of candles marks the end of the prohibition to start a fire.

When you are emotionally involved with the Sabbath, it is hard to say good-bye, but every Sabbath must come to an end. This bittersweet sentiment was no doubt felt by many early Jewish Christians as they transitioned from the old covenant to the new. The relief that the Sabbath has passed is a relief that what it stood for has come, not in part and not in a whisper, but in the fullness and glory of Jesus Christ. Blessed are You, Lord, our God, King of the Universe, who gave us your Son so that the Sabbath blessings follow us every day of the week.

1. Ouaknin, *Symbols of Judaism*, 58–60; Hertzberg, *Judaism*, 120–21.

Appendix One

The Didymous and Septenary Law

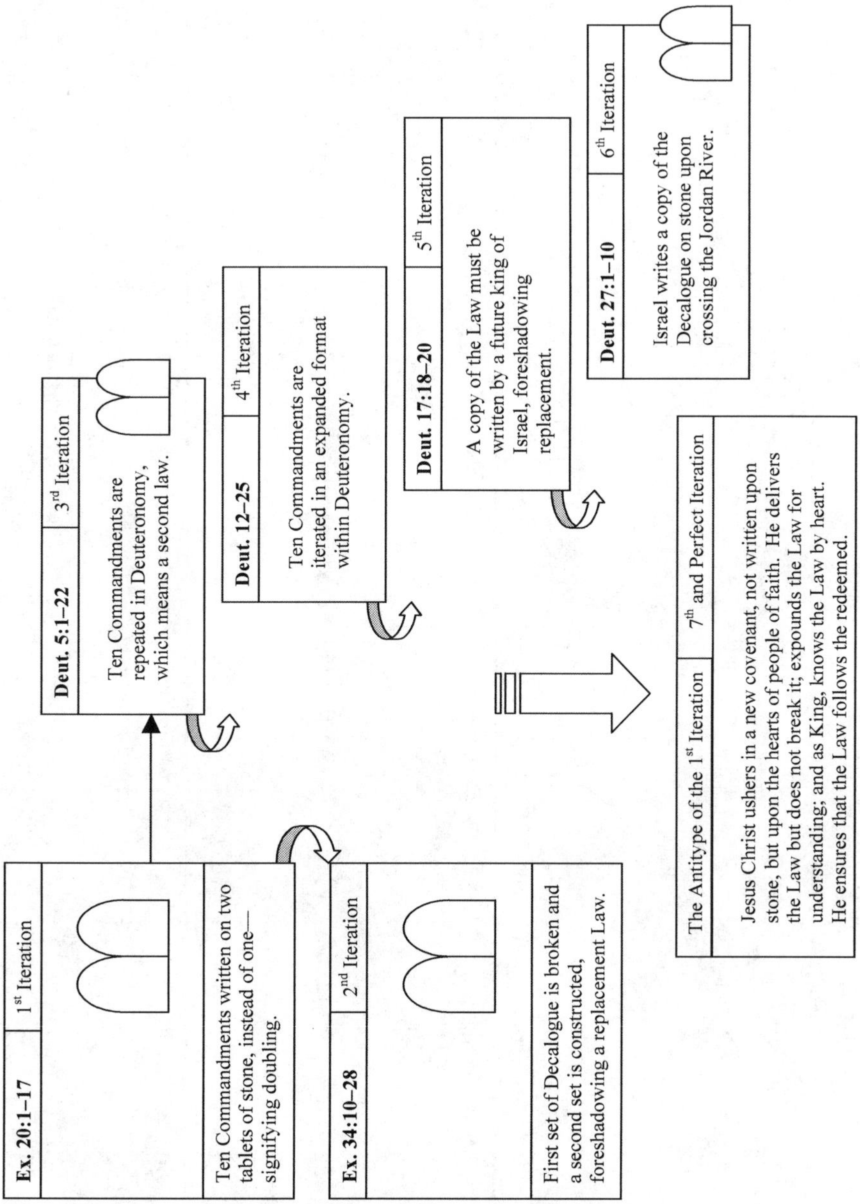

Appendix Two

Summary of Sabbath Law

Duty	Question	External Answer	Fulfilled Answer
•Day and Frequency •Time to begin and end	When	•Every seventh day of the week •Starting PM on sixth day and ending at PM on seventh day	•Perfection of Lord's work in His own time; Lord's work will surely be completed; Redemption as promised will be fulfilled eternally •God's work begins in midst of man's darkness; Man awakens to the promised rest (enlightened to salvation, resurrected to glory)
•In Your Dwellings •Holy Convocation	Where	•In your home throughout Israel •Official national services in Jerusalem specific to that day	•Presence of and fellowship with God in us, the personal temple; Communion with family of God •Christ, our representative, makes the requisite propitiation before God in heaven

Duty	Question	External Answer	Fulfilled Answer
•Consider Creation	Why	•Imitate the Lord in his seventh-day rest; meditate on His lordship of time and space	•The creation events and pattern are redemptive types; God's rest was disrupted by sin, yet it was only a shadow of a future eternal glory; That rest is only provided by the work of God through the Seed
•Remember slavery		•Through ritual recollection, each Israelite must reckon himself as having been delivered from Egypt; Treat fairly all those in servitude	•Redemption of man implies a previous master: Sin is the bondage from which man must be redeemed
•Do no work	How	•No manner of work: such as, meal preparation; picking up sticks; conducting business transactions; buying and selling, bringing commercial products through the Jerusalem gates, treading winepresses; ensuring that children, servants or animals do no work	•Salvation not by works and not for purchase; not of yourself or the laurels of others; redemption not only for man but the whole world, and not only for Israel, but strangers to their land; the redeemed are not burdened with the guilt of their sin
•Rest		•Physical rest at home and around adjoining community; maintenance works are acceptable, such as dressing and eating	• Relational rest in Jesus Christ, the sum of all rest figures; a present soulical rest in salvation by grace through faith; an expected bodily resurrection rest at the end of the ages; the death-rest of Jesus Christ which fulfilled the Sabbath

Duty	Question	External Answer	Fulfilled Answer
•Light no fire •Prepare beforehand	How	•Do not make a fire or use combustion •Make preparations the day prior to avoid even accidental breaches of Sabbath law; cook the day prior	•Free from the eternally severe judgment of God for our sins; made acceptable to God by Christ •Our redemption was foreordained before the creation of the world and therefore, forever sure
•Official Sacrifices •Official Showbread	How	•Two lambs in addition to the continual burnt offering, meal offering with oil, and drink offering •Twelve loaves baked and placed on table in holy place in the morning in exchange for the old loaves; old loaves removed and eaten by priests	•Sin-payment exacted for Adam and Eve through whom the promised Seed should come •Heavenly bread is sufficient for the life of all the redeemed; All the redeemed are one before the face of God
•Cut Off from Israel •Exact Death Penalty	What if	•Nonparticipation signifies dissociation from commonwealth of Israel •Stone to death convicted Sabbath-breakers on testimony of 2–3 witnesses	•Living death of unregenerate souls apart from God •Second death of the wicked (who do not obtain eternal rest)

Appendix Three

Redemption Analogies of Sabbath Law

Cook Day Prior Spiritual preparation 6th day double portion Word of God	Commemorated the eternal plan of God to send His Son to earth Commemorated the double-portion sixth day of creation in the creation of Adam and Eve Commemorated God's provision of a double portion of manna on the sixth day Prefigured the preparations for the incarnation of Christ, the God-Man Prefigured the heavenly origin of Christ who appeared at the appointed time in history Prefigured God's work in our heart by His word prior to salvation Anticipates a double portion event before the day of eternity
Seventh Day Completion Perfection Redemption	Commemorated the completion of God's work of creation Commemorated the holy fellowship of God and man Commemorated the Sabbath institution and other seventh-day signs Typified the perfection of all that God accomplishes, especially in redemption Anticipates the re-creation of a new heavens and earth, especially the final sanctification of His elect, and the summation of His divine plan to bring them into eternal rest
Rest Place Person Faith	Commemorated the post-creation rest of God that existed prior to the fall as well as those hours that Adam walked in faith Commemorated the sleep of Adam necessary to the life of Eve Commemorated the emancipation from bondage under Egypt Typified faith in God unto salvation Typified the salvation of God when sin has been done away with Typified Christ who should restore mankind to the original rest Typified the restoration of the cosmos under God's perfect will Typified post-mortem burial of Jesus Christ necessary for our salvation Anticipates the completion of plan of redemption Anticipates the heavenly rest

No Work God alone	Commemorated the creation rest for which mankind did not labor Commemorated the redemption of Israel by God that He alone provided without their assistance Typified that salvation is not by works, not by the will of man or anything else, but by God alone Anticipates the single-handed culmination of God's work for the redemption of mankind
As Well As Thou Gospel call	Commemorated the liberation of Israel, as well as Gentiles Commemorated the hardship of slavery and the benefits of freedom Typified that there were others who were slaves to sin who also desired spiritual freedom Typified the grace of God to be extended beyond national confines to provide true freedom in salvation Anticipates the coexistence of nations, tribes, and families in harmony with God
Evening to Evening Conversion	Commemorated the union and unity of the Godhead through time Commemorated the creation of Eve and her union with Adam, symbolic of the church and Christ Commemorated the evening of Israel's liberation from Egypt and their encampment around the Shekinah glory Typified that salvation comes in the darkest hour Typified the reunion of the church and her Husband Anticipates a time of extreme wickedness prior to the eschaton Anticipates the sovereign timing of the final union of the elect with God
In Your Dwelling Physical presence of God	Commemorated the pre-fall experience of Adam and Eve in the garden, God's dwelling place with man Commemorated the freedom from Egypt and the dwelling of God within the midst of Israel's camp Commemorated the chosen land of Canaan Prefigured the incarnation of Christ who tabernacled among us Prefigured the residence of the Holy Spirit in human tabernacles Anticipates the final tabernacle of God with men
Kindle No Fire God's wrath	Commemorated the freedom from God's wrath that Adam and Eve enjoyed because of the vicarious death of animals Commemorated the flaming sword to bar reentry into the garden Commemorated the freedom from God's curses upon Egypt Prefigured God's wrath and judgment of our sin on Jesus Christ Anticipates the freedom from the fire of hell throughout all eternity

Two lambs Propitiation	Commemorated the salvation of Adam and Eve, two animals slain at the end of the seventh day Commemorated the Passover sacrifice that secured liberation from Egypt as well as all ceremonial death–payments of the law Typified the sacrificial blood of Christ that was necessary to provide salvation Typified Jesus, our high priest, who works in heaven continuously for the redemption of mankind Anticipates the complete removal of sin and the exultation of the saints in the Lamb of God throughout eternity
Showbread Unity	Commemorated the presence of God in the garden with Adam and Eve as they walked and talked with Him Commemorated God's presence among the twelve tribes of Israel as they encamped around Him Prefigured the incarnation of Jesus Christ on earth and His indwelling of saints through the Holy Spirit Prefigured the unity of all those found in Christ Anticipates the second coming of Jesus Christ and the physical unity of His beloved
Death Penalty Consequence of sin	Commemorated the sin of Adam and Eve that brought death into the world Commemorated the severity of breaking God's law, condemning all men as lawbreakers and worthy of death Prefigured the death of Jesus Christ for those who put their trust in Him Anticipates the eternal death of men who reject the gospel of Jesus Christ

Appendix Four

Comparison of Passover with Supper[1]

Text	Detail	Similar	Dissimilar
Lev. 23:5	Preparations begin on Nisan 10 and end on Nisan 14		First day of the week
Lev. 23:5	Annual or seasonal	Some churches observe annually	Weekly, throughout the year
Ex. 12:6	Commemorates exodus from Egypt and the Mosaic covenant		Commemorates the resurrection and the new covenant
Ex. 12:1–20	Associated with the Feast of Unleavened Bread		No associated feasts
Deut. 16:5–7	At designated place in Jerusalem		Wherever Christians come together in worship
Deut. 16:6 Ex. 12:8	At the going down of the sun; at night	Some churches have closed communion at night	Not specified, but typically observed in the morning
Lev. 23:4–7	Attend by pilgrimage		Locally celebrated
Deut. 26:5–11	Ritual instruction of children		Not specified; and rarely duplicated

1. For the most part, none of the Passover rituals are carried forward into the Lord's Supper. The Lord's Supper was instituted *after* the Passover which better illustrates the fulfillment of the OT sign of the covenant and the institution of the new covenant. The Passover is not the place to look for Lord's Supper traditions. Is there a biblical imperative to create Lord's Supper traditions based on the Passover? Who should decide which Passover rituals should be duplicated in the Lord's Supper? The better question is: Which details of the Passover ritual have been fulfilled in Christ and how, and therefore abrogated in their external form?

Text	Detail	Similar	Dissimilar
Ex. 12:5–6	Select a male yearling lamb without blemish three days prior to killing at twilight		No lamb required
Ex. 12:7	Apply blood to doorposts		No blood required
Ex. 12:8, 11	Eat cooked lamb in haste that night		No lamb required
Ex. 12:8	Eat with bitter herbs		No bitter herbs required
Ex. 12:10	Burn the next morning what lamb is not consumed		No lamb required
Ex. 12:8, 34	Eat with unleavened bread		Eat either leavened or unleavened bread
Ex. 12:3–4	Everyone eats a portion among family and relatives	Paedocommunion	Believers communion among a household of faith
	Wine was not specified, but is required by tradition	Drink wine	Drink wine, but by command
Ex. 12:11	Dress with belt and sandals on, staff in hand, and ready to go		No attire specified
Deut. 16:7	In the morning, return home		May return home immediately after
Num. 9:1–13	Alternative Passover for those ritually unclean		No alternatives specified
Ex. 12:48–49 Num. 9:14	Foreigners and non-Jews could keep Passover if circumcised		Circumcision not required of participants; Non-believers not asked to participate
Ex. 12:14	A memorial forever		Observe until Christ returns

Appendix Five

Similarities Among the Twelve Calendar Feasts

Type	Name	Frequency	Seventh	Duration	Eighth Day	Sabbatic	Pilgrimage
Recurring	Continual	Day					
	Sabbath	Week	7th Day			Yes	
	New Moon	Month					
Annual	Passover	Year					
	Unleavened Bread	Year		7-Day Feast		2 Sabbaths	Appear
	First Fruits	Year			7 Days+1		
	Weeks	Year			7 Weeks+1	Sabbath	Appear
	Trumpets	Year	7th Month			Sabbath	
	Atonement	Year				Sabbath	
	Tabernacles	Year		8-Day Feast		2 Sabbaths	Appear
Periodic	Sabbatic Year	7 Year	7th Year			Yes	
	Jubilee	50 Year			7 Sabyrs+1	Yes	

Appendix Six

Already and Not Yet

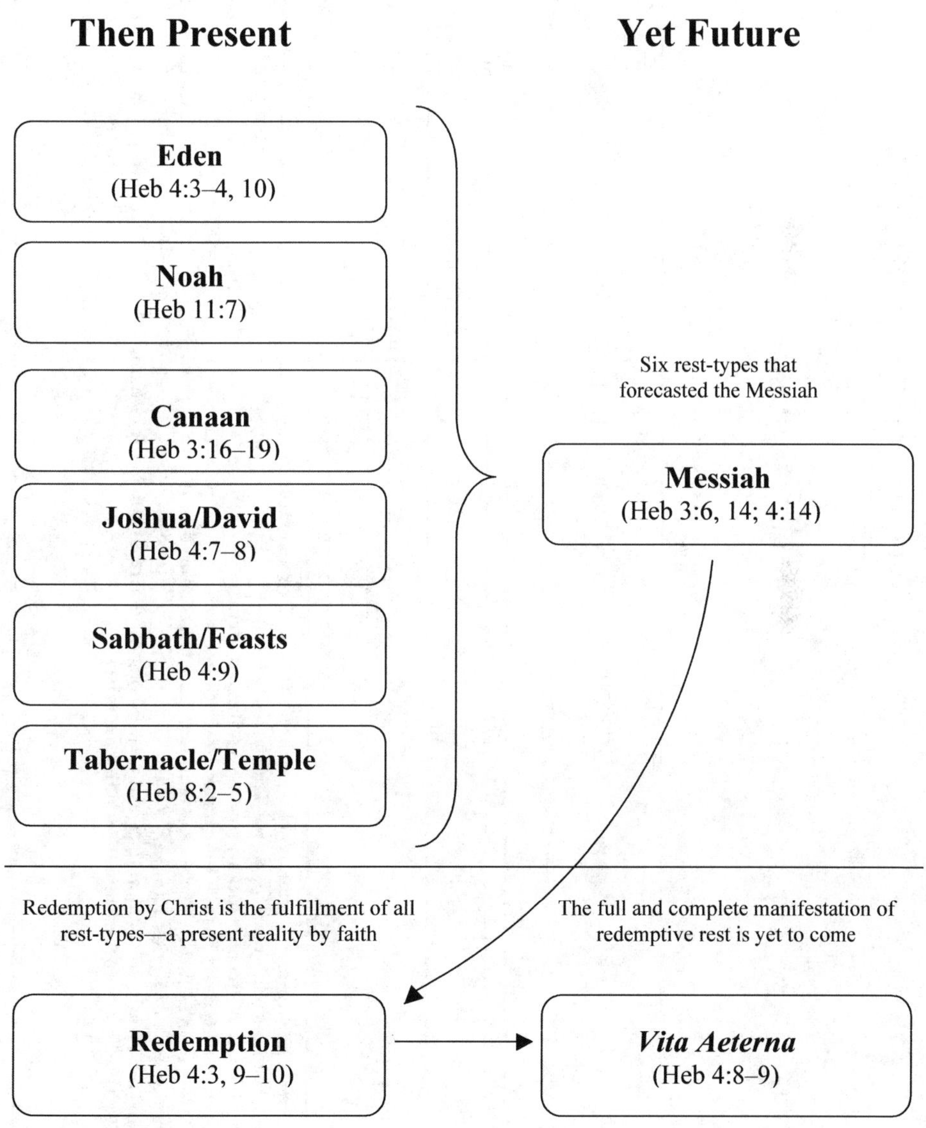

Appendix Seven

Seven Covenants with Man

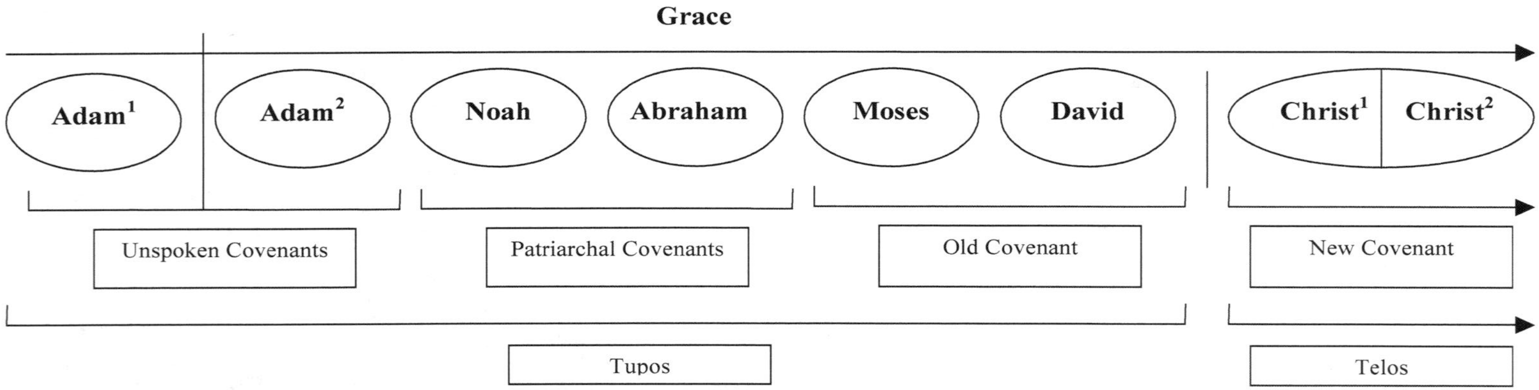

Adam^1: prelapsarian man, works-oriented, type of Federal Head;
Adam^2: lapsarian man, promise-faith oriented, type of righteous remnant
Noah: type of Second Adam; promise-faith oriented
Abraham: type of Father-Son; promise-faith oriented
Moses: type of future Prophet, Mediator, Law Giver, and Priest
David: type of Divine King, Law advocate
Christ^1: 1st advent, Prophet, Priest, Law Giver, Mediator and Kingdom King
Christ^2: 2nd advent, culmination of all promises

Adam comprises two covenants
Christ comprises one covenant

OT reveals 3 pairs of covenants with man (6)
NT reveals final covenant with Son of Man (1)

The new and everlasting covenant of grace in Christ fulfills Adam's original mandate as well as the shadows of the successive covenants

Bibliography

Adler, Elchanan. "The Sabbath Observing Gentile: Halakhic, Hashkafic and Liturgical Perspectives." *Tradition* 36, no. 3 (2002) 14–45.

Andrews, J. N. *History of the Sabbath and First Day of the Week*. Battle Creek, MI: Steam, 1873.

Aquinas, Thomas. *Summa Theologica*. 5 vols. Translated by brothers of the English Dominican Province. Allen, TX: Benziger Bros., 1948.

Archer, Gleason L. Jr. *Encyclopedia of Bible Difficulties*. Grand Rapids: Zondervan, 1982.

Auerbach, Leo, ed. *The Babylonian Talmud in Selection*. Translated by Leo Auerbach. New York: Philosophical Library, 1944.

Bacchiocchi, Samuele. *From Sabbath to Sunday: A Historical Investigation of the Rise of Sunday Observance in Early Christianity*. Rome: Pontifical Gregorian University Press, 1977.

———. *The Sabbath Under Crossfire: A Biblical Analysis of Sabbath/Sunday Developments*. Berrien Springs, MI: Biblical Perspectives, 1998.

Badenhorst, Chris. "What Are New Covenant Ethics?" *Proclamation* 8, no. 4 (July–August 2007) 13–17.

Bahnsen, Greg L. *By This Standard*. Tyler, TX: Institute for Christian Economics, 1985.

———. "The Theonomic Reformed Approach to Law and Gospel." In *Five Views on Law and Gospel*, edited by Wayne G. Strickland, et al., 93–143. Grand Rapids: Zondervan, 1996.

Barcellos, Richard C. *In Defense of the Decalogue*. Enumclaw, WA: WinePress, 2001.

———. "First Timothy 1:8–11 and the Utility of the Decalogue." *Reformed Baptist Theological Review* 1, no. 1 (2004) 3–25.

———. "The Old Testament Theology of the Sabbath—Creation, Old Covenant and Old Testament Prophecy." *Reformed Baptist Theological Review* 3, no. 2 (2006) 27–50.

Barker, William S. "King of Kings and Lord of Commoners: The Westminster Confession and the Relationship of Church and State." In *The Westminster Confession into the 21st Century*. Vol. 1, edited by Ligon Duncan, 413–28. Ross-shire, Great Britain. Christian Focus, 2003.

Barnes, Albert. *Barnes' Notes*. 14 vols. 1884–1885. Reprint, Grand Rapids: Baker, 2001.

Barnhouse, Donald Grey. *Expositions of Bible Doctrines: Taking the Epistle to the Romans as a Point of Departure*, 4 vols. Grand Rapids: Eerdmans, 1964.

Barrett, Michael P. V. *Beginning At Moses: A Guide to Finding Christ in the Old Covenant*, 2nd ed. Greenville, SC: Ambassador-Emerald International, 2001.

Barrow, Reg. Review of *The Psalms in Worship*, by John McNaughter. *Revival Review* (March-June 1992) 20–21.

Barth, Markus, and Helmut Blanke. "Colossians." Translated by Astrid B. Beck. Anchor Bible 34B. New York: Doubleday, 1994.

Bass, Dorothy. "Christian Formation in and for Sabbath Rest." *Interpretation* (January 2005) 25–37.

Bauckham, R. J. "The Lord's Day." In *From Sabbath to Lord's Day: A Biblical, Historical, and Theological Investigation*, edited by D. A. Carson, 222–50. 1982. Reprint, Eugene, OR: Wipf & Stock, 1999.

———. "Sabbath and Sunday in the Post-Apostolic Church," In *From Sabbath to Lord's Day: A Biblical, Historical, and Theological Investigation*, edited by D. A. Carson, 252–98. 1982. Reprint, Eugene, OR: Wipf & Stock, 1999.

———. "Sabbath and Sunday in the Medieval Church in the West," In *From Sabbath to Lord's Day: A Biblical, Historical, and Theological Investigation*, edited by D. A. Carson, 300–309. 1982. Reprint, Eugene, OR: Wipf & Stock, 1999.

Beale, G. K., and D. A. Carson, eds. *Commentary on the New Testament Use of the Old Testament*. Grand Rapids: Baker Academic, 2007.

Beisner, E. Calvin, ed. *The Auburn Avenue Theology, Pros & Cons: Debating the Federal Vision*. Fort Lauderdale, FL: Knox Theological Seminary, 2004.

Benedict XVI. *In the Beginning . . .: A Catholic Understanding of the Story of Creation and the Fall*. Translated by Boniface Ramsey. 1986. Reprint, Grand Rapids: Eerdmans, 1995.

Blakely, William Addison. *American State Papers Bearing on Sabbath Legislation*. New York: National Religious Liberty Association, 1890.

Blomberg, Craig. The Sabbath as Fulfilled in Christ: A Response to S. Bacchiocchi and J. Primus." In *The Sabbath in Jewish and Christian Traditions*, edited by Tamara C. Eskenazi et al., 122–28. New York: Crossroad, 1991.

Boice, James Montgomery. *Genesis: An Expositional Commentary*. Grand Rapids, MI: Baker, 1998.

Bonar, Andrew. *A Commentary on Leviticus*. 1846. Reprint, Geneva Series. Philadelphia, PA: The Banner of Truth Trust, 1989.

Bordwine, James E. "The Doctrine of the Sabbath." *Contra Mundum* 10 (1994) No Pages; 14 (1995) No Pages. Online: http://www.contra-mundum.org/cm/features/ 10_sabbath.pdf; http://www.contramundum.org/cm/features/14_sabbath.pdf

Boston, Thomas. "Of the Fourth Commandment." In *The Commentary on the Shorter Catechism* 1853. Reprint, Edmonton, Alberta: Still Waters Revival, 1993.

Bromiley, G.W. *Zwingli and Bullinger*, 4th ed. Philadelphia: The Westminster, 1953.

Brown, Collin, ed. *The New International Dictionary of New Testament Theology*. 4 vols. Grand Rapids: Zondervan, 1975–1985.

Brown, Michael, ed. *Called To Serve*. Grandville, MI: Reformed Fellowship, Inc., 2007.

Bullock, Richard, and Richard J. Bruesehoff. *Clergy Renewal: The Alban Guide To Sabbatical Planning*. Washington, DC: The Alban Institute, 2000.

Cairns, Earl E. *Christianity Through the Centuries*, 2nd ed. Grand Rapids: Zondervan, 1981.

Calvin, John. *Calvin's Commentaries*. 23 vols. Reprint, Grand Rapids: Baker, 2009.

———. *John Calvin's Sermons on the Ten Commandments*. Edited and Translated by Benjamin W. Farley. Grand Rapids: Baker, 1980.

———. *Institutes of the Christian Religion*. Translated by Henry Beveridge. Reprint, Grand Rapids: Eerdmans, 1995.

Carson, D. A. *Exegetical Fallacies*, 2nd ed. Grand Rapids: Baker, 1996.

———, ed. *From Sabbath to Lord's Day: A Biblical, Historical, and Theological Investigation*. 1982. Reprint, Eugene, OR: Wipf & Stock, 1999.

———. "Jesus and the Sabbath in the Four Gospels." In *From Sabbath to Lord's Day: A Biblical, Historical, and Theological Investigation*, edited by D. A. Carson, 58–42. 1982. Reprint, Eugene, OR: Wipf & Stock, 1999.

Case, Thomas. "Of Sabbath Sanctification" 1674. Photocopy. Edmonton, Alberta: Still Waters Revival, n.d.

Catechism of the Catholic Church. Translated into English. Ligouri, MO: Ligouri, 1994.

Catechism of the Council of Trent. Translated by J. Donovan. Baltimore, MD: Lucas Brothers, [1829?].

Chafer, Lewis Sperry. *Major Bible Themes*. Grand Rapids: Zondervan, 1974.

Chantry, Walter. *Call the Sabbath a Delight*. Carlisle, PA: The Banner of Truth Trust, 1991.

Ciampa, Roy E. and Brian S. Rosner. "1 Corinthians." In *Commentary on the New Testament Use of the Old Testament*, edited by G. K. Beale and D. A. Carson, 695–752. Grand Rapids: Baker Academic, 2007.

Clarke, Adam. *Clarke's Commentary*. 6 vols. New York: Abingdon-Cokesbury, n.d.

Cohen, Gary G. "shābûa`." In *Theological Wordbook of the Old Testament*, edited by R. Laird Harris et al., 899, 2 vols. Chicago: Moody, 1980.

Dabney, Robert Lewis. "The Christian Sabbath: Its Nature, Design and Proper Observance." In *Discussions of Robert Lewis Dabney*. Vol. 1. 496–550. Photocopy. Edmonton, Alberta: Still Waters Revival, n.d.

———. "Lecture 32 (First Table: Fourth Commandment)." In *Lectures in Systematic Theology*. 2nd editon. St. Louis, MO: Presbyterian Publishing, 1878.

———. "The Sabbath of the State." In *Discussions of Robert Lewis Dabney*. Vol. 2. 594–617. Photocopy. Edmonton, Alberta: Still Waters Revival, n.d.

Davidson, Richard M. *Typology in Scripture*. Berrien Springs, MI: Andrews University Press, 1981.

Dawn, Marva J. *Keeping the Sabbath Wholly*. Reprint, Grand Rapids: Eerdmans, 1995.

DeHaan, M. R. *Law or Grace*. Grand Rapids: Zondervan, 1965.

De Lacey, D. R. "The Sabbath/Sunday Question and the Law in the Pauline Corpus." In *From Sabbath to Lord's Day: A Biblical, Historical, and Theological Investigation*, edited by D. A. Carson, 160–95. 1982. Reprint, Eugene, OR: Wipf & Stock, 1999.

Dennison, James T. *The Market Day of the Soul*. Grand Rapids: Reformation Heritage, 2008.

———. "The Perpetuity and Change of the Sabbath." In *Soli Deo Gloria*, edited by R. C. Sproul, 146–55. Phillipsburg, NJ: Presbyterian & Reformed, 1976.

Dever, Mark. *Nine Marks of a Healthy Church*. Wheaton, IL: Crossway, 2000.

Doig, Kenneth F. *New Testament Chronology*. Lewiston, NY: Edwin Mellen, 1991.

Douma, J. *The Ten Commandments*. Translated by Nelson D. Kloosterman. Phillipsburg, NJ: Presbyterian & Reformed, 1996.

Downey, Mark. "The Sabbath." No Pages. Online: http://www.kinsmanredeemer.com/ Sabbath.html.

Downie, Hugh Kerr. *Harvest Festivals*. 1951. Reprint, Grand Rapids: Gospel Folio, 1994.

Drew, Charles D. *The Ancient Love Song: Finding Christ in the Old Testament*. Phillipsburg, NJ: Presbyterian & Reformed, 2000.

Duncan, David Ewing. *Calendar*. New York: Avon, 1998.

Duncan, J. Ligon, III, ed. *The Westminster Confession into the 21st Century*. Vol. 1, Ross-shire, Great Britain. Christian Focus, 2003.

Duncan, J. Ligon, III and David W. Hall. "The 24-Hour View." In *The Genesis Debate*, edited by David G. Hagopian, 21–66. Mission Viejo, CA: Cruxpress, 2001.

Du Preez, Ron. *Judging the Sabbath: Discovering What Can't Be Found in Colossians 2:16*. Berrien Springs, MI: Andrews University Press, 2008.

Durham, James. *A Practical Exposition of the Ten Commandments*. Edited by Christopher Coldwell. 1675. Reprint, Dallas, TX: Naphtali Press, 2002.

Eadie, John. *The John Eadie Greek Text Commentaries*. 5 Vols. 1869. Reprint, Grand Rapids: Baker Book House, 1979.

Ecumenical Creeds and Reformed Confessions. Grand Rapids: CRC Publications, 1988.

Edersheim, Alfred. *The Life and Times of Jesus the Messiah*. 1883. Reprint, Peabody, MA: Hendrickson, 1993.

———. *The Temple: Its Ministry and Services As They Were at the Time of Jesus Christ*. 1874. Reprint, Grand Rapids: Kregel, 1997.

Eells, Walter Crosby. "The Origin and Early History of Sabbatical Leave." *AAUP Bulletin* 48, no. 3 (September 1962) 253–56.

Epstein, I., ed. *Babylonian Talmud*. Translated by H. Freedman. London: The Soncino, 1961.

Eskenazi, Tamara C., et al., eds. *The Sabbath in Jewish and Christian Traditions*. New York: Crossroad, 1991.

Eyres, Lawrence. "The Evening Worship Service" *The Ordained Servant* 6, no. 4 (October 1997) 83–84.

Ewing, Curtis Clair. "Excellent," n.p. Online: http://www.presenttruthmag.com/ mailbox/mailbox18.htm

Ewing, Curtis Clair and Charles Wesley Ewing. "Israel's Calendar and the True Sabbath." 1958. rev. ed. Spokane, WA: Christ's Gospel Fellowship, 1980.

Fairbairn, Patrick. *Typology of Scripture*. 1900. Reprint, Grand Rapids: Kregel, 1989.

Famighetti, Robert, ed. *The World Almanac and Book of Facts 1995*. Mahwah, NJ: Funk & Wagnalls, 1994.

Faulstich, E. W. *Bible Chronology and the Scientific Method*. Spencer, Iowa: Chronology, 1990.

Feazell, J. Michael. *The Liberation of the Worldwide Church of God*. Grand Rapids: Zondervan, 2001.

Finley, Mark A. *The Almost Forgotten Day*. Siloam Springs, AR: The Concerned Group, Inc., 1988.

Finnegan, Jack. *Handbook of Biblical Chronology*, rev. ed. Peabody, MA: Hendrickson, 1998.

Frame, John M. *Worship in Spirit and Truth*. Phillipsburg, NJ: Presbyterian & Reformed, 1996.

Freedman, H. *The Babylonian Talmud*, Vol. 1, Seder Mo'ed. Translated by H. Freedman. London: The Soncino Press, 1961.

Freeman, James M. *Manners and Customs of the Bible*. 1875. Reprint, Plainfield, NJ: Logos International, 1972.

Gaffin, Richard B. *Calvin and the Sabbath: The Controversy of Applying the Fourth Commandment*. Ross-shire, Great Britain: Christian Focus, 1998.

———. "Westminster and the Sabbath." In *The Westminster Confession into the 21st Century*,Vol. 1, edited by Ligon Duncan, 123–44. Ross-shire, Great Britain. Christian Focus, 2003.

Gambel, H. R. *Sunday and the Sabbath*. New York: E. P. Dutton & Company, 1901.

Gamble, Samuel Walter. *Sunday: the True Sabbath of God*. New York: Eaton & Mains, 1900.

George, Timothy, and Denise George, eds. *Baptist Confessions, Covenants, and Catechisms*. Nashville, TN: Broadman & Holman, 1996.

Gilfillan, James. *The Sabbath Viewed in the Light of Reason, Revelation, and History*. New York: American Tract Society, 1862.

Godfrey, Robert. *Pleasing God in Our Worship*. Wheaton, IL: Crossway, 1999.

Goppelt, Leonhard. *Typos, The Typological Interpretation of the Old Testament in the New*. Translated by Donald H. Madvig. 1939. Reprint, Grand Rapids: Eerdmans, 1982.

Griedanus, Sidney. *Preaching Christ from the Old Testament*. Grand Rapids: Eerdmans, 1999.

Gunner, R. A. H. "Number." In *The New Bible Dictionary*, 3rd ed., edited by J. D. Douglas et al., 830–35. Downers Grove, IL: Intervarsity, 1996.

Haack, Margie. "Sabbath Master," *World Magazine* (May 1998) 29.

Habershon, Ada R. *Study of the Types*. 1908. Reprint, Grand Rapids: Kregel, 1997.

Hagen, Karl. "The Egyptian Calendar." No Pages. Online: http://www.polysyllabic.com/ ?q=calhistory/earlier/Egyptian.

Hagopian, David G., ed. *The Genesis Debate: Three Views on the Days of Creation*. Mission Viejo, CA: Crux, 2001.

Harline, Craig. *Sunday: A History of the First Day from Babylonia to the Super Bowl*. New York: Doubleday, 2007.

Harris, R. Laird et al., eds. *Theological Wordbook of the Old Testament*. 2 vols. Chicago: Moody, 1980.

Hart, D. G., and John R. Muether, "The Lord's Supper: How Often?" *Ordained Servant* 6, no. 2 (October 1997) 97–98.

Hendrickson, William. *New Testament Commentary*. 12 vols. Grand Rapids: Baker Academic, 2007.

Henry, Matthew. *Commentary On the Whole Bible*. 6 vols. 1712. Reprint, Peabody, MA: Hendrickson, 1991.

________. "A Serious Address to Those That Profane the Lord's Day," In *The Complete Works of the Rev. Matthew Henry*, Vol 1. 1855. Reprint, Edmonton, Alberta Still Waters Revival, n.d.

Hertzberg, Arthur, ed. *Judaism*. New York: George Braziller, Inc., 1962.

Heschel, Abraham Joshua. *The Sabbath: Its Meaning for Modern Man*. New York: Farrar, Straus & Giroux, 1951.

Hopkins, Mark. "The Sabbath and Free Institutions." New York: Edward O. Jenkins, 1863. No pages. Online: http://www.lettermen2.com/hopkins.html.

Horton, Michael. *A Better Way: Rediscovering the Drama of God-Centered Worship*. Grand Rapids: Baker, 2002.

Howard, Kevin, and Marvin Rosenthal. *The Feasts of the Lord*. Nashville, TN: Thomas Nelson, 1997.

Huey, Mark. "Reflections on Returning." *Outreach Israel News* (September 2006), 5–8.

Hyde, Daniel R. "Table Manners: Whom We Welcome to the Lord's Supper." In *Called to Serve*, edited by Michael Brown, 135–43. Grandville, MI: Reformed Fellowship, Inc., 2007.

Irons, Lee. "Entering God's Rest by Faith: Realized Eschatology in Hebrews 3:7–4:11." No pages. Online: http://www.upper-register.com/papers/rest_hebrews.pdf.

Ironside, H. A. *Addresses on the Gospel of John*. Neptune, NJ: Loizeaux Brothers, 1942.

Jamieson, Fausset, and Brown Bible Commentary, 3 vols. Reprint, Peabody, MA: Hendrickson, 2008.

Jervis, L. Ann. "Galatians." *New International Bible Commentary on the New Testament* 9, Peabody, MA: Hendrickson, 1999.

Jewett, Paul K. *The Lord's Day: A Theological Guide to the Christian Day of Worship*. Grand Rapids: Eerdmans, 1971.

John Paul II, "*Dies Domini*." 1998. No pages. Online: http://www.vatican.va/holy_father/john_paul_ii/apost_letters/documents/hf_jp-ii_apl_05071998_dies-domini_en.html.

Jordan, James B. *Primeval Saints*. Moscow, Idaho: Canon, 2001.

———. *Christianity and the Calendar*. Niceville, FL: Biblical Horizons, 1988.

———. *Creation in Six Days*. Moscow, Idaho: Canon, 1999.

———. *Sabbath Breaking and the Death Penalty: A Theological Investigation*. Tyler, TX: Geneva Ministries, 1986.

Josephus, Flavius. *The Works of Josephus*. Translated by William Whitson. 1736. Reprint, Peabody, MA: Hendrickson, 1987.

Kaiser, Walter C., Jr. "The Law as God's Gracious Guidance for the Promotion of Holiness." In *Five Views on Law and Gospel*, edited by Wayne G. Strickland, et al., 177–99. Grand Rapids: Zondervan, 1996.

———. *Toward Old Testament Ethics*. Grand Rapids: Zondervan, 1983.

Kang, Bai, and Michael T. Miller. "An Overview of the Sabbatical Leave in Higher Education: A Synopsis of the Literature Base." ERIC Document Reproductive Service, No. ED 430 471, 1999.

Kaplan, Aryeh. *Sabbath—Day of Eternity*, 2nd ed. New York: Orthodox Union/NCSY, 1982.

Keddie, Gordon J. *The Lord's Supper is a Celebration of Grace*. Auburn, MA: Evangelical Press, 2000.

Keil, C. F. and F. Delitzsch. *Commentary on the Whole Bible*. 1866–1892. Reprint, Peabody, MA: Hendrickson, 2006.

Kelly, Douglas, et al., eds. *The Westminster Confession of Faith*, 2nd ed. Greenwood, SC: The Attic, 1981.

Kistemaker, Simon J. "Exposition of the Acts of the Apostles," In *New Testament Commentary*. Grand Rapids: Baker, 1990.

Klagsbrun, Francine. *The Fourth Commandment*. New York: Harmony, 2002.

Kleyn, Daniel. "Is Once Enough?" *The Standard Bearer* 77, no. 1. (October 2000).

Kline, Meredith. "The Two Tables of the Covenant." *Westminster Theological Journal* 22 (1960) 133–46.

Knight, George R. *A Search for Identity: The Development of Seventh-day Adventist Beliefs*. Hagerstown, MD: Review and Herald, 2000.

Knight, George W. "1 Corinthians 11:17–34: The Lord's Supper: Abuses, Words of Institution and Warnings." In *The Auburn Avenue Theology, Pros & Cons: Debating the Federal Vision*, edited by E. Calvin Beisner, 282–96. Fort Lauderdale, FL: Knox Theological Seminary, 2004.

Koestlin, Julius. *Life of Luther*. 1881. Reprint, New York: Charles Scribner's Sons, 1911.

Kurtz, J. H. *Offerings, Sacrifices and Worship in the Old Testament*. Translated by James Martin. 1863. Reprint, Peabody, MA: Hendrickson, 1998.

Laband, David N., and Deborah Hendry Heinbuch. *Blue Laws: The History, Economics, and Politics of Sunday-Closing Laws*. Lexington, MA: D.C. Heath and Company, 1987.

Lange, John Peter. *Commentary on the Holy Scriptures*. Translated by Philip Schaff. Grand Rapids: Zondervan, 1960.

Law, Henry. *The Gospel in Exodus*. 1855. Reprint, London: The Banner of Truth Trust, 1967.

Leith, John H., ed. *Creeds of the Churches*, 3rd ed. Louisville, KY: John Knox, 1982.

Letham, Robert. "Given for You." *Tabletalk* (November 2006) 12–15.

———. *The Lord's Supper: Eternal Word in Broken Bread*. Phillipsburg, NJ: Presbyterian & Reformed, 2001.

Lewis, Gordon R. *The Bible, the Christian, and Seventh-day Adventists*. Phillipsburg, NJ: Presbyterian & Reformed, 1966.

Lewis, Richard M. "Minority Report (I)." In Report of the Committee on Sabbath Matters, Fortieth General Assembly, Orthodox Presbyterian Church, 1973. 106–10.

Liethart, Peter J. "A Response to '1 Corinthians 11:17–34: The Lord's Supper.'" In *The Auburn Avenue Theology, Pros and Cons: Debating the Federal Vision*, edited by E. Calvin Beisner, 297–304. Fort Lauderdale, FL: Knox Theological Seminary, 2004.

———. "Worship First and Last." *Credenda Agenda* 11, no. 4, (2000) 16.

———. "Worship is Warfare." *Credenda Agenda* 13, no. 2 (2001) 17.

Lightfoot, J. B. *The Apostolic Fathers*. 1891. Reprint, Grand Rapids: Baker Book House, 1978.

Lincoln, A. T. "Sabbath, Rest, and Eschatology in the New Testament." In *From Sabbath to Lord's Day: A Biblical, Historical, and Theological Investigation*, edited by D. A. Carson, 198–220. 1982. Reprint, Eugene, OR: Wipf & Stock, 1999.

———. "From Sabbath to Lord's Day: A Biblical and Theological Perspective," In *From Sabbath to Lord's Day: A Biblical, Historical, and Theological Investigation*, edited by D. A. Carson, 344–412. 1982. Reprint, Eugene, OR: Wipf & Stock, 1999.

Long, Thomas G. *The Witness of Preaching*. Louisville, KY: Westminster/John Knox, 1989.

Longman, Tremper, III, and David E. Garland. *The Expositor's Bible Commentary*. rev. ed. 13 vols. Grand Rapids: Zondervan, 2006.

Luther, Martin. *The Large Catechism of Martin Luther*, Translated by Robert H. Fischer. Philadelphia: Fortress, 1959.

———. *Luther's Works*. 55 vols. Translated by W. A. Lambert and Martin H. Bertman. Edited by James Atkinson and Helmut T. Lehman. 1915. Philadelphia: Fortress, 1971.

———. *Works of Martin Luther*. 6 vols. Translated by W. A. Lambert. 1915. Reprint, Grand Rapids: Baker, 1982.

MacArthur, John F., Jr. *The MacArthur New Testament Commentary: Colossians and Philemon*. Chicago: Moody, 1992.

Macaulay, Joseph Cordner. *Expository Commentary on Hebrews*. Chicago: Moody, 1948.

MacDonald, Dennis. "A Response to R. Goldenberg and D. J. Harrington, S.J." In *The Sabbath in Jewish and Christian Traditions*, edited by Tamara C. Eskanazi et al., 57–61. New York: Crossroad, 1991.

Maimonides. *Sanctification of the New Moon*. Translated by Solomon Ganz. Yale Judaica Series 11. Forge Village, MA: Yale University Press, 1956.

Marcussen, A. Jan. *National Sunday Law*. Homosassa Springs, FL: Amazing Truth, 1983.

Martin, Ralph P. *Worship in the Early Church*, 2nd ed. Grand Rapids: Eerdmans, 2000.

Martin, Robert P. "The Remaining Sabbath for the People of God." *Reformed Baptist Theological Review* 1, no. 2 (2004) 3–11.

Mathison, Keith A. *Given For You: Reclaiming Calvin's Doctrine of the Lord's Supper*. Phillipsburg, NJ: Presbyterian & Reformed, 2002.

McCartney, Dan, and Charles Clayton. *Let The Reader Understand*, 2nd ed. Phillipsburg, NJ: Presbyterian & Reformed, 2002.

McGee, J. Vernon. *The Sabbath Day or the Lord's Day—Which?* Thru the Bible Radio Network, 2006. Online: http://www.thruthebible.org.

———. *Thru the Bible with J. Vernon McGee*. 5 vols., Nashville, TN: Thomas Nelson, 1983.

McIlhenny, Charles A. "Literal, Six-Day Creation and the Local Church." *Chalcedon Report*. (September 1998).

McKay, Heather A. *Sabbath and Synagogue: The Question of Sabbath Worship in Ancient Judaism*. Leiden, Netherlands: E.J. Brill, 1994.

McKee, J. K. "The Work of the Holy Spirit: Perfection of the Heart." *Outreach Israel News*, (July 2006) 7–15.

———. "The Work of the Holy Spirit: Perfection of the Mind." *Outreach Israel News*, (August 2006) 6–15.

McKee-Huey, Margaret. *Messianic Sabbath Helper*. Kissimmee, FL: TNN Press, 2006.

Meier, Samuel A. "The Sabbath and Purification Cycles." In *The Sabbath in Jewish and Christian Traditions*, edited by Tamara C. Eskenazi et al., 3–11. New York: Crossroad, 1991.

Mikkelson, Barbara, and David Mikkelson. "Blue Laws," No Pages. Online: http://www.snopes.com/language/colors/bluelaws.htm.

Miller, Bryan. "Sabbath Rest for the Christian Life." *The Outlook* 61 no. 1 (2011) 12–14.

Moo, Douglas. "Response to Greg L. Bahnsen." In *Five Views on Law and Gospel*, edited by Wayne G. Strickland et al., 165–73. Grand Rapids: Zondervan, 1996.

Moody, Dwight L. *Twelve Select Sermons*. Chicago: F. H. Revell, 1881.

Morris, Henry M., III. *5 Reasons to Believe in Recent Creation*. Dallas, TX: Institute for Creation Research, 2008.

Morrison, Michael. *Sabbath, Circumcision, and Tithing: Which Old Testament Laws Apply to Christians?* Lincoln, NE: Writers Club, 2002.

Muller, Wayne. *Sabbath: Finding Rest, Renewal, and Delight in our Busy Lives*. New York: Bantam, 1999.

Murray, John. *The Collected Writings of John Murray*. 4 vols. Carlisle, PA: Banner of Truth, 1976.

Needham, Robert. *Keep the Sabbath Holy* (audiocassette) December 1995.

Nelson, Rodney. *A Biblical Study of the Lord's Day*. 1999. No Pages. http://www.ratzlaf.com/product35.html.

New Edition of the Babylonian Talmud. Translated by Michael L. Rodkinson. Edited by Isaac M. Wise. New York: New Talmud Publishing Company, 1901.

New English Bible. Oxford University Press, 1970.

Nichol, Francis D. *Reasons for Our Faith*. Tacoma Park, Washington, DC: Review & Herald Publishing Association, 1947.

Nietzsche, Friedrich. *Beyond Good and Evil*. Translated by: Helen Zimmern. New York: MacMillan [1917?].

North, Gary. "The Economics of Sabbath-Keeping." In *The Institutes of Biblical Law*, 824–36. Phillipsburg, NJ: Presbyterian & Reformed, 1973.

Novak, David. "The Sabbath Day." In *The Ten Commandments for Jews, Christians, and Others*, edited by Roger Van Harn, 69–79. Grand Rapids: Eerdmans, 2007.

Orlinski, Harry M., ed. *The Synagogue: Studies in Origins, Archaeology and Architecture*. New York: KTAV, 1975.

Oord, Wybren, "The Table of Showbread," *The Outlook* 58, no. 6 (June 2008) 6–8.

Orr, Ralph. "From Sunday to Sabbath" No Pages. Online: http://www.wcg.org/lit/law/ sabbath/sun-sab1.htm.

Ouaknin, Mark-Alain. *Symbols of Judaism*. Singapore: Barnes & Noble, 2003.

Owen, John. *Owen's Exposition on the Epistle to the Hebrews*. 1649. Reprint, London: J. Haddon, 1840.

Parker, Richard A. *The Calendars of Ancient Egypt*. Chicago, IL: Oriental Institute of the University of Chicago, 1950.

Philo, Judaecus. *The Works of Philo*. Translated by C. D. Yonge. 1854. Reprint, Peabody, MA: Hendrickson, 1993.

Pinkoski, Jim. *The Truth About The Sabbath*. Frederick, MD: Amazing Facts, Inc., 1988.

Pipa, Joseph A. *The Lord's Day*. Fearn, Ross-Shire, Great Britain: Christian Focus, 1997.

Pipa, Joseph A., Jr. "From Chaos to Cosmos: A Critique of the Non-Literal Interpretations of Genesis 1:1–2:3." In *Did God Create in 6 Days?* edited by Joseph A. Pipa Jr. and David W. Hall, 2nd ed., 151–96. White Hall, WV: Tolle Lege Press, 2005.

Porter, Stanley E., ed. *Hearing the Old Testament in the New Testament*. Grand Rapids: Eerdmans, 2006.

Price, Greg L. *Remember the Sabbath Day to Keep It Holy*. Edmonton, Alberta: Still Waters Revival, n.d. (5 audiocassettes).

———. *When Does The Sabbath Begin? Morning or Evening?* Edmonton, Alberta: Still Waters Revival, 1996.

Primus, John H. *Holy Time: Moderate Puritanism and the Sabbath*. Macon, GA: Mercer University Press, 1989.

———. "Sunday, The Lord's Day as a Sabbath—Protestant Perspectives on the Sabbath." In *The Sabbath in Jewish and Christian Traditions*, edited by Tamara C. Eskenazi et al., 98–121. New York: Crossroad, 1991.

Putnam, C. E. *Sunday Observance or Sinai Seventh-Day Sabbath-Keeping?* Chicago: The Bible Institute Colportage Association, 1924.

Raphael, Chaim. *The Festivals: A History of Jewish Celebration*. London: Weidenfeld & Nicholson Limited, 1990.

Ratzinger, Joseph. *See* Benedict XVI.

Ratzlaff, Dale. *Sabbath in Christ*. Glendale, AZ: Life Assurance Ministries, 2003.

Ray, Bruce A. *Celebrating the Sabbath*. Phillipsburg, NJ: Presbyterian & Reformed, 2000.

Renihan, James M. "'Bound to Keep the First Day'—Covenant Theology, the Moral Law, and the Sabbath among the first English Particular Baptists." *Reformed Baptist Theological Review* 3, no. 2 (2006) 51–76.

Reisinger, John G. *The Believer's Sabbath*. Frederick, MD: New Covenant Media, 2002.

Rice, John R. *False Doctrines Answered*. Murfreesboro, TN: Sword of the Lord, 1970.

Ridgeley, Thomas. "The Sabbatic Institution," In *The Commentary on the Larger Catechism*. Vol. 2. Photocopy in *Sabbath Keeping*. 1855. Reprint, Edmonton, Alberta: Still Waters Revival, n.d.

Ringe, Sharon H. "'Holy, as the Lord Your God Commanded You': Sabbath in the New Testament." *Interpretation* (January 2005) 17–24.

Roberts, Alexander, and James Donaldson. *Ante-Nicene Fathers*. 10 vols. 1885. Reprint, Peabody, MA: Hendrickson, 1995.

Robertson, Archibald Thomas. *Word Pictures in the New Testament*. 6 vols. Nashville, TN: Broadman, 1930–1932.

Robertson, Don W. *The Christian Sabbath*. Coulterville, IL: New Creation, 2001.

Robertson, O. Palmer. *The Christ of the Covenants*. Phillipsburg, NJ: Presbyterian & Reformed, 1980.

———. *The Israel of God*. Phillipsburg, NJ: Presbyterian & Reformed, 2000.

Rome's Challenge: Why Do Protestants Keep Sunday? Reprint, "The Christian Sabbath" in *Catholic Mirror*, (September 1893) n.d.

Rordorf, Willy. *Sunday*. 1962 Translated by A. A. K. Graham. London: SCM, 1968.

Rosen, Ceil, and Moishe Rosen. *Christ in the Passover*. Chicago: Moody Press, 1978.

Runneson, Anders, et al. *The Ancient Synagogue from its Origins to 200 C.E.*, Leiden: Brill, 2008.

Rushdoony, Rousas John. *The Institutes of Biblical Law*. Phillipsburg, NJ: Presbyterian & Reformed, 1973.

———. *Salvation and Godly Rule*. Vallecito, CA: Ross House, 1983.

Sande, Ken. "Taking Church Membership Seriously," *Leadership Journal* (April 2005). Online: http://www.christianitytoday.com/leaders/newsletter/2005/cln50418.html.

Schaeffer, Edith. *Lifelines: The Ten Commandments for Today*. Westchester, IL: Crossway, 1978.

Schaff, Philip. *The Creeds of Christendom: With a History and Critical Notes*. 3 vols. 1931. Reprint, Grand Rapids: Baker, 1996.

Scheifler, Michael. "Exactly Which Pope Changed the Sabbath to Sunday?" No Pages. Online: http://biblelight.net/sylvester-I.htm.

Schwertley, Brian. *The Regulative Principle of Worship and Christmas*. Southfield, MI: Reformed Witness, 1996.

Seiss, Joseph A. *The Apocalypse: Lectures on the Book of Revelation*. 1900. New York: Cosimo, 2007.

Sevier, Melissa Bane. *Journeying Toward Renewal: A Spiritual Companion for Pastoral Sabbaticals*. Herndon, VA: The Alban Institute, 2002.

Shaw, Robert. "Of Religious Worship, and the Sabbath-Day," *The Exposition of the Confession of Faith*. 1845. Photocopy in *Sabbath Keeping*. Edmonton, Alberta: Still Waters Revival, n.d.

Shelly, Bruce L. *Church History in Plain Language*, 2nd ed. Dallas, TX: Word, 1995.

Shepard, Thomas. *Theses Sabbaticae: The Doctrine of the Sabbath*. 1649. Reprint, Dahlonega, GA: Crown Rights, 2002.

Sherman, Robert. "Reclaimed by Sabbath Rest." *Interpretation*. (January 2005) 38–50.

Skarsaune, Oskar. *In the Shadow of the Temple*. Downers Grover, IL: Intervarsity, 2002.

———. "The Ebionites." In *Jewish Believers in Jesus: The Early Centuries*, 2nd ed., edited by Oskar Skarsaune and Reidar Hvalvik, 419–62. Peabody, MA: Hendrickson, 2007.

Spurgeon, Charles H. *Morning and Evening*. Edited by Roy H. Clarke. Nashville, TN: Thomas Nelson, 1994.

Still, Todd D. "Colossians." In *The Expositors Bible Commentary*. Vol. 12, rev. ed. Grand Rapids: Zondervan, 2006.

Stott, W. "Sabbath, Lord's Day." In *The New International Dictionary of New Testament Theology*. Vol. 3, 405–15. 4 vols. Edited by Colin Brown. Grand Rapids: Zondervan, 1975–1978.

Strickland, Wayne G. et al. *Five Views on Law and Gospel*. Grand Rapids: Zondervan, 1996.

Tangelder, Johan D. "Celebrating the Lord's Day," *The Outlook* 56, no. 4 (2006) 11–15; 56, no. 5 (2006) 14–19.

Torrey, R. A. *Ought Christians to Keep the Sabbath?* New York: Fleming H. Revell Company, 1899.

Trepp, Leo. *The Complete Book of Jewish Observance*. New York: Behrman House, Inc., 1980.

Trice, T. Nathan. "'Drink of It, All of You.'" *Ordained Servant* 14, no. 1 (2005) 1–28.

Turner, M. Max B. "The Sabbath, Sunday, and the Law in Luke/Acts." In *From Sabbath to Lord's Day: A Biblical, Historical, and Theological Investigation*, edited by D. A. Carson, 100–157. 1982. Reprint, Eugene, OR: Wipf & Stock, 1999.

Ursinus, Zacharias. *Commentary on the Heidelberg Catechism*. Translated by G. W. Williard. 1852. Reprint, Phillipsburg, NJ: Presbyterian & Reformed, n.d.

Van Harn, Roger, ed. *The Ten Commandments for Jews, Christians, and Others*. Grand Rapids: Eerdmans, 2007.

Varner, William C. "Do We Need Messianic Synagogues? Biblical, Historic, and Pragmatic Issues." *The Masters Theological Journal* 14 no. 1 (2003) 47-62.

Venema, Cornelis, "The Old Testament Evidence Regarding the Participation of Children in Covenant Observances." *The Outlook* 56, no. 4 (April 2006) 26–30; 56, no. 6 (June 2006) 22–27.

Vincent, M. R. *Word Studies in the New Testament*. 2 vols. 1888. Reprint, McLean, VA: MacDonald Publishing Company, n.d.

Vine's Complete Expository Dictionary of Old and New Testament Words. Nashville, TN: Thomas Nelson, 1996.

Walvoord, John F., and Roy B. Zuck. *The Bible Knowledge Commentary*. Wheaton, IL: Victor Books, 1983.

Ward, Rowland S. *God and Adam: Reformed Theology and The Creation Covenant*. Wantirna, Australia: New Melbourne, 2003.

Watson, Thomas. *The Ten Commandments*. 1692. Reprint, Great Britain: The Banner of Truth Trust, 1999.

Webster, Hutton. *Rest Days*. 1916. Reprint, Detroit: Omnigraphics, 1992.

Weilerstein, Sadie Rose. *Jewish Heroes*. Vol. 2. New York: United Synagogue Commission on Jewish Education, 1956.

Weirsby, Warren W. *Real Worship*. Grand Rapids: Baker, 2000.

Weisman, Charles A. *The Sabbath and the Lord's Day: Viewed in the Light of Reason, Revelation, Law, Race and History*, 3rd ed. Apple Valley, MN: Weisman, 2002.

Wesley, John. *Explanatory Notes on the New Testament*. 1754. Reprint, London: Epworth Press, 1954.

Westminster Confession of Faith. 1646. Reprint, Glascow: Free Presbyterian Publications, 1997.

White, Ellen G. *The Desire of Ages*. 1898. Reprint, Wildwood, GA: Family Heritage, 1990.

———. *The Great Controversy*. 1888. Reprint, Mountain View, CA: Pacific Press, 1954.

Williamson, G. I. *The Heidelberg Catechism*. Phillipsburg, NJ: Presbyterian & Reformed, 1993.

———. "The Scriptural Regulative Principle of Worship." Photocopy of pamphlet. Edmonton, Alberta: Still Waters Revival, n.d.

———. *The Shorter Catechism*, 2 Vols. Phillipsburg, NJ: Presbyterian & Reformed, 1970.

Wilson, Larry. "On Weekly Communion—Some Pastoral Reflections." *Ordained Servant* 14, no. 1 (2005) 15–20.

Winner, Lauren F. *Mudhouse Sabbath*. Brewster, MA: Paraclete Press, 2003.

Wisner, Kerry. *Eye of the Sun: The Sacred Legacy of Ancient Egypt*. Nashua, NH: Hwt-Hrw, 2000.

Yadin, Yigael. "The Temple Scroll—The Longest Dead Sea Scroll." In *Understanding the Dead Sea Scrolls*, edited by Hershel Shanks, 87–112. New York: Random House, 1992.

Yang, Yong-Eui. *Jesus and the Sabbath in Matthew's Gospel*. Sheffield, England: Sheffield Academic, 1997.

Zinberg, George. *Jewish Calendar Mystery Dispelled*. New York: Vantage Press, Inc., 1963.

Subject Index

Scripture Index

OLD TESTAMENT

Genesis

NEW TESTAMENT